"The chapters collected here are authored by an all-star cast. They ably explore the many implications of epistemic injustice across philosophical sub-fields and through timely case studies. This Handbook takes the next step in broadening and deepening our understanding of this distinctive form of harm."

– **Michael Brownstein, John Jay College of Criminal Justice (CUNY), USA**

# THE ROUTLEDGE HANDBOOK OF EPISTEMIC INJUSTICE

In the era of information and communication, issues of misinformation and miscommunication are more pressing than ever. *Epistemic injustice* – one of the most important and ground-breaking subjects to have emerged in philosophy in recent years – refers to those forms of unfair treatment that relate to issues of knowledge, understanding, and participation in communicative practices.

*The Routledge Handbook of Epistemic Injustice* is an outstanding reference source to the key topics, problems, and debates in this exciting subject. The first collection of its kind, it comprises over thirty chapters by a team of international contributors, divided into five parts:

- Core Concepts
- Liberatory Epistemologies and Axes of Oppression
- Schools of Thought and Subfields within Epistemology
- Socio-political, Ethical, and Psychological Dimensions of Knowing
- Case Studies of Epistemic Injustice.

As well as fundamental topics such as testimonial and hermeneutic injustice and epistemic trust, the Handbook includes chapters on important issues such as social and virtue epistemology, objectivity and objectification, implicit bias, and gender and race. Also included are chapters on areas in applied ethics and philosophy, such as law, education, and healthcare.

*The Routledge Handbook of Epistemic Injustice* is essential reading for students and researchers in ethics, epistemology, political philosophy, feminist theory, and philosophy of race. It will also be very useful for those in related fields, such as cultural studies, sociology, education, and law.

**Ian James Kidd** is Assistant Professor of Philosophy at the University of Nottingham, UK. With Jonathan Beale he is editor of *Wittgenstein and Scientism* (Routledge, 2017).

**José Medina** is Professor of Philosophy at Vanderbilt University, USA. He is the author of four books, including *The Epistemology of Resistance: Gender and Racial Oppression, Epistemic Injustice, and Resistant Imaginations* (2013).

**Gaile Pohlhaus, Jr.** is Associate Professor of Philosophy and affiliate of Women's, Gender, and Sexuality Studies at Miami University, USA.

# ROUTLEDGE HANDBOOKS IN PHILOSOPHY

*Routledge Handbooks in Philosophy* are state-of-the-art surveys of emerging, newly refreshed, and important fields in philosophy, providing accessible yet thorough assessments of key problems, themes, thinkers, and recent developments in research.

All chapters for each volume are specially commissioned, and written by leading scholars in the field. Carefully edited and organized, *Routledge Handbooks in Philosophy* provide indispensable reference tools for students and researchers seeking a comprehensive overview of new and exciting topics in philosophy. They are also valuable teaching resources as accompaniments to textbooks, anthologies, and research-orientated publications.

*Recently published*

*The Routledge Handbook of Embodied Cognition*
Edited by Lawrence Shapiro

*The Routledge Handbook of Philosophy of Well-Being*
Edited by Guy Fletcher

*The Routledge Handbook of Philosophy of Imagination*
Edited by Amy Kind

*The Routledge Handbook of the Stoic Tradition*
Edited by John Sellars

*The Routledge Handbook of Philosophy of Information*
Edited by Luciano Floridi

*The Routledge Handbook of the Philosophy of Biodiversity*
Edited by Justin Garson, Anya Plutynski, and Sahotra Sarkar

*The Routledge Handbook of Philosophy of the Social Mind*
Edited by Julian Kiverstein

*The Routledge Handbook of Philosophy of Empathy*
Edited by Heidi Maibom

*The Routledge Handbook of Epistemic Contextualism*
Edited by Jonathan Jenkins Ichikawa

*The Routledge Handbook of Philosophy of Pain*
Edited by Jennifer Corns

*The Routledge Handbook of Brentano and the Brentano School*
Edited by Uriah Kriegel

*The Routledge Handbook of Collective Intentionality*
Edited by Marija Jankovic and Kirk Ludwig

*The Routledge Handbook of Libertarianism*
Edited by Jason Brennan, Bas van der Vossen, and David Schmidtz

*The Routledge Handbook of Metaethics*
Edited by Tristram McPherson and David Plunkett

*The Routledge Handbook of Philosophy of Memory*
Edited by Sven Bernecker and Kourken Michaelian

# THE ROUTLEDGE HANDBOOK OF EPISTEMIC INJUSTICE

*Edited by*
*Ian James Kidd, José Medina, and Gaile Pohlhaus, Jr.*

LONDON AND NEW YORK

First published 2017 by Routledge

2 Park Square, Milton Park, Abingdon, Oxfordshire OX14 4RN
52 Vanderbilt Avenue, New York, NY 10017

*Routledge is an imprint of the Taylor & Francis Group, an informa business*

First issued in paperback 2019

Copyright © 2017 Ian James Kidd, José Medina, and Gaile Pohlhaus, Jr., editorial and selection matter; individual chapters, the contributors

The right of Ian James Kidd, José Medina, and Gaile Pohlhaus, Jr. to be identified as the authors of the editorial material, and of the authors for their individual chapters, has been asserted in accordance with sections 77 and 78 of the Copyright, Designs and Patents Act 1988.

All rights reserved. No part of this book may be reprinted or reproduced or utilised in any form or by any electronic, mechanical, or other means, now known or hereafter invented, including photocopying and recording, or in any information storage or retrieval system, without permission in writing from the publishers.

Notice:
Product or corporate names may be trademarks or registered trademarks, and are used only for identification and explanation without intent to infringe.

*British Library Cataloguing-in-Publication Data*
A catalogue record for this book is available from the British Library

*Library of Congress Cataloging-in-Publication Data*
Names: Kidd, Ian James, 1983- editor.
Title: The Routledge handbook of epistemic injustice/edited
  by Ian James Kidd, Josâe Medina, and Gaile Pohlhaus, Jr.
Description: 1 [edition]. | New York : Routledge, 2017. |
Series: Routledge handbooks in philosophy | Includes bibliographical references and index.
Identifiers: LCCN 2016043132| ISBN 9781138828254 (hardback : alk. paper) |
  ISBN 9781315212043 (e-book)
Subjects: LCSH: Justice (Philosophy) | Knowledge, Theory of. |
  Ethics. | Political science—Philosophy.
Classification: LCC B105.J87 R68 2017 | DDC 172/.2—dc23
LC record available at https://lccn.loc.gov/2016043132

ISBN: 978-1-138-82825-4 (hbk)
ISBN: 978-0-367-37063-3 (pbk)

Typeset in ApexBembo
by Apex CoVantage, LLC

*To the silenced, and those who have resisted
(and continue to resist) epistemic injustice*

# CONTENTS

*Notes on contributors*     *xiii*
*Acknowledgements*     *xviii*

    Introduction to *The Routledge Handbook of Epistemic Injustice*     1
    Ian James Kidd, José Medina, and Gaile Pohlhaus, Jr.

## PART 1
## Core concepts     **11**

1  Varieties of epistemic injustice     13
    *Gaile Pohlhaus, Jr.*

2  Varieties of testimonial injustice     27
    *Jeremy Wanderer*

3  Varieties of hermeneutical injustice     41
    *José Medina*

4  Evolving concepts of epistemic injustice     53
    *Miranda Fricker*

5  Epistemic injustice as distributive injustice     61
    *David Coady*

6  Trust, distrust, and epistemic injustice     69
    *Katherine Hawley*

| | |
|---|---|
| 7   Forms of knowing and epistemic resources<br>*Alexis Shotwell* | 79 |
| 8   Epistemic responsibility<br>*Lorraine Code* | 89 |
| 9   Ideology<br>*Charles W. Mills* | 100 |

## PART 2
## Liberatory epistemologies and axes of oppression — **113**

| | |
|---|---|
| 10  Intersectionality and epistemic injustice<br>*Patricia Hill Collins* | 115 |
| 11  Feminist epistemology: the subject of knowledge<br>*Nancy Tuana* | 125 |
| 12  Epistemic injustice and the philosophy of race<br>*Luvell Anderson* | 139 |
| 13  Decolonial praxis and epistemic injustice<br>*Andrea J. Pitts* | 149 |
| 14  Queer epistemology and epistemic injustice<br>*Kim Q. Hall* | 158 |
| 15  Allies behaving badly: gaslighting as epistemic injustice<br>*Rachel McKinnon* | 167 |
| 16  Knowing disability, differently<br>*Shelley Tremain* | 175 |

## PART 3
## Schools of thought and subfields within epistemology — **185**

| | |
|---|---|
| 17  Power/knowledge/resistance: Foucault and epistemic injustice<br>*Amy Allen* | 187 |
| 18  Epistemic injustice and phenomenology<br>*Lisa Guenther* | 195 |

19  On the harms of epistemic injustice: pragmatism and transactional epistemology        205
    *Shannon Sullivan*

20  Social epistemology and epistemic injustice        213
    *Sanford Goldberg*

21  Testimonial injustice, epistemic vice, and vice epistemology        223
    *Heather Battaly*

## PART 4
## Socio-political, ethical, and psychological dimensions of knowing        **233**

22  Implicit bias, stereotype threat, and epistemic injustice        235
    *Jennifer Saul*

23  What's wrong with epistemic injustice? Harm, vice, objectification, misrecognition        243
    *Matthew Congdon*

24  Epistemic and political agency        254
    *Lorenzo C. Simpson*

25  Epistemic and political freedom        261
    *Susan E. Babbitt*

26  Epistemic communities and institutions        270
    *Nancy Arden McHugh*

27  Objectivity, epistemic objectification, and oppression        279
    *Sally Haslanger*

## PART 5
## Case studies of epistemic injustice        **291**

28  Epistemic justice and the law        293
    *Michael Sullivan*

29  Epistemic injustice: the case of digital environments        303
    *Gloria Origgi and Serena Ciranna*

30  Epistemic injustice in science                                           313
    Heidi Grasswick

31  Education and epistemic injustice                                        324
    Ben Kotzee

32  Epistemic injustice in medicine and healthcare                           336
    Havi Carel and Ian James Kidd

33  Epistemic injustice and mental illness                                   347
    Anastasia Philippa Scrutton

34  Indigenous peoples, anthropology, and the legacy of epistemic
    injustice                                                                356
    Rebecca Tsosie

35  Epistemic injustice and cultural heritage                                370
    Andreas Pantazatos

36  Epistemic injustice and religion                                         386
    Ian James Kidd

37  Philosophy and philosophical practice: Eurocentrism as an
    epistemology of ignorance                                                397
    Linda Martín Alcoff

Index                                                                        409

# NOTES ON CONTRIBUTORS

**Ian James Kidd** is Assistant Professor of Philosophy at the University of Nottingham, having previously worked at Durham and Leeds. His research interests include virtue epistemology, philosophy of illness, and philosophy of religion, among other things. His website is https://nottingham.academia.edu/IanJamesKidd

**José Medina** is Professor of Philosophy at Vanderbilt University. His research interests include critical social theory, political philosophy, social epistemology, philosophy of language and mind, and race and gender theory. He is the author of four books, including *The Epistemology of Resistance: Gender and Racial Oppression, Epistemic Injustice, and Resistant Imaginations* (2013).

**Gaile Pohlhaus, Jr.** is Associate Professor of Philosophy and affiliate of Women's, Gender, and Sexuality Studies at Miami University. Her research interests include feminist epistemology, feminist theory, social epistemology, and the work of the later Wittgenstein.

**Linda Martín Alcoff** is Professor of Philosophy at Hunter College and the CUNY Graduate Center, and a former president of the American Philosophical Association, Eastern Division. Her books include *The Future of Whiteness* (2015), *Visible Identities: Race, Gender and the Self* (2006), and *Real Knowing: New Versions of the Coherence Theory* (1996). Her website is www.alcoff.com/

**Amy Allen** is Liberal Arts Research Professor of Philosophy and Women's, Gender, and Sexuality Studies at the Pennsylvania State University. Her research interests include 20th century European philosophy, critical social theory, feminist theory, and psychoanalysis. Her website is http://pennstate.academia.edu/AmyAllen

**Luvell Anderson** is Assistant Professor of Philosophy at the University of Memphis. His research lies principally in philosophy of language, philosophy of race, and aesthetics, and specifically on Black semantics and racial language. He is currently working on a book manuscript tentatively entitled *Black Semantics*.

**Susan E. Babbitt** is the author (most recently) of *Humanism and Embodiment* (Bloomsbury, 2014) and *José Martí, Ernesto "Che" Guevara and Global Development Ethics* (Palgrave MacMillan

2014), does research at Queen's University, Canada in Theravada Buddhism. She writes for *Counterpunch* and *Global Research*.

**Heather Battaly** is Professor of Philosophy at California State University, Fullerton. Her interests include epistemology, ethics, and virtue theory. She is author of *Virtue* (2015). She is currently working on a book on epistemic vice.

**Havi Carel** is Professor of Philosophy at the University of Bristol. Her research interests are in philosophy of medicine, death, and phenomenology of illness. She is the author of *Phenomenology of Illness* (2016) and is currently a Wellcome Trust Senior Investigator on her project, the Life of Breath (www.lifeofbreath.org).

**Serena Ciranna** is a PhD student at the Institut Nicod (www.institutnicod.org). She holds a Masters degree in Philosophy and Social Sciences at the *Ecole des Hautes Etudes en Sciences Sociales* in Paris and works on the epistemological and moral problems raised by the Big Data society.

**David Coady** is Senior Lecturer in Philosophy at the University of Tasmania. His research interests include rumour, conspiracy theory, blogging, expertise, democracy, causation, climate change, legal philosophy, cricket ethics, police ethics, and horror film ethics. His website is www.utas.edu.au/profiles/staff/humanities/David-Coady

**Lorraine Code** is Distinguished Research Professor Emerita at York University in Toronto. She works in epistemology with particular interests in feminist, post-colonial, and ecological epistemology. Her books include *Ecological Thinking: The Politics of Epistemic Location* (2006).

**Patricia Hill Collins** is Distinguished University Professor at the University of Maryland whose research examines issues of race, gender, social class, sexuality, and/or nation. She is the author of several books, including *Black Feminist Thought* (1990). Her website is https://socy.umd.edu/facultyprofile/Collins/Patricia%20Hill

**Matthew Congdon** is Senior Lecturer in Philosophy at Vanderbilt University. He specializes in ethics and is currently working on the normative status of pain, ethical issues in social epistemology, and the propositional structure of moral emotions. His website is https://vanderbilt.academia.edu/MattCongdon

**Miranda Fricker** is Professor of Philosophy at CUNY Graduate Center. Her research is mainly in social epistemology and ethics. She served as Director of the Mind Association 2010–2015. She is an Associate Editor of the *Journal of the American Philosophical Association* and a Fellow of the British Academy.

**Sanford Goldberg** is Professor of Philosophy at Northwestern University. He works in epistemology, philosophy of language, and philosophy and mind, and his recent books include *Anti-Individualism* (2007), *Relying on Others* (2010), and *Assertion* (2015). His website is www.philosophy.northwestern.edu/people/continuing-faculty/goldberg-sanford.html

**Heidi Grasswick** is the George Nye & Anne Walker Boardman Professor of Mental and Moral Science in the Department of Philosophy at Middlebury College. Her research interests span questions of feminist epistemology and philosophy of science, and social epistemology. Her website is http://sites.middlebury.edu/drheidigrasswick/

**Lisa Guenther** is Associate Professor of Philosophy at Vanderbilt University. She is the author of *Solitary Confinement: Social Death and its Afterlives* (2013) and co-editor of *Death and Other Penalties: Philosophy in a Time of Mass Incarceration* (2015) with Geoffrey Adelsberg and Scott Zemon.

**Kim Q. Hall** is Professor of Philosophy and Director of Gender, Women's, and Sexuality Studies at Appalachian State University. Her areas of research interest include feminist philosophy, disability studies, queer theory, philosophy of race, continental philosophy, and environmental philosophy.

**Sally Haslanger** is Ford Professor of Philosophy and affiliate in the Women's & Gender Studies at Massachusetts Institute of Technology and a former president of the American Philosophical Association, Eastern Division. Her interests include social and political philosophy, feminist theory, and critical race theory, and her books include *Critical Theory and Practice* (forthcoming) and *Resisting Reality* (2012).

**Katherine Hawley** is Professor of Philosophy at the University of St Andrews, Scotland. She is the author of *Trust: A Very Short Introduction* (2012) and of articles on trust, practical knowledge, and injustice; she has also published extensively in metaphysics.

**Ben Kotzee** is Senior Lecturer in the School of Education at the University of Birmingham. He applies insights from contemporary epistemology to topics in the philosophy of education and is editor of *Education and the Growth of Knowledge* (2013).

**Nancy Arden McHugh** is Professor and Chair of Philosophy at Wittenberg University. She is the author of *The Limits of Knowledge: Generating Pragmatist Feminist Cases for Situated Knowing* (2015) and *Feminist Philosophies A-Z* (2007). She teaches philosophy courses as part of the Inside-Out Prison Exchange Program at London Correctional Institute in London, Ohio, where she also writes with the LoCI-Wittenberg University Writing Group. Her website is www.nancyamchugh.org

**Rachel McKinnon** is Assistant Professor in the Department of Philosophy at the College of Charleston. Her research focuses on the relationship between knowledge and action, and she is the author of *Norms of Assertion* (2015). Her website is www.rachelmckinnon.com/

**Charles W. Mills** is a Distinguished Professor at the CUNY Graduate Center. His research interests focus on oppositional political theory, particularly critical philosophy of race. He is the author of six books: *The Racial Contract* (1997), *Blackness Visible: Essays on Philosophy and Race* (1998), *From Class to Race: Essays in White Marxism and Black Radicalism* (2003), *Contract and Domination* (co-authored with Carole Pateman) (2007), *Radical Theory, Caribbean Reality: Race, Class and Social Domination* (2010), and *Black Rights/White Wrongs: The Critique of Racial Liberalism* (2017).

**Gloria Origgi** is senior researcher (Directeur de recher) at the Institut Nicod, CNRS in Paris: www.institutnicod.org/. Her main areas of interest are social epistemology, philosophy of social science, and web studies. She is author of *La Réputation* (2015), due to be published in English translation as *Reputation* (2017).

*Notes on contributors*

**Andreas Pantazatos** is Teaching Fellow in Philosophy at Durham University and has research interests in the ethics of cultural heritage, philosophy of archaeology, and business ethics. He is co-editor of *Cultural Heritage, Ethics, and Contemporary Migrations* (2016).

**Andrea J. Pitts** is Assistant Professor of Philosophy at the University of North Carolina at Charlotte. Her research interests include social epistemology, philosophy of race and gender, and Latin American philosophy. Her website is https://uncc.academia.edu/AndreaPitts

**Jennifer Saul** is Professor of Philosophy at the University of Sheffield. She directed the Leverhulme Implicit Bias and Philosophy Network 2011–2013, and she co-edited (with Michael Brownstein) *Implicit Bias and Philosophy* (Volumes 1 and 2, 2016).

**Anastasia (Tasia) Philippa Scrutton** is Associate Professor in Philosophy of Religion at the University of Leeds. Her research interests include philosophy of religion, emotion, and psychiatry, sometimes individually and sometimes in combination. Her website is www.leeds.ac.uk/arts/profile/20042/958/anastasia_philippa_scrutton_

**Alexis Shotwell** is Associate Professor at Carleton University, on unsurrendered Algonquin territory. Her academic work addresses impurity, environmental justice, racial formation, disability, unspeakable and unspoken knowledge, sexuality, gender, and political transformation. Website: alexisshotwell.com

**Lorenzo C. Simpson**, Professor of Philosophy at Stony Brook University, has published in the areas of hermeneutics, Critical Theory, philosophy of science, African American philosophy, and musical aesthetics. He is completing a book entitled *Towards a Critical Hermeneutics: Interpretive Interventions in Science, Politics, Race and Culture*.

**Michael Sullivan** is Associate Professor of Philosophy at Emory College of Arts and Sciences. He works in ethics, legal theory, critical theory, pragmatism, and social and political philosophy and is author of *Legal Pragmatism* (2007).

**Shannon Sullivan** is Professor and Chair of Philosophy at UNC Charlotte. Her most recent books include *Good White People: The Problem with Middle-Class White Anti-Racism* (2014) and *The Physiology of Sexist and Racist Oppression* (2015).

**Shelley Tremain** has a PhD in philosophy and specializes in philosophy of disability, feminist philosophy, and Foucault. She has published widely on ableism in philosophy, disability and Foucault, and disability and bioethics. She is the editor of *Foucault and the Government of Disability* (2015).

**Rebecca Tsosie** is a Regent's Professor at the James E. Rogers College of Law at the University of Arizona, and previously a Regent's Professor of Law and Vice Provost at Arizona State University. Her work focuses on the rights of Indigenous peoples under U.S. domestic law and international human rights law.

**Nancy Tuana** is DuPont/Class of 1949 Professor of Philosophy and Women's Studies at Penn State University and founding Director of the Rock Ethics Institute. Her research interests include feminist philosophy and theory and coupled epistemic-ethical issues in scientific practice, with particular emphasis on climate science. Her website is: http://philosophy.la.psu.edu/directory/nat3

**Jeremy Wanderer** is Associate Professor of Philosophy at the University of Massachusetts, Boston. He is the author of *Robert Brandom* (2008) and co-editor of *Reading Brandom: On Making It Explicit* (2010). His website is https://um-boston.academia.edu/JeremyWanderer

# ACKNOWLEDGEMENTS

The editors offer their thanks to the contributors for their support and patience. Ian James Kidd's research was supported by an Addison Wheeler Fellowship. B. Rosen kindly gave permission to use 'Listen' for the cover. We also thank Adam Johnson for first proposing this volume and to the team at Routledge for their work in bringing it to press.

# INTRODUCTION TO *THE ROUTLEDGE HANDBOOK OF EPISTEMIC INJUSTICE*

*Ian James Kidd, José Medina, and Gaile Pohlhaus, Jr.*

Since the first three chapters of the volume (authored by Gaile Pohlhaus, Jr., Jeremy Wanderer, and José Medina) survey the varieties of epistemic injustice (especially in their testimonial and hermeneutical variants, although not exclusively), we will devote this introduction to elucidating the significance of epistemic injustice issues and clarifying the structure of the volume and its contents.

In the era of information and communication, issues of misinformation and miscommunication are more pressing than ever. Who has voice and who doesn't? Are voices interacting with equal agency and power? In whose terms are they communicating? Who is being understood and who isn't (and at what cost)? Who is being believed? And who is even being acknowledged and engaged with? *Epistemic injustice* refers to those forms of unfair treatment that relate to issues of knowledge, understanding, and participation in communicative practices. These issues include a wide range of topics concerning wrongful treatment and unjust structures in meaning-making and knowledge producing practices, such as the following: exclusion and silencing; invisibility and inaudibility (or distorted presence or representation); having one's meanings or contributions systematically distorted, misheard, or misrepresented; having diminished status or standing in communicative practices; unfair differentials in authority and/or epistemic agency; being unfairly distrusted; receiving no or minimal uptake; being coopted or instrumentalized; being marginalized as a result of dysfunctional dynamics; etc.

The topic of epistemic injustice is a very rich one, in at least three ways. The first is that it brings together, often in innovative ways, many topics, debates, and traditions in philosophy. These include issues concerning authority, credibility, justice, power, trust, and testimony as explored within areas like ethics, epistemology, political philosophy, and philosophy of language (and sometimes within related areas such as philosophy of science, philosophy of mind, and aesthetics). The distinctively ethico-epistemic and socio-epistemic framing of those issues as provided by epistemic injustice resonates, in turn, with many deep themes that run through major philosophical traditions, such as pragmatism, phenomenology, and critical theory. The second is that epistemic injustice, as both a phenomenon and a topic of study, obviously connects to and interpenetrates with major social and intellectual movements, such as feminism, hermeneutics, critical race theory, disability studies, and decolonialising, queer, and trans epistemologies. The third source of richness for epistemic injustice lies in the fact of its status as a pervasive feature of our social and professional lives – where issues of authority, credibility, and testimony take on distinctive forms. Much of the emerging interest in epistemic injustice comes from theoreticians and practitioners in different professional fields, areas of study, and areas of social interaction where problems of epistemic injustice take distinctive shapes.

Here is a quick overview of the five sections in which the volume is divided, followed by a fuller description of each section. In **Part I: Core concepts**, the volume begins with essays that lay out and clarify the central concepts used in the growing field of epistemic injustice. In **Part II: Liberatory epistemologies and axes of oppression,** authors explore the rich traditions and bodies of literature that have discussed epistemic injustices and offered critical tools to resist them. These are liberatory epistemological frameworks that were developed to denounce and resist the epistemic side of oppression even before the contemporary vocabulary of epistemic injustice was available. **Part III: Schools of thought and subfields within epistemology** elucidates the conceptual resources available in some schools of thought and identifies the critical tools available in some subfields of epistemology that can prove particularly fruitful for discussions of epistemic injustice. **Part IV: Socio-political, ethical, and psychological dimensions of knowing** uses concepts from psychology, social philosophy, ethics, and political philosophy to elucidate the nature and various dimensions of epistemic injustice. **Part V: Case studies of epistemic injustice** examines particular domains, identifying distinct sorts of epistemic injustices that arise within them.

**Part I: Core concepts** offers tools to navigate the rich and broad debates on issues of epistemic injustice that have taken place in various fields – in epistemology, ethics, and political philosophy, but also in related fields in philosophy and outside philosophy. The first three chapters look retrospectively at the different ways in which issues of epistemic injustice have been debated in recent years after the publication of Miranda Fricker's 2007 book, but also prior to that in the long-held discussions of the epistemic aspects of oppression and marginalization in feminist, critical race, and decolonial philosophies (more on this in Part II: Liberatory epistemologies and axes of oppression). Gaile Pohlhaus, Jr. offers four different lenses for examining the varieties of epistemic injustice and relations among epistemic injustices. Because our knowledge practices, including those that map concepts, orient epistemic attention simultaneously toward some and away from other aspects of the world, she cautions against using only one lens (or even one set of lenses) for thinking about epistemic injustices.

Jeremy Wanderer's and José Medina's chapters critically review different conceptions of two of the most prominent kinds of epistemic injustice: testimonial and hermeneutical injustice. Wanderer examines different kinds of testimonial injustices ("transactional" and "structural"), and he distinguishes them from a different kind of normative failure in testimonial dynamics in "thick" relations, what he terms "*testimonial betrayal*". Medina critically reviews the different ways of thinking and categorizing varieties of hermeneutical injustice, offering an argument for having a pluralistic approach to this concept (which calls for an open-ended list of possible classifications rather than a closed and definitive list). He also calls attention to an extreme form of hermeneutical injustice, which he terms "*hermeneutical death*". In her essay in this section, Miranda Fricker discusses evolving notions of epistemic injustice, looking not only retrospectively at her own work and the debates it has sparked, but also prospectively to future work ahead. Drawing a contrast with cases of conscious manipulation and deliberate distortion or silencing, Fricker offers an argument for restricting the notion of (what she is now labelling) "discriminatory epistemic injustice" to unfair treatments in epistemic practices that are produced unintentionally although not always non-culpably. She calls attention to issues of powerlessness that are involved in discriminatory epistemic injustice, and she emphasizes that these issues demand that our philosophical analyses of epistemic practices become more socially alive and engaged. In this respect, she calls particular attention to the pressing research needed on discriminatory epistemic injustice in "new terrains of social experience", such as in the domain of physical and mental health care in which the paradigm of discriminatory epistemic injustice can shed light on the epistemic dysfunctions that arise in doctor-patient communicative interactions (more on this in Section V: Case studies of epistemic injustice). As Fricker acknowledges in her essay, her notion of "discriminatory epistemic injustice" leaves plenty of conceptual space for other notions of epistemic injustice, such as that of "distributive epistemic injustice" coined by David Coady. Coady's chapter – "Epistemic injustice as distributive injustice" – challenges Fricker's distinction between discriminatory and distributive epistemic injustice, arguing that both testimonial and hermeneutical injustices can be conceived as forms of distributive injustice and that, by treating them as such, considerable insight can be gained into the nature of these injustices and into their interrelations.

Going beyond the specific varieties and dimensions of the wide array of phenomena that can be described as epistemic injustices, the next four chapters in Part I elucidate fundamental concepts that appear in the diagnoses and analyses of and in the work of resistance against epistemic injustices: trust and distrust, kinds of knowledge and epistemic resources, epistemic responsibility, and ideology.

Katherine Hawley analyzes the roles played in epistemic injustices by the notions of trust and distrust (by contrast to the notion of reliance) and by the related notions of trustworthiness and untrustworthiness. According to Hawley's analysis, different ways of trusting and distrusting are different ways of exercising social (or socio-epistemic) power, and she clarifies how those exercises can lead to epistemic injustices in testimony and in action. In "Forms of Knowing and Epistemic Resources", Alexis Shotwell elucidates the importance of the distinctions between knowing-that and knowing-how, and between propositional and non-propositional knowledge, to settle disputes about knowledge and understanding. She argues that privileging one kind of knowledge as the only form of knowing worth considering is itself a form of epistemic injustice, for it leads to the marginalization and neglect of epistemic resources that can help oppressed subjects craft more just worlds. More specifically, Shotwell argues that the work of redressing epistemic injustice can benefit from attention to the epistemic resources involved in implicit understanding and knowing. In the next chapter, "Epistemic responsibility", Lorraine Code takes a retrospective look at the genesis and evolution of the notion of epistemic responsible agency in her own pioneering work and in the debates around this notion in the last three decades. Code critically examines the philosophical obstacles posed to the formulation, development, and uptake of this notion by certain philosophical assumptions and views (in particular, *individualism*). Code argues for situating discussions of epistemic responsibility within particular *epistemic imaginaries*, drawing inspiration from Michèle Le Dœuff and Cornelius Castoriadis, and basing her argument on the claim that "there is no intellectual activity that is not grounded in an imaginary". Finally, Part I concludes with Charles W. Mills' examination of the concept of ideology and the key role it can play in the diagnosis, analysis, and treatment of epistemic injustices. Mills first identifies the ways in which recent discussions of epistemic injustices in feminist epistemology and standpoint theory are indebted to the concept of ideology in Marxist and Post-Marxist theories and their claims about distorted perspectives on social reality. In the second place, Mills analyzes racism as a form of ideology. Following Tommie Shelby in expanding the scope of "ideology" to include "forms of consciousness" (and not just formalized intellectual systems), he calls attention to how anti-black racist ideology works in different ways through moral legitimation, social reification, and metaphysical mystification. Mills underscores the implications of these ideological mechanisms for epistemic injustices in testimonial dynamics and in the hermeneutical resources available to and circulating across different racialized publics.

**Part II: Liberatory epistemologies and axes of oppression** contains chapters that investigate how discussions of epistemic injustices emerge from and can be further enriched by major social and intellectual movements of liberation, such as feminism, critical philosophy of race, indigenous and decolonial movements and theories, disability studies, and queer and trans epistemologies.

The section opens with a chapter on *intersectionality* by Patricia Hill Collins, where the author elucidates the contours of intersectionality as the project of connecting resistant knowledges and using these connections, both in theory and in praxis, to navigate, survive, and subvert heterogeneous social contexts of multiple oppressions. Focusing on Black feminism, Hill Collins emphasizes that intersectional analyses and proposals cross political, social, and epistemological borders, and that this border-crossing is multi-directional and not reducible to a one-way traffic, either from social movements into the academy or vice versa. Offering an analysis of "epistemic violence within intersectionality", Hill Collins issues some critical warnings for the future of the paradigm of intersectionality and echoes academics and activists who have recently expressed reservations about the ways in which intersectionality has become misrecognized, rigidified, impoverished, and misappropriated within the academy, resulting in the deterioration or neutralization of its emancipatory possibilities.

In the next chapter, Nancy Tuana brings to the fore the emancipatory possibilities within feminist epistemologies and the critical tools and resources that these epistemologies have to offer for discussions of epistemic injustice. Tuana analyzes how feminist epistemologists have called into question "the subject of knowledge" in a variety of fields and topics (from philosophy, science, and technology to popular culture, from the domain of domesticity to that of public life and policy-making, from the study of sexuality to the study of climate change or the global economy, etc.). As Tuana emphasizes, feminist critical questioning of "the subject of knowledge" accomplishes two things simultaneously: first, it calls critical attention to how dominant interests and values set the epistemic agendas and heavily influence what (and in what way) something counts as a proper "subject" of discussion and investigation, and secondly, it calls critical attention to what kind of subject one must be in order to be (seen as) a knowing subject. In her analysis Tuana underscores the emancipatory potential of feminist (and other liberatory) epistemological approaches that are informed by multifaceted ways of critically questioning "the subject of knowledge" along multiple axes of oppression, paying attention to the interactions among gender, sexuality, ability/disability, race, ethnicity, class, nationality, religion, etc.

Focusing on the epistemic side of racial oppression and the fight against it, in the next chapter of Part II, Luvell Anderson puts to use the critical and analytic tools that we find in the fields of philosophy of race, speech act theory, and the literature on epistemic injustice to shed light on contemporary discussions around *post-racial* ideals. Anderson argues that the pursuit of post-racial ideals (in their assimilationist, eliminativist, or colorblind varieties) produces hermeneutical injustices by "illocutionarily flipping" or by silencing the utterances of members of marginalized racial groups and he illustrates his argument brilliantly by analyzing the ways in which the slogan "Black Lives Matter" is neutralized and disarmed by post-racial sensibilities. In "Decolonial praxis and epistemic injustice", Andrea J. Pitts examines how (what Walter Mignolo refers to as) the global *geopolitics of knowledge* produces, hides, and protects epistemic injustices from resistant knowledge practices. As Pitts' analysis underscores, decolonial thought and praxis critically unveil the production and dissemination of knowledge (implicating universities, academic presses, research institutes, and a wide range of networks and agencies involved in "intellectual production") within the material context of colonialism, imperialism, and capitalism. Acknowledging different threads of decolonial thought and praxis, Pitts' chapter focuses on discussions among Latin American, U.S. Latina, and Caribbean decolonial theorists, linking these critical discourses with the growing body of literature on epistemic injustice to address the following problem: "how to produce disciplinary discourses from Anglophone North American academic institutions on the topic of a *decolonial* geopolitics of knowledge without perpetuating an Occidentalism and 'othering' of communities whose existences require a perpetual struggle against neoliberal economic expansion and epistemic hegemony".

Focusing on sexual and gender oppression, the next two chapters by Kim Q. Hall and Rachel McKinnon connect queer and trans epistemology with discussions of epistemic injustice. Exploring queer theory's influential claim that "sexuality delineates an epistemic rather than a primarily erotic space in western contexts", Hall's chapter elucidates the ways in which queer epistemology explains the production of testimonial and hermeneutical injustices in the domain of sexuality. Hall underscores that queer epistemology identifies different forms of sexual testimonial and hermeneutical injustices, which include the sexual silencing of those deemed deviant, but also the epistemic violence of compulsory testimony about one's sexuality and gender – i.e. being forced to "come out" and to speak in a particular way about one's gender and sexuality. Using the critical tools of queer epistemology, Hall analyzes "a fraught epistemic terrain in which the epistemic authority of sexually minoritized people is contested", and she elucidates the testimonial and hermeneutical mistreatments that result from being forced to understand oneself as a certain kind of person because of one's desires, embodiment, and actions. Hall's chapter discusses the meaning and significance of queer epistemology for issues of epistemic injustice in connection with four themes: (1) sexuality as a problem for truth, (2) queer epistemology and self-knowledge, (3) queer epistemologies and standpoint, and (4) queer and crip epistemologies. Next, in "Allies behaving badly", Rachel McKinnon analyzes the phenomenon of *gaslighting* – that is, the phenomenon of systematically discounting another's experiences or concerns as having a basis in reality – as a form of testimonial injustice. More specifically, McKinnon considers cases of well-meaning cisgender subjects who, while acting as an "ally" to a trans★ subject, may nonetheless minimize the experiences and concerns of the trans★ subject as having little or no significance or as meaning something quite different from what the trans★ subject claims. McKinnon identifies problems with "ally culture" and how, far from helping mitigate epistemic injustices, an "ally culture" can contribute to their perpetuation. She argues that, instead of working on becoming "a good ally", we should focus our efforts on becoming "active bystanders".

Finally, in 'Knowing disability, differently', Shelley Tremain concludes Part II with a discussion of the failure of feminist epistemologists and theorists of epistemic injustice to incorporate a critical understanding of "the *apparatus* of disability" into their philosophical analyses. This failure, Tremain argues, constitutes an epistemic injustice that, among other things, seriously distorts our understanding of such concepts as identity, oppression, privilege, and even epistemic injustice itself. To make her argument, Tremain examines gaps and oversights in discussions of hermeneutical and testimonial injustice such as those contained in Fricker's notion of "epistemic bad luck" and in the absolute failure to reflect upon disability in one of the cases that has received much discussion in the literature, that of Tom Robinson in Harper Lee's *To Kill a Mockingbird*. Analyzing this case with attention to the apparatus of disability in conjunction with those of race, gender, and sexuality, Tremain demonstrates the critical importance of robustly intersectional approaches to epistemic injustice.

**Part III: Schools of thought and subfields within epistemology** examine particular philosophical approaches that are resourceful for thinking about epistemic injustice. The chapters by Amy Allen, Lisa Guenther, and Shannon Sullivan demonstrate the ways in which specific figures and schools of thought greatly enhance our understanding of epistemic injustice. In the opening chapter to this section, Amy Allen argues that Foucault's work is indispensable for analyzing reason's entanglements with power. Specifically, she identifies three areas of Foucault's work that complicate and enrich our understanding of epistemic injustices: his theorization of distinct forms of power (constitutive and agential), his analysis of power/knowledge or the political economies of truth, and his genealogical method as resistance to regimes of truth through counter-memory. Given the degree to which Foucault examined and offered ways of resisting reason's entanglements in power, Allen notes that it is surprising that his work is not used more often within current discussions of epistemic injustice. In the second chapter to this section, Lisa Guenther contrasts Fricker's colloquial use of "phenomenological" as a description of first person experience to the phenomenological method first developed by Edmund Husserl and later advanced by such figures as Maurice Merleau-Ponty and Frantz Fanon. Guenther argues that there are gaps in the literature on epistemic injustice that can be filled through the use of specific insights from the phenomenological tradition and contemporary critical phenomenologists, for example through phenomenology's attention to consciousness as relational, its rich account of the embodied dimensions of social cognition, and (particularly within the critical form Guenther advocates) its emphasis on not only reflecting upon the structures of experience but also collectively transforming them. Drawing on the pragmatist tradition, and the work of John Dewey in particular, Shannon Sullivan considers what a transactional epistemology would bring to conversations about epistemic injustice. By transactional she means an epistemology that recognizes knowing as an "activity undertaken by a bodily organism-in-the-world who helps shape what is known". Utilizing such an approach, she argues, greatly enhances our understanding of the harms of epistemic injustice.

The chapters by Sanford Goldberg and Heather Battaly situate the notion of epistemic injustice and the concerns it raises within particular subfields of epistemology, demonstrating how these subfields are enhanced through discussions of epistemic injustice and identifying features of these subfields that are helpful for thinking about epistemic injustice. Sanford Goldberg considers epistemic injustice in light of social epistemology, understood as "the systematic investigation into the *epistemic significance of other minds*". Such an epistemology, he notes, will consider not only various forms of epistemic dependence, but also the norms that underwrite our epistemic expectations of others and the epistemic assessments implied when beliefs are socially acquired. Within this framework, Goldberg identifies three ways in which social epistemic practices can function illegitimately, leading to epistemic injustice: through unjust exclusions from epistemic practices, when a practice itself contains a normative expectation that treats people unfairly, and when a practice is structured or directed in such a way that treats people unfairly. Examining the subfield of virtue epistemology and the growing subfield of vice-epistemology, Heather Battaly distinguishes among three ways in which epistemic vice can be understood as a bad cognitive disposition: (1) as a disposition that results in bad epistemic effects (effects-vice), (2) as a bad cognitive character trait for which an epistemic agent is responsible (responsibilist-vice), and (3) as a bad cognitive character trait that is not necessarily under the epistemic agent's control (personalist-vice). She argues that testimonial injustice can take the form of either an effects-vice or a personalist-vice, even when it falls short of responsibilist-vice.

**Part IV: Socio-political, ethical, and psychological dimensions of knowing** contains chapters that analyze epistemic injustice through a variety of perspectives that focus on different dimensions of knowing. The first two chapters examine what might be considered non-epistemic concepts in relation to epistemic injustice. In the first chapter, Jennifer Saul analyzes the psychological concepts of implicit bias and stereotype threat, which at first glance might appear simply to be instances of epistemic injustice. However, Saul argues that there are important distinctions to be recognized between these concepts and the concept of epistemic injustice. Her chapter outlines the convergences and divergences between implicit bias and stereotype threat on the one hand and testimonial and hermeneutical injustice on the other hand. Matthew

Congdon utilizes the tools of normative ethics and critical theory to address the question: what is wrong with epistemic injustice? While noting ways in which consequentialist, Kantian, and virtue approaches certainly enrich our understanding of the wrong of epistemic injustice, ultimately Congdon argues that we ought to understand this wrong utilizing Hegelian recognition theory of the sort found in the work of Axel Honneth. Taking this approach in the latter part of his chapter, Congdon develops the notions of epistemic love, epistemic respect, and epistemic esteem as well as epistemic neglect, epistemic disrespect, and epistemic disesteem.

The third and fourth chapters in Part IV take up the relationship between a political concept and its epistemic counterpart. Lorenzo C. Simpson utilizes a hermeneutical approach to consider the complexities of agency, drawing a distinction between first-order agency, or the ability to implement action, and second-order agency, or the ability to identify and access the conditions that facilitate first order agency. This distinction disaggregates the volitional and epistemic dimensions of agency, which, Simpson argues, helps us to understand and identify particular sorts of epistemic injustice. Simpson's analysis further reveals that in order to understand and address certain forms of political injustice, we must engage a hermeneutical investigation under a constraint he calls "narrative representability" such that we ask "how do things appear from the first person perspective from which these choices were made?" Susan E. Babbitt uses Cuban political philosophy and history to investigate the nature of and relationship between epistemic and political freedom. In particular, she notes that understanding the nature of ideas is critical for political freedom; that epistemic freedom is constituted socially, materially, and through action; that as such epistemic freedom requires more than reason; and that consequently epistemic freedom is undermined when epistemic injustice is named and analyzed without transforming the conditions that explain it. Babbitt's analysis suggests that epistemic injustices committed against other cultures and epistemic resources (such as Latin-American philosophy) obscure and impoverish the concept of "epistemic injustice" as understood and deployed in Western academic contexts.

In the final two chapters, Nancy Arden McHugh and Sally Haslanger examine the notions of epistemic community and epistemic objectivity respectively in conjunction with epistemic injustice. In her chapter, Nancy Arden McHugh analyzes debates concerning the locus of knowledge in either the individual epistemic agent or epistemic communities, arguing that attention to epistemological communities of resistance gives us a more robust understanding of epistemic injustice. She closes her chapter with an examination of one such community, a prison writing group with which she developed an epistemology of incarceration. In the final chapter to this section, Sally Haslanger examines the notion of epistemic objectivity and its relation to epistemic objectification, and oppression. Haslanger argues that certain models of objectivity support what she calls *status quo* reasoning, which both enables epistemic injustices and is an epistemic tool of oppression. Her analysis reveals three distinct forms of objectification that qualify as epistemic injustices: ideological, projective, and Kantian. Furthermore, Haslanger identifies a focus on individual as opposed to structural explanations and a bias toward stability as culprits that facilitate epistemically unjust forms of objectification, marginalization, and their use as epistemic tools of oppression through *status quo* reasoning.

**Section V: Case studies of epistemic injustice** explores forms of epistemic injustice that can emerge and manifest within specific professional, disciplinary, and social domains. The assumption is that epistemic concepts and practices take distinctive forms within such domains that complicate and variegate the forms of epistemic injustice that can occur within them.

Michael Sullivan explores the ways that epistemic injustice can occur within legal systems and practices, which, after all, ideally aim at truth as well as justice. Since testimony, credibility, and a capacity to make sense of other's social experiences *matters* so much in legal cases, Sullivan identifies four ways to combat epistemic injustice in trials that invoke practical reform, diversification of juries and judges, and greater collection and disclosure of evidence. Gloria Origgi and Serena Ciranna propose that the transformations of our epistemic lives by digital technologies can both exacerbate existing forms of epistemic injustice and also generate new and distinctive ones. Indeed, these new forms may be more centrally epistemic than others, since they pertain to our very epistemic capacities, by challenging guiding assumptions about confidence, credibility, and epistemic authority and agency.

Heidi Grasswick's chapter examines epistemic injustice within the institutions and practices of one of our most powerful forms of knowledge production: science. Drawing on the history, sociology, and philosophy of science, Grasswick identifies two broad categories of epistemic injustice within this domain: participatory epistemic injustices, or those that systematically marginalize and unfairly exclude particular knowers from contributing to collective scientific pursuits, and epistemic trust injustices, or those that unjustly alienate particular groups of knowers from scientific institutions so that they cannot reasonably rely upon those institutions in the ways that others can. Ben Kotzee explores the many points of contact between epistemic injustice and educational institutions, practices, and ideals, including the ways that unfairness or bias can affect the credibility teachers assign to students qua developing epistemic agents, whose social experiences are selected for inclusion in curricula, and important political questions about policies promoting epistemic and social diversity in classrooms.

The relation of epistemic injustice to medicine, healthcare, and illness is the theme of chapters 32 and 33. Havi Carel and Ian James Kidd argue that many ill persons are often vulnerable to epistemic injustices due to negative stereotyping and structural features of healthcare systems. An omnipresent feature of critical discourse about "modern medicine" are reports of feeling "silenced", "ignored", and "not listened to", all of which are apt for analysis in terms of epistemic injustice and resonate with recent developments in the philosophy of healthcare and the phenomenology of illness. Continuing this theme, Anastasia Scrutton investigates epistemic injustices in the context of psychiatric diagnosis and treatment, which can occur through both credibility-deflating stereotypes and the entrenched focus on medical perspectives on experiences of mental illness. Such injustices can be counteracted by recognition of the distinctive forms of epistemic privilege that a person with a mental illness might possess, and the ways this recognition can enhance clinical practice in more epistemically just ways.

Chapters 34 and 35 consider epistemic injustices in the context of morally, politically, and epistemically charged interactions between cultures. Rebecca Tsosie places the concept of epistemic injustice into the complex interplay of law and ethics in the context of anthropology as it pertains to the historic and ongoing harms suffered by Indigenous peoples. The legacies of colonialist and imperialist history continue to disadvantage those peoples in a variety of ways, many of which have overt epistemic aspects – for instance, by privileging the social and epistemic practices of academic and scientific disciplines whose conceptions of testimonial credibility and hermeneutical resources are often insensitive or hostile to the values, sensibilities, and interests of Indigenous peoples. Andreas Pantazatos focuses on epistemic injustices and cultural heritage. The tangible and intangible heritage of a culture – including objects, sites, biological remains, music, literature, and so on – are richly epistemic: testimonies from the past, perhaps from one's ancestors, preserving and transmitting experiences, events, values, and "forms of life" and shared ways of making sense of them. But for these reasons, heritage is complexly contested by ethicists, scientists, cultural resource managers, museums and other institutions, political leaders, and aboriginal communities. Pantazatos identifies a specific form of *participant perspective epistemic injustice*, that occurs when the authoritative institutions constitutive of modern heritage management are charged with failing to select, preserve, interpret, present, transmit, or otherwise control (aspects of) cultural heritage in ways that fail to properly include the perspectives of those whose heritage it is. Pantazatos argues that this generates a complexly layered epistemic injustice – one affecting whole cultures, rather than individuals or groups.

Ian James Kidd describes a variety of ways that religious persons and traditions can be both perpetrators and victims of epistemic injustices, including in "generic" and religiously inflected forms. Religious communities and traditions can perpetrate epistemic injustices by depriving certain groups of credibility and hermeneutical authority, which is a latent theme within feminist, liberation, and queer theologies. But religious persons and groups can also be victims of epistemic injustices, if, as some critics argue, the prevailing sensibilities of late modern societies tend to deny credibility and intelligibility to religious testimonies and experiences. In the final chapter of the volume, Linda Martín Alcoff argues that modern European philosophies themselves emerged from, and continue to perpetuate, epistemic injustices against non-European societies. Those philosophies often evince a form of "Eurocentrism" that reflects a "transcendental delusion", a conviction that thought is separable from its spatially and culturally specific sources, such that social and historical considerations can be safely neglected. Unfortunately, the sociohistorical contexts of the European philosophical traditions, and the wider cultures in which they are embedded, were and are rife with epistemic injustices, many of which have affected philosophizing. Epistemic justice might therefore require not just closer engagement with philosophical traditions and ideas from the wider non-European worlds, but also a difficult form of self-critical reflexivity – a task informed by feminist, postcolonial, decolonial, and critical race theories that might offer not only pluralism and perspective, but also epistemic justice.

# PART 1

# Core concepts

# 1
# VARIETIES OF EPISTEMIC INJUSTICE[1]

*Gaile Pohlhaus, Jr.*

The idea of "epistemic injustice" draws together three branches of philosophy – political philosophy, ethics, and epistemology – to consider how epistemic practices and institutions may be deployed and structured in ways that are simultaneously infelicitous toward certain epistemic values (such as truth, aptness, and understanding) and unjust with regard to particular knowers.[2] Examining the ethics and politics of knowledge practices is, of course, not new; for example, feminist, critical race, and decolonial philosophers have done so for quite some time (Anderson 2017; Babbitt 2017; Collins 2017; Pitts 2017; Tuana 2017). As Patricia Hill Collins notes, where there is oppression, there is also resistance to oppression (1991: 12–13, 2000: 22). Likewise, where there has been epistemic injustice there has also been resistance to epistemic injustice. One form of this resistance has been the explicit identification and analysis of epistemic injustices offered by those experiencing them. For example, as Vivian May notes, Anna Julia Cooper, writing in 1892, highlighted the suppression of Black women's ideas through epistemic violence and interpretive silencing (May 2014: 97). Sojourner Truth, speaking in 1867, highlighted the denial of Black women as knowers via asymmetries in cognitive authority and via men's habitually constrained imaginations (May 2014: 98). Gayatri Chakravorty Spivak, writing within a (post-)colonial context, identifies what she calls 'epistemic violence' in claims to know the interests of subaltern persons that preclude the subaltern from formulating knowledge claims concerning their interests and speaking for themselves (Spivak 1988). These examples are part of a broader history of epistemic resistance through identifying and calling attention to ways in which knowers have been wronged in their capacities as knowers.

Importantly, there is often an implicit sense that these kinds of wrongs are perpetuated from within epistemic practices or are the result of how epistemic institutions are structured. Epistemic injustices can therefore be understood as epistemic in at least three senses. First, they wrong particular knowers *as* knowers, for example by suppressing a knower's testimony (Dotson 2011) or by making it difficult for particular knowers to know what it is in their interest to know (Fricker 2007: 147–175). Second, they cause epistemic dysfunction, for example by distorting understanding or stymieing inquiry. Third, they accomplish the aforementioned two harms from within, and sometimes through the use of, our epistemic practices and institutions, for example, when school curricula and academic disciplines are structured in ways that systematically ignore, distort, and/or discredit particular intellectual traditions (Minnich 1990; Mohanty 2004; Outlaw

2007). Consequently, an epistemic injustice not only wrongs a knower as a knower, but also is a wrong that a knower perpetrates *as* a knower and that an epistemic institution causes *in its capacity as* an epistemic institution.

Given that epistemic injustices are something that occur within the activities and institutions knowers engage in order to know, and given that a chapter that seeks to convey knowledge concerning the varieties of epistemic injustice does, by definition, engage in epistemic activity, we would do well to consider at the outset the ways in which this essay might itself participate in and perpetuate epistemic injustice. With this concern in mind, I will begin by first considering some specific ways in which a chapter on the varieties of epistemic injustice might perpetuate or contribute to epistemic injustice. In doing so, I provide an argument for why I will *not* offer readers an exhaustive list of the varieties of epistemic injustice nor prescribe a definitive set of categories with which to classify them, but rather provide some initial examples of epistemic injustices so that readers may begin to understand the *grammar* of the term 'epistemic injustice' for future and new uses. I will then sketch four (although not the only) lenses with which to think about varieties of epistemic injustice. I do so with the aim of giving readers a sense of some ways epistemic injustices can take shape without foreclosing the possibility of thinking about epistemic injustices along other trajectories, and especially along trajectories that may be more readily noticed by those who are differently located than I am.

## On the dangers of defining the field of epistemic injustice

In her essay, "A Cautionary Tale," Kristie Dotson warns that "when addressing and identifying forms of epistemic oppression one needs to endeavor not to perpetuate epistemic oppression" (2012a: 24). For Dotson, epistemic oppression occurs when exclusions produce deficiencies in social knowledge that unjustly infringe upon particular knowers' "ability to utilize persuasively shared epistemic resources within a given epistemic community in order to participate in knowledge production and, if required, the revision of those same resources" (2012a: 24). In other words, epistemic oppression occurs when particular knowers are precluded from making an impact, not just *with* shared epistemic resources, but also *on* shared epistemic resources. The danger of perpetuating epistemic oppression in this manner seems significant in a discipline that seeks to define concepts of concern to all knowers (such as "truth," "knowledge," and "reality"), but is oriented by a *culture of justification*. Following the work of Gayle Salamon, Dotson defines a culture of justification as one that "requires the practice of making congruent one's own ideas . . . with some 'traditional' conception of philosophical engagement" (2012b: 6), and argues that this kind of culture is pervasive in philosophy. To this I would add that while one is encouraged in philosophy to make one's own ideas congruent with those that have already dominated the field, the "best" kind of philosophy is often defined as establishing and preserving norms to which others must now make themselves congruent, where those persons regarded as capable of establishing norms worth preserving have historically been dominantly situated (Cherry and Schwitzgebel 2016).[3] As Amy Olberding points out, this dynamic, as it is embedded in philosophical institutions, puts non-dominant philosophers and non-dominant philosophical traditions in a double-bind: if their philosophical contributions conform to what is already established, they appear to be an unnecessary addition to philosophy as typically conceived, but if they do not conform to what is already established, they are deemed un- or less than philosophical (Olberding 2015: 14–15). Either scenario frames European and Euro-American philosophical traditions as wholly representative of experienced reality toward which all other experiences of reality must bend – surely a kind of epistemic injustice insofar as it simultaneously hierarchizes without warrant what is epistemically significant or worthy of epistemic attention (i.e. the world as experienced by this particular set of knowers and not another) and who counts as an ideal epistemic agent (i.e. those who experience the world in this particular way, not another).[4]

With these initial cautions in mind, there are at least two dangers I should like to avoid in introducing the reader to particular varieties of epistemic injustice. First is the danger of participating in what Kristie Dotson calls a "rhetoric of beginnings" (2014b: 3). The second danger is of generating what David Owen calls "aspectival captivity" (2003: 88). These two dangers, which I will explain below, are related insofar as engaging a rhetoric of beginnings is one way of generating aspectival captivity. Nonetheless, it is not the only way. Both dangers carry the risk of wronging particular knowers as well as distorting epistemic activity. Explaining how will help to illustrate some of the ways epistemic injustices can manifest.

In her introduction to the special issue of *Hypatia* on *Interstices: Inheriting Women of Color Feminist Philosophy*, Dotson challenges the notion that the issue represents a beginning or entry of women of color into philosophy, indicating that to frame the intellectual work contained in the volume as a beginning would ignore (and encourage readers to ignore) the history of women of color thought that precedes its publication and upon which authors within the volume draw (Dotson 2014b: 3).[5] Moreover, to frame the issue as an epistemic beginning would treat an historically white epistemic institution (i.e. the journal) as that which confers legitimacy to women of color philosophers, a move that Dotson actively resists in her introduction. A "rhetoric of beginnings" also carries the pitfalls associated with "coinage" discussed by Patricia Hill Collins in this volume. For example, when epistemic practices and resources honed within communities resistant to social oppression move from those communities into institutions that have been shaped to serve the interests of those with social power, they can become distorted and made to serve dominant interests in these distortions (Collins 2017).

The danger of "beginnings," then, is that in offering an account of the varieties of epistemic injustice I might proceed by, or be taken as, offering an "origin" story that represents a "new" development in philosophy beginning to be explored. Proceeding in this manner disrespects and perpetuates harm against particular knowers in ways that can be considered epistemically unjust. First, it perpetuates ignorance regarding the prior existence, as well as the resilience and creativity, of those who have historically experienced and called attention to epistemic injustices, thereby disrespecting whole groups of knowers and encouraging habits of attention that disregard certain knowers as knowers. Second, in failing to acknowledge the epistemic labor that precedes me, I would encourage habits of mind that deflect attention away from the interdependence of knowers, while simultaneously relying upon that interdependence, thereby exploiting the epistemic labor of others to perpetuate the appearance of my own epistemic labor as singular. I can only think and communicate the thoughts I offer here owing to the epistemic labor of those who have worked so hard before me to call attention to injustices in our practices of knowing. Finally, an "origin" story would likely distort understanding of at least some epistemic injustices insofar as it would encourage readers to view all epistemic injustice solely in relation to the account given here, thereby establishing my own account as primary or central. There is a presumption in thinking that the wide range and long history of various groups of marginalized knowers' resistances and protestations concerning epistemic injustices could be captured in one essay or by one sort of person or within one particular frame. Instead, I encourage readers to read this essay alongside the multiple accounts of epistemic injustices offered in the section on liberatory epistemologies with the knowledge that even these accounts are not the final word on the forms that epistemic injustices might take (Anderson 2017; Collins 2017; Hall 2017; McKinnon 2017; Pitts 2017; Tremain 2017; Tuana 2017).

This last concern is connected to the second danger, generating what David Owen calls "aspectival captivity," by which he means the tendency to repress alternate ways of reflecting on a given topic (2003: 85–88). Calling attention to particular epistemic activities and institutions, necessarily downplays and omits others.[6] Doing so, even in the service of identifying particular epistemic injustices, has the potential of fixating attention in ways that might render inconceivable other epistemic injustices as yet unarticulated and best understood by attending to altogether different aspects of epistemic life. For example, if focusing on epistemic injustices that pertain to propositional knowing, I might neglect those that pertain to knowing how (Hawley 2011) and other forms of non-propositional knowing (Shotwell 2011, 2017). Or, if focusing on the acquisition and transfer of knowledge, I might draw attention away from injustices that pertain to other sorts of epistemic activities such as attending, perceiving, questioning, imagining, and acknowledging (Hookway 2010). As Kristie Dotson has argued, one way of navigating these sorts of difficulties is to utilize open conceptual structures "that signify without absolute foreclosure" (Dotson 2012a: 25). Still even adding the proviso, "and there may be other forms, too," leaves the possibility that other forms of epistemic injustice may be misperceived if rendered in the terms established by my own account (Lugones 2003: 68–69), particularly given the homogenizing tendencies often operative when regarding multiple resistances to dominance (Roshanravan 2014: 41–42). Any account of the varieties of epistemic injustices must, therefore, be rendered polyvocally or with what José Medina calls a *kaleidoscopic sensibility* (Medina 2013: 297–308).

This need not, however, lead to an epistemic relativism where an injustice is only an injustice if one cares to envision our epistemic lives one particular way and not another. Attending to these difficulties *does* call attention to the situatedness of the philosopher and to the fact that her accounts will be useful in some ways while not at all useful in others. Even so, the very idea of epistemic injustice entails the notion that knowers can be *harmed* or *wronged* in their capacity as knowers, suggesting that knowers owe and ought to be able to reasonably expect some things from one another insofar as they are knowers. In other words, our epistemic lives are fundamentally intertwined with one another such that one cannot simply ignore other knowers and *know well*. Hence my attempt to avoid establishing a set of definitive categories of epistemic injustice is motivated precisely by a desire to leave my account open to other knowers with the understanding that as finite temporal beings, "we simply do not have the capacity to track all the implications of our positions on any given issue" (Dotson 2012a: 24–25). Whether any given knower engages in epistemic activities (such as knowing, inquiring, imagining, and considering) well is not up for grabs, but rather navigated and evaluated within the thick of our epistemic lives together.

Holding onto both concerns (that we ought to attend to epistemic injustices *and* that we ought not consider any one approach to understanding epistemic injustice as foundational or definitive of all), I instead discuss varieties of epistemic injustice through four possible lenses. Each lens provides a way to distinguish and trace relations among ways that epistemic agents and institutions can simultaneously harm knowers and distort epistemic values. However, these four lenses are not the only way to do so.[7] In addition, it should be noted that some epistemic injustices appear within more than one lens; however the light shed on them will refract differently depending upon the lens with which they are viewed.

## Social contract and coordinated ignorance

One lens with which to think about varieties of epistemic injustice is to consider how persons may be systematically subject to injustice generally speaking and to understand epistemic injustices as intertwined with (and reinforcing) relations of dominance and oppression. Charles Mills' analysis of the nonideal conditions that maintain white supremacy in the United States as a racial contract provides such a lens. In the *Racial Contract*, Mills notes that typically philosophers recognize the moral and political dimensions of social contract theory, but neglect its epistemic dimensions: that signatories and beneficiaries of (real or hypothetical) social contracts not only submit to political institutions and oblige themselves to standards of behavior for mutual benefit, but also bind themselves to epistemic institutions and habituate themselves to standards of epistemic behavior, so as to mutually recognize and maintain the terms of the social contract (Mills 1997: 17–18). With this lens, epistemic injustices take the form of epistemic institutions and cognitive practices that maintain and enforce unjust power relations.

First, just as the racial contract creates two classes, one of persons and the other of sub-persons (Mills 1997: 16–17), so too does it create two epistemic classes, one of (purportedly ideal) knowers, the other of sub-knowers. In other words, the racial contract establishes terms under which white European men are regarded as "generic" prototypical knowers collectively on a progressive path toward knowing the world and deems those it categorizes as non-white as incapable of intellectual achievement and progress (Mills 1997: 44–46). Feminist philosophers have also identified and discussed the manner in which systems of dominance and oppression create two distinct classes of knowers, arguing that patriarchy relies upon and sustains networks of asymmetrical authority that harmfully position women as less than competent knowers (e.g. Code 1991; Collins 1991; Jones 2002; Tuana 2006). Because the feminist literature on these harms often emphasizes the interpersonal aspects of epistemic activity, this same literature will appear in a different light in the next section; whereas I draw attention here to the structural aspects of these relations. Practices and institutions that create and maintain a class of sub-knowers are clear candidates for the label epistemic injustice insofar as they wrong those knowers deemed "sub-knowers" and constitute an epistemic dysfunction in their treatment toward them. A classic example of this form of epistemic injustice within an institution would be laws prohibiting blacks from testifying against whites in a court of law as was upheld by the U.S. Supreme Court in *Blyew vs. U.S.* (1871). A corresponding cognitive practice to this institution would include implicit biases that render certain groups of people less credible than others, i.e. as sub-knowers (Saul 2017). Long-standing practices of this type of epistemic injustice would include the systematic dismissal and ignorance of Black American intellectual traditions as properly philosophical (Outlaw 2007). All of these examples, insofar as they create a class of sub-knowers in the service of oppression, harm and disrespect particular knowers as knowers from within dominantly sanctioned epistemic institutions and practices.

Second, in service of the unjust social contract, the epistemic contract creates what Mills' calls "an inverted world" in which those who have created and benefitted from injustice remain largely ignorant of the unjust arrangements through which they benefit (1997: 18).[8] The creation of a sub-class of knowers goes a long way toward achieving this goal, for one way to remain ignorant of injustice is to disqualify those in a position to call attention to it from doing so. In addition to disqualifying those who suffer from injustice from calling attention to it, under the terms of the racial contract, dominantly situated knowers are encouraged to ignore structural injustices through the cultivation of particular habits that direct their attention away from racial injustice through epistemic vices. For example, those dominantly situated may be encouraged to develop a kind of epistemic arrogance in order to maintain that their experience of the world is generalizable to the entirety of reality, a close-mindedness to the possibility that others may experience the world in ways they cannot, and an epistemic laziness with regard to knowing the world well in light of those oppressed by the racial contract (Medina 2013: 30–40). These vices may manifest in and be supported by what I have called "willful hermeneutical ignorance," or the propensity to dismiss whole aspects of the experienced world by refusing to become proficient in the epistemic resources required for attending to those parts of the world well (Pohlhaus, Jr. 2012). Importantly, this is a matter of not only individual vice, but also epistemic institutions and collective behaviors that enable, encourage, and incentivize particular epistemic vices in groups of individuals. Targeted ignorances are only sustainable when they are collective and supported by the kind of social power dominant institutions confer.

## Interdependence and epistemic relations

While the lens of the racial contract highlights the ways in which knowers can be unjustly treated and harmed by epistemic institutions and practices in a systematic way, it does not highlight the degree to which knowers are intersubjectively constituted. In other words, just as feminist philosophers have noted that social contract theories eclipse the degree to which nurturing relations are necessary in order to become rational agents capable of assenting to a social contract, so too have traditional epistemologies typically neglected to acknowledge the degree to which knowers become knowers in relation to those who raise them and teach them how to know (Code 1993). If care is the relation that binds moral agents, trust is the relation that binds epistemic agents. To the degree that infants trust (and are able to trust) those who nurture and cultivate them into beings capable of engaging mutually relied upon epistemic practices and institutions, they become epistemic agents (Code 1993). Moreover, mutually relied upon institutions and practices are integral to our knowing (Code 2006; McHugh 2017; Nelson 1990, 1993). As Lorraine Code notes, "[e]ven the simplest of observational knowledge claims depend, more than people ordinarily realize, on corroboration and acknowledgment" (1991: 216).

Through this lens, epistemic injustices fall into two broad categories: first, exclusions that keep epistemic agents isolated from one another without warrant and, second, fractures in epistemic trust. Examples of the former include formal and informal refusals to allow certain knowers to participate in various areas of communal epistemic life, such as education, healthcare, politics, and science (Carel and Kidd 2017; Grasswick 2017; Kotzee 2017). Such exclusions wrong the individual knowers excluded and stymie the development of knowledge along particular trajectories. For example, participation in a wide variety of epistemic practices is necessary for developing one's capacities as an epistemic agent (Hookway 2010), such that unfair exclusion from them can impede individual epistemic growth. In addition, epistemic communities from which certain knowers are unfairly excluded lack the beneficial *epistemic friction* that might be provided by their participation (Medina 2013). The need for epistemic friction in such cases will be complicated when considering epistemic injustice through the lens of epistemic labor, bringing this lens in tension with the fourth lens I discuss below.

Epistemic interdependence, while manifest in epistemic communities, is not reducible to them. Consequently, epistemic injustice is not simply remedied by allowing participation in epistemic communities. Where there are serious and systematic breakdowns in trust, epistemic injustice still prevails (Hawley 2017). This can be seen on the individual level, interpersonally, and on the level of institutions. As Karen Jones has argued, proper self-trust is both necessary for knowing the world well and something that is developed interactively with others (Jones 2012: 245). It is therefore something that may be seriously hampered by such things as epistemic gaslighting or the systematic denial by others of an epistemic agent's lived experiences (McKinnon 2017). Moreover, disempowering structures of cognitive authority can make it difficult for those groups disempowered to place their trust wisely (Code 1991: 186); for example, when women are systematically taught to distrust their own instincts and to defer to the cognitive authority of men, it can be difficult not only to develop appropriate self-trust, but also proper trust in others. Finally, this lens brings into focus that even *warranted* distrust may signal a kind of epistemic injustice, for example in institutions that have historically failed particular populations such as the justified mistrust by women in psychiatric authority or by African-Americans in pre-dominantly white medical institutions. In such cases, the problem is not the withholding of trust or improper distrust, but rather the *breach* of trust caused by the institutions, leading to the inability to trust (Carel and Kidd 2017; Grasswick 2017; Hawley 2017; Scrutton 2017). Communities that have historically been harmed in the past by specific epistemic institutions may understandably be less trusting of them and so less able to benefit epistemically from a trusting reliance on them that is available to others for whom there has been no historical breach in trust. In such cases, the breach of trust that leads to a population's inability to trust in communal epistemic institutions constitutes an epistemic trust injustice (Grasswick 2017).

## Degrees of change and/in epistemic systems

While the lenses provided above treat epistemic injustice as inextricable from social and political forms of oppression, Dotson utilizes a degree of change lens to argue that there are distinct forms of epistemic oppression that are not reducible to social and political factors, but rather derive from epistemic systems themselves (2014a: 116). In other words, there are features of our epistemic lives that can hold epistemic injustices in place independently of social and political relations of power. This need not mean epistemic injustices cannot serve or do not very often serve social and political injustice, including those that originate from epistemic systems. Nor does it mean that epistemic injustices that are irreducible to social and political injustices are somehow more worthy of our attention. Rather, it demonstrates the need to refrain from utilizing only one sort of lens when thinking about epistemic injustice. There are legitimate and important reasons for utilizing lenses that *do* focus on epistemic injustices that stem from social and political injustices.[9] However, if these are the *only* approaches we take to epistemic injustice, we may very well miss other sorts of epistemic injustices such as those that can exist solely within the epistemic realm. In addition, Dotson's account provides reason to refigure the field of epistemology insofar as her account brings attention to epistemic injustice as an ongoing contingent possibility, always to be determined in possibly new and unforeseen ways within any given social historical context, and not once and for all.

Dotson begins with some basic features of epistemic life: that our epistemic lives are social, that this sociality gives rise to epistemic systems from which individuals may be excluded to greater and lesser extents, and that epistemic systems must have a certain degree of resilience (2014a: 120–122). Given these features of epistemic life, Dotson asks: what are the various ways in which knowers can be unwarrantedly excluded from contributing to epistemic systems, and in each kind of exclusion what degree of change is necessary in order to rectify the exclusion? With a degree of change lens, she identifies three distinct levels of exclusions from epistemic systems that may occur, *first-*, *second-*, and *third-order* exclusion, each with a corresponding degree of change that would be necessary to rectify the exclusion (2014a: 123–133).

A first-order epistemic exclusion "results from the incompetent functioning of some aspect of shared resources with respect to some goal or value" (Dotson 2014a: 123). In other words, there are types of epistemic exclusions that do not signal anything wrong with the epistemic system; instead, what is needed to remedy the exclusion is to utilize the system more proficiently (Dotson 2014a: 125). Dotson identifies unwarranted devaluations of credibility and the creation of epistemically disadvantaged identities as first-order exclusions (2014a: 125). Examples of first-order exclusions include testimonial injustice, whereby knowers attribute less credibility to a knower's testimony due to an identity prejudice (Fricker 2007: 28) and other sorts of exclusions from non-testimonial epistemic practices such as those involved in querying, conjecturing, and imagining, owing to deflated perceptions of competency (Hookway 2010). In such cases, an epistemic agent is unfairly prevented from participating fully within epistemic systems owing to an unfair distribution of epistemic power due to unwarranted credibility deficits and assessments of competency. However, there is nothing about the exclusion that indicates a problem with the epistemic systems themselves. In such cases, actions like offering testimony and entertaining a possibility are still beneficial practices; indeed if they were not, then the exclusion from such practices would not so clearly be a wrong. What is needed to rectify the situation in first-order cases is to more faithfully and consistently engage the systems themselves, for example, by applying the rules consistently such that epistemic agents are not unfairly excluded from epistemic participation.

Second-order epistemic exclusions require more than ensuring equitable participation in epistemic systems. In such cases, there is something wrong with the epistemic system itself: it is insufficient in a way that leads it to function less well with regard to certain experiences or aspects of the world as experienced by certain persons (Dotson 2014a: 126–127). The sorts of cases that Miranda Fricker identifies as hermeneutical injustice whereby a significant area of one's experience is obscured from collective understanding (2007: 154–155) would be a second-order exclusion (Dotson 2014a: 127). However, there are other sorts of exclusions that result from the use of insufficient resources. For example, some (although not all) cases of what Dotson calls "testimonial smothering" would fall in this category. Testimonial smothering occurs when one "perceives one's immediate audience as unwilling or unable to gain the appropriate uptake of proffered testimony" and so must truncate one's testimony (Dotson 2011: 244). Those instances of testimonial smothering where one's audience is unable to give proper uptake owing to a lack of particular epistemic resources would qualify as second-order exclusions so long as all that would be needed to rectify the situation would be an adjustment or addition to epistemic resources for proper testimonial uptake. In cases where more than adding and adjustment are required, we turn to third-order exclusions.

Third-order epistemic exclusions are exclusions that occur when an epistemic system is functioning properly and is sufficiently developed, but the system itself is altogether inadequate to a particular epistemic task (2014a: 129–131). As such, Dotson argues that third-order epistemic exclusions are *irreducible* to social and political factors given that these sorts of exclusions can be perpetuated by the very systems themselves, given the need for such systems to be resilient (2014a: 132–133). These sorts of exclusions require third-order change, or the ability to think what a given epistemic system does not allow one to think, revealing the system itself to be not just insufficient (and so remediable by adding and adjusting) but rather *inadequate* to certain epistemic tasks (and so in need of a new epistemic system). Dotson identifies what she calls "contributory injustice" as an epistemic injustice that requires third-order change (2012a: 31–32). Contributory injustices occur when knowers utilize epistemic resources that are inapt for understanding the potential contributions of particular knowers to our collective knowledge pool and thereby engage in a form of willful hermeneutical ignorance that refuses to employ more apt epistemic resources for receiving and appropriately responding to those contributions (Dotson 2012a: 31–32). In such cases, the knower who commits the wrong may treat other knowers as competent and trustworthy. Moreover, the knower who commits the wrong may be open to adjusting and developing currently shared epistemic resources. For example, rather than shift one's conception of workers and the workplace to more adequately attend to workers who are also child-bearers, one might seek to understand the concerns of this group of workers by further developing already existing systems such as understanding maternity leave as a sort of disability leave. But these remedies mistake the problem. Instead, a whole new approach is required, one in which axiomatic features of the previous collective epistemic resources may need to be abandoned. Indeed, Dotson argues that in such cases, something akin to what María Lugones calls "world"-travelling is necessary to rectify the exclusion (2012a: 35), otherwise the contributions of particular knowers will continue to be distorted and misapprehended.

## Epistemic labor and knowledge production

Finally, we can view epistemic injustices through the lens of epistemic labor and knowledge production. This lens captures much (although not all) of what has been discussed with the previous lenses. Nonetheless, as I will demonstrate below, focusing on epistemic labor and knowledge production distinguishes among some cases that other lenses group together. In addition, thinking about epistemic injustices through the lens of epistemic labor draws attention to sorts of epistemic injustice not contained in the previous sections. By focusing on epistemic labor and knowledge production, we can discern (at least) three broad categories of epistemic injustice: *epistemic agential injustices*, those that directly and unfairly thwart epistemic labor; *epistemic labor invalidation*, those that disregard or systematically fail to acknowledge the epistemic labor of some; and *epistemic exploitation*, those that unjustly exploit epistemic labor.

Epistemic agential injustices, or those that unfairly thwart epistemic labor, may come in many forms. For example, some (although not all) testimonial injustices can be seen to do so. As I have argued elsewhere, within certain contexts, not only must knowers work together, but also they have a right to expect that knowers will work together to develop epistemic pursuits (Pohlhaus 2014). When one is subject to testimonial injustice in such contexts, this unfairly stymies epistemic agency insofar as it is through engagement with epistemic communities that one's epistemic labor bears fruit. As Ishani Maitra points out, within the context of certain relationships (including, but not only, those pertaining to particular epistemic institutions such as a court of law), even simply suspending judgment (neither believing nor disbelieving) may constitute a kind of epistemic injustice (2010: 200–201). In addition, the phenomenon of stereotype threat, insofar as it has ill effects on epistemic activity by way of unfairly increasing epistemic labor for some and not others (Steele 2010), signals an epistemic agential injustice.[10] In other words, pernicious stereotypes, or what Patricia Hill Collins aptly calls "controlling images" (2000: 69–96), add to the cognitive labor of particular groups, since these images bring to the knower's awareness the potential unfair bias through which their epistemic activities may be received. Contending with this ever present possibility adds to the cognitive labor of those stereotyped in ways that can impede their epistemic activity in comparison to those who are not perniciously stereotyped and so do not need to engage in such additional epistemic labor. Consequently, the imposition of this extra epistemic labor for some and not others can be identified as an epistemic agential injustice.

In contrast to epistemic injustices that impede epistemic agency by making it disproportionately harder to complete epistemic tasks, there are epistemic injustices that disregard and devalue certain sorts of epistemic activity, invalidating the epistemic labor necessary for completing epistemic tasks; these kinds of epistemic injustice I will call "epistemic labor invalidations." For example, epistemic labor that attends to affect and knowing people well is both expected of women while simultaneously downplayed as "real knowledge" or engaging in actual epistemic labor. As Uma Narayan points out, third-world scholars are often expected to be fountains of knowledge concerning the groups to which they are perceived as belonging in a way that disregards the actual cognitive labor necessary for knowing what is expected of them insofar as this knowledge is regarded as automatically present in virtue of group membership and not through actual cognitive effort (Narayan 1997: 121–157). Furthermore, as Lisa Heldke argues, hierarchies in what counts as worthy of being known may lead some people to be regarded as less competent precisely because of what it is they know (2006). Similarly, Amy

Olberding points out that knowledge of non-Western philosophy is invalidated within the discipline of philosophy to such an extent that knowing something about it can reduce one's credibility as a philosopher (2016).

Finally, epistemic exploitation occurs when epistemic labor is coercively extracted from epistemic agents in the service of others. Attention to this kind of epistemic injustice highlights the Foucauldian insight that power not only suppresses, but also *produces* (Allen 2017; Hall 2017). Likewise, epistemic injustices can not only stymie epistemic activity, but also exploitatively produce it. For example, epistemic and social coercion may be used to *produce* testimony that is subordinating. Rachel McKinney calls this form of produced testimony *extracted speech* (McKinney 2016). Examining cases such as the Central Park Five, in which five male juveniles of color were compelled to give false confessions and were consequently wrongly convicted of sexually assaulting and attacking a white woman jogging in New York City's Central Park, McKinney shows how social and epistemic power may be used to extract or produce testimony from persons that is both untrue and self-damaging (McKinney 2016). Nora Berenstain calls attention to another sort of epistemic exploitation where those who are harmed by axes of oppression are continually called upon to educate those who benefit from their oppression. As Berenstain argues, the repeated calls to those who are oppressed to "prove" the harm they endure produce double binds from which it is extraordinarily difficult to extract oneself (Berenstain 2016). In other words, solicitations to "prove" that things like sexism and racism exist leave one with the choice of either engaging in fruitless and tiresome epistemic labor or appearing to be complicit in the view that one's experiences simply do not exist. Moreover, responding to such solicitations can have the effect of reinscribing epistemic hierarchies insofar as the continuing effort to "prove" and scientifically document the harms of oppression reinforces the background assumption that the experience of harm by some groups is not plausible or reliable on its own (Schroer 2015). Epistemic exploitation can be maintained not only through credibility deficits, but also via credibility surpluses as when non-dominantly situated knowers are expected to act as epistemic tokens, being called upon continually to provide "raw experience" and to "represent" for the groups to which they are perceived as belonging (Davis 2016). Given the pervasive nature of epistemic exploitation, one form of resistance is for non-dominantly situated knowers to withdraw from epistemic interactions they justifiably assess to be exploitative (Henning 2015).

## Conclusion

Each of the four lenses used above to identify epistemic injustices leads to different ways of categorizing and understanding varieties of epistemic injustice. Beginning from the insight that under conditions of oppression "epistemic relations are screwed up" (Medina 2013: 27), the first lens sorts epistemic injustices into two broad categories: those that structure inequitable relations among knowers (for example, by creating a class of sub-knowers in relation to dominantly situated knowers) and those that divert epistemic attention in the service of dominance (for example, by actively ignoring the injustices that privilege members of dominant groups). If we begin from the insight that knowers are constituted in relation, different varieties of epistemic injustice emerge: those that stymie epistemic relations and those that manifest in breaches of trust. Using an order of change lens focuses attention not only to three distinct levels through which we can classify epistemic injustices, but also highlights that a fundamental aspect of epistemic systems, namely the resilience required for efficacy, can itself maintain some epistemic injustices (i.e. third-order) on its own. Finally, through the lens of epistemic agency as labor, other varieties of epistemic injustice emerge, not only those that stymie knowers, but also those that devalue particular sorts of epistemic labor and those that exploitatively extract epistemic labor from particular knowers. Moving among these lenses demonstrates that attention to different aspects of epistemic life will bring different sorts of epistemic injustice in and out of focus. Moreover, shifting attention will highlight different ways of conceiving the relations among various epistemic injustices. It is, therefore, critical when attending to the ethical and political aspects of epistemic life neither to foreclose the possibility of identifying and tracking new forms of epistemic injustice nor to preclude other knowers from calling attention to them as they arise.

**Related chapters**: 2, 3, 4, 5, 6, 9, 10, 11, 12, 13, 14, 15, 16, 34, 37

## Notes

1 I would like to thank Ian James Kidd, José Medina, Michael R. Hicks, and especially Madelyn Detloff for helpful comments and suggestions on earlier drafts of this chapter.
2 In this chapter, I take a broader sense of the term 'epistemic injustice' than forwarded in Miranda Fricker's *Epistemic Injustice: The Power and Ethics of Knowing* in order to call attention to the larger body of work preceding the book that analyzes the political and ethical aspects of epistemic activity and to broaden epistemological attention to a wider range of epistemic activities than the acquisition of propositional knowledge.
3 In addition, as Kathryn Hutchison points out, since (unlike other disciplines) philosophy lacks "an independently accessible body of subject matter" (2013: 111), there is a high likelihood that implicit biases will lower the credibility of work by persons from traditionally underrepresented groups thereby making it even more difficult for such persons to be recognized as forwarding new and innovative ideas within the discipline (Hutchison 2013).
4 See Alcoff (2017) for a related but distinct argument concerning the epistemic injustice of the almost exclusive attention given to European and Euro-American thought in professional philosophy.
5 I owe thanks to Dotson, whose work has helped me to keep in mind that there have been Black women and other women of color practicing philosophy for centuries; one need only as capacious a view of philosophy when regarding the intellectual work of Black women and women of color as is granted to European men regarding their work to see that this is so.
6 Shannon Sullivan makes a similar observation when she notes that some ignorances are produced by knowledge. These types of ignorances she refers to as "ignorance/knowledge," to keep in mind that ignorance is not always simply the absence of knowledge but can very much be produced by what one does know (2007: 154).
7 Because Miranda Fricker gave the name "epistemic injustice" to the various sorts of phenomena now being identified with the term, rehearsing her own lens here has the real danger of overdetermining the concept. It is for this reason that I do not do so, but rather situate the sorts of epistemic injustice she has identified, testimonial and hermeneutical injustice, where appropriate within the four lenses I discuss. Nonetheless, the impact of her work on bringing attention to the ethical and political dimensions of knowing has been enormous. For more detailed consideration of testimonial and hermeneutical injustices, I direct readers to the essays by Fricker (2017), Medina (2017), and Wanderer (2017).
8 Since the publication of Mills' *Racial Contract*, there has been a growing body of literature that analyzes this and related sorts of active ignorance. See for example volume 21 issue 3 of *Hypatia*; Proctor and Schiebinger (2008); Sullivan and Tuana (2007).
9 Indeed, Dotson herself acknowledges that there are definite limitations to the order-of-change approach she develops in order to distinguish reducible from irreducible epistemic injustices (2012a: 35–36).
10 Jennifer Saul analyzes the convergences and divergences between stereotype threat and the forms of epistemic injustice identified by Fricker, testimonial and hermeneutical injustices (Saul 2017). Given her use of Fricker's lens to think about the relation between stereotype threat and epistemic injustice, the convergences she finds differ from what I identify here.

## References

Alcoff, L.M. (2017) "Philosophy and Philosophical Practice: Eurocentrism as an Epistemology of Ignorance," in I.J. Kidd, J. Medina, and G. Pohlhaus, Jr. (eds.) *Routledge Handbook of Epistemic Injustice*, New York, NY: Routledge.

Allen, A. (2017) "Power/Knowledge/Resistance: Foucault and Epistemic Injustice," in I. J. Kidd, J. Medina, and G. Pohlhaus, Jr. (eds.) *Routledge Handbook of Epistemic Injustice*, New York, NY: Routledge.

Anderson, L. (2017) "Epistemic Injustice and the Philosophy of Race," in I. J. Kidd, J. Medina, and G. Pohlhaus, Jr. (eds.) *Routledge Handbook of Epistemic Injustice*, New York, NY: Routledge.

Babbitt, S. (2017) "Epistemic and Political Freedom," in I. J. Kidd, J. Medina, and G. Pohlhaus, Jr. (eds.) *Routledge Handbook of Epistemic Injustice*, New York, NY: Routledge.

Berenstain, N. (2016) "Epistemic Exploitation," *Ergo*, 3(22): 569–590.

Carel, H. and I. J. Kidd (2017) "Epistemic Injustice in Medicine and Healthcare," in I. J. Kidd, J. Medina, and G. Pohlhaus, Jr. (eds.) *Routledge Handbook of Epistemic Injustice*, New York, NY: Routledge,.

Cherry, M. and E. Schwitzgebel (2016) "Like the Oscars, #PhilosophySoWhite," *Los Angeles Times* March 4, 2016. www.latimes.com/opinion/op-ed/la-oe-0306-schwitzgebel-cherry-philosophy-so-white-20160306-story.html accessed March 14, 2016.

Code, L. (2006) *Ecological Thinking: The Politics of Epistemic Location*, New York, NY: Oxford University Press.

Code, L. (1993) "Taking Subjectivity Into Account," in L. Alcoff and E. Potter (eds.) *Feminist Epistemologies*, New York: Routledge.

Code, L. (1991) *What Can She Know? Feminist Theory and the Construction of Knowledge*, Ithaca: Cornell University Press.

Collins, P.H. (2017) "Intersectionality and Epistemic Injustice," in I. J. Kidd, J. Medina, and G. Pohlhaus, Jr. (eds.) *Routledge Handbook of Epistemic Injustice*, New York, NY: Routledge.

Collins, P.H. (2000) *Black Feminist Thought: Knowledge, Consciousness, and the Politics of Empowerment*, 2nd ed., New York, NY: Routledge.

Collins, P.H. (1991) *Black Feminist Thought: Knowledge, Consciousness, and the Politics of Empowerment*, New York, NY: Routledge.

Davis, E. (2016) "Typecasts, tokens, and brands: Credibility excess as epistemic vice," *Hypatia*, 31(3): 485–501.

Dotson, K. (2014a) "Conceptualizing epistemic oppression," *Social Epistemology*, 28(2): 115–138.

Dotson, K. (2014b) "'Thinking familiar with the interstitial': An introduction," *Hypatia*, 29(1): 1–17.

Dotson, K. (2012a) "A cautionary tale: On limiting epistemic oppression," *Frontiers: A Journal of Women Studies*, 33(1): 24–47.

Dotson, K. (2012b) "How is this paper philosophy?," *Comparative Philosophy*, 3(1): 3–29.

Dotson, K. (2011) "Tracking epistemic violence, tracking practices of silencing," *Hypatia*, 26(2): 236–257.

Fricker, M. (2017) "Evolving Concepts of Epistemic Injustice," in I. J. Kidd, J. Medina, and G. Pohlhaus, Jr. (eds.) *Routledge Handbook of Epistemic Injustice*, New York, NY: Routledge.

Fricker, M. (2007) *Epistemic Injustice: Power and the Ethics of Knowing*, New York: Oxford.

Grasswick, H. (2017) "Epistemic Injustice in Science," in I. J. Kidd, J. Medina, and G. Pohlhaus, Jr. (eds.) *Routledge Handbook of Epistemic Injustice*, New York, NY: Routledge.

Hall, K. (2017) "Queer Epistemology and Epistemic Injustice," in I. J. Kidd, J. Medina, and G. Pohlhaus, Jr. (eds.) *Routledge Handbook of Epistemic Injustice*, New York, NY: Routledge.

Hawley, K. (2017) "Trust, Distrust, and Epistemic Injustice," in I. J. Kidd, J. Medina, and G. Pohlhaus, Jr. (eds.) *Routledge Handbook of Epistemic Injustice*, New York, NY: Routledge.

Hawley, K. (2011) "Knowing How and Epistemic Injustice," in J. Bengson and M. Moffet (eds.) *Knowing How: Essays on Knowledge, Mind, and Action*, New York: Oxford University Press.

Heldke, L. (2006) "Farming made her stupid," *Hypatia*, 21(3): 151–165.

Henning, T. (2015) "Valid Disengagements: The Case for Epistemic Insensitivity," Paper presented at *Exploring Collaborative Contestations and Diversifying Philosophy Conference* May 28–30, 2015.

Hookway, C. (2010) "Some varieties of epistemic injustice: Reflections on Fricker," *Episteme*, 7(2): 151–163.

Hutchison, K. (2013) "Sages and Cranks: The Difficulty of Identifying First-Rate Philosophers," in K. Hutchison and F. Jenkins (eds.) *Women in Philosophy: What Needs to Change*, New York, NY: Oxford University Press.

Jones, K. (2012) "The politics of intellectual self-trust," *Social Epistemology*, 26(2): 237–251.

Jones, K. (2002) "The Politics of Credibility," in L. Antony and C. Witt (eds.) *A Mind of One's Own: Feminist Essays on Reason and Objectivity*, Cambridge, MA: Westview Press.

Kotzee, B. (2017) "Education and Epistemic Injustice," in I. J. Kidd, J. Medina, and G. Pohlhaus, Jr. (eds.) *Routledge Handbook of Epistemic Injustice*, New York, NY: Routledge.

Maitra, I. (2010) "The nature of epistemic injustice," *Philosophical Books*, 51(4): 195–211.

Mason, R. (2011) "Two kinds of unknowing," *Hypatia*, 26(2): 294–307.

May, V.M. (2014) "'Speaking into the void'? Intersectionality critiques and epistemic backlash," *Hypatia*, 29(1): 94–112.

McHugh, N. (2017) "Epistemic Communities and Institutions," in I.J. Kidd, J. Medina, and G. Pohlhaus, Jr. (eds.) *Routledge Handbook of Epistemic Injustice*, New York, NY: Routledge.
McKinney, R. (2016) "Extracted speech," *Social Theory and Practice*, 42(2): 258–284.
McKinnon, R. (2017) "Allies Behaving Badly," in I.J. Kidd, J. Medina, and G. Pohlhaus, Jr. (eds.) *Routledge Handbook of Epistemic Injustice*, New York, NY: Routledge.
Medina, J. (2017) "Varieties of Hermeneutical Injustice," in I.J. Kidd, J. Medina, and G. Pohlhaus, Jr. (eds.) *Routledge Handbook of Epistemic Injustice*, New York, NY: Routledge.
Medina, J. (2013) *The Epistemology of Resistance: Gender and Racial Oppression, Epistemic Injustice, and Resistant Imaginations*, New York: Oxford University Press.
Mills, C.W. (1997) *The Racial Contract*, Ithaca: Cornell University Press.
Minnich, E. (1990) *Transforming Knowledge*, Philadelphia, PA: Temple University Press.
Mohanty, C.T. (2004) *Feminism without Borders: Decolonizing Theory, Practicing Solidarity*, Durham: Duke University Press.
Narayan, U. (1997) *Dislocating Cultures: Identities, Traditions, and Third World Feminism*, New York: Oxford University Press.
Nelson, L.H. (1993) "Epistemological Communities," in L. Alcoff and E. Potter (eds.) *Feminist Epistemologies*, New York: Routledge.
Nelson, L.H. (1990) *Who Knows? From Quine to Feminist Empiricism*, Philadelphia, PA: Temple University Press.
Olberding, A. (2016) Comments to "When Someone Suggests Expanding the Canon. . ." on *Daily Nous* May 13, 2016, http://dailynous.com/2016/05/13/when-someone-suggests-expanding-the-canon/ accessed August 20, 2016.
Olberding, A. (2015) "It's not them, It's you: A case study concerning the exclusion of non-western philosophy," *Comparative Philosophy*, 6(2): 14–34.
Outlaw, L. (2007) "Social Ordering and the Systematic Production of Ignorance," in S. Sullivan and N. Tuana (eds.) *Race and Epistemologies of Ignorance*, Albany, NY: SUNY Press.
Owen, D. (2003) "Genealogy as Perspicuous Representation," in C. Heyes (ed.) *The Grammar of Politics*, Ithaca: Cornell University Press.
Pitts, A. (2017) "Decolonial Praxis and Epistemic Injustice," in I.J. Kidd, J. Medina, and G. Pohlhaus, Jr. (eds.) *Routledge Handbook of Epistemic Injustice*, New York, NY: Routledge.
Pohlhaus, Jr, G. (2014) "Discerning the primary epistemic harm in cases of testimonial injustice," *Social Epistemology*, 28(2): 99–114.
Pohlhaus, Jr., G. (2012) "Relational knowing and epistemic injustice: Toward a theory of willful hermeneutical ignorance," *Hypatia*, 27(4): 715–735.
Proctor, R. and L. Schiebinger, eds. (2008) *Agnotology: The Making and Unmaking of Ignorance*, Stanford, CA: Stanford University Press.
Roshanravan, S. (2014) "Motivating coalition: Women of color and epistemic disobedience," *Hypatia*, 29(1): 41–58.
Saul, J. (2017) "Implicit Bias, Stereotype Threat, and Epistemic Injustice," in I.J. Kidd, J. Medina, and G. Pohlhaus, Jr. (eds.) *Routledge Handbook of Epistemic Injustice*, New York, NY: Routledge.
Schroer, J.W. (2015) "Giving them something they can feel: On the strategy of scientizing the phenomenology of race and racism," *Knowledge Cultures*, 3(1): 91–110.
Scrutton, A.P. (2017) "Epistemic Injustice and Mental Illness," in I.J. Kidd, J. Medina, and G. Pohlhaus, Jr. (eds.) *Routledge Handbook of Epistemic Injustice*, New York, NY: Routledge.
Shotwell, A. (2017) "Forms of Knowing and Epistemic Resources," in I.J. Kidd, J. Medina, and G. Pohlhaus, Jr. (eds.) *Routledge Handbook of Epistemic Injustice*, New York, NY: Routledge.
Shotwell, A. (2011) *Knowing Otherwise: Race, Gender, and Implicit Understanding*, University Park: Penn State Press.
Spivak, G.C. (1988) "Can the Subaltern Speak?," in C. Nelson and L. Grossberg (eds.) *A Marxism and the Interpretation of Culture*, Champaign: University of Illinois Press.
Steele, C. (2010) "In the Air between Us: Stereotypes, Identity, and Achievement," in H.R. Markus and P.M.L. Moya (eds.) *Doing Race*, New York: Norton Press.
Sullivan, S. (2007) "White Ignorance and Colonial Oppression or Why I Know So Little about Puerto Rico," in S. Sullivan and N. Tuana (eds.) *Race and Epistemologies of Ignorance*, Albany, NY: SUNY Press.
Sullivan, S. and N. Tuana, eds. (2007) *Race and Epistemologies of Ignorance*, Albany, NY: SUNY Press.
Townley, C. (2003) "Trust and the curse of Cassandra (an exploration of the value of trust)," *Philosophy and the Contemporary World*, 10(2): 105–111.

Tremain, S. (2017) "Knowing Disability, Differently," in I.J. Kidd, J. Medina, and G. Pohlhaus, Jr. (eds.) *Routledge Handbook of Epistemic Injustice*, New York, NY: Routledge.
Tuana, N. (2017) "Feminist Epistemology: The Subject of Knowledge," in I.J. Kidd, J. Medina, and G. Pohlhaus, Jr. (eds.) *Routledge Handbook of Epistemic Injustice*, New York, NY: Routledge.
Tuana, N. (2006) "The speculum of ignorance: The women's health movement and epistemologies of ignorance," *Hypatia*, 21(3): 1–19.
Wanderer, J. (2017) "Varieties of Testimonial Injustice," in I.J. Kidd, J. Medina, and G. Pohlhaus, Jr. (eds.) *Routledge Handbook of Epistemic Injustice*, New York, NY: Routledge.

# 2
# VARIETIES OF TESTIMONIAL INJUSTICE

*Jeremy Wanderer*

Suppose that my testifying at a disciplinary tribunal leads to my unfair dismissal. This would be an instance of injustice that is the result of an act of testimony, but not a case of testimonial injustice in the sense under investigation in this essay. Why not? Because we are interested here in investigating the possibility that there is a categorical connection between certain instances of injustice and the social practice of testimony, where the connection is such that an understanding of the injustice in these specific instances emerges from a consideration of the general practice. It seems clear, in contrast, that one can understand the injustice of my unfair dismissal without any consideration of the social practice of testimony whatsoever.

A glimpse of what is meant by the proposed categorical connection can be had through a preliminary characterization of its key terms, one that will be further developed (and modified) in the ensuing discussion.

In the broadest terms, a *social practice* is a norm-governed pattern of meaningful interaction between people. Participants within a social practice interact with each other through their socially significant performances and hold each other responsible for performing according to the norms integral to such a practice. Such practices are internally diverse and typically include a wide variety of performance-kinds that are recognized by its practitioners. From an explanatory point of view, not all performance-kinds within a practice need be equal; some performances can be seen as more central to the practice, in that they are capable of explaining other performances within the practice. For example, a performance-kind within a practice could be viewed as deviant if it can be seen as subverting other performance-kinds thereby deemed more central to the practice.

The social practice of interest here is that of *testimony*, an internally diverse pattern of norm-governed interactions that includes the speech act of telling someone something close to its explanatory center. Related performances-kinds within this practice include acts such as querying, challenging, listening and conjecturing, as well as 'pathological' performance-kinds such as lying, gossiping and rumor-mongering.[1] (A fuller characterization of this practice, especially its relationship to epistemic matters, will emerge in the ensuing discussion). As with all social practices, the social practice of testimony will take on thicker and culturally-specific forms in different places, times and contexts, including their different functioning in regulated institutional public fora (such as legal settings) and more relaxed, informal everyday exchanges.

It is the social practice of testimony as a whole that stands in a categorical connection to certain cases of injustice, i.e. cases of *testimonial injustice*. The term *injustice* here is used very broadly to include any instance in which a person is maltreated, and is not limited to just those cases involving the unfair distribution of goods or capacities, nor to cases in which someone is denied what is their due. Our focus is thus on those cases in which a person is maltreated and where a full understanding of what makes this an instance of maltreatment will invoke the social practice of testimony. In such a case, one can say there is a *categorical connection* between the social practice and the maltreatment. Think away the social practice, perhaps by imagining a social grouping that has no such practice, and one thinks away the possibility of cases of testimonial injustice arising within such a social grouping.

It is possible to describe the social practice of testimony from a variety of different perspectives, with each perspective bringing a different variety of injustice into view. In what follows, I distinguish three such perspectives and suggest that each sheds light on a different variety of testimonial injustice – *transactional testimonial injustice*, *structural testimonial injustice* and *testimonial betrayal*. This should not be taken to imply that these varieties exhaust the category of testimonial injustice, nor is the order of presentation of these varieties intended to convey their relative importance. Rather the suggestion under investigation here is that these three are distinct varieties of testimonial injustice, in that they are distinguishable from each other in ethically significant ways, while still standing in a categorical connection with the social practice of testimony. We will begin by outlining a much-discussed example of testimonial injustice (Part 1), and explore this same example from three differing perspectives in the remaining sections (Parts 2–4).

## 1. Fricker's account of testimonial injustice

Let us begin with what has become the *locus classicus* for contemporary Anglophone discussions of testimonial injustice, Miranda Fricker's path-breaking book *Epistemic Injustice*,[2] with the aim of relating her work to the general characterization of testimonial injustice just noted.

According to Fricker's seminal account, testimonial injustice occurs when, following an act of telling someone something, a Speaker is accorded insufficient credibility by a Hearer due to a prejudicial stereotype held by the Hearer.[3] More specifically, the Hearer subscribes, at some cognitive level and in a manner that is relatively resistant to counter-evidence, to a widely-held belief that links a salient aspect of the Speaker's social identity to a disparaging attribute, as a result of which the Hearer accords the Speaker less credibility than she deserves.[4] One of Fricker's signature examples is a critical moment towards the end of Anthony Minghella's screenplay 'The Talented Mr. Ripley', where Herbert Greenleaf dismisses the testimony of Marge Sherwood by saying "Marge, there's female intuition, and then there are facts."[5] Drawing on a prejudicial stereotype that female opinion is more often the result of emotion rather than intellect, Greenleaf accords Sherwood insufficient credibility and thus does not take her testimony seriously.

What makes this a case of testimonial injustice, as opposed to an injustice that is the result of an act of testimony? This query needs to be handled with some care as Greenleaf's prejudicial orientation could indeed lead to many instances of maltreatment of Sherwood and others for which we would not need to invoke the social practice of testimony by way of understanding. For example, we could view this as an instance of the prejudice unfairly thwarting Sherwood's ambitions or simply failing to respect her, neither of which need involve appeal to the practice of testimony *per se*. What then does consideration of the social practice of testimony add to our understanding of the injustice in this case?

Understanding Fricker's response requires a detour through the distinctive account of the relationship between the social practice of testimony and the concept of knowledge that she derives from the work of Edward Craig.⁶ Craig tells a State of Nature story involving a stripped-down social community, whose agents lack our epistemic concepts such as 'knowledge' but share certain needs and cognitive resources with us. Specifically, they need true beliefs about the environment, which can be had either through their own on-board sources (e.g. via perception) or from other informants in a community who have a positional advantage over themselves. Imagine a community member, an inquirer, who does not yet have a belief about p but wants to acquire one from a prospective informant, and consider what general properties this inquirer would want their informant to have. On Fricker's retelling, the desired properties are threefold: the inquirer wants an informant who: i) is likely enough in the context to be right as to whether p, ii) is willing and able to convey whether p to the inquirer, and iii) bears indicator properties such that the inquirer can recognize the presence of the first two features.

In such a minimal epistemic community, we can easily imagine inquirers introducing a concept whose function it is to flag good informants, i.e. informants with just that trio of properties indicated. On the one hand, the concept of a good informant is not the same as our concept of a knower: we can, for example, easily think of cases in which we would treat a person as a knower but not as a good informant – such as my son who damn well knows where the remote control is but will not divulge. On the other hand, we can see the concept of a knower emerging from the concept of a good informant via an inevitable process of objectification. The notion of a good informant is initially tied to the inquirer's own powers of recognition; it is a label attached to someone who is not only capable of, and willing to, answer the inquirer's query whether p, but whom the inquirer can recognize as so capable and willing. The process of objectification then works to extend the idea of a good informant beyond something that the inquirer can recognize in the here and now. The inquirer will come to realize that there can be good informants whose indicator properties they cannot identify, and that there can be a good informant as to whether p, even though they have no current interest in answering the question or even if no one has any current interest in answering the question. The result is an objectivized conception of the good informant, the knower, who is now no longer tied to the particular relationship of inquiry between inquirer and informant, yet is involved in the social practice of pooling information.

According to Craig, then, the concept of a good informant is a response to certain identifiable epistemic needs in the State of Nature, and the concept of a knower is a response to further identifiable needs and everyday processes operating on the concept of a good informant. The notion of being a knower, and with it the social practice of testimony, thus emerges, of necessity as it were, from the practice of identifying good informants. On this way of thinking, there is a close conceptual tie between knowledge and testimony, one that rules out the possibility of being able to comprehend what knowledge is but yet have difficulty in grasping how one may come to acquire that knowledge via the say-so of another. As it has been provocatively put elsewhere, "the concept of knowledge contains an account of the possibility of knowing from others".⁷ The concepts of the knower and the testifier appear as one in the newly emerged practice of pooling information.

An actual performance within the social practice of pooling information will involve agents who are socially-situated, including each having specific social identities and standing in various power relations to one another. For some theoretical purposes, however, it is useful to abstract away from socially-situated subjects and to consider the practice as involving agents who are not conceived as standing in relations of social identity and power. Since Fricker's focus is on cases of prejudice, it may seem obvious that the relevant description of the social practice for bringing out an understanding of testimonial injustice is the situated one. This suggestion, however, is only partly right. What is right is the contention that the cases of injustice that we hope to understand through a consideration of the practice of testimony will only come into view if we consider agents who are socially-situated. It does not, however, follow that the insight into these cases cannot be provided by a consideration of the social practice of testimony in the abstract.[8]

As Fricker's extended discussion of Craig's State of Nature reveals, an important feature of her account is the contention that an understanding of the distinctive character of testimonial injustice emerges from a consideration of the social practice of pooling information, abstractly conceived. As she puts it, "[g]iven Craig's account, what the recipient of a prejudicial credibility deficit is excluded from is the single practice that dramatizes the origin of what it is to be a knower at all".[9] So, when Greenleaf's prejudices lead him to dismiss Sherwood's testimony, he maltreats her in various ways – including excluding her from the social practice of pooling information. The categorical connection between the social practice of pooling information and the injustice in this instance is what makes this a case of testimonial injustice as opposed to an injustice connected to an act of testimony. Think away the social practice of pooling information, such as by imagining a State of Nature community that has no such practice, and one thinks away this injustice.

Following Fricker's lead, the case of Sherwood and Greenleaf will provide a useful focus for our own investigation into the possibility of there being a categorical connection between certain instances of injustice and the social practice of testimony. That said, as with all the primary examples of testimonial injustice that Fricker considers in her book, the Sherwood-Greenleaf example is complex, involving the interplay between different features worth distinguishing. One such feature is that the case involves a direct linguistic interaction between Speaker and Hearer, with one explicitly rejecting the testimony proffered by the other. A second feature is that, by invoking sexist prejudicial stereotypes, the case involves reference to socio-historically extended patterns of oppression and injustice that range far beyond this particular interaction alone. A third feature is that the case involves an intense personal relationship between the protagonists. Rather than lump these three features together, our investigation here will consider each in turn (in the next three sections). This is because each feature provides a different perspective on the social practice of testimony, and it is by considering these perspectives separately that the possibility of there being different varieties of testimonial injustice comes into view.

## 2. Transactional testimonial injustice

Theorists interested in the notion of justice have distinguished between two different ways of approaching their subject matter, either by focusing on the normative character of *acts of exchange* between people or on the *distribution of relevant goods*.[10] According to the former, an exchange is just when it lives up to certain normative standards governing exchanges of that type, including both generic norms governing all such exchanges and/or norms specific to the particular kind of exchange under consideration. According to the latter, a structure is just when each person in the structure gets their due in terms of an appropriate distribution of relevant goods. In both cases, injustice involves a certain arbitrariness, either the arbitrary rule of one party of the exchange over the other in the former case (the proverbial 'foot on the neck') or an arbitrary distribution of the relevant good in the latter (the proverbial 'disproportionate slice of the pie'). Let us call the former *transactional injustice* and the latter *structural injustice*. Although one could debate the possible relations of dependence between the transactional and structural, I propose here to treat these as two potentially independent varieties of injustice, varieties that come into view depending on what aspects of the abstract social practice one focuses on: transactional episodes between practitioners or the distribution of goods within the system at a given time.

As the exchange between Greenleaf and Sherwood exemplifies, Fricker's primary examples of testimonial injustice all involve exchanges between people, leaving the strong impression that her main focus is on the transactional variety of testimonial injustice. Granted, she explicitly elects to concentrate on what she dubs 'systematic testimonial injustice', i.e. on "those prejudices that 'track' the subject through different dimensions of social activity – economic, educational, professional, sexual, legal, political, religious, and so on".[11] Such systematicity, however, merely serves to ensure that testimonial injustice is not isolated by linking it to other kinds of actual or potential injustice and does not involve a structural variety of testimonial injustice.[12] In this section, I will develop the idea of transactional testimonial injustice in a manner that is inspired by Fricker's use of Craig's framework as outlined above; in the next section I will evaluate Fricker's reasons for the apparent focus on the transactional variety.

A transaction, as used here, is a special kind of social act.[13] Not only does the very idea of the act implicate more than one person, but the act has a structure that serves to place those persons in a particular relation to one another, such that the act is done from one (agent) towards the other (patient). Any act with this structure can be described in two ways, one from the perspective of the agent and one from the perspective of the patient; self-conscious awareness of this structure by both parties is part of the very idea of the act itself. A successful instance of a transaction serves to yoke the two parties together in a distinctive order of justice, such that an inappropriate response of either party to the act counts as an injustice done towards the other.[14] In our case, the transaction that Fricker focuses on is that of testimony, i.e. the act of telling someone something. The act implicates two people, such that in the successful case, one person is self-consciously aware of telling someone something, and the other is self-consciously aware of being told something by someone. In a successful case of testimony, self-conscious recognition by both parties of the transaction creates an order of justice between them, one delineated by a certain set of appropriate actions in response by both parties under certain conditions, and testimonial transactional injustice occurs when one party responds inappropriately under some of those conditions.

The relevant transaction-type involved in testimonial transactions has thus far been described interchangeably as the act of 'testimony' or 'telling someone something'. Insight into this transaction-type can be had by extending Craig's account of the emergence, via objectification, of the practice of pooling information. In the minimal epistemic community of the State of Nature, inquirer and informant are acquaintances who both recognize each other and are responsive to each other's immediate needs. The same process of objectification that extends the idea of a good informant beyond the *inquirer's* immediate recognitional powers (as described by Craig) also serves to create an addressed act that extends beyond the *informant's* immediate recognitional powers as well, such that the relationships between participants in the emerging social practice of pooling information cease to be that between acquaintances. Testifying is an addressed speech act (as opposed to the mere verbal expression of thought), but the audience to whom it is addressed is potentially anyone and everyone. Thus, the process of objectification that brings about the concept of a knower from the concept of a good informant also gives rise to a distinctive kind of impersonal yet interpersonal speech act, the speech act of testifying, and it is the presence of this act that ensures that the practice in question can be characterized as that of pooling information.

This characterization of the speech act of testimony is a departure from Fricker's own characterization, which limits the audience to whom the act of testimony is addressed to those acquaintances intended by the Speaker.[15] Neither characterization denies that a Speaker can target her speech act towards fulfilling the perceived epistemic needs of an already familiar audience (Hearers) and not others (Over-Hearers). Fricker takes this notion of *targeting* as defining the scope of those *addressed* by the act. On our characterization, in contrast, the scope of those *addressed* depends on the structure of the act of which both Speaker and Hearer are self-consciously aware, and does not depend on those *targeted* by the Speaker. Of course, even on our characterization, acts of testimony typically take place in the context of the perceived epistemic needs of extant relationships, and the Speaker is not absurdly portrayed as making testimonial pronouncements to the universe as it were. Nevertheless, in thinking of the transaction as testimonial, both parties are sensitive to the fact that the scope of those *addressed* extends beyond those *targeted* by the Speaker. Whilst it may be contextually impolite for an Over-Hearer to query or challenge the Speaker, the Over-Hearer too is included in the transaction, and this fact is sometimes exploited to create a heightened sense of intimacy between Speaker and Hearer by, for example, whispering in a way that extrudes the Over-Hearer from fully participating in a testimonial transaction to which she is party (on our characterization).

Fricker's characterization, one that focuses on a relationship of acquaintance between informer and inquirer, is surprising given her own understanding of the social practice of testimony as pooling information. 'To pool' used as a verb denotes the cooperative activity of putting some good into a common fund. If the common fund into which the information is pooled by an act of telling is limited to that between acquaintances alone, as implied by Fricker's characterization of the act of telling, we lose the advertised link between knowing and telling. We will thus persist with our characterization of the act of telling, one that treats informant and inquirer as bound together in an order of justice established by a transaction, all the while remaining possible strangers to each other, in that both potentially stand outside each other's sphere of recognition.

However the act is best understood, Fricker's own discussion of the social practice of pooling information as it is relevant to testimonial injustice concentrates on this one transaction alone, the speech act of testifying. This limited focus, as I understand it, stems simply from the explanatory centrality of the act of telling someone something in characterizing the social practice and does not reflect a parallel limitation of the notion of testimonial injustice to cases involving testimony alone. The social practice of pooling information extends beyond the speech act of telling someone something, and includes an array of different activities, including those related to the activities of inquiring, questioning, discussing, speculating and deliberating, as well as the myriad of thicker and culturally-specific forms that such activities take in differing contexts. Consider the following example from Christopher Hookway, in which a teacher, due to a prejudicial stereotype, does not take seriously the questions put forward by a particular student in the course of a classroom discussion.[16] Hookway argues that here we have a case of injustice akin to those Fricker discusses, even though the teacher's maltreatment of the student does not involve the attribution of insufficient credibility to the student following an act of telling. On the reading proffered here, this is a case of what Fricker would call testimonial injustice even without an act of testimony, since it involves maltreatment of someone that can be explained by appeal to the social practice of testimony, broadly construed to include the activity of participation in discussion from which the student is excluded.

This is admittedly an expansive conception of the social practice of testimony. It is not, for example, limited to what Hookway calls an "informational perspective" in which the relevant "interactions are all concerned with the possession and transmission of information or knowledge from one person to another" but also includes what he terms a broader "participant perspective" that is "involved when we think of [practitioners] as trying to participate in activities such as discussion, inquiry, deliberation, and so on."[17] That said, the conception is not so broad as to conflate the testimonial with the epistemic, and there are forms of epistemic inquiry involving the say-so of others that do not fall within the social practice of testimony even on this expanded conception.

Consider forms of inquiry in which the Hearer gains knowledge from the Speaker by treating their say-so as evidence of a belief in much the same ways as he may treat a yelp as evidence of predator-proximity. The Hearer may indeed gain knowledge via such an inquiry, but this is not achieved by treating the Speaker's say-so as the undertaking of a socially significant performance towards the Hearer in the context of a norm-governed transaction.[18] Craig's way of marking this contrast is in terms of a distinction between somebody's functioning as a 'good informant' and their functioning merely as a 'source of information'. As Craig explains, "What I have in mind is the special flavor of situations in which human beings treat each other as subjects with a common purpose, rather than as objects from which services, in this case true belief, can be extracted".[19] There are many ways of developing this pregnant contrast,[20] but one way of understanding the special flavor of treating someone as a good informant is in terms of the Hearer entering into an order of justice with the Speaker through transacting with her, as opposed to merely treating her utterance as evidence for something. Contra Hookway, the key contrast is thus not between the informational and participant perspectives, but between the deliberative perspectives of the potentially solitary inquirer extracting information from objects and the participant in the social practice of testimony via engagement in transactions such as telling/being told something to/by someone.

Here, then, is our first variety of testimonial injustice: transactional testimonial injustice. The injustice is brought into view by focusing on a breach of the order of justice established between the parties to a testimonial transaction. If the source of the breach is one that yields a systemic pattern of maltreatment of people across an array of different transactions and contexts, such as the widespread maltreatment that results from the sexist prejudices exhibited by Greenleaf, then the injustice may well be termed 'systemic transactional testimonial injustice'.

## 3. Structural testimonial injustice

At the beginning of the previous section we distinguished between transactional and structural varieties of injustice and noted that Fricker's work on testimonial injustice tends to focus on the former. It is not that Fricker is unaware of the possibility of there being a structural variety. Indeed, she begins her book by flagging a way of thinking about epistemic injustice in terms of the "distributive unfairness in the distribution of epistemic goods such as information or education. In such cases we picture social agents who have an interest in various goods, some of them epistemic, and question whether everyone is getting their fair share".[21] This suggestion is, however, flagged by Fricker only to be dismissed, since "there is nothing very distinctively epistemic about [this way of thinking of injustice] for it seems largely incidental that the good in question can be characterized as an epistemic good".

What does Fricker here mean by labelling this 'incidental'? Two possibilities suggest themselves. A more substantive reading takes this as dismissive of the very idea of structural testimonial injustice: even if one can talk of injustice in terms of an inappropriate distribution of goods such as information or education, the injustice does not stand in a categorical connection to the social practice of testimony. A less substantive reading is to take this as conceding that there is a structural variety of testimonial injustice but to dismiss its relevance to her overall project. In what follows, I aim to reject the more substantive reading and to offer a qualified defense of the less substantive one.[22]

To see why one should reject the more substantive reading, consider the following example, due to Elizabeth Anderson, in which a Hearer accords insufficient credibility to the Speaker's say-so on a matter that requires an educated judgment, and the Hearer's primary reason for according a low level of credibility is the Speaker's use of non-standard grammar in formulating their judgment.[23] The context here is crucial: Speaker and Hearer live in a society in which certain social groups are systematically deprived of decent educational opportunities, and the Hearer takes the use of standardized grammar as a marker of education, and hence of credibility. As Anderson points out, there is indeed a significant injustice here, but it is not a transactional testimonial injustice. Assuming the Hearer is not drawing on a prejudicial stereotype that is resistant to counter-evidence in making his credibility judgment, then it is possible that the Hearer is following a sound epistemic procedure that could even be justified to (and perhaps shared by) the Speaker herself. The injustice here is thus not transactional but structural, viz. the unfair distribution of certain epistemic goods within the society. As Anderson puts it, "[a]n original structural injustice – denial of fair opportunities for education – generates additional structural inequalities in opportunities for exercising full epistemic agency, which is an injustice to the speakers".[24]

A proponent of the more substantive reading need not deny that there is an injustice here, though will reject the contention that insight into the injustice is afforded by the social practice of testimony. Anderson's point, however, is that an understanding of the injustice here, as well as ways of overcoming the injustice, requires broadening our conception of the social practice of testimony itself, from a narrower focus on transactions alone to a broader one that incorporates the institutions within which such transactions have their home. In the example above, unfair distribution of institutional markers of credibility undermines the possibility of some to participate in the practice of pooling information, a maltreatment of those persons that would remain out of view if we merely focus – as Fricker does – on the normative standing of testimonial transactions between participants. In other words, insight into the injustice in this case is afforded by the social practice of testimony, since the injustice of a skewed distribution of credibility markers can only be understood by reference to "the single practice that dramatizes the origin of what it is to be a knower at all".[25] Thus it is a case of testimonial injustice in the sense under investigation in this essay, albeit one that requires a focus on structural aspects of the social practice, as opposed to a focus on transactions alone. We should therefore reject the more substantive reading and endorse the claim that there is a structural variety of testimonial injustice.

Earlier we floated a less substantive reading of Fricker's dismissal of structural testimonial injustice as incidental, one that concedes the possibility of a structural variant but provides principled reasons for focusing on the transactional variant alone, independent of structural considerations. What principle could motivate such a narrowed focus, especially when it is conceded that structural features play an important role in a full understanding of the injustice involved in Fricker's own examples of unjust testimonial transactions, such as that between Greenleaf and Sherwood?

One possible response points to the following key difference between the transactional and structural varieties: only the transactional variety of testimonial injustice need be available to the self-understanding of the maltreatment by the practitioners themselves. We have said that a transaction is a social act for which the self-conscious awareness by both agent and patient of their respective and complementary roles that comprise the act's structure is part of the very idea of the act itself. This is not to say that such awareness always accompanies any actual instance of the transaction, but that both parties to the transaction have available an understanding of the structure as part of their participation in the relevant social practice, which includes such a transaction. This means that recognition of the order of justice established between them by the transaction, as well as the possibility of injustice through breaking the order, is part of the self-understanding of the transaction that is available to both agent and patient. The experience of transactional testimonial injustice when it occurs is thus internal to the self-understanding of the transaction of the participants themselves. There is simply no parallel to this in the case of structural testimonial injustice. That is, it is perfectly possible to fully and reflectively participate in the social practice of testimony and have no understanding of the structural injustice whatsoever. Unlike the transactional variant, structural testimonial injustice is not internal to the perspective of the participants in the practice themselves.

A corollary of this difference is that if anyone is interested in understanding testimonial injustice as it is intelligible from within the perspective of those involved in the practice, then there is good reason for limiting oneself to the transactional, and not the structural, variant. There are some indications in Fricker's own writings that her overall concern accords primacy to such an internal perspective. For example, she begins her discussion of epistemic injustice pleading for a parallel reorientation in epistemology to that in ethical theorizing where "a moribund region of philosophy was revivified by a closer attention to lived experience" by "renewed attention to what we may broadly call ethical psychology – that is, to human beings' real experience of ethical value".[26] Although this is not fully developed in the remainder of the book, a parallel attention to what could be called 'epistemic psychology' pervades many of her subsequent discussions of testimonial injustice, paying close attention to the ways in which such injustice is experienced and understood by the agents themselves. Whether this accurately reflects Fricker's own motivations or not, there remains an important sense in which taking seriously the epistemic psychology of testimony, construed as taking seriously the participant's self-understanding of the social practice of testimony, provides a reason for limiting one's theorizing to the transactional variant of testimonial injustice, and not the structural one.

Earlier I called this a 'qualified' defense of the less substantive reading. What makes this defense 'qualified' is just how limited the conclusion of this line of thought is, even if successful. The upshot of the less substantive reading is merely to affirm that not every explanation of an instance of testimonial injustice need appeal to both structural and transactional varieties, and that there may be principled reasons (such as an interest in epistemic psychology) in any case for limiting one's focus on just one of them. The less substantive reading does not, however, imply that the transactional variant is somehow more pervasive or important than the structural one, or that it is more central in an overall account of testimonial injustice. Far from it: in rejecting the more substantive reading, we have affirmed the need to take seriously the possibility of structural testimonial injustice, since the institutional structures that facilitate participation in the practice of pooling information can lead to injustices within the practice that both extend far beyond the framework of transactions between participants, as well as alter the character of the transactions themselves. As a result, even one sympathetic to the less substantive reading would concede that a full understanding of many cases of testimonial injustice, including many of Fricker's own examples, requires consideration of both structural and the transactional varieties, as well as the interplay between them.

## 4. Testimonial betrayal

Perhaps you – like me – harbor the nagging suspicion that our investigation thus far has missed something central to the agent's self-understanding of the maltreatment experienced in central cases of testimonial injustice. The relationships forged by the transactional interactions that we have focused on thus far are thin, in the sense that they involve recognition of each other solely in terms of the interpersonal roles played by their participation in the practice, and the maltreatment involves abrogation of role-responsibilities in these formal relationships. The nagging suspicion is that many key cases critically involve thick relations of intimacy between acquaintances, and the maltreatment involves a rupture of, or disloyalty within, those thick relationships.[27] Put differently, the suspicion is that whilst we have been portraying the injustice as a breach, it is often far better portrayed as a betrayal.

Take Fricker's signature case, Greenleaf's dismissal of Sherwood's say-so. Sherwood's world is rapidly collapsing around her. The death of her fiancée, and the sense of uncertainty surrounding it, leaves her grief-stricken, vulnerable and isolated. Part of her isolation stems from the disparity between Sherwood's belief that her fiancée was murdered by a mutual acquaintance (Ripley) and everyone else's belief that this was a suicide. As her would-be father-in-law, Greenleaf provides a direct link to her deceased fiancée, and as a wealthy male benefactor in that society, Greenleaf provides the security and stability she craves, as well as a source of power to act and investigate that she lacks. Greenleaf's sexist attitudes towards Sherwood's testimony do not just exclude her from participation in the pooling of information; it constitutes a betrayal of their (proxy) relationship and serves to highlight Sherwood's humiliating powerlessness in the social sphere. The viewer's final glimpse of Sherwood in the screenplay highlights these themes. Sitting in a launch, accompanied by Greenleaf, she lunges at Ripley, accusing him of murdering her fiancée. Sherwood is physically restrained by Greenleaf's henchman, who exchanges a knowing glance with Ripley. ("Ripley looks at him as if to say: what can you do, she's hysterical"). The last shot sees Sherwood escorted away in Greenleaf's protective company, passive and alone, all too aware – as we are – of Greenleaf's erroneous complicity in siding with Ripley over herself.

The term 'betrayal' does not appear in Fricker's book-length treatment of epistemic injustice, although it does feature prominently in her more recent work, especially in the context of exploring the possible role played by trust in the epistemology of testimony.[28] At the center of this more recent discussion is a distinction that Fricker makes between second- and third-personal stances of trust. Applied to the testimonial context, her suggestion is that there are two ways of treating someone as an informant as opposed to a source of information. One way (adopting a 'second-personal stance of trust') involves the Speaker and Hearer's mutual awareness of, and acting upon, the Hearer's manifest trust in the Speaker on this occasion. Another way (adopting a 'third-personal stance of trust') involves the Hearer trusting the Speaker, albeit without assuming the Speaker is herself treating the Hearer's trust as the reason for striving to be a sincere and competent testifier towards him. In both cases, the Hearer trusts the Speaker, and that trust is directed towards the Speaker as a person – an active informant – as opposed to cases of mere reliance where the Hearer treats the Speaker as a passive source of information. A clear difference between these three attitudes (reliance, second- and third-personal stances of trust) can be seen when the attitude turns out to be misplaced. As Fricker puts it: "second personal trust creates the possibility of betrayal; third personal trust creates the possibility of ethical let-down; and the ethical attitudes involved in both kinds of trust are still to be contrasted with mere reliance, whose disappointment incorporates no ethical dimension".[29]

I concur that "[t]here is a difference of perspective here that wants philosophical capture",[30] and it seems that our discussion thus far provides a way of doing just that.[31] Earlier we distinguished between the deliberative perspectives of the potentially solitary inquirer extracting information from objects, and the participant in the social practice of testimony via engagement in transactions. Transacting with someone involves adopting a thin stance of trust towards them. Although the person thereby recognized is conceived second-personally ("*I* am telling/being told by *you*"), the stance of trust (and the subsequent relationship) is thin in that it need not involve any recognition of the distinctiveness of the second-person beyond that formally required by the transaction. This is why such thin recognition on its own does not create rivalry: my recognizing you in a transaction on its own does not in any way detract from my recognizing any other person in such a transaction.[32] The order of justice created by the transaction can be culpably breached, and a 'kind of ethical resentment' towards the informant may be properly experienced, unlike the mere disappointment properly experienced in a case of misplaced reliance on a source of information. The breach in the transactional case will not, however, be properly experienced as betrayal, which requires a thicker stance of trusting recognition between persons that creates rivalry. The thin stance of trust adopted towards each other in a transaction thus differs from the thick stance of trust adopted between intimates (in the very broad sense of non-strangers), where the thick stance involves recognition of distinctive features of the personality of the one trusted in a way that creates and maintains rivalries.

Should we therefore admit a third variety of testimonial injustice, in addition to the transactional and structural variants already considered, viz. a betrayal of the intimate relationships established by a thick stance of trust between Speaker and Hearer in certain testimonial encounters? An affirmative response requires further elaboration, as betrayal does not appear to fall under our overall definition of testimonial injustice. Testimonial injustice, we have said throughout, is not merely an injustice associated with an act of testimony, but an injustice that stands in a categorical connection with the social practice of testimony. As we have seen, the act of testimony at the explanatory center of the practice of pooling information does not solely operate between intimates or acquaintances, and thus is not one that necessarily involves a thick stance of trust between Speaker and Hearer. It seems possible to fully understand the sting of betrayal experienced when a Hearer appears to be disloyal to a supposed special relationship with the Speaker without any recourse whatsoever to insight afforded by reflection on the practice of testimony.[33]

This concern is deepened when one considers the difference in the standing accorded to the speech performance itself in establishing the thin trust of transactions, when compared to the thick trust of intimacy. In a transaction, the speech performance plays an ineliminable role in establishing the transactional relationship: even if the Hearer has good reason for being sure what it is that the Speaker thinks on a particular matter, there is no order of justice established between them unless the Speaker expresses this in a testimonial speech act (that is recognized as such by the Hearer). Further, the relationship in the transactional case is fixed at the moment of the transaction: subsequent failure by the Speaker to perform as she ought to perform given the norms established by the transaction is treated by the Hearer as a breach of the transaction, and gives no reason on its own for the Hearer to query whether such a transaction took place to start off with.[34] In contrast, establishing thick relations of intimacy and acquaintance do not require a specific speech performance by one party, and subsequent failures to live up to the expectations of that thicker relationship may well leave one party questioning whether such a thicker relationship was actually in place in the first place. These differences cast further doubt on the suggestion that we should treat betrayal of the relationships involved in the thick stance of trust as an additional variety of testimonial injustice, as the differences appear to reveal the manner in which the ethical intrigue of such thicker relationships potentially floats free from the speech act of testifying.

One response to these concerns is to concede that though betrayal is a central feature of the experience of testimonial injustice in many key cases, it is best construed as an injustice that is associated with an act of testimony rather than a testimonial injustice. A more ambitious response explores the interplay between thick and thin trust relations in the context of a transaction so as to reveal a distinctive notion of betrayal.

Let us provide a thumbnail sketch of the more ambitious response.[35] In intimate relationships forged by thick relations of trust, parties seek each other's approval, often including recognition of their opinions on matters arising in the course of their interactions. In the context of such relationships, seeking approval need not take the form of an explicit request for approval; one party may just assume that the other party will take their opinion seriously given their purported relationship. Failure by one party to accord the recognition sought implicitly may be experienced by the other party as a betrayal of that thick relationship. Matters are subtly different when approval is sought via a transactional engagement between the parties, such as by one party telling the other something. A transaction, we have said, includes the self-conscious awareness of the structure by both parties as part of the very idea of a transaction itself. As a result, once the transaction has taken place, either party can try to ignore the normative implications of the performance, but to ignore these implications in the context of a transaction is to actively reject them.[36] A transaction between intimates thus has the effect of turning a failure to accord the recognition sought into a rejection of the requested approbation. It is not just that one party does not provide the recognition that the other party seeks, but that the one party throws the request for recognition back to the other party. The experience of betrayal following an unsuccessful transaction between intimates thus takes on the distinctive form of the sting of rejection. When Sherwood tells Greenleaf of her suspicions about Ripley, she seeks out his approbation. His failure to believe her is experienced by her as rejection of their relationship, a rejection that exacerbates her own sense of isolation and powerlessness.

Although it needs to be developed further, this more ambitious response opens the possibility for recognition of yet another variety of testimonial injustice – testimonial betrayal. It is admitted that if one thinks of the social practice of testimony abstracted away from agents who are socially-situated, then the sting of betrayal will simply not feature in cases where there is a breach in testimonial transactions. But the actual social practice of testimony does involve socially-situated agents, and this means not just that they stand in varying forms of power relations with one another, but they also stand in varying relations of intimacy and acquaintance with each other. In such a socially situated practice, people seek out recognition and/or approval as believers and testifiers from certain individuals and not others, and experience the sting of betrayal when this recognition is perfidiously accorded to others instead. When seeking approval takes a transactional form, such as through telling someone something, then betrayal takes the form of rejection. The social practice of testimony thus allows us to understand the distinctive kind of betrayal experienced when one has one's testimony rejected in the context of intimate relationships.

## 5. Summary

This essay has been an investigation into the possibility of there being a categorical connection between the social practice of testimony and certain instances of injustice. By focusing on different aspects of the social practice, we have managed to identify three potential varieties of testimonial injustice. The first variety – *transactional testimonial injustice* – emerges when one focuses on the character of the self-conscious, interpersonal transactions that take place within the practice, most centrally the act of telling someone something. The injustice here involves a breach of the order of justice established between the parties by the transactions that fall within the social practice of testimony. The second variety – *structural testimonial injustice* – emerges when one focusses on the social institutions within which the practice of testimony operates. The injustice here stems from structural inequalities within such institutions that lead to diminished possibilities of participation in the social practice of testimony. More tentatively, a third variety – *testimonial betrayal* – emerges when one focuses on the thick trust relations between acquaintances within the practice. The injustice here includes the experience of humiliating rejection felt as part of the sting of betrayal.

We have used the seminal work of Miranda Fricker as both inspiration and foil throughout our investigation. Whilst broadly endorsing her understanding of testimonial injustice, we have made three suggested emendations. The first is to extend the scope of those addressed by the speech act of testimony beyond those targeted by the Speaker. The second is to read her earlier work as focusing on a transactional testimonial injustice, whereas her more recent writings on trust as focusing on testimonial betrayal. The third is to view her relative inattention to structural testimonial injustice as stemming from a principled commitment to the importance of 'epistemic psychology'.

The discussion here has been limited to the diagnostic dimension of Fricker's work on testimonial injustice, the attempt to make theoretical sense of the very idea of testimonial injustice itself. This leaves open the task of exploring the therapeutic dimension of her work, the attempt to consider ways to mitigate and ameliorate such injustice. Further work in both dimensions will no doubt be enhanced by greater sensitivity to the varieties of testimonial injustice brought into view by considering differing aspects of the social practice of testimony, including at least some of the variants distinguished here.[37]

**Related chapters**: 1, 3, 4, 5, 6, 20, 21, 23

# Notes

1 The trio, and the pathological tag, is due to Gelfert (2014: 193–214).
2 Fricker (2007).
3 As per convention, I have used terms Speaker and Hearer as labels for the two parties to a testimonial transaction, even though there need be no actual speaking or hearing going on. Further, unless context dictates otherwise, the Speaker is treated as female and the Hearer as male to aid comprehension.
4 Fricker (2007: 20–21) argues for limiting testimonial injustice to those cases involving a credibility deficit alone and not extending this analysis to cases involving an excess of credibility. For a convincing argument against such a limitation, see Medina (2011).
5 Minghella and Highsmith (2000: 130), cited in Fricker (2007: 9).
6 Craig (1990).
7 Rödl (2014: 292).
8 This is clearest in Fricker (2008).
9 Fricker (2007: 145).
10 In addition to Anderson (2012) discussed below, see – for example – Young (2007), Forst (2012) and Laden (2013).
11 Fricker (2007: 27).
12 Coady (2010) and Anderson (2012) are particularly clear on this point.
13 The notion of a transaction is more fully developed in Wanderer (2014).
14 Cf. Descombes (2014: 243).
15 Fricker (2012).
16 Hookway (2010).
17 Hookway (2010: 156).
18 This point is developed more fully in Moran (2005).
19 Craig (1990: 36).
20 See, esp., Fricker (2012).
21 Fricker (2007: 1).
22 Fricker herself rejects the more substantive reading in Fricker (2010), in response to related concerns raised by David Coady (2010). In subsequent work (Fricker 2013), she explicitly marks the difference between these two varieties under the headings 'discriminatory' and 'distributive' epistemic injustice.
23 Anderson (2012).
24 Anderson (2012: 169).
25 Fricker (2007: 145), cited above.
26 Fricker (2007: vii).
27 Maitra (2010) raises a concern along these lines – see especially her comparison of Marge Sherwood with the case of Zara on pages 198–200. In response, Maitra proposes a modification of Fricker's account, one that supplements it with explicit reference to obligations to believe the say-so of certain others that arise in the context of special interpersonal relationships. As will emerge in the ensuing discussion, such a modification is rejected here as it blurs the difference between transactional testimonial injustice and testimonial betrayal.
28 Fricker (2012).
29 Fricker (2012: 257).
30 Fricker (2012: 257).
31 Fricker's own way of capturing the difference invokes her own understanding of the speech act of testimony as personal, rejected above.
32 Cf. Markovits (2011: 304) for a similar point about promising.
33 Given limitations of space, I am relying here on an assumed familiarity with the sting of betrayal and a tacit understanding of why it is experienced as a form of maltreatment. I have found Simmel (1950: 333–334) and Shklar (1984: 138–191) helpful in this regard.

34 I am drawing here on the discussion of promises in Markovits (2011), which has shown me ways of developing an earlier – and cruder – version of the distinction put forward in Wanderer (2013).
35 My thinking in this paragraph is deeply indebted to discussions with Byron Davies, and to a paper he presented at UMass Boston in April 2015 on 'The Insult in Not Being Believed'.
36 Cf. Wanderer (2012).
37 An earlier version of this chapter was presented at the 'Between Ethics and Epistemology' workshop on Miranda Fricker's work at UMass-Boston in April 2015, and I am indebted to the comments of my co-presenters and members of the audience on that occasion. In addition, I have benefitted from generous feedback from Byron Davies, Miranda Fricker, Henry Lara-Steidel, Richard Moran, Lisa Rivera and Leo Townsend, as well as from the editors of this volume.

## References

Anderson, Elizabeth. 2012. 'Epistemic Justice as a Virtue of Social Institutions'. *Social Epistemology* 26 (2): 163–173.
Coady, David. 2010. 'Two Concepts of Epistemic Injustice'. *Episteme* 7 (2): 101–113.
Craig, Edward. 1990. *Knowledge and the State of Nature*. Oxford: Clarendon Press.
Descombes, Vincent. 2014. *The Institutions of Meaning*. Cambridge, MA: Harvard University Press.
Forst, Rainer. 2012. *The Right to Justification: Elements of a Constructivist Theory of Justice*. New York: Columbia University Press.
Fricker, Miranda. 2007. *Epistemic Injustice: Power and the Ethics of Knowing*. Oxford: Oxford University Press.
Fricker, Miranda. 2008. 'Scepticism and the Genealogy of Knowledge: Situating Epistemology in Time'. *Philosophical Papers* 37 (1): 27–50.
Fricker, Miranda. 2010. 'Replies to Alcoff, Goldberg, and Hookway on Epistemic Injustice'. *Episteme* 7 (2): 164–178.
Fricker, Miranda. 2012. 'Group Testimony? The Making of a Collective Good Informant'. *Philosophy and Phenomenological Research* 84 (2): 249–276.
Fricker, Miranda. 2013. 'Epistemic Justice as a Condition of Political Freedom?'. *Synthese* 190 (7): 1317–1332.
Gelfert, Axel. 2014. *A Critical Introduction to Testimony*. London, UK: Continuum.
Hookway, Christopher. 2010. 'Some Varieties of Epistemic Injustice: Reflections on Fricker'. *Episteme* 7 (2): 151–163.
Laden, Anthony. 2013. 'Learning to Be Equal: Just Schools as Schools of Justice', in D. Allen and R. Reich (eds.), *Education, Justice, and Democracy*, 62–79. Chicago, IL: University of Chicago Press.
Maitra, Ishani. 2010. 'The Nature of Epistemic Injustice'. *Philosophical Books* 51 (4): 195–211.
Markovits, Daniel. 2011. 'Promises as an Arms-Length Relation', in H. Sheinman (ed.), *Promises and Agreements: Philosophical Essays*, 295–326. Oxford: Oxford University Press.
Medina, José. 2011. 'The Relevance of Credibility Excess in a Proportional View of Epistemic Injustice: Differential Epistemic Authority and the Social Imaginary'. *Social Epistemology* 25 (1): 15–35.
Minghella, Anthony, and Patricia Highsmith. 2000. *The Talented Mr. Ripley*. London: Methuen.
Moran, Richard. 2005. 'Getting Told and Being Believed'. *Philosophers' Imprint* 5 (5): 1–29.
Rödl, Sebastian. 2014. 'Testimony and Generality'. *Philosophical Topics* 42 (1): 291–302.
Shklar, Judith N. 1984. *Ordinary Vices*. Cambridge, MA: Belknap Press of Harvard University Press.
Simmel, Georg. 1950. *The Sociology of Georg Simmel* (trans. K.H. Wolff). London: Free Press.
Wanderer, Jeremy. 2012. 'Addressing Testimonial Injustice: Being Ignored and Being Rejected'. *The Philosophical Quarterly* 62: 148–169.
Wanderer, Jeremy. 2013. 'Testimony and the Interpersonal'. *International Journal of Philosophical Studies* 21 (1): 92–110.
Wanderer, Jeremy. 2014. 'Alethic Holdings'. *Philosophical Topics* 42 (1): 63–84.
Young, Iris Marion. 2007. *Structural Injustice and the Politics of Difference*. Cambridge: Cambridge University Press.

# 3
# VARIETIES OF HERMENEUTICAL INJUSTICE[1]

*José Medina*

### Introduction: defining hermeneutical injustice and hermeneutical death

In her pioneering book *Epistemic Injustice* (2007), Miranda Fricker gave explicit formulation to a phenomenon that oppressed subjects had been experiencing and calling attention to for a long time: the expressive and interpretative side of their oppression, that is, *hermeneutical injustice*. Hermeneutical injustice is the phenomenon that occurs when the intelligibility of communicators is unfairly constrained or undermined, when their meaning-making capacities encounter unfair obstacles, or, as Fricker puts it, "when a gap in collective interpretive resources puts someone at an unfair advantage when it comes to making sense of their social experience" (2007: 1). Hermeneutical harms should not be minimized or underestimated, for the interpretative capacities of expressing oneself and being understood are basic human capacities. Meaning-making and meaning-sharing are crucial aspects of a dignified human life. Hermeneutical injuries can go very deep, indeed to the very core of one's humanity. Fricker asked: "Is hermeneutical injustice sometimes so damaging that it cramps the very development of self"? (2007: 163)

In answer to Fricker's question, I want to suggest that there are forms of hermeneutical injustices that are so damaging that they can result in what I call *hermeneutical death*,[2] that is, in phenomena that radically constrain one's hermeneutical capacities and agency such as the following: the loss (or radical curtailment) of one's voice, of one's interpretative capacities, or of one's status as a participant in meaning-making and meaning-sharing practices. This is something that oppressed groups have denounced for a long time. In particular, it has been poignantly expressed by women of color – from Maria Stewart[3] and Sojourner Truth to Audre Lorde and Gloria Anzaldúa – who have felt systematically silenced and misheard by multiple publics. Hermeneutical harms can run so deep as to annihilate one's self, so as to produce *hermeneutical death*. On my view, this occurs when subjects are not simply mistreated as intelligible communicators, but prevented from developing and exercising a voice, that is, prevented from participating in meaning-making and meaning-sharing practices. Gloria Anzaldúa described the predicament of hermeneutical death in forceful and dramatic ways when she writes about Anglo White privilege as killing her voice and her capacity to be heard and understood in her own terms, as using (what she called) 'linguistic terrorism' to annihilate her self: "*El Anglo con cara de inocente nos arranco la lengua*. Wild tongues cannot be tamed, they can only be cut out" (1987: 76). "Repeated attacks on our native tongue diminish our sense of self" (1987: 80).

Hermeneutical injustices of this extreme form not only demand special attention, but also call for a response that is different in kind to the response appropriate for addressing *non-fatal* hermeneutical injustices in which one's status and agency as a communicator and interpreter is preserved even if seriously constrained. Desperate times call for desperate measures and, I will suggest, hermeneutical death calls for a particular kind of hermeneutical struggle with radical features that other hermeneutical struggles do not have. But the different kinds of preventive and reparative work that hermeneutical death and non-fatal hermeneutical injustices demand will have to wait until the final section of this essay. In the next section I will elucidate different versions and dimensions of the concept of hermeneutical injustice and how it relates to issues of epistemic responsibility. The following section will address different possible classifications of hermeneutical injustices and how these classifications offer conceptual resources for diagnosing cases of hermeneutical injustices and for identifying ways of resisting hermeneutical marginalization. Finally, in the concluding section, I will come back to the notion of hermeneutical death outlined by philosophers of color, gesturing toward possible paths of resistance and hermeneutical liberation.

## Hermeneutical injustices and hermeneutical responsibilities

The last decade has produced a rich literature on hermeneutical injustice, trying to understand the nature of the phenomenon, its causes and consequences, and its varieties. Fricker characterizes hermeneutical injustice as a structural, large-scale phenomenon that happens at the level of an entire culture. There are important advantages in emphasizing the *structural* elements of hermeneutical injustice – this emphasis calls attention to the fact that there can be hermeneutical wrongs built into the very structure of our communicative practices, and that people can be hermeneutically disadvantaged in unfair ways even when we cannot point to particular persons acting in ways that are identifiably wrong. Hermeneutical injustices are indeed very often impersonal, widespread, and systematic. But the structural elements of hermeneutical injustice should not be emphasized at the expense of disregarding its *agential* components. In her 2007 book, Fricker argued that hermeneutical injustices are epistemic wrongs that simply happen, without perpetrators,[4] without being committed by anyone in particular, for they result from lacunas or limitations in 'the collective hermeneutical resource' of a culture. Consequently, Fricker contended that when it comes to hermeneutical injustices, unlike testimonial injustices, issues of responsibility do not arise. I have developed two kinds of arguments intended to show that responsibility is in fact a crucial aspect of hermeneutical injustices (see Medina 2012, 2013).

In the first place, I have argued, when we consider the issue of responsibility with respect to hermeneutical injustice, it would be wrong to restrict ourselves to purely *individual* forms of responsibility such as individual culpability. It is also important to consider here collective and shared forms of responsibility. An entire culture can be held responsible for not trying to understand a particular kind of experience or a particular kind of subjectivity, and, more importantly, different groups and publics within a hermeneutically unjust culture can bear different kinds of responsibility for their hermeneutical neglect in certain areas and/or for their hermeneutical resistance to certain expressive or interpretative efforts. Moreover, I have also argued, when it comes to individuals, their responsibility may be highly limited and diffused, but it does not disappear completely. When it comes to hermeneutical injustices, individuals cannot be left off the hook; that is, they cannot (at least not always and completely) be allowed to hide behind the shortcomings of their culture. There are important issues of *complicity* with respect to hermeneutical injustices that need to be theorized. We can identify degrees of complicity in how individuals respond to the lacunas and limitations in the hermeneutical resources they have inherited and in how they participate (or fail to participate) in expressive and interpretative dynamics.

In the second place, I have also developed arguments against a monolithic conception of culture and its shared hermeneutical resources that called into question blanket statements about the *impossibility* of expressing, understanding, or interpreting an experience, a problem, an identity, etc. It is important to call attention to the inner diversity of a collective, to pay attention to its subgroups and subcultures, and to highlight the diversity and heterogeneity of expressive capacities and resources that collectives typically exhibit. For a pluralistic conception of social groups and cultures, it is problematic to say that it is simply *impossible* for an experience to be understood within a particular culture. Instead of focusing on complete success or failure of understanding, it is important to appreciate that intelligibility is a matter of more or less: doing better or worse in understanding oneself and others is a matter of trying as hard as one can, of paying attention to the emerging expressive and interpretative possibilities, no matter how inchoate or embryonic. Typically, in an expressive community, there are meanings and interpretations that are well established and widely shared, but there are also meanings and interpretations that have a more limited and precarious circulation, and there are also those meanings and interpretations that are still struggling to be formed and to be accepted – struggling for full expression and for full understanding. Poorly understood and inchoate meanings, interpretations, and expressive styles are the site of hermeneutical struggles, struggles in which there are interpretative achievements and break-throughs (new experiences are named, new phenomena understood), but also struggles in which people become silenced, misunderstood, and hermeneutically marginalized.

When it comes to hermeneutical harms and injustices, the question is not simply whether or not there are expressive and interpretative resources available for meaning-making and meaning-sharing, but how those resources are used, by whom, and in what ways. In this sense, when we recognize that a phenomenon or experience is not talked about or is poorly understood in a culture, and we think that a group of people is unfairly disadvantaged as a result, and we label it a hermeneutical injustice, this should be the beginning – not the end! – of a diagnostic process. This process proceeds by asking more and more specific questions: exactly by whom and in what way is the phenomenon or experience poorly expressed/understood?, in what contexts and for what purposes?, what are the dynamics that contribute to halt any expressive and interpretative progress in this area?, etc. With these more specific questions, crucial issues of positionality and relationality with respect to hermeneutical injustice arise, and they enable us to calibrate complex issues of shared and collective responsibility (which also make room for limited forms of individual responsibility). Calling attention to the crucial role of the epistemic agency of privileged subjects in the production and perpetuation of hermeneutical injustices, Gaile Pohlhaus, Jr. (2012) has articulated the notion of 'willful hermeneutical ignorance' to describe instances in which, despite the availability of alternative conceptualizations put forth by marginalized, resistant knowers, "dominantly situated knowers nonetheless continue to misunderstand and misinterpret the world" (2012: 716).[5]

In her recent work, Fricker has recognized the importance of 'localized hermeneutical practices' and has called attention to agential elements in the production of hermeneutical injustices. She has argued that patterns of testimonial injustice can contribute to the production and perpetuation of hermeneutical injustice: "where it is persistent and socially patterned", testimonial injustice "will tend to create or increase *hermeneutical marginalisation*. That is to say, it will tend to create and sustain a situation in which some social groups have less than a fair crack at contributing to the shared pool of concepts and interpretive tropes that we use to make generally share-able sense of our social experiences" (2016: 163). Instead of talking about "the collective hermeneutical resource", Fricker now calls attention to the "*shared* pool" of hermeneutical resources, which contains "meanings that just about anyone can draw upon and expect those meanings to be understood across social space by just about anyone else" (2016: 163). And with this more qualified view, she makes room for dissonant meanings and interpretations that are not widely shared. In this sense, Fricker talks about "localised hermeneutical practices": "fully functioning yet insufficiently widely shared hermeneutical practices"; "localised or in-group hermeneutical practices that are nonetheless not shared across further social space" (2016: 166 and 167). By pluralizing her view of hermeneutical resources and how they enter into hermeneutical dynamics, Fricker's current view becomes polyphonic and converges with my own, as she herself points out:

> Medina is right to emphasise that the intersectional ignorances created by the possession and non-possession of this or that cluster of interpretive concepts growing out of this or that area of social experience tell a 'polyphonic' or multi-voiced story of power *and* resistance, societal conceptual impoverishment *and* localised interpretive sophistication and creativity.
>
> (2016: 167)

Although Fricker accepts the agential production of hermeneutical injustices, she considers it "a purely structural phenomenon with no individual perpetrator" (2016: 172). But in some cases there seem to be such perpetrators, for example, in the case of racial hermeneutical injustices. There are hermeneutical attitudes inscribed in *white ignorance* (Mills 2007) that seem complicit with white privilege and with the perpetuation of hermeneutical disadvantages for racially oppressed groups. Fricker argues that white ignorance often functions as the source of epistemic injustices, but not of distinctively hermeneutical injustices, since it typically concerns "a dysfunction at the level of belief and evidence rather than the level of conceptual repertoire and intelligibility" (2016: 173). However, she acknowledges that there can be cases of white ignorance ("albeit non-standard") that include "the suppression of concepts" and result in "a genuine *deficit in hermeneutical resources* for the white community" (2016: 174). Despite the availability of the relevant meanings and interpretations in localized hermeneutical practices, the "white-ignorant" subject (who may or may not be white) cultivates hermeneutical attitudes that close his/her mind to alternative expressive or interpretative resources and make him/her remain oblivious to or dismissive of these resources. White ignorance includes what Pohlhaus, Jr. (2012) calls racialized "willful hermeneutical ignorance". The victims of racially motivated concept suppression are typically not the hermeneutically dispossessed subjects: they often do have the conceptual resources to communicate properly, but they are simply not being adequately heard or understood because of their interlocutors' hermeneutical deficits. Although privileged subjects are the ones hermeneutically deprived, oppressed subjects are in the end the ones who suffer the most epistemic harms (including hermeneutical harms) as a consequence: non-dominantly situated people often find their meanings and communicative contributions not taken seriously, improperly heard, deemed deficient, reinterpreted, distorted, and too quickly dismissed, and in these ways they are hermeneutically disrespected and wronged. It is important to note that there are cases of white ignorance in which victim and perpetrator coincide: for example, cases in which racially oppressed subjects do not understand some of their own experiences and problems due to internalized white ignorance, and also cases in which underprivileged white subjects are unable to understand predicaments they share with racially oppressed subjects due to a racial ignorance that is not in their own benefit despite their whiteness – think, for example, of white subjects living under conditions of poverty and being seduced by white ignorance to understand their situation as resulting from illegal immigration or from non-whites abusing a welfare system.

Fricker acknowledges that the racially motivated concept-suppression cases are cases in which white ignorance and hermeneutical injustices overlap: cases "in which one group's communicative attempts meet with failure owing to a paucity of concepts on the part of an out-group and therefore in the shared hermeneutical resource" (Fricker 2016: 174–5). But Fricker still objects against using white ignorance as an agentially produced form of hermeneutical injustice. She argues that individuals can only be considered the cause of particular hermeneutical failures; they can only be blamed for "failing to be virtuous hearers"; but they cannot be deemed the "perpetrator of the broader injustice itself" (2016: 172, note 16).

The debates about hermeneutical injustice will surely go on. There is no doubt that there is something conceptual at stake in these debates: how to understand the phenomenon, how to diagnose it and analyze it, etc. But it is important to notice that there is also (and perhaps more fundamentally) something *practical* at stake – how to fight hermeneutical injustices, how to prevent them before they occur, and how to repair hermeneutical practices and dynamics when they occur. We will come back to this practical side in the last section before we survey the wild variety of cases of hermeneutical injustices in the next section.

## Classificatory pluralism: navigating a heterogeneous terrain

Hermeneutical injustices are indeed wildly heterogeneous phenomena, and we can identify indefinitely many varieties depending on the classificatory lenses we use. There are many different ways of classifying varieties of hermeneutical injustice, depending on the aims of our classification. Classifications are useful for what they enable us to accomplish; they are not simply an idle academic exercise of intellectual dexterity; they are, rather, a conceptual exercise that enable us to navigate the world and to find ways to change it. Instead of aiming at a single, all-encompassing classification that covers all possible varieties in a single list, it would be advantageous to avail ourselves of as many classifications as possible so that we can highlight different elements and dimensions in the phenomenology of hermeneutical wrongs committed against individuals, groups, and publics. It is important to have a rich and broad conceptual toolbox for diagnosing hermeneutical wrongs and finding ways of resisting them and repairing them. In this section, I will elucidate possible classifications of hermeneutical injustices according to four different angles or parameters, inviting others to add to this preliminary list of possible classifications, which should remain forever open and growing. The four parameters or criteria I want to focus on are the *source* of the problem, the *dynamics* of the problem, the *breadth* of the problem, and the *depth* of the problem.

In the first place, when it comes to the *source* of the problem, we can distinguish two different kinds of hermeneutical injustice: those that are *semantically produced* and those that are *performatively produced*. The semantically produced hermeneutical injustices are the paradigmatic cases on which Fricker and her followers have tended to focus: cases in which hermeneutical disadvantages and harms result from the unavailability of labels; cases where understanding fails because words are lacking, where we find "a lacuna where the name of a distinctive social experience should be" (2007: 150–151). A powerful example Fricker examines concerns the hermeneutical obstacles that the Women's Movement encountered to address experiences of sexual intimidation when labels such as 'sexual harassment' were not available. As Fricker remarks, women activists found themselves in the peculiar situation of organizing 'speak-outs' in which "the 'this' they were going to break the silence about had no name" (2007: 150). Semantically produced hermeneutical injustices also occur when words and concepts are available, but they are not allowed to be used to express certain things. This is what Sojourner Truth powerfully called attention to in her address at the Ohio Women's Rights Convention in 1851, when she denounced the fact that crucial aspects of black femininity were blocked from entering the meaning of 'woman'. When Sojourner Truth poignantly asked, "And ain't I a woman?", she was unmasking and denouncing the racial biases underlying mainstream conceptions of femininity – whited conceptions of femininity that marginalized black women in the US.

There are also performatively produced hermeneutical injustices, which occur when subjects are judged as unintelligible or less intelligible than other subjects not because of the words they use but because of their communicative performance or expressive style (Fricker 2007: 160ff). So, for example, in certain contexts and for certain audiences, a subject's accent, unorthodox demeanor, or flamboyant style may be perceived as indicative of defective intelligibility – s/he may be perceived as less articulate or clear than other speakers, her/his interpretations and perspectives may be less likely to be understood in their own terms, and s/he may be more likely to be taken as unable to make full sense of certain topics or areas of experience.[6] Fricker calls attention to the performative aspects of hermeneutical injustice when she shifts from semantic contents to voices and expressive styles: "a hermeneutical gap might equally concern not (or not only) the content but rather the form of what can be said" (2007: 160). When we pay attention to unfair disadvantages and obstacles that arise for the development of dissonant or eccentric voices under adverse hermeneutical climates, we need to shift the focus from the semantics of experiential contents to the pragmatics of meaning-making and meaning-sharing activities.

In the second place, hermeneutical injustices can also be classified according to the particular kinds of *dynamics* in which they surface. In particular, we can distinguish between *structural* or *institutional* dynamics and *interpersonal* dynamics. Hermeneutical injustices are committed structurally or institutionally when there are structural conditions or institutional designs that prevent the use of certain hermeneutical resources and expressive styles, or simply when those conditions or designs favor certain hermeneutical communities and practices and disadvantage others. We encounter hermeneutical injustices of this sort when institutions refuse to accept certain categories and expressive styles to the detriment of particular publics, as for example when questionnaires (of e.g. a university or a state agency) force individuals to self-describe in ways they don't want to because of the limited options (e.g. the binary male/female categories when it comes to gender identity, without offering 'transgender' as an option), or because certain categories are not provided, and the closest one involves a mischaracterization (e.g. 'Hispanic' versus 'Latina/o'). On the other hand, hermeneutical injustices are also often committed in and through interpersonal dynamics. This occurs, for example, when there are hermeneutical intimidations in interpersonal exchanges, as it is well illustrated by the literature on micro-aggressions. Although the silencing effects of micro-aggressions have been analyzed as causing testimonial injustices (Dotson 2011), they can also be shown to function as intimidations that cause hermeneutical marginalization: "skeptical stares; looking confused, puzzled, or unable to follow; constantly interrupting or questioning one's meaning, are some of the subtle (sometimes not so subtle) communicative intimidations and micro-aggressions that can silence people or implicitly encourage them to limit their speech or take a discursive detour" (Medina forthcoming: 14). By calling into question one's intelligibility, not only can micro-aggressions unfairly constrain one's testimonial capacities, but they can also put unfair pressures on one's meaning-making and meaning-sharing capacities, thus producing hermeneutical injustices through interpersonal dynamics.

In the third place, we can also classify instances of hermeneutical injustice according to their *breadth*, considering how far the injustice reaches across the social fabric. From the beginning, Fricker distinguished between incidental and systematic cases of hermeneutical injustice, that is, between isolated and widespread cases of unfair failures of understanding and interpretation. Fricker has emphasized that there are 'radical' or 'maximal' cases in which nobody, not even the concerned communicator herself, can achieve understanding because the meanings and expressive/interpretative resources in question are beyond the reach of that community. But she also points out that there are also 'minimal' cases of hermeneutical injustice in which there are communicators who can make sense of the phenomenon, experience, or problem in question, but nonetheless when they try to express themselves in that area, they encounter incomprehension and/or misinterpretation: although able to communicate her experience in principle, "she is unable to render it intelligible across social space to some significant social other to whom she needs to convey it" (Fricker 2016: 165). Fricker has underscored that between 'maximal' and 'minimal' cases of hermeneutical injustice, there is "a continuum of possibilities [. . .] – i.e. a range of cases in which there is shared intelligibility across an increasingly large group or groups" (Fricker 2016: 165). In particular, she has emphasized the importance of "*midway* cases of hermeneutical injustice":

> cases in which there are sophisticated interpretive practices [. . .], but not shared with at least one out-group with whom communication is needed. Members of such hermeneutically self-reliant groups are vulnerable to hermeneutical injustices whose form does not involve any confused experiences whatever, but only frustratingly failed attempts to communicate them to members of an out-group.
>
> (Fricker 2016: 167)

Finally, in the fourth place, we can also classify hermeneutical injustices according to their *depth*, that is, according to how deep the hermeneutical harm goes in undermining or destroying the meaning-making and meaning-sharing capacities of the victims of such harm. Here too we can identify a continuum of cases: from skin-deep cases, in which subjects may face unfair uptake in an isolated aspect of their life without leaving any mark in their interpretative powers and hermeneutical agency (leaving intact even whatever epistemic privileges they may have), to marrow-of-the-bone cases, in which the hermeneutical harms become so pervasive that they compromise one's epistemic life and status as a meaning-making subject in expressive and interpretative practices. In the latter, marrow-of-the-bone cases, the effects of hermeneutical injustice are totalizing, and they reverberate across all the corners of one's epistemic life, affecting one's entire hermeneutical subjectivity, that is, one's voice and capacity to make sense and be understood. The most radical case would be the one in which one's voice is *killed* – what I have called *hermeneutical death*. Although of course it may be extremely rare to find cases in which a subject completely loses her voice and standing as a meaning-making subject, under conditions of extreme epistemic oppressions in which one's status as a subject of knowledge and understanding is barely recognized, we can find cases that approximate hermeneutical death. Women have found themselves in a predicament that approximates hermeneutical death in the lowest cultural moments of sexist societies, and so have ethnic and racial minorities under conditions of extreme racism – a good illustration of measures that contribute to hermeneutical annihilation can be found in slave traders' practice of separating African slaves who spoke the same language to maximize communicative isolation and in US slaveholders' practice of punishing slaves caught speaking African languages.[7] We will come back to extreme cases of hermeneutical injustice in the next section.

These are simply some tentative and preliminary ways in which we can introduce some distinctions and conceptual orders in the vast and heterogeneous field of hermeneutical injustices. The different classifications we can entertain should have a practical pay-off: they should enable us to see different aspects and dimensions of the diverse cases of hermeneutical injustice, and, accordingly, they should enable us to respond to those cases in diverse ways. This is very important because the responses that may be appropriate and effective for some forms of hermeneutical injustice may be inappropriate or ineffective for other kinds of hermeneutical injustice. For example, expanding the available vocabulary may meliorate some hermeneutical injustices, but it will not do when what is needed is more attunement or sensitivity to an expressive style. Hermeneutical courage and self-trust on the side of those trying to articulate a new experience may be what is needed in some cases, but it will not help with cases in which what creates the problem is a resistance on the listener's side, not the expressive limitations of the speaker. Improving ways of listening and giving uptake may meliorate hermeneutical injustices produced by interpersonal dynamics, but it will not be sufficient when we need to change structural and institutional conditions of communication that go beyond those dynamics. I want to emphasize, in particular, the distinctiveness of totalizing cases of hermeneutical injustice that approximate hermeneutical death, because these cases require special forms of resistance: what I have called *hermeneutical insurrection* (forthcoming), that is, forms of disobedience to and revolt against expressive/interpretative norms and expectations in order to pave the way to a new hermeneutical order.

## Fighting against hermeneutical injustice and hermeneutical death: resistance and insurrection

Hermeneutical injustices are complex phenomena that are very difficult to prevent and eradicate, but, as Fricker points out, the fight against them has as a prerequisite that we develop "alertness or sensitivity to the possibility that the difficulty one's interlocutor is having as she tries to render something communicatively intelligible is due not to its being nonsense or her being a fool, but rather to some sort of gap in collective hermeneutical understanding. The point is to realize that the speaker is struggling with an objective difficulty and not a subjective failing" (2007: 169). As Fricker goes on to emphasize, in order to mitigate hermeneutical injustices and work toward hermeneutical justice, we need to cultivate *virtuous listening*. The preventive and reparative work that hermeneutical injustices call for requires the constant improvement of our hermeneutical sensibilities. We need to cultivate hermeneutical openness and self-critical hermeneutical capacities that can make us more attentive to blind-spots, lacunas, and interpretative failures. Active listening and pro-active attitudes of hermeneutical charity can include things such as: knowing when to shut up, knowing when to suspend one's own judgment about intelligibility,[8] calling critical attention to one's own limited expressive habits and interpretative expectations, listening for silences, checking with others who are differently situated,[9] letting others set the tone and the dynamics of a communicative exchange, etc.

But fighting hermeneutical injustices may require more than virtuous listening; it may require encouraging and facilitating *hermeneutical resistance*, that is, exerting epistemic friction against the normative expectations of established interpretative frameworks and aiding dissonant voices in the formation of alternative meanings, interpretations, and expressive styles. As I have argued elsewhere (2012, 2013), communicative contexts are always polyphonic, and there are typically dissonant voices, embryonic formulations of alternative meanings, and resistant hermeneutical practices even in the most adverse hermeneutical contexts. Fricker has called attention to experiences of *dissonance* between one's meaning/understanding and the interpretative horizon one has inherited, and I have argued that these experiences can function as the source of an important form of 'resistance', *hermeneutical resistance*. I have further argued that we all have a *prima facie* hermeneutical responsibility to resist unfair hermeneutical climates. Although this responsibility will take different configurations depending on one's positionality and relationality in hermeneutical communities and practices, we should all feel responsible to facilitate, in any way we can, the hermeneutical agency of eccentric voices and perspectives that *resist* established meanings and communicative dynamics, and work toward the formation of original meanings, alternative expressive styles, and new horizons of interpretation.

Should we always be expected to contribute to the expansion of expressive and interpretative resources? Should we always promote the sharing of hermeneutical repertoires? Fighting hermeneutical injustices typically involves improving communication across hermeneutical practices and communities, and making dissonant meanings and eccentric interpretative frameworks available through the social fabric. However, an important caveat needs to be issued here. Although the default attitude in working toward hermeneutical justice is that of cooperation and sharing hermeneutical resources, that is not always the most appropriate attitude and response for fighting against hermeneutical injustices. Drawing from the recent literature on hermeneutical injustice in critical race theory, Fricker remarks that there are "cases in which it may not be in the interests of an oppressed group to fight immediately for the introduction of local meanings into the wider collective hermeneutical resource" (2016: 168-9). As Fricker explains, this is a point that has been forcefully made by Charles Mills by echoing an African-American folk poem: "Got one mind for white folks to see / Another for what I know is me" (Mills 2007: 18). Under conditions of oppression, sometimes there can be advantages in keeping things local or even private, so as to prevent dangers and vulnerabilities that may come with visibility and exposure for oppressed subjects (see Bailey 2007). Not sharing one's expressive and interpretative resources may be required for self-protection and for resisting the hermeneutical imperialism or hermeneutical expansiveness[10] that demands access to all resources and take it as legitimate the appropriation of all expressive practices, no matter where they come from or where they are going. In this sense, Fricker has pointed out that in certain contexts it is important to appreciate "the value of maintaining hermeneutical privacy" (2016: 169; my emphasis), citing as an example Alice Walker's descriptions of how in the segregated American South, black parents "inculcated in their children a way of understanding racial oppression that might be read as incorporating a certain security in on-going hermeneutical separation" (2016: 169). This 'hermeneutical separation' can be sometimes the only way to safeguard the hermeneutical resources and practices of one's community and a necessary strategy for survival as well as "a source of in-group solidarity and strength" (2016: 170). Although *non-fatal* hermeneutical injustices can typically be resisted through dissenting or eccentric hermeneutical agency geared toward more cooperation and more sharing of hermeneutical resources, this is not the case when we are dealing with cases that approximate hermeneutical death.

In some cases, the conditions of hermeneutical marginalization can be so extreme that more than regular hermeneutical resistance may be required; near-death hermeneutical marginalization calls for *insurrection*. As I said at the beginning of this chapter, I want to give center-stage to the extreme case of hermeneutical death because it reveals something important about the depth and disabling power that hermeneutical injustice can reach, but also because it reveals that in the difficult and uphill battle of fighting hermeneutical injustices, sometimes radical hermeneutical measures may be needed. As I have argued elsewhere (forthcoming), epistemic death calls for epistemic disobedience and epistemic insurrection: besides relaxing and suspending obligations, situations of testimonial and hermeneutical death also create a right (if not a duty) to fight epistemically by any means necessary (including the right to lie, to hide, to sabotage, to silence others, etc.), demonstrating loyalty and solidarity only with alternative epistemic communities (communities of resistance). This is the rationale for the notions of 'epistemic disobedience' (Mignolo 2009) and 'epistemic insurrection' (Medina forthcoming) that we can apply here to the case of radical hermeneutical injustice or hermeneutical death. Under conditions of hermeneutical death, subjects owe nothing to those expressive practices and communities that contribute to the annihilation of their meaning-making capacities: communicative obligations (such as making meanings accessible to others, sharing expressive and interpretative resources, listening charitably, aiding others in their attempts to speak, etc.) are suspended because one should not be expected to cooperate with practices that undermine one's own status and agency or that of one's fellows. (And note that you don't have to be hermeneutically oppressed to justifiably engage in 'hermeneutical disobedience'!)

As Pohlhaus, Jr. (2011: 228) has argued, it is justified for oppressed subjects to engage in "strategic refusals to understand", that is, in refusals to enter into oppressive 'rhetorical spaces'[11] and to cooperate hermeneutically with oppressive meanings and perspectives that constrain their agency. As Pohlhaus, Jr. insists, refusing to entertain certain meanings and to work with certain hermeneutical frameworks and perspectives should not be confused with disengaging and refusing to cooperate altogether. In fact, such refusals are often the prerequisite for opening up new forms of communicative engagement: they are exercises in *hermeneutical resistance* aimed at disrupting complicity with hermeneutical injustices and at facilitating the articulation of resistant meanings and alternative rhetorical spaces.

Sometimes in order to clear the path for the development of a new language or a new expressive style, we need to make some oppressive expressive styles and interpretative frameworks explode, or at least we need to subject them to sufficient friction – or insurrectionary resistance – so as to feel pressured to change or to learn to co-exist with other styles and frameworks. Sojourner Truth's explosive interrogation of the meaning of 'woman',[12] James Baldwin's or Audre Lorde's poetic uses of black English, and Gloria Anzaldúa's persistent use of Spanglish, dialectical differences and linguistic hybridization, should all count as acts of hermeneutical disobedience and insurrection, attempts to disrupt oppressive linguistic habits and expectations and to form alternative expressive communities. Obviously most of us are not a Sojourner Truth, a James Baldwin, an Audre Lorde, or a Gloria Anzaldúa, but we can help in small ways to rebel against hermeneutical injustices by disobeying oppressive communicative norms and expectations, and by deploying communicative moves that facilitate paths of resistance for eccentric voices, expressive styles, and interpretative perspectives. When we hear someone unfairly constraining someone's voice by saying, for example, "I don't think those words can be used in that way" (or some other pronouncement that calls into question the speaker's intelligibility by unfairly policing her voice), interlocutors (and not just the speaker being targeted) can justifiably object to the norm or expectation ("Why don't you let me/her talk and see where I/she go/es with my/her words?"); they can call critical attention to the unfair questioning and redirect the hermeneutical challenge ("Why are you assuming that this is nonsense?"), and they can also simply ally their voices and join hermeneutical forces so as to change the communicative dynamics, shift the hermeneutical expectations, and empower the eccentric voice(s) in question. These ordinary ways of resisting hermeneutical marginalization in everyday communication can amount to *hermeneutical insurrection* if they involve the dismantling of entire expressive styles or interpretative frameworks and the shift to new ones – e.g. when people in professional venues, such as philosophy conferences, refuse to articulate and justify their meanings according to some unique, narrow standard, and they move to more inclusive ways of negotiating meanings and interpretations. As I have argued elsewhere (forthcoming), our *micro-resistance* to hermeneutical intimidations in micro-aggressions can not only help mitigate the negative impact of hermeneutical injustices, but it can also forge paths of hermeneutical resistance – and even insurrection! – and slowly work toward more liberating hermeneutical climates and dynamics.

**Related chapters:** 12, 16, 19, 28, 29, 31, 32, 33, 34, 36

## Notes

1 I would like to thank Ian James Kidd, Gaile Pohlhaus, Jr., and Miranda Fricker for helpful comments and suggestions on earlier drafts of this chapter.
2 This is part of my concept of epistemic death, which can take the form of testimonial death and of hermeneutical death. See Medina (forthcoming).
3 Stewart developed an understanding of epistemic oppression as a form of 'deadening' and 'numbing' of mental capacities that can 'kill' oneself as a subject of knowledge and understanding. She wrote: "There are no chains so galling as the chains of ignorance – no fetters so binding as those that bind the soul, and exclude it from the vast field of useful and scientific knowledge". (1932/1987: 45)
4 For Fricker, hermeneutical injustice is not a harm perpetrated by an agent (159) but "the injustice of having some significant area of one's social experience obscured from collective understanding owing to a structural identity prejudice in the collective hermeneutical resource" (155).
5 Kristie Dotson has used Pohlhaus, Jr.'s notion to identify a third category of epistemic injustice that combines features of testimonial and hermeneutical injustice, which she calls 'contributory injustice': an agentially produced form of epistemic injustice in which "an epistemic agent's willful hermeneutical ignorance in maintaining and utilizing structurally prejudiced hermeneutical resources thwarts a knower's ability to contribute to shared epistemic resources within a given epistemic community by compromising her epistemic agency" (2012: 32).
6 In other cases, unorthodox demeanors, styles, or dictions may not trigger a negative judgment of intelligibility, but they may provoke reluctance or refusal to engage, resulting in communicative marginalization. I am thankful to Ian James Kidd for pointing this out to me.
7 As Carnavale (2012) points out, "African language groups were separated by slave traders in an attempt to thwart any uprising"; and, "once in the New World, slave owners punished those who were caught speaking African languages: in at least a few cases, by removing their tongues" (Carnavale 2012: 45). I am grateful to Gaile Pohlhaus, Jr. for calling my attention to this illustration.
8 A directive in this direction is Louise Antony's suggestion of a policy of *epistemic affirmative action*, which recommends that interpreters operate with the "*working hypothesis* that when a woman, or any member of a stereotyped group, says something anomalous, they should assume that it's *they* who don't understand, not that it is the woman who is nuts" (1995: 89). While seeing merits in this proposal, Fricker has argued persuasively that 'the hearer needs to be *indefinitely context sensitive* in how he applies the hypothesis', and that 'a policy of affirmative action across all subject matters would not be justified.' (2007: 171; my emphasis)
9 See Ortega (2006). I am grateful to Gaile Pohlhaus, Jr. for helping me think through this preliminary list of things to be included in active listening and pro-active attitudes of hermeneutical charity.
10 I owe these apt formulations to Gaile Pohlhaus, Jr., who pointed out to me the connection between the problematic epistemic expectation of dominantly situated subjects to have access to everything and Shannon Sullivan's (2006) discussion of *white ontological expansiveness*.
11 Pohlhaus, Jr. borrows this notion from Lorraine Code (1995) and explains it as follows: "Just as the arrangement of material space can enable and disable whole groups of people, so, too, can the arrangement of 'rhetorical space' (to use Lorraine Code's apt phrase)". (2011: 228).
12 I would say that one of the best examples of hermeneutical defiance and insurrection can be found in Truth's discourse, "Ain't I a Woman?" (1851), in which she exercised hermeneutical disobedience in refusing to accept established meanings of femininity and in insisting on the inclusion of alternative contents in the very meaning of 'woman'.

## References

Antony, Louise (1995), "Sisters, Please, I'd Rather Do It Myself: A Defense of Individualism in Feminist Epistemology", *Philosophical Topics* 23 (2): 59–94.
Anzaldúa, Gloria (1987), *Borderlands/La Frontera: The New Mestiza*. New York: Aunt Lute Books.
Bailey, Alison (2007), "Strategic Ignorance", in Shannon Sullivan and Nancy Tuana (eds.), *Race and Epistemologies of Ignorance*. New York: SUNY Press, pp. 77–94.
Carnavale, Nancy (2012), *A New Language, A New World*. Champaign: University of Illinois Press.
Code, Lorraine (1995), *Rhetorical Spaces: Essays on Gendered Locations*. New York: Routledge.
Dotson, Kristie (2011), "Tracking Epistemic Violence, Tracking Practices of Silencing", *Hypatia: A Journal of Feminist Philosophy* 26 (2): 236–257.

Dotson, Kristie (2012), "A Cautionary Tale: On Limiting Epistemic Oppression", *Frontiers: A Journal of Women's Studies* 33 (1): 24–47.
Fricker, Miranda (2007), *Epistemic Injustice: Power and the Ethics of Knowing*. Oxford and New York: Oxford University Press.
Fricker, Miranda (2016), "Epistemic Injustice and the Preservation of Ignorance", in Rik Peels and Martijn Blaauw (eds.), *The Epistemic Dimensions of Ignorance*. Cambridge: Cambridge University Press, pp. 160–177.
Medina, José (2012), "Hermeneutical Injustice and Polyphonic Contextualism: Social Silences and Shared Hermeneutical Responsibilities", *Social Epistemology* 26 (2): 201–220.
Medina, José (2013), *The Epistemology of Resistance: Gender and Racial Oppression, Epistemic Injustice, and Resistant Imaginations*. New York: Oxford University Press.
Medina, José (forthcoming), "Epistemic Injustice and Epistemologies of Ignorance", in Linda Alcoff, Paul Taylor, and Luvell Anderson (eds.), *Routledge Companion to the Philosophy of Race*. London and New York: Routledge.
Mignolo, Walter (2009), "Epistemic Disobedience, Independent Thought and Decolonial Freedom", *Theory, Culture & Society* 26 (7–8): 159–181.
Mills, Charles (2007), "White Ignorance", in Shannon Sullivan and Nancy Tuana (eds.), *Race and Epistemologies of Ignorance*. New York: SUNY Press, pp. 11–38.
Ortega, Mariana (2006), "Being lovingly, knowingly ignorant: White feminism and women of color", *Hypatia: A Journal of Feminist Philosophy* 21 (3): 56–74.
Pohlhaus, Jr., Gaile (2011), "Wrongful Requests and Strategic Refusals to Understand", in Heidi Grasswick (ed.), *Feminist Epistemology and Philosophy of Science: Power in Knowledge*. New York: Springer, pp. 223–240.
Pohlhaus, Jr., Gaile (2012), "Relational Knowing and Epistemic Injustice: Toward a Theory of Willful Hermeneutical Ignorance", *Hypatia: A Journal of Feminist Philosophy* 27 (4): 715–735.
Stewart, Maria W. (1932/1987), "Why Sit Ye Here and Die?", in Marilyn Richardson (ed.), *Maria W. Stewart: America's First Black Woman Political Writer*. Bloomington, IN: Indiana University Press, pp. 45–49.
Sullivan, Shannon (2006), *Revealing Whiteness: The Unconscious Habits of Racial Privilege*. Bloomington: Indiana University Press.

# 4
# EVOLVING CONCEPTS OF EPISTEMIC INJUSTICE

*Miranda Fricker*

What does the concept of epistemic injustice do for us? What should we want it to do? If meaning is use, then there is no point trying to put precise boundaries on the concept in advance; indeed its use has already evolved, spreading slightly more widely than originally intended, and for good reason. My chief purpose in invoking the label was to delineate a distinctive class of wrongs, namely those in which someone is ingenuously downgraded and/or disadvantaged in respect of their status as an epistemic subject. A first point to make is that this kind of epistemic injustice is fundamentally a form of (direct or indirect) discrimination. The cause of testimonial injustice is a prejudice through which the speaker is misjudged and perceived as epistemically lesser (a direct discrimination). This will tend to have negative effects on how they are perceived and treated non-epistemically too – secondary aspects of the intrinsic wrong. The cause of a hermeneutical injustice is a background inequality of hermeneutical opportunity – specifically, hermeneutical marginalisation in relation to some area of social experience. This puts them at an unfair disadvantage in comprehending and/or getting others to comprehend an experience of that kind (a somewhat indirect discrimination). It might therefore be a good idea to explicitly label both these phenomena as forms of '*discriminatory* epistemic injustice'; for as David Coady (2010, 2017) has rightly emphasised, we should leave room for something called 'epistemic injustice' that is primarily a distributive injustice – someone's receiving less than their fair share of an epistemic good, such as education, or access to expert advice or information.[1] In this kind of epistemic injustice too, after all, someone is indeed *wronged in their capacity as an epistemic subject*, and so it fits the generic definition originally given (Fricker 2007).

But following on the heels of this welcome broadening of the remit of 'epistemic injustice' in general, I would like to advocate continued strictness with regard to the remit of (what I am now labelling) 'discriminatory epistemic injustice', for I believe the category will only be useful if it remains bounded and specific, not relaxing outwards to embrace the generality of unfair interpersonal manipulations or, again, systemic riggings of the epistemic economy. The many and various forms of these things will tend to merit their own classifications, and that is how we will best continue the business of bringing to light the different ethical and political dimensions of our epistemic lives.[2]

## Theorising the unintended

Strictness in what respect? Essentially I have in mind the question of intention, or rather its absence. In testimonial injustice the absence of deliberate, conscious manipulation is definitive, at least in my conception. I was trying to bring out a phenomenon that is easy to miss, and in need of a name. In this kind of epistemic injustice, the hearer makes a special kind of misjudgement of the speaker's credibility – one actually clouded by prejudice. And this is importantly different from any deliberate misrepresentation of someone's true or reasonable beliefs as false or rationally unfounded, for when that happens, the perpetrator herself need not misjudge the other's epistemic status at all. Precisely not – rather she sees that he knows, or has reasons, but she intends to cause *others* to doubt these things and to downgrade his epistemic status in their eyes. Testimonial injustice by contrast happens by way of a discriminatory but ingenuous misjudgement, and it will, I believe, be useful to continue keeping this separate from the closely related kind of injustice that involves the deliberate manipulation of others' judgements of credibility.

This is in no measure to downplay the importance of deliberate interpersonal manipulations of credibility relations. On the contrary, it is a pervasive epistemic, ethical, and political phenomenon – political not only with a small 'p' but with a capital too, for manipulating credibility relations is the stock in trade of professional political campaigns, in which one side will try to get the electorate to think the other side doesn't have a clue, or cannot be trusted, or both. Furthermore, such deliberate manipulations of credibility relations will often be causally connected with the mechanism of a testimonial injustice. Looking to the movie of *The Talented Mr. Ripley*, for example, if we consider again for a moment the testimonial injustice which I argued (Fricker 2007) Greenleaf senior does to Marge Sherwood in misperceiving her as a hysterical lovelorn woman whose 'female intuition' that Ripley is Dickie's killer is evidentially unfounded, then we confront a telling example. Here Ripley has deliberately manipulated the sexist prejudices of the day in order to induce in Greenleaf a certain misperception of Marge and her suspicions, and the result is that Ripley successfully causes Greenleaf to do Marge a grave testimonial injustice. Thus we see that the deliberate manipulation of others' prejudices is likely to be an effective way of producing an authentic testimonial injustice – a way of inducing in another a prejudiced judgement of credibility in respect of a speaker. Ripley's repeated dismissive or faux sympathetic remarks to Greenleaf about Marge do the trick very nicely, and they are deliberately designed to cause Greenleaf to be impervious to the rationality of Marge's suspicions, thereby doing her a testimonial injustice. But we don't want our concept of testimonial injustice to blur what Ripley does and what Greenleaf does, because the point of the concept was to bring into focus a certain class of epistemic misjudgements, and Ripley does not epistemically misjudge Marge at all. For this reason I would advocate continued strictness about 'testimonial injustices' being unintentional: a species of ingenuous epistemic misjudgement. (We perhaps need another label for Ripley's wicked puppetry – a third-personal intentional gaslighting.[3])

Second, and in the case of hermeneutical injustice now, the hearer who cannot understand because she lacks sufficiently shared concepts with the speaker might be trying in earnest to understand but is unable because of an objective difficulty. She is not deliberately manipulating, concealing, or blanking anything. Again, I think it is worth emphasising this, simply because otherwise one walks away with the impression that so long as we all make reasonable efforts and avoid bad faith, no one will suffer a hermeneutical injustice. Not so, for the cause of the injustice is structural – the background hermeneutical marginalisation – and so the injustice will tend to persist regardless of individual efforts. Hermeneutical injustice is the actualisation of unequal hermeneutical opportunity, which can be somewhat mitigated by especially virtuous epistemic and communicative conduct on the part of any individual hearer. Any such virtuous listening will somewhat erode hermeneutical marginalisation, because the more actively a hearer listens, the more the speaker's hermeneutical marginalisation is *thereby* eroded – they are thereby enabled to contribute more than before to the shared hermeneutical resource. But insofar as hermeneutical marginalisation is a product of social powerlessness (and is a form of it), the actual eradication of this kind of injustice will require significantly more than such slight interpersonal hermeneutical empowerments; it will require sufficient social equality in general, to ensure that new areas of hermeneutical marginalisation do not keep re-emerging with new patterns of unequal power.

Quick on the heels of emphasising the non-deliberate nature of both these kinds of epistemic injustice, however, I would also like to join others in emphasising the importance of recognising the role of our agency in sustaining them, and to point out that non-deliberateness does not entail non-culpability. (On the contrary, in connection with testimonial injustice, I assume prejudiced thinking is almost always culpable in some degree – it's just also very ordinary.) And there are many intriguing interim cases where it is unclear, even indeterminate, how far the hearer in a moment of either testimonial or hermeneutical injustice may be colluding with the forces of prejudice or of hermeneutical marginalisation to prevent the speaker's words being properly received. The slippery slope to bad faith, and self-interested or plain lazy denial, is an ever-present factor in situations where the nascent content of the attempted communication is potentially challenging to the hearer's status or, for whatever other reason, outside of their epistemic comfort zone. A number of authors have rightly emphasised and explored this point in illuminating ways (Mason 2011; Dotson 2012; Medina 2012, 2013; Pohlhaus, Jr. 2012). But I trust it is compatible with their developments of this aspect that discriminatory epistemic injustice might remain a normative concept that carves out a space in which people are wronged in their status as a knower without that ever being a wrong done simply on purpose. The interesting thing about denial, or other kinds of motivated or willful ignorance or non-knowing, is of course that it is not quite on purpose, or not in the normal conscious way. If, on the other hand, a hearer really does straightforwardly dissemble, pretending not to understand when in fact she understands perfectly well, then that is a closely related but distinct injustice from hermeneutical injustice.

In thinking about the point of the concepts of epistemic injustice, it might help to glance briefly back to the aetiology of the concepts of testimonial and hermeneutical injustice: what were these categories a response to? Through the nineties feminist philosophy was a developing field of energised contention between two intellectual inheritances. The first was Marxism – much of feminist consciousness and the women's movement, after all, had grown out of class consciousness and socialist politics.[4] This critical theoretical store supplied invaluable bold abstractions such as *ideology, false consciousness*, and particularly the concept (from Lukàcs 1971[5]) of a *standpoint* (of the proletariat), which was epistemically privileged – this standpoint being a position or role in the relations of production that made available, false consciousness notwithstanding, an epistemically privileged viewpoint on the social world. The general idea was that the more hands-on involvement someone had in the close-to-nature processes of production that are necessary for keeping society going, the more they are in a position to see social reality in its true colours.

The second intellectual inheritance, in sharp contrast, was not from the past but was very much present in the burgeoning academic and cultural *zeitgeist*. Postmodernism was taking hold in the humanities, and many feminist theorists saw in it an ally. The philosophical aspects of this culture-wide movement originated in various sources and took different forms, but its philosophical notes included most sonorously Foucault's refusal to separate power and truth, the exhilarating ring of which harmonised with Lyotard's (1984) definitive postmodernist claim that 'grand narratives' had had their day, so that projects of 'legitimation' were over and there was consequently now only *de facto* legitimation of knowledge. Rorty's special brand of pragmatism with its air of dismissive scepticism about the truth as nothing more than 'what people around here think' also made a powerful philosophical presence felt (Rorty 1990). Here and there philosophers with an interest in these cultural currents and 'endist' themes debated how far epistemology was 'dead'.[6]

Against this backdrop, what I hoped for from the concept of epistemic injustice and its cognates was to mark out a delimited space in which to observe some key intersections of knowledge and power at one remove from the long shadows of both Marx and Foucault, by forging an on-the-ground tool of critical understanding that was called for in everyday lived experiences of injustice – experiences that sometimes might be inconsequential, or sometimes by contrast a matter of life and death – and which would rely neither on any metaphysically burdened theoretical narrative of an epistemically well-placed sex-class, nor on any risky flirtation with a reduction of truth or knowledge to *de facto* social power. As regards Marxism, for my purposes the monolithic social ontology of class – or its gender or race counterparts – remained at that time riskily insensitive to other dimensions of difference, even if it was recognised to be an abstraction rather than an empirical generalisation.[7] And as regards Foucault, on whose conception of power I explicitly drew, the reductionist drift that inevitably attends any view characterised by a refusal to separate truth from power (though I would not read Foucault as positively committed to any bald reductionism on this score) made it unhelpfully provocative in its rhetoric: if there is no separation between truth and power, then it at least *sounds* like you are saying there is nothing more to knowledge than having the power to count as having knowledge, but if that were so then there could never be any injustice in being deemed not to know. On such a reductionist view there could be no distinctively epistemic injustice, for there could be no contrast between the way power deems things to be and how they are. (On Foucault's actual view, see Allen 2017). Somehow the reductionist challenge, essentially frivolous though it always was, had established itself as a benchmark of politically conscious intellectual activity, its bogus radical rhetoric enjoying some considerable sway at the time.

What was needed, I believed, was something much more easily recognisable as making sense of the lived experience of injustice in how a person's beliefs, reasons, and social interpretations were received by others, even conscientious well-meaning others. And although feminist standpoint theory at the time remained too beholden to the sweeping abstractions of Marxism to be viable, it contained a lasting methodological insight that was usefully sloganised by Sandra Harding (1991): 'start thought from marginalized lives'. Start with the experience of powerlessness and show that it raises philosophical questions. That was the primary phenomenological drive behind the notion of epistemic injustice, and it is why I continue to think it important in any broadly social philosophy to build up slowly from an account of what goes on at the interpersonal level.[8] In this sense, the interpersonal is political.

All this, moreover, is entirely compatible with the thought that there might be forms of testimonial injustice that are not interpersonal – not, as Elizabeth Anderson has helpfully labelled it, 'transactional' – but rather 'structural' (Anderson 2012). In making the distinction between transactional and structural testimonial injustice, Anderson elaborates the following imagined example of structural testimonial injustice. We imagine a list of expert witnesses that no one has refreshed for a good while, so that (through no one's fault, let us add) the same old white male witnesses tend to be drawn on time and time again, and all those whose names would have made it onto the list if any official had been keeping more of a vigilant eye on updating it are effectively silenced. They are, perhaps unwittingly, on the receiving end of what I call 'pre-emptive testimonial injustice' (Fricker 2007, ch. 6). Their views are not sought, and this is owing to a structural prejudice (the un-refreshed list). It is worth noting that any such structural testimonial injustice would have to be *pre-emptive*, for as soon as anyone actually said anything (perhaps they speak uninvited and formally out of turn in the courtroom), it would become transactional as well as structural, since there would be a speaker whose word was prejudicially received by another party. We cannot really get a grip on the phenomenon of testimonial injustice without anchoring it in transactional possibilities, but the extension of the idea of testimonial injustice to structural forms is very helpful.

## The interpersonal is political

There are two immediate upshots of starting one's philosophical thinking from the (partly imagined) experience of marginalisation or powerlessness. The first is that the initial focus is bound to be interpersonal, or transactional. The experiences in question are concrete, tending to involve individuals reacting to one another, standing in relations of power to one another. To focus on such experiences is to bring into view all the micro aggressions and injustices that instantiate and indicate more structural, macro formations of power. The second is that the initial focus is also bound to be on dysfunction rather than well-functioning, failures of justice or of reason rather than successes.

Taking the first upshot first, around the same time that Foucault was writing about micro power, feminists were declaring 'the personal is political'. They were both right. If you want to identify the operations of power in, say, practices through which people attempt to put their beliefs, knowledge, opinions, and interpretations into the shared pool of ideas, then you should look to the micro, the transactional. The interpersonal pushes and pulls in daily life encode the larger social structures one hopes to understand, and while I would not commit to the (perhaps Foucauldian) idea that the micro is always prior, certainly it can be. In any case, the micro is generally a good place to start, for one does not really understand the structural or know how to combat it unless one also understands a good deal about how it is played out at the micro level. Start thought from marginalised lives.

Taking the second upshot, the idea that it might be philosophically fruitful to focus on dysfunction rather than well-functioning has become increasingly popular, especially with the help of the independent and more general notion of non-ideal theory. Sometimes, as back-up to the general idea that the dysfunctional is interesting, instructive, and ripe for theorising, authors offer the well-known, striking opening sentence of Tolstoy's *Anna Karenina*: 'All happy families are alike; each unhappy family is unhappy in its own way'. But I believe the real lesson from starting philosophy with the dysfunctional is precisely *not* that the functional forms of institutions, practices, or experiences, or indeed families, are blandly the same as one another. Quite the opposite. The lesson, rather, is that the functional forms of things need to be seen as successfully staving off or coping with endemic problems and difficulties. The real difference between a happy family and an unhappy one is that the happy family has found a way to cope with its tensions and difficulties, at least not letting them eclipse family life, whereas the unhappy one has not. And the difference between a functional epistemic practice and a dysfunctional one is that the functional practice contains certain counter-pressures or mechanisms by which to stave off anti-veridical forces of various kinds, such as prejudice, for example. The interest in the dysfunctional and the non-ideal need not stem from an intrinsic interest in these things (though they are indeed interesting); rather it may stem simply from a realistic interest in how to achieve functionality in any given practice. Thus a philosopher who only aimed to understand and represent epistemic practices in their most functional forms, perhaps even in some notionally ideal form, would still need to do so by looking first at what potential collapses into dysfunctionality are being perpetually staved off, and by what mechanisms.

Starting philosophical theorising from (real or imagined) experiences of powerlessness, then, tends to encourage a focus on interpersonal dysfunctions, and possibilities for correcting for them. This I believe can be philosophically fruitful, though I would never pretend it delivers all the answers, or makes other perspectives redundant. Rather it represents a historically situated commitment to a certain set of philosophical priorities and a certain set of hopes for what philosophy may yet become – a more humanistic,[9] more socially enlivened, and above all more interesting version of itself.

## New terrains of social experience

The measure of the slogan 'start thought from marginalised lives' (and it is strictly as an enlivening methodological slogan that I believe in it, not as part of any general *theory* of what kinds of social experience may or may not systematically produce any epistemically privileged perspectives) must be in the philosophy that it produces. A new area in which this can be seen is in the philosophy of healthcare.

When a doctor talks to a patient, asking questions about his symptoms or his preferences regarding alternative forms of treatment, things can easily go awry. Pressures of time, the high stakes and burden of responsibility, plus the need for technical or otherwise professional language, all conspire to make it all too easy for a doctor to either fail to solicit her patient's relevant epistemic input (his relevant beliefs and experiences regarding his own illness) and instead she may inadvertently end up talking down to her patient, or giving short shrift to legitimate questions and concerns, and so on. Ian James Kidd and Havi Carel (2017a) have written about the way negative stereotypes of ill persons can lead to epistemic injustices of various kinds, including the testimonial injustice of finding that their relative expertise in the matter of their lived experience of illness is not recognised or utilised adequately by healthcare professionals. Their aim is to open up 'an epistemic space for the lived experience of illness' (Carel & Kidd 2016, p. 16). (See also the contribution to this volume by Carel & Kidd 2017b, and by Anastasia Scrutton 2017, who explore this issue in relation specifically to mental illness.)

In the domain of psychiatry, recent work by two psychiatrists, Michaelis Kyratsous and Abdi Sanati, reveals the applicability of concepts of epistemic injustice to the diagnostic moment. In 'Epistemic Injustice in Assessment of Delusions' (Kyratsous & Sanati 2015), they argue that sometimes in diagnosing a patient as delusional, a prejudicial stereotype of delusional persons as generally irrational can lead to an over-generalisation. In effect their delusionality is seen as affecting all their cognitive behaviour rather than just affecting more local regions of it. By way of two case studies, they show that this all-too-easy prejudicial over-generalisation can lead to secondary concrete unfair disadvantages for the person diagnosed, such as being 'treated in a coercive manner' (p. 5). Thus the effect of the prejudicial over-generalisation fits exactly the theoretical structure of testimonial injustice: the intrinsic injustice of being judged as epistemically lesser owing to prejudice, plus a secondary associated disadvantage.

As regards hermeneutical injustice in the healthcare context, Carel and Kidd have argued that:

> In the case of illness, hermeneutical injustice arises because the resources required for the understanding of the social experiences of ill persons are not accepted as part of the dominant hermeneutical resources. Most ill persons are capable of describing their experiences in non-expert terms, but such experiences are (a) largely considered inappropriate for public discussion and (b) play little or no role in clinical decision making.
> *(Kidd and Carel 2017a: 184)*

So ill people tend to be hermeneutically marginalised in the sense that the non-expert terms in which they naturally and effectively understand their experiences of illness are not sufficiently shared across social space as regards the decision-making of the professionals whose judgements they rely on. When a resultant failure of shared intelligibility takes place, a hermeneutical injustice occurs and the patient's perspective goes missing from the process of care itself. (See also Carel & Kidd 2017b).

These new applications of the concepts of testimonial and hermeneutical injustice exemplify the ground-up energies that will no doubt somewhat evolve the concepts themselves, perhaps ultimately broadening them out in unforeseen ways. The use-driven evolution of the concepts will I hope continue to be fuelled by these sorts of real interests in explaining the experiences of those on the less powerful end of various relationships. If so, that will reflect a widening commitment to the usefulness of starting philosophical thinking from experiences of powerlessness, chiefly because that is a good way to arrive ultimately at a philosophical account of how things should be, even ideally. Such developments would also encourage a continued hope that philosophy really is gradually becoming a more humanly intelligent and more socially inflected discipline.[10]

**Related chapters** 1, 2, 3, 5, 15, 17, 32, 33

## Notes

1 The distinction between 'discriminatory' and 'distributive' is not intended as a deep and/or exclusive demarcation, of course, since most cases of one will have aspects of the other. Not getting your fair share of a good will often be the cause and/or the result of discrimination of some kind.
2 See, for instance, Fricker (2016) 'Epistemic Injustice and the Preservation of Ignorance', in which I argue that for the most part Charles Mills' category, 'white ignorance', is I believe designed to distinguish an importantly different category from 'hermeneutical injustice'; though I also argue that the two phenomena overlap wherever white ignorance comes in the form of a poverty of shared concepts or social meanings, as opposed to non-sharedness of beliefs and priorities of epistemic attention. I take both to be important phenomena meriting their own categorisation.
3 In this connection, see Rachel McKinnon (2017), who shows how there can also be gaslighting that is unintentional, even specifically well-meaning, and which can constitute a form of testimonial injustice.
4 With reference to the UK women's movement and its roots in socialism, see Sheila Rowbotham, *Woman's Consciousness, Man's World* (London: Pelican, 1973).
5 See the section entitled 'The Standpoint of the Proletariat' in Lukàcs (1971, pp. 149–209).
6 For a compelling contemporary feminist philosophical response to these complex issues, see Sabina Lovibond (1989).
7 Subsequently, however, it has been re-developed in new ways – for an overview of various forms of standpoint theory and their relation to feminist empiricism, see Kristen Intemann (2010).
8 See Jeremy Wanderer (2017).
9 See Bernard Williams' essay, 'Philosophy as a Humanistic Discipline' (Williams, 2006).
10 I am grateful to the editors of this volume for very helpful comments on an earlier draft of this chapter; and to the Leverhulme Trust for its support of this work as part of a Major Research Fellowship.

## References

Allen, Amy (2017) 'Power/Knowledge/Resistance: Foucault and Epistemic Injustice'. In *The Routledge Handbook of Epistemic Injustice*, eds., I.J. Kidd, J. Medina, and G. Pohlhaus, Jr. (New York: Routledge).
Anderson, Elizabeth (2012) 'Epistemic Justice as a Virtue of Social Institutions', *Social Epistemology* 26.2: 163–173.
Kidd, Ian James and Carel, Havi (2017a) 'Epistemic Injustice and Illness', *Journal of Applied Philosophy* Special Issue Applied Epistemology, eds., D. Coady and M. Fricker, 33.2: 172–190.
Kidd, Ian James and Carel, Havi (2017b) 'Epistemic Injustice in Medicine and Healthcare'. In *The Routledge Handbook of Epistemic Injustice*, eds., I.J. Kidd, J. Medina, and G. Pohlhaus, Jr. (New York: Routledge).
Coady, David (2010) 'Two Concepts of Epistemic Injustice', *Episteme: A Journal of Social Epistemology* 7.2: 101–111.

Coady, David (2017) 'Epistemic Injustice as Distributive Injustice'. In *The Routledge Handbook of Epistemic Injustice*, eds., I. J. Kidd, J. Medina, and G. Pohlhaus, Jr. (New York: Routledge).
Dotson, Kristie (2012) 'A Cautionary Tale: On Limiting Epistemic Oppression', *Frontiers* 33.1: 24–47.
Fricker, Miranda (2007) *Epistemic Injustice: Power and the Ethics of Knowing*, Oxford: Oxford University Press.
Fricker, Miranda (2015) 'Epistemic Contribution as a Central Human Capability'. In *The Equal Society: Essays on Equality in Theory and Practice*, ed. George Hull (Lanham, MD: Lexington Books).
Fricker, Miranda (2016) 'Epistemic Injustice and the Preservation of Ignorance'. In *The Epistemic Dimensions of Ignorance*, eds. M. Blaauw and R. Peels (Cambridge: Cambridge University Press).
Harding, Sandra (1991) *Whose Science? Whose Knowledge?*, Milton Keynes: Open University Press.
Intemann, Kristen (2010) '25 Years of Feminist Empiricism and Standpoint Theory: Where Are We Now?', *Hypatia* 25.4: 778–796.
Kyratsous, Michaelis and Sanati, Abdi (2015) 'Epistemic Injustice in Assessment of Delusions', *Journal of Evaluation in Clinical Practice* 21.3: 479–485.
Lovibond, Sabina (1989) 'Feminism and Postmodernism', *New Left Review* 1.178: 5–28.
Lukàcs, Georgy (1971) *History and Class Consciousness: Studies in Marxist Dialectics*, trans. Rodney Livingstone, London: Merlin Press.
Lyotard, Jean-François (1984) *The Postmodern Condition: A Report on Knowledge*, trans. G. Bennington and B. Massumi, Manchester: Manchester University Press.
Mason, Rebecca (2011) 'Two Kinds of Unknowing', *Hypatia* 26.2: 294–307.
McKinnon, Rachel (2017) 'Allies Behaving Badly: Gaslighting as Epistemic Injustice'. In *The Routledge Handbook of Epistemic Injustice*, eds., I. J. Kidd, J. Medina, and G. Pohlhaus, Jr. (New York: Routledge).
Medina, José (2012) 'Hermeneutical Injustice and Polyphonic Contextualism: Social Silences and Shared Hermeneutical Responsibilities', *Social Epistemology* 26.2: 201–220.
Medina, José (2013) *Epistemologies of Resistance: Gender and Racial Oppression, Epistemic Injustice, and Resistant Imaginations*, Oxford: Oxford University Press.
Mills, Charles (2007) 'White Ignorance'. In *Race and Epistemologies of Ignorance*, eds., Shannon Sullivan and Nancy Tuana (New York: State University of New York Press).
Mills, Charles (2015) 'Global White Ignorance'. In *Routledge International Handbook of Ignorance Studies*, eds., Matthias Gross and Linsey McGoey (London and New York: Routledge).
Nussbaum, Martha (1999) *Sex and Social Justice*, Oxford and New York: Oxford University Press.
Pohlhaus, Jr., Gaile (2012) 'Relational Knowing and Epistemic Injustice: Toward a Theory of Willful Hermeneutical Ignorance', *Hypatia* 27.3: 715–735.
Rorty, Richard (1990) *Contingency, Irony, and Solidarity*, Cambridge: Cambridge University Press.
Scrutton, Anastasia Philippa (2017) 'Epistemic Injustice and Mental Illness'. In *The Routledge Handbook of Epistemic Injustice*, eds., I. J. Kidd, J. Medina, and G. Pohlhaus, Jr. (New York: Routledge).
Williams, Bernard (2006) 'Philosophy as a Humanistic Discipline'. In *Philosophy as a Humanistic Discipline*, ed., A. W. Moore (Princeton: Princeton University Press).

# 5
# EPISTEMIC INJUSTICE AS DISTRIBUTIVE INJUSTICE[1]

*David Coady*

Is epistemic injustice a form of distributive injustice? In her early, profoundly influential work on epistemic injustice Miranda Fricker makes it clear that she does not think it is. In a recent article, however, she has expanded her conception of epistemic injustice to include something she calls *distributive epistemic injustice*, which she characterizes as "the unfair distribution of epistemic goods such as education or information" (Fricker 2013: 1318).[2] She contrasts this with her earlier, narrower, conception of the subject, which she now prefers to call *discriminatory epistemic injustice*. In what follows I will challenge Fricker's distinction between discriminatory and distributive epistemic injustice; each of the forms of epistemic injustice that Fricker describes is a form of distributive injustice (or at any rate can be fruitfully treated as such) and that considerable insight into the nature of these injustices, and into the interrelations between them, can be gained from recognizing this fact.

Epistemic injustice in the original, and still most widely used, sense of the term is divided by Fricker into two categories: testimonial injustice and hermeneutic injustice. I will consider them separately.

## Testimonial injustice

Testimonial injustice "occurs when prejudice on the part of the hearer leads to the speaker receiving less credibility than he or she deserves" (Fricker 2003: 154). The most obvious case of this would be when the prejudice in question leads the hearer to disbelieve the speaker, even though the speaker deserves to be believed. However Fricker makes it clear that this is only the limiting case of a broader phenomenon, which would include situations in which there is an unjust reduction in credibility, even if it doesn't actually result in disbelief. Now, as Fricker notes, it is tempting to think of testimonial injustice as a form of distributive injustice, a concept that will be familiar to anyone with a passing acquaintance with recent Anglo-American political philosophy. If we think of credibility as a good (like wealth, healthcare, education or information), then it is natural to think that testimonial injustice consists in an unjust (or unfair) distribution of this good and that there is a philosophical problem of specifying what a just distribution of credibility would be.

Fricker has two arguments against this idea. The first of which is in the following passage:

> Credibility is not a good that belongs with the distributive model of justice. Unlike those goods that are fruitfully dealt with along distributive lines (such as wealth or health care), there is no puzzle about the fair distribution of credibility, for credibility is a concept that wears its proper distribution on its sleeve. Epistemological nuance aside, the hearer's obligation is obvious: she must match the level of credibility she attributes to her interlocutor to the evidence that he is offering the truth.
>
> (Fricker 2007: 19)

Like Fricker, I will put aside epistemological nuance and agree, at least for the sake of argument, with her "obvious" principle governing the obligations of hearers. Nonetheless this principle does not take us very far. Suppose, by way of analogy, that someone were to say that there is no puzzle about the fair distribution of wealth, since it is obvious that everyone should receive the wealth that he or she deserves. The correct response to this principle, I suggest, is to accept it but point out that it leaves the real issue, namely how much wealth people deserve, unanswered. Do they deserve equal wealth or do they deserve wealth in proportion to the hours they have worked, their intelligence, their moral virtue, their good luck or are all attempts to achieve such patterns of distribution themselves unjust?[3]

In a similar way, I suggest that Fricker's principle in the above passage does not address the most important questions about the just distribution of credibility, questions about the nature of the hearer's obligations to seek out and interpret evidence that a speaker is offering the truth, especially in situations in which the speaker has less social power than the hearer. Fricker herself has had much to say about these issues, and I don't think I can add anything worthwhile to her discussion of them here. It is enough to note that this argument does not establish a disanalogy between credibility on the one hand, and goods such as wealth and healthcare, etc., such that the latter, but not the former, are suited to the distributive model of injustice.

Fricker's second argument for the same conclusion occurs in the following passage:

> Goods best suited to the distributive model are so suited principally because they are finite and at least potentially in short supply [. . .] Such goods are those for which there is, or may soon be, a certain competition and that is what gives rise to the ethical puzzle about the justice of this or that particular distribution. By contrast, credibility is not generally finite in this way, and there is no analogous competitive demand to invite the distributive treatment.
>
> (Fricker 2007: 19–20)

But this seems to be clearly wrong. Credibility is finite. It would clearly be irrational (and probably psychologically impossible) to believe every piece of testimony one comes across, still less, as José Medina notes (2012: 62), to assign them all maximum credibility. Furthermore credibility is, unfortunately, often in short supply, and, as a result, there is often competition for it.[4] Indeed the two main examples of testimonial injustice that Fricker discusses illustrate this point very clearly. One of these examples comes from Harper Lee's novel, *To Kill a Mockingbird*. The all-white jury in that novel commit a testimonial injustice against Tom Robinson when they fail to believe his testimony because he is black. Fricker's discussion of this case is subtle and illuminating, but it largely ignores the fact that the unjustifiably low credibility that the jurors assign to Tom Robinson's testimony is inextricably linked to the unjustifiably high credibility they assign to the testimony of his accusers, especially Mayella and Bob Ewell. The trial of Tom Robinson, like most trials, especially in the adversarial Anglo-American legal system is, to a very great extent, a competition over credibility. Indeed this is a point Fricker herself seems to acknowledge in the following passage:

> The trial is a zero-sum contest between the word of a black man against that of a white girl ... and there are those on the jury for whom the idea that the black man is to be epistemically trusted and the white girl distrusted is virtually a psychological impossibility.
>
> (Fricker 2007: 25)

None of this should be taken to imply that the business of assigning credibility is always a zero-sum game; it is sometimes possible for one person or group of people to gain credibility without a corresponding loss of credibility for anyone else.[5] But this is also true of wealth; sometimes it is possible for one group of people to become wealthier at no cost to anyone else, but this fact is not normally taken to imply that questions about economic injustice should not be thought of in distributive terms.[6] There is no disanalogy between credibility and wealth here. Nor does there seem to be any disanalogy here between credibility and healthcare, education or information, all of which are goods that Fricker does think are suited to the distributive model of injustice.

Fricker's other main example of testimonial injustice, drawn from Anthony Minghella's screenplay of *The Talented Mr. Ripley*, in which Herbert Greenleaf refuses to take seriously Marge Sherwood's suspicions that Tom Ripley has murdered his son because he has internalized certain prejudicial stereotypes against women, illustrates the same point. Fricker's otherwise admirable discussion of this example strikingly neglects the fact that Greenleaf gives too little credibility to Sherwood, to a large extent, because he gives too much credibility to Ripley. His undervaluing of the testimony of women (at least in certain contexts) is inextricably linked with his overvaluing the testimony of men, just as the jury's undervaluing of the testimony of black people in *To Kill a Mockingbird* is inextricably linked with their overvaluing of the testimony of white people.

To summarize, competition for credibility is a pervasive feature of much of our social and political life. The unjustifiably low credibility often assigned to the testimony of oppressed groups, which Fricker rightly emphasizes, is inextricably linked with the unjustifiably high credibility that privileged groups often enjoy. Fricker's attempt to distinguish between "distributive goods" such as wealth and healthcare on the one hand and credibility on the other hand, on the grounds that the latter "is not generally finite" (i.e. it is generally infinite), is mistaken.

Fricker's view that testimonial injustice should not be thought of in distributive terms is built into her definition of the phenomenon, according to which it consists in a speaker receiving less credibility than he or she deserves.[7] We can see the limitations of this account if we compare testimonial injustice with economic injustice. Suppose someone were to claim that economic injustice consists in someone getting less wealth than he or she deserves. That is certainly part of the story, but it doesn't really get to the heart of the matter. It would be better to characterize it as someone getting less wealth than he or she deserves as a result (at least partially) of others getting more wealth than they deserve. It seems to me that testimonial injustice parallels economic injustice in having this kind of relational, and more specifically causal, structure. In neither case is it a simple one way causal relation. Rather, it is true, in both cases, that some have less than they deserve of the good in question because others have more of it than they deserve, and it is also true that some have more than they deserve because others have less than they deserve. In short, in both cases there is a relation of mutual reinforcement between deficits of a certain good and excesses of it.[8]

Fricker does consider broadening the concept of testimonial injustice to include credibility excesses as well as credibility deficits. A person whose testimony is routinely given too much credence may, she reasons, be wronged by being rendered incapable of developing certain intellectual virtues, such as open-mindedness.[9] In the end, however, she decides that the concept of testimonial injustice should not be extended to such cases:

> I do not think it would be right to characterise any of the individual moments of credibility excess that such a person receives as in itself an instance of testimonial injustice, since none of them wrongs him sufficiently in itself.
>
> *(Fricker 2007: 21)*

There is surely something to this. We may grant that such a person has, in some sense, been wronged, but it would be deeply misguided to characterize him as a victim of injustice (or, at any rate, as a victim of the same kind of injustice as a person who suffers from an unjust credibility deficit).[10] Fricker is right about this. But she is wrong to leave credibility excesses out of her analysis altogether. This is not, or at least not primarily, because individual instances of credibility excess can be unjust as well as individual moments of credibility deficit. Rather it is because, as José Medina says, any analysis which "focuses exclusively on the individual moments of testimonial exchanges among particular subjects" (2012: 59) is inevitably short-sighted. I would add that the reason it is short-sighted is that it fails to do justice to the fact that testimonial injustice is fundamentally a form of distributive injustice. It is an injustice in the distribution of a particular good: credibility.

## Hermeneutical injustice

Fricker does not explicitly argue that hermeneutical injustice should not be understood in distributive terms; nonetheless, as we have seen, it is classified by her, along with testimonial injustice, as a form of discriminatory epistemic injustice, which is explicitly contrasted with distributive epistemic injustice. I will argue that hermeneutical injustice, like testimonial injustice, should be conceived, at least partially, in distributive terms. Indeed, I will argue that a particular substantive principle of just distribution is implicit in her account of the phenomenon.

Fricker says that hermeneutical injustice, unlike testimonial injustice, occurs "prior to communicative activity". She defines it as "the injustice of having some significant area of one's social experience obscured from collective understanding owing to hermeneutic marginalization" (2006: 99). The concept of *hermeneutic marginalization* in turn is explained as a matter of belonging "to a group which does not have access to equal participation in the generation of social meanings" (Fricker 2013: 1319).[11]

What is it to be denied access to equal participation in the generation of social meanings? I cannot hope to do justice to Fricker's subtle discussion of this matter, but some of her examples give a rough idea of the kind of thing she has in mind. One is that of "a woman suffering from sexual harassment prior to the time when we had this concept and word to name the experience" (Fricker 2007: 151). Another is that of a homosexual man who is unable, because of a lack of collective conceptual and linguistic resources, to understand or explain his sexual experiences in positive terms (Fricker 2006: 105–7). These examples make it clear that the generation of social meaning includes (though it may not be limited to) both the coining of words and phrases to explain one's social experiences and the practices that give words and phrases the public meaning that they have.[12] Certain social groups (e.g. journalists, academics, politicians, men, white people, heterosexuals) are in a better position to generate these meanings than others, and as such, they have greater hermeneutical power. Other social groups, those with less hermeneutical power, have their social experience misunderstood (sometimes, but not always, by themselves and/or other members of their social group) to one degree or another, and are unjustly harmed as a result.

In what follows, I will argue that Fricker's account of hermeneutical injustice in terms of hermeneutic marginalization is (at least implicitly) a principle of distributive justice: the egalitarian principle according to which it is a requirement of justice that everyone should have equal access to participation in the generation of social meanings. That is, everyone should have equal hermeneutic power. To be marginalized with respect to a certain good is just to have less than an equal share of it. We may call the distributive principle that everyone should have equal hermeneutic power "hermeneutic egalitarianism." Fricker's examples of hermeneutical injustice encourage us to think that hermeneutic egalitarianism is obviously correct. It is because women have not had equal hermeneutic power that the kinds of encounters we now recognize as sexual harassment were (and often still are) dismissed as harmless flirting. Likewise, it is because homosexual men have not had equal hermeneutic power that they have often been (and in some cases still are) unable to understand or explain their sexual experiences in positive terms.

These examples may make it seem that hermeneutic egalitarianism is obviously correct and hence that there is no puzzle about the correct distribution of hermeneutic power, just as Fricker argued there is no puzzle about the correct distribution of credibility. However, the analogy with credibility should give us pause. Fricker, quite rightly, does not countenance any form of credibility egalitarianism. There is nothing unjust about distributing credibility unequally. On the contrary, justice requires credibility to be distributed unequally.[13] Something similar may be true of hermeneutic power.

This seems to be more than a hypothetical possibility. Take neo-Nazis, for example. They appear to be a hermeneutically marginalized social group. They have very little impact on the generation of social meanings. They understand the words "Jew" and "Muslim" quite differently from the wider society in which they live, and their attempts to popularize certain expressions, such as "Jewish conspiracy" and "Islamization", to explain their social experiences have been largely unsuccessful. It seems in short that they are victims of hermeneutical injustice, on Fricker's definition, because they have had some significant areas of their "social experience obscured from collective understanding owing to hermeneutic marginalization" (Fricker 2006: 99). If I am right, hermeneutic marginalization in this case is not an injustice. It is a good thing. Even if I am wrong, and it is not true that neo-Nazis have been hermeneutically marginalized, there seems to be a very good case that they should be. Some groups of people, I suggest, do not deserve to have as much hermeneutic power as others.

Neo-Nazis are, of course, a very extreme case, so I will consider another example, which makes the same point in a somewhat different way. In the past, proponents of same-sex marriage were hermeneutically marginalized. They were members of a group that did not have equal access to the generation of social meaning. In particular, they did not have an equal say in the social (and, more specifically, legal) meaning of the word "marriage." But increasingly the tables are turning, with large majorities in most Western countries in favour of marriage equality and more and more countries legislating to keep pace with public opinion. What are we to make of this? Certainly opponents of same-sex marriage have lost their hermeneutic monopoly, but more than this, it seems clear that they have themselves become hermeneutically marginalized (at least in Western countries). Their claims and arguments are (rightly, in my opinion) given scant consideration in the public domain, and, as a result, they are often not heard and have little or no influence on the social meaning of "marriage." If hermeneutic egalitarianism were correct, their hermeneutic marginalization would constitute an injustice. But it seems to me that this is not an injustice. There is an egalitarian principle that is relevant here: that gays and lesbians should have the same rights and privileges (including marriage) as everyone else. But it seems to me that this example makes it clear that there is no right to equal hermeneutic power. Those who insist that the traditional definition of "marriage" is the right one are just wrong, and they were wrong all along.

This example also makes it clear that hermeneutic power, like credibility, is a finite resource and, as a result, there can be competition for it. The political and social struggle over the meaning of the word "marriage" is a zero-sum game. To the extent that one party wins, the other party loses. Hence, hermeneutic power seems to be the kind of good which, on Fricker's own account, raises a problem of distributive justice.

I have argued that hermeneutical injustice can be fruitfully treated as a form of injustice in the distribution of a certain good: namely hermeneutic power. I have also argued against the idea, implicit in Fricker's work, that justice requires this good to be distributed equally. Unfortunately, I don't have a plausible alternative principle governing its just distribution to offer in its place.

It could be argued that some neo-Nazis and some proponents of traditional marriage are victims of an injustice of the kind Fricker now calls "distributive epistemic injustice," i.e. injustice in the distribution of education and information.[14] After all, many of them do appear to be under-educated and ill-informed. Hence some of these people may be victims of a form of injustice[15] that is, in a sense, epistemic, but they are not victims of hermeneutic injustice.

## Conclusion

There are people who have no time for the concepts of distributive justice and injustice at all. Robert Nozick, for example, has argued that these concepts imply "a central distributing authority" (1974: 149), and that any such person or entity is inherently unjust. I don't intend to go into the details of Nozick's position here; however, it does suggest a disanalogy between credibility and hermeneutic power on the one hand, and goods that are standardly thought of as raising problems of distributive justice and injustice on the other. A lot of people are, I think rightly, undisturbed by the idea of a central distributing authority for some of these goods (healthcare, for example), but would baulk at the idea of a central distributing authority for either credibility or hermeneutic power. The idea of such an authority for credibility conjures up Orwellian visions of thought crime. It is surely not the State's business to tell us whom we should believe, nor, more generally, how much credibility we should give to people's testimony. Similarly, though perhaps not so obviously, it is not the State's job to distribute hermeneutic power. In both cases it seems that any attempt by the State to impose a just distribution of the good in question would itself be unjust. So if you think of distributive justice, as some people do, as presupposing some kind of State-imposed distribution, then you may think that Fricker is right (albeit for the wrong reasons) not to treat testimonial and hermeneutical injustice as examples of distributive injustice after all.

Having said that, I don't think we should think of distributive justice and injustice as necessarily involving a centralized distributer. It is perfectly possible to think that the distribution of a certain good is unjust, but also to think that any attempt by the State to impose a more just distribution of it would be undesirable either because it would itself be unjust or because it is objectionable in some other way which in this case trumps considerations of justice. All that is needed for a good to raise a problem of distributive justice is that it be limited and, as a result, for there to be at least the possibility of competition over it. I have argued that credibility and hermeneutic power are both goods of this kind, and hence that testimonial injustice and hermeneutical injustice can fruitfully be treated as forms of distributive injustice. What principles would govern the just distribution of these goods is a further question.

**Related chapters**: 1, 2, 3, 4, 8

## Notes

1 I would like to thank Ian James Kidd, José Medina and C.A.J. Coady for their helpful comments on an earlier draft.
2 I have argued elsewhere (Coady 2010) that these two concepts of epistemic injustice are interrelated in important ways.
3 Some people (e.g. Nozick 1974) argue that the distributive model of justice (and injustice) should be rejected altogether. I will return to this position later. For now, I am considering only whether there is a good reason for accepting it in the case of certain goods, such as wealth, education, etc., while rejecting it in the case of credibility.
4 José Medina (2011 and 2012) also emphasizes the phenomenon of competition for credibility; however he does not argue, as I do, that we should think of testimonial injustice as a form of distributive injustice.
5 Medina (2012: 63–4) argues that credibility judgements are always comparative and contrastive. I think they often are, but not always.
6 Probably the best known example of a distributive principle of justice, John Rawls' Difference Principle (1972), is explicitly motivated by the idea that the accumulation of "primary social goods" such as wealth, is sometimes, but not always, a zero-sum game.
7 According to Fricker, not all cases of speakers receiving less credibility than they deserve are cases of testimonial injustice. The credibility deficit must be a result of an identity prejudice, rather than (say) bad luck.
8 Economic injustice and testimonial injustice are closely related in more ways than one. They are not only structurally similar, they are also themselves in a relation of mutual reinforcement. To a great extent, testimonial injustice is caused by economic injustice, and economic injustice is caused by testimonial injustice.
9 Fricker seems to take the contemporary view that open-mindedness is an intellectual (or epistemic) virtue for granted. I'm not so sure. I tend to agree with G.K. Chesterton that an open mind, like an open mouth, is really a mark of foolishness, and that the purpose of opening one's mind, like that of opening one's mouth, is to close it on something solid (Chesterton 1937: 223–4).
10 Once again the economic analogy seems good. Someone who is unjustly wealthy may as a result be unable to develop a range of moral and epistemic virtues, but it would be somewhat perverse to characterize such a person as a victim of economic injustice.
11 I am only considering Fricker's definition of "hermeneutic marginalization" here. Havi Carel and Ian James Kidd (2017) write that hermeneutic marginalization should be understood to include not only unequal participation in the generation of social meanings, but also unequal participation in authoritative practices by which social meanings are legitimated. I believe that my argument would be largely unaffected if we were to broaden the concept of hermeneutic marginalization in this way.
12 It is worth emphasizing that "meaning" should be understood very broadly here. It is certainly not restricted to the extensions of words and phrases; it also includes their connotations, whether positive or negative.
13 Justice requires us (at least presumptively) to distribute credibility in accordance with the available evidence (see Fricker 2007: 25). This entails that an equal distribution would be unjust.
14 See Kotze (2017).
15 This will depend of course on the reasons for their lack of education and/or information.

## References

Carel, Havi and Ian James Kidd (2017) 'Epistemic Injustice in Medicine and Healthcare', in Ian James Kidd, Jose Medina, and Gaile Pohlhaus, Jr. (eds.), *The Routledge Handbook of Epistemic Injustice* (New York: Routledge).
Chesterton, G.K. (1937) *Autobiography*, London: Hutchinson.
Coady, David (2010) 'Two concepts of epistemic injustice,' *Episteme* 7(2): 101–113.
Fricker, Miranda (2003) 'Epistemic injustice and a role for virtue in the politics of knowing,' *Metaphilosophy* 3–4(1–2): 154–173.
Fricker, Miranda (2006) 'Powerlessness and social interpretation,' *Episteme* 3(1–2): 96–108.
Fricker, Miranda (2007) *Epistemic Injustice: Power and the Ethics of Knowing*, Oxford: Oxford University Press.
Fricker, Miranda (2013) 'Epistemic injustice as a condition of political freedom?,' *Synthese* 190(7): 1317–1332.

Kotzee, Ben (2017) 'Epistemic Injustice and Education', in Ian James Kidd, Jose Medina, and Gaile Pohlhaus, Jr. (eds.), *The Routledge Handbook of Epistemic Injustice* (New York: Routledge).

Medina, José (2011) 'The relevance of credibility excess in a proportional view of epistemic injustice: Differential epistemic authority and the social imaginary,' *Social Epistemology* 25(1): 15–35.

Medina, José (2012) *The Epistemology of Resistance: Gender and Racial Oppression, Epistemic Injustice, and Resistant Imaginations*, Oxford: Oxford University Press.

Nozick, Robert (1974) *Anarchy, State, and Utopia*, New York: Basic Books.

Rawls, John (1972) *A Theory of Justice*, Oxford: Clarendon Press.

# 6
# TRUST, DISTRUST, AND EPISTEMIC INJUSTICE

*Katherine Hawley*

## Introduction

There are many overlapping concepts of trust within philosophy. These are multiplied still further when we look to other disciplines – such as psychology, economics, and sociology – and when we reflect upon our ordinary ways of thinking and talking about trust. Sometimes trust is thought of as an emotionally thrilling leap into the dark; sometimes it is pictured as a bloodless pragmatic choice, based on cost-benefit analysis. Paradigmatic settings for trust vary from our most intimate personal relationships to our interactions with government, media, or corporate brands. And we talk of trusting what someone says, trusting someone to do something, or simply trusting someone, all to varying degrees.

Absence of trust, likewise, is multi-faceted. It inherits all the conceptual variety associated with trust. Moreover, for any given notion of trust, there are at least three different ways in which trust can be absent. First, we may lack trust in a given situation because we think that neither trust nor distrust is merited, that trustworthiness is not at stake. For example, my neighbour is not a philosopher and has not offered to write this chapter for me. So I do not trust my neighbour to write this chapter for me, but nor do I distrust her in that respect: I recognise that neither of these attitudes fits the situation. Second, we may lack trust through lack of evidence: we think that a situation is one in which either trust or distrust is appropriate, but we can't tell which of these is the right attitude. For example, suppose my neighbour has offered to care for my garden whilst I'm away, but I don't know whether she is trustworthy in such matters. I think that either trust is appropriate here, or else distrust is appropriate, but I don't know which.

Third, we may lack trust when we think that trust-or-distrust is appropriate, i.e. that trustworthiness is at stake, and moreover that trust is inappropriate. For example, suppose my neighbour has promised to turn off her music at midnight, but I know from bitter experience that she never keeps such promises. In such a situation, my lack of trust amounts to distrust. Thus distrust should be distinguished from mere lack of trust, and from mere agnosticism about trust. The relationship between trust and distrust is in some ways analogous to that between justice and injustice: it is fruitful to examine justice through the lens of injustice, and likewise it is fruitful to examine trust through the lens of distrust (I pursue this project in Hawley 2014a).

On any understanding of trust and distrust, these attitudes are intertwined with issues of social power (Allen 2017). Trusting, distrusting, being trusted, and being distrusted can all flow from the exercise of social power, and all can have consequences for social power. When you trust someone, you make yourself dependent upon her, giving her a certain power over you: a trusted person enjoys a great deal of discretion in her actions. But, as Spiderman reminds us, with great power comes great responsibility: when you place your trust in someone, that can be a way of imposing responsibilities upon her. Placing your trust can give you the power to tug at the other person's conscience and the power to represent the trusted person as untrustworthy if your expectations are unmet. For these sorts of reasons, trust is not always welcomed by the trusted person.

Distrusting, or withholding trust, is also an exercise of social power: you may deny other people important opportunities when you fail to trust them, both through the practical consequences of your distrust and through its symbolic power. But these exercises of social power stand in complicated relationships to privilege and security: whilst those with few resources may be forced to trust others, since they have no alternative, those who are more comfortably situated can afford to be more trusting, since they can more easily bounce back if they get things wrong. Dimensions of privilege, security, resources, and comfort here include emotional stability, health, strong relationships, and access to reliable information, not just access to money or material goods.

Where there is social power, there is the potential for injustice, and there are many ways of linking discussions of trust and distrust with discussions of injustice. In this chapter, I focus on issues of trust and distrust, which seem especially relevant to epistemic injustice, and in particular on issues where thinking about trust and distrust may help us crystallise questions that we might have missed otherwise; the chapter should of course be read in the context of the many complementary chapters which make up this *Handbook*.

## Trust, distrust, and reliance

What kind of attitude is trust? Following Annette Baier (1986), recent philosophical literature has focused on a rich, normatively-laden attitude of trust, an attitude that is properly adopted towards other people, but not towards inanimate objects. This is the attitude I have when I trust my friend to show up for our habitual coffee date, rather than the attitude I have when I trust the coffee itself to keep me awake. Such discussions of trust typically focus on trusting people to act as we expect, in practical situations. As such, we might wonder how they can raise issues of distinctively epistemic injustice. But trusting people to do things often involves trusting them to be competent or skilful, i.e. evaluating them on epistemic grounds, so there is potential for epistemic injustice here. (I return to the contrast between 'epistemic trust' and 'practical trust' in the section that follows.)

Philosophers disagree about how exactly to characterise the difference between these attitudes (McLeod [2015] surveys the options, whilst Holton [1994] influentially connects this debate to Strawson's [1974] account of 'reactive attitudes'). But some common themes are as follows. If my friend does not show up, I am likely to feel resentful, to feel she owes me an apology, and if the stakes are high, I may even feel betrayed. If my coffee does not keep me awake, I may feel disappointed, frustrated, and sleepy, but it would be an anthropomorphising confusion to resent the coffee, or feel betrayed by it. (I might reasonably feel that way towards the barista, however, if I was mistakenly served decaf.) If my friend is a regular no-show, we regard this as a moral flaw, a kind of selfishness or failure to meet obligations, whereas if the coffee regularly sends me to sleep, we look for a different brand, rather than moralising about its vices. Moreover there may be a distinctive phenomenology or emotional colour involved when I trust my friend, one which is absent when I rely upon the coffee (Jones [1996] emphasises emotion, whilst Medina [2013: 79–80] makes the connection to injustice).

Analogously, we can distinguish between a normatively-laden attitude of distrust and a more mundane attitude of low expectations. I distrust certain politicians, but I merely have low expectations regarding the reliability of my clapped-out car. Distrust embodies a moral criticism, involving attitudes such as resentment, and may have a distinctive emotional colour. Mere low expectations lack those features and seem more like a pragmatic accommodation to an imperfect material world rather than a bruised response to moral inadequacy.

The richer attitudes of trust and distrust are appropriately adopted towards people and not towards cups of coffee or clapped-out cars. But the thinner attitudes of reliance or low expectations can sometimes be appropriately adopted towards people, as well as towards inanimate objects. I might rely on the noisy teenagers in the café to keep me awake, but I don't think they are obliged to do this, and I can't reasonably resent them if they do not. Similarly, I might have low expectations about my neighbour's dress sense, but it would be a mistake for me to distrust her in this respect: dressing badly is not a moral failing, and my neighbour doesn't owe me anything on this front.

When we regard other people in these ways, there is a sense in which we treat them impersonally, as sources of noise or of sartorial displeasure. But often this is the appropriate, indeed the respectful thing to do: I would be absurdly presumptuous if I treated my neighbour's sense of style as a personalised issue between us, regarding her as untrustworthy when she wears that dowdy jacket, demanding apologies, or feeling resentful. However we can wrong other people when we go too far in the opposite direction, treating them impersonally in situations when we should recognise them as deserving something richer. If my friend promises to meet me for coffee, I should take her seriously as making a personal commitment to me. I may trust her or indeed distrust her, depending on her habits of punctuality. But if instead I simply make a practical estimation of whether she is likely to turn up, and do not engage my reactive attitudes, this is a way of failing to treat my friend as a mature adult. (This is why it is painfully diminishing to be told 'I'm not angry, I'm just disappointed'.) If this is my general approach to our interactions, then we are not really friends.

When thinking about the ways in which trust and distrust can allow for injustice, it is often useful to think about a two-part structure and, correspondingly, two opportunities for justice or injustice. In situations where trust or distrust may be appropriate attitudes, we need to get two different things right. We need to grasp whether the situation is one where trust-or-distrust is appropriate: 'no' for my neighbour's dress sense, 'yes' for my friend's promise to meet for coffee. And then if trust-or-distrust is appropriate, we need to grasp which of these is correct: should I trust my friend to show up, or should I distrust her? Getting things wrong at either stage has the potential to harm others. At the first stage, I might mistakenly fail to take my friend's promise seriously as a promise, or I might mistakenly think that my neighbour's outfits are a matter of trust-or-distrust for me. At the second stage, I might take my friend's promise seriously, but mistakenly distrust her, rather than giving her the trust she deserves. And at either stage our judgments may be guided by prejudice and biases.

## Epistemic trust and practical trust

We trust people's words, and we trust their actions; to put things somewhat differently, we trust people as *speakers* (or as writers, as signers, etc.), and we trust people as *actors*. These contrasts are sometimes marked as distinctions between 'epistemic' and 'practical' trust. But the labels are unhelpful for several reasons, and the underlying distinction itself is often blurry. First, speaking is itself a way of acting, so when we trust people as informants, this is an instance of trusting them as actors. Second, our trust in people's actions often involves trusting them to act as they said they would: I trust my friend to meet me for coffee as she promised.

Third, our trust in people's words can have both epistemic and practical consequences, likewise for our trust in people's actions. When someone offers me information, and I trust what she says, if all goes well I thereby gain testimonial knowledge; there may also be practical consequences, whether things go well or badly. When I trust someone to act in a certain way, then likewise if all goes well, her behaviour can provide me with knowledge. For example, if a ship's captain trusts the lookout to warn her of icebergs, then the captain can know that there are no icebergs on the basis of the lookout's silence.

Fourth, even paradigmatic cases of trust in a speaker's words involve more than trust in her knowledgeability; trusting the speaker involves trust that she knows what she is talking about, trust that she is sincere, and potentially much more. As Miranda Fricker reminds us (2007: 45), accepting someone's testimony requires us to have faith in the speaker's competence but also in her sincerity; conversely, we can recognise incompetence and dishonesty as two different forms of untrustworthiness. I myself am inclined to regard competence, but not sincerity, as an epistemic matter: that's to say, I think that when we judge someone to be insincere, we do not thereby judge her as a knower. But Fricker regards both competence and sincerity as epistemic: this is because, inspired by Edward Craig (1990), she takes the capacity to convey one's knowledge to others as essential to the very possession of knowledge. If one is regarded as chronically insincere, then one is not regarded as trustworthy. For Fricker, this means one is not in fact a knower.

Despite my complaints about the distinction between so-called 'epistemic' and 'practical' trust, it is clear that testifying – purporting to offer information to others – is an action with a special social significance both for the speaker and for the audience. Testifying is not the only way in which speech can have epistemic significance. Nevertheless, it is a type of speech – a type of action – which creates distinctive normative concerns, and distinctive opportunities for both justice and injustice. With that in mind, I will discuss injustice first in the context of trust and distrust in testimony, and then in the context of trust and distrust in action more generally.

## Testimony

In ordinary language, the term 'testimony' is reserved for significant first-person reports of witnessing, often in religious, legal, or journalistic contexts. But for philosophers, 'testimony' encompasses the multitudinous ways in which we purport to provide information to one another, taking in idle gossip, scientific papers, encyclopaedia articles, and kindergarten teaching, amongst much else. When somebody testifies, seeming to tell me something, I may believe or fail to believe what I am told. Many contextual factors will combine to determine how much credibility I give to a speaker. And, as Fricker so powerfully articulates (2007), sometimes I give a speaker less credibility than she deserves, because of my prejudices about her social identity, perhaps as a woman, as a refugee, or as an octogenarian. Then I perpetrate a testimonial injustice upon her.

Other chapters in this *Handbook* discuss testimonial injustice (e.g. Battaly 2017; Wanderer 2017). What difference does it make if we think of this in terms of trust and distrust, rather than simply in terms of giving and withholding credibility? We could use 'trust' and 'distrust' as mere synonyms for giving and withholding credibility, in which case it would make no difference at all. But to make life more interesting, let's use those terms in a way that respects the distinction between rich, normatively-laden trust and distrust on the one hand, and mere reliance or low expectations on the other hand.

Which of these is the attitude we take to other people's testimony? Do we feel resentful or just disappointed when testimony turns out to be false? Do we understand the offering and accepting of testimony in richly normative terms? Perhaps it depends: testimony about important matters, or within a personal or professional relationship, can feel more significant than testimony about trivia from strangers. Indeed, Wanderer (2017) argues that a pre-existing relationship can mean that epistemic injustice constitutes an epistemic betrayal. Nevertheless, even in the most low-stakes scenarios, we tend to moralise both intentional deception and reckless speculation disguised as sober fact (or 'bullshit' as it is technically known, following Frankfurt (2005).

Some epistemologists argue that when a speaker offers her personal assurance to an audience, who then reward her with their trust, this improves the epistemic status of the beliefs formed by the audience (Hinchmann 2005; Moran 2005). In this picture, the intended audience acquires a distinctive epistemic justification that is unavailable to mere eavesdroppers, no matter how clearly they overhear the testimony. Other epistemologists deny the epistemic significance of trust (e.g. Lackey 2008). But even sceptics such as Lackey accept that testimony is typically intertwined with interpersonal normative expectations, opening up opportunities for resentment and gratitude, justice and injustice, whether or not these are epistemically significant.

Following Craig (1990), Fricker distinguishes between treating someone as an informant, part of a community with common purposes, and treating that person as a mere source of information (2007: 132). She argues that systematic testimonial injustice treats a speaker as a mere *source* of information, and is thereby a form of objectification. I would suggest instead that objectification arises when we disrespect people by offering them either mere reliance or low expectations, where trust or distrust would be more appropriate. Sometimes we are prepared only to feel pleased or disappointed, when it would be more respectful to feel grateful, angry or betrayed. Systematic testimonial injustice – systematic unfair distrust – is wrong, but not because it treats others as mere objects.

## Trustworthiness and untrustworthiness

Epistemological discussions of testimony typically start by assuming that a speaker testifies that $p$, and is recognised as doing so, whether or not the audience believes what she says. Discussions of testimonial injustice often inherit that starting point. But there are also opportunities for injustice that arise before that point, as a potential audience decides who to ask and where to direct their attention, as a potential speaker decides whether and how to speak, and as an audience interprets both the meaning of a speaker's words and the force with which she utters them.

For example, Kristie Dotson (2011) identifies the phenomenon of 'testimonial smothering', in which a potential speaker decides to remain silent, recognising the potential audience's unwillingness or inability to appreciate what she might have said: perhaps the speaker fears the consequences of miscommunication, or perhaps she simply thinks the struggle is not worth her effort on this occasion. Similarly, Rebecca Kukla (2014) shows how social structures can unfairly determine whether a speaker manages to testify, or merely to suggest, speculate, or joke when she uses her words; Kukla calls this 'discursive injustice' (see also Anderson 2017). And Andrew Peet (2015) shows how prejudicial stereotypes can help determine the meaning we attribute to other people's words, generating what Peet calls 'interpretative injustice'.

This rich array of work – of which these three papers are just a sample – illustrates the complexity of our social interactions around the offering, receiving, and evaluating testimony (Hookway [2010] explores this complexity further). Whilst no single theoretical tool can neatly handle all this, we can make some progress by thinking in terms of trustworthiness and untrustworthiness, not just trust and distrust. When we think about trust and distrust in the context of testimony, we easily slip into an undue focus on situations in which a speaker is recognised as testifying that $p$, for some definite $p$, and an audience responds with either trust or distrust.

But we also judge one another's trustworthiness in more general terms, not just in respect of particular instances of testimony. When we judge someone to be trustworthy, we do not assume that they are omniscient, able to provide us with whatever information we need. But we do assume that a trustworthy person is able to judge her own competence, so that she will testify only in areas where she is indeed competent. Perhaps also we assume that a trustworthy person will speak up whenever her testimony is potentially relevant; this assumption is undermined by Dotson's account of testimonial smothering. Kukla's work shows how someone who is not taken seriously as testifying – someone who is heard as merely speculating – does not have opportunities to demonstrate her trustworthiness, since she is not viewed as a proper target of either trust or distrust. And Peet shows how, through audience misinterpretation, speakers can falsely appear to misjudge their own competencies in untrustworthy ways.

In my view, these phenomena around trustworthiness present us with a disturbing theoretical dilemma. On the one hand, we can think of trustworthiness (and of untrustworthiness) as an intrinsic feature of an individual, or at least as a disposition of the individual to respond in trustworthy fashion to various external challenges. We can then try to understand the ways in which such trustworthiness can be misunderstood, misperceived, or intentionally ignored by others. On this approach, injustices arise from the way in which an individual is unfairly and inaccurately represented by others as being untrustworthy.

These kinds of judgments of untrustworthiness can become a self-fulfilling prophecy. The various processes through which an individual comes to be regarded as untrustworthy may in turn damage her self-confidence, limit her access to sources of information, and/or render her less able to articulate her thoughts and opinions (Carel and Kidd 2017; Saul 2017). This is a *causal* mechanism via which unfair treatment can reduce someone's trustworthiness, even when we recognise that being trustworthy is not the same as being regarded as trustworthy.

Alternatively, we can think of an individual's trustworthiness (or untrustworthiness) as not merely caused but *constituted* by the ways in she interacts with others, including the ways in which others perceive and represent her words and actions. Crudely speaking, we can identify trustworthiness with being regarded as trustworthy. We can then try to understand the ways in which people are rendered untrustworthy – or less trustworthy – by other people's interactions with them, or by other people's failures to offer opportunities of interaction. On this approach, injustices arise from the way in which an individual is unfairly made untrustworthy by others' interactions with her – not just through the causal consequences of others' interactions, but in virtue of the fact that trustworthiness is constituted by the regard of others.

Testimonial smothering again provides a useful illustration. As Dotson writes, '[i]n testimonial smothering, a speaker smothers her/his own testimony [i.e. decides not to speak] when an audience demonstrates testimonial incompetence for unsafe, risky testimony owing to pernicious ignorance' (2011: 250). When a speaker is smothered, does she merely disguise her own trustworthiness, or does she thereby actually become less trustworthy in virtue of her 'failure' to testify? This is an uncomfortable dilemma, since we seem forced to choose between a picture of the heroic individual unjustly misunderstood by others, and a picture of injustice so pervasive that it even undermines individual character traits, constitutively as well as causally. It is not yet clear which of these theoretical approaches will be most fruitful for the practical struggle against injustice; nor is it clear which of these is more respectful of the experiences of those who suffer most from injustice.

## Trust in action

Gerald Marsh (2011) identifies testimonial injustice as a special case of a more general phenomenon of injustice in trusting, arguing that understanding the significance of trust more generally is key to understanding the nature of testimonial injustices. He points out that, just as we assess informants in terms of their competence (knowledge) and sincerity, we also assess agents in terms of their competence to act, and their sincerity or good intentions in acting. Marsh explores the centrality of trust to social life, arguing that we owe one another a baseline level of trust, simply as fellow human beings, and that we harm one another when we do not offer this baseline trust.

Not every aspect of other people's behaviour is the proper target of our trust or distrust. My neighbour's habits of dress may reflect her taste, intentions, and competencies, but I misunderstand our relationship if I make this an issue of trust or distrust between us, or regard this as evidence of my neighbour's trustworthiness or untrustworthiness. Much of our engagement in the social world is bound up with questions about when our behaviour is a matter for ourselves alone, and when it becomes an issue of trust or distrust for others; these boundaries can shift over time, and between different communities, making it difficult for an outsider to assimilate.

There is empirical controversy about whether multi-ethnic neighbourhoods typically have lower levels of social trust, and about what mechanisms might promote or reduce trust in such contexts (Schmid et al. 2014 is an interesting recent contribution): lack of shared conventional expectations may make it more difficult to establish trustworthiness, or even to establish what trustworthiness requires of us. Again, we face the uncomfortable theoretical dilemma I outlined above: does moving to an unfamiliar setting render us untrustworthy in virtue of other people's attitudes towards us, or does it instead make it more difficult for people to recognise our underlying and authentic trustworthiness?

Assuming that we can fairly identify those situations in which others' behaviour is a test of their trustworthiness, how might epistemic injustice arise here? We often understand other people's behaviour as grounded in their practical competencies, skill, or knowledge-how; where we think behaviour is not competence-based, we often regard this as problematic. This suggests that there are opportunities for epistemic injustice arising from systematic unfairness in the ways in which we attribute knowledge-how to the people around us, just as there can be systematic unfairness in our attributions of knowledge in testimonial contexts.

Unfairly underestimating other people's practical knowledge on the basis of their behaviour can take at least two forms. Prejudice may lead us to misjudge the quality of an action or performance: Goldin and Rouse (2000) showed that, when American orchestras began to audition players from behind an opaque screen, the proportion of women admitted rose significantly. Moreover prejudice may lead us to attribute evidently high-quality action to luck rather than to skill or knowledge: Biernat and Kobrynowicz (1997) showed that, in simulated job applications, women and black people found it more difficult to prove that their successes were due to their own abilities.

Unfair distrust in practical contexts may arise from these sorts of prejudices in attributing success or knowledge-how. However, distrust is often focused not upon competence but upon the other person's intentions, sincerity or goodwill. We may judge someone to be highly skilled, yet deeply untrustworthy: 'Machiavellian' characters deserve this verdict, as do classic evil geniuses. Where such judgments are unfair, due to systematic identity prejudices of the type discussed by Fricker (2007), is the resulting injustice a distinctively epistemic injustice, which harms the person in her capacity as a knower? I believe it is not, and I attempt to justify this claim in Hawley (2011). But setting this disagreement aside, considering trust and distrust in practical, not just testimonial, contexts can more generally give us fresh insights into the possibilities for epistemic justice and injustice.

## Uniqueness, rationality, and choice

What is the difference between trusting someone in some respect and believing her to be trustworthy in that respect? One important difference between trust and belief is that, in certain circumstances, we can freely choose whether to trust, whereas we cannot simply choose whether to believe. Richard Holton (1994) has influentially argued that although evidence may sometimes require us to trust, or to distrust, we are often in a middle ground where each of trust and distrust seem permissible, and both options are available to us, though we cannot simultaneously choose both.

This is a complex issue, but in short there seems to be a smaller gap between genuinely trusting and 'merely' acting as if you trust, than there is between genuinely believing and 'merely' acting as if you believe: someone who systematically behaves as if she trusts is not merely pretending to trust, she is in fact trusting. In this context, philosophers sometimes write of 'therapeutic' trust, i.e. trust that is extended to someone who does not appear positively trustworthy, in the hope that such trust will in its turn encourage trustworthiness (Horsburgh 1960).

There are two complementary ways of thinking about this middle ground where trust seems to be a matter of choice; depending on which we endorse, there seem to be different consequences for issues of injustice. First, we can understand this as a psychological point about our thought processes: in such circumstances, we do not inevitably find ourselves either trusting or distrusting, but instead these are attitudes we can actively and consciously adopt. In contrast, we do not typically experience belief formation in this active, conscious way.

Second, we can understand this as a normative point about rationality or justification for trust: in certain circumstances trust is justified, and distrust is justified (though holding both attitudes simultaneously is not justified), as is withholding from either trust or distrust. This contrasts with standard epistemological ways of thinking about belief, according to which in any given evidential situation, only one attitude can be rationally justified, even if it is difficult for us to tell which attitude that is (this principle is sometimes known as 'uniqueness'; White 2005). The psychological claim and the normative claim are distinct: we may experience ourselves as choosing between options, even though one of these is rationally mandated, and conversely we may feel compelled to take one option even though others are rationally permissible.

Consider the psychological claim, that we can exercise control over our trusting and distrusting, and suppose this to be accurate in at least some cases. This would seem to have consequences for the ways in which we blame ourselves and others for injustices in trust and distrust: it seems easier and more fruitful to attribute blame for actions, which seem to be under the actor's direct control. Moreover, the psychological claim of control may have consequences for which strategies we should adopt to remedy such injustices, both in ourselves and in others: changing our conscious actions is a different task from changing what seem to be unconscious habits (Saul 2017).

Now consider the normative claim, that in certain circumstances there is no unique rationally-mandated degree of trust, but rather a permissible range of more-or-less trusting attitudes. If this is accurate, we face an intriguing challenge to the way in which epistemic injustice is standardly characterised. For Fricker, the central case of testimonial injustice is identity-prejudicial credibility deficit (2007: 28). Credibility deficit is defined both in counterfactual terms – by reference to the credibility the speaker would have received in the absence of prejudice (2007: 17) – and in terms of the audience's obligations. Fricker writes 'there is no puzzle about the fair distribution of credibility . . . the hearer's obligation is obvious: she must match the level of credibility she attributes to her interlocutor to the evidence that he is offering the truth' (2007: 19).

This notion of credibility deficit seems to presuppose a unique 'right' level of credibility in any given situation; this is problematic if in certain situations trust is rationally permissible, but so is distrust (Hawley 2014b). One response would be to limit epistemic injustice only to those cases where prejudice takes us beyond what is rationally permissible, cases in which we distrust although trust is mandated. But this concedes too much: someone who always decides borderline cases in favour of men, and against women, may be systematically unjust even if any individual decision is within the bounds of reasonableness, since trust is not mandated in any individual case.

Some people are cautious about trusting, whilst others are quicker to trust: these differences may be due to varying past experiences (including experiences of injustice), to varying significance of the stakes, or just to differences in personality. Some of us are willing to rely on our gut instincts about when to trust, whilst others of us are not: again, these differences may be explained in various different ways, including our past history of interaction with others, justly or unjustly. Trust typically involves risk, and we are familiar with the idea that people vary in their levels of risk aversion, so this should come as no surprise. Indeed, within certain limits, we can regard quite a large range of different attitudes to trust as both morally and rationally acceptable. But it does not seem acceptable to vary even within that 'acceptable' range based on considerations of race, gender, or class. Even if it is epistemically permissible to be somewhat mean-minded and epistemically permissible to be fairly charitable, it is not morally permissible to switch between these doxastic policies on grounds of social identity. If and when we engage in such switching, we perpetrate epistemic injustice without breaking any epistemic rules.[1]

**Related chapters**: 2, 12, 17, 21, 22, 32

## Acknowledgement

This chapter was written during leave supported by a Leverhulme Major Research Fellowship, which I gratefully acknowledge.

## Note

1 Further reading: C. McLeod provides an excellent overview of philosophical work on trust in her 'Trust' in *The Stanford Encyclopaedia of Philosophy* (Fall 2015 Edition), Edward N. Zalta (ed.), URL = http://plato.stanford.edu/archives/fall2015/entries/trust/>. K. Hawley's *Trust: A Very Short Introduction* (Oxford: Oxford University Press, 2012) draws on several academic disciplines and is aimed at a general reader. J. Medina's *The Epistemology of Resistance: Gender and Racial Oppression, Epistemic Injustice, and Resistant Imaginations* (New York: Oxford University Press, 2012) explores many relevant issues in depth. K. Jones "The Politics of Credibility," in L.M. Antony and C.E. Witt (eds.) *A Mind of One's Own* (Boulder, CO: Westview Press, 2002), 154–176, is a rich investigation of epistemic injustices written by a leading philosopher of trust. R. Putnam's *Bowling Alone: The Collapse and Revival of American Community* (New York: Simon and Schuster, 2000) is a classic sociological study of trust, social capital, and inequalities.

## References

Allen, Amy (2017) 'Power/Knowledge/Resistance: Foucault and Epistemic Injustice', in Ian James Kidd, Gaile Pohlhaus, Jr., and José Medina (eds.) *The Routledge Handbook of Epistemic Injustice*. New York: Routledge, 424–40.
Anderson, Luvell (2017) 'Epistemic Injustice and the Philosophy of Race', in Ian James Kidd, Gaile Pohlhaus, Jr., and José Medina (eds.) *The Routledge Handbook of Epistemic Injustice*. New York: Routledge, 319–42.
Baier, Annette C. (1986) 'Trust and Antitrust', *Ethics* 96: 231–60.
Battaly, Heather (2017) 'Testimonial Injustice, Epistemic Vice, and Vice Epistemology', in Ian James Kidd, Gaile Pohlhaus, Jr., and José Medina (eds.) *The Routledge Handbook of Epistemic Injustice*. New York: Routledge, 506–25.
Biernat, Monica and Kobrynowicz, Diane (1997) 'Gender- and Race-Based Standards of Competence', *Journal of Personality and Social Psychology* 72: 544–57.
Carel, Havi and Kidd, Ian James (2017) 'Epistemic Injustice in Medicine and Healthcare', in Ian James Kidd, Gaile Pohlhaus, Jr., and José Medina (eds.) *The Routledge Handbook of Epistemic Injustice*. New York: Routledge, 755–77.

Craig, Edward (1990) *Knowledge and the State of Nature*, Oxford: Clarendon Press.
Dotson, Kristie (2011) 'Tracking Epistemic Violence, Tracking Practices of Silencing', *Hypatia* 26.2: 236–57.
Frankfurt, Harry (2005) *On Bullshit*, Princeton, NJ: Princeton University Press.
Fricker, Miranda (2007) *Epistemic Injustice*, Oxford: Oxford University Press.
Goldin, Claudia and Rouse, Cecilia (2000) 'Orchestrating Impartiality: The Impact of 'Blind' Auditions on Female Musicians', *American Economic Review* 90: 715–41.
Hawley, Katherine (2011) 'Knowing How and Epistemic Injustice', in John Bengson and Marc A. Moffett (eds.) *Knowing How*. Oxford: Oxford University Press, 283–99.
Hawley, Katherine (2014a) 'Trust, Distrust and Commitment', *Noûs* 48: 1–20.
Hawley, Katherine (2014b) 'Partiality and Prejudice in Trusting', *Synthese* 191: 2029–45.
Hinchmann, Edward S. (2005) 'Telling as Inviting to Trust', *Philosophy and Phenomenological Research* 70.3: 562–87.
Holton, Richard (1994) 'Deciding to Trust, Coming to Believe', *Australasian Journal of Philosophy* 72: 63–76.
Horsburgh, H. J. N. (1960) 'The Ethics of Trust', *Philosophical Quarterly* 10: 343–54.
Jones, Karen (1996) 'Trust as an Affective Attitude', *Ethics* 107: 4–25.
Kukla, Rebecca (2014) 'Performative Force, Convention and Discursive Injustice', *Hypatia* 29.2: 440–57.
Lackey, Jennifer (2008) *Learning From Words*, Oxford: Oxford University Press.
Marsh, Gerald (2011) 'Trust, Testimony and Prejudice in the Credibility Economy', *Hypatia*, 26.2: 280–93.
Medina, José (2013) *The Epistemology of Resistance: Gender and Racial Oppression, Epistemic Injustice, and Resistant Imaginations*, Oxford: Oxford University Press.
Moran, Richard (2005) 'Getting Told and Being Believed', *Philosophers' Imprint* 5.5: 1–29.
Peet, Andrew (2017) 'Epistemic Injustice in Utterance Interpretation', *Synthese*, DOI 10.1007/s11229–015–0942–7.
Saul, Jennifer (2017) 'Implicit Bias, Stereotype Threat, and Epistemic Injustice', in Ian James Kidd, Gaile Pohlhaus, Jr., and José Medina (eds.) *The Routledge Handbook of Epistemic Injustice*. New York: Routledge, 528–45.
Schmid, Katharina, Al Ramiah, Ananthi, and Hewstone, Miles (2014) 'Neighborhood Ethnic Diversity and Trust: The Role of Intergroup Contact and Perceived Threat', *Psychological Science* 25.3: 665–74.
Strawson, P.F. (1974) 'Freedom and Resentment', in P.F. Strawson (ed.) *Freedom and Resentment*, London: Methuen, 1–25.
Wanderer, Jeremy (2017) 'Varieties of Testimonial Injustice', in Ian James Kidd, Gaile Pohlhaus, Jr., and José Medina (eds.) *The Routledge Handbook of Epistemic Injustice*. New York: Routledge, 75–105.
White, Roger (2005) 'Epistemic Permissiveness', *Philosophical Perspectives* 19: 445–59.

# 7
# FORMS OF KNOWING AND EPISTEMIC RESOURCES

*Alexis Shotwell*

There is a thought experiment well-known in philosophy of mind but not particularly elsewhere, in which Frank Jackson imagined 'Mary,' a fabulous scientist imprisoned since birth in a black-and-white room. Mary has made her life's work the study of color and knows all the facts there are to know about color and perception. In two papers, Jackson argued that Mary would learn something, something *new*, if she were ever freed into the world of color – and thus that physicalism, constituted for him as the thesis that 'complete physical knowledge is complete knowledge *simpliciter*' (Jackson 1986: 291) is false. If everything in the world is physical, we should be able to describe that world in truth-verifiable propositions.

In this chapter I start from one strand of the conversation Jackson's initial papers about Mary initiated: perhaps, commentators argued, Mary had complete *propositional* knowledge, *knowledge that* color was various things, but she lacked *knowledge how* to see color. This dichotomy, between knowledge that and knowledge how, has structured much of the discussion of what forms of non-propositional knowledge there might be, to the extent that settling the know how/know that question is sometimes understood to be sufficient to settle the question of whether there is any knowledge that is not propositional. I argue that, indeed, there are forms of understanding and knowledge that are not propositional, and that acknowledging these forms is a central piece of any project working for epistemic justice.

My central argument is that focusing on propositional knowledge as though it is the only form of knowing worth considering is itself a form of epistemic injustice. Such a focus neglects epistemic resources that help oppressed people craft more just worlds. We should not understand epistemic resources as the sorts of things that help us acquire only propositional knowledge (though such knowledge will, for sure, be useful to us). I suggest that there are several forms of knowing useful to the work of redressing epistemic injustice, and that implicit or nonpropositional forms are in ordinary practice intertwined with propositional forms in epistemically salient ways. Grappling with epistemic injustice benefits from attention to the epistemic resources involved in implicit understanding and knowing.

Second, I argue that the use of fictional thought experiments ascendant within conventional philosophy forms a kind of epistemic injustice, reducing the philosophically relevant 'ingredients' to propositionally evaluable knowledge and ignoring resistant or difficult-to-say knowledge that might reveal quite a lot about the political stakes of our knowing practices. Taking a more expansive and nuanced approach to our epistemic situation is not only more adequate to the world we know (and thus epistemically to be preferred); it also offers a richer approach to discovering and redressing epistemic injustice.

Jason Stanley and Timothy Williamson have been instrumental in re-starting a conversation about the know how/know that distinction, starting from an argument against Gilbert Ryle's work in this area (Ryle 1949; Stanley 2011; Stanley and Williamson 2001). They argue that all putative know how is actually a form of knowing-that, resting their account on a thought experiment. They say: 'a master pianist [call her "Maestra"] who loses both of her arms in a tragic car accident still knows how to play the piano. However, she has lost the ability to do so' (Stanley and Williamson 2001: 6). Stanley and Williamson offer this example with this brevity and understand it as one good illustration of their claim that Ryle's account of knowing-how is 'demonstrably false': Maestra's capacities to play are hampered by the loss of her hands, but they take it that our intuitions will tell us that her knowledge of piano playing is intact. Stanley has gone on to substantially elaborate his intellectualist view of know how, which claims that it is, in fact, knowledge-that (Stanley 2010, 2011).

The Maestra example brings together key moves in the intellectualist argument against know how; the case is reprised in an astonishing range of philosophical work on know how. Helpfully for my argument here, this thought experiment shows us both how impoverished standard philosophical views of knowing really are, and how limited and potentially unjust fictional thought experiments can be. Thinking more broadly about the forms of knowing manifest in fictional and real cases of bodily transformation helps us have better accounts of what we should hold in mind in thinking about epistemic justice.

The argument has four parts:

1. When we talk about know how (for example, Maestra's piano-playing knowledge), there is a far richer story to tell than has been captured so far, and we get one piece of that story through attending to the relation between ability and skill.
2. However, the effect of losing her arms on her 'Maestra-ness' (thus described) is more complex even than an expanded account of our skilled abilities. Her life, including important aspects of her epistemic life, is changed more deeply than it would have been had she lost all the pianos in the world, for example. We benefit from an account of what **more** would be lost, and I offer such an account through enriching the categories we might use to understand Maestra's knowledge. All of us partake in forms of knowledge that include propositional knowledge and skilled capacities; we also engage affective knowing, knowledge by acquaintance, tacit knowledge, and more.
3. Attending to the social and political features of bodily transformation through the stories of real people who live with acquired disabilities gives us a richer picture of the philosophical stakes and effects of this life experience. Rather than the usual thought experiments in which philosophers imagine brutal scenarios for fictional women – life imprisonment in black-and-white rooms for brilliant scientists studying color or catastrophic car accidents for brilliant pianists – we ought to attend to these complex political and interpersonal aspects of consciousness in theorizing knowledge.
4. Understanding the forms of knowing manifest in more adequate accounts of what is at stake in experiencing bodily change and disability opens corollary space for better understanding of epistemic resources.

Standard philosophical narratives iterate and re-iterate pervasive patterns of epistemic injustice, both in the tunnel-vision focus on propositional knowledge that is used to discount forms of knowing that cannot be put into truth-verifiable claims, and in the artificial and impoverished focus on thought experiments that actively bracket out much experience relevant to non-dominantly situated knowers. A richer account of forms of knowing and a richer attention to people's lived experiences in the world helps us identify, analyze, and redress epistemic injustices.

## 1. Know how and ability

Moving beyond Maestra's case offers us more interesting epistemic terrain than the distinction between knowledge how and knowledge that can encompass. There are some things one can say about even that narrow question, however, that are more adequate than what Stanley and Williamson give us. Stanley closes his 2010 article with a reassertion of the claim that 'knowing how can be defined in terms of propositional knowledge.' He writes:

> One would only think that there is a tension here only if one antecedently identified knowing how to do something with having certain dispositions or abilities. But knowing how to do something is not simply a matter of having certain dispositions. It is a matter of having the right propositional knowledge; of knowing the right answer to the question 'How could you do it?'
>
> (Stanley 2010: 29)

This raises the questions of how, in Stanley's view, we ought to understand abilities, their distinction from dispositions, and the relationship between ability and propositional knowledge.

Absent a compelling argument for why we ought to see ability and knowing how as different in relevant ways, the argument that knowing how is a species of propositional knowledge is of considerable technical interest, but less able to speak to the questions that motivate consideration of skillful activity and corollary accounts of know how. In other words, when Ryle and others write about know how, they are interested more in the question of what it means to know how to do something and less in the question of how people talk about knowing how to do something. Stanley and affiliates give a good account of the latter, but no account of the former. There is interest, of course, in giving accounts of how people talk about how to do things – and this is what Stanley treats. But there is also justifiable interest in what it is to know how to do something and not just talk about it.

Alva Noë's critique of the intellectualist approach is useful here. First, as Noë points out, you can be unable to exercise an ability in at least two ways.[1] You may simply lack the ability in question (I, for example, do not know how to play the piano). Or, circumstances might not allow you to exercise an ability that you might be able to practice (you might know how to play a piano but have no piano around). Noë thinks that the loss of Maestra's arms is comparable, 'in the relevant sense', to the loss of her piano, explaining the intuition one might have that she does still know how to play the piano although she cannot now do so. Second, he points out that there are degrees of know how, just as there are variations on what someone knows propositionally about something like piano playing. Know how can wax and wane based on many factors – time, physical condition, practice. As many musicians report, failing to practice a skill affects one's ability to do it in ways that are complexly physical, emotional, conceptual, and practical. Noë offers us the physical aspect of this kind of linkage of know how and ability, noting that temporal considerations should be important to how we think about Maestra's capacities for piano-playing: the longer it has been since she played piano at the expert level, the less likely she is to be able to play at that level were her arms magically returned to her. Further, in the case of amputees, 'deafferance of hand-related cortical areas leads to cortical reorganization, a reorganization which may destroy the brain-basis of the relevant practical knowledge' (Noë 2005: 6). Finally, the relations between knowing how and knowing that might be sufficiently intertwined that there isn't an easy distinction between them. Noë argues: 'Possession of abilities enables us to detect significance where there would otherwise be none. In this way, the body, the world and our practical knowledge open up a meaningful realm of experience to us' (Noë 2005: 8). Following Noë and others, we can see that it may be important – if we are interested in thick, accurate accounts of knowledge – to think about meaning and experience as well. As I will argue, the meaning of experience matters to how we understand the question of epistemic justice.

## 2. Epistemic features beyond and entangled in ability

Noë argues that practical knowledge, along with our embodied situation in the world, *opens a meaningful realm of experience*. But what does it mean to have a meaningful realm of experience open to us? What do we know in the space of that opening? Answering this question requires us to think about epistemically salient aspects of Maestra's knowledge that are not encompassed by the know how/know that binary, or, indeed, by the concept or fact of having the ability to do something.

My sister is an opera singer. It is evident in her use of her voice as an instrument – and its development over time – that she has a complex, rich relationship to being a singer. One part is simply what we call 'knowing how to sing' – a skill that she has spent years working on developing. Complexly related to her developing the skills associated with singing has been her development as a singer: someone who loves a particular kind of music, who is conversant in its masters and its forms, who understands the social practices of being a singer, who moves through the world with an appreciation of vocal sound, whose apprehension of sound itself is related to being a singer, and who projects herself into the future in terms of her self-understanding as a singer. Among other things, this means that she looks forward to singing in particular contexts, learns languages in order to sing them more fluidly, appreciates dating people who like music, and writes convincing fiction about people and music (Shotwell 2015). Much of her life is organized around music. All of these aspects of her life are complexly intertwined with a racist, classist scaffolding that implicitly render some people (white, middle-class) as appropriate subjects for opera. Body shaming and monitoring is rife in opera worlds, producing as if by accident opera singers who are not disabled, who are reasonably thin, and who are conventionally attractive. There are substantive epistemically relevant social features involved in the praxis of being a singer.

Surely my sister is different from Maestra in degree more than kind. Maestra, as defined, is a 'master pianist.' My sister is a still-developing opera singer. But presumably Maestra's relationship to the piano and to herself as a piano player would involve similarly complex habits, affects, tacit knowledge, and more. It is this complex of things – manifesting at the level of what I call her 'implicit understanding' – that would be thrown into relief in the context of an accident sufficiently violent to cause her to lose her arms. We can distinguish five different sorts of understanding at play here, though perhaps there are more. First, there is a level of *propositional knowledge*, through which Maestra thought and thinks about music, musicians, technique, history, and so on. Propositional knowledge is amenable to what is often understood as the 'traditional account' of knowledge – claim-making activity about the world that is truth-verifiable. When did Mozart live? What is the key of this sonata? What time does the concert start? This aspect of her understanding of playing the piano may indeed be relatively intact regardless of the availability of pianos or of arms to play them. There are at least four kinds of implicit understanding also in play, however, and these would be far more violently wounded in this accident than her propositional knowledge: first, her ability to execute the skill in question – in this case, to actually play the piano; second, her socially-situated embodiment as someone who moves through the world as a master piano player; third, her potentially propositional tacit or distal knowledge; and fourth, her affective or emotional understanding (see Shotwell 2011, 2015).

First, then, consider having the ability to play the piano at all – or, especially, to play well. This kind of embodied ability is one of the central things a fictional Maestra must have possessed, practiced, and developed as part of her being a master pianist. As anyone who knows a serious musician knows, active practice is central to making the movements and habits of making music fluid and expert. These habits are not entirely non-conceptual: teachers can communicate propositionally how to change musical habitus. Among other things, learning to make music well involves bodily practices that are consciously practiced and shifted. Integral to playing the piano, then, is the complex social-physical practice of piano playing. Skilled understanding, know how, involves the capacity to enact a practice; developing such an ability using arms and then having to transform a piano-playing practice is one way I regard the loss of her arms as importantly different than the loss of an available piano. Even in a world in which someone with a real hatred for pianos and a lot of resources destroyed every extant piano, one can imagine Maestra 'playing' on a fake piano painted on her kitchen table. One can imagine her using her understanding of pianos to construct new, furtive pianos for backroom concerts. Her own skilled understanding of piano playing would not be fully engaged without an actual piano, but there would be the potential to enact it. There are important ways that her experience of not having her arms is not similar to not having a piano ready to hand. The fact that these two ways of being unable to exercise a capacity are *different* in relevant ways requires us to think about skilled knowledge as a key piece of Maestra's identity. With varying degrees of ability, all of us develop know how as a key form of knowledge practiced in our everyday life.

Second, consider the idea of a category of understanding that is currently tacit but potentially propositional. If a central part of Maestra's becoming a master pianist involved developing embodied skills enacted in a world, another piece is a process of evolving subjectivity – her incorporated and assumed history as a master pianist. Most musicians develop their musical ability in conversation with understanding and internalizing potentially propositional knowledge, which Michael Polanyi and others have termed 'tacit knowledge'(Polanyi 1967, 1969). This kind of knowing would include discovering the history of a particular piece of music, the style of the composer, how to relate to the audience as she played, and how to carry herself as 'Maestra.' Most of these ways of being could be articulated and described, but in order for someone to enact them in everyday life, they must go without saying. Tacit, potentially-propositional knowledge is that form of knowing that has come, over time, to go without saying. It is perhaps most perceptible at points of change – after an accident that has transformed the possibilities for a master pianist to exercise her skill, perhaps key points of her tacit knowledge would come into explicitness, while others would remain implicit.

Finally, consider the involvement of affective understanding with Maestra's piano playing ability. Why do we as listeners enjoy seeing someone play music live? Why do musicians work perhaps unreasonably hard in order to play music? Perhaps we can imagine what losing arms would mean to someone whose identity is deeply tied to the particular use of them. My contention, then, is that grief, confusion, anger, loss, along with other complex emotions for which we do not have names, would attend Maestra's loss of her arms, and that the braiding together of these emotions with the other forms of implicit understanding I have laid out is important to the kind of epistemic story we tell about her. Although I think it is important to schematize different sorts of implicit understanding, in order to avoid the kinds of wooly evocations of a category for everything-that-is-not-now-in-words, Maestra's case shows us that separating out these sorts of knowing is, ultimately, a conceptual experiment. To get at what that experience would really be

## 3. Experiencing profound bodily change

It is a truism in disability theory that all of us will have bodily experiences currently identified as disabled – this is the subtext of the Maestra anecdote. But what *counts* as profound change does not have to be socially identifiable as disabled experience to illuminate the socially and politically important aspects of forms of knowledge beyond the propositional. Consider actor Julie Andrews, of *The Sound of Music* and *Mary Poppins* fame. Andrews lost much of her singing range during surgery to remove polyps from her vocal cords, a relatively common but unpredictable condition that interferes with singing. Her case substantiates the argument I'm making for a more multi-layered account in thinking about knowledge. Growing up a performer in a musical family, by fifteen Andrews was the primary financial support for her mother, her alcoholic, abusive step-father, and her siblings. She says about her voice, 'I had a kind of freak, four-octave voice that I could sort of do all sorts of calisthenics with it.' After the surgery that destroyed this range, Andrews says: 'I've got about five good bass notes. So if you wanted a rendition of "Old Man River," I can manage it. But the amazing thing is, it was quite devastating. And I was fairly depressed for a while. And then, it was either stay that way for the rest of my life, or get on and do something' (CBSNews 2009).

Notice a few things about this example: First, like many successful musicians, Andrews's voice gave her an identity, a way of being, and a set of social relations that attended that doing. Her voice grounded her, provided money to her family, and offered a way out of an abusive family situation. Second, her voice was something extraordinary: she could do things with it that very few singers can, and this capacity opened forms of life to her that exceeded the financial and practical effects of being a successful singer. Finally, the loss of the kind of voice she had was sufficiently devastating that she characterizes herself as needing to make a life-choice – to 'stay that way' or 'get on and do something.' The issue is not, or not primarily, whether she still knows how to sing: it is an issue of how to re-construct a selfhood that had been formed around an identity grounded in an ability that was physical, cognitive, socially-situated, affective, and more. Andrews' amazement at the degree of devastation she felt in the wake of her lost octaves speaks against the two-fold intuition Stanley and Williams expect us to endorse: that in considering the knowledge involved in a profound bodily change, we ought to only bring into mind the possibilities of knowing that and knowing how, and that we ought to reduce the scope of what is considered epistemically salient.

I am suggesting that we look to the example of Andrews to give us a richer account of the effects of a profound bodily change on someone who had shaped their subjectivity around the socially-situated embodiment at issue. Andrews's experience of the reduction of her singing voice from four octaves to half an octave shows the inexactitude of holding the view that being able to enact an ability is the same as propositional knowledge of a way to do something. This inexactitude constitutes an epistemic injustice because it disregards important affective and life-shaping features of, in this case, singing. Beyond that, we can consider epistemically salient parts of our everyday knowing practices that cannot be understood with a focus on propositional knowledge.

One might argue that focusing on subjectivities grounded in expertise of the sort required to be an accomplished musician obfuscates the understanding at issue here. Consider then an example that may dis-entangle the philosophical issues important here. Claudia Mitchell is a former US Marine who lost an arm in a motorcycle accident. She joins Jesse Sullivan, a former electrical linesman who lost both arms to a jolt of 7200 volts of electricity, as a subject in a $48.5 million

Defense Advanced Research Projects Agency (DARPA) project to improve the functionality of upper body prostheses. Neither Mitchell nor Sullivan are, it is useful to note, experts in the way that the fictional Maestra is; we may not think that their subjectivities were built around the presence of their arms in the ways that Maestra's subjectivity may have been.

Sullivan has become known as the world's first 'bionic man'; he and Mitchell have both had nerves pertaining to their amputated limbs transferred into newly unused muscles – in their cases, arm nerves now occupy some space in their pectoral muscles. With a lot of training and resources, they are able to move prosthetic arms and hands by thought. This process more closely approximates non-prosthetic arm use than any other technology currently available – though, of course, they lack the proprioceptive capacity to convey information about what is touched, lifted, and so on with the prosthetic arm. The *New Yorker* article about Mitchell's case concludes with the observation that:

> Historically, the demands and rigors of war may have provided the impetus for scientific and medical progress, but domestic life is often where the significant advancements are felt first. In Mitchell's case, she said that occasionally she now finds herself reclining on the sofa at home, watching television, and will suddenly realize that the arm propping up her head is her left arm.
>
> (McGrath 2007: 45)

That she can forget that her left arm is prosthetic – that it has been come 'ready-to-hand' in Heidegger's sense – complexly involves the ways that forms of implicit knowing receded into the background when everything is 'working well.' There is much we don't know about Mitchell's process of becoming able to forget that her left arm, on which she props her head, is a prosthesis. There are some things to notice, though.

First, it's unlikely that having the 'bionic' prosthetic feels the same as having an arm back, primarily because without meaningful biofeedback apparatus, there is no proprioception involved in even very advanced prostheses. Still, note that in the process of re-innervation, teaching Mitchell to use her arm again is based in a pedagogy appropriate to the domestic: she trains her 'arm,' and is trained in its use, by practicing cooking, ironing shirts, and making salad with it – all in a research lab. In more daily ways, she says, the prosthetic 'has changed my life dramatically . . . I use it to help with cooking, for holding a laundry basket, for folding clothes – all kinds of daily tasks' (Brown 2006). That these are the kinds of daily tasks this arm is trained for, and, indeed, required for, is significant: Mitchell's implicit understanding, disrupted and then partially reconditioned in the use of the bionic arm, is thoroughly gendered, raced, and classed. The very availability of the arm to her is situated in a dense webbing of material conditions, which we might not ordinarily think of as important to the epistemic work of being an amputee. DARPA's research into prosthetics is saturated with complex considerations about what it means for the military to be simultaneously responsible for injuries inviting prosthetic response and also a mover in prosthetics research. We do well to attend to the vast material and epistemic resources that go into war and its ongoing aftermath; the differential distribution of injury and death, as well as of medical resources and prosthetics, should itself be a matter of politically and morally-saturated epistemic concern.

All of this floats, iceberg-massive, under the ease Mitchell finds folding laundry with the prosthetic arm DARPA funds. Her integration of the prosthetic into her daily practice involves a complex of feelings, presuppositions, socially-situated embodiment, skills, and propositional knowledge that we need to acknowledge if we are going to do justice to what's involved in everyday life. Current research in bioethics and critical disability studies speaks to the experience of acquiring and then living with impairment and socially-shaped disability. One thing the cases like Claudia

Mitchell's and Julie Andrews's show is a limitation in the solely linguistic account Stanley and Williamson, and later Stanley, give of knowing how. Inquiring into the epistemic salience of a multi-faceted implicit understanding gives us, I hope, more adequate answers to questions about what Maestra knew – and, indeed, how we all know, even now.

Taking examples from the world proliferates the possibilities for what we can attend to, epistemically, ethically, and politically. In this way, it is understandable that philosophers frequently aim to pare away things extraneous to their main point in order to focus on what is putatively philosophically salient. With a compassionate view toward the difficulties of philosophizing in the actually existing world, let me underline that such paring away will almost certainly participate in unjust social relations.[2] The injustice of proceeding as though the only epistemically relevant part of the 'Maestra' case is the know how/know that question is perceptible in attending to actual cases of people experiencing bodily transformations.

## 4. Epistemic resources and implicit understanding

Heidi Grasswick has productively discussed the ways that feminist epistemologists, in responding to what Miranda Fricker identifies as hermeneutic injustice, have appealed to the need for a meaningful normative stance for knowledge work. As she argues, ethical considerations might be important to epistemic success: 'Feminist epistemologists are questioning our ability to answer epistemically normative questions without reference to the ethical' (Grasswick 2014: 236). In similar ways, I next consider how forms of knowing that are not conceptual or propositional may be significant epistemic resources. For the most part, the people thinking about epistemic resources within the context of epistemic injustice focus on concepts and the availability of good or better concepts for adequate knowing. In understanding the epistemic resources knowers draw on in pursuing social justice, we need also to account for forms of knowing that do not take propositional or conceptual form.

In contrast, Kirstie Dotson offers a broader conception of epistemic resources by drawing attention to epistemic systems. As Dotson writes: 'One's epistemic resources and the epistemological system within which those resources prevail may be wholly inadequate to the task of addressing the persisting epistemic exclusions that are causing epistemic oppression' (Dotson 2014: 116). The collective epistemic resources on which we depend to make sense of and engage the world may be both impoverished and harmed by systemic oppression. Dotson clarifies that '[e]pistemological systems, here, refers to our overall epistemic life ways. It includes operative, instituted social imaginaries, habits of cognition, attitudes towards knowers and/or any relevant sensibilities that encourage or hinder the production of knowledge. An epistemological system is a holistic concept that refers to all the conditions for the possibility of knowledge production and possession' (121). I read my above account of implicit understanding as including skills, affect, implicit knowledge, and socially-situated embodiment to be congruent with Dotson's rendering here of epistemological systems.

As my discussion of the fictional example of Maestra and the real examples of my sister, Julie Andrews, and Claudia Mitchell has illustrated, forms of knowledge beyond the propositional should be included as part of knowledge production and possession. Dominant practices of epistemology, focusing on propositional knowledge, are deficient in part because they delimit the scope of epistemic resources. Even liberatory projects such as Fricker's focus on *conceptual* resources in pursuing epistemic justice. So, when Fricker articulates testimonial injustice as the case of speakers receiving deflated credibility because of their social position in an unjust world and hermeneutic injustice as 'the injustice of having some significant area of one's social experience obscured from collective understanding owing to hermeneutical marginalization' (Fricker 2007: 158), she retains a paradigmatic focus on propositional knowledge. Not having the concepts and language to account for an experience, or not having one's words taken seriously are certainly forms of epistemic injustice. But it is also a form of epistemic injustice to have access to the insufficient epistemic resources expressed in a vision of knowledge confined to language and concepts. Pursuing better worlds benefits from including the rich epistemic resources of attending to our feelings, presuppositions, embodied practice, and skilled behavior as salient to our lives.

In thinking with the thought experiments imagining Mary, or Maestra, we do well to move the question of their knowledge beyond the propositional. What would happen if we understood knowledge-that as perpetually and meaningfully connected to forms of knowledge that include emotion, skill, social situation, embodiment, and more? How would our pursuit of epistemic justice expand if we considered more than the adequacies of our concepts and language to our experience? And what might happen when the examples we take up to think about can speak back to our use of them? This question is significant, because simply attending to cases from the real world does not do away with epistemic injustice, as when people's experiences are simplified or instrumentalized to 'make a point.' Still, I believe that expanding our epistemic accounts to include the rich epistemic resources we draw on in our most everyday knowing practices will be of benefit for work on knowledge, as well as for more just worlds in which to know.

**Related chapters**: 1, 3, 8, 16, 26, 32, 33, 37

## Notes

1 Note that these are forms of being unable to play the piano that seem to be just practical, and do not have much to do with epistemic injustices that could contribute to a lack of piano playing. However, there are substantive social contexts to these seemingly simple circumstances that involve epistemic injustices: not having social access to the potential passion for piano playing, not having the confidence or training, being seen as 'not the right sort' to play piano, the prohibitive expense of pianos and the concomitant assumption that people who play piano own a piano and a place to put it, which (given the difficulty of moving and tuning pianos) usually means owning a house.

2 Onora O'Neill's early engagement with the use of examples in moral reasoning (taking up Peter Winch's 1972 paper 'The Universalizability of Moral Judgment') is important, as she critiques 'lurid' and 'schematic' examples while simultaneously rejecting both Wittgensteinian and contemporary analytic 'problem-centred' moral theorizing. She makes the argument that we need to have both a real assessment of the actual situations in which we find ourselves, as well as a principled approach to moral reasoning (O'Neill 1986). Iris Marion Young's discussion of Anita Silvers' work on non-disabled people's difficulty imagines the lives of disabled people as anything other than tragic, racist appropriations of Indigenous experiences, and other difficulties involved in perceiving accurately across difference (Young 1997: 42–43). In cases like these, we do well to be careful about the epistemic assumptions underlying our thought experiments, because they may well carry along unjust implications. Susan Brison observes that philosophers frequently turn to outlandish scenarios of split-brains, teletransporters that destroy an original self, and so on, rather than taking up actual people's experiences of profound self-transformation, including experiencing the destruction and reconstitution of the self (Brison 2002: 38–39).

## References

BBC News. 2006. Woman is fitted with 'bionic' arm. *BBC*, September 15, sec. Health. http://news.bbc.co.uk/2/hi/health/5348458.stm.

Brison, S. 2002. *Aftermath: Violence and the Remaking of a Self*. Princeton: Princeton University Press.

Brown, David. 2006. For 1st woman with bionic arm, a new life is within reach. September 14. www.washingtonpost.com/wp-dyn/content/article/2006/09/13/AR2006091302271.html?nav=E8.

CBS News. 2009. The rise of Dame Julie Andrews. February 11. www.cbsnews.com/stories/2008/04/06/sunday/main3996615.shtml.

Dotson, Kristie. 2014. 'Conceptualizing epistemic oppression', *Social Epistemology* 28.2: 115–138.

Grasswick, Heidi. 2014. "Understanding Epistemic Normativity in Feminist Epistemology." In *The Ethics of Belief*, edited by Jonathan Matheson and Rico Vitz, 216–243. Oxford: Oxford University Press.

Jackson, Frank. 1982. 'Epiphenomenal qualia', *The Philosophical Quarterly* 32.127: 127–136.

Jackson, Frank. 1986. 'What Mary didn't know', *The Journal of Philosophy* 83.5: 291–295.

McGrath, Ben. 2007. 'Muscle memory: The next generation of bionic prostheses', *The New Yorker*, July 30: 40–45.

Noë, Alva. 2005. 'Against intellectualism', *Analysis* 65.4: 278–290.

O'Neill, Onora. 1986. 'The power of example', *Philosophy* 61.235: 5–29.

Polanyi, M. 1967. *The Tacit Dimension*. Garden City, NY: Anchor Books.

Polanyi, M. 1969. *Knowing and Being; Essays*. Chicago: University of Chicago Press.

Ryle, Gilbert. 1949. *The Concept of Mind*. London and New York: Hutchinson.

Shotwell, Vivien. 2015. *Vienna Nocturne*. Toronto: Anchor Books.

Stanley, Jason. 2010. 'Knowing (How)', *Noûs* 45.2: 207–238.

Stanley, Jason. 2011. *Know How*. Oxford: Oxford University Press.

Stanley, Jason, and Timothy Williamson (2001) 'Knowing how', *Journal of Philosophy* 98: 411–444.

Young, Iris Marion. 1997. *Intersecting Voices: Dilemmas of Gender, Political Philosophy, and Policy*. Princeton: Princeton University Press.

# 8
# EPISTEMIC RESPONSIBILITY

*Lorraine Code*

I begin with a certain temerity on an autobiographical note, sketching some of the reasons that prompted me to write a book called *Epistemic Responsibility* in the 1980s, after completing a PhD with a dissertation titled 'Knowledge and Subjectivity'. The dissertation topic did not lead directly into thoughts about epistemic responsibility since the concept was not then so central a part of the philosophical lexicon as it briefly came to be, and as it is again reclaiming explanatory space. Yet a rigorous if short-lived exchange assessing its 'scope and limits', in the late 1970s and early 1980s, prompted me to take it up in ways its then-articulators subsequently ceased to pursue, perhaps because of its apparent fluidity, its lack of conceptual rigour, and/or its uneasy fit within then-current epistemological orthodoxy. For my work, it was the missing piece in a range of issues I was thinking about without the conceptual resources to articulate them.

Briefly to rehearse some moments in a relatively short-lived debate in Anglo-American philosophy then, consider the following: In 1974, asking 'How Do You Know?' Ernest Sosa suggests that, on occasion, a resort to neglectful data collection resulting in lack of knowledge 'could be traced back to epistemic irresponsibility' (1974: 117), to substandard performance attributable to the investigator.[1] More centrally inspirational for how I continued is Laurence Bonjour's (1978) observation:

> Cognitive doings are epistemically justified, on this conception, only if and to the extent that they are aimed at this goal – which means roughly that one accepts all and only beliefs which one has good reason to think are true. To accept a belief in the absence of such a reason, however appealing or even mandatory such acceptance may be from other standpoints, is to neglect the pursuit of truth; such an acceptance is, one might say, *epistemically irresponsible*. My contention is that the idea of being epistemically responsible is the core concept of epistemic justification.
>
> *(1978: 5)*

Yet, according to Hilary Kornblith, Bonjour seems to presuppose that there is a free choice of belief: thus, fulfilling one's epistemic responsibilities is a matter of following certain rules of ideal reasoning – an assumption he rejects (Kornblith 1983: 34 fn.1). But he argues persuasively in favour of judging epistemic conduct responsible or irresponsible: he is a principal contributor to this line of thinking. In this 1983 essay, Kornblith suggests that often when someone wonders whether a belief is *justified*, she/he is asking 'whether the belief is the product of *epistemically responsible action*' (1983: 34). Such questions, he notes, are about the ethics of belief. He stops short, however, of claiming that beliefs are freely chosen *tout court*, concentrating rather on questions about how 'truth seekers ought to comport themselves' (1983:34). Similarly, John Heil focuses on a tension between regarding believers as active doxastic agents who are responsible for what they believe, and believers as being 'at the mercy of their belief-forming equipment' (1983: 357): apparently, they are passive. Referring to the epistemically responsible agent, he argues: 'It is not that one has a choice in the beliefs that one forms, but that one has a say in the procedures one undertakes that lead to their formation' (1983: 363). Hence he is critical of an epistemological focus on proper reasoning to the exclusion of considering *how* evidence is gathered, maintaining that being epistemically responsible is about engaging in appropriate knowledge-seeking procedures. He addresses neither the criteria of 'appropriateness' nor the nature of responsibility as *praxis*. He concludes that a need to avoid voluntarism in knowledge/belief formation leaves space for speaking of epistemic responsibility and agency only if the focus shifts to the ways in which 'agents . . . select belief-generating procedures' (1983: 363).

As this small sampling indicates, discussions of epistemic responsibility did claim a place, then, in mainstream American epistemology. They may have failed to play a more central part in consequence of their uneasy positioning in relation to the post-positivist rigour that continued to govern epistemology, or in consequence of their departure from deductive-nomological analysis. More plausible an explanation is/was their stark *individualism*, which sustains settled practices of failing to take subjectivity into account: indeed, of avoiding the compromises doing so would entail.[2] It is difficult – even incongruous – to talk about responsibilities in relation to knowing chairs and tables, even though in some situations it could matter. But once knowledge-seeking is recognized as a cooperative-collaborative, textured human practice, it is vital to keep in mind Anne Seller's emblematic affirmation: 'As an isolated individual, I often do not know what my experiences are' (1988: 180). These, in condensed form, are among the ideas that, in my view, affirmed the centrality of such issues.

In writing *Epistemic Responsibility*, I was attempting to fill a gap I could neither name nor describe – a gap where evaluative and interpretive judgments could find no place, seemingly because they could not 'boil down' to simple true-or-false empirical propositional claims, nor did they admit of evaluation – say, of nuance or relevance. Most crucially, inquiry that starts from (perhaps tacit) questions about epistemic responsibility requires engaging with subjectivity/ subjectivities: it is about working to understand, assessing, and (often hermeneutically) engaging with issues about the place of subjectivity in knowledge-making, constructing, and evaluating practices. It is about the ethics and politics of knowledge, and indeed about epistemic subjectivity in its multiple instantiations. Hence given that talk of responsibility in its literal modalities commonly, if implicitly, refers to human agency, it clearly requires 'Taking Subjectivity Into Account' (Code 1996): starting from understandings of epistemic *subjectivity/subjectivities* more diverse and more complex than working from the standard unidentified occupant of the S place, in '*S* knows that *p*' assertions, allows. My aim was to claim space for the concept and the practices it could inform in knowledge acquisition, development, evaluation, and circulation by bringing the epistemic subject out of hiding:[3] acknowledging the incongruity embedded in working from a systemic failure to recognize that talk about responsibility without reference to a responsible epistemic subject – to *the knower(s)*, the potentially responsible or irresponsible epistemic agents involved – is indeed futile.

Space did have to be claimed, for in the then (and often still now) 'instituted' Anglo-American epistemic imaginary, talk about responsible epistemic conduct and its implications for knowing well was conceptually at odds with established epistemic practice.[4] This incongruity is apparent in the examples I cite from epistemologists who were working on such issues, then. In an entrenched concentration on determining how $S$ can know that $p$, there was no ready conceptual framework for assessing the variability, tonality, and situation-specificity of a range of putative knowers or of certain kinds of claim that nonetheless, I maintain, merit the label 'knowledge'. Nor was it easy to detach references to subjectivity from a then-pressing worry about inquiry reducing to a defence of subjectivism or to a chapter in the sociology of knowledge. In short, appeals to necessary and sufficient conditions were inadequate to naming the task that investigations into such situated, contextualized responsibilities required.

Thus, in claiming significance for 'epistemic responsibility', the book brings a sideways/ oblique conceptual framing into the going discourse, albeit tentatively and uneasily: uptake was, and persisted in being, rare. There was no space within the going conceptual repertoire to introduce, and anticipate a hearing for, matters of responsibility within the formal apparatus of analytic/Anglo-American theories of knowledge, then. In part owing to an implicit yet firm separation of epistemology from ethics, politics, and ontology, such proposals were read as heralding a descent into incoherence. Again, in part owing to the principled absence of any real 'knower(s)', it seemed that to achieve objectivity, knowledge-claims had to be made from nowhere and into a void, with no hearers, validators, deliberators, or naysayers participating in the scenario: no-one appropriately nameable as responsible or otherwise. In short, the received Anglo-American epistemic imaginary lacked the conceptual resources to bring matters of responsibility into focus or to follow so unorthodox a line of reasoning. The very idea of epistemic responsibility unsettles the self-certainty of an orthodoxy for which, to avoid a pernicious subjectivism, knowers are replicable space-holders whose circumstances are irrelevant to processes of verification or falsification.

Nonetheless, working within a conceptual frame for which responsible or irresponsible epistemic practices – of knowing, and *a fortiori* of responsible knowing *as* conduct are pervasive goals – can move toward closing a conceptual-interpretive lacuna that holds a range of issues *hors de question* in epistemology and its cognate practices, even as the politics of knowledge claims increased epistemic legitimacy. Pivotal are matters of subjectivity that are integral to thinking about responsibility, but could claim no place in Anglo-American epistemology, then. Yet these matters are integral to issues, practices, and puzzles that exceed the assertive scope and legitimacy of '*S* knows that *p*' declarations. They direct attention to the activity – the human *praxis* of knowing, inquiring, deliberating – in an ongoing quest that resists premature closure.

Questions about responsible epistemic conduct have met with impatience or disdain from mainstream Anglo-American epistemologists, no doubt because it is difficult to establish definitive criteria for or against judging how well an act/process/practice of knowing fulfills or evades these requirements. Moreover, sufficiently elaborated examples of epistemic (mis)conduct face charges of committing the *ad hominem* fallacy. Yet such acts are not so different from practices of judging *moral* conduct good or bad, which are integral to virtue ethics: apart from strict adherence to a utilitarian calculus or facsimile thereof, ethical/moral conduct *is* amenable to interpretive-evaluative judgments, which admit of degree. The parallel is plausible. But, given the tenacious legacy of logical positivism and its derivatives, Anglo-American epistemologists were less than prepared to think analogously about knowing. Silently, it was conceived as an all-or-nothing phenomenon which, in striving for objectivity, presupposes and preserves the anonymity and/or the absence of the knowing subject(s).

Hence, although the knower is generally absent from articulated knowledge claims, other than as a place-holder in relatively trivial, empirically-derived assertions, epistemology prior to *social* epistemology persisted as a more rigorously individualist activity/practice than moral-political practices could be. When paradigmatic knowledge claims draw on everyday events and equipment in (presumptively) materially replete scenarios with a single but replicable player, the act of knowing that a cup is on the table needs no additional substance to establish its exemplary status. Yet this status is an artefact of the localized specificity and limited reach of the putative universality of standard epistemic exemplars and of the invisibility of knowers beyond their role as mere place-holders. To invoke a tired yet still pertinent example, even so venerated an empiricist as Bertrand Russell withdrew the paradigm status he presupposed for 'All swans are white' in the aftermath of colonizers' 'discovering' black swans in Australia. The example points to the limitations of generalizing from local experiences and to the challenges colonialism, at home and abroad, poses to taken-for-granted epistemic habits and practices.[5] Are such practices thereby rendered irresponsible? The question is unsettling for Anglo-centered evaluations of responsibility in 'mainstream' epistemology: clearly, their paradigm status, not just as specific utterances but as constitutive of settled epistemic practices and precepts, needs to be reevaluated.

The difficulty in bringing matters of responsible epistemic conduct into the then-going (late 1980s) conceptual frame is thus consequent upon the conception of subjectivity that has silently sustained the 'instituted' Anglo-American epistemic imaginary. Then, and still now, '*S*' was an infinitely replicable place-holder: the invisible knower '. . . that *p*'. When the influence of British empiricism and logical positivism was strongest, S was rarely named. Yet *he* was presumptively adult (but not old), male, white, educated, and sufficiently affluent to have cups, tables, and other 'standard' material accoutrements of 'everyday life' in the social-economic circumstances that formed the presumed backdrop of *his* being, knowing, and doing. Exemplary knowledge claims were commonly uttered 'outwards', into an empty or universally presupposed space: thus neither deliberatively nor interactively. The discursive spaces (written or spoken) into which they are spoken, heard, written, or read were rarely taken into account. Such assumptions infused the social-epistemic *imaginary* of Anglo-American philosophy then – and still, if less persistently, now. Silently yet firmly, they establish the scope and limits of human knowledge worthy of the name and of epistemological investigation.

Reasons for or against the uptake of such projects are difficult to substantiate, but to catch a sense of the opposition they generated, consider two early reviews of *Epistemic Responsibility*, by Elizabeth Fricker (1989) and Susan Haack (1991). The former is cautiously yet helpfully critical; the latter vociferously excoriating. For Fricker (and I agree), a serious flaw is the book's (the author's) failure to spell out exactly what a 'responsibilist' epistemology is. She notes its indebtedness to Aristotelian virtue theory, is uneasy about its appeal to a Kantian idea of the active role of the subject in synthesizing experience, and suggests that the epistemic responsibilities an agent is to fulfill are insufficiently articulated in the text. These points are well taken.[6] They suggest that a principal flaw is in my attempt to position the book in relation to analytic epistemology then, some of whose major contributors I cite. With respect to Haack's review, evidently the hermeneutic style of much of the book's presentation – its quasi-narrative articulation – offends her: plainly, she is deeply offended. She elaborates her reaction in extensive examples of places where I am less than exact, where the writing is allusive rather than expository-argumentative, where I fail to observe settled distinctions. Many such criticisms may be warranted, yet the review's mockingly dismissive tone is at best grossly insulting, at worst, nastily mocking. Its purpose is unclear: seemingly, it is meant to discipline an undisciplined – and ignorant – would-be philosopher. In so doing, it speaks from a closed, hard-edged epistemic position where the epistemic 'engagement' these criticisms suggest is characteristic, in Kristie Dotson's words, of a 'culture of justification'. The contrast as I understand it is with a deliberative, dialogical culture. Whereas the justificatory approach has no space for representing philosophers as engaged in ongoing dialogic inquiry, in a culture of praxis the aim is to work collegially, collaboratively – if not harmoniously – toward evaluating, understanding, interpreting guiding beliefs, both superficial and sedimented.⁷ Epistemic friction may well be integral to the process, but it need not be negatively or aggressively conceived.

As *Epistemic Responsibility* moves into a more explicitly *hermeneutic* dimension, there is – I think – a clearer sense of what is at stake, as also in its appeals to quasi-Wittgensteinian cautions about asking not for meaning, but for use: its *situating* knowledge.⁸ That said, I do not spell out necessary and sufficient conditions for achieving responsibility in epistemic practice, mainly because there are none. Nor do I offer a guide or rule-book. This absence, for some (including Haack), may leave the book in something of a criterion-less limbo. But such an approach is not so different from how a putative *doer* will endeavour to engage in virtuous moral-political conduct. Although there may be no established rules, epistemic agents learn, communally and interactively, to work toward, and embody, responsible epistemic practices: to navigate situations where trust, deliberation, and debate are their principal resources, and accountability requires careful deliberative practices.⁹ Would-be knowers need not be dogmatic or rigidly rule-bound in so doing: often, and appropriately, there *are* no rules, and arguments may work from example and/or analogy. Nonetheless, thinking how knowers might achieve such a goal is an ongoing project in social epistemology, as is evaluating epistemic responsibility in its basic connections with trust. The conclusion may be that analytic epistemology, given the fixity of its formal conceptual apparatus, cannot make space for epistemic responsibility and is impoverished in consequence. Such a conclusion is not mine.

When Fricker's and Haack's reviews appeared, the conceptual resources may indeed have been lacking for assessing the meaning and value of responsible epistemic conduct. Hence it would be challenging – akin to a category mistake – to spell out rules or necessary and sufficient conditions for its achievement. Fricker's puzzlement is apt. There was no conceptual space where knowers could find 'the minds prepared' to take its potential seriously (recalling Louis Pasteur: *Dans les champs de l'observation le hasard ne favorise que les esprits préparés*: chance, or fortune, favours only the prepared mind). Now, social epistemology is creating spaces where such projects can claim a voice:¹⁰ spaces hospitable to understanding knowledge-seeking as a *social practice* in communicative-interpretive frameworks where discussion, deliberation, debate claim a pivotal place. Conditions of situation and uptake claim a new centrality, and hermeneutic-interpretive-deliberative practices a renewed pertinence, even though the subjectivity of the subject remains unaddressed. Yet Elizabeth Fricker, with many Anglo-American epistemologists then, found a quasi-oxymoronic uneasiness in the very idea that so putatively inexact a practice could claim the label 'epistemology' while offering no objective (contrasted with situation-specific) criteria that, for bona fide epistemologists, are definitive of epistemic practice. But 'responsibilists' need not eschew such criteria: respect for empirical evidence, commitment to truth-seeking and objectivity, adherence to public standards of inquiry remain. Still, responsible epistemic conduct requires even more challenging practices: communicative, deliberative, evaluative, temporally extended practices such as are rarely engaged by knowers as isolated, solitary place-holders making punctiform knowledge claims.

Social epistemology involves more than adding a concept, or another variation, to a conceptual orthodoxy. It marks a radical shift in practices of understanding and evaluating knowledge as integral to, constitutive of ways of being in the world. Like all human practices, knowing is situated within and enabled or thwarted by material, political, geographical, situational, cultural, and other factors, many of which are integral to assessing and/or implementing knowledgeable beliefs and actions, and many of which evoke matters of responsibility. Feminist, antiracist, multicultural, and other 'difference sensitive' theories and practices are acutely aware of them. By this feature alone, in its multiple modalities, they depart from the bland neutrality of Anglo-American orthodoxy. Nor do all such factors figure in every instance of social epistemology *per se*, so to speak, but their insistent (if tacit) affirmation unsettles the scope and limits of pre-social epistemic projects while adding urgency to developing responsible knowledge-making practices.

Situating this discussion within an *epistemic imaginary*,[11] is more than and different from adding one more piece to an established conceptual apparatus. As I have indicated, in advocating such a relocation I am drawing indirectly and variously on the work of Michèle Le Dœuff and Cornelius Castoriadis. While neither of these thinkers makes explicit reference to epistemic responsibility, their (admittedly diverse) conceptions of an *imaginary* prepare the way to developing a framework for loosening the constraints inherent in locating inquiry within rhetorical spaces where the power of such a conceptual reconstruction is unacknowledged. Hence I am endorsing Le Dœuff's contention that 'there is no intellectual activity that is not grounded in an imaginary'(2003: xvi), while insisting that working within an *imaginary* is emphatically not equivalent to appealing to 'imagination' as fantasy – individual or collective – as an explanatory contributor to knowledge making and circulating. Such thought experiments have no place here. Yet neither is the point to discount the contributions of 'imagination' to knowing well: as José Medina (2013) shows, the language of a social 'imagination', also, claims space in these deliberations, if differently.

In understanding inquiry/knowing as grounded in an imaginary, I follow Castoriadis, who refers to a widespread, often imperceptible yet multifaceted world-view or framework, a complex of ideas, expectations, presuppositions, implicit assumptions which are by no means beyond articulation or debate, although they rarely enter everyday discourse. An imaginary thus conceived is (distantly) analogous to a Kuhnian paradigm or a Foucauldian *epistêmê* in shaping, framing, conferring legitimacy and/or its opposite, on quotidian knowing in its particularity and generality. With Kuhn, a paradigm refers to standard-setting exemplars of scientific legitimacy within a powerful if often tacit worldview, which confer or withhold judgments of scientific achievement. With Castoriadis, Le Dœuff, and Foucault (albeit variously for each), the effects of an imaginary can be more quotidian than domain specific. For example, as the rhetoric of 'public man, private woman' signals, the implicit imaginary from which it derives is integral to a western-northern white middle-class social imaginary that women (of a certain class, age, race) should comport themselves 'decorously' in ways which, *inter alia*, were stifling, inhibiting, damaging. Certain areas of activity, study, or employment were known to be 'unsuitable' for a woman. Likewise, received values – epistemic, social, moral, political, ontological – deeply if silently embedded in, yet constitutive of the dailiness (*allgemeine Alltäglichkeit*) of 'everyday life', carry a normative force whose (often tacit) power demands recognition in thought and action. Violations occasion disapproval or worse, yet their manifestations are less than explicit, despite the power they exert. The social imaginary characteristic of white middle-class North America, as of much of the affluent western-northern world in the twentieth and twenty-first century, has silently condoned and perpetuated such coercive practices, shaping the assumptions that hold 'neutral' examples in place, whose 'neutrality' often masks an endorsement of variably unjust yet entrenched ways of thinking, being, and knowing. Nor were/are these assumptions always negative, restrictive. In their evolving modalities, they open space for hitherto unacceptable policies and practices: women's and non-white people's admission to higher education in many countries is a telling example. Analogous claims pertain, diversely, to assumptions that hold approval or disapproval in place across the social-political-everyday world in most societies and situations: albeit gradually and tacitly, they are sufficiently powerful to effect hitherto unimaginable shifts in social practices.

Writing *Epistemic Responsibility* in the early 1980s, I knew neither Le Dœuff's nor Castoriadis's work: their rich – diverse – thinking about *the imaginary*. In consequence, my analysis was too slender in its articulation of the conceptions of subjectivity and epistemic agency that informed it, and of the powerful, if often hidden, forces that conferred or withheld attributions of responsibility. Processes of understanding thinking, knowing, living within an imaginary relocate this way of thinking, now (if less clearly then) off-side from an epistemological orthodoxy with its presuppositions that formal analyses couched in a language of anonymity (*S* knows that *p*) or generic assertions about knowers and the known will best achieve objectivity and explanatory clarity, uncluttered by the specificities of subjects and situations: by *particularities*. With such presuppositions this analysis parts company. One reason for this shift derives from the exclusionary power, then (if less starkly now) of a divide between Anglo-American and 'Continental' philosophical thinking about knowledge. It manifests vividly in a widespread (erstwhile) Anglo-American philosophical reluctance to acknowledge and draw upon the *interpretive-hermeneutical* resources integral to the practice of such philosophers as Martin Heidegger, Simone de Beauvoir, Maurice Merleau-Ponty, Jean-Paul Sartre, Luce Irigaray, Franz Fanon, and their 'post-modern' contemporaries and descendants.[12] Most of these philosophers neither represent themselves nor are represented as epistemologists (owing perhaps to a resistance to Anglo-American orthodoxy or to convictions about the interrelatedness of diverse 'branches' of philosophy). Their engagements with 'being in the world' investigate ways of experiencing and knowing that world in its singularities, sociality, multiplicity, and unevenly distributed power structures. They work, albeit variously, with practices of explicitly embodied knowing that are responsive and responsible, or the reverse, in their interactive relations with their 'subject matters'.[13] From such holistic approaches *the imaginary* achieves its power as a resource, where epistemological questions may not be labelled as such, but are woven into larger interpretive/hermeneutical analyses. Knowing, being, doing appear as integrated *practices*: 'situated knowledges' in Donna Haraway's words attest to analogous assumptions and practices, even though the terminology would not be hers.

Thinking-knowing within an epistemic imaginary in its contrasts with an imaginary of mastery and control, eschewing any goal of achieving a 'view from nowhere', are integral to Castoriadis's conception of an *instituted social imaginary*, which 'carries within it the normative social meanings, customs, expectations, assumptions, values, prohibitions, and permissions – the habitus and ethos – into which human beings are nurtured from childhood and which they internalize, affirm, challenge, or contest as they make sense of their place, responsibilities, options within a world, both social and physical, whose 'nature' and meaning are also instituted within these imaginary significations'.[14] This conceptual framing owes a debt to phenomenology, especially in its hermeneutic modalities, while drawing on and engaging with approaches in Anglo-American epistemology that are, perhaps in spite of themselves, hospitable to such readings. The consequent position need be neither static nor dogmatic. To it, Castoriadis counter-poses the *instituting* imaginary: the critical-creative activity of a society whose autonomy is apparent in its capacity to put itself in question, recognizing that as a society, it is incongruous with itself, with scant reason for self-satisfaction.[15] Feminist, post-colonial, anti-racist, and other 'new' epistemologies are often informed by what amounts to an implicit recognition of such incongruities.

Relating these thoughts to epistemic responsibility, I suggest that working toward its realization – cognizant of its questions as both urgent and difficult – requires no mere adjustment of certain basic assumptions of mainstream epistemology: it re-situates its projects and practices. Thus to José Medina's question – 'When is partaking in a body of social ignorance a form of irresponsibility? . . . And is the failure in responsibility an ethical failure of the individual or a political failure of society'? (2013: 133) – my response is that, despite its seeming to fall outside the purview of standard epistemology *tout court*, the failure is both ethical and political. Thus, appeals to epistemic responsibility, which has been something of a sleeper since my 1987 book appeared,[16] are now enriching the conceptual repertoire of Anglo-American social epistemology, opening new rhetorical-discursive spaces. In consequence, epistemic inquiry moves toward wide-ranging *reconceptions* of the place and purpose of responsibility in knowledge-making and knowledge-conveying practices. One of its effects is evident in the spaces it opens for taking subjectivity seriously into account in projects of evaluating knowledge claims, both punctiform and extenuated. Indeed, for this project to succeed, a fundamental restructuring of going assumptions about epistemic subjectivities is urgently required. Such appeals acquire an enhanced urgency in relation to *knowing* – and understanding – the epistemic implications of racism, sexism, classism, homophobia, and multiple other 'otherings' from an entrenched and powerful social norm.

As its early critics note, epistemic responsibility does not come complete with a set of accompanying rules for the direction of the mind. Like many virtues, it names a precept, a principle whose effects are diffuse, unpredictable, and open to ongoing, collaborative-contestatory deliberation. Often they do not speak for themselves but require collective processes of evaluation/negotiation. I do not spell out necessary and sufficient conditions for achieving epistemic responsibility, and for good reasons: there are none. But guidelines can be sketched: impressionistic though they may be. In this respect they are akin to other articulations of virtue theory as for example, in Alasdair MacIntyre's *After Virtue*, where he affirms the significance of *narrative* and *tradition* for understanding human lives. He emphasizes that virtue is not a one-off phenomenon: that it manifests as part of 'a concept of self whose unity resides in the unity of a narrative which links birth to life and death as narrative beginning to middle to end' (1981: 191). He is not claiming narrative as the only route to understanding, nor that narrative will tell of a single, isolated protagonist, but its contribution to engaging with complex moral (and epistemological) questions can be vital.[17]

For reasons such as these, it is increasingly clear why such socially grounded and enacted capacities as responsible knowing found no easy uptake in Anglo-American philosophy, prior to the development of social epistemology. Now, more than thirty years after *After Virtue*, and in consequence of the proliferation of social media as sources of information, in the early twenty-first century, the issues are still more complex. So, for example, in response to a question about what he expected students to know about climate-ecological issues, a colleague observed: 'Virtually nothing: their main source of information is Fox News'.[18] Does these students' putative ignorance in these matters invite condemnation, understanding, and tolerance? Such questions are increasingly urgent as people's reliance on social media as sources of knowledge/information increases in western/northern societies, where epistemological counter-arguments often struggle to claim a hearing. Here matters of epistemic responsibility claim a renewed urgency. A new epistemology of listening, interpreting, deliberating will need to claim a larger place than it has hitherto occupied, in philosophy and in the world, and the inadequacy of epistemic individualism will be increasingly evident.

Still pertinent, then, is Medina's observation: 'The mistake of intellectualism is to think that by changing the epistemic, the ethical and political will follow, whereas . . . people's concepts and cognitions may not control all their emotions, moral characters, and political attitudes' (2013: 90). The going social imaginary makes space for such a thought. Medina, citing Miranda Fricker on epistemic injustice, rightly insists that 'such a contextual approach has to be pluralized and rendered relational in more complex way . . . [its] assumptions . . . about the pervasiveness of hermeneutical lacunas and their influence on entire collectivities have to be interrogated' (90). But *whose* collective understanding is at issue? *Whose* collective hermeneutical resource? Of particular interest, especially in relation to climate change, is how certain 'epistemic identities' and social-structural positionings enable and restrict projects of bringing *epistemic responsibility* into conversation with questions about hermeneutic and testimonial (in)justice.

In his chapter 'Epistemic Responsibility and Culpable Ignorance', Medina asks: 'When is partaking in a body of social ignorance a form of irresponsibility? . . . And is the failure in responsibility an ethical failure of the individual or a political failure of society'? (2013: 133). The questions are timely now that appeals to epistemic responsibility are currently unsettling – and enriching – the conceptual repertoire of Anglo-American social epistemology: opening new rhetorical-discursive spaces. Medina's book exemplifies this reengagement. Such appeals acquire enhanced urgency in relation to climate change skepticism, with the doubts that feed it and are nurtured to preserve it. Participating in such skeptically generated social ignorance is indeed, and always, a form of irresponsibility: at once an ethical and a political failure, with ethics and politics reinforcing one another. It is, primarily, an egregious failure of epistemic responsibility, with cultivated-manufactured ignorance and doubt sustaining the ethics and politics that require contestation.[19] The question of *whose* irresponsibility is at issue, and how it could/should be discerned and addressed, is fraught in a time of conflicting information which few 'ordinary people' are equipped to disentangle from the vested interests and unstable expertise that often infuse it. Answering the question in the affirmative presupposes that ignorance is recognizable and that its 'partakers' acknowledge it as such. How could they justify doing so?

I have noted Castoriadis's references to the social unrest that follows when a society where a certain imaginary has prevailed comes to realize that it is *incongruous with itself*: that a struggle to preserve an impoverished imaginary would be ethically and politically unworthy. Especially pertinent in this regard are ongoing, often vicious debates in/about the epistemology and ethics of climate change inquiry. Large epistemic injustices are widely enacted against bringing to public-social attention matters that challenge fixed self-presentations to overinflate an epistemic exaggeration that positions certain findings *'dans le faux'* (to distort the Foucauldian idea *'dans le vrai'*). This inquiry, then, is involved in working to discern how certain 'epistemic identities' and social-structural positionings simultaneously enable and restrict projects of bringing *epistemic responsibility* into the conversation with matters of hermeneutic and testimonial (in)justice. Difficult to articulate in this regard are injustices performed against hard-won public reasons that generate a certain credibility in favour of scientific research stereotypically presumed to be 'neutral' (in a now superseded imaginary!). They unsettle assumptions that accord quasi-inviolate standing to 'science has proved' assertions, without asking 'whose science' (with a nod to Sandra Harding).[20] Hence an imaginary of complacency and comfort seeks reassurance from its own persistence, so long as practitioners look away from empirical events that, increasingly, strike at the core of their lives – and their theories. Taking some of these ideas as my starting point, I am currently examining events of denial and refusal in response to climate change, which the social imaginary of the affluent western world still strives to accommodate.[21] At issue, still, are questions of individual and collective epistemic responsibility.

**Related chapters**: 3, 7, 11, 20, 21

# Notes

1 See also Sosa (1980).
2 See in this connection Code (1993).
3 The reference is to Medina (2013: 133), with thanks to Gaile Pohlhaus, Jr.
4 Yet owing to Ernest Sosa's (and others') careful reading of the manuscript, *Epistemic Responsibility* found its way into print. It was awarded a Brown University First Book Prize, with a teaching and research fellowship at Brown.
5 The ways that putatively universal and general concepts and convictions are challenged by material, social, and historical realities is explored by Alcoff (2005), especially chapters 1–4.
6 In part, these criticisms indicate the degree to which the notion of epistemic responsibility was under-theorized at the time and the extent to which *Epistemic Responsibility* was forward reaching. Indeed, Aristotelian virtue epistemology arose in response to the need for accounts of epistemic responsibility.
7 See Dotson (2012), with thanks to Gaile Pohlhaus, Jr. See also Moulton (1983).
8 The reference is to Haraway, 'Situated Knowledges', in her 1991 work.

9 See Battaly (2014).
10 I refer to Edward Craig's (1999) innovative approach, moving away from single epistemic agents speaking into a void, to working with the language of speakers and hearers. It is a revolutionary move, whose implications are central to the development of social epistemology.
11 Charles Taylor (2003) also writes about imaginaries in a sense contiguous with, but not identical, to the sense that informs the works I draw upon here.
12 A notable exception is Alcoff (1996), where she draws on the work of Gadamer and Foucault and, relevant to my thinking here, on hermeneutics.
13 Pertinent is Barad (2007). Rather than 'interactive', Barad says 'intra-active'.
14 See Code (2006, especially pp. 29ff).
15 See Castoriadis (1998, 1994).
16 See Code (1987).
17 Relevant here is Code (2011). This appeared in a special issue on *Social Cognitive Ecology and its Role in Social Epistemology*, edited by Mikkel Gerken, Jesper Kalelstrup, Klemens Kappel, and Duncan Pritchard.
18 I cite this example in Code (2014).
19 See Code (2013).
20 See, for instance, Harding (1991).
21 See Code (2015).

# References

Alcoff, Linda Martín, *Real Knowing: New Versions of the Coherence Theory* (Ithaca, NY: Cornell University Press, 1996).

Alcoff, Linda Martín, *Visible Identities: Race, Gender, and the Self* (Oxford: Oxford University Press, 2005).

Barad, Karen, *Meeting the Universe Halfway: Quantum Physics and the Entanglement of Matter and Meaning* (Durham, NC: Duke University Press, 2007).

Battaly, Heather, 'Intellectual Virtues', in Stan van Hooft (ed.), *The Handbook of Intellectual Virtues* (Durham, UK: Acumen, 2014), 177–187.

Bonjour, Lawrence, 'Can empirical knowledge have a foundation?', *American Philosophical Quarterly* 15:1 (1978): 1–13.

Castoriadis, Cornelius, 'Radical Imagination and the Social Instituting Imaginary', in Gillian Robinson and John Rundell (eds.), *Rethinking Imagination: Culture and Creativity* (London: Routledge, 1994), 136–154.

Castoriadis, Cornelius, *The Imaginary Institution of Society*, trans. Kathleen Blamey (Cambridge: MIT Press, 1998).

Code, Lorraine, *Epistemic Responsibility* (Hanover, NH: University Press of New England, 1987).

Code, Lorraine, 'Taking Subjectivity into Account', in Linda Alcoff and Elizabeth Potter (eds.), *Feminist Epistemologies* (New York: Routledge, 1993). Reprinted in Ann Garry and Marilyn Pearsall, eds., *Women, Knowledge and Reality*, 2nd edition (New York: Routledge, 1996), 15–48.

Code, Lorraine, 'Taking Subjectivity into Account', in Ann Garry and Marilyn Pearsall (eds.), *Women, Knowledge, and Reality*, 2nd edition (New York: Routledge, 1996), 191–221.

Code, Lorraine, *Ecological Thinking: The Politics of Epistemic Location* (New York: Oxford University Press, 2006).

Code, Lorraine, 'An ecology of epistemic authority', *Episteme: A Journal of Social Epistemology* 8:1 (2011): 24–37.

Code, Lorraine, '"Manufactured Uncertainty": Epistemologies of Mastery and the Ecological Imaginary', in Peg Rawes (ed.), *Relational Architectural Ecologies: Architecture, Nature and Subjectivity* (London: Routledge, 2013), 73–90.

Code, Lorraine, 'Culpable ignorance?', *Hypatia* 39:3 (2014): 670–676.

Code, Lorraine, 'Doubt and Denial: Epistemic Responsibility Meets Climate Change Scepticism', in Anna Grear and Evadne Grant (eds.), *Thought, Law, Rights and Action in the Age of Environmental Crisis* (Northampton: Edward Elgar Publishing, 2015), 25–45.

Craig, Edward, *Knowledge and the State of Nature* (Oxford: Oxford University Press, 1999).

Dotson, Kristie, 'How is this paper philosophy?', *Comparative Philosophy* 3:1 (2012): 3–29.

Fricker, Elizabeth, 'Review of *Epistemic Responsibility* by Lorraine Code and *The Theory of Epistemic Rationality* by Richard Foley', *Mind* 98:391 (1989): 457–461.

Haack, Susan, 'Review of *Epistemic Responsibility* by Lorraine Code', *Canadian Journal of Philosophy* 21:1 (1991): 91–107.
Haraway, Donna, 'Situated Knowledges', in Donna Haraway (ed.), *Simians, Cyborgs, and Women: The Reinvention of Nature* (New York: Routledge, 1991), 183–201.
Harding, Sandra, *Whose Science? Whose Knowledge? Thinking from Women's Lives* (Ithaca, NY: Cornell University Press, 1991).
Heil, John, 'Doxastic agency', *Philosophical Studies* 43:3 (1983): 355–364, at p. 357.
Kornblith, Hilary, 'Justified belief and epistemically responsible action', *The Philosophical Review* 92:1 (1983): 33–48.
Le Dœuff, Michèle, *The Sex of Knowing*, trans. Kathryn Hamer and Lorraine Code (New York: Routledge, 2003).
MacIntyre, Alasdair, *After Virtue: A Study in Moral Theory* (London: Duckworth, 1981).
Medina, José, *The Epistemology of Resistance: Gender and Racial Oppression, Epistemic Injustice, and Resistant Imaginations* (New York: Oxford University Press, 2013).
Moulton, Janice, 'A Paradigm of Philosophy: The Adversary Method', in Sandra Harding and Merrill Hintikka (eds.), *Discovering Reality: Feminist Perspectives on Epistemology, Metaphysics, Methodology, and Philosophy of Science* (Dordrecht: Reidel, 1983), 149–174.
Seller, Anne, 'Realism versus Relativism: Toward a Politically Adequate Epistemology', in Morwenna Griffiths and Margaret Whitford (eds.), *Feminist Perspectives in Philosophy* (Bloomington: Indiana University Press, 1988), 169–186.
Sosa, Ernest, 'How do you know?', *American Philosophical Quarterly* 11:1 (1974): 113–122.
Sosa, Ernest, 'The Raft and the Pyramid: Coherence versus foundations in the theory of knowledge', *Midwest Studies in Philosophy* 5 (1980): 3–26.
Taylor, Charles, *Modern Social Imaginaries* (Durham, NC: Duke University Press, 2003).

# 9
# IDEOLOGY

*Charles W. Mills*

The academy, no less than any other institution – and certainly the radical academy – is subject to the vagaries of intellectual fashion. "Ideology" as a concept was a crucial tool for Western progressives in universities in the 1960s and 1970s seeking both to theorize the repressive dimension of ostensibly liberal capitalist states and to challenge their own disciplines as generally complicit with that repression. In the United States in particular, the revival of the Marxist left (albeit "New" rather than "Old") on campus after the purges and witch-hunts of the McCarthyist 1950s would stimulate the formation of radical caucuses in a wide range of subjects (Ollman and Vernoff 1982). Railing against establishment orthodoxies, establishing new journals where they could speak truth to disciplinary power, these radical scholars saw "ideology" at work in both everyday and elite consciousness. Whether drawing on Frankfurt School "critical theory" (Held 1980), Georg Lukács's (1971) "reification," Antonio Gramsci's (1971) "hegemony," or Louis Althusser's (2001) "ideological state apparatuses," they sought to reveal and expose ideology's pervasive and negative influence on social cognition. But the increasing problems, and eventual collapse, of self-describedly Marxist states and movements would take down with it Marx's apparatus, whether justifiably or not. By the mid-1980s or so, and even more glaringly following the 1989–91 East Bloc debacle and accompanying proclamations of "the end of history," talk of *Ideologie* and *Ideologiekritik* began to seem hopelessly old-fashioned, tied to a dubious meta-narrative about capitalist crisis and the coming socialist revolution, and committed to an Enlightenment vision that seemed to some intrinsically "totalitarian." Instead these critical lenses would largely be replaced by Derridaean deconstruction and Foucauldian discourse theory. Postmodernism and post-structuralism would become the new radical orthodoxy for scholars in need of an optic for the emancipatory revisioning of the existing order.

But recent years have seen a shift back to the left and increasing dissatisfaction in at least some quarters with what is now called, in retrospect, "the culturalist turn." A "new" materialism (or materialisms) has been announced, in some respects continuous with, in other respects breaking with, older materialist traditions like Marxism (Coole and Frost 2010). Today, decades later, there are some signs – possibly as part of the same trend – that "ideology" may also be in for a revival as a critical concept, as indicated most recently (as I write) by a very successful January 2016 conference on the subject at Yale University, where indeed the original version of this chapter was presented.

What I want to do in this entry is to try to relate the concept of "ideology" to some of the literature in social epistemology inspired by Miranda Fricker's (2007) *Epistemic Injustice*. Fricker's book was an important intervention in the development of an epistemology nominally more sensitive to the social circumstances of the knower, yet which in actuality marginalized the obvious fact of domination in real-world societies. But the fact of social domination was, of course – though admittedly reduced primarily to its class aspect – the *central* theme of Marxist theory. Late twentieth-century feminist epistemology and feminist standpoint theory, to which Fricker pays brief tribute as precursors of her project, were themselves indebted to late nineteenth-century and early twentieth-century Marxism and its claims, most famously in Lukács (1971), about "bourgeois" and "proletarian" perspectives on social reality. Insofar as "ideology" is taken to be the Marxist concept crucial for illuminating and explaining these cognitive patterns, then it should be a valuable exercise to see whether, or to what extent, "ideology" in some form can provide a useful instrument for engaging current debates in the field.

## 1. "Ideology" in Marxism

What, if historical materialism as a theory of society and history is correct, would the implications be for the realm of the ideational? And even if historical materialism is not correct – acknowledging the greater degree of agnosticism or skepticism on this point in these post-Marxist times – what worthwhile core might still be salvageable from the concept of ideology?

The basic Marxist claim is not at all hard to understand in principle, even if working out the details will be complex and contested in practice. It can, indeed, be expressed in a sentence (and a short one at that): *social class oppression negatively affects social cognition*. More long-windedly: systems of domination will have deleterious cognitive effects on those enmeshed within its relations, both the privileged and the subordinated, via multiple determinants of group location, group identity, group interest, and group power (or its lack). Marx's own focus was limited to class oppression, and these days we would want to broaden it, as I have, to group oppression. But you can immediately see why such a claim anticipates, and should be relevant to, the contemporary epistemic injustice debates. Marxism takes for granted the necessity of a socio-historical account of cognition, one typically shaped by the "materialist" causal dynamics of classes in relations of domination and subordination, and is committed to a non-relativist epistemic perspective on the resulting beliefs and concepts.

Long before mainstream epistemology "discovered" that "testimony" and social circumstances were relevant to actual human cognition, Marxism was rejecting any kind of individualist Cartesian problematic, just as it rejected the social contract picture of asocial individuals coming together to create society. In both areas, theoretical "Robinsonades" – starting from Robinson Crusoe-like figures as the basic building-blocks – were to be dismissed as absurd. As David-Hillel Ruben's (1979, 109) pioneering work from decades ago put it: "knowledge is irreducibly *social*."

But although locating the cognizer in his/her sociohistorical context is a crucial first step, a necessary one, it is certainly not sufficient. The problem many progressives had with the early work on social epistemology was its ignoring or marginalization of social oppression. To use Rawlsian (Rawls 1999) language, issues of the sociopolitical in mainstream philosophy have usually been framed in terms of "ideal theory," "perfectly just" societies. But the reality is that, once humanity exits the hunting and gathering stage, *all* societies have been oppressive on axes of gender, class, ethnicity, religion, or (by the modern period) race. Marxism's concept of oppression is centered one-dimensionally on class – one of its many weaknesses. But its great virtue by contrast with mainstream sociopolitical theory is that it takes for granted that non-ideal theory should be our starting-point.

In her introduction, Fricker (2007, 2) refers to "the relativistic outlook of which postmodernism was the apotheosis" and suggests that this epistemic feature may explain mainstream Anglo-American epistemology's indifference to more "politicized" approaches to the topic. But Marxism is classically committed to Enlightenment objectivism (hence its claims about developing a "science" of history and society), and the rearguard struggle the few Marxist holdouts fought in the radical academy against the post-structuralist triumph from the 1980s onward revolved precisely around this question.

Correspondingly, the epistemic status of "ideology" was clearly *negative* in a presumptively non-relativist way. That is, "ideology" was a critical pejorative term referring to something bad, something that had to be avoided if truth were to be achieved. Self-consciously self-positioned within non-ideal theory, Marxism was claiming to have identified an important social phenomenon in the cognitive realm whose analysis, demystification, and eventual overcoming would be crucial to bringing about a better social order.

But could these claims be backed up in a non-question-begging way, or would it turn out that any set of ideas Marxists didn't like would, simply on their say-so, automatically earn the designation? What is the etiology offered of ideology, what is its relation to "materialism," and can it be made plausible to a non-Marxist audience? And for progressives with a view of oppression broader than class domination, are any of these insights transferable, or are they necessarily tied to a reductionist class analysis?

I have argued elsewhere (Mills 2010) that four crucial socioeconomic ("material") variables can be identified in Marx's writings as shaping social ideation. They are: (i) ruling-class domination, as manifest in intellectual domination (transmitted via the educational system and the mass media), (ii) societal "appearance" (spontaneous patterns of mistaken induction and faulty concept-formation fostered by the opacities of the capitalist system itself), (iii) class interest (whether in maintaining or overturning the system), and (iv) class experience (differential experiential trajectories through the social world influenced by one's class membership).

I suggested that these interacted in a multi-causal way to produce a pattern in which both the privileged and subordinated classes alike tended to be deceived by the "appearances" of capitalism, but that the subordinated classes had a vested interest in seeing through them as well as a differential experience with partially demystifying effects. However, they were handicapped in this cognitive awakening by the cognitive influence of the dominant classes, who had a vested interest in remaining at the level of appearance, a class-privileged experience that reinforced rather than undercut social illusions, and differential power in propagating their worldview. In Gramsci's (1971, 333) famous conclusion, working-class consciousness would thus not be "false" but "contradictory." It would reflect the conflicting cognitive influences, at both the doxastic and the conceptual/theoretical levels, of the workers' own experiences on the one hand, and ruling-class hegemony in the form of crucial assumptions and constraining conceptual framings on the other.

As this brief gloss indicates, many of these concepts can indeed be transferred and many of these moves emulated – perhaps, in fact, with greater plausibility than in the Marxist original – for non-class social groups, especially those, such as genders and races, central to the social structure. Far from being part of Rawlsian "cooperative ventures for mutual advantage," these groups, call them G ("non-voluntary social groups" in Ann Cudd's [2006] terminology), will be hierarchically arranged in relations of domination and subordination. Abstracting away for simplicity's sake from issues of intersectionality and intra-group heterogeneity, then, for any particular pair, the $G1s$ are structurally dominant over the subordinated $G2s$, socio-politically, economically, and, in particular time periods, juridically. But for our purposes, the crucial issue is that this domination is also manifest *cognitively*, in belief systems, conceptual frameworks, and normative assumptions. *G1* ideology is pervasive and justifies or obfuscates (in different ways at different times) *G1* domination. The *G2s* are cognitively influenced by *G1* ideology, so that even though there is resistance and attempts at counter-hegemonic ideation, many or most *G2s* are to a significant extent (again, historically- and group-variant) under its sway. Moreover, because of their social subordination, many *G2s* are likely to have less access to the tools of intellectual development, and may internalize the *G1* view of them as inferior cognizers. So they will be disadvantaged in developing oppositional views. If we distinguish material benefit (the chance at opportunities, status, and wealth) from epistemic benefit (the chance at getting it right, factually and morally), we could say that the *G1s* are generally materially advantaged while in crucial respects (at least in regards to seeing the social truth) epistemically handicapped, while the *G2s* are generally materially handicapped while in crucial respects (at least in regards to seeing the social truth) epistemically advantaged (though this, as standpoint theorists emphasize, is a matter of the *potential* insight afforded from their social location, given the obstacles just cited).[1]

If it can be made convincing, then, such a picture of oppressive societies will obviously have multiple implications for patterns of social cognition and the corresponding norms of epistemic justice we will need to devise to overcome this deep structural biasing. Dominant ideologies of a patriarchal and white supremacist form can be linked not just to the group interests of men and whites, and their respective differential power over the ideational apparatuses of society, but to patriarchy and white supremacy as social systems and the "appearances" (obviously we need a different vocabulary) they generate as matrices of social cognition. That is, one moves (experientially, phenomenologically) in a "male" or "white" world constituted not merely by one's peculiar identity-based social trajectory, but also one's processing (via socialization) of empirical inputs through a conceptual and affective grid that so transforms them as to reinforce rather than challenge dominant framings and narratives. Given our current more conscientious awareness of the need to take different identities into account, all kinds of "intersectionality" issues need to be worked out here, not to mention a necessary updating of Marx's archaic language and an operationalization of his vague metaphors in the light of current research in cognitive psychology, concept formation, etc. But I hope it is nonetheless evident that some useful insights can indeed be gained by bringing ideology theory into the conversation.

## 2. Racism as an ideology

So let us investigate some of these implications. I will use racism and racial domination as my examples, both because race is under-discussed in the literature and because, over several articles, Tommie Shelby (2002, 2003, 2014) has provided one of the most detailed analytical philosophical reconstructions ever of ideology and of racism as an ideology.

Shelby works with the concept of belief-sets as *forms of social consciousness*, an epistemically neutral concept that allows for both ideological and non-ideological versions. (So being a form of consciousness is a necessary, but not sufficient, condition for being ideological.) Four features characterize forms of consciousness: (i) the beliefs are widely shared (as against limited to a few); (ii) they form a seemingly coherent descriptive and/or normative system (in networks of apparent explanatory or justificatory power); (iii) they shape group outlooks (e.g., as part of "common sense"); and (iv) they significantly impact social action, interaction, and institutions, constituting part of our "life-world."

So forms of consciousness as such are not intrinsically problematic and in fact are obviously necessary for us to navigate the world. Ideological forms of consciousness, however – the epistemically negative subset – are marked by (i) epistemic deficiencies of various kinds, for example false factual or normative claims, or tendentious framings and theoretical misrepresentations even when true claims are involved; (ii) problematic origins, that is belief-formation and norm-uptake by the epistemic agent for bad reasons; and (iii) functionality for the establishment (when not yet existing), or reinforcement (when already existing), of systems of social oppression, via the epistemically deficient aspect of these forms of consciousness. (Epistemically respectable sets of beliefs can also serve the interests of privileged groups, so the role of this feature needs to be specified to avoid committing a version of the genetic fallacy.)

Ideologies thus serve to justify, rationalize, legitimize, and/or obfuscate wrongful social domination. And what makes this account a *materialist* one is the crucial explanatory role played in the genesis and reproduction of these ideologies by group power and group interests within socio-economic structures and conditions. Vested group interests provide a causal explanation for the endurance of ideologies even when the evidence clearly refutes them.

Shelby then demonstrates how racist ideology fits this characterization very readily. During slavery, anti-black racist ideology justified treating blacks differently because they were not equal individuals worthy of white respect; in the post-Emancipation period, anti-miscegenation taboos justified "separate but equal"; today, racial profiling reinforces stereotypes of blacks as differentially prone to crime and needing societal surveillance. Shelby points out that ideologies work in different ways, through moral legitimation (depicting existing power relations as just), social reification (representing as natural what is actually the product of social causality), and metaphysical mystification (resorting to supernatural explanations of subordination). Thus if blacks are inferior, they do not deserve the same opportunities as whites; if blacks have a racial essence that limits their capabilities, remedial social policy past a certain point will be fruitless; if blacks are doomed by Noah's curse on Ham, empirically this-worldly argumentation about their situation is pointless.

Finally, note that this account is not a conspiracy theory, since the agents of such ideologies will generally accept these illusions themselves (so they are not consciously promoting false beliefs). In the case of racism, for example, there is no reason to believe that most racist theorists were not quite sincere in their racist assumptions. The bottom line is that a critique of ideologies that does not address their material roots in oppressive social structures will ultimately fail. Ideologies are illusions, but illusions whose power and resistance to elimination are based in material conditions.

## 3. Racist ideology and epistemic injustice

Against this background, let us now turn to the question of how bringing ideology into the debate on epistemic injustice might contribute to the conversation, using racist ideology as our specific example.

Fricker's (2007) book differentiated two main varieties of epistemic injustice, testimonial and hermeneutical, and spent most time focusing on the former (hermeneutical injustice only gets the final chapter). Dominant-group ideologies typically derogate the cognitive capacities of the subordinated, as racism certainly did, but I think it is the understanding of hermeneutical injustice that could most benefit from engagement with the ideology literature. Fricker characterizes hermeneutical injustice as follows: "the injustice of having some significant area of one's social experience obscured from collective understanding owing to a structural identity prejudice in the collective hermeneutical resources" (155; italics removed). Her key illustrative example is the naming of the concept of "sexual harassment," as a result of which women subjected to this experience were now better equipped to identify what was happening to them and protest it: "extant collective hermeneutical resources can have a lacuna where the name of a distinctive social experience should be" (150–1).

Consider now some implications for this issue of the foregoing analysis of ideology. We can readily see how ideology as an epistemically deficient form of consciousness serving to reproduce group domination fits here. Sexist ideology provides a descriptive and normative worldview in which male access to women is legitimized, so that any contrary framing is to be resisted. Yet at the same time, one wonders whether "collective hermeneutical resources" best characterizes the cognitive situation, or whether it concedes too much to the Rawlsian idea of society as a "cooperative venture for mutual advantage." If one is taking the competing non-ideal, group domination picture of society as one's starting-point, then conflictual and adversarial relations, whether open or submerged, are *central* to the social order, thereby shaping the doxastic and hermeneutical. It will generally be the case, then, that such "lacunae" are integral to the ideology of domination, functional for the reproduction of the existing order. It is not a matter of an innocent misunderstanding or gap, but of a misrepresentation generated organically, materially, from the male perspective on the world, motivated by their group interests and phenomenologically supported by their group experience. And depending on how pivotal this misrepresentation or non-representation is to the preservation of the status quo, its reformist naming or renaming will be vigorously resisted by the system's male beneficiaries. So in assessing the likelihood of a cooperative pooling of "collective hermeneutical resources," we will need to take into account the group interests at stake, and how the *G1s* will respond to the putting into jeopardy of their group domination.

Relatedly, in the case of at least some systems of domination, the *G1s* can be argued to bear some collective responsibility for the prevalence of *G1* ideology. Marx seems to suggest that capitalism is intrinsically opaque, even if "bourgeois" ideology contributes to reinforcing this opacity. But can the same be said about male or racial domination? While causal responsibility for sexist and racist ideology should not be voluntarized, reduced to the ill-will or deliberate misperception of individual male and white *G1* members, collective responsibility surely cannot be altogether denied here. In one sense, Fricker (159) is of course correct to write, "In contrast, however, to the case of testimonial injustice, hermeneutical injustice, whether incidental or systematic, involves no culprit. No agent *perpetrates* hermeneutical injustice – it is a purely structural notion." But structures are created by humans and maintained through human actions and inactions. In ill-ordered societies, where these structures privilege some groups at the expense of others, some moral responsibility must be seen as falling on the beneficiaries of injustice, even if teasing out individual from collective guilt is very difficult. The growing body of literature on the subject of group moral complicity usually focuses on wrongful material benefit – think, for example, of the large body of work in critical race theory on "white privilege." But a case can be made for extrapolating these arguments to wrongful *cognitive* benefit also, involving both testimonial and hermeneutical injustice.

In the case of white racial domination/white supremacy, for example, one has extra believability not merely *as* a white person but because one is operating within a framework of cognitive interactions that is *itself* shaped in tendentious ways by an overarching hermeneutic of "whiteness" (Dyer 1997). Thus sociologist Joe Feagin (2010) speaks of "the white racial frame," an interpretive prism whose conceptual deficiencies and biased refractions are not at all contingent but an artifact of white racist ideology. "Whiteness" and "Eurocentrism" – ideological "forms of consciousness" – constitute a pervasive worldview generated and maintained over several hundred years of European domination, and embedded in the social structure. So one virtue of putting the social epistemology discussions into dialogue with an ideology framework is that it brings out more clearly that in at least some instances of group domination it will not be so easy to conceptually separate testimonial and hermeneutical injustice, since a case can sometimes be made that the hermeneutical problems come from the collective "testimony" of the *G1s*. As

Fricker (2016) herself points out in a recent article, in such instances of "hermeneutical marginalization," "we see how closely the two kinds of epistemic injustice are related" (164), since "the concepts and meanings that are shared by all are bound to reflect, in the broad view, the perspectives and experiences of those groups with more social power generally . . . [who] are very likely to be over-contributors to the shared hermeneutical resource" (166).

In *The Eighteenth Brumaire of Louis Bonaparte*, for example, Marx (Marx and Engels 1979, 128) writes that: "Upon the different forms of property, upon the social conditions of existence, rises an entire superstructure of different and distinctly formed sentiments, illusions, modes of thought and views of life. The entire class creates and forms them out of its material foundations and out of the corresponding social relations." Thus one would speak – in a vocabulary now antiquarian – of a *bourgeois* perspective on social reality. It is not a matter of deliberate misrepresentation (for the doxastic) or deliberately engineered conceptual bias (for the hermeneutical). Rather, it is a matter of *the world seeming that way* from the perspective of the G1s, and this perspective then being imposed on the G2s. And just as it would seem odd to speak of bringing together in a collective enterprise to fill lacunae and remedy distortions a "bourgeois" and a Marxist perspective, considering their polar opposition, so we would not expect to be able to integrate a white-supremacist and a racially egalitarian perspective. Rather, it is a matter of rejecting one and accepting the other.

Relatedly, another implication an ideology framework has for current debates is the potential for counter-hegemonic G2 thought. In the critical dialogue stimulated by Fricker's (2007) book, various philosophers (Mason 2011; Medina 2012; Pohlhaus, Jr. 2012) expressed concern that Fricker's original formulation seemed to underestimate the possibilities for hermeneutical resistance. Thus José Medina (2012) would offer a book-length exploration of what he called "the epistemology of resistance." The danger of generalizing from the case of (white) women (the sexual harassment example) is that one may lose sight of the greater possibilities for developing oppositional ideas in other populations who are differently, and in a sense more favorably (at least epistemically), located in the social order. Gaile Pohlhaus, Jr. (2012, 724) emphasizes the importance of not ignoring the cases of geographically segregated racial groups and social classes and points out that "[M]arginally situated knowers [may] actively resist epistemic domination through interaction with other resistant knowers" (716), thereby constituting themselves as an oppositional epistemic community capable of generating counter-hegemonic cognitions.

In her more recent response, Fricker (2016, 164–7) has suggested that while her book did distinguish between different varieties of hermeneutical injustice, "maximal" and "minimal," the category of "midway cases of hermeneutical injustice" could, she now agrees, have been "centre-staged" more. In these (midway) cases of "relatively powerless" marginalized groups, "in-group intelligibility is doing just fine" (167), operating "perfectly functioning and sophisticated sets of interpretive practices" (165). The real problem here is "frustratingly failed attempts to communicate them" (167) to the socially powerful. This diagnosis is particularly pertinent, I would contend, in the case of race.

Marx's hope – if generally unrealized – was that the proletarian experience of factory work and unionization would lead to a class consciousness that would eventually become revolutionary. But in the case of race, the greater intensity and greater transparency of white group subordination of blacks meant that black oppositional ideation (with its nascently alternative belief-systems, conceptual frameworks, and normative challenges) was far more easily cultivated. During slavery and into the post-bellum period, whites were, of course, constantly watchful about what slaves and later the freedmen were up to. But precisely because whites generally shunned rather than seeking to integrate with black communities, it did mean that there were far greater possibilities after Emancipation for developing a collective counter-hegemonic worldview than in the circumstances of white women largely isolated in individual households under the patriarchal male gaze, or white workers for whom race generally trumped class. At the end of the day, blacks are returning to *black* households. And in the days, when not working in Jim-Crowed jobs, they are going to black churches and black barbershops and black colleges and black organizational meetings, because though whites want to keep them under control, they emphatically do not want to mix with them. A black alternative public sphere was in existence even before the Civil War and would come into its own in the late nineteenth century onward. Not only would a thriving black press be established – a history of *The Defender* (Michaeli 2016), the most famous of all African American newspapers, has just been published – but various Negro scholarly journals (as they were then called) would be founded to contest the misrepresentations of the mainstream white academy.

In the opening essay of his most celebrated book, the 1903 *Souls of Black Folk*, W.E.B. Du Bois captures the cognitive situation through the doubly-signifying metaphor of the veil. On the one hand, he discovers as a child that blacks are cognitively "shut out from their [whites'] world by a vast veil." Black Americans are not seen as equal human beings but as "a problem." But Du Bois has "no desire to tear down that veil, to creep through." Rather, he "held all beyond it in common contempt" (44), knowing that entering this white cognitive world would only mean remaining permanently in a state of "double-consciousness": "[Such a world] yields him no true self-consciousness, but only lets him see himself through the revelation of the other world . . . looking at one's self through the eyes of [white] others . . . measuring one's soul by the tape of a world that looks on in amused contempt and pity." (45)

This, then, is a very different case from a hermeneutical gap or lacuna in the "collective" epistemic resources of a "community." Rather, it is a white-supremacist vision, a racist optic that must be resisted in its framing doxastic and conceptual perspective on reality. Du Bois inverts the metaphor of the veil so as to positively valorize, so to speak, the *meta-perspective* of blacks seeing whites seeing whitely, and gaining a corresponding cognitive insight into their vision: "[T]he Negro is a sort of seventh son, born with a veil, and gifted with second-sight in this American world" (45). And this second sight – not spontaneously, to be sure, but through conceptual labor, and in company with others – will eventually enable blacks to *see through* the white distortions and illusions constituted by the white veil.[2] So the idea of common epistemic resources would in this case understate the adversarial dynamic and conflicting group interests involved, and obscure the fact that the subordinate black worldview (proposing much more than a simple conceptual supplementation) cannot simply be brought additively into relation with the ideology of white domination, since it is in fundamental opposition to it.

Correspondingly, under the non-ideal circumstances of systemic group domination, the *G1s* are not generally going to be receptive to such challenges, since of course what is at stake is the legitimacy of the system itself. In another oft-quoted Du Bois passage from decades later, this one in his autobiographical *Dusk of Dawn* (2007), he modifies Plato's Cave – the most renowned image of cognitive imprisonment in the Western philosophical tradition – to illustrate the non-responsiveness of whites to black protests about the experience of "caste segregation":

> It is as though one, looking out from a dark cave . . . sees the world passing and speaks to it; speaks courteously and persuasively, showing them how these entombed souls are hindered in their natural movement, expression, and development; and how their loosening from prison would be a matter not simply of courtesy, sympathy, and help to them, but aid to all the world. One talks on evenly and logically in this way, but notices that the passing throng does not even turn its head, or if it does, glances curiously and

walks on. It gradually penetrates the minds of the prisoners that the people passing do not hear; that some thick sheet of invisible but horribly tangible plate glass is between them and the world. . . . [The passing white world] either do not hear at all, or hear but dimly, and even what they hear, they do not understand.

(66)

Note how differently Du Bois frames his own account of "epistemic injustice." Those in the darkness of the cave *already* know the social truth, viz. that they are living in an unjust society of white supremacy, and that its founding principle (nonwhite inferiority) is false. They do not need to be illuminated, nor are there hermeneutical gaps in their cognitive apparatus and mappings of the world. The cognitive problems are on the other side – the heedless whites who, walking in the bright sunlight, exist in a cognitive darkness, a white ignorance (Mills 2007).

I suggest that this scenario is more typical of the epistemic injustice involved in situations of racial domination. The racially subordinated – victims, after all, of genocide, expropriation, and slavery! – are often quite well able to recognize their situation. It is not (or not always) that the imprisoned lack the concepts, the hermeneutical resources, to understand their situation, but that the *privileged* lack the concepts and find them incredible or even incomprehensible, because of their incongruity with white-supremacist ideology. Even if they were to "hear" what blacks were saying, they still would not be able to "hear" them because of the conceptual incoherence of the black framework of assumptions with their own dominant framework. Whites are imprisoned (reversing the metaphor) in a cognitive state which both protects them from dealing with the realities of social oppression and, of course, disables them epistemically. As Pohlhaus, Jr. (2012, 725–6) suggests, in commenting on Fricker's analysis of *To Kill a Mockingbird*:

> [I]t is more complicated than just not believing someone when one ought due to identity prejudice. . . . This difficulty in the transfer of knowledge is not just because the jury won't believe him, but because the members of the jury are using epistemic resources that do not allow for the intelligibility of what Robinson [the black defendant] has to say. . . . The jury commits an epistemic injustice in this scene because it has not, does not, and will not enter into a relation of true epistemic interdependence with Robinson.

As earlier emphasized, following Shelby, if we expand the scope of "ideology" to include "forms of consciousness" and not just formalized intellectual systems, then we get a broader notion which is more useful in tracking deficient cognition since it includes affect, sensibility, ingrained patterns of response, racialized perceptions and operationalizations of putatively abstract concepts, and so forth. "Whiteness" (as internalized white superiority) becomes a particular way of being in the world – whiteness as a form of life and understanding (Dyer 1997). And it then means that the resistance to seeing or hearing the black cave dwellers (those who are in the social darkness but the epistemic light) is far greater because their claim poses an ontological threat. One could not continue to be "white" in this way if one were to accept what is being said, but would have to reshape one's life and existence in the light of this new understanding. Not just the material racial interests at stake, then, or the incongruity of blacks' claims with the white narrative, but also the vertiginous threat to one's very sense of reality, one's lived white experience of the world – these factors all cumulatively militate against the uptake of knowledge from such a source.

A third version of the Cave, Kristie Dotson's (2014), illustrates the obstacles involved. Dotson imagines, within the iconography of the cave metaphor, three varieties of epistemic exclusion, the first two (in ascending order of difficulty of overcoming) being "reducible" (capable of being addressed by using epistemic resources within the system), the third being "irreducible" (needing resources from outside the system):

> The third kind of epistemic exclusion, a third-order exclusion is a compromise to epistemic agency caused by *inadequate* dominant, shared epistemic resources. . . . This kind of epistemic exclusion is different than first- or second-order exclusion. . . . Third-order epistemic exclusion proceeds from the "outside" of a set of epistemic resources to throw large portions of one's epistemological system into question as a result of the goals of a given inquiry. . . . This kind of recognition, which can be seen as akin to a broad recognition of one's "cultural traditions systems," is extraordinarily difficult.
>
> *(129, 131)*

I suggest that this picture captures very well the epistemic situation of whites socialized into a white "cultural traditions system" with overt or tacit racist assumptions. The feat of cognitive estrangement required for them to liberate themselves, to see themselves and these "forms of consciousness" from outside, will thus be very demanding indeed. They will have to draw on the denied and/or stigmatized "third-order" resources of the oppositional traditions of people of color who have, for their own sanity and survival, been forced both to understand this worldview and to develop the "second sight" to see through it. And just as the injustice of the society is far more pervasive than local wrongdoings, so the epistemic injustice infecting the cognitive realm is, in a sense, global.

Since I began by referencing the 1960s–70s challenge to the academy by the left theorists of the time, I want to close by looking at how the "epistemic exclusions" of white-supremacist ideology have shaped mainstream ("white") thought in the disciplines themselves, problematizing their identity as neutral "collective hermeneutic resources." Consider the general category of the sociopolitical, both nationally and internationally, and the disciplines that study it: sociology, political theory (whether as a section of political science or as political philosophy), and international relations. If the analysis of the black cave-dwellers is correct, white racial domination has in modernity been central to U.S. social structure, U.S. political dynamics, and U.S. relations to the rest of the world. Once this would have been admitted, and positively valorized (i.e., white racial domination is a good thing, or does not count as "domination" because it is rule over natural inferiors). But in the postwar period, of course, especially in the post-civil rights epoch, this could no longer be acknowledged. What one would expect, then, is fanciful histories in all three of these subjects, which whitewash both the racial past and their own racial past, and construct alternative genealogies of modernity and their own disciplinary evolution that erase the shaping role of race on both.

And this is in fact – *mirabile dictu* – exactly what one finds. Moreover, the recognition of Du Bois' pioneering work in all three areas has been central to the new revisionist literature exposing this whitewashing. Aldon Morris's (2015) book on Du Bois, *The Scholar Denied*, makes the strongest case yet for the longstanding black American claim that he rather than Robert Park should be seen as the father of American sociology, and that, at a time when Park and mainstream sociology were still operating with overt or tacit social Darwinist assumptions, the "Atlanta School" created a social science on the assumption of racial equality rather than racial hierarchy. Similarly, Robert Vitalis' *White World Order, Black Power Politics* (2015) has recovered the role of the "Howard School" of international relations (IR), which indicted a white supremacy that was not merely national but global, in keeping with Du Bois's vision (1969, xi) of a global "color line." International Relations was originally predicated on the imperative of maintaining global white domination – the journal we now know as *Foreign Affairs* was originally titled the *Journal of Race Development*. Whites saw themselves as ruling a world of colored races and were preoccupied with staving off the danger of a global race war. But of course in the postwar, post-colonial period, such a past became too embarrassing to be avowed – hence the need for a disciplinary purging and self-reinvention. Finally, work on Du Bois's political thought by various theorists – Robert Gooding-Williams (2009), Lawrie Balfour (2011), and others – is beginning to establish "Afro-Modern Political Thought" as a respectable category, whose foundational assumptions are the recognition of white supremacy and the struggle against it *as* political, and the rejection of what has come to be called the "anomaly" view of American racism (Smith 1997).

The point, then, is that in all three cases, it is the black perspective on social reality that has been vindicated, or that is well on its way to being vindicated, contesting its erasure by the white mainstream, whether in sociology (the Atlanta School is barely acknowledged), in IR (the Howard School has been so thoroughly "disappeared" that even Vitalis was shocked to discover its existence), or in political theory and political philosophy (where, whether in Alexis de Tocqueville, Gunnar Myrdal, and Louis Hartz, or in Rawls and Rawlsianism, race is either confined to the status of an anomaly in U.S. political culture or denied recognition as an appropriate subject for the remit of social justice).

I suggest that it is in examples like these that we have the most profound variety of epistemic injustice, since it is here that we have the formal disciplinary study and erasure of the racial realities of the United States. But by the same token, it is difficult to recast these disciplines because of the implications of such a recasting for the legitimization of the existing racial order. Social injustice and epistemic injustice thus remain deeply intertwined. Bringing the concept of ideology back to the center of our theoretical attention can help us to understand this deep connection, and, one hopes, show us the way to overcome both.

**Related chapters**: 11, 12, 13, 17, 24, 34, 37

## Notes

1 Most of this paragraph comes from Mills (2013, 38–9).
2 For a detailed analysis of this famous text, see Gooding-Williams (2009).

## References

Althusser, Louis. 2001 [1971]. *Lenin and Philosophy, and Other Essays*. Trans. Ben Brewster. New York: Monthly Review Press.
Balfour, Lawrie. 2011. *Democracy's Reconstruction: Thinking Politically with W.E.B. Du Bois*. New York: Oxford University Press.
Coole, Diana, and Samantha Frost, eds. 2010. *New Materialisms: Ontology, Agency, and Politics*. Durham, NC: Duke University Press.
Cudd, Ann E. 2006. *Analyzing Oppression*. New York: Oxford University Press.
Dotson, Kristie. 2014. "Conceptualizing Epistemic Oppression." *Social Epistemology* 28/2: 115–38.
Du Bois, W.E.B. 1969 [1903]. *The Souls of Black Folk*. New York: Signet Classic/New American Library.
Du Bois, W.E.B. 2007 [1940]. *Dusk of Dawn: An Essay toward an Autobiography of a Race Concept*. New York: Oxford University Press.
Dyer, Richard. 1997. *White*. New York: Routledge.
Feagin, Joe R. 2010. *The White Racial Frame: Centuries of Racial Framing and Counter-Framing*. New York: Routledge.
Fricker, Miranda. 2007. *Epistemic Injustice: Power and the Ethics of Knowing*. New York: Oxford University Press.

Fricker, Miranda. 2016. "Epistemic Injustice and the Preservation of Ignorance." In Rik Peels and Martijn Blaauw, eds., *The Epistemic Dimensions of Ignorance*. New York: Cambridge University Press.

Gooding-Williams, Robert. 2009. *In the Shadow of Du Bois: Afro-Modern Political Thought in America*. Cambridge, MA: Harvard University Press.

Gramsci, Antonio. 1971. *Selections from the Prison Notebooks*. Ed. and trans. Quintin Hoare and Geoffrey Nowell Smith. New York: International Publishers.

Held, David. 1980. *Introduction to Critical Theory: Horkheimer to Habermas*. Berkeley: University of California Press.

Lukács, Georg. 1971. *History and Class Consciousness*. Trans. Rodney Livingstone. Cambridge, MA: MIT Press.

Marx, Karl, and Frederick Engels. 1979. *Collected Works*. Vol. 11. New York: International Publishers.

Mason, Rebecca. 2011. "Two Kinds of Unknowing." *Hypatia* 26/2: 294–307.

Medina, José. 2012. *The Epistemology of Resistance: Gender and Racial Oppression, Epistemic Injustice, and Resistant Imaginations*. New York: Oxford University Press.

Michaeli, Ethan. 2016. *The Defender: How the Legendary Black Newspaper Changed America*. Boston: Houghton Mifflin Harcourt.

Mills, Charles W. 2007. "White Ignorance." In Shannon Sullivan and Nancy Tuana, eds., *Race and Epistemologies of Ignorance*. Albany, NY: SUNY Press.

Mills, Charles W. 2010 [1989]. "Determination and Consciousness in Marx." In Charles W. Mills, *Radical Theory, Caribbean Reality: Race, Class and Social Domination*. Mona, Kingston, Jamaica: University of the West Indies Press.

Mills, Charles W. 2013. "White Ignorance and Hermeneutical Injustice: A Comment on Medina and Fricker." *Social Epistemology Review and Reply Collective* 3/1: 38–43.

Morris, Aldon D. 2015. *The Scholar Denied: W.E.B. Du Bois and the Birth of Modern Sociology*. Oakland, CA: University of California Press.

Ollman, Bertell, and Edward Vernoff, eds. 1982. *The Left Academy: Marxist Scholarship on American Campuses*. New York: McGraw-Hill.

Pohlhaus, Jr., Gaile. 2012. "Relational Knowing and Epistemic Injustice: Toward a Theory of *Willful Hermeneutical Ignorance*." *Hypatia* 27/4: 715–35.

Rawls, John. 1999. *A Theory of Justice*. Rev. ed. Cambridge, MA: Harvard University Press.

Ruben, David-Hillel. 1979. *Marxism and Materialism: A Study in Marxist Theory of Knowledge*. Rev. ed. Atlantic Highlands, NJ: Humanities Press.

Shelby, Tommie. 2002. "Is Racism in the 'Heart'?" *Journal of Social Philosophy* 33/3: 411–20.

Shelby, Tommie. 2003. "Ideology, Racism, and Critical Social Theory." *The Philosophical Forum* 34/2: 153–88.

Shelby, Tommie. 2014. "Racism, Moralism, and Social Criticism." *Du Bois Review: Social Science Research on Race* 11/1: 54–74.

Smith, Rogers M. 1997. *Civic Ideals: Conflicting Visions of Citizenship in U.S. History*. New Haven, CT: Yale University Press.

Vitalis, Robert. 2015. *White World Order, Black Power Politics: The Birth of American International Relations*. Ithaca, NY: Cornell University Press.

# PART 2

# Liberatory epistemologies and axes of oppression

# 10
# INTERSECTIONALITY AND EPISTEMIC INJUSTICE

### *Patricia Hill Collins*

Intersectionality constitutes a provocative site for examining how ideas are taken up by different sets of social actors, but also how resistant knowledges change as they navigate heterogeneous social contexts. As a knowledge project, intersectionality repeatedly crosses an important political, social and epistemological border: its social actors are distributed within both social movement settings and academic venues. This border-crossing is not unidirectional – either from social movements into the academy or vice versa – and placement within these overlapping and often contentious fields of power means that intersectionality is always under construction. Neither inherently beneficial nor harmful, travelling across academic borders generates new opportunities and constraints (Carbado 2013). Yet increasingly, academics and activists have expressed reservations about the ways in which intersectionality has changed, specifically, the deterioration of the emancipatory possibilities of Black feminism and intersectionality within the academy (Alexander-Floyd 2012), and the academic misrecognition and misappropriation of intersectionality (Mohanty 2013).

No agreed-upon definition currently characterizes intersectionality, yet a general consensus exists about its general contours. The term *intersectionality* references the critical insight that race, class, gender, sexuality, ethnicity, nation, ability and age operate not as unitary, mutually exclusive entities, but rather as reciprocally constructing phenomena that in turn shape complex social inequalities (Collins 2015). In prior work, I have examined the contours of intersectionality as a form of critical inquiry and praxis (Collins and Bilge 2016, 31–63); analyzed intersectionality's ideas core within scholarly research (Collins and Chepp 2013); provided an overview of how social actors in human rights, social media, social movements and similar non-academic settings use intersectionality (Collins and Bilge 2016, 88–114, 136–159); and compared how conceptions of intersectionality differ in social movement and academic settings (Collins 2015). In this essay, I explore one component of this larger venture by examining how intersectionality's travels into academia shed light on two different forms of epistemic injustice: (1) the epistemic injustices that intersectional approaches are responding to, diagnosing, and offering critical tools to address and fight, and (2) the epistemic injustices that are committed within the academy against scholar-activists who claim intersectionality.

## Crossing epistemic borders: intersectionality and Black feminism

Contemporary narratives routinely identify Kimberlé Crenshaw's 'Mapping the Margins: Intersectionality, Identity Politics, and Violence against Women of Color' as an important point of origin for intersectionality (Crenshaw 1991). Yet Crenshaw's 1991 article also highlights a significant juncture where the fluid borders that distinguished the epistemic communities of social activists and academics in the 1980s solidified and became increasingly difficult to traverse. As Crenshaw's analysis reminds us, the term *intersectionality* emerged in this border space between Black feminism and similar social movements and a desegregating of colleges and universities that incorporated African Americans, Latinos/as, women and other historically excluded groups. The term intersectionality seemingly captured the border crossing of the times. Yet Crenshaw's positioning of intersectionality in an ever-changing border zone of social activism and academic politics has been overshadowed by the increasingly common practice of situating intersectionality's origins *within* academia. Crenshaw's name is appropriated and circulated as a decontextualized brand for intersectionality, one invoked by oft-repeated statements that Crenshaw 'coined' the term intersectionality. The overreliance on a 'coining' metaphor belies the importance of intersectionality before its academic discovery and assigns value to intersectionality when it became an academic commodity.

Crenshaw's work constitutes neither an end point nor a point of origin for intersectionality, but rather an important turning point in intersectionality's engagement with social action within academic settings. Intersectionality was changed by its entrance into academic epistemic communities, primarily its engagement with practices of epistemic injustice. Moreover, African American women and similarly situated subjects encountered strategies of epistemic injustice that questioned their authority as knowers.

## Black feminism, social justice and political activism: social movement frameworks

Examining the treatment of social justice within mid-twentieth century Black feminism in social movement settings sheds light on this turning point for intersectionality and its engagement with epistemic injustice. Despite African American women's heterogeneous understandings of Black feminism, the idea of social justice was paramount. Toni Cade Bambara's groundbreaking edited volume, *The Black Woman*, illustrates how African American women conceptualized social justice from different points of view (Bambara 1970). Building on this foundation, in 1982, the Combahee River Collective's 'A Black Feminist Statement' laid out a more comprehensive statement of the framework that had permeated Black feminist politics (Combahee-River-Collective 1995 [1977]). This innovative document argued that race-only or gender-only frameworks advanced partial and incomplete analyses of the social injustices that characterize African American women's lives, and that race, gender, social class and sexuality all shaped Black women's experiences. The Statement proposed that what had been treated as separate systems of oppression were interconnected. Because racism, class exploitation, patriarchy and homophobia collectively shaped Black women's experiences, Black women's liberation required a comprehensive response to multiple systems of oppression. The Statement also developed a comprehensive argument about the necessity of identity politics for Black women's empowerment (Collins and Bilge 2016, 67–71).

Works such as *The Black Woman* and the CRC Statement foreshadowed important ideas within intersectional knowledge projects, namely, the interconnections among truth, ethics and politics. What sense would it make for Black women to understand the truth of their lives without social justice as an ethical touchstone for action and political action to foster social justice in their lives?

Moreover, because social justice was intricately linked to epistemic justice, testifying on one's own behalf within Black feminism not only produced new knowledge from Black women's standpoint, but this exercise of epistemic agency challenged prevailing practices of epistemic injustice.

During the 1980s, Black women, many of whom were political activists, obtained academic positions and brought ideas from Black feminist politics with them (Collins 2000). Joining other social actors with similar social, political and epistemological aspirations, these social actors established an array of interdisciplinary fields with social justice at their core (Parker and Samantrai 2010). This context catalyzed a nascent race/class/gender studies with a dual epistemological focus – responding to academic norms about what constituted credible scholarship and who was authorized to do it, and responding to the patterns of similarities and differences of heterogeneous social justice projects concerning race, class, gender and sexuality (Dill 2009).

Scholar-activists within race/class/gender projects in the academy found themselves explaining and often defending three taken-for-granted assumptions from social movement settings. First, a commitment to *social justice* constituted a foundational premise of race/class/gender studies that needed neither justification nor explanation. Social justice could not be imagined as a thing, but rather constituted an essential ethical goal to which individuals could commit in the here and now in working toward a better future. Second, understanding and reducing social inequality constituted a core objective of race/class/gender studies. Because social problems such as violence, hunger, illiteracy, poor health and unemployment were indicators of social inequality across individual and group difference, addressing social problems both lay at the heart of the field and served as an important site for coalitions among social actors who historically had worked in separate venues. Finally, the belief in political action to bring about social change had to be defended in academic venues. If social justice was less a finished ideological product than a process, then moving toward social justice required political action. Social problems and social inequality were the catalysts, social justice the ethical principle, and political action the action strategy.

Like similar interdisciplinary social justice projects, race/class/gender studies found itself fighting for space and legitimation within academic venues (Parker and Samantrai 2010). During this period, race/class/gender studies served as a sort of clearing house for an array of projects that brought new ideas to the field from scholar-activists working on sexuality, ethnicity, ability and citizenship. The prospects for coalitional politics among such disparate groups and projects transcended the fuzzy borders of race/class/gender studies. The term intersectionality might bring an array of scholar-activists and traditional academic actors together under one rubric.

## Institutional incorporation: intersectionality, social justice and political activism

Few dispute intersectionality's appearance as an important discourse as well as Crenshaw's significance in elevating intersectionality's visibility and importance. Initially, the crystallization of the far-flung set of ideas and actors associated with race/class/gender studies under the rubric of intersectionality showed promise. Intersectionality's claimants could move beyond open-ended yet cumbersome race/class/gender frameworks and toward greater clarity and new ideas. Moreover, because the term intersectionality seemingly addressed a certain set of intellectual and political challenges within academia in the 1990s, it survived.

The term intersectionality simultaneously created possibilities for new ways of thinking, yet homogenized the field by silencing, erasing and thereby marginalizing some perspectives. Neoliberal influences on higher education may have set the stage for intersectionality's complex border crossing, yet epistemic injustice contributed to the specific trajectories that intersectionality actually took. Social actors who crossed the borders from social movement to academic settings encountered contradictory epistemological frameworks that distinguished social activism from academic politics. In social movement settings, social actors could continue to link intersectionality with politics and to claim a social justice mandate as a core principle of intersectionality itself. Yet once inside the academy, these actors discovered that political action and taking principled positions became objectionable because they seemingly opposed norms of scholarly objectivity. Moreover, intersectionality seemed to travel more smoothly through the academy when Black women and other subordinated social actors minimized forms of knowing that empowered them in social movement settings. Ignoring intersectionality's roots in social activism, social actors eschewed direct confrontation with Black women and similar social actors but rather used indirect but effective epistemic arguments to attack the identity politics of social activism. What remained was pressure to produce a depoliticized version of intersectionality that was individualized and fragmenting. How did this happen?

## Intersectionality and epistemic injustice

Epistemology may appear to be the great equalizer within academic settings, yet placing epistemology beyond the boundaries of politics and ethics militates against seeing how hegemonic understandings of intellectual work reproduce social inequality. Once within the academy, intersectionality had to navigate contradictory epistemological frameworks. It drew from both expansive understandings of epistemology within Black feminism and race/class/gender studies that laid claim to social justice and political action, as well as storied and more proscribed academic definitions of epistemology that elevated the search for truth above ethics and politics. As Medina points out, 'a narrow conception of epistemology restricted to issues of justification of knowledge claims . . . is impotent, ineffectual, and always arrives too late' (Medina 2013, 253).

Three important dimensions of epistemic injustice shed light on intersectionality's trajectories within academia. First, when it comes to social inequality, epistemologies are not epiphenomena but rather constitute core structuring dimensions of social institutions and practices. Second, hegemonic epistemologies are not situated outside of politics, but rather are embedded within and help construct the political. Third, accomplishing social inequality relies upon strategies of epistemic injustice that collectively reproduce epistemic oppression. Collectively, these dimensions of epistemic injustice provide different lenses for analyzing why and how intersectionality changed as it travelled into the academy.

Epistemic oppression constitutes a core defining feature of intersecting systems of power, a fact made visible by intersectionality's border-crossing from epistemic communities of social activism to those defining academic norms. The construct of epistemic oppression identifies how epistemology constitutes a structuring dimension of social injustice beyond actual ideas of racism, sexism and similar ideological systems (Dotson 2014). This concept has been fertile ground for intersectional scholar-activists: Barbara Tomlinson analyzes how a dominant racial frame that denies the continuation of racism suppresses the conceptual tools for analyzing racism and contributes to a colonization of intersectionality (Tomlinson 2013a), and Vivian May examines how often deeply entrenched ways of thinking are used to critique intersectionality, even as intersectionality scholars have criticized these same tools as fostering misrepresentation, erasure and violation (May 2014). By providing the frames that shape all aspects of scholarly processes, epistemic oppression go beyond the simpl bias of any group of social actors.

Epistemic oppression relies on specific strategies that reproduce social inequality. Both explicit but more often implicit within colorblind and gender-neutral social relations of post-raciality and post-feminism, these recurring strategies of epistemic injustice discipline social actors into taken-for-granted epistemological frameworks. Intersectional scholars have questioned this disciplinary process, more recently identifying specific practices of constructing truths about intersectionality itself misrepresent and thereby restrain its radical potential (Tomlinson 2013b). Joining this literature with that of the tactics of epistemic oppression, for example, epistemic violence and how epistemic agency is quieted or smothered adds to the growing tool kit of analyzing intersectionality's current status and future prospects. This broader landscape of epistemic oppression and epistemic injustice provides new tools for understanding intersectionality.

## Epistemic violence within intersectionality: identity politics and standpoint epistemology

In a context of legal equality, discrediting Black women and similarly subordinated people as epistemic agents happens less by direct confrontation and increasingly by eroding their epistemic authority by indirectly attacking their credibility. In the 1990s, intersectionality gained legitimacy within the academy, yet its claims regarding social justice and political action remained antithetical to academic norms. Painting identity politics as an inferior form of politics and standpoint epistemology as a limited and potentially biased form of knowing illustrates this general practice of discrediting the epistemic agency of oppressed subjects. Excising these forms of epistemic agency from intersectionality enabled a more acceptable and sanitized intersectionality to emerge that was more closely aligned with academic epistemic norms.

Identity politics and standpoint epistemology constitute two important forms of authorization for people of color, women, poor people and new immigrant populations that constitute sources of epistemic authority (Collins 1998, 201–228). Identity politics claims the authority of one's own experiences and social location as a source of epistemic agency. Standpoint epistemology asserts the right to be an equal epistemic agent in interpreting one's own realities within interpretive communities. Standpoint theories claim, in different ways, that it is important to account for the social positioning of social agents. Within standpoint epistemology, the process of approximating the truth is part of a dialogical relationship among subjects who are different situated (Stoetzler and Yuval-Davis 2002, 315).

Misinterpreting the robust understanding of identity politics expressed by the Combahee River Collective, Kimberlé Crenshaw and others by recasting these ideas as essentialized and self-serving not only misreads the intent of social movement actors, it undercuts an important source of epistemic agency for oppressed groups. Crenshaw's groundbreaking article on intersectionality ironically contains an extensive, analytical examination of identity politics that takes it seriously. Crenshaw's article engages intersectionality in relation to identity politics, interrogating its strengths and limitations for social action by and behalf of women of color. Yet the discourse on identity politics that potentially empowers subordinated groups disappears within a linguistic shift from collective identity to multiple subjectivities. Individualizing identities reduces race, class, gender and sexuality to dimensions of intersecting subjectivities managed by each unique individual. This substitution shorn of historic context of racism or sexism, for example, first replaces a robust framework of identity politics with individualistic and non-structural analysis of social inequalities, then criticizes intersectionality's emphasis on identity as problematic.

This persistent erasure and misrecognition of Crenshaw's work, e.g., claiming the 'coins' yet rejecting the identity politics, constitutes epistemic violence, namely,

> a refusal, intentional or unintentional, of an audience to communicatively reciprocate a linguistic exchange owing to pernicious ignorance. Pernicious ignorance should be understood to refer to any reliable ignorance that, in a given context, harms another

person (or sets of persons). *Reliable ignorance* is ignorance that is *consistent* or follows from a predictable epistemic gap in cognitive resources.

(Dotson *2011, 238–239*)

Persistent, reliable ignorance neither occurs in a vacuum nor is it a harmless expression of free speech among scholars who agree to disagree. Dotson points out that determining whether a situation constitutes epistemic violence requires 'an analysis of power relations and other contextual factors that make the ignorance identified *in that particular circumstance or set of circumstances* harmful' (Dotson 2011, 239). The stock story of intersectionality that *ignores* the agency of Black women prior to intersectionality's naming serves the vested interests of people who are empowered by different epistemic practices. Similarly, the misreading of a collective identity politics within settings of social activism enables academics to advance a politics of individual identity that depoliticizes intersectionality by rendering its social justice politics suspect. Through bait and switch, an emphasis on individual identities severed from collective politics increasingly dominates intersectional discourse, with many of intersectionality's practitioners thinking that intersectionality is a theory of multiple identities (Collins and Bilge 2016, 114–135). In this context, the shrinking emphasis on social justice passes virtually unnoticed.

The related attacks on standpoint epistemology in the 1990s stem from similar epistemic sources yet illustrate a different path of deflection. Again, the attacks cannot be made via direct confrontation with Black women and women of color who were clearly central to intersectionality's inception because that would call the standpoints of more privileged academics into question. Instead, the criticisms of standpoint epistemology operate in the abstract terrain of epistemology itself. Such standpoints were accused of suffering from limited vision and bias, and being a compromised way of moving toward truth. Yet the purpose of standpoint epistemology was never to become a theory of truth. Rather, it valorized the role of reflective, analytical thought that was grounded in power relations. Elite academics feared being displaced by standpoints that they could not have or control. So the entire endeavor of having standpoints at all had to be discredited.

Versions of intersectionality's stock story that discredit identity politics and standpoint epistemology perform epistemological gate keeping that erases and sanitizes the radical potential of a more-unruly intersectionality and installs a more orderly, recognizable, disciplined intersectionality in its place. Within intersectionality, some scholars want to claim the legitimacy of intersectionality as a recognized scholarly perspective while leaving the subordinated people who created it behind (see, e.g., Nash 2008). In its place, they wish to install a new narrative of intersectionality that privileges academic norms of objectivity and truth. More importantly, just as tactics of violence police political and social borders between privileged and disadvantaged people, epistemic violence emerges to police the border between academics and activism. Intersectionality could not be evicted from the academy. Instead, it had to be contained and changed. Claiming the ethical position of intersectionality's ties with social justice without doing the political work to bring it about suggests that intersectionality need not do anything about social injustice, rather be seen as an icon of social justice.

## Who gets to tell intersectionality's story? Testimonial practices of quieting and smothering

Epistemic oppression suppresses the epistemic agency of some members of the group while elevating that of others, thus producing privileged and derogated categories of knowers. Within interpretive communities that express a shared commitment to social justice, all members theoretically have equitable access to testimonial recognition. They should participate equitably albeit differently in intersectionality's knowledge production and, if required, enjoy access to epistemic authority to shape intersectionality's definitions (Dotson 2012, 24). Yet this theoretical model of democratic communities of scholars based on testimonial inclusivity bears little resemblance to actual academic communities characterized by epistemic injustice. Through their epistemic practices, interpretive communities regulate and reproduce relationships of unequal epistemic agency among group members.

Because intersectionality has long been associated with social justice, if not assumed to be essentially about social justice, the question of intersectionality's contributions to epistemic oppression by its own epistemic agents becomes especially important. Intersectionality within the academy faces a conundrum: its legitimation and success privilege some epistemic agents – the case, for example, of epistemic agents who enjoy an elevated status because they reject identity politics and/or standpoint epistemology – and increasingly marginalize and subsequently silence epistemic agents within intersectionality as an interpretive community who claim these same sources of epistemic empowerment. What epistemic tools regulate these unequal power relations within intersectionality as an epistemic community? Specifically, what tactics or strategies foster the suppression of the epistemic agency of Black women, women of color and similar social actors who brought the ideas of intersectionality into the academy and fought for the institutionalization of those ideas?

Interpretive communities organized by the testimonial practices of its members socially construct intersectionality. Testimonial practices can occur through face-to-face interaction, but because interpretive communities within academia are typically imagined communities of putative equals, testimonial interactions often happen in more mediated ways. Practices such as patterns of citation, themes of journal articles, articles selected for, invitations to deliver keynote addresses and the composition of panels at academic conferences collectively shape the testimonial contours of intersectionality's interpretive community. Through these mechanisms, and not primarily through face-to-face interaction, being able to control the narrative about intersectionality enables some actors to endorse aspects of intersectionality that reinforce their own point of view while ignoring and suppressing alternative perspectives. Some actors become more authoritative to speak or testify about intersectionality because they silence others. Epistemic violence operates through practices of silencing (Dotson 2011).

Intersectionality's travels from social movement settings into academia not only reveal epistemological assumptions concerning social justice and political action, they also suggest how established testimonial relationships within the academy reproduce epistemic inequality, for example, those identifying white males as more authoritative than everyone else, and theoretical knowledge as better than practical experience. Social movements fostered an important epistemic upheaval regarding testimony concerning oppressions of race, gender, class and ethnicity. The metaphor of gaining 'voice' versus achieving visibility speaks to the connections between speech and epistemic agency. People who had been deemed objects of academic knowledge reclaimed epistemic agency in their own behalf.

In the academy, social actors who have been rendered voiceless within established patterns of epistemic oppression confront the challenge of exerting epistemic agency within intersectionality's big academic tent. Because academics are neither equal in their ability to give testimony nor do they receive testimony in the same way, speaking from the bottom takes more skill and effort than speaking from the top. Race, gender, class, ethnicity and sexuality, singularly and in varying combinations, structure social interactions, not solely in the abstract, but also by structuring the social inequalities within colleges and universities. As a result, normative and ostensibly normal epistemological practices privilege the epistemic agency of well-established social actors.

Two practices of epistemic violence illuminate how and why some aspects of intersectionality became so well-known, thus rendering other aspects virtually unknown. One consists of testimonial quieting that fundamentally ignores what less powerful epistemic agents say: 'A speaker needs an audience to identify, or at least recognize, her as a knower in order to offer testimony. This kind of testimonial oppression has long been discussed in the work of women of color' (Dotson 2011, 242). The other, testimonial smothering, occurs by 'the truncating of one's own testimony in order to insure that the testimony contains only content for which one's audience demonstrates testimonial competency' (Dotson 2011, 244). Testimonial quieting and smothering go hand in hand – those who are repeatedly told to 'be quiet' by more powerful social actors quickly learn the protections of self-censorship.

In intersectionality's case, deciding that began when Crenshaw 'coined' the term in the early 1990s simply stopped the clock. Thirty years of social movement activism was off the table, thus suppressing the epistemic agency of many Black women and making Crenshaw intersectionality's designated academic spokesperson. This is a stunning example of testimonial quieting – simply ignoring the historical record and letting it drop from sight to allow other issues to come to the forefront.

Moreover, because testimonial quieting and smothering together reinforce reliable and pernicious ignorance about intersectionality itself, it's hard to tell how many Black women, Latinas and similar social actors self-censor themselves in response to the repeated calls to 'explain' intersectionality itself. Because intersectionality is so vast, a thorough analysis of practices of coerced silencing within it awaits completion. Tactics of testimonial smothering within intersectionality can best be traced by the thematic mapping of scholarly publications that claim intersectionality in some fashion since its naming. This mapping would embed a thematic analysis within the testimonial community of intersectionality as evidenced by how this idea unfolded within journals, textbooks, conference proceedings, edited volumes and solo-authored monographs. This analysis would take note of certain stylistic practices, for example, the 'mentioning' of Crenshaw's work as an agreed upon proxy. The challenge is to shift Dotson's analysis of coerced silencing and testimonial smothering as a form of self-censorship from the level of the individual to the structural group processes of intersectionality as an interpretive community.

## An obligation to resist? Social injustice and epistemic resistance

Neither social justice nor political action have vanished from intersectionality in the academy. Despite epistemic violence and practices of quieting and smothering, many social actors both inside and outside the academy refuse to relinquish a commitment to social justice and to the political action required to bring it about. For many subordinated people, identity politics and the distinctive standpoints on social inequality that it engenders remain important tools of empowerment, especially outside the academy (see, e.g., the discussion of hip hop and intersectionality in Collins and Bilge 2016, 116–123).

Intersectionality within the academy currently has a heterogeneous testimonial community with differently empowered epistemic actors expressing various forms of agency. On the one hand, some community members interpret the waning focus on social justice and political action as a good thing, in much the same way that the shift from race, class and gender studies to the broader and seemingly more universal construct of intersectionality moved this field of inquiry away from its particularistic roots. Dominant epistemologies value decontextualized, abstract, objective and ostensibly universal knowledge, and historically fields that have proven their connections to these constructs have gained legitimacy over those that do not. Moreover, within an academy that seemingly valorizes objectivity as the antidote to bias, knowledge that seems unduly political or politicized (unless it represents the interests of those in power) is typically delegitimized. For those who strive for academic legitimation, intersectionality's ties to an ethics of social justice and a politics of action weaken it.

On the other hand, academic norms that interpret political action as biased and outside the purview of the academy make it more difficult to argue that intersectionality should examine epistemic injustice. Why worry about epistemic injustice within intersectionality's own practices if social justice is no longer central to its academic mission? Intersectionality's commitment to truth is certainly worth-while. Yet this pressure to sever truth from ethics and politics can in fact reduce intersectionality to a 'buzzword,' a discourse that is popular precisely because it can be so easily incorporated in academic norms yet with boundaries maintained by tactics of testimonial quieting and smothering dissent.

Given these contested relations, do social agents who lay claim to intersectionality from diverse social locations within the field have an obligation to resist social inequality? Medina argues that those of us who claim intersectionality are interconnected, and that we are each responsible for resisting oppression: 'those who live under conditions of oppression – however they happen to inhabit contexts of domination (as victim, as a bystander, as both victim and oppressor, etc.) – have an obligation to resist' (Medina 2013, 16). Yet because we each stand in a different relationship to intersectionality, we have an obligation to resist differently. Assuming that oppressed people bear the burden of making changes, by themselves, and that everyone else can either study the efforts of the oppressed or cheer them on from the sidelines undermines the field. Paying lip service to social justice is easy – figuring out how to do the hard political work of challenging epistemic inequality within epistemic practices requires far more diligence.

**Related chapters**: 2, 3, 8, 11, 13, 14, 15, 16, 37

# References

Alexander-Floyd, Nikol G. 2012. 'Disappearing acts: Reclaiming intersectionality in the social sciences in a post-Black Feminist Era', *Feminist Formations* 24: 1–25.
Bambara, Toni Cade, ed. 1970. *The Black Woman: An Anthology*. New York: Signet.
Carbado, Devon. 2013. 'Colorblind intersectionality', *Signs* 38: 811–845.
Collins, Patricia Hill. 1998. *Fighting Words: Black Women and the Search for Justice*. Minneapolis: University of Minnesota Press.
Collins, Patricia Hill. 2000. *Black Feminist Thought: Knowledge, Consciousness, and the Politics of Empowerment*. New York: Routledge.
Collins, Patricia Hill. 2015. 'Intersectionality's definitional dilemmas', *Annual Review of Sociology* 41: 1–20.
Collins, Patricia Hill and Sirma Bilge. 2016. *Intersectionality*. London: Polity.
Collins, Patricia Hill and Valerie Chepp. 2013. 'Intersectionality', in Georgina Waylen, Karen Celis, Johanna Kantola, and Lauren Weldon (eds.), *The Oxford Handbook of Gender and Politics* (New York: Oxford University Press), 31–61.
Combahee-River-Collective. 1995 [1977]. 'A Black Feminist Statement', in Beverly Guy-Sheftall (ed.), *Words of Fire: An Anthology of African-American Feminist Thought* (New York: The New Press), 232–240.
Crenshaw, Kimberlé Williams. 1991. 'Mapping the margins: Intersectionality, identity politics, and violence against women of color', *Stanford Law Review* 43: 1241–1299.
Dill, Bonnie Thornton. 2009. 'Intersections, Identities, and Inequalities in Higher Education', in Bonnie Thornton Dill and Ruth Enid Zambrana (eds.), *Emerging Intersections: Race, Class, and Gender in Theory, Policy, and Practice* (New Brunswick, NJ: Rutgers University Press), 229–252.
Dotson, Kristie. 2011. 'Tracking epistemic violence, tracking practices of silencing', *Hypatia* 26: 236–257.
Dotson, Kristie. 2012. 'A cautionary tale: On limiting epistemic oppression', *Frontiers* 33: 24–47.
Dotson, Kristie. 2014. 'Conceptualizing epistemic oppression', *Social Epistemology* 14: 1–23.
May, Vivian M. 2014. '"Speaking into the void": Intersectionality critiques and epistemic backlash', *Hypatia* 29: 94–112.

Medina, Jose. 2013. *The Epistemology of Resistance: Gender and Racial Oppression, Epistemic Injustice, and Resistant Imaginations*. New York: Oxford University Press.

Mohanty, Chandra Talpade. 2013. 'Transnational feminist crossings: On neoliberalism and radical critique', *Signs* 38: 967–991.

Nash, Jennifer C. 2008. 'Rethinking intersectionality', *Feminist Review* 89: 1–15.

Parker, Joe and Ranu Samantrai. 2010. 'Interdisciplinarity and Social Justice: An Introduction', in J. Parker, R. Samantrai, and M. Romero (eds.), *Interdisciplinarity and Social Justice: Revisioning Academic Accountability* (Albany, NY: State University of New York Press), 1–33.

Stoetzler, Marcel and Nira Yuval-Davis. 2002. 'Standpoint theory, situated knowledge and the situated imagination', *Feminist Theory* 3: 315–333.

Tomlinson, Barbara. 2013a. 'Colonizing intersectionality: Replicating racial hierarchy in feminist academic arguments', *Social Identities* 19: 254–272.

Tomlinson, Barbara. 2013b. 'To tell the truth and not get trapped: Desire, distance, and intersectionality at the scene of argument', *Signs* 38: 993–1017.

# 11
# FEMINIST EPISTEMOLOGY
## The subject of knowledge[1]

*Nancy Tuana*

Once upon a time scholars assumed that the knowing subject in the disciplines is transparent, disincorporated from the known and untouched by the geo-political configuration of the world in which people are racially ranked and regions are racially configured.

*(Mignolo, 2009)*

The subject of knowledge has been a central concern of feminist epistemological analyses since their inception. Early work in standpoint theory, for example, focused on the links between privilege/power and the nature and limits of knowledge. Informed by Marxian analyses of the shaping of knowledge by dominant interests, standpoint theory addressed the inextricable connections between politics and knowledge production. As early as 1983 standpoint theorist Nancy Hartsock argued that "feminist theorists must demand that feminist theorizing be grounded in women's material activity and must be part of the political struggle necessary to develop areas of social life modeled on this activity" (Hartsock, 1983, 304). Patricia Hill Collins' standpoint analysis in *Black Feminist Thought* (1990) focused on how feminist theorizing must attend to the way "social phenomena such as race, class, and gender . . . mutually construct one another" (1998, 205) rather than assume that there is a somehow neutral "women's standpoint." Standpoint theory was designed to be a method that would render transparent the values and interests, such as androcentrism, heteronormativity, and Eurocentrism, that underlie allegedly neutral methods in science and epistemology, and clarify their impact. Such attention to the subject of knowledge illuminated the various means by which oppressive practices can result in or reinforce epistemic inequalities, exclusions, and marginalizations. In this way, feminist and other liberatory epistemologists aimed to transform the subject of knowledge in the sense of *focusing on knowledge obscured by dominant interests and values* and thereby to identify and provide tools for undermining the knowledges and practices implicated in oppression. "Androcentric, economically advantaged, racist, Eurocentric, and heterosexist conceptual frameworks," Sandra Harding argues, "ensured systematic ignorance and error about not only the lives of the oppressed, but also the lives of their oppressors and thus about how nature and social relations in general worked" (2004, 5). Feminist and other liberatory epistemologies aimed not only to diagnose and contest epistemic injustices, but also to provide resources for more just epistemic practices. One of my aims in this essay is to provide a genealogy of the concept of epistemic injustice by tracing its origins in feminist and other liberatory epistemological attention to the relations between power, knowledge, and difference. This historically informed understanding provides a lens for both understanding and expanding upon later deployments of the concept of epistemic injustice as we find it developed, for example, in the work of Miranda Fricker (2007). Rather than footnoting and potentially downplaying my coupling of feminist and other forms of liberatory epistemologies in this essay, I would like to acknowledge the frequently parallel, sometimes fraught, but often interactive genealogies of feminist and other forms of liberatory epistemologies. As highlighted in the quote from Harding, gender oppression does not happen in a vacuum but is complexly linked to colonialism, racism, heterosexism, as well as class biases, Eurocentrism, androcentrism, ableism, and other manifestations of power/privilege. Feminist epistemologies emerge with awareness of and attention to these linkages, some of which I will highlight in this essay. I will drop the "other" in my use of the locution, "feminist and liberatory," for stylistic reasons, but it is essential to see the "and" coupling them as a both/and, not an either/or. These epistemologies are *liberatory* in the sense that they aim to reveal the workings of power in the governance and disciplining of knowledge practices and institutions in order to generate paths to freedom (cf. Tuana, 2001, 18).

In addition to focusing attention onto knowledge obscured by dominant interests and values, feminist and liberatory epistemologists were attentive to the subject of knowledge through a second lens, namely, *attention to what kind of subject one must be in order to be (seen as) a knowing subject*. Through this lens, questions about who counted as a knowing subject and who did not led feminist and liberatory epistemologists to examine what qualities were deemed necessary to be a knowing subject and how the social situations of groups impacted who counted as a knowing subject and who did not. Lorraine Code's "Is the Sex of the Knower Epistemically Significant?" and Sandra Harding's "Is Gender a Variable in Conceptions of Rationality: A Survey of Issues" appeared in 1981 and 1982 respectively and broached the topic of the relevance of the situation of knowers to their epistemic capacities. This is also a position developed by Donna Haraway in "Situated Knowledges" in 1988. Code's *What Can She Know?* (1991), Lynn Hankinson Nelson's *Who Knows?* (1990), and Harding's *Whose Science? Whose Knowledge?* (1991) aimed to critique and offer alternatives to traditional "S knows that p" epistemologies that posited a knowing subject as singular and unmarked in the sense of assuming that perception and cognition would be invariant. On traditional accounts, knowers were viewed as distinct but not distinctive, and subjective qualities of knowing subjects, their affective and material dimensions, were deemed irrelevant at best, contaminating at worst. In contradistinction to this view, feminist and liberatory epistemologists demonstrated the ways that a knower's situatedness affects not just *what* she or he knows, but also *how* she or he knows. Knowers, then, far from the disinterested, interchangeable subjects of knowing, are "social, embodied, interested, emotional, and rational and whose body, interests, emotions, and reason are fundamentally constituted by her particular historical context" (Jaggar and Bordo, 1989, 6).

## Who knows?

Genevieve Lloyd's classic 1979 article, "The Man of Reason", and her eponymous 1984 book brought to light the historical linkage of maleness and masculinity with conceptions of reason and rationality. Lloyd argues that the view of reason as manly was more than symbolic. She demonstrates that accounts of reason throughout the history of Western philosophy systematically exclude capacities historically deemed feminine and often attributed to women and marginalized men.[2] The underlying argument is that the Western epistemic *tradition* itself, due to its biased conceptions of reason, is epistemically unjust. These conceptions of reason, and corresponding social arrangements, resulted not only in conceptions of the maleness of reason, but in women and marginalized men being viewed as less capable of reason and more fitted for emotional or manual labor. As Donna Haraway explained, these are "the embodied others, who are not allowed *not* to have a body, a finite point of view, and so an inevitably disqualifying and polluting bias in any discussion of consequence" (1988, 575). Lloyd argues that the linkage between reason and the attainment of freedom and the capacity for an ethical life further distances all but privileged men from the capacities required for the realization of full humanity. This coupling sets the stage for some groups of people being seen as less than fully human. The subject of knowledge thus involves not only whose knowledge is deemed worthy, *but whose lives are so deemed.* As Judith Butler queries, "Who counts as human? Whose lives count as lives?" (2004, 20).

Early feminist epistemological work thus identified the ways that traditional conceptions of knowers as distinct, but not distinctive, occluded the fact that the qualities required to be a knower – objectivity, disinterestedness, lack of emotionality – excluded all but privileged individuals from full achievement of that ability. In other words, traditional epistemology was based on the false assumption that a particular standpoint was neither particular, nor a standpoint, and thereby obscured the linkages between knowledge and power. "What we have," Naomi Scheman explains, "are sets of complex interactions among (at least) social, economic, cultural, pedagogical, and familial structures that, in thoroughly circular fashion, shape the world, shape people to occupy different positions in that world, and shape the norms in terms of which some of the beliefs those people have about that world will count as justified" (1995, 183). Clarification and analysis of the mechanisms through which those not in privileged positions are unjustifiably excluded from the domain of knowers are key themes of early liberatory epistemological work. Adrienne Rich, for example, refers to the practice of "gaslighting" as a mechanism for invalidating the experiences and knowledges of those not in privileged positions. "Women have been driven mad, 'gaslighted,' for centuries by the refutation of our experience and our instincts in a culture which validates only male experience. The truth of our bodies and our minds has been mystified to us" (Rich, 1979, 190).

Through the growing recognition of the epistemic salience of the *situatedness* of knowers, liberatory epistemologists argued for the importance of reconsidering and often reclaiming dimensions of human capacities that had been excluded from the domains of reason and rationality. Philosophical accounts of reasoning and rationality were shown to be exceedingly narrow and serving to demarcate as irrational beliefs, habits, affective dispositions, behaviors, or inferential patterns that are outside those narrow boundaries that include affective, relational, and material dimensions. As Phyllis Rooney emphasized in relation to the male-female opposition: "The problem is not simply that a male-female division is set up but that the loci of voice, of agency, of subjectivity, of (rational) power and knowledge are all located within the male mode. The dialectic of rational discourse is such that the female is given the minimal agency of interference or simply the voice of silence" (1991, 95).

## Whose knowledges?

Attention to neglected ways of knowing provided a venue for attending to and valuing the experiences and knowledges of oppressed groups, a vehicle for what Patricia Hill Collins termed *oppositional consciousness* (1989). Collins argued that oppositional consciousness provided an epistemic resource for those who were often ignored or treated as the object of research to become subjects of knowledge in both senses. Oppositional consciousness contests the exclusion of marginalized groups from the category of knowers and serves as the wellspring of knowledge to displace oppressive practices. "Those who do the devalued work in a society, or who are oppressed and exploited in other ways, can learn how to use their oppressed social position as a source of insight about how social relations work – insight unavailable or at least hard to come by within the conceptual frameworks of dominant institutions, including research disciplines" (Harding, 2006, 25). Lisa Heldke brings in a class dimension by examining why "some forms of knowledge [are] actually regarded as leaving one incapable of other forms of rational thought" through "an attempt to show why and how defining entire classes of people – in this case rural people and farmers – as 'stupid knowers' ensures their marginalization and subordination, clever resistance moves on their part notwithstanding" (2006, 155).

Kimberle Crenshaw's analysis of *intersectionality* (1991) illustrates both sides of liberatory transformations of the subject of knowing. Crenshaw's attention to the marginalization of the issue of violence against women of color is a good example of oppositional consciousness. Shifting attention to this neglected area of concern through the lens of the experiences of women of color serves to transform both *who* knows and *what* is known. Intersectionality's transformative impact on the field of liberatory epistemologies is well described by Vivian May as the effort "to account for how knowledge derived from and crafted in marginalized locations entails a double struggle: the struggle to articulate what cannot necessarily be told in conventional terms, and the struggle to be heard without being (mis)translated into normative logics that occlude the meanings at hand" (2014, 99).

Feminist attention to affect played an important role in giving liberatory attention to a crucial aspect of experience that traditional epistemic frameworks have excluded from the epistemic domain. Some have turned to what Alison Jaggar (1989) called *outlaw emotions* as an epistemic resource for what May called the double struggle. One such outlaw emotion, that of anger, has been seen by feminists as particularly fruitful for providing insights into the ways in which those of us who have been marginalized have been epistemically oppressed, and it has served as a vehicle for reasserting our epistemic agency. What María Lugones called *hard to handle anger* has been embraced by many liberatory epistemologists as a wellspring for knowledge about ways in which oppressive practices are formulated and work upon us. It has functioned as a resource to unveil "gaslighting" and serves as a way of asserting our epistemic agency (e.g., Campbell, 1994; Frye, 1983a; Lorde, 1984b; Lugones, 2003; McKinnon 2017; McWeeny, 2010; Narayan, 1988; Scheman, 1980; Spelman, 1989).

## Systematic epistemic silencing

Liberatory epistemological attention to the interrelated issues of who knows and what is known gave rise to a virtual explosion of concerns about epistemic silencing and violence. Gayatri Chakravorty Spivak in 1985 deployed the conception of *epistemic violence* to illustrate "the remotely orchestrated, far-flung, and heterogeneous project to constitute the colonial subject as Other." (1988, 280–281). Spivak's conception of epistemic violence has been developed to illuminate the complex silencing of marginalized groups through appropriation and homogenization. Kevin Ayotte and Mary Husain (2005) show this complex silencing by delineating the representation of the women of Afghanistan through arguing "that representations of the women of Afghanistan as gendered slaves in need of 'saving' by the West constitute epistemic violence, the construction of violent knowledge of the third-world Other that erases women as *subjects* in international relations" (113). They provide an analysis of Western discourses concerning the burqa arguing that "the use of the burqa as a generalized symbol of female oppression performs a colonizing function" (118) in which Afghan women are rhetorically constructed as *objects* of knowledge that legitimize U.S. military intervention to liberate, but in a way that "creates the epistemological conditions for material harm" (113). Ayotte and Husain detail the epistemic violence inflicted by such discourses in that they "unwittingly obliterate vital aspects of feminist agency for Afghan women" (119), occlude the diversity of Islamic practices, amplify "the distinction between 'liberated' U.S. women and 'unenlightened' Afghan women" (120), and cause "the reduction of Afghan women's agency to their conformity to popular U.S. notions of feminist liberation" (121). Such (mis)translation into normative logics mischaracterize, standardize, and silence marginalized groups, contributing to distorted knowledges about them.

The theme of *systematic silencing* is central to postcolonial epistemological perspectives. "One of the supposed characteristics of primitive peoples," Linda Tuhiwai Smith explains, "was that we could not use our minds or intellects. We could not invent things, we could not create institutions or history, we could not imagine, we could not produce anything of value, we did not know how to use land and other resources from the natural world, we did not practice the 'arts' of civilization" (1999, 25). Smith explains that the epistemic violence of such misconceptions was to deny full humanity to such groups. "In other words, we were not 'fully human': some of us were not even considered partially human" (25). Through such epistemic violence, certain lives, indeed entire populations are conceived of as less valuable. "If certain lives do not qualify as lives within certain epistemological frames," Butler explains in *Frames of War*, "then these lives are never lived nor lost in the full sense" (2010, 1).

Systematic silencing not only happens through means that render some groups of people less than fully human. It can happen even to those who are members of so-called "privileged" groups by practices that violate their credibility in certain domains. Jennifer Hornsby and Rae Langton (1998) provide an early analysis of epistemic violence involving hearers not giving credibility to a speaker's testimony, in this case a woman's statement that she is refusing sex. Taking up Catharine MacKinnon's claim that pornography interferes with women's freedom of speech in that it silences women, Hornsby and Langton develop an analysis of the nature of this form of silencing, arguing that pornography can have the result of making "certain speech acts unspeakable for women" (1998, 27). Hornsby and Langton's claim is that one of the harms of pornography is that it silences women through what they term *illocutionary disablement*. Their focus is on those cases in which women say "No" to sex, but the hearer fails to recognize the utterance as a refusal. The problem they identify is a form of what Austin (1962) referred to as "uptake" failure, namely that the hearer does not understand the illocutionary force of her statement, her intention to refuse. "The point is that a woman's liberty to speak the *actions* she wants to speak has been curtailed: her liberty to protest against pornography and rape, to refuse sex when she wants to, to argue about violence in court, or to celebrate and promote new ways of thinking about sexuality. The point is that women cannot *do things* with words, even when we think we know how" (Langton, 1993, 328). Their point is that there is a *systematic uptake failure* in this domain due to pornographic images of women's sexuality through which women as a group are being silenced.

Kristie Dotson develops the concept of *epistemic violence* to illuminate the impact of such silencing. "To communicate *we all need an audience willing and capable of hearing us.* The extent to which entire populations of people can be denied this kind of linguistic reciprocation as a matter of course institutes epistemic violence" (2011, 238). Dotson develops the notion of *pernicious ignorance* to develop a robust account of epistemic violence, identifying two practices of silencing involving testimony that are the result of an audience's failure to offer communicative reciprocity, namely, *testimonial quieting*, in which the audience fails to identify a speaker as a knower and *testimonial smothering*, in which there is coercion not to introduce risky testimony.

More recently, Mary Kate McGowan builds on this work by identifying a different type of silencing, what she calls *sincerity silencing*. McGowan argues that in addition to the cases identified by Hornsby and Langton, sincerity silencing occurs when there is a failure to recognize a speaker's sincerity. She illustrates sincerity silencing through the following example:

> A woman says "No," sincerely intending to refuse sex but, although the man recognizes her intention to refuse, he mistakenly believes that she is doing so insincerely . . . and he proceeds to rape her. In this case, the addressee recognizes the speaker's illocutionary intention (to refuse) but fails to recognize that the speaker is doing so sincerely. Assuming that the hearer's failure (to recognize that the speaker's sincerity condition is met) is brought about in some systematic manner, this is a case of sincerity silencing.
>
> *(2014, 463)*

She stresses the importance of understanding sincerity silencing by arguing that it is a relatively widespread phenomenon that is implicated in various forms of discrimination. McGowan's claim that this is a widespread phenomenon is developed through Rebecca Kukla's conception of *discursive injustice*, where she examines how already marginalized speakers can be disempowered due to a distortion of their intended speech act in which "the performative force of [their] utterances is distorted in ways that enhance disadvantage" (2014, 441).

Akin to sincerity silencing are the various ways in which members of marginalized groups are systematically seen as epistemically untrustworthy. Nancy Daukas argues that

> Where unjust power relations are in play, the link between individual epistemic agency and social epistemic practices forged by attitudes about the epistemic capacities of self and diverse others, creates a mutually supporting "feedback loop" between a widespread, socially inculcated habitual failure of epistemic trustworthiness, on the one hand, and patterns of epistemic interactions, on the other, which perpetuate those power relations. Since these retrograde patterns of epistemic interaction are structurally in line with normal modes of social/epistemic interaction, they easily become normalized. As a result, their hold on an epistemic community is easily concealed, and difficult to break.
>
> *(2006, 116)*

Daukas analyzes, for instance, the feedback loop between the tacit assumption that people of color are not-fully-rational leading to their systematic under-representation in roles where rationality is a primary qualification, which then is argued to evince that they are "cognitively, psychologically, or emotionally unsuited to those fields and roles" (2006, 116). In this way, the attribution of epistemic untrustworthiness is reinforced with modes of social/epistemic interaction and become normalized.

The link between trust and epistemic justice has been a key theme of feminist and liberatory epistemologies. Karen Frost-Arnold identified three types of trust essential to epistemic justice:

> (1) self-trust – members of oppressed groups must trust themselves (Daukas, 2011; Jones, 2012a; Mills, 1997, 119), (2) trust in others – they must be trusted by fellow community members (Daukas, 2006, 2011; Fricker, 2007), and (3) trust in practices – community members must trust the practices, institutions, and social structures that create avenues for critical discourse (Scheman, 2001).
>
> *(2014, 793)*

If oppressive practices or structures undermine the trustworthiness of oppressed groups in any of these ways, they are thereby unjustly excluded from full membership in the epistemic community.

Even efforts by those who see themselves as allies can unintentionally undermine an individual's or group's trustworthiness. For example, a particularly problematic form of systematic silencing is cloaked within the well-intentioned efforts of some members of privileged communities to fight against oppression by engaging in what Linda Martín Alcoff (1991–1992) refers to as "the problem of speaking for others." Rather than reinforcing the importance of creating spaces for those who have been marginalized to speak for themselves and to be seen as trustworthy speakers, Alcoff cautions that the practice of speaking for others is often grounded in a desire for mastery and power. bell hooks warns that "[o]ften this speech about the 'Other' is also a mask, an oppressive talk hiding gaps, absences, that space where our words would be if we were speaking" (1990, 151). Mariana Ortega develops a related analysis of a form of ignorance that she calls "being lovingly, knowingly ignorant," in which members of privileged communities, although often well-intentioned, "are actively involved in the production of knowledge about women of color – whether by citing their work, reading and writing about them, or classifying them – while at the same time using women of color to the perceiver's own ends" (2006, 61). Ortega argues that the "result of this ignorance is that women of color continue to be misunderstood, underrepresented, homogenized, disrespected, or subsumed under the experience of 'universal sisterhood' while 'knowledge' about them is being encouraged and disseminated and while feminism claims to be more concerned and more enlightened about the relations between white women and women of color" (2006, 63).

In addition to such systematic silences of oppressed groups, there are also systemic epistemic silences of knowledges and knowings. As Walter Mignolo explains, "geo- and body-politics of knowledge has been hidden from the self-serving interests of Western epistemology and that a task of de-colonial thinking is the unveiling of epistemic silences of Western epistemology and affirming the epistemic rights of the racially devalued" (2009, 4). His goal is to unmask the "epistemic privilege of the First World" in framing the *terms* of knowing and not just the *content* of knowledge. "In the . . . distribution of scientific labor, the First World had indeed the *privilege of inventing the classification and being part of it*" (2009, 8). The theme of epistemic privilege is central to what María Lugones calls *the monologism of the colonizer*, which "is a way of silencing all contestatory interlocution. There is no place for conversation that includes the colonized tongue – the one you and I hold in our mouths – as a centrifugal force altering the society's language and its map of reality" (2006, 81–82). For Lugones, resistance must happen in a borderlands, what she calls the limen. Sabelo J. Ndlovu-Gatsheni and Walter Chambati in *Coloniality of Power in Postcolonial Africa: Myths of Decolonization* detail "the processes of universalizing Western particularism through epistemological colonization (colonization of the mind) that decentered pre-existing African knowledge systems" and argue that "the worst form of colonization of a people is that which created epistemological mimicry and intellectual dependency" (2013, 38).

Ramón Grosfoguel reminds us, in a related vein, of the way epistemic racism

> operates through the privileging of an essentialist ("identity") politics of "Western" male elites, that is, the hegemonic tradition of thought of Western philosophy and social theory that almost never includes "Western" Women and never includes "non-Western" philosophers/philosophies and social scientists. In this tradition, the "West" is considered to be the only legitimate tradition of thought able to produce knowledge and the only one with access to "universality," "rationality" and "truth".
>
> *(2010, 29)*

His critique of this form of "identity politics" is echoed in the work of André Keet, who talks about the "epistemic othering" that occurs in the academy. He argues that it emerges from a lack in collective interpretive resources as a structurally anchored prejudice. This anchor is the disciplines, because they help us produce a work where voids in hermeneutical assets are falsely regarded as equally distributed . . . these "otherings" are legitimized by knowledge and are thus rendered, for the most part, invisible to the academy itself.

(2014, 24)

## Epistemologies of ignorance

Charles Mills' conception of the *epistemologies of ignorance* has been particularly fruitful in uncovering such systematic epistemic silences. In *The Racial Contract* (1997), Mills introduced the concept to refer to the active production and preservation of ignorance by those in privileged positions about the mechanisms of racism and the ways in which they benefit the privileged. Mills views the racial contract as resting upon an inverted epistemology in which those in privilege are ignorant of the privileges they reinforce and benefit from. Such instances of ignorance are not simple "gaps" in knowledge, but rather what Marilyn Frye (1983b) identified as "determined ignorances" and what I have labeled "willful ignorance" (Tuana, 2006, 10) that involve an effort to willfully misrepresent in ways that sustain privilege.

Linda Martín Alcoff develops the concept of epistemic ignorance through tracing the origins and implications of three different liberatory frameworks for understanding epistemologies of ignorance: i) Lorraine Code's analysis of the significance of our situatedness as knowers, ii) Sandra Harding's standpoint analysis of ignorance as emergent from the systematic experiential differences among social groups, and iii) Charles Mills' structural account of the nature of oppressive systems and the desire, and perhaps need, to "see the world wrongly." Her conclusion is that "to truly understand the cause of the problem of ignorance, we also need to make epistemology reflexively aware and critical of its location within an economic system" (2006, 57). Understanding the epistemic function and the mechanisms for cultivating ignorance has been a valuable resource for liberatory epistemology in both domains of the subject of knowledge demarcated in this essay. Work on epistemologies of ignorance has provided valuable insights into how power gets complexly woven into the subject of knowledge – both in terms of what we do (and do not) know and in terms of who is (and is not) deemed a knower (Sullivan and Tuana, 2007; Tuana and Sullivan, 2006).

Miranda Fricker's work in *Epistemic Injustice: Power and the Ethics of Knowing* builds on such efforts to identify the mechanisms of epistemic ignorance that serve to maintain systematic unknowing. She identifies two such mechanisms: *hermeneutical* and *testimonial injustice*. While testimonial injustice arises from the undermining of epistemic trustworthiness, hermeneutical injustice is "the injustice of having some significant area of one's social experiences obscured from collective understanding owing to a structural identity prejudice in the collective hermeneutical resource" (2007, 155). She argues that there are gaps in hermeneutical resources that prevent members of marginalized groups from fully understanding their experiences, thereby obstructing the knowledge of such experiences by privileged groups as well. Unlike willful ignorance, where privileged individuals actively maintain ignorance about racist or other oppressive structures and the ways they benefit from them, Fricker identifies injustices that do not (yet) have a name (comparable to what Betty Friedan dubbed "The problem that has no name" [1963]) and which impair the ability of such groups to make sense of their experiences or to communicate them to members of other groups. Understood in this light, Fricker's understanding of hermeneutical injustice functions primarily to identify ways in which marginalized individuals can be epistemically disabled, while Mills' conception of epistemologies of ignorance frames what privileged groups effect to not know, or what Alison Bailey labeled "the ignorance of internalized oppression," in which the privileged are ignorant of their role in oppressive practices, and oppressed groups internalize the negative images of themselves created through oppressive practices (2007, 85), or what Mills called the *epistemology of victims* (1997, 109).

The systematic exclusion or distortion of the experiences of marginalized groups that preclude members of such groups from full hermeneutical membership due to meanings being "unduly influenced by more hermeneutically powerful groups" (Fricker, 2007, 155) locates such accounts of epistemic injustice in the lineage of standpoint, postcolonial, and other liberatory epistemologies that attend closely to the couplings of power and knowledge. Fricker's notion of hermeneutical injustice is akin to Lorraine Code's account of *rhetorical spaces* (1995) and Sarah Lucia Hoagland's analysis of *conceptual coercion* in which "those working to preserve the sense of a dominant paradigm employ an array of strategies to appropriate, coopt, and erase distinct worlds of sense" (Hoagland, 2001, 127). In *Rhetorical Space: Essays on Gendered Locations,* Code develops an analysis of how "territorial imperatives structure and limit the kinds of utterances that can be voiced within them with a reasonable expectation of uptake and "choral support": an expectation of being heard, understood, taken seriously" (1995, ix–x). Consider, she explains, "trying to have a productive public debate about abortion in the Vatican in 1995, where there is no available rhetorical space, not because the actual speech acts involved would be overtly prohibited, but because the available rhetorical space is not one where ideas on such a topic can be heard and debated openly, responsively" (1995, x). Devonya Havis brings a similar lens to traditional practices of philosophy when she asks, "Do our practices as philosophers overtly or covertly exclude the possibility that philosophies derived from some Black women's experiences can be intelligible?" (2014, 240). Writing from the situated location of Africa, André Keet explains that "given the Eurocentric nature and practices of the disciplines in African higher education, it is plausible to argue that what is systematically obscured by the 'structural prejudice in the collective interpretive resource' [Fricker's hermeneutical injustice] is that which is designated 'African' . . . in relation to a discourse that presents Africa as that which is 'incomplete, mutilated, and unfinished'" (2014, 25).

Rebecca Mason offers an important corrective to the conception of hermeneutical injustice. She argues that reading Fricker's conception of hermeneutical injustice through the lens of Mills' analysis of ignorance "reveals an epistemic asymmetry," namely that the hermeneutical lacuna may not be symmetrical. Some hermeneutical lacunas, say in the case of sexual harassment, may only be in the domain of the harasser, in which the "harasser was cognitively disabled by ethically bad epistemic practices that maintained (to his benefit) his ignorance of her experiences" (2011, 304). Gaile Pohlhaus, Jr. (2012) labels this form of epistemic injustice *willful hermeneutical ignorance*, which describes instances where "marginally situated knowers actively resist epistemic domination through interaction with other resistant knowers, while dominantly situated knowers nonetheless continue to misunderstand and misinterpret the world" (2012, 716). Kristie Dotson develops Pohlhaus, Jr.'s conception of willful hermeneutical ignorance to identify a third category of epistemic injustice, what she labels *contributory injustice* (2012).

> Contributory injustice, in this analysis, is defined as the circumstance where an epistemic agent's willful hermeneutical ignorance in maintaining and utilizing structurally prejudiced hermeneutical resources thwarts a knower's ability to contribute to shared epistemic resources within a given epistemic community by compromising her epistemic agency.
>
> *(2012, 32)*

Dotson argues that addressing contributory injustice will demand a form of what María Lugones (1987) called "world"-traveling.

## Epistemologies of resistance and liberation

The liberatory responses to active ignorances, epistemic occlusions, and systemic silences are numerous. Efforts to identify the various ways in which subjects can be systematically silenced have led to various strategies to address such injustices. However, some liberatory theorists caution against unwittingly reinscribing a logic of purity by seeing all silences or all ignorances as oppressive. Aída Hurtado (1996), for example, argues that silence can be a strategic act of resistance.

> Silence is a powerful weapon when it can be controlled. It is akin to camouflaging oneself when at war in an open field: playing possum at strategic times causes the power of the silent one to be underestimated . . . the knowledge obtained by remaining silent is like a reconnaissance flight into enemy territory that allows for individual and group survival.
>
> *(382)*

Hurtado calls attention to what she calls "subjugated knowledge," or strategic suspensions that constitute a positive and productive domain of not knowing. "*Subjugated knowledge* is knowledge that is temporally suspended or subjugated to resist structures of oppression and to create interstices of rebellion and potential revolution" (386).

María Lugones deploys the concept of the trickster to analyze how ignorance can be deployed strategically by those who take advantage of the ignorances of the privileged. Lugones' trickster functions at times to more safely or effectively navigate worlds in which the groups or perspectives they represent are oppressed. Alison Bailey provides the example of Frederick Douglas using such ignorance strategically to trick white boys into teaching him how to write (2007, 88). But the trickster can also engage in epistemic disobedience by challenging the privileged to unlearn their ignorance and become aware of their oppressive norms. There are "truths that only the fool can speak and only the trickster can play out without harm" (Lugones, 2003, 92).

Walter Mignolo argues that awareness of epistemic violence requires that we engage in *epistemic disobedience*. He argues that "the task of de-colonial thinking and the enactment of the de-colonial option in the 21st century starts from epistemic de-linking: from acts of epistemic disobedience" (2009, 15). In a similar vein, Sarah Lucia Hoagland calls for *epistemic resistance*, which involves

> a double operation: (1) finding resistant logics, and (2) resisting the logic/language-games of hegemonic medical, legal, and scientific models, exploring how those at the center keep the center by rendering the resistance of others invisible as resistance . . . I am interested in strategies of resisting rationality both in the sense of resisting (dominant) rationality and also of finding nondominant resisting rationalities.
>
> *(2001, 140)*

As Karen Frost-Arnold argues, "in epistemic communities structured by oppression, betrayal of epistemic norms is sometimes virtuous" (2014, 791).

José Medina (2013) develops this theme by developing *epistemologies of resistance* that engage epistemic disobedience that are, as Eduardo Mendieta explains "fueled by epistemic outrage at the production, the making of new inequalities, new injustices, new forms of 'expulsion'"

(2013, 97). Medina calls for epistemic resistance through using "our epistemic resources and abilities to undermine and change oppressive normative structures and the complacent cognitive-affective functioning that sustains those structures" (2013, 3). Medina reanimates the links between the affective and the epistemic often found in the work of feminist epistemologists. Code, for example, critiqued the traditional epistemic position that would "accord no epistemic worth to the attunement, the sensitivity, that certain kinds of knowing demand" (1995, 122). Medina invokes a similar epistemic role for empathy, arguing for the importance of those in privileged groups overcoming their "impoverished affective structures" in order to develop the empathy and trust required to undermine willful ignorances against such groups. He sees epistemic resistance as a mode of relationality essential to democratic sociability. Mary Jeanne Larrabee argues that resistance epistemologies move away from the epistemic violence of seeing "knowledge as primarily mentally cognitive and . . . epistemology as a reasoned reflective enterprise" (2006, 456). She turns instead to Cherrie Moraga's and Gloria Anzaldúa's conception of "theories in the flesh" (1983, 23) as a type of resistance epistemology. Larrabee deploys Sarah Hoagland's conception of resistant logics as a lens for seeing forms of resistance that have been silenced and rendered invisible by dominant logics (2001, 140).

María Lugones' conception of "world"-travelling (1987) and the importance of "world"-travelling for those in privileged groups is similarly based on the link between responsible knowing and affective connection. In her dialogue with Elizabeth Spelman, Lugones (1983) argues that genuine dialogue between groups will require recognition, comprehension, respect, and love. Liberatory epistemologists have begun to explore whether the various forms of epistemic injustice can be ameliorated through such encounters (Butnor and McWeeny, 2014; Code, 2013; Hoagland, 2007; Ortega, 2006; Potter, 2013; Sullivan, 2004).

> Through travelling to other people's "worlds" we discover that there are "worlds" in which those who are the victims of arrogant perception are really subjects, lively beings, resistors, constructors of visions, even though in the mainstream construction they are animated only by the arrogant perceiver and are pliable, foldable, file-awayable, classifiable.
> *(Lugones, 1987, 18)*

Medina underscores the importance of challenging epistemic silencing through respectful exchanges between dominant and marginalized groups, enabling "mutual resistance and beneficial friction and not a mere overpowering of one perspective by the other (which would simply reproduce internally the relation of subordination and cognitive domination that characterizes oppression)" (2013, 198).

In closing, let me acknowledge at least some of the limitations of this essay that animate the critical importance of attention to the complex interchanges of power/knowledge. My efforts to include nonwestern perspectives was impacted by the limitations of language – both my own abilities as well as the decisions of others about which theorists are worthy of translation. It was also limited by access and the politics of library collections. As just one example, many important African academic journals are not included on the shelves or in the electronic databases of even the top research libraries. Furthermore, important work arising from continental philosophical attention to power/knowledge gets marginalized by the very category and practices of what counts as epistemological inquiry. My efforts to frame this essay in light of liberatory epistemologies was also limited by the paucity of epistemic analyses of the import of class on issues of ignorance and knowing, as well as my personal limitations regarding queer or disability perspectives on these topics.

**Related chapters**: 10, 13, 15, 27, 37

## Notes

1 This chapter was enriched and improved thanks to feedback from the editors.
2 While racism functions differently at different historical periods, the linkage between denigrated traits and marginalized men has been tightly coupled, a coupling that results in nonprivileged women often being doubly "othered."

## References

Alcoff, Linda Martín, 1991–1992. 'The problem of speaking for others.' *Cultural Critique*, 20: 5–32.
Alcoff, Linda Martín, 2006. 'Epistemologies of ignorance: Three types.' *Hypatia: A Journal of Feminist Philosophy*, 21/3: 39–57.
Austin, John L., 1962. *How to Do Things with Words*, London: Oxford University Press.
Ayotte, Kevin J. and Mary E. Husain, 2005. 'Securing Afghan women: Neocolonialism, epistemic violence, and the rhetoric of the veil.' *NWSA Journal*, 17/3: 112–133.
Bailey, Alison, 1998. 'Locating traitorous identities: Toward a view of privilege-cognizant white character.' *Hypatia: A Journal of Feminist Philosophy*, 13/3: 27–42.
Bailey, Alison, 2007. 'Strategic Ignorance.' In Shannon Sullivan and Nancy Tuana, eds., *Race and Epistemologies of Ignorance*. Albany: State University of New York Press, 77–94.
Butler, Judith, 2004. *Precarious Life: The Powers of Mourning and Violence*, London: Verso.
Butler, Judith, 2010. *Frames of War: When Is Life Grievable?*, London: Verso.
Butnor, Ashby and Jennifer McWeeny, 2014. 'Feminist Comparative Methodology: Performing Philosophy Differently.' In Jennifer McWeeny and Ashby Butnor, eds., *Asian and Feminist Philosophies in Dialogue: Liberating Traditions*. New York: Columbia University Press, 1–36.
Campbell, Sue, 1994. 'Being dismissed: The politics of emotional expression.' *Hypatia: A Journal of Feminist Philosophy*, 9/3: 46–65.
Code, Lorraine, 1981. 'Is the sex of the knower epistemologically significant?' *Metaphilosophy*, 12: 267–276.
Code, Lorraine, 1991. *What Can She Know? Feminist Theory and Construction of Knowledge*, Ithaca: Cornell University Press.
Code, Lorraine, 1993. 'Taking Subjectivity into Account.' In Linda Alcoff and Elizabeth Potter, eds., *Feminist Epistemologies*, New York: Routledge, 15–48.
Code, Lorraine, 1995. *Rhetorical Space: Essays on Gendered Locations*, New York and London: Routledge.
Code, Lorraine, 2013. 'Feminist Epistemology.' In Byron Kaldis, ed., *Encyclopedia of Philosophy and the Social Sciences*, Los Angeles: Sage, 353–356.
Collins, Patricia Hill, 1989. 'The social construction of black feminist thought.' *Signs: Journal of Women in Culture and Society*, 14/4: 745–773.
Collins, Patricia Hill, 1990. *Black Feminist Thought: Knowledge, Consciousness, and the Politics of Empowerment*, Boston: Unwin Hyman.
Collins, Patricia Hill, 1998. *Fighting Words*, Minneapolis: University of Minnesota Press.
Crenshaw, Kimberle, 1991. 'Mapping the margins: Intersectionality, identity politics, and violence against women of color.' *Stanford Law Review*, 43/6: 1241–1299.
Daukas, Nancy, 2006. 'Epistemic trust and social location.' *Episteme: A Journal of Social Epistemology*, 3/1–2: 109–124.
Daukas, Nancy, 2011. 'Altogether now: A virtue-theoretic approach to pluralism in feminist epistemology.' In Heidi Grasswick, ed., *Feminist Epistemology and Philosophy of Science*. New York: Springer, 45–67.
Dotson, Kristie, 2011. 'Tracking epistemic violence, tracking practices of silencing.' *Hypatia: A Journal of Feminist Philosophy*, 26/2: 236–257.
Dotson, Kristie, 2012. 'A cautionary tale: On limiting epistemic oppression.' *Frontiers: A Journal of Women's Studies*, 33/1: 24–47.
Fricker, Miranda, 2007. *Epistemic Injustice: Power and Ethics in Knowing*, Oxford: Oxford University Press.
Friedan, Betty, 1963. *The Feminine Mystique*, New York: WW Norton.
Frost-Arnold, Karen, 2014. 'Imposters, tricksters, and trustworthiness as an epistemic virtue.' *Hypatia: A Journal of Feminist Philosophy*, 29/4: 790–807.
Frye, Marilyn, 1983a. 'A Note on Anger.' In Marilyn Frye, eds., *Politics of Reality: Essays in Feminist Theory*. Freedom, CA: The Crossing Press, 84–94.
Frye, Marilyn, 1983b. 'On Being White: Thinking Toward a Feminist Understanding of Race and Race Supremacy.' In Marilyn Frye, ed., *Politics of Reality: Essays in Feminist Theory*. Freedom, CA: The Crossing Press, 110–127.

Grosfoguel, Ramón, 2010. 'Epistemic Islamophobia and colonial social sciences.' *Human Architecture: Journal of the Sociology of Self-Knowledge*, 8/2: 29–38.
Haraway, Donna, 1988. 'Situated knowledges: The science question in feminism and the privilege of partial perspective.' *Feminist Studies*, 14/3: 575–599.
Harding, Sandra, 1982. 'Is gender a variable in conceptions of rationality: A survey of issues.' *Dialectica*, 36/2–3: 225–242.
Harding, Sandra, 1991. *Whose Science? Whose Knowledge? Thinking from Women's Lives*, Ithaca, NY: Cornell University Press.
Harding, Sandra, 2004. *The Feminist Standpoint Reader: Intellectual and Political Controversies*. New York and London: Routledge.
Harding, Sandra, 2006. 'Two influential theories of ignorance and philosophy's interests in ignoring them.' *Hypatia: A Journal of Feminist Philosophy*, 21/3: 20–36.
Hartsock, Nancy, 1983. *Money, Sex, and Power: Toward a Feminist Historical Materialism*, New York: Longman.
Havis, Devonya N., 2014. '"Now, how you sound": Considering a different philosophical praxis.' *Hypatia: A Journal of Feminist Philosophy*, 29/1: 237–252.
Heldke, Lisa, 2006. 'Farming made her stupid.' *Hypatia: A Journal of Feminist Philosophy*, 21/3: 151–165.
Hoagland, Sarah Lucia, 2001. 'Resisting Rationality.' In Nancy Tuana and Sandra Morgen, eds., *Engendering Rationalities*. Albany: State University of New York Press, 125–150.
Hoagland, Sarah Lucia, 2007. 'Denying Relationality: Epistemology and Ethics and Ignorance.' In Shannon Sullivan and Nancy Tuana, eds., *Race and Epistemologies of Ignorance*. Albany: State University of New York Press, 95–118.
Hooks, bell, 1990. Yearning: Race, Gender, and Cultural Politics, Boston: South End Press.
Hornsby, Jennifer and Rae Langton, 1998. 'Free speech and illocution.' *Legal Theory*, 4: 21–37.
Hurtado, Aída, 1996. 'Strategic Suspensions: Feminists of Color Theorize the Production of Knowledge.' In J. Tarule, B. Clinchy, and M. Belenky, eds., *Knowledge, Difference, and Power: Essays Inspired by "Women's Ways of Knowing"*. New York: Basic, 372–392.
Jaggar, Alison M., 1989. 'Love and knowledge: Emotion in feminist epistemology.' *Inquiry: An Interdisciplinary Journal of Philosophy*, 32/2: 151–176.
Jaggar, Alison M. and Susan R. Bordo, 1989. 'Introduction.' In Alison M. Jaggar and Susan R. Bordo, eds., *Gender/Body/Knowledge: Feminist Reconstructions of Being and Knowing*. New Brunswick, NJ and London: Rutgers University Press, 1–10.
Jones, Karen, 2012a. 'The politics of intellectual self-trust.' *Social Epistemology*, 26/2: 237–251.
Jones, Karen, 2012b. 'Trustworthiness.' *Ethics*, 123/1: 61–85.
Keet, Andre, 2014. 'Epistemic othering and the decolonization of knowledge.' *Africa Insight: Development Through Knowledge*, 44/1: 23–37.
Kukla, Rebecca, 2014. 'Performative force, convention, and discursive injustice.' *Hypatia: A Journal of Feminist Philosophy*, 29/2: 440–457.
Langton, Rae, 1993. 'Speech acts and unspeakable acts,' *Philosophy and Public Affairs*, 22/4: 293–330.
Larrabee, Mary Jeanne, 2006. '"I know what a slave knows": Mary Prince's epistemology of resistance.' *Women's Studies*, 35: 453–473.
Lloyd, Genevieve, 1979. 'The man of reason.' *Metaphilosophy*, 10/1: 18–37.
Lloyd, Genevieve, 1984. *The Male of Reason: "Male" and "Female" in Western Philosophy*. Minneapolis: University of Minnesota Press.
Lorde, Audre, 1984a. 'Eye to Eye: Black Women, Hatred, and Anger.' In *Sister Outsider*. Berkeley: The Crossing Press, 145–75.
Lorde, Audre, 1984b. 'The Uses of Anger: Women Responding to Racism.' In *Sister Outsider*. Berkeley: The Crossing Press, 124–133.
Lugones, María C., 1987. 'Playfulness, world-traveling, and loving perception.' *Hypatia: A Journal of Feminist Philosophy*, 2/2: 3–19.
Lugones, María C., 2003. *Pilgrimages/Peregrinajes: Theorizing Coalition against Multiple Oppressions*, Lanham, MD: Rowman & Littlefield.
Lugones, María C., 2006. 'On complex communication.' *Hypatia: A Journal of Feminist Philosophy*, 21/3: 75–85.
Lugones, María C. and Elizabeth V. Spelman, 1983. 'Have we got a theory for you! Feminist theory, cultural imperialism, and the demand for the woman's voice.' *Hypatia: Women's Studies International Forum*, 1: 573–581.
Mason, Rebecca, 2011. 'Two kinds of unknowing.' *Hypatia: A Journal of Feminist Philosophy*, 26/2: 294–307.

May, Vivian M., 2014. '"Speaking into the void"? Intersectionality critiques and epistemic backlash.' *Hypatia: A Journal of Feminist Philosophy*, 29/1: 94–112.

McGowan, Mary Kate, 2014. 'Sincerity silencing.' *Hypatia: A Journal of Feminist Philosophy*, 29/2: 458–473.

McKinnon, Rachel, 2017. 'Allies Behaving Badly: Gaslighting as Epistemic Injustice.' In Ian James Kidd, José Medina, and Gaile Pohlhaus, Jr., eds., *The Routledge Handbook of Epistemic Injustice*. New York: Routledge, 167–174.

McWeeny, Jen, 2010. 'Liberating anger, embodying knowledge: A comparative study of María Lugones and Zen Master Hakuin.' *Hypatia: A Journal of Feminist Philosophy*, 25/2: 295–315.

Medina, José, 2013. *The Epistemology of Resistance: Gender and Racial Oppression, Epistemic Injustice, and Resistant Imaginations*. New York: Oxford University Press.

Mendieta, Eduardo, 2013. 'Beyond epistemic injustice, toward epistemic outrage: On Saskia Sassen's analytical destabilizations.' *The Pluralist*, 8/3: 96–100.

Mignolo, Walter D., 2009. 'Epistemic disobedience, independent thought and decolonial freedom.' *Theory, Culture & Society*, 26/7–8: 159–181.

Mills, Charles, 1997. *The Racial Contract*, Ithaca, NY: Cornell University Press.

Moraga, Cherríe and Gloria Anzaldúa, 1983. *Entering the Lives of Others: Theory in the Flesh*. This Bridge Called my Back: Writings by Radical Women of Color. 2nd Ed. New York: Kitchen Table: Women of Color.

Narayan, Uma, 1988. 'Working together across difference: Some considerations on emotions and political practice.' *Hypatia: A Journal of Feminist Philosophy*, 3/2: 31–47.

Ndlovu-Gatsheni, Sabelo J. and Walter Chambati. 2013. *Coloniality of Power in Postcolonial Africa: Myths of Decolonization*, Oxford: African Books Collective.

Nelson, Lynn Hankinson, 1990. *Who Knows: From Quine to a Feminist Empiricism*, Philadelphia: Temple University Press.

Ortega, Mariana, 2006. 'Being lovingly, knowingly ignorant: White feminism and women of color.' *Hypatia: A Journal of Feminist Philosophy*, 21/3: 56–74.

Pohlhaus, Jr., Gaile, 2012. 'Relational knowing and epistemic injustice: Toward a theory of willful hermeneutical ignorance.' *Hypatia: A Journal of Feminist Philosophy*, 27/4: 715–735.

Potter, Nancy Nyquist, 2013. 'Empathic Foundations of Clinical Knowledge.' In K.W.M. Fulford, Martin Davies, Richard Gipps, George Graham, John Sadler, Giovanni Stanghellini, and Tim Thornton, eds., *The Oxford Handbook of Philosophy and Psychiatry*. Oxford: Oxford University Press, 293–306.

Rich, Adrienne, 1979. *On Lies, Secrets, and Silence: Selected Prose 1966–1978*, New York: Norton.

Rooney, Phyllis, 1991. 'Gendered reason: Sex metaphor and conceptions of reason.' *Hypatia: A Journal of Feminist Philosophy*, 6/2: 23–45.

Scheman, Naomi, 1980. 'Anger and the politics of naming.' In Sally McConnell-Ginet, Ruth Borker, and Nelly Furman, eds., *Women, Language, and Society*. New York: Praeger, 174–187.

Scheman, Naomi, 1995. 'Feminist epistemology.' *Metaphilosophy*, 26/3: 177–190.

Scheman, Naomi, 2001. 'Epistemology Resuscitated: Objectivity as Trustworthiness.' In Nancy Tuana and Sandra Morgen, eds., *Engendering Rationalities*. Albany: State University of New York Press, 23–52.

Smith, Linda Tuhiwai, 1999. *Decolonizing Methodologies: Research and Indigenous Peoples*, London: Zed Books.

Spelman, Elizabeth V., 1989. 'Anger and Insubordination.' In Ann Garry and Marilyn Pearsall, eds., *Women, Knowledge, and Reality*. Boston: Unwin Hyman, 263–273.

Spivak, Gayatri Chakravorty, 1988. 'Can the Subaltern Speak?' In Cary Nelson and Lawrence Grossberg, eds., *Marxism and the Interpretation of Culture*. London: Macmillan, 271–314.

Sullivan, Shannon, 2004. 'White world-traveling.' *Journal of Speculative Philosophy*, 18/4: 300–304.

Sullivan, Shannon and Nancy Tuana, eds. 2007. *Race and Epistemologies of Ignorance*, Albany: State University of New York Press.

Tuana, Nancy, 2001. 'Introduction.' In N. Tuana and S. Morgen, eds., *Engendering Rationalities*. Albany: State University of New York Press, 1–20.

Tuana, Nancy, 2006. 'The speculum of ignorance: The women's health movement and epistemologies of ignorance.' *Hypatia: A Journal of Feminist Philosophy*, 21/3: 1–19.

Tuana, Nancy and Shannon Sullivan, 2006. 'Feminist Epistemologies of Ignorance.' Special issue of *Hypatia: A Journal of Feminist Philosophy*, 21/3, 1–183.

Tuana, Nancy, and Sandra Morgen, eds. 2001. *Engendering Rationalities*. Albany: State University of New York Press.

# 12
# EPISTEMIC INJUSTICE AND THE PHILOSOPHY OF RACE

*Luvell Anderson*

## 1. Introduction

The Black Lives Matter movement (BLM) emerged recently in the U.S. in response to what many view as the continued use of state-sanctioned violence against Black bodies and the impunity with which state agents operate. It has been noted that police killed more than 100 unarmed Black people in the U.S. during 2014 alone (Unarmed Victims, n.d.). Also, the *Washington Post* reported that "blacks were killed at three times the rate of whites or other minorities" (Kindy, 2015). It is not surprising, then, that communities who find themselves disproportionate victims of such violence would respond in protest.

For many, the meaning of the phrase "Black Lives Matter" is quite clear. There is an implicit "too" attached to the end of the phrase so that it should read "Black lives matter, too!" We can call this an *inclusive reading*. A central message of the movement is that we as a society have historically treated Black lives as if they are valueless and expendable, and that this should no longer be the case. Not everyone interprets the phrase in this way, however. A common retort to "Black Lives Matter" is "All Lives Matter," expressing the idea that by singling out Black lives, the former phrase represents a devaluing of non-Black lives. Thus, the elliptical element in the phrase is more like "*Only* Black lives matter." We might call this an *exclusive reading*. For instance, we find this sentiment expressed in a column for conservative website *Townhall*. The author, Bill Murchison, contrasts the "morally incontestable claim" that "all lives matter," with what he says is pushed by BLM and the media as the *real* issue, i.e. "Black Lives Matter" (Murchison, 2015). The title of the article, "Do 'All Lives Matter' or Not?" further reinforces the notion that the BLM slogan is exclusively about Black lives and a dismissal of all others.

Murchison and his ilk could very well be part of a propagandizing conspiracy to undermine any potential effectiveness of the BLM movement, and so could be regarded as disingenuously expressing moral objections.[1] But it seems clear that many ordinary U.S. citizens sincerely share the same sentiment.[2] That is, many ordinary citizens are inclined to attribute an exclusive reading to "Black Lives Matter." One could say that this is simply a misreading, perhaps an uncharitable one. I think the proper response goes deeper than this, however. I want to argue that the misreading wrongs the protestors in their capacity as knowers, a phenomenon that has been referred to as *epistemic injustice*. In this particular case, there is a gap in the collective interpretive resources that unjustly disadvantages the protestors' ability to express themselves intelligibly, i.e. what is called a hermeneutical injustice. We find plenty of examples of this phenomenon, for instance, in letters sent to Martin Luther King, Jr., in which some "concerned citizen" accuses King of starting trouble "between the races." In these instances King is read as a rabble-rouser and not a protesting citizen with a legitimate concern.[3]

In what follows, I aim to show that hermeneutical injustices remain even as we pursue strategies intended to get us beyond the corrupting influence of race and racism. In Section 2, I provide a brief summary of the concept of hermeneutical injustice. Section 3 discusses the so-called post-racial ideal. I argue that pursuing a post-racial strategy not only fails to produce racial justice, but it perpetuates the sorts of hermeneutical injustices previously mentioned by obscuring our resources for referring to distinctively racial wrongs. In Section 4, I draw on resources from the philosophy of language to illuminate some of the ways speech can be marshaled to produce hermeneutical injustices. I conclude in Section 5 by clarifying how post-racialism gives rise to hermeneutical injustices via the linguistic mechanisms outlined in Section 4.

## 2. Hermeneutical injustice

In her book, *Epistemic Injustice: Power and the Ethics of Knowing* (2007), Miranda Fricker describes two kinds of epistemic injustice: *hermeneutical injustices* and *testimonial injustices*. Testimonial injustices arise when a hearer, due to prejudice triggered by the speaker's social identity, attributes a credibility deficit to the speaker's utterance. Hermeneutical injustices, on the other hand, are described as occurring "when a gap in collective interpretive resources puts someone at an unfair disadvantage when it comes to making sense of their social experiences" (1). Due to limitations of space, I will restrict my attention to injustices of the hermeneutical variety in what follows.[4]

In chapter 7 of her book, Fricker notes that certain social groups often face an inequality in hermeneutical participation. There are some situations ("hermeneutical hotspots" in Fricker's parlance) in which it serves the interests of the socially powerful to maintain ignorance or a misinterpretation of certain social experiences. Contributions to interpretations of those experiences by members of marginalized groups are excluded or evaded through misinterpretation. Fricker describes this scenario as *hermeneutical marginalization*, which she defines in the following way: "when there is unequal hermeneutical participation with respect to some significant area(s) of social experience, members of the disadvantaged group are *hermeneutically marginalized*" (153). In particular social situations, members of disadvantaged groups are "prevented from generating meanings pertaining to some areas of the social world" (153–4). This might be evident, for instance, in the cases presented in the introductory section. BLM protestors are being prevented from successfully describing the manner in which Black lives are taken as reflective of a general devaluation of Black lives in general.

Of course, to get a fuller sense of hermeneutical marginalization we would need to delve deeper into the details. For instance, we might need an account of "hermeneutical participation" and the particular ways it happens, or perhaps a fuller account of what constitutes a "hermeneutical hotspot." But let's not allow the details to detain our attention; the intuitive sense of the notion will suffice for our purposes. Having provided a description of hermeneutical marginalization, Fricker uses it to define *hermeneutical injustice*: "the injustice of having some significant area of one's social experience obscured from collective understanding owing to hermeneutical marginalization" (158). Fricker notes that this is the generic definition meant to cover both systematic and incidental cases. What makes a case systematic, according to Fricker, is that the hermeneutical marginalization is "persistent and wide-ranging," triggered by prejudice that tracks a "subject through different dimensions of social activity" (27). Incidental cases, on the other hand, are ones in which hermeneutical marginalization occurs in "a highly localized patch of the subject's experience," which are reflective of "one-off moment[s] of powerlessness" (156).

To be sure, Fricker is not the first to think through issues concerning the harms done to persons as givers and receivers of knowledge or the difficulties and injustices experienced by individuals denied a place in the production of social meanings. For instance, Audre Lorde (2007), in her essay "The Master's Tools Will Never Dismantle the Master's House," takes white feminists to task for failing to include the voices of Black women and women of Color in a substantial way in discussions concerning the fate of women in general. Lorde's criticisms certainly map onto discussions of hermeneutical marginalization. Patricia Hill Collins (1999) discusses the exclusion of Black women's voices in knowledge production and the perpetuation of "controlling images" that contribute to the "ideological dimension of U.S. Black women's oppression." And Anna Julia Cooper also discusses the importance of Black Women's voices in conversations concerning racial uplift in "A Voice From the South" (Cooper, 1990, 5). These are but a few of the many women of Color who have contributed valuable insights with respect to marginalized persons and epistemic oppression. Thus, while Fricker is widely recognized in "mainstream" philosophical circles as shining a light on these issues, it is important not to perpetuate exclusionary practices that render the voices of women of Color invisible, even while attempting to give them voice.[5]

## 3. Post-racialism

Having provided a brief overview of hermeneutical injustice, we can now consider some ways race intervenes in our epistemic practices. There are several points of entry for intersections involving the literature on epistemic injustice and the philosophy of race. For instance, we might talk about the role of education found in the work of Carter G. Woodson as a means of bridging epistemic gaps for members of marginalized groups. Alternatively, we could visit the thoughts of thinkers like W.E.B. Du Bois or Frantz Fanon to investigate the ways the experiences of individuals in marginalized groups shape their cognitive lives and the resulting epistemic consequences in terms of double-consciousness (Du Bois) and racial interpellation (Fanon).[6] However, I will restrict my attention to the idea of *post-racialism*, a notion that has garnered discussion recently from critical philosophers of race such as Kathryn Gines, Ron Sundstrom, Howard McGary, Paul C. Taylor, Falguni Sheth, and sociologist Eduardo Bonilla-Silva. In this section I briefly review a few ways post-racialism has been characterized. My ultimate aim is to argue that pursuing post-racialism as a strategy for creating a society in which race no longer unduly affects people's lives ends up producing hermeneutical injustices.

What exactly is *post-racialism*? Ron Sundstrom (P. Taylor, Alcoff, & Anderson, forthcoming) suggests that conceptualizations of the notion can be divided into two broad categories: *descriptive* and *prescriptive*. The first type is illustrated by some thoughts about America in the age of Obama. There has been a lot of talk about post-racialism in recent years, especially after the election of Barack Obama as president of the United States. News stories and headlines emerged proclaiming the arrival of a post-racial America. The claim that we now live in a post-racial America represents the notion of post-racialism as an achieved status or state of affairs, perhaps a state in which race no longer matters politically, economically, or socially. We can call this version, as Paul C. Taylor dubs it, "idiot post-racialism" (2014). On this naïve account, as Taylor characterizes it, we are said to be in a state in which we've "moved beyond race" as evidenced by some significant event that would not have happened in more racially dark times, in this case the election of a Black man named Barack Obama. The event is supposed to show the obsolescence of race-thinking.

Taylor quickly dispenses of idiot post-racialism by pointing out that racism and the effects of past racial injustices are still with us. For example, social psychologists have presented evidence of pervasive implicit biases that continue to influence people's actions (Greenwald & Pettigrew, 2014; Nosek & Banaji, 2009). There are also significant racial disparities in housing (Elmelech, 2004; Kirk, 2006), wealth (Oliver & Shapiro, 2006; Shin, 2015), and the criminal justice system (Clemons, 2014; Lynch, Patterson, & Childs, 2008) that persist due to past racial injustices. Even the treatment of the figure whose election was supposed to serve as our epochal shift into "postrace-dom," i.e. President Obama, belies the veracity of this naïve view.[7] As a descriptive claim about the state of race in America, this version of post-racialism is manifestly false and thus not something we should waste time entertaining.

Whereas descriptive characterizations of post-racialism focus on demographics and the role that race actually plays in the present states of affairs, prescriptive notions direct their attention towards the realization of an ideal. Kathryn Gines (2014) represents the content of that ideal in the following forms: (i) assimilationism, (ii) eliminativism, (iii) color-blindness, and (iv) post-racism. Assimilationism, according to Bernard Boxill, maintains that "a society in which racial differences have no moral, political, or economic significance . . . is both possible and desirable in America" (119). Presumably, this would mean that in a post-racial society, racial differences would be insignificant along moral, political, and economic dimensions. On this view one gets a picture of a society in which people no longer see themselves as subdivided into their own special groups, but as members of one group, at least when it comes to race.[8]

An eliminativist version of post-racialism views the elimination of racial categories as paramount. Advocates of eliminativism typically regard race as one of the sources of the injustices we are fighting against. Thus, we can only move beyond racial ills if we jettison race altogether. At least, this is the picture presented by the strongest variant of the view. Josh Glasgow (2008) identifies two weaker versions: *political eliminativism*, which calls for the erasure of race from political documents, policies, proceedings, and institutions, and *public eliminativism*, which seeks to erase race from our public, as opposed to our private, lives. The strongest form, which he calls *global eliminativism*, is the one I've already discussed. Thus, on the strongest version, a post-racial society will be one in which race no longer plays any role in our discursive or cognitive practices, both publicly and privately.

Some propose a colorblind version of post-racialism. The spirit of the principle is captured in the sentiment that policies should not be designed to treat people differently because of their race (Boxill, 1992, 10). Race is not something one achieves – i.e. it has no meritocratic value. In our purported meritocratic society, race is not the kind of thing that should advantage some while disadvantaging others. Thus, policy should be "colorblind" with respect to how it is constructed and applied. The colorblind principle can be broadened to apply to all of social life. A post-racial society of the colorblind variety would be one in which race makes no moral, legal, political, or social difference to how people are treated.

Gines points out that Howard McGary (2012) considers each of the proposed versions just presented to be assimilationist views. One might think there exists no real distinction between the aforementioned versions of post-racialism. The reasoning might go as follows. Each view calls for the jettisoning of race in moral, political, social, and economic decisions. Each view also seems to suggest that acknowledging or encouraging racial difference generates unwelcome moral and social problems. Thus, the best course, perhaps the most just one, is to come to a place where everyone shares the same values and, in some sense, identity.

I want to acknowledge the skepticism, but I do think there is reason to recognize a distinction, at least between the eliminativist position and the others. Assimilation and possibly colorblindness conceivably allow for the continued existence of racial categories, whereas the eliminativist version does not. On the assimilation and colorblind positions, we can conceive of the preservation of racial identities, though they may function differently, perhaps much the way other voluntary identities – e.g. "Cardinals fans," "soccer moms," "academics," "blue collar workers," etc. – do. In contrast, eliminativism calls for the obliteration of race and racial identities. There may not be much of a distinction to make between the assimilationist and colorblind versions, however. It is not important to settle these issues in this essay.

One final form post-racialism might take is as *post-racism* (Gines, 2014; Joseph, 2009; Pettigrew, 2009). According to this version, a post-racialist society is one in which racist structures and institutions no longer exist. As a purely future-oriented ideal, post-racialism as post-racism desires much of what the previously mentioned forms do, namely a society in which race no longer disadvantages some while unjustly advantaging others. The post-racist variety of post-racialism, as opposed to the others, focuses on the institutional structures that perpetuate racism rather than targeting race and racial identities.

As a claim about the current state of affairs, post-racialism as a post-racist society would obviously be false. There are also those who think we should not conflate post-racialism and post-racism. Both Kathryn Gines (2014) and Ron Sundstrom (P. Taylor et al., forthcoming), for instance, see a clear distinction between the two notions. Just to point out one problem, we could quite easily imagine a world that was post-racist but not post-racial: a world that has moved beyond racism, perhaps in both its interpersonal and institutional varieties, while still holding onto racial distinctions. Thus, if the idea of post-racialism must carry with it the disappearance of race, and post-racism lacks this element, then we might concur with Gines and Sundstrom that post-racialism and post-racism should be kept conceptually distinct.[9]

Given the reservations about "post-racialism as post-racism," we can ignore it for what follows. I will argue that whichever of the three remaining forms post-racialism takes, the pursuit and/or realization of them would result in the production of hermeneutical injustices for members of marginalized groups. Before doing so, I turn next to the linguistic mechanisms underlying the hermeneutical injustices generated by the pursuit of post-racial strategies.

## 4. Illocution and silencing

How might post-racialism result in the production of hermeneutical injustices? Recall the responses to the "Black Lives Matter" slogan mentioned in the introduction. It is plausible to think that at least some of these responses are motived by something like a post-racial ideal. The post-racial response to the slogan has at least two effects. First, there is an obscuring of what the speaker intends to be the import of her speech. And second, there is a loss in the ability of certain speakers to both produce certain utterances and be interpreted correctly. In this section I will provide a brief description of the linguistic mechanisms that underlie these effects in order to prepare the ground for establishing, in the final section, the claim that post-racial discourse perpetuates hermeneutical injustice.

Language is a complex social practice with various moving parts. Some of those parts involve the speaker, some involve the recipient/hearer/audience, and others concern the circumstances surrounding the interaction between speaker and audience. When two or more people wish to communicate with each other, there is an exchange that occurs between them. To take as our starting point a simple exchange, a speaker has a thought she wants to share with her interlocutor, and she translates that thought into words she believes her audience will understand. This simple picture already suggests quite a few things. Firstly, it assumes the existence of a system of meaningful strings of symbols and sounds commonly shared by our interlocutors. Secondly, it also presupposes a relatively facile ability on the part of speaker and audience to coordinate in such a way that communication is successful, i.e. the speaker is able to "get across" the message she wants to share.

J.L. Austin, in his famous William James Lecture *How To Do Things With Words* (1975), investigated the various ways in which we use language to perform various actions. He made a distinction between three types of linguistic acts: *locutionary acts*, *illocutionary acts*, and *perlocutionary effects*. One performs a locutionary act when one makes a meaningful utterance. Illocutionary acts are actions that have a specific kind of *force*, e.g. making a request, issuing a command, asking a question, etc. Perlocutionary acts are acts that achieve certain effects in a hearer by making an utterance with a particular force, e.g. getting an audience to laugh at a joke or the feelings of offense provoked by an insult.

Austin focused most of his attention on the illocutionary act, and that is where our focus will be as well. In a typical exchange between speaker and hearer (and/or audience), the speaker makes an utterance with an intended force. The hearer/audience receives or understands the utterance in part by recognizing the intended force. When this transaction goes smoothly, communication is successful. But it can also go wrong in several ways. Sometimes the illocutionary act fails due to certain background conditions not being met. For instance, no matter how sincere, a pronouncement of marriage by a speaker who is not licensed in the proper way does not succeed in changing a couple's marital status. An intended act might also fail because the hearer/audience does not recognize the intended force. In some of those cases, the speaker is at fault in some way. In others, the fault lies with the audience. For the purposes of this essay I will be concerned with a subset of cases of the latter sort.

I want to briefly highlight two ways speech can fail to register with its intended force. The first way involves the systematic undermining of the very ability to perform certain speech acts because of the speaker's social identity, what Rebecca Kukla refers to as a *discursive injustice* (Kukla, 2014). Kukla understands speech acts in terms of *inputs* and *outputs*. Pragmatic inputs are entitlement conditions like contextual constraints, constraints concerning the speaker/audience relationship, and the instantiation of conventions that must obtain before a speech act can have "its characteristic performative force" (442). Pragmatic outputs are the sets of normative statuses instituted by the speech act. On Kukla's account, in order for a speech act to have performative force, it must make a difference to people's behavioral dispositions. For instance, marriage pronouncements change the couple's tax status and family relationships and how people previously unrelated now relate to one another.

The failure Kukla highlights is one in which a speaker sets out to perform one speech act – while being entitled to perform it in that context and use the conventionally appropriate words, tones, and gestures – but the kind of uptake given constitutes an entirely different act.[10] With these cases the incapacity to perform an act with its characteristic force is due to the speaker's social identity. For instance, a woman trying to resist the sexual advances of another might say, "No," which characteristically has the force of denial, but be read as performing an act with the force of affirmation. Let us call this *illocutionary flipping*.

The second kind of failure of illocution has been discussed in the work of philosophers such as Jennifer Hornsby (2012), Rae Langton (1993), Langton and Hornsby (1998), Ishani Maitra (2009), and Mary Kate McGowan (2014). The case in view here is what has come to be known as *silencing*, and the way it is discussed in the literature is basically as a short-circuiting of illocution. In the example above concerning the woman being misread as affirming rather than denying sexual advances, her illocution is silenced just in case her speech act is not given uptake as a denial. That is, it is not read as a different speech act, i.e. affirmation, but rendered inert – what Langton and Hornsby (1998) have referred to as "illocutionary disablement."

Both of these kinds of failure, when systematically applied to members of marginalized social groups, constitute oppressive harm. Whether caused through illocutionary flipping or silencing, the gap in shared interpretive resources creates the occasion for misinterpreting or dismissing the experiences of the members of marginalized groups.

## 5. The post-racial ideal and hermeneutical injustice

Having set in place some key concepts from the epistemic injustice literature and speech act theory, I will conclude with a brief expansion of and support for the claim that pursuit of the post-racial ideal results in hermeneutic injustices. It achieves this by either illocutionarily flipping or silencing the utterances of members of marginalized groups concerning racial injustice. The post-racial ideal, in either of the assimilationist, eliminativist, or colorblind forms, seeks to establish a society in which we've "moved beyond race" in some significant fashion. How would we achieve such a state?

Presumably, the journey involves ceasing to think, act, and feel in terms of race. One would have to alter one's perceptions of oneself and others as raced beings on the eliminativist, colorblind, and assimilationist accounts. This would seem to involve a change not only in how we think, but also in how we speak. In fact, one might think that the way to effectively change how we think is via our discursive practices. We find support for such an argument, for example, in Lera Boroditsky (2001), where she discusses the effects of language on English and Mandarin speakers' conceptions of time. Boroditsky claims that the way we speak, shapes the way we think.[11] If she is right, then the way to achieve a post-racial state will necessarily involve new discursive practices surrounding race.

Quite often we find proponents of post-racialism endorsing the elimination of race-talk, at least from the public square. One example of this move is California Proposition 54, the so-called "Racial Privacy Initiative." The proposition, if passed, would have "restricted state and local governments in California from collecting or using information on a person's race, ethnicity, color, or national origin for the purposes of public education, public contracting, public employment, and other government operations" (California Proposition 54). This policy, exemplifying either the more restricted *political* or *public eliminativist* positions, or the broader *global* eliminativist position, would rob our ordinary discursive practices of linguistic and hermeneutic resources for identifying racial harms. It naively assumes the absence of race-talk means the elimination of racism. But as Eduardo Bonilla-Silva (2013) has argued, explicitly racist animus or beliefs are not necessary for the continuation of racial inequality. Bonilla-Silva points out the various apparently non-racial ways racial discrimination takes place. Therefore, eliminating race from our discourse does not necessarily lead to a deflated importance of race for orchestrating our lives. Indeed, such elimination obscures the role race plays and impoverishes our shared hermeneutical resources. Given our discussion in sections 2 and 3, we can now see that this impoverishment constitutes a hermeneutical injustice.

I think we end up in much the same place on the assimilationist and colorblind versions of post-racialism as well. Each views the use of race or racial distinctions as irrelevant for moral, political, economic, and social decision-making. But if the strategy is to rid our vocabularies of racial terms and categories, this leaves the various non-verbal ways we communicate race unaccounted for.[12] It is likely that an erasure of race-talk would lull us into falsely believing we've undone the significance of race in decision-making, while in reality we've simply obscured the presence of race still at work in our everyday practices. Thus, it is not difficult to see that creating such a lacuna would result in the production of hermeneutical gaps that in turn give rise to hermeneutical injustices. If we do indeed communicate things about race non-verbally as well as verbally, then reordering our verbal behavior does not automatically adjust the non-verbal behavior.

Race would still be operative in our decision-making processes – even deleteriously so in many instances – while our post-racial vocabulary would rob us of the shared hermeneutical resources to describe them. My view thus represents an extension of Fricker's analysis. Hermeneutical gaps arise not only due to the lack of development of certain concepts for certain speakers—i.e. hermeneutical marginalization—but also from the suppression of existing concepts. Hermeneutical gaps are also actively maintained through the use of alternative concepts such as, e.g. 'postracial.'

The chant of "Black Lives Matter" being met with the response "All Lives Matter" also displays the kind of hermeneutical injustice that results from a post-racial understanding. The most plausible reading of "Black Lives Matter," as I stated in the introductory section, is an inclusive one; that is, one that implores us not to exclude the value of Black lives. In fact, the misreading of this phrase underscores the lack of understanding concerning the structural epistemic injustices endured by Black Americans.[13] Those who give an exclusive reading to the slogan are belittling, downplaying, or ignoring the turbulent history of how Black people have been treated in the United States.[14] I submit that the inclusive reading is the most natural if one considers the context in which it is uttered (i.e. suspicious killings by police officers of Black individuals without indictments in many cases, or conviction in others), the broader historical context of the treatment of Black people in the U.S., and the contrary treatment of White people in this same historical and present context. In order for someone to interpret the phrase as an exclusionary one, i.e. "Only Black lives matter," that person has to either accept the idiot post-racialism Taylor describes or believe the use of racial terms is inappropriate because it provokes division and upsets the path to a post-racial society. In either case, it has the effect of blocking the marginalized speaker's contribution to making sense of social reality. And because this hermeneutical blocking results in further material disadvantages beyond discursive ones, it is – channeling Fricker – a systematic rather than incidental harm.

Ultimately, the pursuit of a post-racial society by means of a change in our discursive practices leaves in place the social structures that fuel racial injustices. Rather than achieving a state of post-racial harmony, pursuit of the post-racial ideal entrenches existing disharmony while creating hermeneutical lacunae that make harmony even more difficult to achieve.

**Related chapters**: 3, 9, 10, 13, 23, 24, 27

## Notes

1. For an argument supporting this interpretation, see (Patterson, 2015).
2. For an argument that propaganda can be sincere, see (Stanley, 2015).
3. Examples of such letters can be found at The Archive at the King Center website: http://thekingcenter.org/archive.
4. Certainly, the slogan "Black Lives Matter" and responses to it can be analyzed in terms of both hermeneutical and testimonial injustice. Testimonial injustice, on Fricker's account, "occurs when prejudice causes a hearer to give a deflated level of credibility to a speaker's word" (2009, 1). Fricker notes the possibility of a speaker being "doubly wronged," i.e. "once by the structural prejudice in the shared hermeneutical resource, and once by the hearer in making an identity-prejudiced credibility judgement [sic]" (2009, 159). She intimates that this double wrong is possible but not inevitable. José Medina (2012), however, suggests a tighter connection between hermeneutic and testimonial injustice, that the two become "intertwined," feeding and deepening the effects of each other (96).
5. For a nice discussion of this point, cf. (Dotson, 2012). Additionally, many chapters in this handbook include discussions of the rich "prehistory" of concerns surrounding issues of epistemic injustice across various traditions, disciplines, and communities, some of which informed Fricker's account.
6. One might also make the case that the Negritude and *Africanité* movements were attempts by African and Afro-Caribbean intellectuals to enrich shared hermeneutical resources. Thanks to Ian James Kidd for this suggestion.

7   For instance, see (Davis, 2015).
8   It could be argued that racial assimilation is compatible with the continuance of other types of social groups, e.g. political affiliations, professional identities, or nationality. Thus, assimilationism should be understood in a restricted sense, i.e. as referring only to the racial dimension.
9   I suspect the two ideals aren't as distinct as it might appear. As I understand it, the purpose for assimilation, eliminativism, or adoption of the colorblind principle is the wresting of the grip of race on our social, moral, political, and economic decision-making, presumably because it results in racist societies. That is, a non-racist society is the end game. Thus, in a sense, these strategies could be read as ultimately pursuing a post-racist society. But I will leave this fight for another day.
10  An interesting alternative analysis that might complement Kukla's is presented in Andrew Peet (forthcoming).
11  It is important to note here that the view Boroditsky advocates – the idea that language influences thought, so-called *linguistic relativism thesis* – is weaker than the view commonly known as the Sapir-Whorf hypothesis, encapsulated in the following quote by Edward Sapir: "Human beings . . . are very much at the mercy of the particular language which has become the medium of expression for their society . . . The fact of the matter is that the "real world" is to a large extent unconsciously built up on the language habits of the group" (1929).
12  For a nice review of the literature on nonverbal behavior in intergroup contexts, see (Dovidio, Hebl, Richeson, & Shelton, 2006).
13  Thanks to Ian James Kidd for pointing out this insight.
14  Gaile Pohlhaus, Jr. makes a good case for willful hermeneutical ignorance occurring in dominantly situated knowers with respect to the epistemic tools marginally situated knowers develop to make sense of social experiences. See Pohlhaus, Jr. (2012).

## References

Austin, J. L. (1975). *How to Do Things with Words: Second Edition* (2 edition). Cambridge, MA: Harvard University Press.
Boroditsky, L. (2001). Does Language Shape Thought?: Mandarin and English Speakers' Conceptions of Time. *Cognitive Psychology*, *43*(1), 1–22. http://doi.org/10.1006/cogp.2001.0748
Boxill, B. R. (1992). *Blacks and Social Justice*. Lanham, MD: Rowman & Littlefield.
California Proposition 54. (n.d.). Retrieved October 11, 2015, from http://ballotpedia.org/California_Proposition_54,_the_
Clemons, J. T. (2014). Blind Injustice: The Supreme Court, Implicit Racial Bias, and the Racial Disparity in the Criminal Justice System. *The American Criminal Law Review*, *51*(3), 689–713.
Collins, P. H. (1999). *Black Feminist Thought: Knowledge, Consciousness, and the Politics of Empowerment* (Revised, 10th Anniv., 2 edition). New York: Routledge.
Cooper, A. J. (1990). *A Voice from the South*. New York: Oxford University Press.
Davis, J. H. (2015, May 21). Obama's Twitter Debut, @POTUS, Attracts Hate-Filled Posts. *The New York Times*. Retrieved from www.nytimes.com/2015/05/22/us/politics/obamas-twitter-debut-potus-attracts-hate-filled-posts.html
Dotson, K. (2012). A Cautionary Tale: On Limiting Epistemic Oppression. *Frontiers*, *33*(1), 24–47.
Dovidio, J. F., Hebl, M., Richeson, J. A., & Shelton, J. N. (2006). Nonverbal Communication, Race, and Intergroup Interaction. In *The SAGE Handbook of Nonverbal Communication* (pp. 481–500). Thousand Oaks CA: SAGE. Retrieved from http://knowledge.sagepub.com/view/hdbk_nonverbalcomm/n25.xml
Elmelech, Y. (2004). Housing Inequality in New York City: Racial and Ethnic Disparities in Homeownership and Shelter-Cost Burden. *Housing, Theory and Society*, *21*(4), 163–175. http://doi.org/10.1080/14036090410026338
Fricker, M. (2007). *Epistemic Injustice: Power and the Ethics of Knowing*. Oxford and New York: Oxford University Press.
Gines, K. T. (2014). A Critique of Postracialism: Conserving Race and Complicating Blackness Beyond the Black-white Binary 1. *Du Bois Review*, *11*(1), 75–86. http://doi.org/http://dx.doi.org.ezproxy.princeton.edu/10.1017/S1742058X1400006X
Glasgow, J. (2008). *A Theory of Race* (1 edition). New York: Routledge.
Greenwald, A. G., & Pettigrew, T. F. (2014). With Malice Toward None and Charity for Some: Ingroup Favoritism Enables Discrimination. *American Psychologist*, *69*(7), 669–684. http://doi.org/10.1037/a0036056

Hornsby, J. (2012). Subordination, Silencing, and Two Ideas of Illocution. *Jurisprudence*, *2*(2), 379–385.

Joseph, R. L. (2009). "Tyra Banks Is Fat": Reading (Post-)Racism and (Post-)Feminism in the New Millennium. *Critical Studies in Media Communication*, *26*(3), 237–254. http://doi.org/10.1080/15295030903015096

Kindy, K. (2015, May 30). Fatal Police Shootings in 2015 Approaching 400 Nationwide. *The Washington Post*. Retrieved from www.washingtonpost.com/national/fatal-police-shootings-in-2015-approaching-400-nationwide/2015/05/30/d322256a-058e-11e5-a428-c984eb077d4e_story.html

Kirk, J. A. (2006). Housing, Urban Development, and the Persistence of Racial Inequality in the Post-Civil Rights Era South. *Souls*, *8*(1), 47–60. http://doi.org/10.1080/10999940500516967

Kukla, R. (2014). Performative Force, Convention, and Discursive Injustice. *Hypatia*, *29*(2), 440–457.

Langton, R. (1993). Speech Acts and Unspeakable Acts. *Philosophy and Public Affairs*, *22*(4), 293–330.

Langton, R., & Hornsby, J. (1998). Free Speech and Illocution. *Legal Theory*, *4*(1), 21–37.

Lynch, M. J., Patterson, E. B., & Childs, K. K. (2008). *Racial Divide : Racial and Ethnic Biases in the Criminal Justice System*, edited by Michael J. Lynch, E. Britt Patterson and Kristina K. Childs. Monsey, NY: Criminal Justice Press.

Maitra, I. (2009). Silencing Speech. *Canadian Journal of Philosophy*, *39*(2), 309–338.

McGary, H. (2012). *The Post-Racial Ideal (Aquinas Lecture)*. Milwaukee: Marquette University Press.

McGowan, M. K. (2014). Sincerity Silencing. *Hypatia*, *29*(2), 458–473.

Medina, J. (2012). *The Epistemology of Resistance: Gender and Racial Oppression, Epistemic Injustice, and Resistant Imaginations*. Oxford and New York: Oxford University Press.

Murchison, B. (2015, September 1). Bill Murchison – Do "All Lives Matter" or Not? Retrieved September 12, 2015, from http://townhall.com/columnists/billmurchison/2015/09/01/do-all-lives-matter-or-not-n2046218

Nosek, B. A., & Banaji, M. R. (2009). Implicit Attitude. In B. Tim, C. Axel, & W. Patrick (Eds.), *The Oxford Companion to Consciousness* (pp. 84–85). Oxford: Oxford University Press.

Oliver, M. L., & Shapiro, T. M. (2006). *Black Wealth, White Wealth : A New Perspective on Racial Inequality* (10th anniversary ed.). New York: Routledge.

Patterson, B. Ellington. (2015, September 4). Here's the conservative playbook for tearing down Black Lives Matter. Retrieved December 13, 2015, from www.motherjones.com/mojo/2015/09/conservative-record-criminalizing-black-social-movements

Peet, A. (forthcoming). Epistemic Injustice in Utterance Interpretation. *Synthese*, 1–23.

Pettigrew, T. F. (2009). Post-Racism? Putting President Obama's Victory in Perspective. *Du Bois Review: Social Science Research on Race*, *6*(2), 279–292.

Shin, L. (2015, March 26). The Racial Wealth Gap: Why A Typical White Household Has 16 Times The Wealth Of A Black One. Retrieved December 17, 2015, from www.forbes.com/sites/laurashin/2015/03/26/the-racial-wealth-gap-why-a-typical-white-household-has-16-times-the-wealth-of-a-black-one/

Stanley, J. (2015). *How Propaganda Works*. Princeton, NJ: Princeton University Press.

Taylor, P. C. (2014). Taking Post-Racialism Seriously: From Movement Mythology to Racial Formation. *Du Bois Review*, *11*(1), 9–25.

Taylor, P. C., Alcoff, L. M., & Anderson, L. (forthcoming). *Routledge Companion to Philosophy of Race*. London: Routledge.

Unarmed Victims of 2014. (n.d.). Retrieved September 12, 2015, from http://mappingpoliceviolence.org/unarmed/

# 13
# DECOLONIAL PRAXIS AND EPISTEMIC INJUSTICE

*Andrea J. Pitts*

For our cognitive edge cannot be defined in *moralistic* terms – that is, we ourselves as intellectuals are not the "victims" of oppression, nor of wicked exploiters, and it is neither our intention to set out to "reclaim the true value" of our "minority" being nor, indeed, to establish a "dictatorship of the Minoriat." Such a *moralistic* approach is the logical result of taking our *isms* as isolated rather than systemic facts. Rather we are constituted as a negative ontological category by the systemically functioning directive signs of an order of discourse generated from the descriptive statement of man on the model of a natural organism, an order of discourse that it is our task to *disenchant*.

(*Wynter 1987*)

My homeland was desert until they started irrigating and turned the desert into a subtropical paradise, a garden that grows everything from papayas, to avocados, to sugar cane, to . . . whatever . . . all in the space of my lifetime. The straight world, the gay world, the literary world, the world of academia . . . I go in and out of these worlds. I think that's why I picked this topic tonight, so I could give you a different perspective.

(*Anzaldúa 2009 [1986]*)

In a 2009 essay, Walter Mignolo asks his readers to consider "[For whom] and when, why, and where knowledge is generated" (Mignolo 2009, 2). He continues:

Asking these questions means to shift the attention from the enunciated to the enunciation. And by so doing, turning Descartes's dictum inside out: rather than assuming that thinking comes before being, one assumes instead that it is a racially marked body in a geo-historical marked space that feels the urge or get[s] the call to speak, to articulate, in whatever semiotic system, the urge that makes of living organisms "human" beings.

(*Mignolo 2009, 2*)

For Mignolo, inverting the Cartesian presupposition of rationality as a requirement for knowing the self is an attempt to "de-link" knowledge practices from the dominant macro-narratives of modernity.[1] One such narrative of modernity is common to Anglophone academic philosophy:

that the beginnings of civilization were founded in ancient Greek thought, and accordingly, that distinct intellectual developments and trajectories from this seat of civilization can be tracked through Western Europe and eventually to Anglo-America. The second macro-narrative stems from a critique of capitalism developed by sociologists during the Cold War. Theorists in this vein of sociological critique, such as Immanuel Wallerstein (Wallerstein 1983) and Fernand Braudel (Braudel 1992 [1979]), describe modernity as the rise of a "modern world-system," developing since the fifteenth century. They propose that it was neither mere national projects nor intellectual developments arising from particular geopolitical locations that came to stand in for the narrative of "civilizing" national identities such as "the Dutch," "the Portuguese," "the Belgian," "the Spanish," "the French," and "the English." Rather it was the emergence of a capitalist world-economy through conquest and imperial expansion that became the basis for a densely interrelated socioeconomic network known as the "modern world-system." Classical Marxist theory had, according to world-systems theory, an epistemic "blind spot" in the sense that a great deal of Marxist analysis did not view imperial expansion as itself constitutive of modern capitalism. Instead, classical Marxism held that colonialism could be explained "as a collateral effect of global European expansion and was in this sense a necessary route toward the advent of communism" (Castro-Gómez 2008, 260–264). The sociologists of world-systems theory then provided a way to link capital expansion to the expansion of knowledge production, which later thinkers, including Edward Said (1978) and Gayatri Chakravorty Spivak (1988), would take up in their respective writings.

In these critical veins, the subject matter of Western/Global Northern knowledge practices and the disciplinary philosophical discourses of epistemology have never existed merely as forms of abstract argumentation about belief, truth, justification, or cognition. Rather, as is a common theme among decolonial thought and praxis, knowledge production itself – implicating universities, academic presses, research institutes, and the range of other associated networks comprised of those who concern themselves with "intellectual" production – is a materially embedded set of social and historical phenomena. In addition, the wide-ranging practices that concern themselves with the production and dissemination of knowledge are themselves located in differing political and cultural sites of enunciation, each with differing relations to histories and realities of colonialism, imperialism, and capitalism.

This framing of epistemology – what Mignolo refers to as a *geopolitics of knowledge* – will be the starting point for this examination of the relationship between decolonial approaches to "epistemology" and the topic of epistemic injustice. While there are many distinct threads of decolonial thought and praxis,[2] this essay attends primarily to discussions among Latin American, U.S. Latina, and Caribbean decolonial theorists to bring these critical discourses into conversation with the growing body of scholarship in Anglophone academic philosophy that is the organizing theme of this volume. As such, the focus of this chapter is the following problem: how to produce disciplinary discourses from Anglophone North American academic institutions on the topic of a *decolonial* geopolitics of knowledge without perpetuating an Occidentalism and "othering" of communities whose existences require a perpetual struggle against neoliberal economic expansion and epistemic hegemony. For example, Mignolo states this problem in two related ways:

> One is the political agenda of those of us (an empty category to be filled) born in North or South America, India, Iran, or Africa but writing and teaching here in the United States who are concerned with colonial discourse. The other issue is the agenda of those (an empty category to be filled) born or writing there in India, Iran, Africa, or South America who are struggling to resist modern colonization, including the academic one from here.
> 
> *(Mignolo 1993, 122)*

Given North American Anglophone and Western European institutional dominance, a decolonial geopolitics of knowledge from such centralized sites will require a careful set of strategies to de-link it from the homogenizing and totalizing trends of neocolonial expansion that characterize so much academic production in the U.S., Canada, and Europe.

In what follows, in the first two sections, I provide a brief history of decolonial thought and several related fields of study, including dependency theory and subaltern studies. This history importantly demonstrates that the concern with just and ethical knowing, as well as resistance to colonial epistemic violence predates the contemporary literature on epistemic injustice within academic Anglophone philosophy. Accordingly, in the final section of the chapter, I examine how the contemporary discourse of epistemic injustices might converge with the aims of a decolonial praxis in the Anglophone Western/Global Northern academy.

## 1. Colonialism, postcolonialism, coloniality, and the Bandung Era

Edward Said's groundbreaking 1978 work *Orientalism* emerged out of what David Scott and Samir Amin describe as the "Bandung Era." The Bandung Era was the period of roughly 1955 to 1977 when many newly independent nations and collective nationalist movements struggling for independence in Asia and Africa began collaborating with other global movements in the hope of developing tools for anticolonial and anti-imperial resistance (Amin 1994; Scott 1999). In this vein, the Bandung Conference of 1955 and the Cuban Revolution of 1959 marked the beginnings of various efforts by world leaders in the newly labeled "Third World" to undertake anti-capitalist paths toward socialism (Young 2005). However, despite the national projects of Salvador Allendé in Chile, Michael Manley in Jamaica, or Sirimavo Bandaranaike in Sri Lanka, efforts to combat capitalism during this era were confronted with a number of obstacles. Scott attributes the "failure" of these projects to the dismantling of the Soviet Union and to the rise of global neoliberalism, including the structural adjustment programs of the World Bank and the International Monetary Fund. As such, the anti-imperialist and anti-capitalist momentum springing from these historical junctures gradually waned after the 1970s (Scott 1999, 144).

Also emerging from this era was a series of intellectual debates about knowledge and knowledge production that sought to question the significance and challenges of the various anticolonial and anti-capitalist movements that circulated throughout the twentieth century. The work of Edward Said, in this sense, serves as a landmark piece in the development of a rich theoretical discourse on the epistemic and disciplinary implications of imperialism, colonialism, and economic globalization. Said's main contribution in *Orientalism*, according to Scott, is his criticism of "the Orient's special place in European Western experience" (Said 1978, 1). He refers not merely to the geographic location of various Asian nations relative to Western European nations, but primarily to the Orient as one of Western Europe's "deepest and most recurring images of the Other" (Said 1978, 1). Orientalism, for Said, refers to three aspects of this construction of this "Other" to Occidental Europe: 1) European intellectual institutions are dedicated to the mastery and dissemination of information about "the Orient," 2) such institutions maintain a commitment to an ontological and epistemological distinction made between "the Orient" and "the Occident," and 3) this distinction functions through "a Western style for dominating, restructuring, and having authority over the Orient" (Said 1978, 2–3).

These features of Orientalism also come with three important qualifications according to Said. The first is that the Orient is not merely an idea with no corresponding reality. Said states "There were – and are – cultures and nations whose location is in the East, and their lives, histories, and customs have a brute reality obviously greater than anything that could be said about them in the West" (Said 1978, 5). However, Said states that he has little to contribute to that fact. Second, Orientalism requires an implicit analysis of the configurations of power between the West and non-Western geopolitical contexts, i.e. such analyses of power enable the treatment of the Orient as an object of study. Finally, Said states that Orientalism is not a mere "structure of lies and myths, which, were the truth about them to be told, would simply blow away" (Said 1978, 6). Instead, Said locates Orientalism within various socioeconomic and political institutions that retain a vested socioeconomic interest in preserving the validity and relevance of the placement of "the East" or "the Orient" as the Other to "the West."

In concert with Said's critical interventions on these epistemic issues, a rich set of theoretical resources on the relationship between knowledge practices and colonialism has been circulating in various Latin American disciplinary trajectories as well.[3] Many of these theories connected various philosophical notions of modernity and scientific progress with emerging global networks of economic and political development. Through the work of theorists such as Fernando Henrique Cardoso and Enzo Faletto (1969), Andre Gunder Frank (1969), and Aníbal Quijano (1977), dependency theory, for example, offered critical positions against narratives about the so-called "Third World" that had been circulating extensively throughout the Cold War period. These authors, through various means, sought to explain conceptions of "development" and "underdevelopment" through relational theories of imperial and economic expansion from Western Europe and later through the economic and political expansion of the United States. According to dependency theorists, center-periphery relations of economic and political influence that functioned through the colonization of the Americas, Asia, and Africa (via the extraction and exploitation of laboral and natural resources) were responsible for the demarcation of the boundaries that supported the logic of "stages of development" and the current global political situation.

However, as Ramón Grosfoguel has argued regarding the *dependentistas*, "most dependentista analyses privileged the economic and political aspects of social processes at the expense of cultural and ideological determinations" (Grosfoguel 2008, 326). Rather than relegating the explanation of colonialism to the expanding dynamics of capitalism as classical Marxism had, many dependentistas relegated colonialism solely to the machinations of political and economic processes. One notable exception Grofoguel mentions is the work of Aníbal Quijano, whose writings foreground both political and economic dependency relations, as well as the racial and sexual hierarchies that functioned through capitalist and colonial cultural expansion (Grosfoguel 2008, 326–327). As I will elaborate below, this understanding of the relationship between modernity and coloniality refers to an understanding of modern conceptualizations of freedom, progress, civilization, development, and democratic capitalism as themselves epistemic products of the subjugation and exploitation of colonized and enslaved peoples (Mignolo 2016, 2–3).

## 2. Articulating an academic geopolitics of knowledge

Here, following dependency theory and theories of modernity/coloniality, including understandings of racial, sexual, and gendered dimensions of coloniality, we can begin to link the current discourse of epistemic injustices to decolonial theory. First, as Mignolo notes, Quijano's notion of the "coloniality of power" should be distinguished from the notion of "colonialism." Mignolo writes:

> Colonialism is a concept that inscribes coloniality as a derivative of modernity. In this conception modernity comes first, with colonialism following it. On the other hand, the colonial period implies that, in the Americas, colonialism ended toward the first

quarter of the nineteenth century. Instead coloniality assumes, first, that coloniality constitutes modernity. As a consequence, we are still living under the same regime.

*(Mignolo 2008 [2002], 248–249)*

This conception of coloniality thus establishes the onto-epistemic dimensions of racial hierarchies that functioned through conquest narratives for European imperial expansion and that remain entrenched within contemporary philosophical discourses today. While dependency theory offered conceptual and pragmatic resources for articulating the functionings of "the underside of modernity" (Dussel 1996), theories of race and racial hierarchy, as well as some variants of gender and sexual theory (Lugones 2007; Mohanty 1984; Wynter 1990), are thus able to enrich academic understandings of the social field of coloniality. Moreover, if the modern/colonial world system has required the homogenization of vast numbers of distinct cultural histories as racialized non-Europeans (e.g. "Indians," "Blacks," and "Orientals") for the purposes of global capital, this entails a number of complex interrelated patterns of knowledge production and distribution to sustain those prevailing conceptualizations. Such patterns, according to both decolonial theory and the epistemic injustice literature as well, need to be analyzed, resisted, and overturned.

However, this insight, regarding the intimate relationship between capital expansion and the homogenization of distinct histories and ways of being, speaks to the imbrications of the coloniality of power within Anglophone academia in the United States, Canada, and Western Europe. In this vein, Mario Roberto Morales has argued that the initial invocation of "subalterity" into academic discourses in the 1980s through the writings of the South Asian Subaltern Studies Group was a "'strategic' intellectual construct" employed by theorists to articulate an outside to the intellectual hegemony of "Western lettered culture" (Morales 2008, 482). This strategic set of maneuvers, Morales proposes, was thereby a temporary effort to place a limit onto academic discourses in the Western world until a more "emancipatory" end could be met. This goal would be "to free not only the oppressed from his chains, but also the oppressor from his power, so as to not just limit ourselves to flipping the coin of authoritarianism and thus lose the emancipatory nature of the struggle" (Morales 2008, 483). The irony was that many academicians in the United States did not interpret subalterity as a strategy or temporary maneuver. Rather, through "subaltern" figurations such as the debate surrounding the testimonial credibility of Rigoberta Menchú, Anglophone theorists in Latin American area studies began seeking ways to "provide a voice" to subaltern subjectivities in the academy.[4] Morales describes this shift in the following passage:

What had been a political act of national democratic transformation in the view of Third World intellectuals . . . was, when appropriated by North American professors, made into a careerist dilemma regarding how to deal with the budgetary cuts that neoliberalism was perpetuating against the humanities.

*(2008, 483)*

Speaking here of the early markings of the impact of austerity measures across U.S. and Canadian campuses, Morales pinpoints an important lesson that should be linked to the development of the discourse of epistemic injustices in the Anglophone world. Namely, as the epigraphs that frame this essay suggest, Western academia has never been at a loss for how to reproduce itself and its own mirror-image through displacing an Other. In this sense, bringing the literature of epistemic injustices into conversation with a decolonial geopolitics of knowledge must not seek to merely add another layer to epistemology-qua-philosophy as an already-dominant set of institutional practices in the Western academy. As I outline below, drawing from the writings of several intellectuals who have existed both in the liminal spaces of "minority discourse" in the U.S. and as critics of their own placement within academia of the Global North, I propose in the following section a cautionary note regarding the potential recentering of the geopolitics of knowledge in academic Anglophone philosophy through the discourse of epistemic injustices.

## 3. Decentering epistemic injustices as decolonial praxis

Before attempting to connect epistemic injustice literature in academic philosophy with decolonial thought and praxis, in the spirit of decolonial critique we may ask: toward what end or for whom is this theoretical collaboration a performative invocation? We may, on the one hand, situate the unification of these disparate fields of study as a disciplinary hail that seeks to find points of contact between literatures in the hope of giving rise to new ideas and areas of study for both fields. However, to move behind the invocation of "innovation," we can return to the two epigraphs above. The "disenchantment" heralded by Sylvia Wynter's disapprobation of the proliferation of minority literatures is a call to reject the temptation to merely add one's "truer" voice to the already circumscribed set of hermeneutical possibilities for writing in a new field of study (Wynter 1987, 237–238). Moreover, Wynter guides our attention to the role of the figure of "intellectuals" within our social spaces and the various onto-epistemic stances that we occupy as such. In this vein, in an afterword to the first edited collection of its kind in Anglophone literature dedicated to critical essays written by Caribbean women (*Out of the Kumbla* 1990), Wynter urges her readers that more work must be done to shift the sedimented layers of historical degradation and "existential weightlessness" that have reified perceptions of Caribbean and Black women (Wynter 1990, 365). For those who are invested in revaluing and resituating Caribbean and Black women authors within a literary canon, she states that "all theoretical models function both as 'knowledge' and as the water-with-berries strategy sets of specific groups" (Wynter 1990, 370 n. 53). Wynter offers an endnote referring to the following lines delivered by Caliban to Prospero in Shakespeare's *The Tempest*:

> This island's mine, by Sycorax my mother,
> Which thou takest from me. When thou camest first,
> Thou strokedst me and madest much of me, wouldst give me
> Water with berries in't, and teach me how
> To name the bigger light, and how the less,
> That burn by day and night: and then I loved thee
> And show'd thee all the qualities o' the isle,
> The fresh springs, brine-pits, barren place and fertile:
> Cursed be I that did so!
>
> (Shakespeare, 1.2.332–340)[5]

In effect, Caliban's enchantment with Prospero's offerings was his self-described downfall. By providing the knowledge necessary for survival on the island, Caliban became subject to the ordering constraints and laboral demands of Prospero. In this sense, Wynter is calling her readers, through figurations of *The Tempest* to resist the "'water with berries' strategy sets, of all our present hegemonic, theoretical models in their 'pure' forms" (Wynter 1990).[6]

For our present concerns with the call to explore points of convergence among decolonial discourses and the recent literatures of epistemic injustices, such "water-with-berries" strategies are enacted by relatively centralized discourses that offer an opening in their respective discursive spaces for non-Western or non-white intellectuals working toward decolonial politics and praxis.

Yet, Wynter's suggestion is to refuse "present hegemonic models in their '*pure*' forms" and to seek "demonic grounds" which can reexamine how the absences of specific forms of "knowledge" and "experience" structure the functioning of already-existent discourses. This point thus connects us to other writings, primarily by women of color and other marginalized and "existentially weightless" authors who have been attempting, from epistemic positions *within* various Anglophone academic and literary discourses, to mark the limits of disciplinary fields of meaning.

Consider Gloria E. Anzaldúa's discussion of varying "modes of consciousness" that allow for differing forms of cognition, creativity, and feeling.[7] In a 1986 lecture given at Vermont College, Anzaldúa outlines her thinking on the topic of the imagination. She offers brief autobiographical excerpts from her life to sketch how shifting modes of consciousness displace and place our creative capacities and stability within a given social order. In the epigraph I mention above, Anzaldúa's location both within and outside of various social orders – i.e. the straight world, the gay world, the literary world, the world of academia – provide her the ability to critically shift through differing modes of consciousness. Much like her notion of the *borderlands* or *nepantla*, Anzaldúa points to the often uncomfortable and precarious positioning of herself within these varying discourses. Moreover, by describing her homeland as an agriculturally developed space that produces non-native and mass-produced food products, she notes the rich and tempting ways in which the manipulations of coloniality can offer modes of being/feeling/knowing that may nourish and delight us.[8]

As Anzaldúa, Wynter, and Mignolo each point out through their respective works, however, it is the possibility of producing counter-knowledges and critiques from these liminal loci of enunciation that differentiate them from dominant racial, gendered, classed, able-bodied, sexual, and religious ways of being/feeling/knowing. This liminality, however, will fail to trace an onto-aesthetic mark within academic philosophy if the discourse of epistemic injustices does not engage primarily through the writings of marginalized and subjugated authorial positionings. Thus, the test for how such an emergent discourse in academic philosophy will converge with decolonial theory, and praxis will be how it de-centers, what Catherine Walsh describes as, "the white racialized intellectual paradigm – of who intellectuals are and who are intellectuals – and the intellectual authority of the academy and its ties to the State" (Walsh 2010, 209). Accordingly, many of the theorists in this volume, whose work draws from spaces of liminality and who thereby attempt to push philosophy's disciplinary production beyond its intellectualized circulations in the academy, are developing the possibility for connecting decolonial praxis to the terrain of epistemic injustices. Yes, such a proposal is grand and invariably invokes a novel form of transnational and pluriversal being/feeling/knowing. However, to view the intellectual struggles of academia as isolated rather than systemic runs the risk of enchanting us once again by Prospero's pleasures. Rather, as Anzaldúa suggests, perhaps it is the memory's imagination of a non-irrigated desert that will endow us with the perspective of disenchantment for our academic pursuits today.

**Related chapters**: 9, 10, 11, 12, 34, 37

# Notes

1 "Delinking" refers to the attempts to shift away from the presumed universality of a dominant hegemonic frame of reference (e.g. "modernization," "the West," etc.) and shift toward the universality of non-dominant worldviews with a pluralized conception of being/knowing as a universal project (Mignolo 2007, 543).

2 Other trajectories of decolonial thought and praxis include those of African, African-American, Arabic, Caribbean, First Nations, Native American, Muslim, and South Asian knowledge traditions.

3 These include notable works by Orlando Fals-Borda (1971), Enrique Dussel (1977), Edmundo O'Gorman (1991 [1958]), and Leopoldo Zea (1957).

4 The academic controversy surrounding Rigoberta Menchú erupted following David Stoll's publication of a series of criticisms about the factual accuracy of Menchú's autobiographical account or *testimonio*. In Stoll's work, he proposed both a critique of the truth of Menchú's recounting of events affecting her and her family in *Me llamo Rigoberta Menchú* (1983), and a critique of leftist academic attempts to commodify and recirculate her testimonio as an example of subaltern literature. Defenders of her work, however, such as John Beverley, have argued that *Me llamo Rigoberta Menchú* is not an attempt to make present a subaltern voice in the academia, but rather that the appropriate target of critique should be the multicultural politics within academia that have presumed a form of epistemic egalitarianism that minimizes the authorial agency of Menchú (See Arias 2001; Beverley 2004; Menchú Tum 1985; Morales 1999; Stoll 1999).
5 Wynter may have also been indirectly calling to mind with this reference George Lamming's (1971) novel *Water with Berries*, although her footnote makes reference to Shakespeare's *The Tempest*.
6 Wynter's primary focus in this piece is the absence of "Caliban's woman" in *The Tempest*. Wynter figures the absence of a desirous native feminine counterpart to Caliban as a consequence of the dominance of Miranda's onto-aesthetic presence in the play. According to this reading, Miranda dramatically enacts the dynamics of white feminism's displacement of women of color.
7 Mignolo also cites Anzaldúa as a pivotal figure exhibiting a method of decolonial praxis (Mignolo 2000).
8 The phrase "being/feeling/knowing" is derived from Wynter's articulation of the ontological, aesthetic, and epistemic dimensions of articulating "the self." See, for example, Wynter (1987).

# References

Amin, Samir. 1994. *Re-Reading the Postwar Period: An Intellectual Itinerary*. New York: Monthly Review Press.
Anzaldúa, Gloria E. 2009 [1986]. 'Creativity and Switching Modes of Consciousness.' In *The Gloria Anzaldúa Reader*, edited by AnaLouise Keating. Durham: Duke University Press.
Arias, Arturo. 2001. *The Rigoberta Menchú Controversy*. Minneapolis: University of Minnesota Press.
Beverley, John. 2004. *Testimonio: On the Politics of Truth*. Minneapolis: University of Minnesota Press.
Braudel, Fernand. 1992 [1979]. *The Perspective of the World: Vol. 3 of Civilization and Capitalism, 15th-18th Century*. Translated by Sian Reynolds. Berkeley: University of California Press.
Cardoso, Fernando Henrique and Enzo Faletto. 1969. *Dependencia y desarrollo en América Latina*. Mexico City: Fondo de Cultura Económica.
Castro-Gómez, Santiago. 2008. '(Post)Coloniality for Dummies: Latin American Perspectives on Modernity, Coloniality, and the Geopolitics of Knowledge.' In *Coloniality at Large: Latin America and the Postcolonial Debate*, edited by Mabel Moraña, Enrique Dussel, and Carlos A. Jáuregui. Durham: Duke University Press.
Dussel, Enrique. 1977. *Filosofía de la liberación*. Mexico City: Editorial Edicol.
Dussel, Enrique. 1996. *The Underside of Modernity: Apel, Ricoeur, Rorty, Taylor, and the Philosophy of Liberation*. Translated and edited by Eduardo Mendieta. New York: Humanities Press.
Fals-Borda, Orlando. 1971. *Ciencia propia y colonialismo intelectual: Los nuevos rumbos*. Bogotá: C. Valencia Editores.
Frank, Andre Gunder. 1969. *Latin America: Underdevelopment or Revolution*. New York: Monthly Review Press.
Grosfoguel, Ramón. 2008. 'Developmentalism, Modernity, and Dependency Theory in Latin America.' In *Coloniality at Large: Latin America and the Postcolonial Debate*, edited by Mabel Moraña, Enrique Dussel, and Carlos A. Jáuregui. Durham: Duke University Press.
Lamming, George. 1971. *Water with Berries*. London: Longman.
Lugones, María. 2007. 'Heterosexualism and the Colonial/Modern Gender System.' *Hypatia* 22 (1): 186–209.
Menchú Tum, Rigoberta. 1985. *Me llamo Rigoberta Menchú y así me nació la conciencia*, edited by Elisabeth Burgos-Debray. Mexico City: Siglo XXL.
Mignolo, Walter D. 1993 'Colonial and Postcolonial Discourse: Cultural Critique or Academic Colonialism?' *Latin American Research Review* 28(3): 120–134.
Mignolo, Walter D. 2000. *Local Histories/Global Designs: Coloniality, Subaltern Knowledges, and Border Thinking*. Princeton: Princeton University Press.
Mignolo, Walter D. 2007. 'Delinking.' *Cultural Studies* 21 (2): 449–514.
Mignolo, Walter D. 2008 [2002]. 'The Geopolitics of Knowledge and the Colonial Difference.' In *Coloniality at Large: Latin America and the Postcolonial Debate*, edited by Mabel Moraña, Enrique Dussel, and Carlos A. Jáuregui. Durham: Duke University Press.

Mignolo, Walter D. 2009. 'Epistemic Disobedience, Independent Thought, and De-colonial Freedom.' *Theory, Culture & Society* 26 (7–8): 1–23.

Mignolo, Walter D. 2016. 'Global Coloniality: Decolonality after Decolonization and Dewesternization after the Cold War.' Paper for the 13th Rhodes World Public Forum, World Public Forum Dialogue of Civilizations.org. January 29, 2016. http://wpfdc.org/images/2016_blog/W.Mignolo_Decoloniality_after_Decolonization_Dewesternization_after_the_Cold_War.pdf.

Mohanty, Chandra Talpade. 1984. 'Under Western Eyes: Feminist Scholarship and Colonial Discourses.' *Boundary 2* 12 (3) *On Humanism and the University I: The Discourse of Humanism*. (Spring–Autumn): 333–358.

Morales, Mario Roberto. 1999. *La articulación de las diferencias, o, El síndrome de Maximón : Los discursos literarios y polítocos del debate interétnico en Guatemala*. Guatemala: FLASCO.

Morales, Mario Roberto. 2008. 'Peripheral Modernity and Differential *Mestizaje* in Latin America: Outside Subalternist Postcolonialism.' In *Coloniality at Large: Latin America and the Postcolonial Debate*, edited by Mabel Moraña, Enrique Dussel, and Carlos A. Jáuregui. Durham: Duke University Press.

O'Gorman, Edmundo. 1991 [1958]. *La invención de América: Investigación acerca de la estructura histórica del Nuevo Mundo y el sentido de su devenir*. Mexico City: Fondo de Cultura Económica.

Quijano, Aníbal. 1977. *Imperialismo y marginalidad en América Latina*. Lima: Mosca Azul.

Said, Edward. 1978. *Orientalism*. New York: Vintage Books.

Scott, David. 1999. *Refashioning Futures: Criticism after Postcoloniality*. Princeton: Princeton University Press.

Shakespeare, William. 2012 [1611]. *The Tempest*, edited by Grace Tiffany. Boston: Wadsworth, Cengage Learning.

Spivak, Gayatri Chakravorty. 1988. 'Can the Subaltern Speak?' In *Marxism and the Interpretation of Culture*, edited by Lawrence Grossberg and Cary Nelson. Champagne: University of Illinois Press.

Stoll, Davis. 1999. *Rigoberta Menchú and the Story of All Poor Guatemalans*. Boulder: Westview Press.

Wallerstein, Immanuel. 1983. *Historical Capitalism and Capitalist Civilization*. London: Verso.

Walsh, Catherine. 2010. 'Political-Epistemic Insurgency, Social Movements, and the Refounding of the State.' In *Rethinking Intellectuals in Latin America*, edited by Mabel Moraña and Bret Gustafson. Madrid: Iberoamericana.

Wynter, Sylvia. 1987. 'On Disenchanting Discourse: '"Minority" Literary Criticism and Beyond,' *Cultural Critique*, no. 7 (1987): 207–244.

Wynter, Sylvia. 1990. 'Beyond Miranda's Meanings: Un/silencing the "Demonic Ground" of Caliban's "Woman".' In *Out of the Kumbla: Caribbean Women and Literature*, edited by Carole Boyce Davies and Elaine Savory Fido. Trenten: Africa World Press, Inc.

Young, Robert J. C. 2005. 'Postcolonialism: From Bandung to the Tricontinental.' *HISTOREIN* 5: 11–21.

Zea, Leopoldo. 1957. *America en la Historia*. Mexico City: Fondo de la Cultural Económica, Universidad Nacional Autónoma de México, Centro de Estudios Filosóficos.

# 14
# QUEER EPISTEMOLOGY AND EPISTEMIC INJUSTICE

*Kim Q. Hall*

One of queer theory's most influential claims is that sexuality delineates an epistemic rather than a primarily erotic space in western contexts (Foucault 1990; Sedgwick 1990; McWhorter 1999: 40–41). Queer theory challenges two prevailing assumptions about sexuality in Western contexts: (1) sexuality is a stable, fixed part of innate human nature and (2) sexual identities and acts exist prior to and independent of the need to know and catalogue them as such. Thinking queerly about sexuality denaturalizes sexual identities and acts and the presumed inevitability of connections between them.

Emerging as a scholarly field in the United States in the early 1990's and departing from the then-named gay and lesbian studies' emphasis on making visible and revaluing gay and lesbian people and experience, queer theory is a field whose genealogical approach to gender and sexual identity places the coherence of those identities in question. Queer theorists ask: what are the conditions for the possibility of the emergence of gender and sexual identities, and how does power operate as both an oppressive, repressive force and as that which enables resistance in the name of sexual subjects (Foucault 1990)? Queer theory is influenced by Michel Foucault's reconceptualization of power as both repressive and productive, as that which not only oppresses those deemed "perverse," but also produces a "reverse discourse," the possibility of those deemed "perverse" to resist and demand recognition (101).

A concern for testimonial injustice has been a foundational and abiding concern for queer epistemology. For example, within western contexts, compulsions to reveal one's sexuality (to "come out" and make known one's sexual identity) generate a fraught epistemic terrain in which the epistemic authority of sexually minoritized people is contested. As Eve Sedgwick points out, even when one announces the truth of one's sexuality (or gender) by coming out, that announcement is often met with questions like "How do you know?" or "Are you sure?" and it is not uncommon to be told that one is mistaken in what one thinks one knows about oneself (1990: 79). Furthermore, in the absence of any claim to sexual identity, one becomes the recipient of various forms of pressure to announce the truth of one's desire (Sedgwick 1990; McWhorter 1999). To be situated as gender or sexually deviant is to experience the truth about one's gender or sexuality as not in one's control.

Queer epistemology points to another form of testimonial injustice, namely the epistemic violence of compulsory testimony about one's sexuality and gender. Rachel Ann McKinney analyzes the productive role of power on extracted or compelled speech, especially the injustice of forced confession in assigning criminal responsibility in racist contexts (2016). A queer epistemological approach to testimonial injustice attends not only to the silencing of those deemed deviant but also the epistemic violence perpetuated by the compulsion to occupy an identity category, to understand oneself as a certain kind of person because of one's desires and actions. The imperative to know one's own or others' sexuality has given rise to numerous forms of surveillance, all geared toward revealing the truth of sexuality. Regardless of how one might understand oneself, every minute aspect of one's behavior, appearance, and interests are taken as signs of the truth of one's sexuality (McWhorter 1999: 24–25). Testimony is not optional.

A queer epistemological approach to testimonial injustice contributes another perspective on hermeneutical injustice. Gaile Pohlhaus, Jr. (2012) addresses the limitations of Miranda Fricker's (2007) account of hermeneutical injustice, noting that the problem is not only the absence of conceptual resources among marginalized knowers; the problem is also the refusal of dominant knowers to allow their interpretations of the world to be informed by the knowledge of those who are marginally situated. This is a form of injustice Pohlhaus, Jr. calls "willful hermeneutic injustice" (2012: 722). Willful hermeneutic injustice is an apt name for some forms of response to queer critiques of assimilationist politics, normalization, and binary conceptions of identity. As Pohlhaus, Jr. puts it, "those who are situated in positions for which epistemic resources are underdeveloped are well situated to know this: that there are whole parts of the world for which dominantly held resources are not very suitable" (719–720). From a queer epistemological perspective, binary conceptions of gender and sexuality are woefully inadequate for knowing the complex experiences and realities of gender and desire.

While some have questioned the political usefulness of queer theory, queer theorists contend that a critically queer position, one attuned to the exclusions of unifying tendencies in political movements and the contingency of subject positions in whose name political resistance occurs, enables a more democratized politics (Butler 1993: 231). In this chapter I discuss the meaning and significance of queer epistemology by focusing on the following themes: (1) sexuality as a problem for truth, (2) queer epistemology and self-knowledge, (3) queer epistemologies and standpoint, and (4) queer and crip epistemologies. I highlight some of the questions and problems a queer epistemology strives to address, as well as some of the forms of epistemic injustice that a queer epistemic framework reveals and attempts to undo.

## Sexuality as a problem for truth

Queer theorists approach sexuality and sexual identity as effects of what Foucault calls a "regime of power-knowledge-pleasure" (1990: 11). Thus understood, sexuality is reconceived as a site of the operation of power and not merely an inner, repressed truth (1990). Foucault uses a genealogical approach to sexuality and shows how sexuality is a problem for truth, not a fixed, innate truth of human nature waiting for discovery. Following Foucault, the history of sexuality in western contexts is a history of sexuality's emergence as a problem for truth, as something that can and must be known. One historical effect of this "will to knowledge" about sexuality was the emergence of the "homosexual" as a species, a kind of person.

Influenced by Foucault's understanding of sexuality, Eve Sedgwick contends that the problem of the homo/heterosexual definition is central to Western institutions and societies, so much so that any scholarly project that fails to critically contend with the homo/heterosexual binary will fail to understand whatever aspect of Western culture it seeks to know (1990: 1). The emergence of the term homosexual in the late nineteenth century, followed by the emergence of the term heterosexual inaugurated

> the world-mapping by which every given person, just as he or she was necessarily assignable to a male or a female gender, was now considered necessarily assignable as well to a homo- or hetero-sexuality, a binarized identity that was full of implications, however confusing, for even the ostensibly least sexual aspects of personal existence. It was this new development that left no space in culture exempt from the potent incoherences of homo/heterosexual definition.
>
> *(1990: 2)*

The crisis generated by the notion that something possibly unknown to oneself nonetheless pervasively influences behaviors and interests fueled intense interest in creating systems of surveillance devoted to cataloguing all evidence of a person's sexuality. Everything from the length of one's ring finger relative to one's middle finger, to one's gait and one's interest in music, could be taken as evidence of one's true underlying sexuality. As a result, one learned to monitor one's own and others' behavior for the least sign of sexual deviance (Foucault 1990; Sedgwick 1990; McWhorter 1999).

Sedgwick's turn to the implications of the "crisis of homo/heterosexual definition" questions the epistemological ground of what she calls "minoritizing" and "universalizing" discourses of sexuality. A minoritizing conception, Sedgwick explains, understands the question of homo/heterosexual definition as pertinent only for a distinct group of homosexuals; whereas, a universalizing conception of sexuality understands the question of homo/heterosexual definition as bearing on all sexual subjects (1990: 1, 11). According to Sedgwick, these two conflicting approaches constitute the "common sense" about sexuality in Western culture, and both take for granted the possibility of knowing the truth of sexuality.

In *Epistemology of the Closet*, Sedgwick adopts a deconstructive approach to the homo/heterosexual binary, exploring the implications of how each term's definitional solidity is contingent upon the other term. What results, for Sedgwick and for queer theorists generally, is an appreciation of the ignorance at the core of knowledge about sexuality, an understanding of how "relations of the closet" put into play an ultimately unresolvable tension between knowledge and ignorance about sexuality (1990: 3, 8, 71, 81).

Sedgwick's framing of the closet as central to the circulation of knowledge and ignorance about sexuality is important for queer epistemology. From an Enlightenment perspective on knowledge, the closet functions as a source of possible certain knowledge. That is, behind its closed door, lies a truth waiting to be revealed. Thinking queerly about the closet suggests that any truth supposedly concealed there is actually contingent upon ignorance both inside and outside the closet. One implication for queer epistemology is the view that knowledge is not the opposite of ignorance.

The co-constitutive relation between knowledge and ignorance initiated by the closet is a site of epistemic injustice and harm. The relations of the closet present the truth of sexuality as a revelation of coming out and breaking silence, and at the same time coming out requires adopting sexual and gender categories and speaking in particular ways about one's erotic experiences and identity. The requirement to categorize one's erotic experiences in a particular way and, as a result, to understand one's self as having a particular sexuality constitutes an epistemic harm.

Critical attention to sexuality as an epistemic space questions the assumption that more and better knowledge can eradicate prejudice by disarming erroneous beliefs. Instead, Sedgwick points to a double bind between knowledge and ignorance that structures the closet's relation to sexual identity. Whatever truth is known about sexuality is dependent upon the ignorance of the closeted person and the people from whom the truth is concealed. As Foucault explains, one of the legitimating claims of the science of sexuality is that the truths it reveals are unknown to the individuals themselves. Queer epistemology aims to understand how relations of power, truth, desire, and identity are deployed from above and from below, as well as the implications of those deployments.

## Queer epistemology and self-knowledge

In addition to critiquing what can be known about sexuality, queer epistemology raises questions about the nature and limits of self-knowledge. Far from offering a position from which one can glean a stable and unifying truth about oneself, queer self-knowledge is a critical position from which one must manage truths about sexuality and their implications for one's well-being. Such fraught negotiations are an inevitable part of the path to understanding oneself as queer (McWhorter 1999). Having a queer conception of identity means understanding one's identity as contingent and always revisable. It means understanding that one's authority and certainty as a knowing subject are perpetually at risk of being undone (56–57). While some may perceive this insight as self-defeating, Ladelle McWhorter contends that it is empowering precisely because it reveals that current social, political, and economic hierarchies are not inevitable consequences of an immutable nature; things can be otherwise (2009: 295–296).

A queer understanding of the heteronormative context in which one is forced to come out and claim a sexual and gender identity that purportedly matches one's erotic life reveals that the particular identity one is forced to claim is not historically inevitable; it is possible that the identity one is forced to claim in a particular time and place can be replaced by a category that does not yet exist (31). This awareness acknowledges the significance of experiences that exceed social categories. It also presents a different perspective on questions of epistemic authority and credibility. Queer epistemology cautions that more self-understanding does not necessarily entail more justice. Rather than shoring up epistemic authority in response to its denial, queer epistemology emphasizes greater epistemic humility in the evaluation of one's own and others' knowledge claims (McWhorter 1999; Medina 2013; Chen 2014). From a queer epistemological perspective, queer self-knowledge is a hard-won critical perspective. While one occupies (more or less comfortably) an identity category and thus has an identity, that identity is not reflective of a fixed, innate nature (McWhorter 1999: 30). Purported sexual truths do not mirror an individual's essential being; instead, knowledge about sexuality produces the very thing it supposedly discovers and describes.

Queer knowing risks the certainty of self-knowledge promised by fitting into identity categories. Risking self-certainty does not necessarily entail a rejection of identity itself or its political usefulness. After all, identity is an important part of people's lived experience. Rather than reject identity, queer ways of knowing identity understand it as historically contingent rather than an inevitable result of one's behavior, biology, or appearance. As Judith Butler's notes, the use of identity categories, while necessary, is always risky (1993: 227–228). In addition, José Medina notes the importance of attunement to *epistemic friction* within and between groups. Epistemic friction, he asserts, importantly decenters one's own perspective in ways that enable transformation of one's understanding of self, others, and the world (2013: 7, 10). Attention to the risks entailed in the use of identity categories, attention to what or whom they include and exclude, can be a source of queer epistemic resistance that denaturalizes dominant narratives and reconceptualizes, rather than rejects, identity.

E. Patrick Johnson describes queer epistemology as a way of knowing something again and differently that resists "narrative closure in relation to a knowable 'I'" (2011: 430). To know again and differently is to know genealogically, a process that enacts a fierce knowing underscored in McWhorter's declaration that those who have been discredited and stigmatized as abnormal must "know actively and adamantly *what we know*" (2009: 326). This fierce knowing includes unmasking the networks of power-knowledge that structure dominant accounts of the world *and* exploring alternative knowledges unearthed by a genealogical approach to knowledge (295). Paying attention to discredited and unauthorized forms of counter-knowing and counter-remembering is empowering because it reveals that things can be otherwise, not because it enables a substitution of an account that is more truthful than the dominant account (295–296).

As McWhorter powerfully states, "The truth does not make deviants free" (1999: 13). Instead, as those who are deemed deviant know, the truth will lock you up (13). A genealogical approach to knowledge is not a failure to know; it is instead an account of what it means to know (and to ignore), of what knowledge (and ignorance) is. McWhorter thus also distinguishes between a genealogical conception of truth and relativism (42–43). As she points out, a genealogical description of knowledge does not deny the existence or possibility of truth claims; rather it understands truth as produced by contingent standards of justification (49).

One implication of queer epistemology's denaturalization of sexuality is the dominant conception of heterosexuality as normal and natural is revealed to be a product of contingent power-knowledge networks. Another implication is a critique of the notion of "born gay" (that being gay is also natural and thus normal) as a political strategy that reinforces dominant discourse of sexuality and thus fuels the very tactics of surveillance, containment, and normalization that have oppressed all labeled sexually deviant, including "homosexuals." From a queer epistemological perspective, adopting an epistemically resistant rather than an epistemically assimilationist strategy involves changing how one understands the normal and the natural.

The risk of losing self-certainty in queer epistemic space is the condition for the possibility of democratized knowing and politics, a space in which the meaning of queer is used critically and refers to "a site of collective contestation" and a "point of departure for a set of historical reflections and futural imaginings" (Butler 1993: 228). This suggests the question: is the conception of queer as a critical point of departure similar to a standpoint as conceived in feminist standpoint epistemology?

## Queer epistemology and the question of standpoint

Given queer critiques of identity, one might assume that queer epistemology necessarily rejects standpoint epistemologies. Such a stance, in my view, oversimplifies the meaning of standpoint within feminist standpoint epistemology. While it would be a mistake to equate queer epistemology and feminist standpoint epistemology, there are interesting areas of overlap between the two.

Feminist standpoint epistemology points out that knowledge is socially situated and that there is a relationship between knowledge and power that works to authorize the perspectives of dominantly situated knowers and de-legitimate the perspectives of marginally situated knowers (Collins 1991; Harding 2004). Importantly, standpoint is not another name for a perspective that automatically follows from one's identity; rather standpoint, as feminist standpoint epistemologists use the term, is a collective "achievement" founded on political struggle (Harding 2004: 6, 8). Within feminist standpoint epistemology, identity is a point of departure for the achievement of a standpoint, but identity alone does not ensure that a critical standpoint will be achieved. A standpoint results from the development of a politicized consciousness of the situatedness of one's group within structures of power in society. It is for this reason that Sandra Harding describes the achievement of a standpoint as a moment of epistemic empowerment for members of oppressed groups, an empowerment that is based on a collective realization of "oppositional and shared consciousness in oppressed groups" (3). And it is why Patricia Hill Collins describes a black feminist standpoint as a "shared angle of vision" among Black women and "a key to Black women's survival" (1991: 26).

With this brief summary of feminist standpoint epistemology in mind, we are better placed to carefully reflect on similarities and differences between feminist standpoint epistemology and queer epistemology. Sandra Harding asserts that queer movements have themselves generated "standpoint themes" in their opposition to heterosexism and homophobia (2004: 3). Queer epistemology shares feminist standpoint theory's critique of dominant epistemic paradigms and the entanglement of knowledge and power. Nonetheless, there are important differences between the two concerning how each conceives of the relationship between a standpoint and political transformation.

As previously discussed, queer theory critically negotiates, rather than rejects, identity. Nonetheless, while queer theory has defined itself as a field attentive to the exclusions of identity categories, queers of color point out that the field itself has been largely shaped by an unacknowledged whiteness framing its analyses (José Muñoz 1999; E. Patrick Johnson 2001). Queers of color critique the persistence of epistemic exclusions even in scholarship (like queer theory) that aims to make visible and dismantle epistemic exclusions. Disidenification is a concept that emerged from queer-of-color critique and names a queer critical relation to identity that neither uncritically claims nor rejects but "works on and against" identity (Muñoz 1999: 11–12; Johnson 2001: 12). While this position seems to reflect a "standpoint theme," queer critique of the relation between standpoint and political transformation shouldn't be ignored.

Consider, for example, Gloria Anzaldúa's conception of the epistemic space of mestiza consciousness. Mestiza consciousness is a queer epistemic space between worlds that questions the terms of authentic identity and loyalty that define membership in worlds. Importantly, borderlands are not, in Anzaldúa's account, stable points of reference or departure; they are "vague and undetermined" and constantly shifting (1987: 3). Anzaldúa writes, "*Los astrevesados* live here: the squint-eyed, the perverse, the queer, the troublesome, the mongrel, the mulatto, the half-breed, the half-dead; in short, those who cross over, pass over, or go through the confines of the 'normal'" (3). In this well-known passage, Anzaldúa articulates a queer (and crip) epistemology that is critical of norms that inform boundaries surrounding group identity.

Anzaldúa describes the borderland as "created by the *emotional residue* of an unnatural boundary" (3). In so doing, she characterizes the epistemic space of the borderland as an affective space, a space where queer knowing is an affective register cultivated in the fraught and shifting place between worlds. As an affective attunement, queer knowing in her account does not proceed from the stable ground of identity or belonging; instead, it is a feeling attuned to that which is below the surface (or to the side) of dominantly conceived realities. As Sara Ahmed explains, affective attunement to exclusions that structure dominant institutions illuminates how those institutions persist despite their claims of inclusiveness (2012: 14).

Attuned to the affective dimensions of queer knowing, it is possible to understand where queer epistemology differs from standpoint epistemology. Queer affective knowing does not have the certainty of identity as a point of departure for shared consciousness. Instead, affectively attuned knowing is inchoate, a sensibility of something other than shared understanding. As Alexis Shotwell puts it, affective knowing is not best understood as propositional knowledge claims; instead, affect is embodied involvement in the world that enables one to know otherwise (2011: ix, xii–xiii).

*La facultad*, "the capacity to see in surface phenomena the meaning of deeper realities, to see the deep structure below the surface," is Anzaldúa's concept for the affective epistemic sensibility available to those who do not conform to the norms of group belonging (1987: 38). Rather than a source of counter-beliefs, the queer affective knowing Anzaldúa describes opens space for a different sensibility attuned to that which is outside the bounds of the known in dominant and marginalized contexts.

Within standpoint epistemology, achieved identity generates perspectives on reality that make possible group solidarity and liberation (Harding 2004: 2). However, within queer epistemology, identity is an achievement that is always fraught, even if politically expedient. A queer epistemology is sensitive to that which lies beyond the edges of identity, to that which remains unknown and possibly unknowable but nonetheless beckons as an affective register of the experience of ambiguity in the face of identity. Queer epistemology does not offer oppositional knowledge. Oppositional knowing, Anzaldúa reminds us, attends only to two sides of the river, enabling reaction rather than resistance (1987: 78). Instead, queer epistemology desires possibilities for being and knowing otherwise (Shotwell 2011). A queer epistemology is a haunted epistemology alive to that which is outside the frame of intelligibility (Butler 2009). Thus understood, a queer epistemic space makes possible the cultivation of resistant imaginations necessary for personal, social, and political transformation (Medina 2013). Within queer epistemology, knowing is not democratized as a result of collecting dominant and marginal perspectives; instead, queer knowing understands those perspectives themselves as sites of "collective contestation" (Butler 1993: 228).

## Queer and crip epistemologies

Crip theory is an area of disability studies influenced, in part, by queer theory's critique of identity (Sandahl 2003; McRuer 2006). Crip theory calls into question normalizing, neoliberal assumptions within disability studies' understanding of disability, ableism within queer theory, and the systematic, interdependent institutions of compulsory ablebodiedness and ablemindedness (McRuer 2006; Kafer 2013). Crip theorists understand disability identity as "contested terrain," while cautioning against an uncritical assumption of identity's fluidity that characterizes at least some understandings of queer theory (Kafer 2013: 16–17). For example, Alison Kafer offers a political/relational model that both conceives of disability as "a site of questions rather than firm definitions" (11) and attends to the lived experiences of impairment (7). In their guest-edited special issue of the *Journal of Literary and Cultural Disability Studies*, Robert McRuer and Meri Lisa Johnson invited reflection on the possible meaning of cripistemology, a term they coined for an approach to disability informed by queer, feminist, and disability epistemologies (McRuer and Johnson 2014: 149).

In his contribution to the virtual roundtable, Jack Halberstam associates the "crip" in cripistemology with forms "not knowing, unknowing, and failing to know" and "a refusal to inhabit the realm of action and activation at all" (152). Halberstam imagines that "any cripistemology worthy of its name" must negate the possibility of knowledge (152). Nonetheless, one might question the assumption that a crip or disability epistemology must always fail to know. In her critique of Halberstam's use of mental disability as a spectacular example of queer failure, Meri Lisa Johnson asserts that uncritical appropriations of mental disability as an example of radical queer failure undermine the epistemic authority of mentally disabled people (2015: 251). Johnson critiques Halberstam's embrace of failure as a radical queer practice (or art) from the standpoint of borderline personality disorder, thus forging a feminist queer crip epistemic perspective on failure. From this epistemic vantage point, Johnson critiques Halberstam's inattention to the realities of lived bodymind failure and his "rush to metaphor" rather than critical reflection informed by attending to disabled people's experiences (256).

While Johnson uses the term "standpoint" for the epistemic vantage point she describes, I suggest that hers is a standpoint that does not take itself for granted but instead works on and against itself and remains open to revision and transformation. A feminist queer crip epistemology (or a cripistemology) is not a failure of knowledge. It deconstructs the ablebodyminded/disabled binary (Kafer 2013: 13) and is a critical position from which knowledge and identities are known differently.

In addition, a crip epistemology considers the epistemic significance of unthinkability, comprehension, and agency and challenges ableist assumptions about these concepts. For example, ableist norms of sexuality cast as unthinkable disability as the object of erotic attention and desire (Wilkerson 2011; McRuer and Mollow 2012). The unthinkability of disabled people's erotic flourishing informs various forms of injustice against disabled people, including sterilization, euthanasia, and lack of access to sexual partners and sexual health information. One implication is the tendency to ignore disabled women's sexual agency and sexual health care needs in medical institutions (Wilkerson 2011). Crip epistemology challenges the norms that make sex in the context of disability unthinkable and contributes to a reconceptualization of sex and sexiness that does not perpetuate disability stigma (McRuer and Mollow 2012).

Cognitive differences, including the experience of an inability to think, are unthinkable within academia and are presumed to be epistemic obstacles (Price 2011; Chen 2014, 177). However, cripistemology considers how cognitive differences can be epistemic resources for developing resistant, transformative knowledge. Comprehension, as Mel Chen explains, suggests that to know fully is to know comprehensively, but such comprehension "feels impossible when brains are foggy" (2014: 172–173). Taking cognitive differences seriously means abandoning the myth of comprehensive knowledge and recognizing that the reality of partial perspectives necessitates greater epistemic humility and epistemic collaboration (174). For Chen, these epistemic collaborations "amongst our diverse embodiments and cognitions" result in a "hopeful blurring," not comprehension (174, 181). Thus, knowing, from a cripistemological perspective, is not the result of the comprehensive grasp of an individual rational epistemic agent; knowing is importantly "shared cognitive labor" (180).

The unknowability and not knowing that characterize queer and crip epistemologies are modes of reframing what one thought one knew without leading to any stable, unproblematically unifying ground from which to know. Queer and crip knowing is always in progress, always revisable. As Anzaldúa writes, "Because your reconstructions are always in progress, the world, society, and culture are always compositional/decompositional states" (2015, 43). Although she is writing before the emergence of crip theory as a scholarly field, Anzaldúa's characterization of "other epistemologies" that enable transformation reflects a queer crip feminist sensibility, a sensibility poised between life and death, between that which is allowed to exist within dominant epistemic frameworks and that which is disavowed and cast into the realm of impossible or nonexistent within dominant epistemic frameworks (Butler 2009).

**Related chapters**: 1, 2, 3, 7, 10, 11, 12, 13, 16, 17

# References

Ahmed, S. (2012) *On Being Included: Racism and Diversity in Institutional Life*. Durham: Duke University Press.
Anzaldúa, G. (2015) 'Flights of the Imagination: Rereading/Rewriting Politics.' In Ana Louise Keating (ed.), *Light in the Dark/Luz En Lo Oscuro: Rewriting Identity, Spirituality, Reality*. Durham: Duke University Press.
Anzaldúa, G. (1987) *Borderlands/La Frontera: The New Mestiza*. San Francisco: Aunt Lute Books.
Butler, J. (2009) *Frames of War: When Is Life Grievable?* New York: Verso.

Butler, J. (1993) *Bodies That Matter: On the Discursive Limits of 'Sex'*. New York: Routledge.

Chen, M.Y. (2014) 'Brain fog: The race for cripistemology.' *Journal of Literary and Cultural Disability Studies* 8(2): 171–184.

Collins, P. (1991) *Black Feminist Thought: Knowledge, Consciousness, and the Politics of Empowerment*. New York: Routledge.

Foucault, M. (1990) *The History of Sexuality Volume 1: An Introduction*, trans. Robert Hurley. New York: Vintage.

Fricker, M. (2007) *Epistemic Injustice: Power and the Ethics of Knowing*. New York: Oxford University Press.

Harding, S. (2004) 'Introduction: Standpoint Theory as a Site of Political, Philosophic, and Scientific Debate.' In S. Harding (ed.), *The Feminist Standpoint Theory Reader: Intellectual and Political Controversies*. New York: Routledge.

Johnson, E.P. (2011) 'Queer epistemologies: Theorizing the self from a writerly place called home.' *Biography: An Interdisciplinary Quarterly* 34(3): 429–446.

Johnson, E.P. (2001) '"Quare" studies or (almost) everything I know about queer studies I learned from my grandmother.' *Social Text* 21(1): 1–25.

Johnson, M.L. (2015) 'Bad romance: A crip feminist critique of queer failure.' *Hypatia: Journal of Feminist Philosophy* 30(1): 251–267.

Kafer, A. (2013) *Feminist Queer Crip*. Bloomington: Indiana University Press.

McKinney, R.A. (2016). 'Extracted Speech.' *Social Theory and Practice* 42(2): 258–284.

McRuer, R. (2006) *Crip Theory: Cultural Signs of Queerness and Disability*. New York: New York University Press.

McRuer, R. and Merri Lisa Johnson (2014). 'Proliferating cripistemologies: A virtual roundtable.' *Journal of Literary and Cultural Disability Studies* 8(2): 149–169.

McRuer, R. and Anna Mollow, eds. (2012) *Sex and Disability*. Durham: Duke University Press.

McWhorter, L. (2009) *Racism and Sexual Oppression in Anglo-America: A Genealogy*. Bloomington: Indiana University Press.

McWhorter, L. (1999) *Bodies and Pleasures: Foucault and the Politics of Sexual Normalization*. Bloomington and Indianapolis: Indiana University Press.

Medina, J. (2013) *The Epistemology of Resistance: Gender and Racial Oppression, Epistemic Injustice, and Resistant Imaginations*. New York: Oxford University Press.

Muñoz, J. (1999) *Disidentifications: Queers of Color and the Performance of Politics*. Minneapolis: University of Minnesota Press.

Pohlhaus, Jr., G. (2012) 'Relational knowing and epistemic injustice: Toward a theory of willful hermeneutical ignorance.' *Hypatia: Journal of Feminist Philosophy* 27(4): 715–735.

Sandahl, C. (2003) 'Queering the crip or cripping the queer? Intersections of queer and crip identities in solo autobiographical performance.' *GLQ: A Journal of Lesbian and Gay Studies* 9(1–2): 25–56.

Sedgwick, E. (1990) *Epistemology of the Closet*. Berkeley: University of California Press.

Shotwell, A. (2011) *Knowing Otherwise: Race, Gender, and Implicit Understanding*. University Park: Pennsylvania State University Press.

Wilkerson, A. (2011) 'Disability, Sex Radicalism, and Political Agency.' In K.Q. Hall (ed.), *Feminist Disability Studies*. Bloomington: Indiana University Press.

# 15
# ALLIES BEHAVING BADLY
## Gaslighting as epistemic injustice

*Rachel McKinnon*

### 1. Trans* epistemology and "allies"

There isn't a great deal of work that we might call "trans* epistemology," although there is certainly increasing attention being given to epistemological insights to be gained by considering trans* perspectives.[1] Taking trans* perspectives seriously allows us to shed light on some problems, particularly with how "allies" behave towards those they claim to support. Talk of "allies" is everywhere in queer politics and activism.[2] There are "safe spaces" and "ally" training programs at most universities and colleges. In many cases, one can acquire a sticker, sign, or plaque to display, maybe even a button, badge, or pin that denotes one as an "ally." However, the concept of an "ally" and how this concept has translated into what we might call "ally culture" has started receiving increasing attention and criticism, mostly by the very people it's meant to support. One prominent example is Mia McKenzie's 2013 blog post (reprinted in McKenzie 2014) "No More 'Allies,'" where she discusses some problems endemic to the behavior of allies. In many cases, allies have been behaving badly. In some cases, "allies" are further harming victims.

My focus in this chapter is the bad *epistemic* behaviors of "allies," approached from a trans* perspective. One common form of bad behavior is that when "allies" are confronted with their bad behavior, they use their identity as an "ally" as a defense; other times, people will do so on an "'ally's' behalf': "Dave couldn't have behaved that badly, he's an ally!" Another bad behavior I will focus on is known as *gaslighting*. I'll argue that we can best understand gaslighting as an instance of epistemic injustice – more specifically, as an instance of testimonial injustice. I'll discuss this through the lens of trans women's experiences with "allies," since a common form of epistemic injustice that trans* people face is gaslighting at the hands of "allies."[3] I'll close with some considerations on what this means going forward for "allies" and "ally culture." In short, I'll argue that we should abandon "allyship" and replace it with a focus on cultivating active bystanders.

For the purposes of this chapter, I should briefly comment on what I mean by "allies." I take it as given that "[e]ach person has a complicated intersectional identity, composed of various socially and biologically constructed factors.[4] These factors include race, gender and gender identity, sexual orientation, socioeconomic status, education, religious affiliation, nationality, and so on" (McKinnon 2015a: 428). Following Brown and Ostrove (2013), "[a]cross these various settings and identities, allies are generally conceived as dominant group members who work to end prejudice in their personal and professional lives, and relinquish social privileges conferred by their group status through their support of nondominant groups" (2013: 2211). On this view of "allies," a cisgender person may act as an "ally" to a trans★ person, a white person can act as an "ally" to a person of color, a man can act as an "ally" to a woman, and so on.[5]

## 2. Gaslighting as epistemic injustice

There's been a recent resurgence in interest in a kind of behavior called *gaslighting*.[6] It generally takes one of two forms: a psychological abuse form and a more subtle epistemic form. The term originates from a 1938 Patrick Hamilton play and subsequent 1944 film called *Gaslight*. In it, the protagonist engages in psychological warfare on his wife with the aim of having her hospitalized for mental instability. He does this by trying to convince his wife that she's crazy and suffering delusions.[7] He wants her to doubt her memory and sense perceptions. And it works. However, this isn't the form of gaslighting that I'm interested in for the purposes of this chapter. Instead, I'm interested in the more subtle form, often unintentional, where a listener doesn't believe, or expresses doubt about, a speaker's testimony. In this epistemic form of gaslighting, the listener of testimony raises doubts about the speaker's reliability at perceiving events accurately. Directly, or indirectly, then, gaslighting involves expressing doubts that the harm or injustice that the speaker is testifying to really happened as the speaker claims.

Here's the sort of case I want to focus on.[8] Let's say that a trans woman, Victoria, is at a department holiday party. Victoria uses the feminine pronouns she/her/hers. It's the end of a long semester, and a long week for everyone. So people are looking forward to cutting loose a little. After a couple drinks, she's in conversation with a few people, when one of her colleagues, James, begins telling an amusing anecdote about her. The story is about how she didn't notice a particular feature about his house at a previous department party. James continues the story: when Victoria gets into an involved conversation about her field of work, she gets a sort of tunnel-vision focus. He then says, "So of course *he* wouldn't notice something like that. When *he* gets talking epistemology, *he* doesn't notice anything about *his* surroundings. *He*. . ." In rapid-fire fashion, James mispronouns Victoria five times. Mispronouning is a serious offence for trans people: it's one of the most common forms of harassment that they face. In many jurisdictions where gender identity is included as a protected class with respect to harassment, mispronouning counts as gender harassment.[9]

We don't yet have our case of gaslighting, though. Suppose that Victoria goes to a mutual colleague, Susan, to complain about James's mispronouning her at the party and to raise worries about the workplace climate given that this isn't the first time James has done this. And suppose that they have this conversational exchange:

*Susan:* "I'm sure you just misheard him: you're on edge and expect to hear mispronouning. I just don't believe that James would do that. He won a university diversity award for his supporting queer issues, after all. Besides, he's been a supporter of yours in the past too. He really is your ally."
*Victoria:* "Well, he's done it a bunch of times in the past few months. The last time was two weeks ago in his office."
*Susan:* "You say that he's done it before, and maybe he has, but *I've* never heard him do it before."

At first, many cases of gaslighting don't seem clearly to arise from a speaker identity prejudice or stereotype. And in order to properly count as testimonial injustice – following Fricker's (2007) framework – the credibility deficit that Victoria suffers would have to be due to an identity prejudice.[10]

Two things are happening in Victoria's case when Susan discounts Victoria's testimony. First, one common stereotype of trans women is that they're overly emotional, perhaps particularly if they're on estrogen-based hormone replacement therapy.[11] And since it's also a common view, particularly in many Western patriarchal societies, that emotionality is at odds with rationality, a common way of discounting a woman's testimony (whether cis or trans*) is to point to her being emotional.[12] This is at play when Susan responds by doubting Victoria's perceptual reliability: Victoria is probably hearing things she expects to hear because she expects mispronouning and discriminatory behavior, for example. Victoria suffers a credibility deficit due to an identity stereotype or prejudice: (trans) women are emotional, and emotionality undermines rationality and perceptual reliability. This is classic testimonial injustice, then.

As a short detour, though, one pattern that I notice is what I often refer to as the "epistemic injustice circle (of hell)." This happens when something such as an identity prejudice based on emotion is treated as a reason to discount a speaker's testimony, whereby a normal response to this testimonial injustice is to become *more* emotional (e.g., angry, frustrated, etc.). But this subsequent emotionality is treated as a *further* reason to discount the speaker's testimony. And so on: it's a positive feedback loop. Testimonial injustice tends to cause victims to become emotional, which is often used as a reason to further victimize them. Drawing on one of Fricker's examples, observe Marge Sherwood's behavior in *The Talented Mr. Ripley*, particularly the last scene where we see Marge. She has an emotional outburst, crying (while hitting Tom Ripley), "I *know* it was you! I know it was *you*!!" But Herbert Greenleaf shuttles her away: she's just another distraught woman lashing out. "Allies" also engage in this with those they purport to support: their gaslighting of victims tends to cause the victims to become more upset, which the "allies" take as further reason to discount the victim's testimony. In more extreme cases, it leads to writing off the victim as worthy of any credibility at claims of harassment or harm. In Dotson's (2011) terms, this constitutes *testimonial quieting*: the speaker suffers such a severe credibility deficit that it's as if they never spoke at all.

Second, Susan doubts Victoria's testimony – that James mispronounced Victoria repeatedly at a recent party – by appealing to *James'* "identity" as an "ally."[13] Susan thus lends inappropriate weight to her background knowledge[14] of James, particularly in relation to her observation of James's past behavior with respect to Victoria, and thus produces a credibility deficit for Victoria's testimony. And yet it's entirely consistent that James's past behavior has been good with respect to Victoria in other contexts. When Susan says, "You say that he's done it before, and maybe he has, but *I've* never heard him do it before," she is at least expressing the implicature that she doubts Victoria's testimony of James's previous bad acts.[15] But why should the listener privilege her own perceptions, rather than trust Victoria's testimony? I suggest that this is another site of subtle, but deeply troubling epistemic injustice.

In many cases, "allies," when listening to a person's testimony, privilege their own first-hand experience over the testimony of the person they're supposed to be supporting.[16] Probably, the "ally" suspects that the affected person isn't properly epistemically situated – perhaps they're not suitably objective – to properly assess the situation. Maybe the "ally" thinks the person is expecting to see harassment, so they perceive harassment when it's not really there (but, of course, this is used to doubt accurate claims of harassment).

But why would this be a readily observable pattern, one that I know many trans* people have experienced with their "allies"? I suspect that the listener (the "ally") thinks that the speaker is misperceiving events, or maybe that they're reading into situations things that just aren't there. These are taken as good reasons to doubt the speaker's testimony. They may not be taken as reasons to think that the speaker is wrong in what they say, per se, but they'll be taken as reasons not to believe. But this gets things exactly backwards. The affected person is particularly *well* epistemically situated to perceive events properly. In the following section, I turn to some discussions about why.

## 3. Trans* epistemology and first person authority

As I noted at the outset, there isn't a great deal of work that we might call "trans* epistemology," although there is certainly increasing attention being given to epistemological insights to be gained by considering trans* perspectives. Two contributions I want to focus on here involve arguments for taking the assertions of trans persons as *prima facie* reasons for believing what they say. Part of my view is to fail to do this constitutes testimonial injustice. Building on what I argue in McKinnon (2015a), we have strong *prima facie* reason to believe what someone tells us with respect to harassment and discrimination. And combining that with what Bettcher (2009) argues, we have a *moral* responsibility to afford speakers with disadvantaged identities first person authority. My argument is that gaslighting, particularly by "allies," constitutes a failure to afford the first person (epistemic) authority of disadvantaged speakers their appropriate epistemic weight.

Gaile Pohlhaus, Jr. (2012) nicely captures the behavior that I'm highlighting in "allies," which she describes as *willful hermeneutical ignorance*. In short, willful hermeneutical ignorance happens when "marginally situated knowers actively resist epistemic domination through interaction with other resistant knowers, while dominantly situated knowers nonetheless continue to misunderstand and misinterpret the world."[17] Key to this phenomenon is taking seriously the idea that *who* knowers are, and their social situatedness, matters to their epistemic positions with respect to themselves, the world, and others. As Pohlhaus Jr. notes:

> [T]he situations resulting from one's social positioning create "common challenges" that constitute part of the knower's lived experience and so contribute to the context from which she approaches the world (Alcoff 2000, 2006; Collins 2008). Repeated over time, these challenges can lead to habits of expectation, attention, and concern, thereby contributing to what one is more or less likely to notice and pursue as an object of knowledge in the experienced world (Alcoff 2006, 91).
>
> *(2012: 716–717)*

The key here is that one's social situatedness – which involves various social identity features such as gender, race, socioeconomic status, sexual orientation, disability status, and so on – impacts *how and what we perceive* in the world.

The point is that one's situatedness impacts whether one is sufficiently well epistemically positioned to even properly perceive the world – whether one, *e.g.*, is likely to perceive harassment *as* harassment. Applying this to Victoria's case, Victoria, on account of her being a trans woman and marginally situated, is both far better epistemically positioned than her cis "ally" Susan to perceive mispronouning (and to perceive it *as* mispronouning) and to understand the depth of the harm of being mispronouned. Those who don't personally experience a category of harms are likely to underappreciate its severity. There is thus an important epistemic asymmetry between those with marginalized situatednesses and their "allies." The marginalized people tend to be better epistemically situated to *perceive* harassment as harassment.

Willful hermeneutical ignorance, then, is how those with dominant situatednesses fail to develop their epistemic resources in order to better perceive the world and others. I suspect that one mechanism for this is that these people – such as "allies" – fail to give the testimony of marginalized persons' testimony adequate epistemic weight. The "allies" place too much weight on their own first-hand experiences and perceptions of events. And when their perception of things conflicts with the testimony of the marginalized person's, this is taken as a reason to doubt (or reject) the testimony.

There are both epistemic and moral upshots of this. The epistemic upshot is that dominantly situated knowers – *i.e.*, "allies" – ought to place more epistemic weight, credibility, and *trust* in the first person reports of marginalized situated knowers. It was epistemically inappropriate for Susan to treat her perceptions and experiences of James as equally credible or with equal weight as Victoria's testimony that James has mispronouned her in the past, and on more than one occasion.[18] "Allies" ought to put their own perceptions largely aside and *trust* the testimony of the marginalized person. Trusting testimony means believing what's said.[19] However, "allies" are far too often unwilling to simply trust and accept a marginalized person's testimony at face value: they need to see the harm for themselves.

## 4. No more "allies"[20]

I haven't yet said much about what's particularly wrong with gaslighting, above and beyond the harms that Fricker (2007) herself notes as the wrong of testimonial injustice. Fricker argues that the wrong of testimonial injustice is that a central feature of being human is being a knower, and testimonial injustice disrespects people *qua* knower. Thus, testimonial injustice disrespects people *qua* persons. One way to cash this out is that listeners fail to appropriately trust speakers.

However, I find that gaslighting produces possibly unique moral and epistemic harms. First, gaslighting, as a sub-species of testimonial injustice, creates all the same harms as the more generic forms of testimonial injustice. Second, consider the context in which gaslighting occurs: a disadvantaged person (say, a trans woman) reports an injustice to someone she considers an "ally," but the "ally" doesn't afford her testimony appropriate epistemic weight. But more than that, the "ally" responds by raising doubts viz. the speaker's perceptual (and perhaps reasoning) abilities. The claim of being harmed is dismissed or explicitly doubted. In an important sense, the speaker's moral trust of turning to an "ally" has been *betrayed* via the gaslighting. While generic testimonial injustice involves a listener's not appropriately trusting a speaker, gaslighting involves further betraying of a particular moral and epistemic trust of the speaker. This is particularly acute if the "ally" positively identifies themself *as* an ally (perhaps by proudly posting a "Safe Space" sign or some such on their office door).

This betrayal has a variety of consequences. The trans woman, in our case, will likely decrease her trust in the "ally" who gaslit her. One primary function of "allies" is to provide support, in a variety of forms. But if we don't trust our "allies," then we lose a critical source of epistemic and moral support. This can isolate those who are already vulnerable in our societies. Isolation can lead to a variety of harms, including mental health concerns such as depression, but also social harms of exclusion. For example, suppose that Victoria tends to eat lunch in a common room where both James and Susan frequent. If Victoria doesn't feel that she can sufficiently trust Susan to help her out when James, for example, mispronouns her, then Victoria may simply cease to eat lunch with her colleagues. She may even begin to avoid coming into the office when she can, which leads to missing out on important interpersonal interactions with colleagues. In a way, the workplace becomes increasingly toxic for Victoria merely through the betrayal of trust by her "ally," Susan. And these harms can be exacerbated if Victoria is structurally vulnerable by, for example, James and Susan being more senior and thus having institutional power over Victoria's career and economic well-being.[21]

But what should we make, epistemically speaking, of a speaker's claim that, for example, someone has harassed or mispronouned the speaker? While I advocate a default position of epistemic trust for such claims, I'm by no means arguing that one is epistemically required to believe the speaker. While one is epistemically positioned to form a justified belief or, in the case of true assertions, knowledge on the basis of the speaker's say-so, one is free to withhold belief. However, I do think that one ought not respond immediately by expressing doubt or doubt-raiser's of the speaker's testimony. Moreover, one ought not to respond by asking questions about details of events in a way that makes it seem like an interrogation of the victim.[22]

The epistemic and emotional harm of "allies," the people we ostensibly turn to in times of most need, responding to claims of harm by first expressing doubt or, worse, gaslighting can often be worse than the original harm that the person wishes to share. Simply put, those who aim to be a "good ally" ought both to afford appropriate epistemic weight to the testimony of the people for whom one wants to be an "ally" and to be responsive to criticism. I consistently and repeatedly find that "allies" fall far short in both respects. In recent empirical work on "allies," Brown and Ostrove (2013) found that "allies" tend to overestimate how good a job they're doing at being an "ally." Relatedly, I have noticed that "allies" are often insensitive to constructive criticism and, moreover, often react negatively (often going on the attack) to such criticism.

In the space that remains, I want to turn some attention to how we can move forward from many of the problems that I see with "allies" and "ally culture." In short, I argue that we should abandon the concept of "ally" and replace it with a focus on cultivating active bystanders. Active bystander training has been gaining steady momentum in recent years.[23] The idea is that if one develops strategies for how to respond to discrimination and harassment when one sees it happen, one will be more likely to (hopefully) appropriately intercede and assist the disadvantaged person. Importantly, active bystanders can be in-group or fellow out-group members of the disadvantaged person. A trans woman can thus act as an active bystander to another trans woman.

As noted above, one way that "allies" respond poorly to constructive criticism – particularly pointing out gaslighting or cases where they failed to adequately support the disadvantaged person – is by referencing their status as "really" an "ally." One relatively recent high profile instance was Piers Morgan's misgendering Janet Mock (referring to her on his television show and in tweets as "formerly a man," which is often an offensive way to refer to trans women). In response to being called out, instead of contritely apologizing, Morgan went on the attack, demanding that *Mock* be the one to apologize to Morgan. To many, the identity of being an "ally" – whether or not one actually ever appropriately acts as an "ally" – is central to their overall identity.

One way to avoid the ability to point to one's identity as an "ally" as a defense from criticism is to focus on cultivating concrete actions in people, removing the label and – in a sense – *certification* as being an "ally." One cannot claim to be an active bystander unless one is actually appropriately active when one observes discrimination or harassment. Moreover, whether one has been an active bystander in the past isn't a laurel on which one can rest: in the context of a harm, did you act or not? When we observe harm, we're all bystanders (unless we're the one harmed). If you didn't act, then you were a passive bystander; if you did, then you were an active bystander. Active bystanders, by not being so explicitly an identity (no badges or signs), may well be more open to criticism on how to perform better in future instances.

I don't pretend to offer a fully fleshed-out argument for why we would do better with "active bystanders" than with "allies," partly due to space constraints. In an important sense, this is an empirical claim: one could conceivably measure whether people tend to act better with respect to a disadvantaged group as an "ally" or as an "active bystander." I conjecture that abandoning "ally" concepts and terminology – especially badges and certifications – and replacing it with "active bystander" would have better results. However, in this chapter I have identified a number of persistent and seriously harmful aspects of "allies" and their behavior. I suggest that this behavior is partially caused by the appeal to "ally" as an identity. When our identities – ones we strongly identify with – are under attack, it's predictable that we'll respond by counter-attacking. And "allies" tend to hit back with gaslighting and isolating the affected, disadvantaged person.

**Related chapters**: 2, 3, 4, 6, 11

## Notes

1. Some examples include Stone 1987; Namaste 2000 and 2009; Koyama 2003; Spade 2006; Stryker 2006; Hale 2007 and 2015; Serano 2007 and 2013; Bettcher 2009 and 2014; McKinnon 2014, 2015a, and 2016a; McKenzie 2014.
2. You'll note that I consistently use quotation marks for "ally" and its cognates. This is deliberate, for part of the purpose of this chapter is to argue for rejecting the concept and particularly its implementation as "ally culture" and its many attendant problems.
3. As I note in McKinnon 2014 and 2015a, I will generally use the language of "trans women" to refer only to transsexual women ("transsexual" is now strongly dispreferred by many trans people, though) and "trans★ women," which is the current convention, to be the more inclusive term that refers to all forms of transgender women, including genderqueer, genderfuckers, bi-gender, and so on. The generic "trans★" denotes maximal inclusivity, including trans masculine people, agender people, and so on. The primary focus of this chapter, though, is on trans women's experiences. What I have to say will apply, in varying degrees, to other trans★ identities.
4. However, I am of the view that any biological feature, such as race, sex/gender, and so on is also inherently socially constructed. For some of my thoughts on this, see McKinnon (forthcoming). What it means for someone to be black, mixed race, a man, or a woman (or neither!) inherently depends on social decisions, almost always implicit and undisclosed. For some useful discussions of Intersectionality, see Crenshaw (1991) and Garry (2008, 2012).
5. For some criticism of this view, though, and for a discussion of allies, see my blog post: www.metamorpho-sis.com/blog/2013/10/50-empirical-research-on-allies.html Last accessed February 23, 2015.
6. For example, see Abramson (2014) and Ruiz (2014).
7. I recognize that "crazy" is an ableist term, but I use it purposefully because the protagonist aims to have all the negative stigma of "crazy" attach to his wife.
8. This is based on a real case, but the names and some of the details have been changed.
9. For example, here is the Ontario Human Rights Commission 2000 "Policy on Discrimination and Harassment Because of Gender Identity": www.ohrc.on.ca/sites/default/files/Policy_on_discrimination_and_harassment_because_of_gender_identity.pdf
10. For a review of recent developments in epistemic injustice, See McKinnon 2016b.
11. For a discussion of trans women stereotypes, see McKinnon (2014).
12. Indeed, this is at the heart of Fricker's discussion of Marge Sherwood in *The Talented Mr. Ripley*.
13. Another way to explain what's going on is that James is enjoying a credibility *excess*, if only implicitly based on Susan's perceptions of James's identity as an "ally." See Medina (2011).
14. I almost put "knowledge" in quotation marks, since it's likely that the hearer has some false beliefs about James.
15. Implicatures are things that are communicated, though not explicitly said. For the canonical view, see Grice (1989).
16. I raise this phenomenon in McKinnon 2012 and in Chapter 10 of McKinnon 2015b.
17. Pohlhaus, Jr. 2012, p. 716.
18. I hesitate to say that Susan has *mis*perceived things. She may well have never seen James mispronoun Victoria. She's simply giving her past experiences of James too much epistemic weight: she should be giving Victoria's testimony much more weight than she is. Moreover, Susan might be privileging her own perceptions of James *over* Victoria's testimony, which would be doubly bad.
19. For a detailed treatment of the nature and implications of epistemic trust, see Zagzebski (2012).
20. This is the title of Mia McKenzie's blog post (and the associated chapter in her 2014 collection of blog posts and essays).
21. And the stress and harms that this creates can arise even if James and Susan never adversely affect Victoria's career (other than the harm created by the effects of the stress, of course). As I argue in McKinnon (2014), the mere *possibility* of the harm can create harm.

22 My thanks to Luke Barker for raising this point.
23 Here is one good resource: http://web.mit.edu/bystanders/strategies/ Last accessed March 2, 2015.
24 I note that "transgendered" is now a dispreferred term. "Transgender" is far better.

## References

Abramson, Kate. 2014. Turning up the lights on gaslighting. *Philosophical Perspectives* 28, pp. 1–30.
Alcoff, Linda Martín. 2000. On judging epistemic credibility: Is social identity relevant? In Naomi Zack (ed.), *Women of Color and Philosophy*. Malden, MA: Blackwell, pp. 235–262.
Alcoff, Linda Martín. 2006. *Visible Identities: Race, Gender, and the Self*. New York: Oxford University Press.
Bettcher, Talia Mae. 2009. Trans Identities and First-Person Authority. In Laurie Shrage (ed.), *You've Changed: Sex-Reassignment and Personal Identity*. Oxford: Oxford University Press, pp. 98–120.
Bettcher, Talia Mae. 2014. Trapped in the wrong theory: Re-thinking trans oppression and resistance. *Signs* 39(2), pp. 383–406.
Brown, Kendrick and Ostrove, Joan. 2013. What does it mean to be an ally?: The perception of allies from the perspective of people of color. *Journal of Applied Social Psychology* 43, pp. 2211–2222.
Collins, Patricia Hill. 2008. *Black Feminist Thought: Knowledge, Consciousness, and the Politics of Empowerment*. New York: Routledge.
Crenshaw, Kimberle. 1991. Mapping the margins: Intersectionality, identity politics, and violence against women of color. *Stanford Law Review* 43, pp. 1241–1299.
Dotson, Kristie. 2011. Tracking epistemic violence, tracking practices of silencing. *Hypatia* 26(2), pp. 236–257.
Garry, Ann. 2008. Intersections, social change, and "Engaged" theories: Implications of North American feminism. *Pacific and American Studies* 8, pp. 99–111.
Garry, Ann. 2012. Who Is Included? Intersectionality, Metaphors, and the Multiplicity of Gender. In Sharon L. Crasnow and Anita M. Superson (eds.), *Out from the Shadows: Analytical Feminist Contributions to Traditional Philosophy*. Oxford: Oxford University Press, pp. 493–530.
Grice, Paul. 1989. *Studies in the Way of Words*. Cambridge, MA: Harvard University Press.
McKenzie, Mia. 2013. No more allies. *BGD*. 30 September 2013. www.bgdblog.org/2013/09/no-more-allies/
McKenzie, Mia. 2014. *Black Girl Dangerous: On Race, Queerness, Class and Gender*. Oakland, CA: BGD Press.
McKinnon, Rachel. 2012. What I learned in the lunch room about assertion and practical reasoning. *Logos and Episteme* 3(4), pp. 565–569.
McKinnon, Rachel. 2014. Stereotype threat and attributional ambiguity for trans women. *Hypatia* 29(1), pp. 857–872.
McKinnon, Rachel. 2015a. Trans★formative experiences. *Res Philosophica* 92(2), pp. 419–440.
McKinnon, Rachel. 2015b. *The Norms of Assertion: Truth, Lies, and Warrant*. New York: Palgrave Macmillan.
McKinnon, Rachel. 2016a. Gender, identity, and society. In Arthur Zucker and James Petrik (eds.), *Macmillan's Interdisciplinary Handbooks: Philosophy of Sex and Love*. Farmington Hills, MI: Cengage Learning, pp. 175–198.
McKinnon, Rachel. 2016b. Epistemic injustice. Philosophy Compass 11(8), pp. 437–446.
Medina, José. 2011. The relevance of credibility excess in a proportional view of epistemic injustice: Differential epistemic authority and the social imaginary. *Social Epistemology* 25(1), pp. 15–25.
Namaste, Viviane. 2000. *Invisible Lives: The Erasure of Transsexual and Transgendered People*.[24] Chicago, IL: University of Chicago Press.
Namaste, Viviane. 2009. Undoing theory: The "transgender question" and the epistemic violence of Anglo-American feminist theory. *Hypatia* 24(3), pp. 11–32.
Pohlhaus, Jr., Gaile. 2012. Relational knowing and epistemic injustice: Toward a theory of willful hermeneutical ignorance. *Hypatia* 27(4), pp. 715–735.
Ruiz, Elena Flores. 2014. Spectral phenomenologies: Dwelling poetically in professional philosophy. *Hypatia* 29(1), pp. 196–204.
Spade, Dean. 2006. Mutilating gender. In Susan Stryker and Stephen Whittle (eds.), *Transgender Studies Reader*. New York: Routledge, pp. 315–332.
Stone, Sandy. 1987. The empire strikes back: A posttranssexual manifesto. http://sandystone.com/empire-strikes-back.pdf
Stryker, Susan. 2006. (De)Subjugated knowledges. In Susan Stryker and Stephen Whittle (eds.), *Transgender Studies Reader*. New York: Routledge, pp. 1–17.
Stryker, Susan and Whittle, Stephen. 2006. *The Transgender Studies Reader*. New York: Routledge.
Zagzebski, Linda. 2012. *Epistemic Authority: A Theory of Trust, Authority, and Autonomy in Belief*. Oxford: Oxford University Press.

# 16
# KNOWING DISABILITY, DIFFERENTLY[1]

*Shelley Tremain*

## Knowing the apparatus of disability, conceptually

Rare exceptions notwithstanding, the apparatus (*dispositif*) of disability continues to be left out of feminist and other critical philosophical analyses produced across the sub-disciplines of ethics, metaphysics, philosophy of language, aesthetics, political philosophy, cognitive science, and epistemology (Tremain 2013a). Even feminist epistemologists and other philosophers who use the relatively recent and philosophically and politically important notions of epistemic injustice and epistemological ignorance do not consider how the apparatus of disability conditions their examination of phenomena, that is, do not consider how disability conditions what they examine, how they examine what they examine, nor why they examine what they examine. The failure of feminist and other philosophers to incorporate insights and arguments from philosophy of disability and disability studies into their work on epistemic injustice and epistemological ignorance is starkly evident in the abundance of ableist metaphors – such as "epistemic blindness," "epistemic deafness," "meta-blindness," "gender-blind," and "silenced" – that they invoke to bolster their claims, an abundance that attests to their lack of familiarity with or disregard for the arguments that feminist and other philosophers and theorists of disability have articulated in opposition to the use of these metaphors (for instance, see, Tremain 2011a, 2011b; Schalk 2013). In other words, discussions of epistemological ignorance themselves seem to (re)produce a form of epistemological ignorance. Indeed, perhaps the time has come to scrutinize the metaphorical role that the concept of ignorance *itself* plays in feminist and other critical philosophy and epistemology. Is the concept of epistemological ignorance itself a paradoxical and self-contradicting ableist metaphor? Do feminist and other philosophers inadvertently contribute to the harms perpetrated against certain groups of disabled people when they invoke the concept of epistemological ignorance in their work?

The hypothesis that the concept of epistemological ignorance itself is an ableist metaphor suggests a number of ambitious avenues of inquiry to pursue in (feminist) philosophy and epistemology of disability. I set aside this hypothesis in what follows, however, in order to substantiate my earlier claims that feminist and other philosophers have consistently failed to incorporate critical understanding of the apparatus of disability into their philosophical analyses. I want to show that the failure of philosophers to attend to both (the apparatus of) disability and theoretical insights advanced about it comprises a form of epistemic injustice that distorts the ways in which discussions about (among other things) identity, oppression, and privilege are framed within the philosophical literature on epistemic injustice, as well as how the concept of epistemic injustice itself is construed within that body of work.

In order to make my case, I first examine Miranda Fricker's discussion of the conditions that must prevail for a form of epistemic disadvantage to constitute epistemic injustice, that is, the necessary conditions for a form of hermeneutical disadvantage to count as hermeneutical injustice. I show that insofar as Fricker does not account for the apparatus of disability and its political character in the distinction that she draws between hermeneutical disadvantages that result from injustice and hermeneutical disadvantages that result from "bad luck," the motivation for the distinction is unjustified, and the distinction itself remains unsubstantiated. Once I have shown that Fricker does not appropriately account for the apparatus of disability in her discussion of hermeneutical injustice, I turn to consider how disability has been left out of analyses of a now widely-used example of testimonial injustice that she introduced, namely, the trial of Tom Robinson in Harper Lee's 1960 novel *To Kill a Mockingbird*. I focus in particular on claims that Fricker and José Medina advance about the ways in which the character of Robinson is racialized, gendered, and sexualized in the novel's narrative. I am concerned to show that a more complex interpretation of the identities and events that unfold in Lee's novel than these philosophers articulate would consider how the apparatus of disability contributes to the shape of the ways that Robinson is racialized, gendered, and sexualized in that drama, as well as to the ways that he is disabled therein.

My identification of disability as an "apparatus" follows Michel Foucault, who introduced the term *apparatus* to refer to a heterogeneous ensemble of discourses, institutions, architectural forms, regulatory decisions, laws, administrative measures, scientific statements, and philosophical, moral, and philanthropic propositions that respond to an urgent need in a given historical moment (Foucault 1980: 194; Tremain 2015: 8). Foucault's innovative idea of apparatus enables me to move away from dominant understandings of disability that variously construe it as a personal characteristic or attribute, a property of given individuals, an identity, or a form of social oppression. Furthermore, the idea of an apparatus enables an understanding of disability that is culturally relative, historicist, and more comprehensive than are the aforementioned understandings of it. As we shall see, in some respects, the conception of a disability apparatus resembles the notion of "social imaginary" (Medina 2011: 15, 24) that Medina employs in his writing on epistemic injustice.

## Knowing (the apparatus of) disability, politically

In Fricker's *Epistemic Injustice: Power and the Ethics of Knowing* (2007), she argues that the capacity of relatively powerless social groups to adequately and appropriately understand the world is jeopardized if dominant groups disproportionately influence the interpretive resources available at any given time. Fricker thinks that dominant groups should been seen to inflict a form of epistemic injustice when they enjoy such unfair hermeneutical advantages. Thus, she refers to this form of unfair hermeneutical advantage as "hermeneutical injustice" (Fricker 2007: 146–8). Asymmetrical relations of social power, she explains, can skew shared hermeneutical resources in ways that both enable members of powerful social groups to understand their social experiences and prevent members of relatively disempowered social groups from understanding their own experiences. The mid-twentieth-century feminist consciousness-raising groups, in which women publicly articulated and exchanged experiences that had previously been systematically obscured and routinely privatized were, she remarks, a direct response to the fact that such epistemological resources had hitherto been rendered unavailable to women. Within these groups, she notes, women collectively realized resources for meaning and understanding that had previously been only implicit in the social interpretive practices of that historical context (Fricker 2007: 148).

In order to illustrate these claims, Fricker quotes an excerpt from Susan Brownmiller's memoir in which Brownmiller (1990: 182) wrote about one woman's revelatory introduction to feminist consciousness-raising in a group that embarked on a discussion about postpartum depression. In the quoted passage, Brownmiller described how, over the course of the forty-five minute discussion, this woman came to realize that the depression that she had experienced – and for which both she and her husband had blamed her – was not a "personal deficiency" at all, but rather "a combination of physiological things and a real societal thing, isolation" (Brownmiller 1990: 182, in Fricker 2007: 149). As Fricker explains it, the lack of understanding with which the woman had lived up until that life-altering discussion constituted a harm inflicted upon her in her capacity as a knower, that is, constituted a specific sort of epistemic injustice, namely, a hermeneutical injustice.

Fricker is concerned to point out that not all hermeneutical disadvantages constitute hermeneutical injustice. Thus, she aims to identify the features that distinguish hermeneutical disadvantages that inflict epistemic injustice from hermeneutical disadvantages that do not involve injustice. Drawing upon the distinction between justice and luck that is a mainstay of mid-twentieth-century analytic political philosophy and ethics, she remarks that some hermeneutical disadvantages derive from "bad luck," rather than from injustice, a difference that she asserts can be easily recognized (Fricker 2007: 149, 152). In order to illustrate this distinction, she offers the following description as an example of a hermeneutical disadvantage that does not inflict epistemic injustice:

> If, for instance, someone has a medical condition affecting their social behaviour at a historical moment at which that condition is still misunderstood and largely undiagnosed, then they may suffer from a hermeneutical disadvantage that is, while collective, especially damaging to them in particular. They are unable to render their experiences intelligible by reference to the idea that they have a disorder, and so they are personally in the dark, and may also suffer seriously negative consequences from others' non-comprehension of their condition. But they are not subject to hermeneutical injustice; rather, theirs is a poignant case of circumstantial bad luck.
>
> *(2007: 152)*

What, to me, is striking about Fricker's sketch of a hermeneutical disadvantage that derives from circumstantial bad luck, rather than from injustice, is how aptly it describes the hermeneutical disadvantage that only three pages earlier in her book she had associated with a paradigm case of epistemic injustice, that is, the lack of hermeneutical resources that in the not-so-distant past had been unavailable to women who experienced postpartum depression. Fricker argues, however, that the salient difference with respect to epistemic injustice between the situation of women with postpartum depression and the situation of the hypothetical subject in the cited example is that in the former case, but not the latter, "background social conditions" prevailed "that were conducive to the relevant hermeneutical lacuna" (Fricker 2007: 152). She explains that revelations about postpartum depression emerged in feminist consciousness-raising groups during a historical moment in which women were still markedly powerless in relation to men. This powerlessness, Fricker points out, entailed that women had unequal hermeneutical participation, which "provides the crucial background conditions for hermeneutical injustice" (Fricker 2007: 152). She notes, furthermore, that when this kind of unequal hermeneutical participation exists with respect to some area of social experience, members of the relevant disadvantaged group are likely "hermeneutically marginalized" (Fricker 2007: 153).

My argument (*contra* Fricker) is that people with an "undiagnosed condition" whose social behavior is subject to "negative consequences" due to the ways in which others perceive them are also members of a hermeneutically marginalized group; that is, the detrimental consequences that accrue to these people are produced by precisely the sort of background conditions from which Fricker claims that a hermeneutical disadvantage must result in order to qualify as a form of hermeneutical injustice. Certain forms of unequal social power – that is, mechanisms of the apparatus of disability – produce an array of disciplinary norms about proper social behavior and interaction, modes of communication, rationality, emotional self-control, psychological resilience, and so on. These historically-specific forms of unequal power – that is, these "background conditions" – shape the public perceptions and authoritative epistemologies from which the negative social, political, interpersonal, and economic consequences of the sort to which Fricker refers accrue to some people, naturalizing, medicalizing, and depoliticizing these perceptions and epistemologies in ways that conceal their contingent and artefactual character.[2] The medical and juridical classifications that emerge from these background conditions actually produce the kinds of subjects that they are claimed to (merely) identify and name or represent. As Foucault pointed out, people are not naturally – that is, universally and transhistorically – sorted into kinds in accordance with ontologically pre-existing categories such as sane and mad, healthy and sick, normal and pathological. Rather, kinds of people come into being because we make them that way, by and through the practices that we use to describe them and in which they are inserted. Ian Hacking has noted, furthermore, that the practices constitutive of the subject have "looping effects" (Hacking 1995: 351–83): people become aware of how they are perceived and classified, and this in turn changes their self-perceptions and self-understandings. Because the self-perceptions and self-understandings of people subjected to disciplinary classification change by virtue of that subjection, changes to the classifications themselves generally follow. In other words, as more and more people come to identify with a particular normalizing classification, they struggle to exert greater control over its usage and associated meanings.

Nevertheless, the performative and artefactual character of human classifications in general and psychiatric diagnoses in particular does not nullify their disciplinary and punitive effects. As philosophers and theorists of disability have repeatedly shown, people who, for any number of reasons, do not conform to highly-regulated standards of (for instance) social behavior and interaction – such as people who are classified as "mentally ill" or are perceived to be "insane" – are routinely discredited, ignored, vilified, and stigmatized. Until the relatively recent formation and rise of "the mad pride movement" and related social movements, the hermeneutical resources that such disabled people required in order to collectively understand the political character of their situation were unavailable to them. In short, these people have been, and indeed continue to be, habitually subjected to hermeneutical injustice. That Fricker, in her discussion of kinds of hermeneutical disadvantage, neither takes into account the arguments that philosophers and theorists of disability and disabled activists have articulated with respect to the political origins of the "negative consequences" that accrue to these disabled people, nor recognizes the unequal hermeneutical participation that produces these effects, seems itself to be an instance of the form of epistemic injustice that Fricker calls "testimonial injustice." I turn now to more closely consider testimonial injustice in the following sections.

## Knowing Tom Robinson, differently

In her book, Fricker offers the trial of Robinson in Lee's novel as an "extreme example" (Fricker 2007: 26) of the kind of testimonial injustice that she aims to portray philosophically in the book. As she defines it, "a speaker sustains a testimonial injustice if and only if she receives a credibility deficit owing to identity prejudice in the hearer" (Fricker 2007: 28). Fricker wants to show that the events and outcome of the fictional 1935 trial of Robinson exemplify such a credibility deficit due to racist prejudice. To do so, Fricker concentrates on one moment in Lee's depiction of Robinson's testimony to explicate her claims, according to which, given particular social contexts and circumstances, some people will invariably be regarded as less credible due to the identity prejudice against them that certain other people hold: the exchange between Robinson and the county prosecutor, Mr. Gilmer, about why Robinson ran out of and away from the Ewell house and why he was in the house in the first place. Fricker asserts that Lee's depiction of this moment in the trial of Robinson vividly illustrates how testimonial injustices contribute to the production and reproduction of positions of social subordination and oppression (Fricker 2007: 23–9).

Medina, who acknowledges the insightful character of Fricker's arguments, has pointed out nevertheless that, *contra* Fricker, "a proportional, contextualized account" (Medina 2011: 15, 22–8) of epistemic injustice must also attend to the ways in which the credibility deficits that accrue to members of certain social groups due to identity prejudice are inextricably tied to correlative credibility excesses that accrue to members of other social groups due to their identity privilege (Medina 2011: 23, and *passim*). Thus, Medina asserts that, in order to fully capture and adequately understand these sorts of credibility differentials, we must go beyond Fricker's almost-exclusive focus on the utterances of individual speakers to also consider the antecedent social imaginary in terms of which such utterances are produced, including the historical and extant discursive, cultural, political, and economic mechanisms and events that make the disparate interpretations and receptions of the utterances possible.

In the context of Robinson's trial, philosophical inquiry into epistemic injustice that incorporates analysis of how the social imaginary (to use Medina's term) contributes to the production of utterances and the degree of credibility variously attributed to them would consider (for example) how the deeply-seated racist belief according to which all black men are potential rapists who have an uncontrollable desire for white women had already set in place the disparate credibility attributions that determined the inevitable outcome of the trial. As Medina explains it, a proportional, contextualized account of the epistemic injustice that shapes the proceedings and outcome of Robinson's trial would take into account the credibility excesses conferred upon Ewell and her father, Bob Ewell – whose accusations initially led to the charges against Robinson – and the credibility excesses conferred upon both of the white attorneys involved in the trial, as well as the antecedent white supremacist social imaginary that (among other things) conditioned the perceptions and beliefs of the all-white male jury and white spectators in the courtroom even before the trial began. Medina thinks that this kind of proportional, contextualized account of epistemic injustice enables nuanced understanding of the ways in which shifting gradations of credibility attribution contribute to, collude with, and consolidate social and economic hierarchies.

Although Fricker and Medina may disagree about whether the utterances made in this moment of the fictional trial should be the central element in a philosophical analysis of how epistemic injustice is represented in Lee's narrative, their analyses of this moment advance our understanding of how credibility attributions underwrite the constitution of race, gender, and sexuality, as well as, alternatively, how the complicated relations between these social categories influence the differential distribution of credibility attributions. Nevertheless, I want to argue that the analyses of these phenomena that Fricker and Medina have produced remain incomplete insofar as neither philosopher makes more than a passing reference to the fact that Lee's character, Tom Robinson, is disabled. That Robinson is disabled seems to play no role, for Fricker or Medina, in the formation of identity categories within the narrative, nor, for them, does (the apparatus of) disability play a role in the events of the narrative, except to the extent that, and insofar as, Robinson's arm and hand provide tangible evidence that he could not have committed the crime of which he was accused. Nor, furthermore, do there seem to be insights about disability that we can derive from the novel. For Fricker and Medina, that is, Robinson's social positioning as disabled is essentially no more than the rhetorical device that Lee uses to underscore the credibility deficit attributed to him when the guilty verdict is eventually pronounced.

I maintain that the analyses that Fricker and Medina offer with respect to the Robinson trial in *To Kill a Mockingbird* would have been more satisfactory had both philosophers incorporated insights from philosophy of disability into their claims about how gender, race, and sexuality and the credibility differentials incumbent upon these categories are represented through the events and outcome of the trial.

An improved analysis of how social identity categories are produced in the narrative – that is, a more complex intersectional analysis than these philosophers offer – would consider: (1) how the constitution of elements of the apparatus of disability is inextricably interwoven with the constitution of social identities that other apparatuses of power produce and thus contributes to their constitution, (2) how the apparatus of disability is constituted by and through these other identities categories, and, in addition (3) how credibility assessments are conferred and withheld on the basis of the proximity of these identity categories to a conception of normality and hence contribute to the mechanism of normalization that the apparatus of disability produces.

In order to indicate some of the insights about the apparatus of disability that would have been derived from such an expanded analysis, let me turn to consider the exchange between Robinson and Gilmer that pertains to why Robinson was on the Ewell property and went into their house. A portion of their exchange is especially relevant to my argument that Fricker and Medina overlook the precise nature of the way in which Robinson is racialized insofar as they fail to recognize the importance of disability to this exchange (and to the book's narrative in general). This portion of the exchange immediately follows Robinson's testimony that he entered the Ewell property in order to help Mayella Ewell with her chores:

| | |
|---|---|
| *Mr. Gilmer:* | "You're a mighty good fellow, it seems – did all this for not one penny?" |
| *Tom Robinson:* | "Yes, suh. I felt sorry for her, she seemed to try more 'n the rest of 'em." |
| *Mr. Gilmer:* | "*You* felt sorry for *her*, you felt *sorry* for her?" |
| | Mr. Gilmer seemed ready to rise to the ceiling. |
| | The witness realized his mistake and shifted uncomfortably in the chair. But the damage had been done. Below us, nobody liked Tom Robinson's answer. Mr. Gilmer paused a long time to let it sink in. |

(Lee 1960: 263–4)

Fricker writes that this portion of the exchange effectively destroys any epistemic trust that members of the white jury may have allowed themselves to feel for their fellow human being, the black man testifying, Robinson. "For *feeling sorry for* someone," Fricker remarks, "is a taboo sentiment if you are black and the object of your sympathy is a white person" (Fricker 2007: 24, emphasis in Fricker). Within the context of a white supremacist ideology, Fricker explains, "the fundamental ethical sentiment of plain human sympathy becomes disfigured in the eyes of whites so that it appears as little more than an indicator of self-perceived advantage on the part of the black subject" (Fricker 2007: 24). Within the context of white supremacy, she notes, no black man is permitted to have feelings that imply an advantage, of any sort, relative to a white person, regardless of how difficult and desolate that white person's life is. Agreeing with Fricker, Medina remarks that this moment of the trial throws into relief "[t]he comparative and contrastive nature of credibility assignments" (Medina 2011: 21) of the defendant (Robinson), on the one hand, and his interrogator (Gilmer), on the other. As Medina puts it, Robinson's credibility "diminishes to the point of disappearance" (Medina 2011: 23) when his claim about "pity" meets with the mocking disbelief of a far more credible white man, whose powerful and authoritative echo of the white social imaginary renders the plausibility of Robinson's claim "almost unimaginable" (Medina 2011: 24) to the white jurors and spectators in the courtroom. In short, the trial is a zero-sum contest that pits trust in the word of a black man against trust in the word of a white woman, where the former sort of trust amounts to a psychological impossibility. The sense of superiority that Gilmer, the all-white jury, and the white spectators in the courtroom perceive to be at the root of Robinson's expression of sympathy for Mayella Ewell serves to underscore that impossibility (Fricker 2007: 25).

Notice how Fricker and Medina respectively describe why Robinson's explanation for his presence on the Ewell property meets with disdain from the white jurors and courtroom spectators. Fricker attributes their complete distrust and contempt for Robinson to the fact that he expressed "sympathy" for Mayella Ewell. In Medina's terms, Fricker's reference to this sympathy becomes "pity," which is often associated with sympathy, but is not equivalent to it. In any case, both Fricker and Medina recognize that Robinson, as a black man, is not permitted to be an agent of sympathy or pity for a white woman. He is rather, for whites, the personification of a (to use Fricker's unfortunate term) "disfigured" sympathy (pity).

I want to argue, however, that Fricker and Medina fail to recognize that Robinson, as a black man within the context of white supremacy, also is not entitled to be an *object* of sympathy or pity. That he cannot be an object of pity or sympathy, within white supremacy, subjects Robinson as a distinctly black disabled person, that is, distinguishes him as a black disabled person from white disabled people. If Robinson were a white disabled person and expressed sympathy or pity for Mayella Ewell, a nondisabled white woman, Gilmer's surprise and amazement would have conveyed an entirely different meaning. Due to pervasive ableist prejudices and biases, white disabled people are widely perceived to deserve pity or sympathy by virtue of their very existence, that is, their disabled existence is taken to warrant pity or sympathy; they are perceived as the archetypal objects of pity and even tragedy (see Shapiro 1994; Stramondo 2010).

By contrast, black disabled people are not readily identified as the recipients of such sympathy and pity. Had Robinson been a white disabled man who expressed sympathy or pity for a nondisabled white woman, his expression of sympathy or pity likely would have met with exaggerated patience, patronizing condescension, or even amusement. Because Robinson is a black disabled man, he instead confronts contempt when he expresses such sentiments for a white woman. In other words, that Robinson cannot himself be an *object* of pity or even sympathy *racializes him with respect to disability*. Within the racist terms of the apparatus of disability, ableist pity (or sympathy) can be directed only at white disabled people. Insofar as, in the terms of white supremacist ableism, disabled people are the archetypal objects of pity and, given that black men cannot be the objects of pity, a black disabled man is, as Tommy Curry has argued, "a conceptual impossibility" (Curry 2015). "The disabled Black male," Curry remarks, "is configured as a deformity at some distance from the racist stereotype of the Black male savage and, therefore, is unimaginable to most people" (Curry 2015). Although within the system of white supremacy, white disabled people are generally regarded as helpless, genderless, and devoid of sexuality, black men are perceived as superhuman and hyper-masculine, are hyper-sexualized as rapists, and construed as black "bucks," a term that in fact prosecutor Gilmer uses to describe Robinson during his interrogation of him (see Lee 1960: 265). In short, vulnerability, pity, sympathy, and asexuality are "compliments" that white supremacy pays to white (disabled) people only.

The process through which Lee's narrator Scout (Finch), Scout's older brother Jem (Finch), and Mr. Underwood become aware of the white racist social imaginary that convicted Robinson coincides with a distinctive acknowledgement by each of them that Robinson is a disabled person; that is, it is at this point in the narrative that a disabled black man becomes a conceptual possibility for them. Consider how each of them acknowledges that Robinson is disabled. For Jem – the novel's vehicle for the articulation of ideals of justice, impartiality, and fairness, whose exclamation, "Scout, look! Reverend, he's crippled!" (Lee 1960: 248) reminds us of Frantz Fanon's (1952) "Look, a Negro!" – the wide-eyed recognition that Robinson is "crippled" paradoxically underscores the frustrated justice of the novel's narrative according to which every person should be treated equally. By contrast, for Scout, who states that "If [Robinson] had been whole, he would have been a fine specimen of a man" (Lee 1960: 257), the recognition that Robinson is disabled renders him flawed, unfortunate, and tragic, de-masculinizes him and compromises his sexual desirability and prowess. For Underwood, who appeals to the belief according to which the wrongness of Robinson's eventual killing was prior to, and more fundamental, or intuitive, than lofty talk about justice, killing cripples is always wrong, a sin. For Underwood, it seems, Robinson's death is horrible – an act of "senseless slaughter" (Lee 1960: 323) – not simply because he committed no crime, but rather, because he committed no crime *and* he was a cripple. Cripples, Underwood wrote in his newspaper editorial, should be regarded like songbirds: like songbirds, cripples are poignant, helpless creatures subject to the mercy and benevolence of other, more powerful creatures, rather than fully-fledged human beings subject to the values and ideals of justice, fairness, and truth. In short, through their apparently distinct remarks, Scout, Jem, and Underwood variously reinforce *their own* identities as *not* crippled, as *not* disabled, as "able-bodied," in addition to the ways in which they signify Robinson as disabled, that is, as "crippled." Hence, each of these apparently distinct utterances from the characters of Scout, Jem, and Underwood serves to reconsolidate and reproduce the apparatus of disability within the context of Lee's narrative and, in particular, reproduce the ideal of able-bodiedness that has emerged from within that apparatus of power.

## Knowing the apparatus of disability, initially

In this essay, I demonstrated how consideration of disability – that is, consideration of the apparatus of disability – has been left out of analyses of epistemic justice, in particular, and social epistemology, in general. I showed that insofar as feminist and other philosophers have not taken disability into account in their analyses of epistemic injustice, they have circumscribed the political domain too narrowly, obscuring epistemological resources that they ought to acknowledge. When disability is factored into analyses of the epistemic injustice depicted in Lee's novel *To Kill a Mockingbird*, for instance, more complex understandings of how both the apparatus of disability and the white supremacist social imaginary would have shaped dimensions of Lee's characters become available. So long as social epistemologists continue to exclude consideration of the apparatus of disability from their work, the critical scope, political integrity, and transformative potential of this work will remain limited. That the ways in which the apparatus of disability operates in and through Lee's narrative have gone unnoticed and unacknowledged until now is indicative of the pervasiveness of epistemological ignorance and epistemic injustice about disability in both the tradition and contemporary profession of philosophy. My argument, therefore, is that in order to expand the hermeneutical resources and epistemic justice of their theoretical practice, feminist and other philosophers must no longer neglect to consider the apparatus of disability in the analyses of social epistemology that they generate, but rather, must incorporate this political phenomenon into these analyses from the inception of them.

**Related chapters**: 2, 4, 6, 8, 10, 17, 32, 33

## Notes

1 I would like to thank Tommy Curry for feedback on my argument in an earlier draft of this essay and John Drabinski for other advice about the essay. I am also grateful to the editors of this volume for their provocative comments and advice on an earlier draft of the essay.
2 See my remarks about the historical emergence of the "diagnostic style of reasoning" in Tremain 2010, 2013b, and 2015.

## References

Brownmiller, Susan. (1990) *In Our Time: Memoir of a Revolution*, New York: Dial Press.
Curry, T. (2015) 'Dialogues on Disability: Shelley Tremain Interviews Tommy Curry,' *Discrimination and Disadvantage* blog. Online at: http://philosophycommons.typepad.com/disability_and_disadvanta/2015/06/dialogues-on-disability-shelley-tremain-interviews-tommy-curry.html. Last accessed on: August 8, 2015.
Fanon, F. (1952) *Black Skin, White Masks*, Paris: Éditions du Seuil.
Foucault, M. (1980) 'Confessions of the Flesh,' in Colin Gordon (ed.), *Power/Knowledge: Selected Interviews and Other Writings, 1972–1977*, New York: Pantheon Books.
Fricker, M. (2007) *Epistemic Injustice: Power and the Ethics of Knowing*, Oxford: Oxford University Press.
Harper, L. (1960) *To Kill a Mockingbird*, New York: Grand Central Publishing.
Medina, J. (2011) 'The relevance of credibility excess in a proportional view of epistemic injustice: Differential epistemic authority and the social imaginary,' *Social Epistemology* 25 (1) 15–35.
Schalk, S. (2013) 'Metaphorically speaking: Ableist metaphors in feminist writing,' *Disability Studies Quarterly* 33 (4). Online at: http://dsq-sds.org/article/view/3874/3410. Last accessed on: August 8, 2015.
Stramondo, J. A. (2010) 'How an ideology of pity is a social harm to people with disabilities,' *Social Philosophy Today* 26 121–134.
Tremain, S. (2015) 'This is what a historicist and relativist feminist philosophy of disability looks like,' *Foucault Studies* 19 (June) 7–42.
Tremain, S. (2013a) 'Introducing feminist philosophy of disability,' *Disability Studies Quarterly* 33 (4). Online at: http://dsq-sds.org/article/view/3877/3402. Last accessed on: August 8, 2015.
Tremain, S. (2013b) 'Educating jouy,' *Hypatia: A Journal of Feminist Philosophy* 28 (4) 801–817.
Tremain, S. (2011a) 'Ableist language and philosophical associations,' *New APPS: Arts, Politics, Philosophy, Science*. Online at: www.newappsblog.com/2011/07/ableist-language-and-philosophical-associations.html. Last accessed on: August 8, 2015.
Tremain, S. (2011b) 'Bibliography on ableist metaphor,' *New APPS: Arts, Politics, Philosophy Science*. Online at: www.newappsblog.com/2011/08/bibliography-on-ableist-metaphors.html#comments. Last accessed on: August 8, 2015.
Tremain, S. (2010) 'Biopower, styles of reasoning, and what's still missing from the stem cell debates,' *Hypatia: A Journal of Feminist Philosophy* 25 (3) 577–609.

# PART 3

# Schools of thought and subfields within epistemology

# 17
# POWER/KNOWLEDGE/ RESISTANCE
## Foucault and epistemic injustice

*Amy Allen*

Michel Foucault could well be considered a theorist of epistemic injustice *avant la lettre*. As Miranda Fricker makes clear in the introduction to her *Epistemic Injustice: Power and the Ethics of Knowing*, the very notion of epistemic injustice turns on theorizing "reason's entanglements with social power" (2007: 3). But this is precisely the central task of Foucault's work, as he himself indicates in a 1982 interview, where he suggests that

> the central issue of philosophy and critical thought since the eighteenth century has always been, still is, and will, I hope, remain the question: What is this Reason that we use? What are its historical effects? What are its limits, and what are its dangers? How can we exist as rational beings, fortunately committed to practicing a rationality that is unfortunately crisscrossed by intrinsic dangers?
>
> *(2000a: 358)*

For Foucault, the dangers and historical effects of forms of rationality consist primarily in their entanglements with relations of social power, relations that subject individuals in both senses of the term: constitute them as subjects in and through their subjection to prevailing regimes of 'power/knowledge'. Moreover, Foucault interrogates the entanglements of reason with social power while avoiding the kind of reductionism of reason to power that Fricker associates with postmodernism (2007: 2–4). As Foucault emphasizes, his aim is to offer a "rational critique of rationality" (1998: 441); such a project, far from equating rationality or knowledge with power, attempts to study their *relation* (1998: 455).

More specifically, three core features of Foucault's work make his thought an important and productive resource for contemporary discussions of epistemic injustice. These include the following: first, his rich and complex theorization of power, which is one of the most influential analyses in contemporary philosophy and social and political theory. In particular, his account of the relationship between what we might call *constitutive power* and *agential power* helps to highlight the relationship between testimonial and hermeneutical injustices. Second, his specific analysis of power/knowledge regimes and how these shape what it means to be 'within the true' (*dans le vrai*) offers a richer picture of hermeneutical injustices than that provided by Fricker. Third, and finally, his conception of genealogy as a kind of counter-memory that articulates subjugated knowledges provides a compelling model of resistance to epistemic injustices. In what follows,

I take up each of these core features of Foucault's work in turn, with an eye toward showing how Foucault's work intersects productively with the central concerns of theorists of epistemic injustice.

## 1. Power: constitutive and agential

If the goal of theorizing epistemic injustice is to think through reason's entanglements with social power, then it makes sense to start by offering an account of social power.[1] Foucault is perhaps best known for his subtle and nuanced analysis of power, an analysis that combines a constitutive conception of power – that is, a conception of how power works to constitute subjects and tie them to their identities – with an agential conception – that is, a conception of how power is exercised by agents to constrain or act upon the actions of other agents. By theorizing the relationship between these two dimensions of power, Foucault offers important resources for understanding the relationship between testimonial and hermeneutical forms of epistemic injustice.

The classic statement of Foucault's constitutive conception of power is found in his *History of Sexuality*, volume 1. There he defines power as

> the multiplicity of force relations immanent in the sphere in which they operate and which constitute their own organization; as the process which, through ceaseless struggles and confrontations, transforms, strengthens, or reverses them; as the support which these force relations find in one another, thus forming a chain or a system, or on the contrary, the disjunctions and contradictions which isolate them from one another; and lastly, as the strategies take effect, whose general design or institutional crystallization is embodied in the state apparatus, in the formulation of the law, in the various social hegemonies.
>
> *(1978: 92–93)*

In other words, power, for Foucault, is neither an institution nor a structure nor an innate capacity of individuals; rather, "it is the name that one attributes to a complex strategical situation in a particular society" (1978: 93).

Foucault then goes on to articulate five core features of this strategic model of power. First, power is not a metaphysical property possessed by individuals but rather exists only in and through its exercise (Foucault 1978: 94). Second, power is found not only in the sovereign or the state, but rather is spread throughout the social body; hence, when we study power, we should focus on the points where it becomes "capillary" (Foucault 2003: 27). Third, power comes from below, which is to say that it is generated in the myriad mobile force relations that are spread throughout the social body (Foucault 1978: 94). Thus, when we study power, we should not view it, at least not initially, as "a phenomenon of mass and homogeneous domination" (Foucault 2003: 29) or as a "binary and all-encompassing opposition between ruler and ruled" (Foucault 1978: 94). This is not to deny that wide-ranging, systematic relations of domination exist; indeed, Foucault sometimes uses the term 'domination' to capture such broad, structural asymmetries of power.[2] However, he does insist that systematic relations of domination are best understood not as the *causes* but as the *results* of the power relations that are spread throughout the social body; thus, our analysis of power should be ascending rather than descending (Foucault 2003: 30). Fourth, power relations are "intentional and non-subjective" (Foucault 1978: 94). By intentional, Foucault means that power relations have a point or an aim, that they are directed toward a certain end; by non-subjective, he means that they are neither possessed nor controlled by individual subjects. Thus, rather than attempting to discern the intentions of the one who 'has' power, an attempt that would lead us "into a labyrinth from which there is no way out," we should investigate "the multiple peripheral bodies, the bodies that are constituted as subjects by power-effects" (Foucault 2003: 28–29). In other words, rather than viewing power as subjective – as possessed by a subject – we should view the subject as constituted by power relations. Fifth, and finally, "where there is power, there is resistance" (Foucault 1978: 95), and resistance is always internal to power relations.[3]

As far as Foucault's constitutive conception of power goes, the crucial points are the following: power is not a capacity of agents but rather a mobile set of force relations spread throughout the social body that exist only in their exercise and that constitute agents as subjects. Although this constitutive conception has often been taken by Foucault's critics to deny the possibility of subjectivity or agency, and thus to undermine an agential understanding of power, this is a misunderstanding of Foucault's work.[4] In fact, Foucault articulates an agential understanding of power in his late essay, "The Subject and Power." There, he defines power as "a set of actions on possible actions; it incites, it induces, it seduces, it makes easier or more difficult; it releases or contrives, makes more probable or less; in the extreme, it constrains or forbids absolutely, but it is always a way of acting upon one or more acting subjects by virtue of their acting or being capable of action" (2000b: 341). According to his agential conception, power is "exercised only over free subjects, and only insofar as they are 'free'. By this we mean individual or collective subjects who are faced with a field of possibilities in which several kinds of conduct, several ways of reacting and modes of behavior are available" (2000b: 342).

What ties these two apparently conflicting conceptions of power together is Foucault's account of subjection (*assujettissement*). Whereas classical, juridical conceptions of power in political philosophy presuppose "an individual who is naturally endowed . . . with rights, capabilities, and so on" (Foucault 2003: 43) and then ask under what circumstances it is legitimate for such a subject to be subjugated by the state, Foucault, by contrast, begins "with the power relationship itself, with the actual or effective relationship of domination . . . We should not, therefore, be asking subjects how, why, and by what right they can agree to being subjugated, but showing how actual relations of subjugation manufacture subjects" (2003: 45). The aim of this analysis is to uncover the "immense labor to which the West has submitted generations in order to produce . . . men's subjection: their constitution as subjects in both senses of the word" (Foucault 1978: 60).

Foucault's analysis of power is a rich, subtle, and complex account that has proven to be tremendously productive for work in philosophy, the humanities, and the social sciences in the decades since his death. Given the centrality of the concept of social power to the study of epistemic injustice, this fact alone makes his work a potentially productive resource. But more specifically, Foucault's understanding of power as spread throughout the social body through multiple forms of constraint and modes of interaction harmonizes well with the kind of holistic analysis of epistemic injustices as temporally and socially extended called for by José Medina in his critique of Miranda Fricker's account of testimonial injustice (Medina 2013: 58–60). Indeed, one of the central virtues of Foucault's analysis of power is that it is attentive to "complex histories and chains of social interactions that go beyond particular pairs and clusters of subjects" and that it provides "a sociohistorical analysis that contextualizes and connects sustained chains of interactions" (Medina 2013: 60). Moreover, by highlighting the relationship between the constitutive and agential dimensions of power through his account of subjection, Foucault offers a model for thinking through the complex relationships between episodic and agent-centered instances of testimonial injustice and the systemic, constitutive relations of hermeneutical injustice that, for Foucault, provide the former's condition of possibility. This allows not only for a more complex and dynamic conception of testimonial injustice, but also for a more complex and dynamic understanding of the relationship between testimonial and hermeneutic injustice.

## 2. Power/knowledge

Not only does Foucault offer a rich and subtle analysis of social power in its own right, he is also justly famous for his conceptualization of the entanglements of social power with knowledge, truth, and rationality. Indeed, in *Society Must be Defended*, which offers a classic statement of his conception of power/knowledge, Foucault indicates that his aim is to study the 'how' of power, which means studying the triangle of power, right, and truth. But unlike traditional political philosophy, which asks how the discourse of truth sets limits to the legitimate exercise of power (i.e., the right of power), Foucault seeks to invert this question to ask the following questions: "What are the rules of right that power implements to produce discourses of truth" (2003: 24)? In other words, what are power's "truth-effects" (2003: 25)?

What this means concretely is that in our society the multiple and mobile relations of power that traverse the social body are "indissociable from a discourse of truth, and they can neither be established nor function unless a true discourse is produced, accumulated, put into circulation, and set to work. Power cannot be exercised unless a certain economy of discourses of truth functions in, on the basis of, and thanks to, that power" (Foucault 2003: 24). For example, individuals are compelled to discover the truth or tell the truth about themselves; "we are judged, condemned, forced to perform tasks, and destined to live and die in certain ways by discourses that are true, and which bring with them specific power-effects" (Foucault 2003: 25).

On the basis of this conception of power/knowledge, Foucault offers the following conception of truth:

> Truth isn't outside power or lacking in power . . . Truth is a thing of this world: it is produced only by virtue of multiple forms of constraint. And it induces regular effects of power. Each society has its regime of truth, its 'general politics' of truth – that is, the types of discourse it accepts and makes function as true; the mechanisms and instances that enable one to distinguish true and false statements; the means by which each is sanctioned; the techniques and procedures accorded value in the acquisition of truth; the status of those who are charged with saying what counts as true.
> *(2000c: 131)*

According to this analysis, each society would thus have its own distinctive political economy of truth, its own discursive means for determining the political, power-laden conditions of possibility for forming true statements, for being, as Foucault once put it, "*dans le vrai* (within the true)" (1972: 224). For Foucault, the political economy of truth in our society is characterized by two features. The first is the dominance of scientific discourses and institutions in the disciplinary production of the conditions of possibility for truth. The second is the diffusion of the political economy of truth throughout the social body through the operation of educational and informational apparatuses such as the university, the media, and so forth (Foucault 2000c: 131). (Moreover, in late modernity, these two features are closely intertwined, since the educational system is increasingly dominated by scientific discourses.) The goal of analyzing this political economy of truth, however, is not that of "emancipating truth from every system of power (which would be a chimera, for truth is already power) but of detaching the power of truth from the forms of hegemony, social, economic, and cultural, within which it operates at the present time" (Foucault 2000c: 133). The refusal of the attempt to emancipate truth from power is what distinguishes Foucault's analysis of power/knowledge from classical forms of ideology critique.[5]

This refusal carries over to his methodological distinction between genealogy and the history of science. Whereas the latter operates on what Foucault calls "the cognition-truth axis," the former remains within what he calls the "discourse-power axis" (2000c: 178). Thus when we want to examine, for example, 18th century Europe from a genealogical point of view, this requires that we must reject or at least bracket the ideas of "the progress of the enlightenment, the struggle of knowledge against ignorance, of reason against chimeras, of experience against prejudices, of reason against error, and so on" and instead analyze the Enlightenment period as "an immense and multiple battle between knowledges in the plural – knowledges that are in conflict because of their very morphology, because they are in the possession of enemies, and because they have intrinsic power-effects" (Foucault 2000c: 178–179). As an example, Foucault discusses the homogenization, normalization, classification, and centralization of medical knowledge in the second half of the 18th century. This was accomplished through the creation of hospitals, pharmacies, medical societies that established professional codes, and public hygiene campaigns. In other words, the very same operations that Foucault analyzed in his account of disciplinary power – selection, normalization, hierarchization, and centralization – produce both normalized, disciplined subjects and disciplined knowledges.[6] The result of this process of disciplining knowledges was the creation of modern academic and professional disciplines. As Foucault puts it: "The eighteenth century was the century when knowledges were disciplined, or when, in other words, the internal organization of every knowledge became a discipline" (2003: 181). This disciplining of knowledge allowed for the eradication of false or nonknowledge, the homogenization and normalization of the content of knowledge, the centralization of knowledge around core axioms, and the hierarchization of different forms of knowledge production. This process was institutionalized through the emergence of the modern university, which played the role of selecting some knowledges and disqualifying others. The disciplining of knowledges replaced a power/knowledge regime that focused on sorting acceptable from unacceptable statements with one focused on a new problem: "Who is speaking, are they qualified to speak, at what level is the statement situated, what set can it be fitted into, and how and to what extent does it conform to other forms and other typologies of knowledge" (Foucault 2003: 184)? In other words, this process of the "disciplinarization of knowledges" that occurred in 18th century Europe "established a new mode of relationship between power and knowledge" (Foucault 2003: 184).

The goal of Foucault's genealogical analysis of power/knowledge regimes, then, is to provide a "political history of knowledge" or a historical analysis of the "politics of truth" (Foucault 2000d: 13). Foucault's genealogy of disciplines, sketched briefly above, where disciplines are understood as specific, historically emergent, contingent, and culturally specific forms of power/knowledge that set the limits of what can be within the true at a given time and thus serve both as enabling resources for the production of true statements and systems of control and constraint that fix the limits of discourses (Foucault 1972: 224), serves as an example of this kind of political history of knowledge. It also offers some reasons to think that Foucault's conception of power/knowledge might allow for a broader conception of hermeneutical injustice than that provided in existing theories of epistemic injustice. Miranda Fricker defines hermeneutical injustice as "the injustice of having some significant areas of one's social experience obscured from collective understanding owing to a structural identity prejudice in the collective hermeneutical resource" (Fricker 2007: 155). The central case that motivates this definition for Fricker is one in which a member of an oppressed group lacks the conceptual resources to make sense of her situation as a result of structural identity prejudice. An example of such an injustice would be a woman who experienced what we now call sexual harassment prior to the time when this was identified and named by feminists as a distinctive form of gender-based subordination. The harm of such hermeneutical injustice, for Fricker, is that it leaves the oppressed individual unable to make the harm that she has suffered intelligible to others or even to herself; thus, hermeneutical injustice can threaten the very development of the self (Fricker 2007: 163).

What Foucault's work offers is a richer and more complex conception of the intertwined discursive and institutional mechanisms by means of which collective hermeneutical resources are produced, codified, and organized into hierarchies. Foucault's genealogy of the emergence of disciplines in the 18th century provides a contextually and historically specific analysis of how particular knowledges are disqualified by being cast out of the domain of the true while others are organized into disciplines that are codified in social institutions such as the university, the media, and the educational system. Foucault's work also allows for a deeper understanding of the kind of structural epistemic injustice or identity prejudice that is at work in Fricker's central case of hermeneutical injustice. Foucault's genealogical analyses of power/knowledge regimes enable us to see how certain people are first classified into groups (the ill, the insane, the sexually deviant) and then disqualified as knowers by virtue of being members of such groups. These aspects of Foucault's work thus afford a more complex genealogical understanding of the distribution and dispersal of hermeneutical resources throughout societies such as ours, and of the role of academic disciplines in those patterns of distribution.

## 3. Power/knowledge/resistance

Recall Foucault's claim that where there is power, there is resistance. If we extend this claim about social power to his analysis of power/knowledge regimes, we get the corollary that where there is power/knowledge, there is epistemic resistance. Although Foucault is often criticized for failing to give a fully elaborated account of resistance, it is worth noting that one of his more developed discussions of resistance focuses on epistemic resistance and, specifically, on the relationship between genealogical method and epistemic resistance. This discussion thus provides an excellent vantage point on the resources that Foucault's work offers for theorizing resistance to epistemic injustice.

In the opening lecture of his "*Society Must be Defended*" course at the Collège de France, Foucault begins by characterizing his critiques of the prison, the asylum, and the clinic as forms of local critique that are made possible by the "insurrection of subjugated knowledges" (2003: 7). By subjugated knowledges, Foucault means two things: first, the "blocks of historical knowledges that were present in the functional and systematic ensembles, but which were masked", and, second, knowledges "that have been disqualified as nonconceptual knowledges, as insufficiently elaborated knowledges: naïve. . . , hierarchically inferior knowledges. . . that are below the required level of erudition or scientificity" (2003: 7). The former understanding of subjugated knowledges refers to those forms of scholarly knowledge that have been marginalized or rendered inferior by the knowledge hierarchy imposed by disciplines; the latter meaning refers to those forms of knowledge that were disqualified *as* knowledge by the process of disciplinarization that I described in the previous section. As examples of the latter, Foucault offers the knowledge of the nurse, of the psychiatric patient, or of the delinquent. Genealogical analysis, as a kind of local critique, is made possible and given "its essential strength" by the "coupling together of the buried scholarly knowledge and knowledges that were disqualified by the hierarchy of erudition and sciences" (Foucault 2003: 8). At stake in the recovery of both forms of subjugated knowledges is a historical, genealogical knowledge of struggles, and an attempt to make use of that knowledge in the service of a critique of our historical present.

In this sense, genealogies are antisciences. This is not to say that genealogies reject knowledge and celebrate ignorance, nor even that they reject science per se; rather, they enact what Foucault calls "the insurrection of knowledges," (2003: 9) which means an insurrection that challenges the centralizing, normalizing, and hierarchizing features of disciplinary power/knowledge regimes. Such an insurrection does not amount to a straightforward rejection of science or scientific knowledge. Rather, Foucault's aim is to show how the production of scientific knowledge is entangled with relations of power, to reveal scientific truth as a thing of this world. So, for example, when Foucault writes a historical critique of modern psychiatry, his aim is not to reject psychiatry but rather to understand its historical conditions of possibility and its entanglement with relations of power and exclusion (Foucault 2006). Thus, Foucault defines genealogy, the central method of the best known period of his work, as an "attempt to desubjugate historical knowledges, to set them free, or in other words to enable them to oppose and struggle against the coercion of a unitary, formal, and scientific theoretical discourse" (2003: 10). Genealogy is thus a form of counterhistory that disrupts and critiques existing, inherited, but contingent epistemic hierarchies.

As José Medina has argued convincingly, Foucault's conception of genealogy as the insurrection of subjugated knowledges provides a powerful model of resistance to epistemic injustice. As Medina puts it, "the critical goal of genealogy is to energize a vibrant and feisty epistemic pluralism so that insurrectionary struggles among competing power/knowledge frameworks are always underway and contestation always alive" (2011: 12). Although there is always the danger that such insurrections will consolidate into new forms of epistemic hegemony, Foucault's work also views the local critique fueled by the insurrection of subjugated knowledges as an ongoing, endless task. Thus, as Medina explains, it guarantees "the constant *epistemic friction* of knowledges from below, which . . . means guaranteeing that eccentric voices and perspectives are heard and can interact with mainstream ones, that the experiences and concerns of those who live in darkness and silence do not remain lost and unattended" (2011: 21).

Although some theorists of epistemic injustice, such as Fricker, have criticized Foucault's analysis of power/knowledge for dispensing too readily with the notion of truth (Fricker 2007: 55), Medina finds its radicality to be precisely its source of strength for an account of epistemic resistance. In Foucault's work, as Medina explains, "epistemic frictions are sought for their own sake, for the forms of *resistance* that they constitute" (2011: 24). Moreover, Medina argues that Foucault's radical, 'guerrilla pluralism' offers two crucial insights for theorizing the epistemology of ignorance, even though his work has not been widely embraced by theorists working on this topic. These insights are, first, the co-constitution of knowledge and ignorance within power/knowledge regimes and, second, the lack of availability of an epistemically innocent standpoint, that is, an epistemic standpoint outside of power relations (Medina 2011: 30–31). As Medina shows, these two Foucauldian insights are tremendously productive for the critique and resistance of racialized epistemologies of ignorance, insofar as they highlight "the co-constitutive relations between racial knowledge and racial ignorance, and the unavailability of innocent racialized standpoints" (Medina 2011: 31). As such, Foucault's understanding of genealogy as the insurrection of subjugated knowledges enables theorists of epistemic injustice to highlight "the constant epistemic struggles that take place in racialized social fields, calling attention to possibilities of resistance and contestation" (Medina 2011: 31).

## 4. Conclusion

Medina notes that it is surprising that Foucault's work is not more widely cited and discussed in the literature on epistemologies of ignorance in feminist and critical race theory (2011: 29). He speculates that this could be explained by the long-standing but now largely outmoded opposition between standpoint theories and social constructivist theories. It is equally surprising that Foucault's work is not more widely cited and discussed in the literature on epistemic injustice. My best guess is that this can be explained by long-standing but also largely unproductive if not outmoded oppositions between analytic philosophy – from which the field of social epistemology emerged – and continental philosophy. But if we assume, as Fricker does in her groundbreaking work, that our theorizing of epistemic injustice should start not by articulating norms of epistemic justice or non-oppressive rationality but rather by exploring the "negative space" of injustice as it inheres in actually existing social practices (Fricker 2007: viii), then there are profound substantive and methodological resources in the traditions of continental philosophy and critical theory for this kind of project. Theorists of epistemic injustice would do well to make use of them.

**Related chapters**: 9, 11, 12, 14, 37

## Notes

1 To be sure, one might just as well say that we should start by giving an account of reason, but Fricker starts with power because of her methodological commitment to non-ideal theory, a commitment that Foucault would most definitely share.
2 See, for example, Foucault 2000b: 331–332.
3 I discuss resistance in more detail in section three.
4 I argue against this misunderstanding of Foucault's work in Allen 2008 chapter 2.
5 On this point, see also Foucault 2003: 33–34. By 'classical forms of ideology critique,' I have in mind those theorists in the Marxist tradition who presuppose the possibility of emancipating truth from power, at least in principle. As I read him, this would include not only Marx himself, but also critical theorists such as Habermas.
6 For Foucault's account of how these mechanisms work in the disciplining of individual subjects, see Foucault 1977 part III.

## References

Allen, Amy. 2008. *The Politics of Our Selves: Power, Autonomy, and Gender in Contemporary Critical Theory*. New York: Columbia University Press.
Foucault, Michel. 2006. *History of Madness*, ed. Jean Khalfa, trans. Jonathan Murphy and Jean Khalfa. New York: Routledge.
Foucault, Michel. 2003. *"Society Must be Defended": Lectures at the Collège de France, 1975–1976*, trans. David Macey. New York: Picador Press.
Foucault, Michel. 2000a. "Space, Knowledge, and Power," in *Power: Essential Works of Michel Foucault*, volume 3, ed. James D. Faubion. New York: The New Press.
Foucault, Michel. 2000b. "The Subject of Power," in *Power: Essential Works of Michel Foucault*, volume 3, ed. James D. Faubion. New York: The New Press.
Foucault, Michel. 2000c. "Truth and Power," in *Power: Essential Works of Michel Foucault*, volume 3, ed. James D. Faubion. New York: The New Press.
Foucault, Michel. 2000d. "Truth and Juridical Forms," in *Power: Essential Works of Michel Foucault*, volume 3, ed. James D. Faubion. New York: The New Press.
Foucault, Michel. 1998. "Structuralism and Post-Structuralism," in *Aesthetics, Method, and Epistemology: Essential Works of Michel Foucault*, volume 2, ed. James D. Faubion. New York: The New Press.
Foucault, Michel. 1978. *History of Sexuality, volume 1: An Introduction*, trans. Robert Hurley. New York: Vintage.
Foucault, Michel. 1977. *Discipline and Punish: The Birth of the Prison*, trans. Alan Sheridan. New York: Vintage.
Foucault, Michel. 1972. *The Archaeology of Knowledge and the Discourse on Language*, trans. A.M. Sheridan Smith. New York: Pantheon.
Fricker, Miranda. 2007. *Epistemic Injustice: Power and the Ethics of Knowing*. Oxford: Oxford University Press.
Medina, José. 2013. *The Epistemology of Resistance: Gender and Racial Oppression, Epistemic Injustice, and Resistant Imaginations*. Oxford: Oxford University Press.
Medina, José. 2011. "Toward a Foucaultian Epistemology of Resistance: Counter-Memory, Epistemic Friction, and *Guerrilla* Pluralism," *Foucault Studies* 12 (October): 9–35.

# 18
# EPISTEMIC INJUSTICE AND PHENOMENOLOGY

*Lisa Guenther*

What is epistemic injustice, and what might we learn from the phenomenological tradition about how to analyze, critique, and transform the harm done to someone in their capacity as a knower?

Miranda Fricker identifies two kinds of epistemic injustice: testimonial injustice, which harms someone as a "giver of knowledge" (Fricker 2007: 7), for example by silencing them or discrediting their words in advance on the basis of their social identity, and hermeneutical injustice, which harms someone as a "subject of social understanding" (7) by depriving them of the necessary concepts and contexts for making sense of their own experience and becoming intelligible to others. Fricker's work builds on decades of analysis by Women of Color feminists, critical race theorists, and critical disability scholars, and it skirts along the edges of work by continental philosophers such as Michel Foucault and Judith Butler, but there has been little, if any, engagement between the emerging field of epistemic injustice and the phenomenological tradition.[1]

In what follows, I will explore some possibilities for engaging phenomenologically with issues of testimonial injustice and hermeneutical injustice. While these issues do not exhaust the field of epistemic injustice, they offer a productive starting-point for further conversation.

## The phenomenological method

Fricker uses the word "phenomenology" to refer to the feeling of "what it is like" to experience something, rather than to the phenomenological method developed by Edmund Husserl, Martin Heidegger, Maurice Merleau-Ponty, and others. As a method, phenomenology begins with first person experience, but it does not end there; rather, the aim of the phenomenological method is to identify the fundamental structures of experience and signficance presupposed by perception, thought, and language. Put another way, it discloses the conditions for the *possibility* of testimonial and hermeneutical activity at its most foundational level. In reducing phenomenology to subjective feeling, Fricker excludes the resources of a method that begins with a reflection on the lived experience of first person consciousness, but also extends beyond subjective feeling to trace the intersubjective constitution of a sense of the objective world.

The phenomenological method was developed by Husserl as a way of navigating between the radically subjectivist and objectivist epistemologies of psychologism and naturalism. The basic orientation of phenomenology is "Back to the things themselves!" (Husserl 2008: 168). This does not signal a return to pre-Kantian epistemology, but rather a critical rejoinder to Kant's opposition of phenomena to noumena and a reclamation of the phenomenal world as the primary site of meaning. Against theories of perception that posit an immaterial mind, a material world, and a set of representations and/or inferences to mediate between them, phenomenology begins with a thick description of how things actually appear to consciousness in lived experience, bracketing the ready-made theories and assumptions with which we typically explain our experience in what Husserl calls the "natural attitude" (Husserl 1991: 37). The natural attitude is a naïve, unreflective relation to the world as if it existed separately from the consciousness to which it appears. The task of phenomenology is to bracket or suspend the natural attitude through what Husserl calls the *epochē* in order to reflect on the transcendental structures through which the sense of the world is constituted in and by consciousness. This transcendental shift does not signal a retreat from the world or an abstraction from everyday lived experience, but rather a more critical, reflective relation to both.

A key insight of phenomenology is that *consciousness is relational*. By reflecting on our lived experience through the *epochē*, we discover an essential correlation between our intentional acts, or *noesis* (the act of thinking, perceiving, imagining, remembering) and the intentional objects or *noemata* towards which these acts are oriented and whose meaning they constitute (the thought, the perceived, the imagined, the remembered. . .).[2] The process of following the traces of the given world back to the intentional acts in which they are given is called the *phenomenological reduction*. This process is elaborated through further reflection on the transcendental structures of givenness (the transcendental reduction) and through an imaginative variation of one's own singular experience to discover the invariant essence or *eidos* of intentional objects (the eidetic reduction).

For Husserl, the essence of consciousness is transcendental subjectivity: a temporal flow of noetic-noematic correlations unfolding in the first person singular. A key question for phenomenology, then, is solipsism and the possibility of empathy: how does one consciousness experience another, not simply as an intentional object but as another consciousness who experiences itself in the first person, and for whom I too exist as another subject in a common world? Furthermore, how does a shared sense of the world emerge if each consciousness constitutes meaning independently through its own singular, unsharable intentional acts?

For Husserl, embodiment plays a key role in the experience of another consciousness. As an embodied subject, I perceive the world from a certain perspective: a "here" in relation to which everything else appears as "there." This sense of "here" is mobile; I carry it with me as the "zero point" of orientation for consciousness, the "field of localization" for sensory experience, and the seat of the "I can" (Husserl 2002: 166, 156, 159). When I encounter another body who moves and orients itself towards objects in a way that is structurally similar to my own, I spontaneously experience this body as another "here": an embodied consciousness with their own perspective on the world, to whom I appear conversely as "there." For Husserl, this is not an inferential process but rather a structural pairing or "analogical transfer" of sense based on the *apperception* of another transcendental consciousness through the direct *perception* of their living, moving body (Husserl 1991: 108–20). This pairing of self and other forms the basis for my own experience of the world, and even of my own body, as objectively "there for others" and not just an intentional object for me. As such, the sense of objectivity is constituted intersubjectively through a triangulation of self, other, and world.

Feminist phenomenologists have critically engaged Husserl's transcendental orientation, identifying a potential site of epistemic injustice in his assumption of an unmarked, pre-social transcendental I who is theoretically capable of discovering the truth of essences through introspective reflection in the first-person, and who spontaneously recognizes other embodied subjects as similar enough to itself to be perceived spontaneously as another ego.[3] But feminists have also built on Husserl's account of embodied consciousness and the intersubjective constitution of objectivity, along with the work of later phenomenologists such as Merleau-Ponty, to reorient and radicalize the basic methods and concepts of phenomenology towards the concrete social and material contexts within which the lived experience of consciousness unfolds.[4]

How might a critical appropriation of phenomenological method contribute to current discussions of epistemic injustice? In the next section, I will sketch an overview of Fricker's account of social perception in relation to testimonial and hermeneutical injustice, flagging the points at which I think a fruitful conversation with phenomenology could begin to unfold.

## Testimonial injustice and the phenomenology of social perception

Fricker develops an account of social perception as part of her broader account of testimonial virtue. At stake here is the challenge of apprehending the testimony of others without unjustly granting or withholding trust on the basis of the speaker's perceived social status; in order to become virtuous listeners, we need to understand the way social perception shapes our epistemic relation to others, and correct for unjust patterns of silencing or exclusion. Fricker contrasts inferentialist accounts of social perception, which are too clunky to account for its rapid, spontaneous, and unreflective character, with what she calls "phenomenological" claims, which account for the spontaneity of social perception at the expense of critical reflexivity.[5] The phenomenological view, which she attributes to Thomas Reid and Tyler Burge, is based on the assumption that people usually tell the truth, so we can and should grant a "*default* of credulity or acceptance of what others tell us" (Fricker 2007: 61–2). Here, as throughout *Epistemic Injustice*, Fricker equates phenomenology with "felt sense" rather than engaging with the phenomenological tradition and its methods. Fricker's own account of social perception turns on the capacity of the hearer to shift back and forth between unreflective and reflective modes of engagement with the testimony of others. But as I will argue, Merleau-Ponty's phenomenological account of perception both anticipates and enriches Fricker's view, without falling into the uncritical stance that she associates with phenomenology as felt sense.

Fricker grants the non-inferentialist point that our default mode of engagement tends to be an unreflective, uncritical acceptance of what other people say. But she argues that this default mode is also regularly interrupted by "signs, prompts, or cues" that disrupt our unreflective trust and prompt a more reflective critical assessment of the speaker's credibility (2007: 66). Perhaps the speaker avoids meeting my gaze, or some aspect of her testimony contradicts another aspect. I may be prompted to shift from an unreflective trust in her testimony to a more wary, critical, and reflective way of listening in which I seek further evidence of (un)trustworthiness, evaluate this evidence in my own mind, ask the speaker for clarification, and/or express my distrust openly.

Taking this description of the lived experience of conversation as a starting point, Fricker develops a hybrid view to which both inferentialist and non-inferentialist views contribute, but which neither can encompass on its own.[6] The theory turns on the cognitive capacity of the hearer to shift back and forth between unreflective and reflective modes, depending on the context of the conversation. This (re)situation of the philosophical argument from the level of ideal theory to the non-ideal "rough ground" of a discursive situation is crucial for Fricker's argument, and it is a move that resonates with Merleau-Ponty's own approach to the seemingly intractable conflict between rationalism and empiricism (2002: 60–74). In the end, Fricker characterizes moral-epistemic virtue as a "critical openness to the word of others" (2007: 66), which is both pre-reflectively trusting and pre-reflectively attentive to possible grounds for mistrust, and which is capable of shifting into reflective evaluation of the degree to which the speaker should be trusted. Fricker argues that such "credibility judgments" are not made on the basis of a pre-existing theory or set of rules, but rather as an open-ended process of attuning oneself to the situation, adjusting one's comportment to new situations based on past experience, and developing a "sensitivity to patterns of moral salience" (2007: 74).

Fricker draws on Aristotle's account of moral perception to develop a non-inferentialist account of "*testimonial sensibility*" (2007: 71). But she could have just as well drawn on the phenomenological tradition for such an account, while enriching the historical dimensions of moral-epistemic perception that she finds lacking in Aristotle (82). Potential resources for this account include Merleau-Ponty's phenomenological engagement with the figure/ground structure in Gestalt theory[7] (2002: 3–74); his analysis of the complex interplay between spatial, temporal, social, historical, and affective senses of the "background" or field that both shapes the meaning of lived experience and also emerges through the sedimentation of embodied practices and habits of individual and collective Being-in-the-world (77–347); his account of embodiment as the primary site of meaning-making, both through the interplay of pre-reflective and reflective modes of comportment or behavior, and also through the expressive power of gestures and speech (112–70, 202–32); his patient description of the social and historical dimensions of embodied perception (348–425); and his account of the "chiasm" or inter-connected feedback loops between self and other, perceiver and perceived, vision and touch (Merleau-Ponty 1968: 130–55).

All this and more could be brought into conversation with Fricker's account of social perception, and both the discourse of epistemic injustice and the phenomenological tradition would be mutually enriched. In the next section, I will pick up on a few of these possibilities and elaborate them at greater length.

## "Settling the mind" through the body

In giving an account of the harm incurred to those who are systematically and unjustly perceived as less credible, Fricker draws on Bernard Williams' account (2002: 192f) of the role that other people play in the process of "steadying the mind," or creating a stable basis for one's own knowledge of the world. Williams argues that the main process through which the mind steadies itself is "trustful conversation with others" (Fricker 2007: 52). A question posed to me by another calls me into critical reflection on my perception of the world, challenging me to distinguish between my subjective experience and the objective reality of the world. The other's response, in turn, helps me to clarify how much of my subjective experience is corroborated by the experience of others.

This account of steadying the mind resonates with Husserl's phenomenological analysis of the way a sense of objectivity is constituted through the convergence of multiple perspectives in a shared world (1989: 60–95):

> In every case the exhibition of any apprehended Objectivity whatsoever requires a relation to the apprehension of a multiplicity of subjects sharing a mutual understanding. . . Nature is an intersubjective reality and a reality not just for me and my companions at the moment but for us and for everyone who can come to have dealings with us and can come to a mutual understanding with us about things and about other people.
> *(Husserl 1989: 86, 91; 1999: 89–151)*

It also resonates with Merleau-Ponty's more historicist and socially-contextual account of the intersubjective constitution of the sense of the world and of cultural objects (2002: 348–425). What is absent from Williams' and Fricker's accounts, however, is the role that the body plays in this co-constitution of meaning. This point is crucial, both for our understanding of social epistemology and for our account of epistemic injustice, given the degree to which the social identities of race, gender, ability, class, and sexuality are perceived in and through the body and its expressive gestures. The phenomenological tradition offers multiple sources for reflecting on the embodied dimensions of social cognition; I will engage with one such account to highlight the possibilities for further development.

In *Phenomenology of Perception*, Merleau-Ponty develops an account of the phenomenal body as the primary site and medium of one's lived experience as consciousness and one's meaningful comportment as Being-in-the-world. The relation between body and world is reciprocal: "my body is a movement towards the world, and the world my body's point of support" (Merleau-Ponty 2002: 408). For Merleau-Ponty,

> Consciousness is in the first place not a matter of "I think that" but of "I can". . . . In the action of the hand which is raised towards an object is contained a reference to the object, not as an object represented, but as that highly specific thing towards which we project ourselves, near which we are, in anticipation, and which we haunt. Consciousness is being-towards-the-thing through the intermediary of the body. A movement is learned when the body has understood it, that is, when it has incorporated it into its "world", and to move one's body is to aim at things through it; it is to allow oneself to respond to their call, which is made upon it independently of any representation.
>
> *(2002: 159–61)*

Perception is neither the reaction to an objective stimulus nor the classical phenomenological constitution of an object; it is, rather, "our inherence in things" (408), a way of relating to the world to which we belong, and upon which we also have a perspective, in a relation of transcendence within immanence. As an embodied Being-in-the-world, I encounter the bodies of others not just as static objects but as "manifestations of behavior" (Merleau-Ponty 2002: 411), just as I too manifest behavior that remains open to interpretation by others. In this context, "behavior" refers to patterned activity and interactivity, embodied and embedded within and responding to a surrounding world or environment. It is not the stimulus-response of an input-output mechanism, but rather the meaningful comportment of a living, self-organizing being, a being who is born to an other and who continues to grow and learn throughout its life.

Merleau-Ponty describes the structure of an encounter with the behavior of another in terms that recall the core insight that Fricker gleans from Bernard Williams:

> No sooner has my gaze fallen upon a living body in process of acting than the objects surrounding it immediately take on a fresh layer of significance: they are no longer simply what I myself could make of them, they are what this other pattern of behavior is about to make of them. Round about the perceived body a vortex forms, towards which my world is drawn and, so to speak, sucked in: to this extent, it is no longer merely mine, and no longer merely present, it is present to x, to that other manifestation of behavior which begins to take shape in it. Already the other body has ceased to be a mere fragment of the world, and become the theatre of a certain process of elaboration, and, as it were, a certain "view" of the world.
>
> *(Merleau-Ponty 2002: 412)*

For Merleau-Ponty, linguistic meaning presupposes this more basic power to apprehend and make sense of the world through sensory-motor feedback loops between my body and the bodies of others:

> Between my consciousness and my body as I experience it, between this phenomenal body of mine and that of another as I see it from the outside, there exists an internal relation which causes the other to appear as the completion of the system. The other can be evident to me because I am not transparent for myself, and because my subjectivity draws its body in its wake.
>
> (Merleau-Ponty 2002: 410)

These circuits of mutual understanding have existential-ontological implications. I discover in the other:

> a miraculous prolongation of my own intentions, a familiar way of dealing with the world. Henceforth, as the parts of my body together comprise a system, so my body and the other's are one whole, two sides of one and the same phenomenon, and the anonymous existence of which my body is the ever-renewed trace henceforth inhabits both bodies simultaneously.
>
> (Merleau-Ponty 2002: 412)

Language establishes a "common ground" between self and other, "a shared operation of which neither of us is the creator," a "dual being" where myself and the other emerge as "collaborators for each other in consummate reciprocity" (Merleau-Ponty 2002: 413). This does not mean that, as collaborators, we always agree about the meaning of the world, nor that every subject is granted equal power in the "consummate reciprocity" that Merleau-Ponty identifies as the shape of successful communication. Rather, it suggests that the co-constitution of meaning is an intersubjective or intercorporeal practice that must create the common ground upon which it relies for its knowledge claims. To exclude certain perspectives from this collaborative practice is not only to diminish one's access to truth about the world, but also to harm oneself and others as intercorporeal knowers and perceivers.[8]

Merleau-Ponty's phenomenological account of language and behavior helps to articulate the basic structures and (inter)corporeal practices of what Fricker calls "hermeneutical sensibility," in a way that calls for more detailed exploration. For Merleau-Ponty, all perception involves a social dimension; we do not merely perceive others in the world, we perceive *according to others*, slipping in and out of their embodied perspectives in the process of making sense of our own. This intercorporeal dimension of perception (and of existence) also shapes our perception of inanimate objects:

> [T]he spontaneous acts through which man has patterned his life [are] deposited, like some sediment, outside himself and lead an anonymous existence as things. . . In the cultural object, I feel the close presence of others beneath a veil of anonymity. *Someone* uses the pipe for smoking, the spoon for eating, the bell for summoning, and it is through the perception of a human act and another person that the perception of a cultural world could be verified . . . The very first of all cultural objects, and the one by which all the rest exist, is the body of the other person as the vehicle of a form of behavior.
>
> (Merleau-Ponty 2002: 405–6)

Through an engagement with these and other analyses in the phenomenological tradition, discourses of epistemic injustice could find fruitful ground for both the corroboration of its core insights and the critical elaboration of these insights beyond their current scope.

## The existential harm of hermeneutical injustice

Fricker suggests that epistemic injustice may have ontological or existential implications. If it is "an essential attribute of personhood to be able to participate in the spread of knowledge and to enjoy the respect enshrined in the proper relations of trust that are its prerequisite" (Fricker 2007: 58), then to be harmed as a knower is to be harmed in one's essential personhood. Following Bernard Williams, Fricker claims that the "process by which the mind is steadied ... is also the process by which we may become who we deeply, perhaps essentially, are" (2007: 53). This implies an intertwining of epistemic capacities with identity: you are what you know, how you know it, and how others respond to your expression of knowledge. But it is not clear how the epistemic and ontological levels are related, beyond the claim that persons are essentially knowers. Existential phenomenology, in particular the work of social phenomenologists such as Fanon and Beauvoir, can help to clarify this relationship and to sketch an outline of existential and political resistance to epistemic injustice.

Fricker refers in passing to Fanon's concept of "psychic alienation" (via Sandra Bartky) as "the estrangement of separating off a person from some of the essential attributes of personhood" (quoted in Fricker 2007: 58). Let's elaborate this concept in relation to a key passage from Fanon's *Black Skin, White Masks*, in the chapter entitled, "*L'experience vécue du Noir*," or "The Lived Experience of the Black":

> I came into the world imbued with the will to find a meaning in things, my spirit filled with the desire to attain to the source of the world, and then I found that I was an object in the midst of other objects.
>
> Sealed into that crushing objecthood, I turned beseechingly to others. Their attention was a liberation, running over my body suddenly abraded into nonbeing, endowing me once more with an agility that I had thought lost, and by taking me out of the world, restoring me to it. But just as I reached the other side, I stumbled, and the movements, the attitudes, the glances of the other fixed me there, in the sense in which a chemical solution is fixed by a dye. I was indignant; I demanded an explanation. Nothing happened. I burst apart. Now the fragments have been put together again by another self.
>
> *(Fanon 1967: 109)*

This passage could be read as a precise phenomenological description of the lived experience of hermeneutical injustice, which disrupts one's self-understanding and one's sense of being or personhood. The speaker comes into the world as an active, creative epistemic subject, seeking to make sense of the world ("to find a meaning in things") as intentional consciousness ("the source of [the meaning of] the world"). But given his social identity, and the way that privileged others respond prejudicially to this social identity, the speaker finds himself stripped of epistemic agency and reduced to an object. Importantly, the speaker is not just reduced to an object *of knowledge* for others, he is reduced to the *ontological* status of an object, as a thing rather than a consciousness who gives meaning to the world, and so introduces a dimension of nonbeing (or possibility, indeterminacy, and virtuality) into that world.

Other subjects have the capacity to restore the speaker to epistemic agency and ontological subjectivity with their attention, which liberates the speaker from objecthood by engaging with him as another subject. But just as this engagement begins, it "fixes" the speaker – not just with words, but with movements, attitudes, and glances – in a position that leaves the objectified subject nowhere *to be*. The speaker re-asserts his epistemic agency by demanding an explanation, but his question meets with no response; an instance of testimonial injustice compounds and intensifies the hermeneutical injustice that already structures the entire (non)encounter. In response, the speaker bursts apart; not only is he unable to "settle his mind," but his existence as a speaking, knowing subject is radically fragmented, and "another self" emerges to document, analyze, and testify to the process. Who is this other self? Following Lewis Gordon's distinction between Fanon as "the voice of the text (the black) and the voice about the text (the theorist and guide)" (Gordon 2015: 25), I suggest that this other self is the resistant remnant of an epistemic survivor, who is altered but not destroyed by epistemic injustice, and whose testimony holds the key to epistemic virtue for both survivors and perpetrators of epistemic harm, albeit in different ways. For the survivor, testimony about the epistemic injustice s/he has experienced is a practice of resistance that performatively contests the patterns of silencing and discrediting that it describes and analyzes, and for the perpetrator, such testimonies are precisely what s/he needs to hear and understand in order to address the harm of past injustice, to develop a critical awareness of present, ongoing injustice, and to develop more just practices for the future.

Fanon's text offers a vivid example of what Fricker calls hermeneutical injustice, which not only blocks the capacity of certain subjects to make sense of themselves and the world, but also "undermin[es] them in their very humanity" (Fricker 2007: 44). As Fricker acknowledges:

> When you find yourself in a situation in which you seem to be the only one to feel the dissonance between received understanding and your own intimated sense of a given experience, it tends to knock your faith in your own ability to make sense of the world, or at least the relevant region of the world.
>
> *(163)*

> [H]ermeneutical injustice can mean that someone is socially constituted as, and perhaps even caused to be, something that they are not, and which it is against their interests to be seen to be.
>
> *(168)*

Fanon's phenomenological account of (what Fricker calls) hermeneutical injustice makes it clear that the predicament of knowing and being known by others cannot be separated from existential or ontological questions of Being-for-itself (or consciousness) and Being-for-Others (or social existence), even if there is also a conceptual difference between knowing and being, or between epistemology and ontology.

## From epistemic virtue to social justice

For Fricker, testimonial and hermeneutical injustice call for the active cultivation of epistemic habits and practices that correct for prejudice by neutralizing its impact on one's perception and judgment, and by "compensating upwards to reach the degree of credibility that would have been given were it not for the prejudice" (Fricker 2007: 91). She suggests that "plain personal familiarity" (96) can help to break down prejudice through habitual exposure to others with different social identities, and that the reflective correction of one's epistemic prejudices, when practiced regularly, can lead to more virtuous spontaneous habits of moral-epistemic perception as a kind of "second nature," or what Merleau-Ponty might call the "habit body." In the end, Fricker acknowledges that individual virtue is insufficient to address the harm of epistemic injustice; collective political action is also necessary to address the problem of structural epistemic injustice. But, for Fricker, collective action of this sort goes beyond the scope of ethics and of philosophy (174).[9]

This is the point where a critical approach to phenomenology could expand the discourse of epistemic injustice beyond the call for individual correction or accommodation. I understand critical phenomenology as a practice of both reflecting on the structures of meaningful experience and also transforming those structures through collective action in order to make different experiences possible and intelligible. Critical phenomenology is a practice of liberation, not only from the natural attitude but also from the naturalized and normalized forms of oppression that shape our social, epistemic, and existential worlds. As Fanon writes in his critique of the racist, colonial natural attitude: "We shall see that another solution is possible. It implies a restructuring of the world" (1967: 82). Fanon's commitment to the possibility of collective thought and action in resistance to colonial domination moves phenomenology from critical reflection to transformative praxis, and his work offers continuing inspiration for the struggle against epistemic injustice in all its forms. For more contemporary examples of critical phenomenology, see the work of Sara Ahmed, Lewis Gordon, Gayle Salamon, George Yancy, Iris Marion Young, and others

**Related chapters**: 3, 4, 10, 11, 12, 20

## Notes

1. An important aspect of epistemic injustice that remains under-theorized in Fricker's work is the role of willful and/or unconscious ignorance on the part of the privileged in producing and perpetuating a situation in which they are both epistemically advantaged (or over-invested with credibility) and also epistemically deficient (in the sense of refusing to understand and confront the conditions of their own privilege). Charles Mills, Kristie Dotson, W.E.B. Du Bois, Mariana Ortega, Jose Medina, Frantz Fanon, and others have developed nuanced accounts of the dynamics of privileged ignorance.
2. For a more detailed discussion of intentionality, see Ratcliffe (2016).
3. See, for example, Al-Saji (2010), Carel (2016), Heinämaa (2003), and Oksala (2006).
4. See Ahmed (2006), Beauvoir (1964, 2010), Bergoffen (1996), Diprose (2002), Salamon (2010), Weiss (1999), and Young (1990), as well as Merleau-Ponty (1968, 1973, 2002).
5. Fricker uses the term "phenomenological" in a non-technical sense, referring to views that focus on qualia or experiences as felt, and not to the phenomenological method I have described above.
6. This construction of a "middle path" between two mutually-opposed and incomplete views resonates with Husserl's middle path between psychologism and naturalism, and with Merleau-Ponty's middle path between rationalism and empiricism.
7. Later, Fricker writes: "If the adjustment [to a new, more critically-reflexive way of perceiving someone's testimony] is direct, [for example, when a stereotype is disrupted and a re-evaluation of the speaker is provoked,] then she [the hearer] will undergo a kind of *gestalt* switch in how she perceives" that type of person (2007: 84). If the adjustment is indirect, then she will go through a process of "active critical reflection" and "some sort of corrective policy" (84). A fruitful discussion between phenomenology, Gestalt theory, and Fricker's own account of epistemic injustice could emerge from these passages.
8. For a more detailed discussion of intercorporeality, which refers to the constitutive intertwining of embodied subjects, see Diprose (2002), Guenther (2013), and Merleau-Ponty (1968).
9. See, however, Fricker (2013), for an account of the relation between epistemic justice and political freedom, and the importance of contesting domination.

## References

Ahmed, Sara, *Queer Phenomenology: Orientations, Objects, Others*. Durham, NC: Duke University Press, 2006.
Al-Saji, Alia, "Bodies and sensings: On the uses of Husserlian phenomenology for feminist theory," *Continental Philosophy Review* 43:1 (2010): 13–37.
Beauvoir, Simone de, *The Ethics of Ambiguity*. Translated by Bernard Frechtman. New York: The Citadel Press, 1964.
Beauvoir, Simone de, *The Second Sex*. Translated by Constance Borde and Sheila Malovany-Chevallier. New York: Alfred A. Knopf, 2010.

Bergoffen, Debra, *The Philosophy of Simone de Beauvoir: Gendered Phenomenologies, Erotic Generosities*. Albany, NY: SUNY Press, 1996.
Carel, Havi, *Phenomenology of Illness*. Oxford, UK: Oxford University Press, 2016.
Davidson, Donald, "Rational Animals," *Dialectica* 36:4 (1982): 317–328.
Diprose, Rosalyn, *Corporeal Generosity: On Giving with Nietzsche, Merleau-Ponty, and Levinas*. Albany, NY: SUNY Press, 2002.
Fanon, Frantz, *Black Skin, White Masks*. Translated by Charles Lam Markmann. New York: Grove Press, 1967.
Fricker, Miranda, *Epistemic Injustice: Power and the Ethics of Knowing*. Oxford: Oxford University Press, 2007.
Fricker, Miranda, "Epistemic justice as a condition of political freedom," *Synthese* 190 (2013): 1317–1332.
Gordon, Lewis, *Bad Faith and Antiblack Racism*. New York: Humanity Books, 1995.
Gordon, Lewis, *What Fanon Said: A Philosophical Introduction to His Life and Thought*. New York: Fordham University Press, 2015.
Guenther, Lisa, *Solitary Confinement: Social Death and Its Afterlives*. Minneapolis: Minnesota University Press, 2013.
Heinämaa, Sara, *Toward a Phenomenology of Sexual Difference: Husserl, Merleau-Ponty, Beauvoir*. New York: Rowman & Littlefield, 2003.
Husserl, Edmund, *Ideas Pertaining to a Pure Phenomenology and to a Phenomenological Philosophy: Second Book: Studies in the Phenomenology of Constitution*. Translated by R. Rojcewicz and A. Schuwer. Dortrecht: Kluwer Academic Publishers, 1989.
Husserl, Edmund, *Cartesian Meditations: An Introduction to Phenomenology*. Translated by Dorian Cairns. Dortrecht: Kluwer Academic Publishers, 1999.
Husserl, Edmund, *Logical Investigations, Vol. 1*. Translated by J. N. Findlay. New York and London: Routledge, 2008.
Merleau-Ponty, Maurice, *The Visible and the Invisible*. Translated by Alphonso Lingis. Evanston, IL: Northwestern University Press, 1968.
Merleau-Ponty, Maurice, "Dialogue and the Perception of the Other." In *The Prose of the World*, edited by Claude Lefort. Translated by John O'Neill. Evanston, IL: Northwestern University Press, 1973, 131–146.
Merleau-Ponty, Maurice, *Phenomenology of Perception*. Translated by Colin Smith. London: Routledge Classics, 2002.
Oksala, Johanna, "A phenomenology of gender," *Continental Philosophy Review* 39:3 (2006): 229–244.
Ratcliffe, Matthew, "The Integrity of Intentionality: Sketch for a Phenomenological Study." In *Phenomenology for the Twenty-First Century*, edited by J. Aaron Simmons and J. Edward Hackett. London: Palgrave Macmillan, 2016, 207–230.
Salamon, Gayle, *Assuming a Body: Transgender and Rhetorics of Materiality*. New York: Columbia University Press, 2010.
Weiss, Gail, *Body Images: Embodiment as Intercorporeality*. New York: Routledge, 1999.
Williams, Bernard, *Truth and Truthfulness: An Essay in Genealogy*. Princeton: Princeton University Press, 2002.
Yancy, George, *Black Bodies, White Gazes: The Continued Significance of Race*. New York: Rowman & Littlefield, Inc., 2008.
Young, Iris Marion, *Throwing Like a Girl and Other Essays in Feminist Philosophy and Social Theory*. Bloomington: Indiana University Press, 1990.

# 19
# ON THE HARMS OF EPISTEMIC INJUSTICE
## Pragmatism and transactional epistemology

*Shannon Sullivan*

What does pragmatist philosophy have to offer accounts of epistemic injustice? In this chapter, I answer that question by reading Miranda Fricker's groundbreaking *Epistemic Injustice* (2007) through a pragmatist lens. In particular, I examine the type of harms caused by testimonial and hermeneutical injustice and argue that Fricker's account of epistemic harm would be improved by the pragmatist epistemology provided by John Dewey. While Fricker's discussion of epistemic injustice tends to rely on a representational account of knowledge, Dewey's pragmatism understands knowledge as transactional.[1] This means that for Dewey, knowing is not a process of mirroring reality (to borrow Richard Rorty's [1979] Deweyan-inspired words), but instead an activity undertaken by a bodily organism-in-the-world who helps shape what is known. Considering knowledge as transactional rather than representational recasts the harm of epistemic injustice as a harm done to the flourishing of a human organism, rather than as an unfair exclusion from a process of pooling of knowledge. Conceiving the harm of epistemic injustice as a type of ontological-environmental damage can help feminists, critical philosophers of race, and others more effectively understand and counter the harmful effects of testimonial injustice. This notion of harm also better explains what Fricker herself is trying to achieve when she describes the effects of hermeneutical injustice as damaging constructions of selfhood.

## I. Fricker's representational epistemology

Epistemic injustice occurs when a person is treated unjustly in her capacity as a knower, and on Fricker's account, it can take two different forms. The primary form of epistemic injustice is testimonial: when a person is making a claim to knowledge ("testifying"), the credibility of her claim is undercut because of prejudice on the part of the hearer toward the speaker (Fricker 2007, 1).[2] In the case of testimonial injustice, the hearer doesn't bother to weigh the merits of what the speaker is claiming before discounting it, or the hearer perhaps does weigh what the speaker says but in a prejudicial (pre-judging) manner. The hearer already knows, so to speak, that what the speaker is saying is dubious, irrelevant, false, or otherwise easily dismissible, and this is because of who the speaker is. For this reason, Fricker associates testimonial injustice with what she calls identity prejudice (2007, 4). Prejudices concerning gender and race are key contributors to testimonial injustice in many societies, but other status markers such as age, disability, and class also can have similar epistemological effects. A quick example of testimonial injustice is a man ridiculing a woman's claim about why a car's engine is broken because the man "knows" that women don't understand cars (see, e.g., Frye 1983). Exactly how testimonial injustice is at work in any given situation can vary, and the specifics of those different situations as they interplay with different identities deserve careful attention.

The second form of epistemic injustice is hermeneutical, and it occurs when a society or culture lacks the concepts to describe or understand a particular person's experience (Fricker 2007, 6). While testimonial injustice tends to focus on the individual and how she is treated by her interlocutors, hermeneutical injustice occurs on the social level.[3] For example, the concept of marital rape did not come into existence in the United States until the mid-1970s, and it did not gain broader social and legal status until 1993, when marital rape was finally made a crime in all fifty states (www.rainn.org/public-policy/sexual-assault-issues/marital-rape). Lacking a concept of marital rape, American women who were forced by their husbands to have sex could not understand their experience as one of rape even as they might have felt that something about the experience was wrong. Rape wasn't conceivable as happening between a husband and a wife, so the "wrong" in question had to be something else: a miscommunication between two people, a misalignment of their desires, perhaps even a failure on the woman's part to anticipate "properly" her husband's needs, and so on. Raped wives, in other words, could not understand the event that occurred in their own lives as an ethical wrong, which the law in turn should acknowledge and punish.

As this last example demonstrates, even though hermeneutical injustice is social, it also has effects on the individual. The wife who cannot understand her rape as a rape is an individual who is harmed, just as the female auto mechanic is. But the epistemic harm done to the raped wife, unlike that inflicted upon the female auto mechanic, occurs because of "a gap in collective hermeneutical resources" (Fricker 2007, 7). In the case of testimonial injustice, an individual (or possibly a group of people, such as a jury) epistemically harms another individual, whose credibility is undercut. In the case of hermeneutical injustice, a society creates a context in which non-epistemic harm, such as that of sexual violence, takes on an epistemic character. The husband who rapes his wife, physically and emotionally harms her, to be sure, but he does not epistemically harm her when he forces her to have sex. The latter form of harm occurs because of a societal failure, often enacted by particular people in particular interactions, to provide the raped wife with a robust epistemic toolbox of concepts with which to adequately and justly understand her experience.

What precisely is the nature of the epistemic harm produced by testimonial and hermeneutical injustice? Beginning with the first form of epistemic injustice, Fricker argues that testimonial injustice harms a person in two related ways. First, she is harmed in her capacity as a giver of knowledge, as someone who could contribute to the pool of knowledge that a society is accumulating (Fricker 2007, 5, 115). Second, since she is seen as incapable of producing knowledge, she can lose confidence in her epistemic abilities as such, which can harm her capacity to gain knowledge from others and/or herself (2007, 49). I will return shortly to the issue of epistemic self-confidence, focusing for now on Fricker's description of the knower as a giver of knowledge and of the activity of knowing as the pooling of knowledge.

The language of "giving" and "pooling" information shows up repeatedly in *Epistemic Injustice*.[4] For Fricker, "essentially what it is to be a knower is to participate in the sharing of information," that is, to engage in "a co-operative practice of pooling information" (2007, 145). The identity prejudice of testimonial injustice presents an obstacle to this process "either directly by causing the hearer to miss out on a particular truth, or indirectly by creating blockages in the circulation of critical ideas" (2007, 43). Either way, a person can't engage in the activity of knowing and thus has been "wronged in their capacity as a giver of knowledge" (2007, 145). This epistemic capacity, furthermore, is a component of a human being's more fundamental capacity for reason. To undercut a person's capacity as a giver of knowledge thus "can cut deep" because it "undermin[es] them in their very humanity" (2007, 45).

Without naming it as such, Fricker operates with a banking model of knowledge that implicitly relies on a representational epistemology.[5] As pieces of information, knowledge is an accurate representation of the world that can be deposited to and withdrawn from a common account. Knowing, in turn, is the activity either of developing accurate representations to deposit to the bank or of withdrawing knowledge from it that others have contributed. Because of this model, the virtues of Accuracy, Sincerity, and Testimonial Justice are crucial to Fricker's project.[6] Testimonial justice is a virtue in the hearer that counters identity prejudice so that blockages in the circulation of ideas in and out of the pool do not occur. On the speaker's part, the virtues of Accuracy and Sincerity ensure that false pieces of knowledge do not poison the common pool (2007, 116, 120–122). Testimonial justice thus is a simultaneously ethical and epistemological virtue that enables all people to have an equal shot at contributing accurate representations of the world to the common pool (2007, 121).

The loss of epistemic self-confidence sometimes caused by testimonial injustice is connected to the epistemic harms that hermeneutical injustice can produce. All those harms involve a person's self-development and her relationship to herself. First, when a society lacks certain concepts, a person cannot understand adequately or accurately her own experiences. People in this situation cannot develop a "proper understanding" or "proper interpretation" of what is happening, effectively creating a "cognitive disablement" that leaves them troubled and confused (Fricker 2007, 151, 152). Second, hermeneutical injustice – and the crisis of self-confidence that it can produce – can affect the very "formation of self," helping constitute a person as the identity that the prejudice in question assumes her to be (2007, 55). The epistemic damage here is also ontological, constraining "who the person can be" and not merely how she is perceived by other people (2007, 58). In that way, hermeneutical injustice cuts very deep, preventing people "from becoming who they are" (2007, 168).

## II. Dewey's transactional epistemology

Fricker's representational account of knowledge depends problematically on the implicit adoption of a view from nowhere.[7] On this view, the real world can be known only when one has freed oneself from the bias of specific, located perspectives – hence the paradoxical epistemic site of "nowhere." Those perspectives are like dirt on clear glass, clouding a distinct, accurate view of the world.[8] Operating with a sharp distinction between objectivity and subjectivity, this approach to knowledge tends to shun anything associated with the subjective and to assume that human knowers are capable of doing the same. It is this view that virtually all forms of pragmatism reject. Pragmatist philosophies understand human knowers as necessarily embodied and thus as inevitably situated and perspectival beings. Maybe a god can occupy a view from nowhere, hovering outside the world that it seeks to know, but human beings cannot.

Rorty's (1979) particular criticism of the view from nowhere argues for abandoning epistemology, implicitly collapsing the latter into attempts to mirror nature and advocating what he calls hermeneutics in its place. While I share his concerns about the mirror of nature, I find Rorty's avoidance of epistemology to be troubling. This is because by offering no alternative to knowledge as mirroring, Rorty ultimately leaves that definition in place. As Fricker (1994, 95) rightly claims, "we cannot tear down the house and build nothing in its place," and this is precisely what Rorty's criticism of the mirror of nature does. It is devastatingly on-target but stops short. Perhaps this is why Fricker tends to lump Rorty's pragmatism together with postmodern philosophy, the latter of which Fricker considers to be treacherous for feminism.[9] Setting that issue aside here, I agree with Fricker that feminists and others concerned about epistemic injustice need more than Rorty can provide. We need a way to judge some beliefs about the world as true and others as false. Likewise we need a way to judge some actions as just and others as unjust.

Dewey's pragmatism can do just that because his criticism of the view from nowhere also (re)constructs an alternative epistemology, and it does so by means of a particular Darwinian insight that is extremely helpful for feminist and critical race purposes. The most significant influence of Darwin upon philosophy, according to Dewey (1977, 1988), doesn't concern the (in)famous notion of the survival of the fittest. It is instead the full appreciation of human beings as bodily animals in the world, engaged in the human equivalent of burrowing, nesting, foraging, and other animal activities. Human beings don't adapt to their environments; instead they and their various environments co-constitute each other in a dynamic, ongoing fashion (Sullivan 2001). A live organism is a changing organism, just as the world with which it transacts is constantly changing and being changed. What is crucial for the purposes here is that these Darwinian insights about human animals hold just as much for their epistemic activities as for their non-epistemic ones. When human beings seek to know what the subject or any other part of the world really is, we are engaged not in a god-like observation of the world, but in practices and activities of knowing that all animals undertake in order to survive and thrive. Those activities might be different for humans than non-human animals due to the (perhaps) greater political, social, and other complexities of the human world, but this is a difference in degree, not kind. As in the case for all other live organisms, there is no perch outside this world for human knowers to occupy. Genuinely post-Darwinian philosophies must acknowledge that there is no view from nowhere from which to generate knowledge.

This does not mean, however, that knowledge is merely subjective or that anything goes concerning claims about how the world is. Dewey's pragmatism argues that one can judge some claims to be true and others to be false without appealing to the view from nowhere. The criterion with which to make such judgments is not whether a claim accurately mirrors the world. It instead is whether, when acted upon, a claim brings about the desired transformations in the world. If it does, it is true, and if it does not, it is false. Put another way, even if oppressed groups were able to accurately mirror the world in ways that dominant groups could not, it's not clear what good that ability would do them. They would still need a way to change the world so that their needs, interests, and experiences were taken seriously by others. On Deweyan terms, this transformation is what activities of knowing and claims to truth are all about: knowledge and truth become fully answerable to the needs, interests, and practices of all people, including the marginalized (Dewey 1985a, 1985b, 1988).

This definition of truth might sound like just the sort of subjective relativism that Fricker wants to avoid in her rejection of postmodernism, but a couple of concrete examples will help demonstrate the critical, experiential notion of objectivity that Deweyan pragmatism provides.[10] It admittedly is one that is not diametrically opposed to subjectivity, but that is precisely the point: feminists and others interested in epistemic justice need an account of objectivity and truth that doesn't depend on discarding human (particularly women's and other oppressed groups') perspectives, interests, and experiences. Take the simple claim that the table in front of me is 30 inches wide. Is this true? The answer depends upon the interest(s) that drive the need to know, which is not the same thing, I hasten to note, as saying that one answer is as good as any other. There is an objectively true, non-mirroring answer to the question. When I measure the table with a ruler, I discover that its width is 30 inches. So for my purposes and needs – having enough room for my laptop, books, and tea – it is true that the table is 30 inches wide. But this answer is true only to the extent that those particular interests are guiding the quest for knowledge.

If, for example, a carpenter needed to know the width of the table to construct a cozy alcove in which to put it, it might very well be false that the table is 30 inches wide. The table is 29.90 inches wide and that 0.10 inches is a difference that makes a difference to the table's fit with the café's tight contours. In the context of the carpenter's interests – which are complexly material, economic, aesthetic, and perhaps even political, depending on the situation – it is objectively false that the table is 30 inches wide.[11]

What's more to the point is that if someone were to claim that the table *really* is 29.90 inches wide – suggesting a level of accuracy that my rough ruler measurement lacked – this claim wouldn't settle the truth of the matter, at least not once and for all. We could always find a different way to measure the table if a particular set of interests required it. A quantum physicist, for example, would be likely to have an entirely different assessment of the material features of the table, explicitly putting into question, moreover, any account that relied on an observer-independent reality of it (Frenkel 2015; Ringbauer et al. 2015). It's not so much that the carpenter's claim about reality is false – its falsity would be just as difficult to ascertain acontextually as its truth – as that perspective-free claims about reality tend to be red herrings: irrelevant and thus unhelpful.

Jane Addams (2001) provides another example of how attempting to mirror reality can be epistemologically off-target in her account of the Devil Baby that allegedly was housed at Hull House. Older, working-class, immigrant women in particular came in droves to Hull House to see the Devil Baby, who was said to be born in retribution for a husband's neglect of his wife and their household. Initially exasperated by the women's refusal to believe that there was no Devil Baby, Addams came to realize how the women used the Devil Baby as a tool for fighting testimonial injustice (to borrow Fricker's term). The story of the Devil Baby helped them "secure . . . a hearing at home" and to grapple with "their double bewilderment, both that the younger generation was walking in such strange paths and that no one would listen to them" (2001, 16)

Let's return now to the case of a woman's claim that her husband raped her. Determining the truth of this claim does not involve somehow standing outside of a human (whose exactly?) perspective to judge the claim. Its truth is intimately bound up with at least some group of human beings' interests, perspectives, and needs, and on pragmatist grounds, this is not necessarily problematic. It becomes problematic, however, if and when those perspectives and interests are denied in the name of alleged perspective-free objectivity. This denial doesn't transport us to an epistemologically pure view from nowhere; instead it allows a particular set of interests and needs to operate uncritically in the guise of perspective-less objectivity. That set of interests – complexly material, economic, political, psychological, and so on – almost always is that of the dominant group, and thus the chimera of perspective-free objectivity tends to operate as the handmaiden of oppressive practices.

What then to say about the wife's claim, especially if her husband and perhaps also society at large denies that he raped her? To best answer this question, feminists and other epistemologists need to dive deeper into situated interests, perspectives, and experiences, rather than flee from them. This does not reduce the question of the wife's rape to a "mind-[dependent] reality [lacking] normative constraints upon what we may correctly believe about the world" (Fricker 1994, 98–99). The truth of a situation finds its test in experience, not divorced from it, and human experience includes far more than what people's minds think about it. Undergoing this test requires asking, whose experience? Who are the interested parties in a particular situation or conflict, and how do we ensure that all of their perspectives and interests are included in knowing what happened? Pragmatically recasting the issue of truth so that it must reckon with experience has the benefit of insisting that the interests of women and other marginalized groups are included. These interests are part of the "real stat[e] of affairs in the world" (Fricker 1994,

95) that constrains what can be truthfully said. When we include the wife's experience (of pain, confusion, and so on) in the knowledge of what happened between her and her husband, we cannot truthfully say that it was an ethically acceptable sexual encounter.

Nor can we say, however, that the wife's experience alone determines the truth of the situation. That would be merely to turn the mirror of nature upside down, so to speak, rather than to discard it altogether. The marginalized are no more able to occupy a view from nowhere than the dominant are, and so it would be equally problematic from a pragmatist perspective for marginalized groups to claim that they can represent the world independent of any particular point of view. A pragmatist rejection of the view from nowhere is radical because it is complete. Pragmatist reasons for valuing the perspectives of the marginalized do not concern whether they can generate accurate representations of the world, but this is not to say that their perspectives aren't immensely epistemologically valuable. They are valuable because increased human flourishing depends upon their epistemic inclusion.

Fricker likely would ask whether pragmatism can give the wife's claims enough epistemic authority such that they are more than an expression of a personal (or group-based) opinion (Fricker 2000, 150). On Fricker's view, if we can't judge that "some forms of social organization are just plain unjust, or that some beliefs are plain false," then pragmatism is just as "hopelessly indiscriminate" as postmodernism allegedly is (2000, 150, 151). The answer to her question is yes, but only if we do not sneak a quest for certainty and universality into the notion of epistemic authority. One of the reasons it is difficult to let go of the idea of a view from nowhere is that it seems to offer epistemic certainty: a way of knowing that something is unjust or false without any doubt and without any contextual or historical qualifications. It is "just plain unjust" or "plain false," period. But the quest for certainty is misguided (Dewey 1988); human knowing only takes place and makes sense in particular contexts, times, histories, and places. It wouldn't be of any value to us if it didn't.[12] The particular contexts for knowledge need not be narrowly local or personal. We can create knowledge that is knit out of the interests and experiences of wide swaths of people, even across the globe. In that way, a large group of people might be able to agree that a particular social practice – such as raping women, one hopes – is unequivocally unjust. But that knowledge and its authority is a human achievement, a product of human activity and interests, not a static truth that exists prior to and independent of human (again, whose?) experience.

## III. The harms of epistemic injustice

We now can appreciate why it matters whether accounts of epistemic injustice operate with a transactional rather than a representational epistemology. The pragmatist answer – appropriately pragmatist – is not because we have discovered an accurate picture of what epistemology really is. It is because working with a transactional epistemology is more likely to improve human lives by eliminating the harms of epistemic injustice. A Deweyan approach to epistemic injustice would help us understand that the primary harm done by testimonial injustice is not that a speaker without credibility isn't allowed to "pool" knowledge (i.e., represent the world) through her speech like everyone else. The harm instead is that the speaker isn't allowed to epistemologically transact with the world in ways that enable her own, as well as others' flourishing. In a similar fashion, the harm done by hermeneutic injustice is not merely that a speaker operating with a different worldview than a hearer is dismissed as unreasonable or crazy. This approach to injustice also operates with a problematic "pooling" or representational model of knowledge, writ large at the level of a culture or community. The harm is that being dismissed as crazy impacts the perceived reasonableness of the entire culture or community in question. That in turn impacts the culture's or community's ability to be an environment that encourages and enables the flourishing of all its members.

Epistemic injustice conceived as interference with transactional flourishing can happen as a deprivation, in which a person isn't able to epistemologically engage the world. But even more importantly, it also can occur as a production, in which a person is produced as a kind of knower required to epistemologically engage the world in ways that undercut her. In the latter case, a person's epistemic activity is particularly harmful because it is transactionally self-destructive: it forces a person to help shape and build a world that, in turn, tears her down. In the case of the wife who was forced to have sex with her husband, for example, she is epistemically harmed by her co-construction of a marriage in which her desires and needs are insignificant and perhaps even indistinguishable from those of her husband's. This is, in my view, the important insight that Fricker is trying to capture when she points to the epistemic harm caused to constructions of selfhood. She need not back away from it out of a concern that it ushers in postmodernism or that it doesn't make room for the possibility of a subject's distortion. Debates over distortion versus accurate representation don't get at the more relevant question of how to create a world in which everyone, including oppressed groups, can thrive. This question involves "a set of beliefs about real states of affairs," as Fricker (1994, 99) would insist, "and in particular, real experiences had by women (and it makes no difference that these experiences are essentially mediated by culture, language and history)," as Fricker helpfully adds. It's experience that matters, particularly those experiences that have been unjustly excluded from knowledge projects. Including them would go a long way toward achieving epistemic justice.

**Related chapters**: 2, 3, 4, 11, 23

## Notes

1 While other pragmatist philosophers such as Jane Addams also offer resources to conceptualize epistemic harm as ontological and dynamically relational, I focus on Dewey because of the depth of his transactional account. I will return briefly to Addams in section II of this essay.
2 While Fricker uses the term "primary," a debate in the literature is ongoing about the complex relationship of testimonial and hermeneutical injustice and whether one form of epistemic injustice is more foundational than the other (see, e.g., chapters 1–3 of Medina [2012]).
3 On testimonial injustice, especially in the form of speech, as structural rather than individual, see Ayala and Vasilyeva (2015).
4 On "giving," see Fricker (2007, 5, 7, 44, 45, 48, and 145); on "pooling," see (2007, 110, 111, 114, 115, 116, 117, and 145).
5 See, e.g., chapter two of Freire (2000).
6 Fricker draws here on Williams (2002).
7 See, e.g., Nagel (1986). While Fricker might be seen as promoting a situated subject that is devoid of biases rather than a view from nowhere, I would argue that the former effectively is the latter. There is no such thing as a situated, embodied subject without particular biases or perspectives.
8 Fricker (2007, 148–154) explicitly uses the metaphor of dark glass, followed by imagery of occlusion, obscurity, and "hermeneutical darkness."
9 See, e.g., Fricker (1994, 100, note 5); Fricker (2000, 151–152 and 159); and Fricker (2007, 2, 3, 55, and 176).
10 Although I use the language of "experience" rather than that of "standpoint" here, neither Dewey nor I am referring to unmediated experience, e.g., of the variety "I feel or think X, therefore I know X is true." The pragmatist concept of experience is similar to that of a standpoint in feminist standpoint theory; for more on this point, see chapter six of Sullivan (2001, especially page 134).
11 Fricker (2007, 10) comes very close to endorsing a similar account of truth at the end of *Epistemic Injustice*.
12 For additional support of this point, see Medina (2012, 118).

# References

Addams, Jane. 2001. *The Long Road of Women's Memory*. Champaign, IL: The University of Illinois Press.

Ayala, Saray, and Nadya Vasilyeva. 2015. "Explaining Injustice in Speech: Individualistic vs. Structural Explanation." 130–135. mindmodeling.org/cogsci2015/papers/0033/paper0033.pdf, accessed September 10, 2015.

Dewey, John. 1977. "The Influence of Darwin on Philosophy." In *The Middle Works, 1899–1924*, volume 4. Ed. Jo Ann Boydston. Carbondale and Edwardsville, IL: Southern Illinois University Press. 3–14.

Dewey, John. 1985a. "A Short Catechism concerning Truth." In *The Middle Works, 1899–1924*, volume 6. Ed. Jo Ann Boydston. Carbondale and Edwardsville, IL: Southern Illinois University Press. 3–11.

Dewey, John. 1985b. "The Problem of Truth." In *The Middle Works, 1899–1924*, volume 6. Ed. Jo Ann Boydston. Carbondale and Edwardsville, IL: Southern Illinois University Press. 12–68.

Dewey, John. 1988. *The Quest for Certainty*. In *The Later Works, 1925–1953*, volume 4. Ed. Jo Ann Boydston. Carbondale and Edwardsville, IL: Southern Illinois University Press.

Freire, Paulo. 2000. *Pedagogy of the Oppressed*. New York: Bloomsbury Academic.

Frenkel, Edward. 2015. "The Reality of Quantum Weirdness." *The New York Times*, February 22, The Sunday Review, page 9.

Fricker, Miranda. 1994. "Knowledge as Construct: Theorizing the Role of Gender in Knowledge." In *Knowing the Difference: Feminist Perspectives in Epistemology*. Eds. Kathleen Lennon and Margaret Whitford. New York: Routledge. 95–109.

Fricker, Miranda. 2000. "Feminism in Epistemology: Pluralism without Postmodernism." In *The Cambridge Companion to Feminism in Philosophy*. Eds. Miranda Fricker and Jennifer Hornsby. New York: Cambridge University Press. 146–165.

Fricker, Miranda. 2007. *Epistemic Injustice: Power and the Ethics of Knowing*. New York: Oxford University Press.

Frye, Marilyn. 1983. *The Politics of Reality: Essays in Feminist Theory*. Trumansburg, NY: Crossing Press.

Medina, José. 2012. *The Epistemology of Resistance: Gender and Racial Oppression, Epistemic Injustice, and Resistant Imaginations*. New York: Oxford University Press.

Nagel, Thomas. 1986. *The View from Nowhere*. New York: Oxford University Press.

Ringbauer, Martin, Ben Duffus, Cyril Branciard, Eric G. Cavalcanti, Andrew G. White, and Alessandro Fedrizzi. 2015. "Measurements on the Reality of the Wavefunction." *Quantum Physics*. http://arxiv.org/pdf/1412.6213v2.pdf, accessed February 23, 2015.

Rorty, Richard. 1979. *Philosophy and the Mirror of Nature*. Princeton, NJ: Princeton University Press.

Sullivan, Shannon. 2001. *Living across and through Skins: Transactional Bodies, Pragmatism, and Feminism*. Bloomington, IN: Indiana University Press.

Williams, Bernard. 2002. *Truth and Truthfulness: An Essay in Genealogy*. Princeton, NJ: Princeton University Press.

# 20
# SOCIAL EPISTEMOLOGY AND EPISTEMIC INJUSTICE

*Sanford Goldberg*

In this chapter I discuss the nature of various forms of epistemic injustice, as seen from the angle of social epistemology.

## 1

Miranda Fricker's ground-breaking book on epistemic injustice (Fricker 2007) made several very important advances in philosophical discussions. First, it introduced new terminology for identifying a phenomenon that, if implicitly recognized, had not previously been called out by name: what she labels "epistemic injustice" is an injustice that affects individuals in their role *as epistemic subjects*. Second, and relatedly, Fricker's book provided a tremendous impetus for those working in epistemology to speak to issues in fields that had previously been at a great remove from the theory of knowledge, at least as traditionally practiced – fields such as political and social philosophy, ethics, feminism, and critical race theory.[1] While Fricker was not the first to try to make such connections,[2] her work has certainly been extremely successful in attracting ever-greater attention to the relevant topics.[3] Third, the notion of an epistemic injustice has been fruitfully applied in a variety of different areas within philosophy – something to which this volume attests beautifully. In this chapter, I will employ the notion of epistemic injustice in connection with social epistemology. If we think of social epistemology as the study of the social dimensions of knowledge acquisition, storage, dissemination, assessment, and application, then the notion of an epistemic injustice has clear application in this domain. My specific aim is to illustrate several distinctive types of epistemic injustice – ones that come sharply into focus when we take a decidedly social-epistemological vantage point on the phenomena to be discussed.

I begin with my own view of the nature of social epistemology itself. In other work, I have urged that social epistemology ought to be regarded as the systematic investigation into the *epistemic significance of other minds*.[4] Such significance is apprehended when we recognize others as epistemic subjects in their own right – subjects who exhibit various forms of agency relevant to the acquisition, storage, transmission, and assessment of information.[5] A systematic investigation of this significance will investigate three fundamental aspects of our knowledge communities: (i) the various forms taken by our epistemic dependence on others, (ii) the variety of norms that underwrite our expectations of one another as we make our way in the common epistemic environment, and (iii) the distinctive epistemic assessment(s) implicated whenever a doxastic state is the result of a "social route" to knowledge.

This conception of the subdiscipline of social epistemology is admittedly somewhat idiosyncratic. The literature has been dominated by two *other* conceptions of the field. These are associated with the work of Steve Fuller (1988, 2012) and Alvin Goldman (1999, 2001, 2002).[6] To a first approximation, Fuller-style social epistemology derives from Kuhn's work in the philosophy of science (and tends to bring a seriously interdisciplinary approach to the study of our knowledge practices, in ways that share strong affinities with the Science and Technology Studies movement), whereas Goldman-style social epistemology has developed out of the tradition of so-called "analytic" epistemology (and tends to focus on topics that emerge out of the questions of traditional epistemology, in ways that employ the normative epistemic vocabulary of that tradition).[7] In Goldberg (forthcoming a), I advocate for the conception described above as something like a middle ground. With the more interdisciplinary approaches it recognizes the need to incorporate our various knowledge practices and the norms that inform them into a full account of our knowledge in social settings, and with the more traditional approaches it acknowledges the need to acknowledge objective, broadly "reliabilist" standards on knowledge. But whether my "middle ground" conception has this merit or not, it is particularly useful in the present context. Simply put, this conception paves the way for some novel applications of the notion of epistemic injustice.

To bring this out I will focus on the second of the three dimensions capturing the epistemic significance of other minds: (ii) the variety of norms that underwrite our expectations of one another as we make our way in the common epistemic environment. Since the norms pertain to what we expect and what we hold each other responsible for, in connection with our roles in a common knowledge community, I will refer to them as generating "normative expectations" regarding our roles as epistemic subjects. My claim will be that there are a variety of forms of epistemic injustice that arise, or can arise, in connection with these normative expectations. One additional advantage of this angle on the subject is that we can quite naturally highlight the tremendous contributions that feminist epistemology has made to social epistemology, as feminist epistemology is (in Elizabeth Anderson's apt words) "the branch of social epistemology that investigates the influence of *socially constructed conceptions and norms of gender and gender-specific interests and experiences* on the production of knowledge" (Anderson 1995: 54; italics in original).[8]

## 2

Before turning to the epistemic injustices themselves, it will be important to understand the variety of norms and expectations that structure our epistemic communities. One can discern the existence of the norms themselves, and the expectations they underwrite, in our everyday informational exchanges with others.

To begin, consider the variety of expectations we have regarding others' *epistemic condition* – their knowledgeableness, the inquiries they have performed, the evidence they possess, the inquiry-related responsibilities they have, and so forth – as we make our way through the world acquiring information. These expectations are present as we rely on our doctor's medical advice, entrust our children to daycare providers, make business decisions with our partners, enroll in a course to learn about a subject, get expert advice on a matter presently before us, interact with our colleagues at work, buy food in a grocery store, etc. In these and so many other humdrum cases, we expect certain things of one another. The expectations that concern us here are those whose content is *epistemic*: they concern what others know, what evidence they have, what evidence-collecting responsibilities they bear, what reporting procedures they follow when they acquire relevant new information, and so forth.

It is important to see that these expectations are *normative* (as opposed to merely predictive) in nature. It is certainly true that in most or all of these cases, you would predict that the various people do in fact have the knowledge (evidence, etc.) you expect of them, and it is also true that you have a good deal of evidence to back up your expectations. But the expectations themselves are not merely predictive in nature. To see this, suppose that you were to find out that your doctor was not knowledgeable about best treatment practices regarding a common medical condition. If your expectation were merely predictive, then, given what you found out, rationality would require that you surrender your expectation of your doctor's knowledgeableness. But of course this is not how you would react. On the contrary, you would appeal to this expectation *in order to criticize your doctor for not having been relevantly knowledgeable*. It is in this sense that we can speak of *normative* expectations.

Of course, not all normative expectations are legitimate. An imperious boss might normatively expect every one of the workers to know absolutely everything that there is to know about the efficient running of the business, but if this expectation is unreasonable (or otherwise unwarranted or arbitrary), then the expectation itself is illegitimate – it would not be proper for the boss to appeal to this expectation to chastise those who failed to meet the standard. This raises an interesting and difficult question in social philosophy: precisely when are normative expectations *legitimate* (where a legitimate standard is one to which it would be proper to hold others accountable)?

While I have no precise answer to this question,[9] it is worth noting that the expectations described above (in connection with our knowledge communities) appear to be far from unwarranted or arbitrary. These expectations would appear to be underwritten by (the norms of) our social practices. To see this, consider the practices of relying on experts. There are a variety of (educational) ways for people to acquire expertise in a given area and, having done so, to signal their expertise to others (credentialing). In addition, there are various ways by which the experts "police" themselves (i.e., via professional organizations). And finally there are various ways for those who rely on experts to signal that they *are* so relying (i.e., by hiring them in their role as expert in the domain in question), as well as various ways for the experts to communicate what can be expected of them in their role as experts (the publication of professional standards). Similar things can be seen in our reliance on authorities such as doctors or consultants. Here it is perhaps even clearer that the sort of reliance connecting ordinary people to such authorities is itself answerable to various sets of standards: in some cases the standards are explicitly formulated by professional organizations (the American Medical Association, the Institute of Management Consultants); in other cases there is relevant law regulating interactions of these types. So, too, for the norms informing the practices in which we rely on *other* types of professionals (daycare providers, instructors).

The sort of norms and expectations that structure our epistemic communities, as well as the social practices that underwrite these, go beyond our interactions with professionals. Sometimes, such expectations arise in the course of a personal (family, friendship, or acquaintance) relationship between two or more people. Once again, we can account for the legitimacy of these expectations (when they are legitimate) in terms of the legitimacy (and mutual familiarity) of the practices that emerge in the course of these relationships. Consider for example the expectations that two long-term partners in a family might have regarding one another: one partner, S, might expect that the other partner, T, knows of S's interests in X, Y, and Z, so that if T were to acquire any relevant knowledge about such matters, T would report this immediately to S. Here, there is a practice of sharing such information with one another whose familiarity to both S and T is part of what renders the expectations themselves legitimate. Or – sticking with the case of family partners – S and T might have the practice of leaving notes on the refrigerator door whenever they are in need of something from the store, so that when one leaves such a note in the evening for the other, s/he expects the other to have read it and to know its contents by breakfast.[10] Once again, the mutual familiarity of the practice is part of what makes the expectations themselves legitimate.

In short, it is a pervasive feature of our social life in knowledge communities that we have what I call normative expectations of others, that some of these expectations pertain to the epistemic condition of others, and that at least some of these normative epistemic expectations are legitimized by relevant social practices (whether professional, legal, scientific, personal, or familial). That is, the norms of the practices themselves determine standards against which we hold one another accountable, and when those practices are themselves mutually familiar and legitimate, the norms or standards captured by our expectations are legitimate as well. But what should be said about the legitimacy of the practices themselves?

## 3

Not all of our practices (or the expectations they underwrite) are legitimate, of course, and when they are not, they can give rise to certain forms of epistemic injustice. There are at least three ways in which the illegitimacy of social practices can give rise to epistemic injustice. One sort of epistemic injustice occurs when some people are unjustly excluded from participating, or else are treated unjustly when they do participate, in the development and sustainment of a social practice informed by normative epistemic expectations. A second sort of epistemic injustice occurs when the social practice itself "warrants" normative epistemic expectations whose standards themselves would have us treat people unfairly. And a third sort of epistemic injustice occurs when the social practices (and the expectations they generate) are "policed" in a way that treats people unfairly, or else which has effects that are unjust. In what follows, I cite examples of each, borrowing heavily from the literature in feminist epistemology and related parts of critical race theory, as well as recent social science.[11]

Since epistemic expectations help to regulate a practice, it should be open to all individuals who participate in the practice to help shape the practice, and so help shape the expectations "warranted" by the practice. Let us begin, then, with the sort of injustice that occurs when some people are unjustly excluded from participating, or else are treated unjustly when they do participate, in the development and sustainment of a social (epistemic) practice.

Insofar as one is excluded from participation altogether, one is excluded from enjoying the potential benefits of the practice. Insofar as these benefits are epistemic – the acquisition of new knowledge, access to further evidence or sources of evidence, etc. – one has been unfairly excluded from acquiring epistemic goods, rendering the injustice an epistemic one. Injustices of this sort have been emphasized by, among others, Alison Wylie (2011): she notes the noxious effects of climate issues in knowledge communities, among which are the exclusion of women and members of underrepresented minorities.[12] And Carla Fehr (2011) has noted similar things for academic institutions more generally.

Consider next the case in which one does participate in the practice, but is treated unjustly as a participant. As an example, we might focus on the norms and expectations in the practice of science. Many feminist philosophers of science have pointed out that some of these have been sexist in effect, if not (always) in intention. Kristina Rolin (2002), for example, describes the sexist effects of regarding masculine styles of presentation as providing the scientific standard. Early work in feminist epistemology held that the sexist norms and expectations in the practice of science were in fact incompatible with the norms of science itself, and might be addressed by appeal to the latter (Bleier 1984; Hubbard 1983; Longino 1990; Longino and Doell 1983); several others held that sexism was inextricably linked to the scientific perspective itself, leading to a more wholesale critique of scientific practice (Addelson 1983; Keller 1985; Lloyd 1984). But whatever the outcome of this debate, it is clear that both sides agree that – whether intended or not – the norms and expectations informing scientific practice have affected the ways in which female scientists could contribute to the scientific projects in which they were engaged (Grasswick 2017).

The feminist philosophers of science cited above, among others, can be seen as having questioned the legitimacy of the expectations embedded in scientific practice. Their critiques, then, can be usefully understood as advancing an allegation of epistemic injustice (in the hope of establishing a more legitimate set of practices).[13] The allegation focuses on the harms to female scientists as knowers: their perspectives and claims are not taken with the same seriousness as those of their male counterparts, and the opportunities as well as the epistemic rights and privileges accorded to their male counterparts are often not accorded to them (or are accorded in only a diminished way). As a result, there is a corresponding diminishment in the authority granted to their claims regarding what inquiries are worth pursuing or what has been established in the inquiries that have been pursued.[14] For this reason, practices with sexist effects do epistemic harm, not only to women scientists but to science itself and indeed the public at large: the fruitful lines of research that might have been pursued had women been full participants are not pursued, or are pursued only after unfair delays – depriving the public of useful and important knowledge that would have been acquired had the practice been more equitable.[15]

Of course, these kinds of injustices are not restricted to women; similar points have been made by critical race theorists regarding the epistemic harms to members of underrepresented minorities, generated when social practices (whether scientific or not) themselves are illegitimate. Thus Charles Mills (1997, 2007) has suggested that there are various practices (including the norms and expectations informing them) that sustain the domination and privilege of whites.[16] Since these practices can and do have a profound impact on what is investigated and why, they can have a profound impact on what is known and what remains in ignorance – thereby constituting an epistemic harm for those who would be well-served to have the knowledge in question, and an unfair advantage for those who benefit from this arrangement.

Interestingly, the kind of injustice Fricker (2007) labels "hermeneutical injustice" can exemplify an injustice of precisely this kind.[17] As Fricker characterizes it, hermeneutical injustice is a sort of injustice that obtains when we lack the very vocabulary for understanding and describing kinds of harms that are done to people in virtue of their membership in a disadvantaged class. (Her example is sexual harassment prior to the coining of the term "sexual harassment.") Fricker describes this sort of harm as an "asymmetrical cognitive disadvantage" (Fricker 2007: 161) since the lack of relevant vocabulary disadvantages the victim but not the perpetrator. Now it seems clear that this sort of injustice can obtain when certain areas of research aren't pursued out of one or another form of prejudice – as when people aren't included in the research practice, or else are not extended full participation, owing to prejudice against a disadvantaged class of which they are members. Insofar as the research at issue would have developed the vocabulary in question if it had been pursued, neglecting such research out of prejudice would appear to constitute hermeneutical injustice to those who are victims of the harms in question.

Next, let us move on to the sort of epistemic injustice that occurs when a social practice "warrants" normative epistemic expectations whose standards themselves treat people unfairly. A familiar example of this sort of injustice is the "soft prejudice of low expectations" in educational settings. Consider prevailing educational practices in schools whose students are primarily drawn from low-income neighborhoods in the US. Often, classrooms are overcrowded, teachers are not well-supported (and in some cases not well-trained), facilities are poor, and the students themselves typically face additional personal and familial challenges. The result is that educational practices are shaped to conform to the prevailing conditions, and what is "expected" of these students often falls far below what might be expected of students from a school in a wealthy neighborhood. This familiar scenario results in an injustice when the result of these lowered expectations are lowered average performance by the students in the low-income school (relative to the state or national norm), and what makes this injustice an *epistemic* injustice is that the affected students have been harmed epistemically, first, in not having access to the same opportunities to acquire epistemically-relevant skills and the cognitive competences needed for acquiring and assessing knowledge, and second, in not acquiring knowledge that is already possessed within the community (Kotzee 2017).

This sort of injustice is particularly profound as it affects the students' capacities for epistemic agency itself.[18] Nor is this the only case of this sort to arise within a classroom setting. Consider how the imposition of certain standards of "academic excellence" might well have the (no doubt, unintended) effect of ensuring that the emerging academic interests of students from disadvantaged backgrounds might not count for as much, or at all, in determining what to read, or how to guide a conversation, in the classroom. These effects constitute a systematic epistemic harm insofar as the students who are affected are likely to be less engaged with the classroom material, and so less likely to do well in school, than those whose interests are taken to set the agenda, and the harm constitutes an epistemic injustice insofar as the epistemic harms (i) are the result of unfair expectations and (ii) disproportionately affect already-disadvantaged students in their capacities as knowers.

The sorts of cases I have been describing in connection with educational settings are those whereby a social practice "warrants" normative epistemic expectations whose standards themselves in effect treat people unfairly (in ways bearing on their status as knowers). Another source of epistemic injustice – the final one I will explore in this chapter – comes when social practices (and the expectations they generate) are "policed" in a way that treats people unfairly, or that has effects that are unjust. Once again, cases of this sort have been described in educational settings. Thus certain norms of the classroom, which may be perfectly fair when stated abstractly, might nevertheless be enforced in ways that unjustly disadvantage women and people of color. Sally Haslanger (2014) has described cases in which norms of interaction in the classroom (both student-teacher and student-student) can result in situations in which students who come into the class already disadvantaged have their disadvantages reinforced. Consider a classroom situation in which a teacher regularly engages in active debate with the "good" students in the classroom, while largely ignoring those who often fail to bring in their homework. This sort of practice, in itself, need not constitute any sort of injustice. But if practices of this sort regularly fall along already-existing lines of disadvantage – it is the white male students who are regularly engaged, and it is female students or students of color whose only regular interaction with the teacher involves the teacher challenging them regarding whether they did their homework – the practices can have the effect of furthering existing advantages and disadvantages.[19]

In the sort of case just described, the practice-sanctioned expectations themselves are fair and just in the abstract, but their enforcement is not, putting additional burdens on those who are already underprivileged. Another familiar case of this sort has been documented to arise in connection with the assessment of CVs from people whose names are ethnic-sounding:[20] even if the epistemic expectations regarding the successful job candidate are perfectly appropriate, an injustice arises if those CVs with ethnic-sounding names are specially scrutinized in ways that the other CVs are not – in effect, holding the two groups to different standards. Insofar as the committee draws inferences to unwarranted conclusions regarding the epistemic condition of the applicants on the basis of the perusal of the CVs, the harms to those with ethnic-sounding names include epistemic harms, constituting an epistemic injustice. But the results of unfair "policing" of standards can be still more far-reaching: insofar as proper social scrutiny of knowledge claims is part of what renders them worthy of belief as objectively correct (Longino 2002; Scheman 2001), unfair policing of claims can undermine the warrant we have that we are getting things right regarding the objective world – thereby constituting an epistemic harm to all, albeit with particular noxiousness to those whose authority is prejudicially denigrated.

The sorts of injustice that Fricker (2007) herself labels "testimonial injustice" can be seen as an instance of this very sort. Testimonial injustice occurs when a speaker's credibility on an occasion of testifying is downgraded owing to prejudice. Now suppose that the practice of giving testimony (or of making assertions more generally[21]) is one for which there are normative epistemic expectations. For example, many philosophers who write on assertion have supposed that we expect those who make assertions to assert only what they know. Even if we suppose that this standard is legitimate, if the "policing" of this standard is unfair – if some people (women, members of underrepresented minority groups) are systematically downgraded in the assessment regarding whether they know, merely in virtue of their membership in the group in question – then clearly the policing is unfair, giving rise to the epistemic harm Fricker characterizes as "testimonial injustice."[22]

## 4

Social epistemology can be conceived as the systematic investigation of the epistemic significance of other minds. So conceived, the investigation involves a focus on the practices by which knowledge communities acquire, store, transmit, and assess information. These practices reflect aspects of the economic division of labor, but they also include practices that emerge in the course of personal, familial, or business interactions between particular people who have regular opportunities to interact with one another. Whether the practices are professional or personal, participants come to expect things of each other, among which are expectations about each other's epistemic condition – one's state of knowledge, the evidence one has, the epistemic responsibilities one acknowledges, and so forth. When the practices themselves are legitimate, these expectations are legitimate as well. But when the practices themselves prevail despite being unjust (or having unjust effects), we arrive at a situation in which there are normative epistemic expectations that are unjustly imposed on (or used to evaluate) others. This can give rise to various forms of epistemic injustice. In this chapter I have highlighted several kinds of epistemic injustice that might arise in this way. I have noted as well that both of the forms of injustice highlighted by Fricker herself (testimonial and hermeneutic) can be assimilated into this taxonomy; this is perhaps some evidence confirming the utility of the social-epistemic perspective, as conceived here.[23]

**Related chapters**: 1, 2, 3, 4, 6, 8, 21, 26, 31

## Notes

1 It is a personal embarrassment of mine that in my original reaction to Fricker's book (Goldberg 2010), I only gave cursory acknowledgement of the importance of the connections Fricker was making between epistemology and other subdisciplines in philosophy – only to go on in my review to focus exclusively on a narrow question of her treatment of the epistemology of testimony. One must own up to one's own blindness: *mea culpa*.

2  Other seminal work at the intersection of these areas include Alcoff and Potter (1993), Anderson (1995), Antony (1993), Code (1981, 1991), Collins (1990), Grasswick and Webb (2002), Harding (1986, 1991), Harding and Hintikka (1983), Jaggar (1983), Lloyd (1984), Longino (1990, 1999), Mills (1997, 2007), Nelson (1990), Scheman (1995), Tanesini (1999), Tuana (1995), and Wylie (2003). For more recent work, see Dotson (2011a, 2011b, 2012, 2014), Grasswick (2013), and Wylie (2011). See also Fricker (1998) for earlier work on the topic by Miranda Fricker herself.
3  Indeed, Grasswick's "Feminist Social Epistemology" entry in the *Stanford Encyclopedia of Philosophy* (Grasswick 2013) includes an entire subsection dedicated to epistemic injustice.
4  See e.g. Goldberg (2013, forthcoming a).
5  The emphasis on agency is also a characteristic of various forms of feminist philosophy; see especially Code (1991), Jaggar (1983), Nelson (1990), and Scheman (1995).
6  See Fuller (1988, 2012) and Goldman (1999, 2001, 2002, 2004) for representative pieces.
7  For a more detailed characterization from which I drew in this brief one, see Collin and Pederson (forthcoming), which serves as the introduction to a special *Synthese* volume on social epistemology they are editing.
8  For my appreciation of the role of feminist epistemology within social epistemology, I would like to register my deep indebtedness to Grasswick (2013), whose influence throughout this chapter is substantial.
9  What I have had to say is presented in Goldberg (forthcoming b).
10  The example is modeled on a case discussed in Gibbons (2006).
11  In the remainder of this section, I am heavily indebted to Grasswick (2013), whose presentation of feminist social epistemology is extremely helpful.
12  As we will see below, this not only constitutes an epistemic injustice to those excluded, but it also has unhappy effects for the community at large, given the epistemic value of diverse perspectives in "vetting" our claims and in deciding which research to pursue.
13  I thank Heidi Grasswick for noting this point to me (in conversation).
14  Dotson (2011b) distinguishes this case involving a diminishment of credibility ascribed to the speaker, from a related case, which she calls "testimonial smothering," in which the affected speakers "insure that [their] testimony contains only content for which one's audience demonstrates testimonial competence" (Dotson 2011: 244).
15  In addition to the work cited above, see also Heldke (2001) and Tuana (2004, 2006).
16  See also Townley (2011), where a similar claim is made about the privileged more generally.
17  I thank Heidi Grasswick for suggesting this to me (in conversation).
18  Compare Code (1991) on the development of epistemic agency.
19  It is worth noting, as a special case of this sort of epistemic injustice, practices and "policing" policies that are fairminded in design may nevertheless have systematically unfair effects on underprivileged groups. Consider, for example, the evidence from social science for the hypothesis that students of color are disproportionately disadvantaged through "resource depletion" in various interracial interactions (Richeson and Trawalter 2005; Richeson, Trawalter, and Shelton 2005). This raises the possibility that even otherwise "good" practices can inadvertently fail an already disadvantaged population – whether in school settings or beyond.
20  See Bertrand and Mullainathan (2004).
21  See Goldberg (2015).
22  Fricker's points about the epistemic injustice she calls "testimonial injustice" was anticipated in Code's (1991) view that as epistemic subjects, we are dependent on the recognition, support, and affirmation of others – with the implication that when a subject is not properly recognized or affirmed, this can have a substantial impact on her epistemic agency. As Grasswick (2013) notes, other feminist social epistemologists "have investigated the complex links between assignments of credibility and social position," including Alcoff (2001), Code (1995), and Jones (2002).
23  With thanks to Heidi Grasswick, Charles Mills, and José Medina for very helpful comments on earlier drafts of this chapter, and to Miranda Fricker and Kathryn Pogin, for several helpful discussions of these matters.

# References

Addelson, K. 1983: "The Man of Professional Wisdom." In Sandra Harding and Merrill Hintikka (eds.), *Discovering Reality: Feminist Perspectives on Epistemology, Metaphysics, Methodology, and the Philosophy of Science* (Dordrecht: D. Reidel), 165–186.

Alcoff, L. 2001: "On Judging Epistemic Credibility: Is Social Identity Relevant?" In Nancy Tuana and Sandra Morgen (eds.), *Engendering Rationalities* (Albany: State University of New York Press), 53–80.

Alcoff, L. and Potter, E. 1993: "Introduction: When Feminisms Intersect Epistemology." In Linda Alcoff and Elizabeth Potter (eds.), *Feminist Epistemologies* (New York: Routledge), 1–14.

Anderson, E. 1995: "Feminist Epistemology: An Interpretation and a Defense." *Hypatia: A Journal of Feminist Philosophy*, 10(3): 50–84.

Antony, L. 1993: "Quine as Feminist: The Radical Import of Naturalized Epistemology." In Louise Antony and Charlotte Witt (eds.), *A Mind of One's Own: Feminist Essays on Reason and Objectivity* (Boulder: Westview Press), 185–226.

Bertrand, M. and Mullainathan, S. 2004: "Are Emily and Greg More Employable Than Lakisha and Jamal? A Field Experiment on Labor Market Discrimination." *American Economic Review*, 94: 991–1013.

Bleier, R. 1984: *Science and Gender* (New York: Pergamon Press).

Code, L. 1995: *Rhetorical Spaces: Essays on Gendered Locations* (New York: Routledge).

Code, L. 1991: *What Can She Know? Feminist Theory and Construction of Knowledge* (Ithaca: Cornell University Press).

Code, L. 1981: "Is the Sex of the Knower Epistemologically Significant?" *Metaphilosophy*, 12: 267–276.

Collin, F., and Pederson, D. Forthcoming: "Introduction." *Synthese* (special edition on Social Epistemology).

Collins, P. 1990: *Black Feminist Thought: Knowledge, Consciousness, and the Politics of Empowerment* (New York: Routledge).

Dotson, K. 2014: "Conceptualizing Epistemic Oppression." *Social Epistemology: A Journal of Knowledge, Culture, and Policy*, 28(2): 115–138.

Dotson, K. 2012: "How Is This Paper Philosophy?" *Comparative Philosophy*, 3(1): 3–29.

Dotson, K. 2011a: "Concrete Flowers: Contemplating the Profession of Philosophy." *Hypatia: A Journal of Feminist Philosophy*, 26(2): 403–409.

Dotson, K. 2011b: "Tracking Epistemic Violence, Tracking Practices of Silencing." *Hypatia: A Journal of Feminist Philosophy*, 26(2): 236–257.

Fehr, C. 2011: "What Is in It for Me? The Benefits of Diversity in Scientific Communities." In Heidi E. Grasswick (ed.), *Feminist Epistemology and Philosophy of Science: Power in Knowledge* (Dordrecht: Springer), 133–156.

Fricker, M. 2007: *Epistemic Injustice: Power and the Ethics of Knowing* (Oxford: Oxford University Press).

Fricker, M. 1998: "Rational Authority and Social Power: Towards a Truly Social Epistemology." *Proceedings of the Aristotelian Society*, 98: 159–177.

Fuller, S. 2012: "Social Epistemology: A Quarter Century Itinerary." *Social Epistemology*, 26(3–4): 267–283.

Fuller, S. 1988: *Social Epistemology* (Bloomington: Indiana University Press).

Gibbons, J. 2006: "Access Externalism." *Mind*, 115(457): 19–39.

Goldberg, S. Forthcoming a: "A Proposed Research Program for Social Epistemology." In P. Reider (ed.), *Social Epistemology and Epistemic Agency* (Maryland: Rowman and Littlefield).

Goldberg, S. Forthcoming b: "Should Have Known." *Synthese*.

Goldberg, S. 2015: *Assertion: On the Philosophical Significance of Assertoric Speech* (Oxford: Oxford University Press).

Goldberg, S. 2013: "'Analytic Social Epistemology' and the Epistemic Significance of Other Minds." *Social Epistemology Review and Reply Collective*, 2(8): 26–48.

Goldberg, S. 2010: "Fricker's Non-Inferentialism." *Episteme*, 7(2): 138–150.

Goldman, A. 2004: "Group Knowledge vs. Group Rationality: Two Approaches to Social Epistemology." *Episteme*, 1: 11–22.

Goldman, A. 2002: *Pathways to Knowledge: Public and Private* (Oxford: Oxford University Press).

Goldman, A. 2001: "Social Epistemology." In Edward N. Zalta (ed.), *The Stanford Encyclopedia of Philosophy* (Spring 2001 Edition), URL = <http://plato.stanford.edu/archives/spr2001/entries/epistemology-social/>.

Goldman, A. 1999: *Knowledge in a Social World* (Oxford: Oxford University Press).

Grasswick, H. 2017: "Epistemic Injustice in Science." In Ian James Kidd, José Medina, and Gaile Pohlhaus, Jr. (eds.), *The Routledge Handbook of Epistemic Injustice* (London: Routledge).

Grasswick, H. 2013: "Feminist Social Epistemology." In Edward N. Zalta (ed.), *The Stanford Encyclopedia of Philosophy* (Spring 2013 Edition), URL = <http://plato.stanford.edu/archives/spr2013/entries/feminist-social-epistemology/>.

Grasswick, H. and Webb, M. O. 2002: "Feminist Epistemology as Social Epistemology." *Social Epistemology: A Journal of Knowledge, Culture and Policy*, 16(3): 185–196.

Harding, S. 1991: *Whose Science? Whose Knowledge? Thinking from Women's Lives* (Ithaca: Cornell University Press).
Harding, S. 1986: *The Science Question in Feminism* (Ithaca: Cornell University Press).
Harding, S. and Hintikka, M. (eds.), 1983: *Discovering Reality: Feminist Perspectives on Epistemology, Metaphysics, Methodology, and the Philosophy of Science* (Dordrecht: D. Reidel).
Haslanger, S. 2014: "Studying While Black: Trust, Opportunity, and Disrespect." *Du Bois Review*, 11(1): 109–136.
Heldke, L. 2001: "How to be Really Responsible." In Nancy Tuana and Sandra Morgen (eds.), *Engendering Rationalities* (Albany: State University of New York Press), 81–97.
Hubbard, R. 1983: "Have Only Men Evolved?" In Sandra Harding and Merrill Hintikka (eds.), *Discovering Reality: Feminist Perspectives on Epistemology, Metaphysics, Methodology, and Philosophy of Science* (Dordrecht: D. Reidel), 45–70.
Jaggar, A. 1983: *Feminist Politics and Human Nature* (Totowa, NJ: Rowman and Allanheld).
Jones, K. 2002: "The Politics of Credibility." In Louise Antony and Charlotte Witt (eds.), *A Mind of One's Own: Feminist Essays on Reason and Objectivity* (2nd Edition, Boulder: Westview), 154–176.
Keller, E. 1985: *Reflections on Gender and Science* (New Haven: Yale University Press).
Kotzee, B. 2017: "Education and Epistemic Injustice." In Ian James Kidd, José Medina, and Gaile Pohlhaus, Jr. (eds.), *The Routledge Handbook of Epistemic Injustice* (London: Routledge).
Lloyd, G. 1984: *The Man of Reason: 'Male' and 'Female' in Western Philosophy* (Minneapolis: University of Minnesota Press).
Longino, H. 2002: *The Fate of Knowledge* (Princeton: Princeton University Press).
Longino, H. 1999: "Feminist Epistemology." In John Greco and Ernest Sosa (eds.), *The Blackwell Guide to Epistemology* (Malden: Blackwell), 327–353.
Longino, H. 1990: *Science as Social Knowledge: Values and Objectivity in Scientific Inquiry* (Princeton: Princeton University Press).
Longino, H. and Doell, R. 1983: "Body, Bias, and Behaviour: A Comparative Analysis of Reasoning in Two Areas of Biological Science." *Signs: Journal of Women in Culture and Society*, 9(2): 206–227.
Mills, C. 2007: "White Ignorance." In Shannon Sullivan and Nancy Tuana (eds.), *Race and Epistemologies of Ignorance* (Albany: State University of New York Press), 11–38.
Mills, C. 1997: *The Racial Contract* (Ithaca, NY: Cornell University Press).
Nelson, L. H. 1990: *Who Knows: From Quine to a Feminist Empiricism* (Philadelphia: Temple University Press).
Richeson, J. and Trawalter, S. 2005: "Why Do Interracial Interactions Impair Executive Function? A Resource Depletion Account." *Journal of Personality and Social Psychology*, 88: 934–947.
Richeson, J., Trawalter, S., and Shelton, J. 2005: "African Americans' Racial Attitudes and the Depletion of Executive Function After Interracial Interactions." *Social Cognition*, 23: 336–352.
Rolin, K. 2002: "Gender and Trust in Science." *Hypatia: A Journal of Feminist Philosophy*, 17(4): 95–118.
Scheman, N. 2001: "Epistemology Resuscitated." In Nancy Tuana and Sandra Morgen (eds.), *Engendering Rationalities* (Albany: State University of New York Press), 23–52.
Scheman, N. 1995: "Feminist Epistemology." *Metaphilosophy*, 26(3): 177–199.
Tanesini, A. 1999: *An Introduction to Feminist Epistemologies* (Malden, MA: Blackwell).
Townley, C. 2011: *A Defense of Ignorance: Its Value for Knowers and Roles in Feminist and Social Epistemologies* (Lanham, MD: Rowman & Littlefield Publishers).
Tuana, N. 2006: "The Speculum of Ignorance: Women's Health Movement and Epistemologies of Ignorance." *Hypatia: A Journal of Feminist Philosophy*, 21(3): 1–19.
Tuana, N. 2004: "Coming to Understand: Orgasm and the Epistemology of Ignorance." *Hypatia: A Journal of Feminist Philosophy*, 19(1): 194–232.
Tuana, N. 1995: "The Values of Science: Empiricism from a Feminist Perspective." *Synthese*, 104(3): 441–461.
Wylie, A. 2011: "What Knowers Know Well: Women, Work and the Academy." In Heidi E. Grasswick (ed.), *Feminist Epistemology and Philosophy of Science: Power in Knowledge* (Dordrecht: Springer), 157–179.
Wylie, A. 2003: "Why Standpoint Matters." In Robert Figueroa and Sandra Harding (eds.), *Science and Other Cultures: Issues in Philosophies of Science and Technology* (New York: Routledge), 26–48.

# 21
# TESTIMONIAL INJUSTICE, EPISTEMIC VICE, AND VICE EPISTEMOLOGY

## Heather Battaly

In her brilliant *Epistemic Injustice* (2007), Miranda Fricker argues that gender and racial prejudices can distort our perceptions of who is credible and who is not. Fricker contends that gender prejudice prevents Herbert Greenleaf (*The Talented Mr. Ripley*) from seeing Marge Sherwood as a source of knowledge about his son's disappearance (2007: 86–88). Likewise, racial prejudice prevents the jurors in Tom Robinson's trial (*To Kill a Mockingbird*) from seeing Robinson as a source of knowledge about events at the Ewell's home (2007: 23–29). Fricker argues that these are paradigmatic cases of testimonial injustice, in which identity prejudice causes hearers to assign a deflated level of credibility to speakers. Accordingly, when our own gender and racial prejudices cause us to downgrade a speaker's credibility, we too are testimonially unjust. Though it is possible for a hearer to inflict a single instance of testimonial injustice on a speaker as a 'one-off', I will focus on testimonial injustice as a disposition of hearers. Testimonial injustice is a disposition to fail to see speakers as credible when they are credible, due to the hearer's identity prejudice.

Is the disposition of testimonial injustice an epistemic vice? If so, why? What makes it an epistemic vice? These questions fall under the purview of vice epistemology, which is an offshoot of virtue epistemology. Having made its debut in the 1980's (Sosa 1980), virtue epistemology is now a well-established field. It has sought to answer three sets of questions:

(VirtueE1)  What is an epistemic virtue? Which dispositions are epistemic virtues and why? Is there more than one kind of epistemic virtue? Can we give analyses of individual epistemic virtues (e.g., open-mindedness)?

(VirtueE2)  How are epistemic virtues connected to knowledge? Is possessing epistemic virtues necessary for having knowledge? Is it sufficient? Are there weaker connections?

(VirtueE3)  How can we acquire epistemic virtues? What is the role of the individual, the environment, and education in the development of epistemic virtues?

Unsurprisingly, virtue epistemologists have disagreed about the answers to these questions. But what unites the field, and distinguishes it from belief-based epistemology, is its focus on the cognitive dispositions of agents, especially their good cognitive dispositions – their epistemic virtues. In virtue epistemology, *agents* are the primary objects of epistemic evaluation, and epistemic virtues, which are evaluations of agents, are the fundamental building-blocks (Battaly 2008).[1] Whereas, in belief-based epistemology, *beliefs* are the primary objects of epistemic evaluation, and justification and knowledge, which are evaluations of beliefs, are taken to be fundamental. Like virtue epistemology, the nascent field of vice epistemology also focuses on the cognitive dispositions of agents, though it targets their bad cognitive dispositions – their epistemic vices (Cassam 2016). Analogously, it seeks to answer:

*(ViceE1)* What is an epistemic vice? Which dispositions are epistemic vices and why? Is there more than one kind of epistemic vice? Can we give analyses of individual epistemic vices (e.g., closed-mindedness)?

*(ViceE2)* How are epistemic vices connected to knowledge? Do epistemic vices always impede knowledge? Are there weaker connections?

*(ViceE3)* How can we correct, rehabilitate, or eliminate epistemic vices? What is the role of the individual, the environment, and education in curbing epistemic vices?

Here, I pursue ViceE1. I argue that testimonial injustice is an epistemic vice. First and foremost, it is an epistemic vice because it consistently produces *bad epistemic effects* – e.g., it impedes the transmission of knowledge. It does this whether or not it is integrated with the agent's values and motives. When it *is* integrated with the agent's values and motives, testimonial injustice is epistemically vicious in a second way. It is epistemically vicious insofar as it expresses those bad epistemic values and motives – e.g., it expresses the racist values and motives of Tom Robinson's jurors. Below, I ground this analysis in a distinction between three concepts of epistemic vice. I argue that testimonial injustice can take the form of an *effects-vice* or a *personalist-vice*, even if it sometimes – perhaps often – falls short of a responsibilist-vice. Here, the key issue is lack of control over our possession of testimonial injustice. I conclude by suggesting that we can be blameworthy for possessing testimonial injustice despite this lack of control.

## Standard conceptions of epistemic virtue and vice

Is testimonial injustice an epistemic vice? If so, why? What is an epistemic vice? Epistemic vices are bad cognitive dispositions – they make us bad thinkers. But, there is more than one way for cognitive dispositions to make us bad thinkers. For starters, they might produce bad epistemic effects – e.g., they might produce false beliefs, or impede knowledge. Or, they might involve bad epistemic motives for which we are blameworthy – e.g., they might involve motives to believe whatever is easiest, or whatever preserves the status quo, or whatever makes one feel good, instead of motives for truth, knowledge, and understanding.

These two nascent conceptions of epistemic vice correspond to the two conceptions of epistemic virtue that have dominated virtue epistemology: virtue-reliabilism and virtue-responsibilism. Virtue-reliabilism contends that epistemic virtues are *reliable* dispositions – they produce more true beliefs than false ones. It counts any reliable disposition as an epistemic virtue, be it a hard-wired faculty (e.g., 20/30 vision), a cognitive skill, or a cognitive character trait. It argues that dispositions are epistemic virtues because they consistently produce good epistemic effects; here, true beliefs. Virtue-responsibilism conceives of epistemic virtues as structurally analogous to Aristotelian moral virtues. Accordingly, it restricts epistemic virtues to acquired cognitive character traits – e.g., open-mindedness and epistemic humility – for which the agent is (at least partly) *responsible*. It argues that epistemic virtues require dispositions of epistemic motivation and epistemic action, for which the agent is praiseworthy. Roughly, it construes open-mindedness as a disposition of motivation (to care about truth and care about considering alternative ideas) and a disposition of action (to consider alternative ideas) that lies in a mean between the vices of closed-mindedness and naïveté.

Let's develop our two budding conceptions of epistemic vice by exploring the key features of virtue-reliabilism and virtue-responsibilism. Epistemic virtues are cognitive dispositions that make us good thinkers. But, there is more than one way they can make us good thinkers. Virtue-reliabilists argue that epistemic virtues make us good thinkers by producing good epistemic effects – true beliefs. There are five key features of *virtue-reliabilism*. First, the epistemic virtues are instrumentally valuable. Their value comes from the value of the things they produce: they are valuable because they consistently produce true beliefs. For reliabilists, dispositions that don't consistently produce true beliefs aren't epistemic virtues. This means that, second, epistemic virtues are reliable. They need not be perfect, but they must produce a preponderance of true beliefs. Moreover, any stable disposition that produces a preponderance of true beliefs will be an epistemic virtue. In other words, the reliability of a disposition is both necessary *and* sufficient for its being an epistemic virtue. Accordingly, third, epistemic virtues need not be acquired dispositions, they can be hard-wired faculties like 20/30 vision. Thus, Ernest Sosa argues that some of our epistemic virtues are natural, while others are derived: "some . . . come courtesy of Mother Nature and her evolutionary ways, but many others must be learned" (2007: 85). Fourth, reliabilists think that we need not be responsible for our epistemic virtues. After all, we have no control over which hard-wired faculties we end up possessing and thus aren't praiseworthy for ending up with reliable faculties. Nor can we control the operation of hard-wired faculties – they operate involuntarily and automatically – and so we aren't praiseworthy for this either. Fifth, reliabilists think that epistemic virtues need not be personal dispositions; they can be sub-personal. Roughly, personal dispositions express one's character – what one values and cares about. Accordingly, personal *epistemic* dispositions express one's epistemic character – one's epistemic motives and values. HarThey tell us whether one's values and cares about truth and understanding, or about (e.g.) getting good grades, or looking smart, or believing whatever is easiest. But, hard-wired epistemic virtues, like 20/30 vision, are *sub-personal*. They don't express the epistemic characters of the individuals who possess them. Case in point: a person who values and loves truth, and a person who cares solely about protecting his own world-view, can both have the virtue of 20/30 vision (as can non-human animals).

We can use these features to flesh out our first conception of epistemic vice: *effects-vice*. Accordingly, epistemic vices will be cognitive dispositions that produce bad epistemic effects – including (but not limited to) false beliefs. There are five points to note about effects-vices. First, they are instrumentally dis-valuable. They get their negative value from the bad epistemic effects they produce. Consequently, a disposition won't count as an effects-vice unless it consistently produces bad epistemic effects. A student who cares solely about getting good grades, but who has the good luck of being in classes in which this motive consistently produces true beliefs (due to teacher-ingenuity), does not have an effects-vice. Moreover, second, any cognitive disposition that consistently produces bad epistemic effects will count as an effects-vice. A student who values and loves truth, but who nevertheless consistently produces false beliefs – he just can't figure things out no matter how hard he tries – has an effects-vice (Battaly 2014). He has an effects-vice because he ends up with a preponderance of false beliefs (despite his impeccable motives). Third, it follows that effects-vices can, but need not, be acquired dispositions, they can be hard-wired faculties like 20/200 vision. If all cognitive dispositions that consistently produce bad epistemic effects are effects-vices, then (uncorrected) 20/200 vision will be an effects-vice. Relatedly, fourth, we need not be blameworthy for our effects-vices, since their possession and operation may be beyond our control. Finally, effects-vices need not be personal. They can be sub-personal faculties that reveal nothing about our epistemic values or motives (Battaly 2016).

Let's explore *virtue-responsibilism*. One might contend that producing good epistemic effects isn't what makes us good thinkers, or isn't the only thing that does. It also matters *why* one produces, or tries to produce, good epistemic effects. In this vein, Virtue-Responsibilists argue that epistemic virtues make us good thinkers because they require good epistemic motives.

There are five key features of virtue-responsibilism. First, the value of the epistemic virtues is at least partly intrinsic. Epistemic virtues are partly composed of epistemic motives – e.g., caring about truth, knowledge, or understanding – which are themselves intrinsically valuable. Consequently, dispositions whose value is purely instrumental won't be epistemic virtues. Second, responsibilists agree that reliability is insufficient for epistemic virtue but disagree about whether reliability is *necessary* for epistemic virtue. Linda Zagzebski (1996: 99–100) argues that reliability *is* necessary; James Montmarquet (1993: 20) and Jason Baehr (2011: 123–126) argue that it is not. (They all think epistemic virtues like open-mindedness are reliable in the actual world.) Third, responsibilists restrict epistemic virtues to acquired dispositions, ruling out hard-wired faculties. They think epistemic virtues must be praiseworthy, and that we aren't praiseworthy for native faculties since they aren't subject to our control (Baehr 2011: 27). Thus, fourth, they think epistemic virtues must be dispositions for which the agent is (partly) responsible. Though they interpret this requirement differently – Zagzebski and Baehr require responsibility for virtue-possession; Montmarquet requires responsibility for virtue-operation (1993: 34) – they all emphasize control. For Zagzebski: "virtues are qualities that deserve praise for their presence, and blame for their absence" (1996: 104). They are dispositions that one must work (perform voluntary actions) to acquire: "it is part of the nature of a virtue in the standard case that it be an entrenched quality that is the result of moral work on the part of the human agent . . ." (Zagzebski 1996: 125). Crucially, the agent has some control over whether she acquires virtue, and the kind of praiseworthiness that attaches to virtue is said to reflect this control. Agents are praiseworthy for possessing virtues insofar as they are praiseworthy for putting in the requisite work (repeated voluntary actions) to acquire them. Dispositions whose possession doesn't allow for such control are not praiseworthy in this way and thus won't be epistemic virtues. Finally, epistemic virtues are personal. They express the epistemic characters – the epistemic values and motives – of the individuals who possess them. Responsibilists build these values and motives into the epistemic virtues themselves. They argue that dispositions to act appropriately are insufficient for virtue. One could consistently do what an open-minded person would do – consider alternatives – but lack the virtue of open-mindedness; suppose one considers alternatives solely because one values and cares about good grades or looking smart. They argue that the virtue of open-mindedness requires belief and motivational components: one must consider alternatives because one cares about truth and believes truth is important.

We can use these features to flesh out our second conception of epistemic vice: *responsibilist-vice*. Accordingly, epistemic vices will be cognitive character traits – e.g., closed-mindedness, intellectual arrogance – over which the agent has some control and for which she is blameworthy. These character traits will be partly composed of bad epistemic motives. There are five key features of responsibilist-vices. First, they are intrinsically dis-valuable. They get (at least some of) their negative value from intrinsically bad motives – e.g., caring about protecting one's views, or about believing whatever will make one feel good, or fit in with one's group. Second, producing bad epistemic effects will be insufficient for responsibilist-vice. This follows from each of their remaining features. Third, since such vices will be restricted to acquired dispositions, hard-wired faculties that produce bad epistemic effects (20/200 vision) will be excluded. Fourth, responsibilist-vices must be dispositions for which the agent is blameworthy, but an agent need not be blameworthy for producing bad epistemic effects. An agent can produce bad epistemic effects due to bad luck – to constitutive or environmental factors that are beyond her control. She might be hard-wired with a memory impairment or the victim of a Cartesian evil-demon. Crucially, responsibilist-vices require features over which the agent *has* some control, namely, her bad epistemic motives and values. According to this conception of vice, the agent has considerably more control over the motives and values she comes to possess than she does over external effects. She is blameworthy for coming to possess bad motives and values because she is blameworthy for failing to perform the requisite voluntary actions to avoid them and/or blameworthy for performing the voluntary actions that eventually produce them. Crucially here, blameworthiness is keyed to control. Finally, fifth, responsibilist-vices must be personal – they must express the agent's epistemic character. But, producing bad epistemic effects need not be an expression of the agent's epistemic character – one can have impeccable motives and values but produce false beliefs due to an inhospitable (e.g., demon) environment. For this reason, too, bad epistemic motives and values will be required for responsibilist-vice.

## Testimonial injustice and standard conceptions of epistemic vice

Arguably, both of the above conceptions of epistemic vice are legitimate – they simply highlight different ways in which we can be epistemically vicious (Battaly 2014: 65). One way to be epistemically vicious is to produce bad epistemic effects; another way is to have bad epistemic motives, for which one is blameworthy. Is the disposition of testimonial injustice an epistemic vice in either of these ways?

It is at least an effects-vice. Fricker rightly argues that whatever form testimonial injustice takes, it produces a ream of bad effects, both epistemic and moral. Epistemically, it prevents the hearer from getting knowledge from the speaker. It also degrades the speaker "in her capacity as a knower" and as a human, which can cause the speaker to lose confidence in her own beliefs and abilities, and even be prevented from acquiring epistemic virtues and knowledge (Fricker 2007: 44).[2] Importantly, Fricker contends that testimonial injustice can take the form of a perceptual prejudice that operates below the level of belief and motive, and without the agent's permission (2007: 39). This form of testimonial injustice can be "flatly inconsistent with the [agent's] beliefs" (Fricker 2007: 36; see also Carel and Kidd 2014: 535). To illustrate, a card-carrying feminist at the level of belief and motive might still see men as more credible than women due to her prejudiced perception. Here, testimonial injustice gets its negative value from the bad effects it produces. Bad motives are not required – the card-carrying feminist's motives are impeccable. Bad effects are – Fricker suggests that a person (like Huck Finn) with prejudiced motives and values, who nevertheless reliably perceives credibility and thus avoids producing the harms above, likewise avoids testimonial injustice (2007: 93–94). Note also that in the card-carrying feminist, testimonial injustice is sub-personal rather than personal. It does not reveal her motives and values; it operates contrary to them. But, it does reveal the prejudice that is prevalent in her society. On Fricker's view, "human societies have prejudices in the air" that infect our perceptions of speaker-credibility, whether we want them to or not (2007: 96). The card-carrying feminist, along with the rest of us, unwittingly inherits prejudiced perception from her society. This means that we lack control over our initial possession of this form of testimonial injustice; we cannot prevent ourselves from absorbing it. Accordingly, we are not blameworthy for its initial possession. In short, when testimonial injustice takes the form of prejudiced perception, it meets the conditions of an effects-vice. It produces bad epistemic effects, even if it is neither personal nor under the agent's control.

Can testimonial injustice also be a responsibilist-vice? Fricker argues that testimonial injustice can take a second form, in which prejudiced perceptions are integrated with prejudiced beliefs and motives (Fricker 2007: 36). To illustrate, Tom Robinson's jurors fail to see Robinson as credible and do so because of their prejudiced beliefs (e.g., that he and all blacks are inferior) and racial hatred (they are not motivated by the evidence, which exonerates Robinson). They are racists at every level. When testimonial injustice takes this form, it *is* personal – it expresses the agent's prejudiced values and motives. The bad epistemic motives it requires also make it intrinsically bad (its bad effects continue to make it instrumentally bad). Thus far, this form of testimonial injustice meets the conditions for responsibilist-vice. But, does it meet the control and blameworthiness condition? Recall that the responsibilist-vices we are focusing on require the agent to have a considerable degree of control over their *possession*. This is where matters get tricky. Arguably, agents typically lack control over whether they initially come to possess prejudiced beliefs and motives. It is no surprise that children 'raised' by the Hitler *Jugend* (or the Taliban or ISIS) acquire prejudiced beliefs and motives involuntarily, as a product of their environment (Adams 1985). Fricker seems to think this is the norm: it is standard for agents to first acquire prejudiced beliefs and motives by passively and unwittingly inheriting them from their societies (2007: 82, 95). In short, agents who acquire this robust form of testimonial injustice don't typically control their initial possession of it and thus aren't blameworthy for that initial possession. Even so, don't they gain control over its possession as mature adults? This, too, is tricky. After all, (1) some of them are in insular societies – they are not afforded the opportunity to know better. Thus, Fricker argues that although Robinson's jurors were in a position to know better (2007: 89–90; see also Pohlhaus, Jr. 2012: 729–731), Greenleaf was not – he had the "epistemic bad luck" of landing in an historical context in which the requisite gender concepts were unavailable (2007: 103). Moreover, (2) their initial possession of this *robust* form of testimonial injustice impedes their ability to change direction. José Medina argues that Robinson's jurors are "meta-insensitive" – they are insensitive to the fact that Robinson is a source of knowledge *and* insensitive to the fact that they have this limitation (2013: 76). Their prejudiced beliefs and motives prevent them from even recognizing that they have a problem! Relatedly, George Sher contends, "by the time a miscreant-in-training has . . . achieved a degree of maturity, the expectation that he will display the insight, flexibility, and persistence . . . needed to arrest or reverse his incipient corruption may well be unreasonable" (2006: 55). In sum, when testimonial injustice takes this robust form, it sometimes – arguably often – falls short of a responsibilist-vice. It runs afoul of the control and blameworthiness condition with respect to its initial possession. It also frequently runs afoul of this condition in mature adults. Presumably, it *is* sometimes a responsibilist-vice – some agents satisfy the control and blameworthiness condition. But, this happens less frequently than we might think.

## Testimonial injustice and an alternative conception of epistemic vice

Notice that when testimonial injustice is robust, it succeeds in expressing the agent's epistemic character, even when it fails to meet the control and blameworthiness condition on responsibilist-vice. This puts us in a position to argue for a third conception of epistemic vice: *personalist-vice* (Battaly 2016; Battaly and Slote 2015). This conception is a *via media* between effects-vice and responsibilist-vice. Like responsibilist-vice, it requires epistemic vices to be personal traits of character – to express the epistemic values and motives of the agent. And, like effects-vice, it rejects control and blameworthiness as a necessary condition: a disposition can count as a personalist-vice even if the agent lacks control over, and is not blameworthy (accountable) for, its possession. This means that the robust form of testimonial injustice in Robinson's jurors will be a personalist-vice, whether or not its possession is under their control.

There are two advantages to recognizing this robust form of testimonial injustice as a personalist-vice. First, bad epistemic effects aren't the only thing that make this form of testimonial injustice bad. It is also intrinsically bad, due to its bad epistemic motives and values. Robinson's jurors are not motivated by the evidence; they are motivated by racial hatred and by their beliefs in accordance with the status quo, which deems all blacks incompetent. These epistemic motives and values would be bad even if they didn't produce bad effects. As Robert Adams puts the point, "it matters . . . what we are for and what we are against, even if we do not have the power to do much for or against it, and even if it was not by trying that we came to be for or against it" (1985: 12). Recognizing this robust form of testimonial injustice as a personalist vice allows us to capture its intrinsic dis-value.

Second, personalism allows us to hedge our bets, in case we lack control over our possession of this form of testimonial injustice and over our possession of epistemic character traits more generally. As suggested above, we may have less control over our possession of bad motives and values than Responsibilists think. This is the view of non-voluntarists like Sher, who argues that "we rarely exercise effective control over the development of our traits" (2006: 12). Sher contends that exercising such control would require knowingly performing actions that contribute to the development of our traits. But, he thinks that *even as adults*, we aren't usually in a position to know whether an action would make a contribution to our development or what sort of contribution it would make. In his words, the connections between actions and traits are often "transparent only in retrospect" (2009: 38). Of course, responsibilists and other Aristotelians (Jacobs 2001) disagree.³ In short: at best, the jury is still out on whether we usually control the possession of our epistemic character traits; at worst, control has been a red herring. Recognizing this form of testimonial injustice as a personalist-vice allows us to circumvent this debate over control. Whether we have control or not, personalism allows us to count this form of testimonial injustice as a character vice.

## Blameworthiness without control

But, doesn't personalism let Robinson's jurors off too easily? Doesn't it commit us to claiming that they – along with Greenleaf and the Nazis – aren't blameworthy for possessing testimonial injustice? To be sure, it commits us to claiming that they are not accountable for possessing it. But, non-voluntarists have argued that the notion of blameworthiness has "two faces": (1) *accountability*, which requires control, and (2) *attributability*, which does not (Watson 2004). In short, Robinson's jurors, Greenleaf, and the Nazis can be blameworthy in the attributability sense, even though they aren't accountable.

What is attributability-blameworthiness? Unsurprisingly, this is hotly debated (Talbert 2016). Non-voluntarists agree that attributability-blameworthiness does not require control. Along these lines, Fricker has recently argued that we can be blameworthy for behavior and for "bad traits or motives" that are "beyond our ken and control" (2016: 41). But, non-voluntarists disagree about the positive constraints on attributability-blameworthiness. Gary Watson's constraints are relatively strict. Watson endorses a 'self-disclosure' view, according to which an agent is only blameworthy for bad traits that express her 'real self' – the values and motives she has endorsed (Watson 2004: 270). Arguably, Sher's constraints are less strict. He contends that an agent is blameworthy for bad traits that *reflect badly on her*, whether or not they express her 'real self' (2006: 57). In his words, she is blameworthy for bad traits that stem from "the innumerable desires, beliefs, attitudes, and dispositions, many of them unconscious, that together make [her] the individual [she] is" (2009: 20). Fricker's constraints may be less strict still (2016: 42fn21). She argues that an agent is blameworthy for bad traits that have their source either in the agent's epistemic character *or* epistemic system. As she puts the point, these traits need not be restricted to what is characteristic of the agent, much less to his 'real self' since "uncharacteristic acts and motives can still be ours in the relevant sense – features of *our epistemic system*" (2016: 41).

All three of these analyses allow us to count Robinson's jurors, Greenleaf, and the Nazis as blameworthy for possessing testimonial injustice in the attributability sense. Indeed, where the constraints are relatively permissive, there will be plenty of attributability-blame to go around. Permissive constraints allow agents to be blameworthy for possessing both explicit and *implicit* forms of testimonial injustice (and for possessing implicit biases more generally), whereas 'real self' views struggle on this score. But, one might wonder whether permissive analyses cast the net too widely, counting the agent as blameworthy for too many dispositions, thus (ironically) curtailing the role of epistemic bad luck. Their challenge will be distinguishing dispositions that have their source in *the agent's* epistemic character or system from dispositions that "merely flow through" the agent but have their source in the *environment*.[4] I close with three open questions:

1. Is the card-carrying feminist blameworthy for possessing testimonial injustice in the attributability sense?
2. Are an agent's implicit cognitive dispositions part of her epistemic character (see Holroyd and Kelly 2016)?[5]
3. Does personalism allow for epistemic vices that are implicit?

These warrant further exploration. For now, the key point is this. If the notion of attributability-blameworthiness is viable, then debates over control may be a distraction. We don't need control for blameworthiness.[6]

**Related chapters**: 2, 4, 6, 8, 22, 23, 26

## Notes

1 Though virtue epistemology has largely focused on individual agents, recent work on collective agents and distributed agents has helped to expand its focus. On collective agents, see Fricker (2010); on distributed agents, see Battaly (forthcoming).
2 At the institutional level, testimonial injustice produces widespread, reverberating harms. As Anderson (2012) points out, it silences agents who are systematically denied fair access to education. In so doing, it prevents these agents from making a contribution to inquiry and thus further narrows the epistemic resources that are available to the community as a whole. Thanks to Ian James Kidd and Gaile Pohlhaus, Jr. for this point.
3 Holroyd (2012) also disagrees. She endorses an indirect control (tracing) account.
4 Fricker (2016: 42). Relatedly, see Riggs (2012: 154).
5 Saul (2017) discusses the relation of implicit biases and epistemic injustice.
6 I am grateful to Ian James Kidd and Gaile Pohlhaus, Jr. for comments on an earlier draft.

## References

Adams, R. (1985) "Involuntary Sins," *Philosophical Review* 94(1): 3–31.
Anderson, E. (2012) "Epistemic Justice as a Virtue of Social Institutions," *Social Epistemology* 26(2): 163–173.
Baehr, J. (2011) *The Inquiring Mind*, New York: Oxford University Press.
Battaly, H. (2008) "Virtue Epistemology," *Philosophy Compass* 3: 639–663.
Battaly, H. (2014) "Varieties of Epistemic Vice," in J. Matheson and R. Vitz (eds.) *The Ethics of Belief*, Oxford: Oxford University Press, pp. 51–76.
Battaly, H. (2016) "Epistemic Virtue and Vice: Reliabilism, Responsibilism, and Personalism," in C. Mi, M. Slote, and E. Sosa (eds.) *Moral and Intellectual Virtues in Western and Chinese Philosophy*, New York: Routledge, pp. 99–120.
Battaly, H. (Forthcoming) "Extending Epistemic Virtue: Extended Cognition Meets Virtue-Responsibilism," in J. A. Carter, A. Clark, J. Kallestrup, and D. Pritchard (eds.) *Extending Epistemology*, Oxford: Oxford University Press.
Battaly, H. and M. Slote. (2015) "Virtue Epistemology and Virtue Ethics," in L. Besser-Jones and M. Slote (eds.) *The Routledge Companion to Virtue Ethics*, New York: Routledge, pp. 253–269.

Carel, H. and I. J. Kidd. (2014) "Epistemic Injustice in Healthcare: A Philosophical Analysis," *Medical Healthcare and Philosophy* 17: 529–540.

Cassam, Q. (2016) "Vice Epistemology," *The Monist* 99: 159–180.

Fricker, M. (2007) *Epistemic Injustice: Power and the Ethics of Knowing*, Oxford: Oxford University Press.

Fricker, M. (2010) "Can There Be Institutional Virtues?," in T. S. Gendler and J. Hawthorne (eds.) *Oxford Studies in Epistemology*, Oxford: Oxford University Press, pp. 236–252.

Fricker, M. (2016) "Fault and No-Fault Responsibility for Implicit Prejudice," in M. Brady and M. Fricker (eds.) *The Epistemic Life of Groups*, Oxford: Oxford University Press, pp. 33–50.

Holroyd, J. (2012) "Responsibility for Implicit Bias," *Journal of Social Philosophy* 43(3): 274–306.

Holroyd, J. and D. Kelly. (2016) "Implicit Bias, Character, and Control," in A. Masala and J. Webber (eds.) *From Personality to Virtue*, Oxford: Oxford University Press, pp. 106–133.

Jacobs, J. (2001) *Choosing Character*, Ithaca: Cornell University Press.

Medina, J. (2013) *The Epistemology of Resistance*, Oxford: Oxford University Press.

Montmarquet, J. (1993) *Epistemic Virtue and Doxastic Responsibility*, Lanham, MD: Rowman and Littlefield.

Pohlhaus, Jr., G. (2012) "Relational Knowing and Epistemic Injustice: Toward a Theory of Willful Hermeneutical Ignorance," *Hypatia* 27(4): 715–735.

Riggs, W. (2012) "Culpability for Epistemic Injustice: Deontic or Aretetic?," *Social Epistemology* 26(2): 149–162.

Sher, G. (2006) *In Praise of Blame*, Oxford: Oxford University Press.

Sher, G. (2009) *Who Knew? Responsibility without Awareness*, Oxford: Oxford University Press.

Sosa, E. (1980) "The Raft and the Pyramid," *Midwest Studies in Philosophy* 5: 3–25.

Sosa, E. (2007) *A Virtue Epistemology*, Oxford: Oxford University Press.

Talbert, M. (2016) *Moral Responsibility*, Cambridge: Polity.

Watson, G. (2004) "Two Faces of Responsibility," in *Agency and Answerability*, Oxford: Oxford University Press, pp. 260–288.

Zagzebski, L. (1996) *Virtues of the Mind*, Cambridge: Cambridge University Press.

# PART 4

# Socio-political, ethical, and psychological dimensions of knowing

# 22
# IMPLICIT BIAS, STEREOTYPE THREAT, AND EPISTEMIC INJUSTICE

*Jennifer Saul*

Epistemic injustice is, broadly speaking, about ways that members of marginalized groups may be wronged in their capacity as knowers, due to prejudicial stereotypes. Members of marginalized groups are also the main subjects of concern in discussions of implicit bias and stereotype threat. Those writing on implicit bias are primarily concerned with the ways that largely unconscious, largely automatic associations and stereotypes may play a role in how we interact with members of stigmatized groups. And those writing on stereotype threat are primarily concerned with the ways that awareness of negative stereotypes about one's group may impair performance. A key concern in discussions of both implicit bias and stereotype threat has been the effects of these phenomena on academic endeavours. It may seem clear, then, what the relationship is between epistemic injustice, implicit bias, and stereotype threat: at first glance, it would appear that implicit bias and stereotype threat are simply varieties of epistemic injustice.

This thought, however, is a mistake. While there are many interesting relationships between epistemic injustice, implicit bias, and stereotype threat, these relationships are far more complicated than the simple one suggested above. To explore this, we will look at Miranda Fricker's (2007)[1] two main categories – testimonial injustice and hermeneutical injustice[2] – exploring how each relates to implicit bias and stereotype threat.

## 1. Testimonial injustice

According to Fricker, in systematic cases of testimonial injustice (her and our primary concern):

> The speaker sustains such a testimonial injustice if and only if she received a credibility deficit owing to the identity prejudice of the hearer.
>
> *(28)*

A key element of this is often what Kristie Dotson calls 'testimonial quieting', drawing on the work of Patricia Hill Collins (1990). This, she writes, "occurs when an audience fails to identify a speaker as a knower," often due to a 'controlling image' (e.g. welfare mother) or stereotype (Dotson 2011: 242–243).

## *1.1 Testimonial injustice and implicit bias*

While there will be substantial overlap between cases of testimonial injustice and cases of implicit bias, we will see that the two notions come apart in many ways. To see this, we'll need a more precise understanding of implicit bias.[3] Here is a useful outline of the notion, from Brownstein and Saul (2016: 2).

> 'Implicit bias' is a term of art referring to evaluations of social groups that are largely outside of conscious awareness or control. These evaluations are typically thought to involve associations between social groups and concepts or roles such as "violent," "lazy," "nurturing," "assertive," "scientist," and so on. Such associations result at least in part from common stereotypes found in contemporary liberal societies about members of these groups. Substantial empirical support has developed for the claim that most people, often in spite of their conscious beliefs, values, and attitudes, have implicit biases and that those biases impact social behavior in many unsettling ways. For example, implicit racial biases are thought to cause a majority of people to give more favorable evaluations of otherwise identical resumés if those resumés belong to applicants with stereotypically white names (e.g. Emily, Greg) than if they belong to applicants with stereotypically black names (e.g. Jamal, Lakisha). Even more ominously, participants in "shooter bias" tasks are more likely to shoot an unarmed black man in a computer simulation than an unarmed white man, and are more likely to fail to shoot an armed white man than an armed black man.

Comparing Fricker's original discussions of testimonial injustice with discussions of implicit bias, there is an initially rather striking difference. Her central cases, from *To Kill a Mockingbird* and *The Talented Mr. Ripley*, involve quite explicitly expressed and endorsed prejudices. And she writes of the relevant prejudices being things like "the idea that women are irrational, blacks are intellectually inferior to whites, the working classes are the moral inferiors of the upper classes" (Fricker 2007, 23). That is, she seems to be focused on prejudices as propositions explicitly believed/endorsed. Later she writes that "prejudices are judgments, which may have a positive or a negative valence" (Fricker 2007, 35). Again, 'judgment' is suggestive of something explicit and conscious. In the implicit bias literature in philosophy, on the other hand, the focus has been very much on the implicit biases which conflict with explicit beliefs and commitments. The prejudices that are the subject of so much discussion are largely unconscious and automatic ones, that people may be horrified to discover they hold (if they are even willing to face up to this revelation).

However, this contrast is overstated. The philosophical implicit bias literature has focused on cases of conflict because they are the most puzzling ones and the cases in which there seems the most potential for alteration and improvement. But even the most openly bigoted people still have implicit biases – generally ones that fit perfectly with their explicit beliefs. So, for example, the bigoted white people in *To Kill a Mockingbird* almost certainly hold implicit biases against black people that match their explicit biases. And Fricker's discussion of how credibility deficits actually function is in fact a very nice fit with discussions of implicit bias. First, her crucial notion of a negative identity-prejudicial stereotype does not seem to be one that requires consciousness:

> A widely held disparaging association between a social group and one or more attributes, where this association embodies a generalization that displays some (typically, epistemically culpable) resistance to counter-evidence owing to an ethically bad affective investment.
>
> *(35)*

She also notes that "prejudicial stereotypes can sometimes be especially hard to detect because they influence our credibility judgments directly, without doxastic mediation" (36), and notes that they may conflict with the holder's beliefs.

Nonetheless, implicit bias is not simply a subcategory of testimonial injustice. There are at least three ways in which implicit bias might occur without testimonial injustice. First, an epistemic injustice must be *done* to someone. There is no epistemic justice until there is an occasion on which some specific testifier suffers a wrong due to a specific credibility deficit. Implicit bias is not like this – implicit biases are associations that may or may not ever manifest in this way. To see this, imagine the case of someone who lives in an all-white isolated village, with no access to internet, television, or news of the outside world, who has picked up racist implicit biases due to an early acquaintance with racist children's literature. It might in principle happen (though this is increasingly unlikely) that this person is never actually in the position of deciding whether to believe the testimony of a non-white person, and so they never inflict an epistemic injustice on anyone. This would be the case of an implicit bias that does not give rise to an epistemic injustice. It also brings out another significant point: implicit bias is a psychological notion, concerning the state of mind of an individual (albeit in ways very importantly related to their society). Testimonial injustice is a more interactive notion, requiring a speaker, an audience, and an occasion on which an injustice is done. Implicit bias can give us a small bit of this – it can be a part of why a speaker might perpetrate an epistemic injustice. But it will not ever give us the whole of this.

Another way that implicit bias is a broader notion is that it is not just about credibility. There are clearly implicit biases related to credibility: associating men with maths and women with arts may reduce the credibility that a woman mathematician receives, for example. But not all implicit biases are related to credibility. Associating black people with violence is not (straightforwardly, anyway) a matter of credibility, and the devastating effects of this association are quite different from the (also devastating) credibility-related effects of associating black people with lack of intelligence.

A final way that implicit bias is potentially a broader notion than testimonial injustice is that implicit biases may be positive as well as negative. While most literature has focused on negative implicit biases about stigmatized groups, there are also positive implicit biases about valorized groups. Indeed, one standard sort of test for implicit biases (the Implicit Association Test) relies on comparing the accessibility of associations about two different groups. A well-known version of this has demonstrated the tendency to associate white people with 'good' and black people with 'bad.' The extent to which positive credibility-related prejudices may count as testimonial injustice is controversial. Fricker maintains that epistemic injustice only occurs in the case of credibility deficits, but Jose Medina (2013) argues that credibility excesses may also result in epistemic injustices. These two versions, then, come apart in their ability to encompass positive effects on credibility judgments from implicit bias, with only Medina able to include positive implicit biases as (potentially) giving rise to epistemic injustice.

## *1.2 Testimonial injustice and stereotype threat*

Stereotype threat is a phenomenon that occurs when members of a group that are negatively stereotyped at some particular task care about doing well at it, and are reminded of the negative stereotype of their group. The most-discussed effect of this is underperformance, but it can also lead to other effects such as avoidance or disengagement (for an overview, see Steele 2010).

Since stereotype threat may impair performance, it may lead to less credible testimony. If someone is stumbling over their words, forgetting what they want to say, or displaying other signs of hesitation or stress, they may well be seen as less credible. Since members of stigmatized groups are especially (though not exclusively) likely to suffer from stereotype threat, these groups may be especially likely to suffer from lowered credibility in these ways. This does not, however, mean that they therefore suffer a testimonial injustice. A testimonial injustice occurs *only if* the credibility deficit is due to identity prejudice. The belief that people who show signs of great stress while speaking are not to be believed is not an *identity* prejudice, even if its results may be more damaging for members of stigmatized groups.

Boudewijn de Bruin (2014), however, has argued that there is a significant, underexplored relationship between testimonial injustice and stereotype threat. Stereotype threat impairs performance due to awareness of stereotypes that are widespread in the culture. Some of these stereotypes are precisely those identity prejudices that give rise to testimonial injustice. Take, for example, the belief that women are not good at mathematics. This belief may lead to a woman mathematician's testimony being taken less seriously than it should be – a clear case of testimonial injustice. But, crucially, the widespread presence of this belief can also lead the woman mathematician to suffer from stereotype threat and to perform less well. His point is that there may be a self-fulfilling aspect to testimonial injustice, which functions via stereotype threat.

Another example of testimonial injustice causing stereotype threat comes from Audrey Yap (2015), quoting a discussion of Aboriginal rape victims facing hostile questioning in court: "The more hostile and racist the credibility assaults, the more distressing and traumatizing the trial process is for rape complainants, creating a vicious circle such that their very distress undermines their ability to 'hold up' under legal interrogation in a way that is seen to be credible" (Yap 2015: 32). This is quite a complex case, in which stereotype threat may also be causing victims to behave in a way that makes their testimony less believable because it displays what are commonly taken to be non-group-based markers of low credibility. Ishani Maitra (2011) also discusses this sort of case, noting that "(e)ven granting that the stereotype here is genuinely reliable and nonprejudicial, if this police officer dismisses the victim merely because of her shifty manner, without making any further effort to check whether she is really lying, he (intuitively speaking) seems to commit a wrong against the victim" (2011: 203).

## 2. Hermeneutical injustice

Hermeneutical injustice is "the injustice of having some significant area of one's social experience obscured from collective understanding owing to hermeneutical marginalization" (Fricker 2007, 158). A key example Fricker discusses is that of experiencing sexual harassment before the term and concept of sexual harassment existed. This lack of a concept meant that those having this experience had much more difficulty both understanding their own experiences and communicating with others. But that gap alone is insufficient for hermeneutical injustice. It is also crucial that that gap resulted from hermeneutical marginalization – a lack of input into the conceptual resources of the culture, due to the marginalization of a group, which had been kept from the key concept-making roles.

It is not initially obvious that this would bear much relationship to implicit bias and stereotype threat. But as we will see below, there are several interesting avenues for exploration.

One fairly simple point that nonetheless bears making is that both stereotype threat and implicit bias are concepts that are very helpful for making sense of the experiences of members of marginalized groups. They fill important hermeneutical gaps. Prior to the rise in awareness of implicit bias, it was very difficult to call attention to a bias without this being taken to be an accusation of outright, conscious bigotry. This made it very difficult to communicate about a significant portion of the barriers faced by members of marginalized groups. Similarly, the concept of stereotype threat has helped many members of stigmatized groups to communicate about their uncomfortable experiences in certain environments – to be able to explain this, name it, and talk about how to change it. Both concepts, then, have filled important hermeneutical gaps.

Importantly, however, this does not meant that the lack of these concepts itself constituted a hermeneutical injustice. For it to constitute a hermeneutical injustice, it would need to be the case that the gap resulted from hermeneutical marginalization. And this, it seems to me, is a matter for historians of science to determine. The gap was not filled until psychological research on stereotypes advanced to the point of formulating these notions. Perhaps it will turn out that this gap would have been filled much sooner, if there were more psychologists who were not white men. But perhaps it will turn out the demographics of the field did not play a role in this and that the gap could not be filled until certain technological advances were made, for which demographics are irrelevant. Before we can know whether the gap was a hermeneutical injustice, we need to know more than we currently do about its cause.

## *2.1 Hermeneutical injustice and implicit bias*

It is relatively easy to see that implicit biases may play an important causal role in bringing about hermeneutical injustices. This is because implicit biases are likely to play an important role in bringing about hermeneutical marginalization. As Fricker notes, members of certain professions are more able to contribute to our common stock of concepts and ways of understanding ourselves than other people are. Politicians, lawyers, academics, and journalists clearly have more of a role in this than do cleaners, construction workers, and unemployed people. There are *many* factors that have posed barriers to those other than middle-class non-disabled white men advancing in these careers, but surely one factor has been implicit bias. If this is right, then implicit bias is implicated in the production of hermeneutical injustice.

But implicit bias may contribute to hermeneutical injustice in further ways as well, not just by contributing to the hermeneutical marginalization that is a background condition for it. In particular, implicit bias may make it more difficult for people to overcome hermeneutical gaps. Recall that hermeneutical injustice is not just about one's difficulties in self-understanding. It also concerns difficulties in communicating one's experience to others. Such communication is difficult enough with someone who has had very different experiences. But it is of course made more difficult by the presence of hermeneutical gaps. However, it can be overcome through what Fricker calls the corrective virtue of hermeneutical justice, on the part of one's audience: "an alertness or sensitivity to the possibility that the difficulty one's interlocutor is having as she tried to render something communicatively intelligible is due not to its being nonsense or her being a fool, but rather to some sort of gap in the hermeneutical resources" (2007: 169). An audience who possesses implicit biases about the person attempting to communicate may well find it very difficult to exercise this corrective virtue.

## *2.2 Hermeneutical injustice and stereotype threat*

Hermeneutical injustice may also, Stacey Goguen (2016) has argued, be caused by stereotype threat. Goguen argues that stereotype threat undermines one's ability to trust oneself, suggesting that it "can also have subtle but powerful consequences for the very foundations of our epistemic lives: our sense of ourselves as rational and reliable human knowers, and as full persons" (2016: 222). Consider, for example, the case of a woman in a very male field, who frequently finds herself in stereotype threat-provoking situations. In such situations, she is unable to recall and use the knowledge that she worked so hard to acquire, and struggles to articulate her thoughts. As this continues, she comes to doubt that she really is a competent and capable thinker. This lack of self-trust impairs one's ability to make sense of and communicate one's experiences, leading to hermeneutical injustice.

## 3. Remedies for epistemic injustice, stereotype threat and implicit bias

In Section 1, we saw that implicit biases may sometimes, but not always, give rise to testimonial injustices. We also considered ways that testimonial injustice may both cause and be caused by stereotype threat. In Section 2, we considered the ways that implicit bias and stereotype threat may cause hermeneutical injustice. Now we turn to considering the ways that remedies for epistemic injustice may impact on implicit bias and stereotype threat. Fricker devotes considerable attention to the issue of how to develop virtuous hearers. Our question is what impact Fricker's virtuous hearers might be expected to have on the levels of implicit bias and stereotype threat in the world.

Linda Alcoff (2010), drawing on the literature on implicit bias, raises concerns about the very conscious, rational mechanisms that Fricker invokes as ways of becoming a more virtuous hearer:

> These are all volitional practices, or ones we might consciously cultivate and practice. And this raises the first question I would direct to Fricker's account: if identity prejudice operates via a collective imaginary, as she suggests, through associated images and relatively unconscious connotations, can a successful antidote operate entirely as a conscious practice?
>
> *(2010: 132)*

Fricker responds to Alcoff, by citing work in social psychology by Margo Monteith (1993), demonstrating that people who become aware of prejudiced behavior in conflict with their avowed convictions are at least sometimes able to self-regulate and reduce the manifestation of prejudice. The decades since Monteith's paper lend even more support to the thought that self-regulation is possible, though they have complicated this thought as well.

Some of the most effective self-regulation, it turns out, itself takes place at an implicit rather than fully conscious level. Glaser and Knowles (2007) have shown that subjects who have a highly negative implicit attitude toward prejudice and a strong implicit belief that they themselves are prejudiced *are* able to block the manifestations of their implicit bias. Such subjects showed a very low correlation between levels of implicit bias against black people and tendency to "shoot" unarmed black people in the shooter bias task. (Other subjects showed a strong correlation between these.) Moskowitz and Li (2011) showed that consciously egalitarian subjects who reflected on a past instance of prejudice were able to inhibit the activation of stereotypes. Crucially, however, this happens without awareness that they are doing this.

Fully conscious self-regulation is also possible for implicit bias. But, crucially, this must be done in the right way. Simply trying not to be biased (Legault et al. 2011) can backfire, as can reflecting on how objective one is (Uhlmann and Cohen 2007). Instead, there are a variety of indirect measures that one can use – carefully forming the right sort of intentions (Mendoza et al. 2010), calling up images of counterstereotypical exemplars (Blair 2001), undergoing the right sort of training (Kawakami et al. 2005).[4] It is vital, then, not just to reflect upon the problem from the armchair – at the very least, one should use one's laptop to explore the internet for effective interventions. And Fricker notes, in her response to Alcoff, that this might well be an important element in cultivating epistemic virtue: she notes that it may well turn out that one should "go in for some sort of unreflective psychological work-out involving anti-prejudicial priming techniques" (Fricker 2010: 165–166).

The nature of implicit bias and stereotype threat, however, also push us to move away from individualistic solutions. These are due to widespread stereotypes in the culture, and individual efforts can only do a limited amount to combat the problem. To fully address these issues, institutional and cultural solutions are needed.[5] This might seem a disconnect with Fricker's work, which is in its original form mainly focused on individual hearers as cultivators of epistemic virtue. But Fricker notes:

> I am not wedded to reflective self-regulation as our only hope. In institutionalized competitive situations (such as appointments procedures, examinations, and so on), structural mechanisms – such as anonymization and double-blind marking and refereeing – are clearly indispensable.
>
> *(2010: 165)*

I think Fricker would also be very friendly to the thought that what is needed are not just individual solutions (reflective or non-reflective) and not just institutional procedures, but wider cultural change. In the end, we need all of these, a point extremely well-made by Michael Brownstein in his (2015) discussion of implicit bias:

> When conceptualizing the fight against implicit bias, our proximal focus should not be on harmonizing our internal states alone, nor should it be on changing the world in a broad sense, nor should it be on seeking out the right kinds of situations and avoiding the wrong ones as such. What I propose instead is a contextualist approach that blends all three from the get-go. It focuses on precisely those nodes at which our attitudes are affected by features of the ambient environment, and the ambient environment is in turn shaped by our attitudes and behavior.

All of these are also, I would argue, needed to effectively combat epistemic justice.

**Related chapters**: 1, 2, 3, 30, 31

## Notes

1 All references are to this work, unless otherwise indicated.
2 It is worth noting, however, that some have disputed this twofold division. Ishani Maitra (2011) argues that these two varieties are not so separate as they may seem, and Kristie Dotson (2012) argues that two varieties are not enough.
3 For more on implicit bias, see Brownstein's (2015) *Stanford Encyclopedia* entry, and the Kirwan Institute's (2015) *State of the Science* report.
4 For an excellent overview of these, see Madva (in progress). And see Rees (2016) for an argument that this is an excellent fit with virtue ethics, which is of course a part of the framework in which Fricker situates her project.
5 See Saul (2013) for an argument that this is where concern about implicit bias ultimately leads. See also Jacobson (2016) for an argument in favour of non-individual approaches to implicit bias, and Anderson (2012) for a discussion of institutional approaches to epistemic injustice.

## References

Alcoff, Linda. (2010). "Epistemic Identities", *Episteme* 7:2, 128–137.
Anderson, Elizabeth. (2012). "Epistemic Justice as a Virtue of Social Institutions", *Social Epistemology* 26:2, 163–173.

Blair, I. V., Ma, J. E., & Lenton, A. P. (2001). "Imagining Stereotypes away: The Moderation of Implicit Stereotypes through Mental Imagery", *Journal of Personality and Social Psychology*, 81:5, 828–841.

Brownstein, Michael. (2015). "Implicit Bias", in Edward N. Zalta (ed.) *The Stanford Encyclopedia of Philosophy* (Spring 2016 Edition), http://plato.stanford.edu/archives/spr2016/entries/implicit-bias/

Brownstein, Michael and Saul, Jennifer. (2016). "Introduction", in M. Brownstein and J. Saul (eds.) *Implicit Bias and Philosophy Volume 1: Metaphysics and Epistemology*. Oxford: Oxford University Press, 1–19.

Collins, Patricia Hill. (1990). *Black Feminist Thought: Knowledge, Consciousness, and the Politics of Empowerment*. New York: Routledge.

de Bruin, Boudewijn. (2014). "Self-Fulfilling Epistemic Injustice", SSRN: http://ssrn.com/abstract=2588430 or http://dx.doi.org/10.2139/ssrn.2588430

Dotson, Kristie. (2011). "Tracking Epistemic Violence, Tracking Practices of Silencing", *Hypatia* 26:2, 236–257.

Dotson, Kristie. (2012). "A Cautionary Tale: On Limiting Epistemic Oppression", *Frontiers* 33:1, 24–47.

Fricker, Miranda. (2007). *Epistemic Injustice: Power and the Ethics of Knowing*. Oxford: Oxford University Press.

Fricker, Miranda. (2010). "Replies to Alcoff, Goldberg and Hookway on *Epistemic Injustice*", *Episteme* 7:2, 164–178.

Glaser, Jack and Knowles, Eric. (2007). "Implicit Motivation to Control Prejudice", *Journal of Experimental Social Psychology* 44, 164–172.

Goguen, Stacey. (2016). "Stereotype Threat, Epistemic Injustice and Rationality", in M. Brownstein and J. Saul (eds.) *Implicit Bias and Philosophy Volume 1: Metaphysics and Epistemology*, 216–237. Oxford: Oxford University Press.

Jacobson, Anne. (2016). "Reducing Racial Bias: Attitudinal and Institutional Change", M. Brownstein and J. Saul (eds.) *Implicit Bias and Philosophy Volume 2*. Oxford: Oxford University Press, 173–190.

Kawakami, K., Dovidio, J. F., and van Kamp, S. (2005). "Kicking the Habit: Effects of Nonstereotypic Association Training and Correction Processes on Hiring Decisions", *Journal of Experimental Social Psychology* 41:1, 68–75.

Kirwan Institute. (2015). "State of the Science: Implicit Bias Review", http://kirwaninstitute.osu.edu/wp-content/uploads/2015/05/2015-kirwan-implicit-bias.pdf.

Legault, L., Gutsell, J., and Inzlicht, M. (2011). "Ironic Effects of Antiprejudice Messages: How Motivational Interventions Can Reduce (But also Increase) Prejudice", *Psychological Science* 22:12, 1472–1477.

Madva, Alex. (work in progress). "Biased Against Debiasing: On the Role of (Institutionally Sponsored) Self-Transformation in the Struggle Against Prejudice."

Maitra, Ishani. (2011). "The Nature of Epistemic Injustice", *Philosophical Books* 51:4, 195–211.

Medina, Jose. (2013). *The Epistemology of Resistance: Gender and Racial Oppression, Epistemic Injustice, and Resistant Imaginations*. Oxford: Oxford University Press.

Mendoza, Saaid, Gollwitzer, Peter, and Amodio, David. (2010). "Reducing the Expression of Implicit Stereotypes: Reflexive Control through Implementation Intentions", *Personality and Social Psychology Bulletin* 36:4, 512–523.

Monteith, Margo. (1993). "Self-Regulation of Prejudiced Responses: Implications for Progress in Prejudice-Reduction Efforts", *Journal of Personality and Social Psychology* 65:3, 469–485.

Moskowitz, Gordon and Li, Peizhong. (2011). "Egalitarian Goals Trigger Stereotype Inhibition", *Journal of Experimental Social Psychology* 47, 103–116.

Rees, Clea. (2016). "A Virtue Ethics Response to Implicit Bias", in M. Brownstein and J. Saul (eds.) *Implicit Bias and Philosophy Volume 2*. Oxford: Oxford University Press, 191–214.

Saul, Jennifer. (2013). "Scepticism and Implicit Bias", *Disputatio* 5:37, 243–263.

Steele, Claude. (2010). *Whistling Vivaldi: How Stereotypes Affect Us and What We Can Do*. New York: Norton.

Uhlmann, E. and Cohen, G. (2007). "'I Think It, Therefore It's True': Effects of Self-Perceived Objectivity on Hiring Discrimination", *Organizational Behavior and Human Decision Processes* 104:2, 207–223.

Yap, Audrey. (2015). "*Ad Hominem* Fallacies and Epistemic Credibility", in T. Bustamante and C. Dahlman (eds.), *Argument Types and Fallacies in Legal Argumentation*, 19–35. Law and Philosophy Library 112, New York: Springer.

# 23
# WHAT'S WRONG WITH EPISTEMIC INJUSTICE?
## Harm, vice, objectification, misrecognition

*Matthew Congdon*

### Introduction

The question posed in the title of this essay is part of a more general question, namely, how best to situate the concept of "epistemic injustice" within the contested terrain of competing traditions called "normative ethics."[1] As is well known, while differing normative theories might readily agree that some action is wrong, they may nonetheless differ vigorously as to why, with utilitarians emphasizing harmful consequences, virtue ethicists emphasizing a vicious character, and Kantians emphasizing the usurpation of one's standing as free and rational, to name just three amongst many possibilities. In light of this, a preliminary strategy for locating epistemic injustice on the normative map presents itself in the form of the question: what background ethical commitments do we assume when we critique epistemic injustice as, precisely, unjust? However, a cursory glance at the literature reveals the complexities involved in answering this question. In the short period since the publication of Miranda Fricker's *Epistemic Injustice*, a range of normative approaches to the distinctive wrongfulness of unjust epistemic practices have been adopted, with Fricker herself synthesizing multiple traditions, including Kantian, virtue-theoretic, and social contract elements within her own account.

Significant discussion has focused on elaborating the many harms that unjust forms of silencing, ignorance, and false belief generate, thereby operating implicitly with a roughly consequentialist set of assumptions concerning epistemic injustice's wrongfulness. This focus on the local and reverberating harms and losses of epistemic injustice – the loss of epistemic confidence, the marginalization of entire populations from hermeneutical practices, the creation of structural blockages in the circulation of knowledge, and the social suffering generated thereby – has been especially productive for large-scale systemic critiques of dysfunctional socio-epistemic practices (Fricker 2007: 46–51).[2] Yet at the same time it has been a recurrent theme that the wrongfulness of epistemic injustice is "not just a matter of bad consequences," to put it with Sally Haslanger (2014: 120). There is a deeper intrinsic indignity at work in various forms of epistemic injustice, as in, for example, unjustly downgrading one's trustworthiness via testimonial injustice or the forms of racial domination supporting and supported by what Charles Mills calls "epistemologies of ignorance."[3] In fleshing out these claims, both explicit and implicit appeals have been made to Kantian notions of dignity, personhood, moral equality, and other "pro-Enlightenment" ideals (Mills 1997: 129; Fricker 2007: 133–142). Finally, there has been a persistent emphasis on the importance of epistemic and ethical *virtues* in correcting conditions of epistemic injustice. While virtue epistemology in the past has emphasized the kinds of virtues speakers should adopt (such as accuracy and sincerity), work on epistemic injustice has brought increased attention to virtues applying to hearers (e.g., critical openness, humility), oppressed groups (e.g., what José Medina calls "meta-lucidity"), as well as entire institutions (most notably in Elizabeth Anderson's discussions of the virtue of "epistemic democracy") (Fricker 2007; Medina 2013; Anderson 2012). Already in this brief sketch we see resources drawn from each of the three most influential traditions in normative ethics: utilitarianism, Kantianism, and virtue ethics. Add to this various influences that do not fall neatly within these three traditions, such as feminist ethics, critical race theory, pragmatism, discourse ethics, and beyond, and the thought of disentangling this complex network of normative assumptions quickly becomes intimidating. Nevertheless, any critique of epistemic injustice will, at least implicitly, assume some notion of moral truth, as Mills affirms when he writes that epistemologies of ignorance generate "not merely ignorance of facts *with* moral implications but moral non-knowings, incorrect judgments about the rights and wrongs of moral situations themselves" (2007: 22).[4] This, in turn, implies commitments to some normative ethical theory or other. In light of the myriad approaches one might take towards the question of the wrongfulness of epistemic injustice, it is perhaps not surprising that Fricker's own account in *Epistemic Injustice* works by synthesizing rather than choosing between these options.

In this essay I navigate a course through these various normative ethical theories. In sections 1 through 3, I examine the wrong of epistemic injustice by discussing, respectively, (1) its harmful consequences, (2) its standing as an epistemic and ethical vice, and (3) its standing as a degrading objectification of a rational subject. Taking each of these models in turn allows us to illuminate how each of the three most influential strands of mainstream normative ethics – utilitarianism, virtue ethics, and Kantianism – could address the question of the wrongfulness of epistemic injustice. In Section 4, I defend an approach that, though massively influential in its own right, is not usually grouped amongst the standard normative ethical theories, namely, Hegelian recognition theory. I find that a multipronged conception of the wrongfulness of epistemic injustice as involving harm, vice, objectification, and misrecognition is required. My motivating thought is that examining these four approaches to the question, "What's wrong with epistemic injustice?" helps us locate the concept of epistemic injustice within the broader discipline of normative ethics.

## 1. Harmful consequences

An elaboration of the many harmful consequences of epistemic injustice in its various forms is a massive topic in its own right. Here I will focus primarily on *testimonial injustice*, which occurs when a hearer downgrades a speaker's credibility on the basis of an unfair identity prejudice, as when "the police do not believe you because you are black" (Fricker 2007: 1).

A utilitarian, harm-based approach to the wrongfulness of testimonial injustice is not entirely without historical precedent. As J.S. Mill wrote in his famous critique of the suppression of thought and speech in *On Liberty*, "the peculiar evil of silencing the expression of an opinion" consists in its "robbing the human race . . . of the opportunity of exchanging error for truth" (1977: 229). As Mill goes on to elaborate at length, the wrongfulness of silencing opinion can be appreciated to a huge extent by elaborating the concrete forms of epistemic loss and error generated thereby. Straightforwardly, the hearer misses out on information, and the speaker misses out on the chance to express that information. In turn, anyone who may have benefited as a result of the sharing of that knowledge also suffers a loss. These more local harms can generate broader deleterious effects, constituting "a moment of dysfunction in the overall epistemic practice or system" (Fricker 2007: 43). Beyond the epistemic harms and losses generated thereby, Mill might also point out that conditions of epistemic injustice cut us off from knowledge of those "different experiments of living," those forms of life unlike our own, exposure to which promotes the development of human flourishing (1977: 260–261). Though Mill's primary concern was institutional censorship and not the forms of prejudice-based silencing Fricker explores as "testimonial injustice," it would not be difficult to extend the utilitarian critique to the latter.

Indeed, something approximating this is already at work in the notion of "epistemic consequentialism," an approach in social epistemology that judges epistemic norms according to their tendency to maximize basic epistemic goods, such as relevant true belief.[5] In a way that an ethical naturalist like Mill would have found favorable, it follows from the notion of a "naturalized" social epistemology, according to which epistemic practices manifest themselves through a material, social, and historical base, that these epistemic harms entail concrete practical harms beyond the purely epistemic (Quine 1969; Kornblith 1994).[6] Reliance upon a trusting epistemic community seems to be a minimal condition for the successful realization of just about any meaningful project within the social world, from mere survival to higher-order cultural pursuits.[7] Accordingly, epistemic dysfunctions have deeper effects on human action, work, and collective forms of world- and meaning-making. A consequentialist, harm-based critique of epistemic injustice could thus be developed from an assessment of the impact of these deleterious effects upon general social welfare.

This view seems well-equipped to capture the frequently emphasized point that an exclusive focus on isolated acts of testimonial injustice should be rejected in favor of a view that monitors the wider range of harms reverberating temporally and socially outwards from the initial act (Medina 2013: 33–34). Yet several authors, Fricker among them, have suggested that a sole focus on the harmful consequences of testimonial injustice, no matter how grave, leaves something out of the moral picture (Fricker 2007: 43–46, 129–146; Haslanger 2014: 120–121; Wanderer 2012: 148–169; Pohlhaus, Jr. 2014: 99–114). For the wrongfulness of testimonial injustice seems to involve a form of moral injury done to the speaker that is more than the sum of the harms accrued. Discussing this point, Jeremy Wanderer describes a case of testimonial injustice in which a white beachgoer ignores a black lifeguard's warnings about a shark sighted in the vicinity (2012: 149–153).[8] Wanderer asks us to suppose that the swimmer's downgrading of the lifeguard's credibility is the result of unjust racial bias, a fatal mistake leading to his being gobbled up by the shark. Even if we imagine that the swimmer is the primary (or sole) bearer of harms generated by ignoring the lifeguard's warning, it does not eliminate the notion that the swimmer did an injustice *to* the lifeguard by downgrading the latter's credibility on the basis of racial prejudice. There is a lingering feeling that the swimmer wronged the lifeguard in a distinctly "second-personal" sense, to put it with Stephen Darwall (2006).[9] What Wanderer's example makes vivid is that the locations of accumulated harms fail to track the locations of perpetrator and victim in such cases, where the perpetrator-victim relation appears to be a second-personal relation irreducible to direct consequentialist analysis. This has led some, Fricker included, to insist upon separating out the "secondary harms" of epistemic injustice (i.e., those epistemic and practical harms that reverberate outwards from the initial act) from the "primary harm" done to the speaker herself (Fricker 2007: 43–51). This idea (to which I will return in Section 3) moves us beyond a merely consequentialist frame.

## 2. Epistemic and ethical vice

Another reason motivating us to move beyond the consequentialist frame is the wish to give greater weight to the notion that the hearer not only causes various forms of damage and loss, but, more subtly, adopts a morally untoward *stance* towards the speaker that reflects a morally deficient *character*. As Fricker stresses, the root of testimonial injustice lies in an unjust bias that has become second nature, such that the hearer is affectively and culpably resistant to counterevidence. It is thus not surprising that conceptions of virtue and vice have played central roles in discussions of epistemic injustice.

Fricker's own account bridges virtue epistemology and virtue ethics by arguing that credibility judgments (i.e., judgments concerning a speaker's competence and sincerity with regard to a particular bit of testimony) may be viewed as complex forms of ethical perception (Fricker 2007: 60–85). Rather than viewing credibility judgments solely as the result of inferences, a virtue-based account urges that we directly *perceive* speakers as credible or incredible, sincere or deceptive, competent or incompetent. To say that such perception is "direct" is not, however, to say that such perception is unmediated or simply given. Rather, one's capacity for rightly perceiving the credibility of persons is a developed result, mediated by an upbringing and culture that fosters the "critical openness" exhibited by virtuous hearers (Fricker 2007: 69). With this, credibility judgments are modeled on the Aristotelian notion of *phronesis* as a perceptual capacity, in a way that shares deep affinities with neo-Aristotelian accounts of moral perception found in John McDowell, David Wiggins, and Martha Nussbaum.[10]

Testimonial injustice occurs when counter-rational forms of unfair prejudice and identity power distort one's perception of others qua informants. Accordingly, it may be viewed as a vice in an Aristotelian sense: a maldevelopment of capacities necessary for human flourishing. This helpfully brings out the sense in which the typical case of testimonial injustice is not simply an isolated instance of unfair credibility downgrading, but the result of a habituated, socio-historically inculcated prejudice distorting the hearer's judgment. This also usefully accounts for the habituated character of what Mills calls "white ignorance," which distorts one's takes on reality not only at the level of reflective judgment and assertion, but more subtly in memory, unreflective inference, and low-level perception, given one's inheritance of, and upbringing within, a racist culture (2007: 23–24; 1998). The problem consists not simply in a one-off wrongful decision on the part of the hearer, but in a flawed epistemic and ethical character. For this reason, Fricker describes the corresponding virtue of epistemic justice as a critical social awareness that is distinctively reflexive in its operation, enabling the hearer to identify the forms of identity power structuring a communicative engagement and to adjust her credibility judgments accordingly (2007: 98).

A worry frequently raised at this point is that a focus on individual virtue can only serve as a partial remedy for epistemic injustice, insofar as the latter is not only a transactional injustice between individuals but also structurally embedded in social institutions and practices.[11] As Elizabeth Anderson puts the point, "the larger systems by which we organize the training of inquirers and the circulation, uptake, and incorporation of individuals' epistemic contributions to the construction of knowledge may need to be reformed to ensure that justice is done to each knower, and to groups of inquirers" (2012: 165). Interestingly, Anderson takes this to require *not* that we abandon talk of virtues but that we widen our view to include the notion of *institutional* virtues.[12] Anderson's specific suggestions focus on group integration and social equality in fundamental socio-epistemic institutions, particularly education, aiming at the institutional virtue she calls "epistemic democracy" (2012: 172).[13]

Nonetheless, there remains the apparent fact that testimonial injustice is not just *wrong*, but that it *wrongs someone*. Even if the virtue-ethical account is correct, some account is still needed of the indignity suffered by the speaker herself. In Section 4 I will argue that this is best captured as a failure of recognition. First, however, we should consider Fricker's account of the indignity suffered in testimonial injustice as "epistemic objectification."

## 3. Epistemic objectification

Epistemic objectification is meant to articulate the sense in which testimonial injustice does a direct and intrinsic moral wrong to the speaker by treating her as less than a full epistemic subject. Mirroring Kant's *Groundwork* distinction between treating a person as an end in itself and a means to an end, Fricker distinguishes between two senses in which a speaker may be treated as an occasion for knowledge: first, as an "informant," a competent and sincere epistemic agent whose testimony is taken up by others as reason to believe, or at least take seriously, a communicated belief, and second, as a "source of information," an observable feature of others' experienced environment from whom information may be gleaned through perception and inference (Fricker 2007: 132). To be treated as an *informant* is to be treated as an active participant in the epistemic community while to be treated as a *source of information* is to be treated as any other passive observable object. As Fricker notes, these are not mutually exclusive ways of treating persons, and it is a morally innocent feature of epistemic life to treat others (and ourselves) as sources of information, as when I infer the rain outside from your wet clothes or perceive that I am hungry from my own growling stomach. Fricker's Kantian suggestion is that treating someone as a source of information takes a turn towards injustice when one is treated as a *mere* source of information. In laying out his famous "humanity" formulation of the categorical imperative, Kant further distinguished between treating persons as means and treating persons as *mere* means (2012: 4, 429). Just as my leaning on your arm to steady my balance does not imply that I view you simply as a living bannister, my inferring the weather from the wetness of your clothes does not imply that I view you merely as an epistemic object. It is when I treat you *solely* as a means, or *solely* as an epistemic object, that I violate you in your very standing as a rational subject. This degradation from epistemic subject to object is, Fricker argues, precisely the demotion in status that takes place in testimonial injustice.

However, certain instances do not so easily fit the objectification model. The following case illustrates the point: Mr. B, a Bosnian citizen and Muslim, is held without charge in Guantanamo for seven years, where he is subject to interrogational torture.[14] His capture was ordered as part of a preemptive sweep for collaborators in an embassy bomb plot. In fact, however, Mr. B had no part in or knowledge of this plot or related actions. Repeatedly, Mr. B tells his captors that he knows nothing, which only leads to further torture. Mr. B sincerely and competently offers the testimony, "I know nothing," which is discredited on the basis of prejudicial bias concerning his Muslim identity. While multiple injustices are at work here, it is clear that testimonial injustice is among them. Yet characterizing this as epistemic objectification is misleading for at least two reasons. First, the testimonial injustice at work would not be possible unless the interrogators view Mr. B as the bearer of critical information and so treat him as a competent epistemic subject. Second, as soon as Mr. B's captors *admonish* him for being deceptive, they thereby include him within the sphere of potential informants to whom norms of epistemic exchange apply. Mr. B is thus treated as a subject in the dual sense of (1) being the subject of knowledge and (2) being subject to epistemic norms. To be sure, it is nowhere part of Fricker's account of epistemic objectification that the speaker must be viewed *utterly* as an object by the hearer in order for the case to count as an offense.[15] Yet the objection here is not just that some degree of epistemic subjectivity persists beyond the degrading effects of testimonial injustice, but that there exist forms of epistemic injustice that structurally *depend* upon the speaker's epistemic subjectivity, rendering the objectification model at least one-sided.

In a similar criticism of the objectification model, Gaile Pohlhaus, Jr. (2012a; 2012b) has pointed out cases of "epistemic exploitation" in which speakers' claims are not rejected or ignored *en masse* but are selectively affirmed and denied by the hearer according to how well they confirm the hearer's existing doxastic commitments. We may imagine a boss happy to lend credibility to an employee's positive testimony about workplace conditions until that testimony includes reports of sexual harassment. Once again, a hearer's very efforts to epistemically exploit a speaker presuppose as a condition for their success a recognition of the latter's authority as at least an epistemic "semi-subject" (Pohlhaus, Jr. 2012a: 104). At work here is not objectification *per se* but a form of asymmetry between subjects that recalls the structure of exploitation described in Hegel's master-slave dialectic (1977: §§178–196). The master's desire that the slave recognize the former's authority cannot be satisfied without recognizing the latter as bearing an authority of his or her own. Thus, we should refine Fricker's point by clarifying that only *some* instances of testimonial injustice fit the model of epistemic objectification. The broader range of cases involves a failed relation between persons that I will develop as *failures of epistemic recognition*.

## 4. Failures of epistemic recognition

A central thesis of recognition theory is that a positive relation-to-self is dependent upon, and therefore may be undone by, relations with others.[16] According to this thesis, one's self-worth is developed and upheld through acts of recognition, understood as expressive acts through which individuals and institutions convey acknowledgment of the worth or normative standing of others. The experience of injustice is thus understood as a dissonance between one's sense of self-worth and the expressive dimension of an act or practice that withholds or denies validation of that worth. We see that this relates directly to the wrongful denial of one's standing as a knower when we note that "knower" is a *normative concept*, one that refers not only to what someone *is* descriptively, but to what someone can *do*, what roles someone may legitimately assume, in the context of socio-epistemic practices. If "knower" is a value-laden concept in this way, then regarding oneself as a knower is a positive relation-to-self, a way of seeing oneself as bearing worth or normative status.[17] This allows us to connect the experience of epistemic injustice directly to Axel Honneth's description of the moral injury of misrecognition: "Because the normative self-image of each and every individual human being . . . is dependent on the possibility of being continually backed up by others, the experience of being disrespected carries with it the danger of an injury that can bring the identity of the person as a whole to the point of collapse" (1995: 132). This is remarkably close to Fricker's own claims that repeated or severe acts of epistemic injustice work to degrade one's self-confidence as a knower and, even more strongly, may "inhibit the very formation of self" (2007: 55). Hence, epistemic-injustice-as-recognition-failure may be understood as a withholding or denial of forms of social validation that are necessary for the development and maintenance of the specific relation-to-self involved in regarding oneself as a knower.[18]

We can venture beyond this quite general description by offering an elaboration of the specific kinds of epistemic recognition we may justifiably view as owed to one another. In *The Struggle for Recognition*, Honneth differentiates between three fundamental modes of recognition: love, respect, and esteem (1995: 92–130). *Love* refers to those forms of care and attentiveness that express to the beloved that she deserves some degree of support and nurturing from others. Including yet extending beyond intimate familial and erotic relationships, recognition-as-loving-care affirms persons in their neediness and particularity. In contrast to this particularistic form of recognition, *respect* refers to the conferral of moral worth in a universal, egalitarian sense, as in Kantian respect for persons as ends in themselves or as rights-bearing persons. Finally, *esteem* refers to the conferral of worth on the basis of a person's distinctive accomplishments, character, contributions to society, and other praiseworthy attributes. Unlike respect, esteem is indexed to individuality and thus distributed differentially. Love, respect, and esteem each serve as normatively distinct modes of conferring social validation upon others, whether in their neediness, their standing as a moral and legal equal, or in their unique and praiseworthy contributions to social life.[19]

Though it has not been explicitly undertaken in the recognition literature, it would not be difficult to extend this three-part schema of recognition in order to reveal love, respect, and esteem as each bearing a special role in epistemic practice. Indeed, the very fact that social epistemologists like Fricker speak of epistemically distinct forms of "disrespect" and "dishonor" at least implies contrasting concepts of epistemic social validation.[20] *Epistemic respect* could refer to an expressive act conveying the acknowledgment of the minimal set of capacities we grant to any knower whatsoever, irrespective of particular expertise, experience, or situatedness (e.g., a minimal capacity for self-reflexiveness, a minimal capacity to offer and ask for justifications, etc.), as well as a minimal set of rights and responsibilities we afford any knower whatsoever (e.g., the right not to have one's epistemic credentials dismissed on the basis of bad prejudice). *Epistemic esteem* could refer to recognition of more specialized forms of epistemic accomplishment not necessarily shared by others (stemming from, e.g., expertise, a track record of exceptional honesty, or the kinds of situated epistemic advantage highlighted by standpoint theorists). In addition to epistemic respect and esteem, we may even speak of *epistemic love*, referring to those forms of epistemic nurturing and attentiveness that confirm a burgeoning knower's epistemic trust and confidence, as well as epistemic skills like literacy and communication in early childhood.[21] The corresponding form of misrecognition in the case of epistemic love could be termed *epistemic neglect*: one's wrongful exclusion from the community of knowers as a result of poor or non-existent learning conditions in early childhood, in particular the relations of care, patience, and attentiveness characteristic of loving care in a broad sense.[22]

The notion that we owe epistemic respect equally to any knower whatsoever may at first appear perplexing, for the obvious reason that knowers are knowers to varying degrees of competence and sincerity across different areas, implying that no two knowers are "equal" in any straightforward sense. It is not easy to specify a precise list of what goes into the basic normative standing that is confirmed via epistemic respect, yet there is theoretical precedent for the idea. Famously, H.P. Grice (1975) argued for a set of conversational norms derived from a "Principle of Cooperation," norms which "apply to conversation as such, irrespective of its subject matter," and which include the imperatives to be informative, be succinct, not assert things we believe to be false, etc. More recently, Nancy Daukas has defended an *epistemic principle of charity*, derived from the thought that "normal practices of epistemic interaction and cooperation require that members of an epistemic community typically extend to one another the presumption that they meet some threshold level of epistemic credibility" (2006: 110). These cautious moves already begin to elaborate the minimal normative standing owed to *any* knower irrespective of competence or sincerity. It seems fair to assume that this would include, e.g., general prohibitions on associating one's race with deceptiveness or one's gender with irrational emoting. There exist further (though contentious) strategies for elaborating thicker notions of the kinds of rights we tacitly attribute to any being we recognize as a knower, by arguing that implicit commitments to such rights are built into our epistemic and communicative practices themselves, as in Jürgen Habermas' (1990) discourse ethics. Acknowledging some minimal notion of epistemic equality via epistemic respect is, moreover, compatible with simultaneously valuing different knowers differentially according to their epistemic strengths via *epistemic esteem*, a non-egalitarian mode of epistemic recognition indexed to relative competence and sincerity. Hence, my *epistemically esteeming* A more highly than B on a given topic in light of A's expertise and B's lack thereof is consistent with my *epistemically respecting* A and B as epistemic equals and, moreover, on par with the demands of epistemic justice.

Acts of testimonial injustice may be described as involving disrespect and disesteem simultaneously or separately. Consider an instance in which a female professor reads her students' anonymous course evaluations at the end of the semester to find a number of disparagingly sexist comments, including a comment from a student who describes her lecture style as "emoting."[23] Assuming the professor was lecturing on a topic within her expertise and that the student's comment about "emoting" has sexist bias at its root, this case may be viewed simultaneously as an instance of epistemic disesteem *and* epistemic disrespect. It is a form of *disesteem* insofar as the professor's unique and hard-won standing as an intellectual authority on this topic fails to be valued by precisely the kind of hearer who is in a position to validate that standing.[24] It is, moreover, a form of *disrespect*, insofar as associating *any* knower's gender with irrational emoting patently violates the minimal normative expectations we hold simply as knowers, expert or not.

So far I have focused on the case of testimonial injustice. We can briefly gesture towards the possibilities for extending this account to other forms of epistemic injustice by drawing some connections to Charles Mills' notion of an epistemic social contract. On his account, one of the fundamental ways in which white supremacy has both explicitly and implicitly shaped modern society is through a tacit agreement amongst the beneficiaries of racial oppression to a set of norms determining criteria for "factual and moral knowledge" (1997: 17). As a result, an "inverted epistemology" is developed in which social conditions of racial domination create an epistemic milieu that hides from view those very conditions, "producing the ironic outcome that whites will in general be unable to understand the world they themselves have made" (1997: 18). Though the world is persistently seen wrongly, the tacit epistemic social contract works to ensure that certain false beliefs will nonetheless be met with epistemic esteem, while disconfirming testimony and experience will be rejected as incoherent. The inverted epistemology Mills describes may thus be understood as an inverted world of epistemic misrecognition, involving excesses of unwarranted epistemic esteem for its beneficiaries alongside a structural proclivity towards epistemic disrespect, disesteem, and neglect for knowers who speak against it.[25]

## 5. Conclusion

I have explored how four important traditions in normative ethics could treat the wrongfulness of epistemic injustice. The general conclusion we may derive from the above discussion is that a multipronged approach best suits the critical diagnosis of epistemic injustice as simultaneously involving harm, vice, objectification, and misrecognition. As we saw, problems that arise for some of the positions cannot be resolved without reference to at least one of the others. More specifically, however, I have argued that the concept of epistemic recognition is an essential component in our efforts to make explicit the normative underpinnings of the critique of epistemic injustice. When we view "knower" as a value concept that may be conferred or withheld by others, it is not surprising that humans not only by nature desire to know, as Aristotle pointed out, but also desire to be recognized as knowers.

**Related chapters**: 1, 2, 3, 21, 27

## Notes

1 I am grateful to Scott Aikin, Ian James Kidd, José Medina, Karen Ng, Andrea Pitts, Gaile Pohlhaus, Jr., and Francey Russell for comments and conversations regarding this chapter. I am also grateful to the New York Wittgenstein Workshop, which generously hosted a discussion of an earlier draft. Particular thanks go to my commentator, Joel de Lara; the organizers, Eddie Guetti and Cayla Clinkenbeard; as

well as Alice Crary, Adam Gies, Janna van Grunsven, Kathleen Kelly, Mahmoud Hassanieh, and the other participants for a stimulating discussion.
2. Fricker offers an extensive discussion of what she calls the "secondary harms" of epistemic injustice, which take both epistemic and practical forms.
3. The term is introduced in Mills (1997:18), and given further elaboration in Mills (2007) and Alcoff (2007).
4. Others writing on epistemic injustice and epistemologies of ignorance have also defended realist commitments that include moral objectivity. See, e.g., Alcoff, (2007: 53); Fricker (2010b: 168–9). I discuss and defend these realist commitments in Congdon (2015).
5. For a critical discussion of epistemic consequentialism in relation to Fricker's *Epistemic Injustice*, see Coady (2010: 101–113). Coady associates the consequentialist view with Goldman (1999).
6. For a discussion by way of Quine and nineteenth-century Marxism, see Mills (2007).
7. Recent "genealogical" approaches to epistemology have done work to carefully explore the ways in which socio-epistemic practices emerge out of basic survival needs in a "State of Nature" (where, e.g., the advantages of pooling knowledge about which foods are good to eat, which are poisonous, motivate socio-epistemic development). See Williams (2002) and Craig (1990).
8. Wanderer's example occurs in a South African context, and so the use above of 'white' and 'black' is a simplification of the more complex set of social identities at work in Wanderer's original presentation of this scenario (2012: 150, note 3).
9. Cf. Thompson (2004) and Darwall (2013).
10. See, especially, the first three essays in McDowell (1998); Wiggins (1998); Nussbaum (1990).
11. For different versions of this worry, see Alcoff (2010: 132–134); Anderson (2012: 163–173); and Medina (2013: 79–89).
12. Fricker (2010) has embraced this notion as well.
13. Cf. Anderson (2006).
14. This is a simplified version of the now famous case in the Supreme Court decision, Boumediene vs. Bush, which resulted in the plaintiff's release after spending 2002–2009 in military custody (Boumediene: 2012).
15. Fricker is explicit on this point: "[T]here will be few contexts in which a hearer's prejudice is so insanely thoroughgoing that he fails to regard his interlocutor as a subject of knowledge *at all*" (2007: 134–135).
16. For variations on this thesis, see Honneth (1995); Taylor (1994); Brandom (2007); Butler (2004); and Bernstein, (2015).
17. In the sense just sketched, "knower'" is a normative concept in a distinctively *epistemic* sense. One might object that this does not bring us all the way to the *moral* normativity required to claim that failure to recognize someone as a knower counts as a moral violation. Yet the necessary bridge between epistemic and moral normativity can be provided in at least two ways: first, by noting the structural necessity that some minimal sense of epistemic self-worth must play within the broader range of activities that constitute a flourishing life; second, by noting that the capacity to be recognized as a knower is a precondition for successfully offering moral testimony, e.g., when one wishes to voice the existence of wrongdoing. Thanks to Mahmoud Hassanieh for pressing this point. I discuss the latter strand of thought in Congdon (2016).
18. Conceiving of epistemic injustice as a form of recognition failure has some precedent. See McConkey (2004:198–205). Pohlhaus, Jr. also draws on the notion of recognition (by way of Simone de Beauvoir) in her account of epistemic exploitation (2012a: 105–106).
19. Recently, Honneth has suggested adding a fourth form of recognition to his typology which he refers to as "antecedent recognition," a more basic form of recognition that must already be in place in order for love, respect, and esteem to be possible (2008: 40–52 and 90, note 70). Whether or not this fourth type should be acknowledged does not significantly affect the present discussion, so I leave it aside here.
20. For example: "testimonial injustice . . . deprives the subject of a certain fundamental form of respect" (Fricker 2007: 46) and, "When one is wrongfully mistrusted . . . one is dishonoured" (Fricker 2007: 46).
21. Epistemic love could be viewed as extending into adulthood as well with, for example, the practice of extending the "benefit of the doubt" to speakers in special circumstances that warrant it, particularly when basic relations of epistemic trust and confidence are under threat and require repair.
22. For a recent philosophical exploration of epistemic injustice in an educational context, see Haslanger (2014).
23. This kind of example is unfortunately commonplace. Recent empirical studies have confirmed the long suspected fact of gender bias at work in university student evaluations. See, e.g., MacNell, Driscoll, and Hunt (2015).

24 The status of the student *as* a student enrolled in this professor's class is important here, since we would deny that just *anyone*, no matter how far removed from the professor's classroom, has an obligation to recognize her expertise. The student in this scenario is in a privileged position to either confer or deny recognition in this case.

25 This raises difficult questions concerning the relation between recognition and ideology. See, e.g., Axel Honneth (2007).

## References

Alcoff, Linda Martín (2010) "Epistemic Identities," *Episteme* 7(2): 128–137.
Alcoff, Linda Martín (2007) "Epistemologies of Ignorance: Three Types," in S. Sullivan and N. Tuana (eds.) *Race and Epistemologies of Ignorance*, Albany, NY: SUNY Press.
Anderson, Elizabeth (2006) "The Epistemology of Democracy," *Episteme* 3(1–2): 8–22.
Anderson, Elizabeth (2012) "Epistemic Injustice as a Virtue of Social Institutions", *Social Epistemology* 26(2): 163–173.
Bernstein, J.M. (2015) *Torture and Dignity: An Essay on Moral Injury*, Chicago: Chicago University Press.
Boumediene, Lakhdar (2012) "My Guantánamo Nightmare", New York Times, January 7, 2012: SR9
Brandom, Robert (2007) "The Structure of Desire and Recognition: Self-Consciousness and Self-Constitution", *Philosophy and Social Criticism* 33(1): 127–150.
Butler, Judith (2004) *Precarious Life: The Powers of Mourning and Violence*, London: Verso.
Coady, David (2010) "Two Concepts of Epistemic Injustice", *Episteme* 7(2): 101–113.
Congdon, Matthew (2016) "Wronged Beyond Words: On the Publicity and Repression of Moral Injury", *Philosophy & Social Criticism* 42(8): 815–834.
Congdon, Matthew (2015) "Epistemic Injustice in the Space of Reasons", *Episteme* 12(1): 75–93.
Craig, Edward (1990) *Knowledge and the State of Nature: An Essay in Conceptual Synthesis*, Oxford: Clarendon Press.
Darwall, Stephen (2006) *The Second-Person Standpoint*, Cambridge: Harvard University Press.
Darwall, Stephen (2013) "Bipolar Obligation," in *Morality, Authority, and Law: Essays in Second-Personal Ethics I*, Oxford: Oxford University Press.
Daukas, Nancy (2006) "Epistemic Trust and Social Location", *Episteme* 3(1–2): 109–124.
Fricker, Miranda (2007) *Epistemic Injustice: Power and the Ethics of Knowing*, New York: Oxford.
Fricker, Miranda (2010a) "Can There Be Institutional Virtues?," in Tamar Szabó Gendler and John Hawthorne (eds.) *Oxford Studies in Epistemology*, Oxford: Oxford University Press, vol. 3.
Fricker, Miranda (2010b) "Replies to Alcoff, Goldberg, and Hookway on Epistemic Injustice", *Episteme* 7(2): 164–178.
Grice, H.P. (1975) "Logic and Conversation," in Peter Cole and Jerry L. Morgan (eds.) *Syntax and Semantics*, New York: Academic Press, vol. 3.
Goldman, Alvin (1999) *Knowledge in a Social World*, Oxford: Oxford University Press.
Habermas, Jürgen (1990) "Discourse Ethics: Notes on a Program of Philosophical Justification," in *Moral Consciousness and Communicative Action*, trans. Christian Lenhardt and Shierry Weber Nicholson, Cambridge: MIT Press.
Haslanger, Sally (2014) "Studying While Black: Trust, Opportunity, and Disrespect", *Du Bois Review: Social Science Research on Race* 11(1): 109–136.
Hegel, G.W.F. (1977) *Phenomenology of Spirit*, trans. A.V. Miller, Oxford: Oxford University Press.
Honneth, Axel (1995) *The Struggle for Recognition: The Moral Grammar of Social Conflicts*, trans. Joel Anderson, Cambridge: MIT Press.
Honneth, Axel (2007) "Recognition as Ideology," in Bert van den Brink and David Owen (eds.), *Recognition and Power: Axel Honneth and the Tradition of Critical Social Theory* Cambridge: Cambridge University Press.
Honneth, Axel (2008) *Reification: A New Look at an Old Idea*, Oxford: Oxford University Press.
Hookway, Christopher (2010) "Some Varieties of Epistemic Injustice: Reflections on Fricker", *Episteme* 7(2): 151–163.
Kant, Immanuel (2012) *Groundwork of the Metaphysics of Morals*, Revised Edition, trans. Mary Gregor and Jens Timmerman, Cambridge: Cambridge University Press.
Kornblith, Hilary (ed.) (1994) *Naturalizing Epistemology*, 2nd Edition Cambridge: MIT Press.
MacNell, Lillian, Adam Driscoll, and Andrea N. Hunt (2015) "What's in a Name: Exposing Gender Bias in Student Ratings of Teachers", *Innovative Higher Education* 40(4): 291–303.

McConkey, Jane (2004) "Knowledge and Acknowledgment: 'Epistemic Injustice' as a Problem of Recognition", *Politics* 24(3): 198–205.
McDowell, John (1998) *Mind, Value, and Reality* Cambridge: Harvard University Press.
Medina, José (2013) *The Epistemology of Resistance: Gender and Racial Oppression, Epistemic Injustice, and Resistant Imaginations* Oxford: Oxford University Press.
Mill, J.S. (1977) "On Liberty," in J.M. Robson (ed.), *Collected Works of John Stuart Mill* University of Toronto Press, vol. 18.
Mills, Charles (1997) *The Racial Contract* Ithaca: Cornell University Press.
Mills, Charles (1998) "Alternative Epistemologies," in *Blackness Visible: Essays on Philosophy and Race* Ithaca: Cornell University Press.
Mills, Charles (2007) "White Ignorance," in Shannon Sullivan and Nancy Tuana (eds.), *Race and Epistemologies of Ignorance* Albany: State University of New York Press.
Nussbaum, Martha (1990) "The Discernment of Perception: An Aristotelian Conception of Private and Public Rationality," in Martha Nussbaum (ed.), *Love's Knowledge: Essays on Philosophy and Literature* Oxford: Oxford University Press.
Pohlhaus, Jr., Gaile (2014a) "Discerning the Primary Epistemic Harm in Cases of Testimonial Injustice", *Social Epistemology* 28(2): 99–114.
Pohlhaus, Jr., Gaile (2014b) "On Subjects, Objects, and Others", *Social Epistemology Review and Reply Collective* 3(6): 44–50.
Quine, W.V.O. (1969) "Epistemology Naturalized," in *Ontological Relativity and Other Essays* New York: Columbia University Press.
Taylor, Charles (1994) "The Politics of Recognition," in Amy Gutmann (ed.), *Multiculturalism and 'The Politics of Recognition'*, Expanded Edition, Princeton: Princeton University Press.
Thompson, Michael (2004) "What Is It to Wrong Someone? A Puzzle about Justice," in R. Jay Wallace, Philip Pettit, Samuel Scheffler, and Michael Smith (eds.), *Reason and Value: Themes from the Moral Philosophy of Joseph Raz*, Oxford: Oxford University Press.
Wanderer, Jeremy (2012) "Addressing Testimonial Injustice: Being Ignored and Being Rejected", *Philosophical Quarterly* 62(246):148–69.
Wiggins, David (1998) "Deliberation and Practical Reason," in *Needs, Value, and Truth*, 3rd Edition, Oxford: Oxford University Press.
Williams, Bernard (2002) *Truth and Truthfulness: An Essay in Genealogy*, Princeton: Princeton University Press.

# 24
# EPISTEMIC AND POLITICAL AGENCY

*Lorenzo C. Simpson*

These remarks on epistemic injustice are drawn from an account of the hermeneutics of agency. I consider the epistemic injustice implicated in assertions about the agential deficiencies of members of disadvantaged groups, as well as the injustice of withholding what I call "semantic authority" from the interpretations of social life that would underwrite the social agency of such persons.

I argue that to fully understand global injustices, we need a way of making salient the discrepancy between, on the one hand, the historically sedimented conditions that continue to *impede* agency for some and, on the other hand, the enabling, but often hidden or unacknowledged, conditions that *facilitate* agency for others. I claim that drawing a distinction between what I call first-order agency and second-order agency allows us to do this insofar as this distinction disaggregates the volitional and epistemic components of agency. By "second order agency," I refer to the ability to produce, acquire, or to avail oneself of the facilitating conditions of action in the first-order sense. While those conditions may be of both a material/structural and of an epistemic sort, in this essay I concentrate primarily on the latter sorts of condition, the epistemic. And I argue that if persons who suffer under current conditions appear, through their actions or inaction, to be culpable for their own suffering, we ought to heed the aforementioned distinctions, for it may be the case that we do not yet truly understand their choices. To understand a person's choices will require that we engage in a hermeneutical investigation undertaken under what I call the constraint of narrative representability. That is, we must ask: how do things appear from the first-person perspective within which these choices were made? Understanding such choices in this manner can bring into focus cases where the agent making the choices is not culpable for their failure to make life-enhancing choices (while, of course, still leaving open the possibility that in some cases they may be), but where instead an injustice of an epistemic sort is present. By "an injustice of an epistemic sort," I refer to the injustice of failing to acknowledge the agent's epistemic state when that state, or the structural conditions responsible for it, unfairly compromise the agent's ability to act. This is the *compound injustice* of having one's agency compromised by an epistemic limitation for which one bears no culpability and of nevertheless being judged or blamed for that lack of agency.

## On agency, the *politics of memory*, and epistemic injustice

In a recent book, Thomas McCarthy (2009) provides a wide-ranging treatment of matters of global justice. Central among his themes is the claim that global justice requires sustained attention to the repair of the "harmful effects of past injustice." In matters of race, the persistence of perniciously systematic racial stratification in the US – despite the discrediting of the biological significance of race and the formal legal protections afforded by the civil rights movement – is instructively on display in *pre*-Katrina New Orleans. New Orleans, well before the levees broke, was paradigmatically illustrative of the kinds of social practice that reproduce racial formations and in a way that fully warrants McCarthy's application of the term "neo-racism." Among the factors operative in this twenty-first century American city were the mutually reinforcing relationships between public educational expectations (and delivery), the predominance of low-wage service sector employment opportunities for unskilled workers, and the "homestead exemption" tax policy. The latter exempts a designated class of real estate owners from having to pay property taxes which, of course, fund the public schools.

Not only were high levels of truancy among New Orleans' African-American school-aged population not regarded as an aberration, but, worse yet, their *teachers* showed up only infrequently. This too was apparently unexceptional. And it did not seem to matter. Or rather it all worked out "all too well" because the predominance of jobs open to the New Orleans poor were in the service sector of the tourist industry. Too much education would be dysfunctional in this system. In many ways, and almost 150 years after the *legal* end of slavery in the US, New Orleans still seemed a virtual "plantation" society where the inertial effects of that past wound maintained their vise-like grip on the present.

One way of pursuing what McCarthy aptly calls the "politics of public memory," (2009: 103–107) a politics in which a critical theory of global development must engage is to address the hysteretic effects of both racial discrimination at home and colonialism abroad. I adopt the expression, "hysteretic effect" from physics, where it refers to the inability of a disturbed system to return to its original state when the external cause of the disturbance has been removed, to effects that persist in the absence of initiating causes. Because past states of systems remain present in this way, hysteretic effects are those wherein systems retain a "memory" that haunts the present, or in the recent words of Barack Obama, where "past injustices continue to shape the present" (2015). A typical formulation of the refusal to address these effects, and one that is symptomatic of our public amnesia regarding matters of race, is the neoconservatives' well-known "culture of poverty thesis," and in the global arena, the invocation of the "dysfunctional cultural values" of "underdeveloped" societies (McCarthy 2009: 10).[1] In challenging the claim of the neoracists and other like-minded commentators that the social pathology of the poor is the independent variable in accounting for their social wretchedness, McCarthy suggests that social structures and processes, on the one hand, and psychological and cultural patterns, on the other, should rather be understood as being reciprocally related (2009: 11). I endorse this view – with the emendation that structural disparities will often have as their corollaries epistemic disparities, an unfair distribution of epistemic resources – and would like here to develop it a bit further.

The expression "culture of poverty" is a signifier for a weakness of culture and character that manifests itself as an agency deficit, a deficit conceived of either as 1) a values deficit and/or 2) as a species of weakness of will, *akrasia,* lack of discipline, self-control, and so on. In the latter case, the agent is taken to be *culpably* unable – for want of will or discipline – to make good choices. I argue here that the invocation of the culture of poverty thesis may well instantiate a fallacy that some have dubbed "psychologizing the structural" (Khader 2011: 56). This refers to the false assumption that a particular population's failure to flourish is caused primarily by such psychological deficits rather than by that population's structural environment. Such a verdict fails to take into account the agents' conceptions of socially available courses of action. Only a hermeneutic investigation will enable us to know whether or not such a fallacy has been committed. Central to such an investigation is the acknowledgment that an agent's knowledge of the social world is essentially interpretive, that is, that it is knowledge of the social domain *under a particular description*. And structuring any such interpretation will be beliefs about what socially available options there are, beliefs about what can intelligibly be done.

I have addressed the issue of the pathology of valuation elsewhere (Simpson 1987: 164–173). Here I address the second form that an agency deficit might assume and, in so doing, expand the conception of agency that we are typically inclined to hold. It is useful to think of agency as the capacity to direct oneself, with effect, towards the achievement of an end or state, either of oneself or of the world. But often, if not always, the actualization of such what I shall now call first-order capacities is conditioned by what I shall call capacities of the second order, capacities that enable or condition the exercise of capacities of the first order. I find it useful to think of second-order agency as the ability to acquire or avail oneself of the enabling and/or facilitating conditions – especially the epistemic conditions – of action in the first-order sense.

An example of John Locke's can be turned to my purposes here. I have in mind the situation of a person who is put into a cell and is led to believe, falsely, that all the doors are locked (1979: II.xxi.10). Such a person is objectively, from a third-person standpoint, able to leave the cell. But because, given the information made available to him, he cannot avail himself of this opportunity, his ability to do so is compromised. To the extent that the second-order capacity to acquire knowledge of the state of the doors was lacking, he would not be in a position to exercise his first-order capacity to walk out. In what follows, I shall focus on systematic or structural epistemic occlusions that compromise the exercise of first-order agency, occlusions for which the agents cannot be held responsible. Ideologically acquired beliefs furnish examples of such agency-compromising occlusions. But so does the situation of children living in poverty, who may well be fully *willing* to apply themselves to their studies but who are unaware of and/or unable to avail themselves of requisite quiet spaces. Or that of high-achieving and ambitious, but low-income, high school students who fail to even *apply* to selective colleges and universities because they receive little, if any, counseling about how to do so or even that such an option is a real possibility for them (Delbanco 2015: 38–39).

The lesson I draw from such considerations is that a genuine and fair assessment of agency must be informed by the agent's first-person perspective of what is possible, a perspective that informs expectations about outcomes of intentions to act, the likelihood of success. So, the choices open to one will be a function of one's "picture of the world." First-order agency can be compromised in a non-culpable way – in a way that results from a limited hermeneutical horizon for which *the agent cannot be held responsible* – when a choice that could have been made or an action that could have been undertaken was not made or undertaken solely because the agent was systematically deprived of the otherwise socially available agency-enabling picture.

This suggests that we disaggregate two aspects of agency, its volitional component and its epistemic component. This would imply that a particular case of what may *appear* to be a lack of agency did not in fact result from a lack of volitional resources *per se* but rather from a lack of awareness of available courses of action, from epistemic-horizonal limitations.[2] This epistemic component figures centrally in the exercise of what I have called second-order agency, in that the latter entails the ability to acquire the epistemic resources requisite to realizing first-order volitions.

If the conditions for second-order agency are blocked for some due to structural features of the societies in which they live, then it is unjust to demand, and unfair to expect, from them the same exercise of first-order agency as those more favorably positioned. How just is it to expect feats of first-order agency from segments of society bereft of the conditions that most of us can take for granted? It is such external obstacles to the exercise of first-order agency that are typically overlooked in neoconservative and neoimperialist accounts. Given that the sort of case I have in mind here involves a constriction of access to requisite epistemic resources where the agent is not culpable for that restriction, I take this sort of case – cases where agency is thwarted in a way for which the agent cannot be held culpable – to be an instance of an injustice of an epistemic sort. For here the agent is unfairly blamed for a compromise of agency that is caused by an epistemic occlusion that 1) is not acknowledged and 2) that results from structural factors over which the agent has no control.

It is in this sense that social and economic rights, and the material and epistemic conditions they would procure, can be understood to be conditions of first-order agency, say, of civil and political agency, and for this reason alone we incur the moral-political obligation to attend to such rights. The fact that second-order agency can be systematically undermined in such an arbitrary way means that a credible diagnosis of agential pathology will require a hermeneutic investigation aimed at construing the web of beliefs that agents actually have regarding the range of social options available to them as real and intelligible possibilities. And this diagnostic deployment of hermeneutics is essential to underwriting critical social interventions that are guided by an acknowledgment of the manifest injustice of the odious expectations mentioned just above.

The advantage of my account of agency can be further demonstrated if we use it to address one of the central issues in current discussions of the "adaptive preferences" of deprived persons. In order to avoid what I have criticized as the view that such persons necessarily suffer from agency deficits, and to support the view that they are agents in the full sense, some scholars maintain that such persons *are* acting in terms of their interests. For instance, recent trends in feminist scholarship that focus on deprivation emphasize a conception of agency that treats "agency as the capacity to make decisions and shape one's world in accordance with what one cares about, or to act in a way that reveals [one's] sense of what matters" (Khader 2011: 31). And such thinkers go on to claim that one can understand adaptive preferences to be genuine manifestations of agency in this sense. But this way of highlighting the agency of deprived women seems to lead to a dilemma. This agency dilemma takes the following form: should we see oppressed people as agents whose choices – even if they are life-diminishing or fail to be life-enhancing – are worthy of unquestioning respect or as passive victims who cannot make genuine choices? (Khader 2011: 31) In addition to providing me with a riposte to the "developmentalist's" charge of agency deficiency, my disaggregating the volitional and epistemic aspects of agency allows me to avoid this so-called agency dilemma lurking in theories of deprivation. And that is because choices that are life-diminishing can be criticized as being "objectively bad" choices without presuming passivity, volitional deficits, or agential culpability on the part of such persons.

An episode from the history of the practice of genital excision in the West is illustrative here. In the twentieth century, a number of Western women *chose* to undergo clitoridectomies, seeking relief from various "psychopathologies," where those pathologies may well have been ideologically constituted (Meyers 2000: 475). Insofar as they were ideological in nature, i.e., could be understood to have a strategic provenance, this can be understood to be a case of cognitive deformation where there is the *distinct* issue of the epistemic injustice done to these women. That is, to the extent that this construal or construction of psychopathology is ideological, we can view this as a case of epistemic injustice rather than insist that such women were passive victims who lacked agency.

Further, the claim that the volitional component of agency lacks defect in cases of "bad" choices is a fully defeasible claim. It follows as a corollary to my use of Locke's prisoner example that if the prisoner, desirous of freedom, *were* aware that the door was unlocked and with effort could be forced open, but nevertheless failed to exit, then this – all things being equal – *would* count as a culpable lack of agency. There can then, of course, be cases of genuine agential deficit, but my point is that we cannot make that discrimination in a meaningful way without the sort of investigation into the hermeneutic/epistemic situation of the agent that I am here advocating.

I now want to claim that the necessary condition for the meaningful application of the expression "culpable agency deficiency" can be understood in terms of what I shall call the requirement of narrative representability. By this I mean that members of the target group of social concern should, in principle, be able to represent to themselves a narrative that will take them in a continuous way without gaps from where they are, in all their concrete circumstances and identities, to circumstances that permit of life-enhancing behaviors. For a life-enhancing avenue for self-actualization to be concretely, that is, genuinely accessible, it must be credible given the concrete material and psychological/epistemic circumstances within which the agent finds him/herself. In that it is the ability to acquire the enabling conditions of action, second-order agency entails a view of the social world that allows for such narrative representability. It entails the epistemic status of holding warranted beliefs about how to bridge the gap between one's current status and the status that one wills for oneself.

The significance of this "epistemic" component of agency can easily go unremarked as long as its satisfaction can be taken for granted. And for the socially privileged – those for whom its satisfaction is taken for granted, those for whom the bridging of such gaps is effected so fluidly, fluently, and relatively effortlessly that the very existence of such gaps, and hence of the requisite epistemic tools for bridging them, goes virtually unnoticed – the requirement of second-order agency is itself invisible. At its limit, privilege just *is* the luxury of being unaware of the apparatus linking volition to effect. It is a condition of blissful hermeneutic oblivion and, as such, of a distinctive modality through which epistemic injustice can be committed.[3]

The apparatus linking volition to effect – i.e., the enabling condition of agency in the first-order sense – has both a more or less purely epistemic dimension (consisting of both propositional and practical knowledge) and a concrete material dimension. By the latter, I refer to enabling infrastructures. An agent's cognitive relationship to them will manifest itself in that agent's local social ontology or "picture of the social world." Acknowledging this will encourage us to attend both to the social availability of resources and options and to cognitive attitudes towards social availability simultaneously. Access to and knowledge of how to exploit such an apparatus is a second-order capacity.

The significance of this apparatus and of the social ontology in which it is embedded and disclosed is strikingly apparent when we examine the touchstones typically deployed in neoconservative commentaries on agency. In such commentaries, the idea of "the unaided accomplishment of individual persons" serves as the idealization that informs assessments of agency (Loury 1985: 25). The most reasonable interpretation of this expression is that it refers to an accomplishment requiring no aid beyond what *most members of a given society can reasonably take for granted* given that society's material and intellectual resources. Think of these as the "normal conditions" that establish the baseline beyond which accomplishment can meaningfully be viewed as aided in the requisite, and here pejorative, sense. Whether they are acknowledged to be so or not, these normal conditions are *enabling* conditions, enabling conditions that are not created by anyone's individual effort alone. In this context, the question I have been pursuing is: why then charge individuals with agency deficiency when, through no fault of their own, these normal conditions do not obtain for them? Why insist that the least advantaged among us bear the additional burden of "proving" themselves under conditions which most of us do not have to face? This is to question the fundamental consistency, not to mention justice, of expecting, as a matter of social policy, feats from one segment of society that most members of that society are not required to perform. This would be tantamount to burdening some, and invidiously so, with the demand to display supererogatory volitional powers.

Now, this interpretation of "unaided accomplishment," where its use implicitly presupposes that background normal conditions have been satisfied, implicitly treating them as "givens," leads to the following paradox. Social policies whose aim is to ameliorate material conditions and thereby to increase the scope of intelligible options for all – to assure that those conditions and options reach the threshold of "normal conditions" – are viewed as a form of aid in the pejorative sense, while achievements made on the basis of (preexisting and unacknowledged) normal conditions – the "standard" case – are not so viewed. This means that one would be said to have been aided in the relevant negative sense if, absent the normal conditions, one is subsequently provided them, but that one would not be said to have been so aided if one in some sense "inherited" those conditions (scoring a triple in virtue of having been born on third base). Once we have acknowledged the role of normal conditions in human agency, how can a meaningful moral distinction be drawn between cases where normal conditions are in force prior to volitional effort and cases where those conditions are set in place after such effort, especially where we stipulate that the agent in question bears no responsibility for the conditions or the lack thereof? What justification can be given for this view of what does and does not count as unaided accomplishment and hence of the exercise of agency or its lack? So, the burden is on those who would make *this* case for agency deficiency to determine where the line separating agential sufficiency and agential lack should be drawn and to justify drawing it there.

If what I have argued above is sound – i.e., that the aid enabling the "unaided" accomplishments of the well-positioned is *hidden*, while for the poor it is simply lacking – then there is a gap between what existing social systems make available and where the poor, even by their own best efforts, find themselves, a gap that cannot be bridged in the narratives that they can represent to themselves. Granting equal opportunity alone to individuals handicapped by the disadvantage of being non-culpably bereft of the normal conditions of agency does not constitute meeting them where they are or, as one commentator has recently put it, "people at their point of need." For many will lack the wherewithal to make use of those meeting opportunities, will lack what is crucial to productive effort, to agency in the full sense.[4]

Hermeneutic oblivion is one source of epistemic injustice. Another – and one that illustratively emphasizes how second-order agency is a distinctive *capacity* – is the refusal to acknowledge the *interpretive* agency of those at society's margins. The fact that our knowledge of the social world has an essentially interpretive nature has deep implications for our ability to exercise *social* agency. Our failure to acknowledge this fact and its implications can render persons vulnerable to a crippling form of epistemic injustice, to a violation that is distinctively hermeneutical in nature. This fact entails that the social world, its ontology and salient relations, is disclosed to social agents as configured in a specific and distinctive way. And the mode of its disclosure – the particular social phenomena, practices, and relations that can be meaningfully acknowledged in its terms – can determine the scope of our ability to intervene in that world, our social agency. This signals the importance of agency-enabling disclosures, of there being socially acknowledged interpretations that enable genuine agency in that they enable one intelligibly to "name" a problematic social experience and to respond accordingly. I have elsewhere referred to the acknowledgement of such an interpretation as the recognition of its semantic authority.[5] Public acknowledgement places at a putative agent's disposal semantic resources for active response by allowing for the publicly acknowledged disclosure of the "what" to which a response is required.

The significance of this cognitive component of agency – that is, the access or capacity to name that which one's action is to address – underscores the importance of democratically pursued conversational negotiation of interpretive frameworks for representing and articulating social experience. That the appropriate semantic resources are in place for interpreting social life then requires a specifically *hermeneutical* form of agency whose restriction is tantamount to yet another form of epistemic injustice, the injustice of arbitrarily restricting our ability to interpret reality in empowering ways. And this hermeneutical agency, activated in the struggle to win semantic authority for empowering social interpretations, is logically prior to the first-order social agency that depends upon it for its focus. The phenomena that we now describe as sexual harassment, "acquaintance rape," and police brutality can serve to illustrate this. The agency with which women and blacks, respectively, are able to oppose such practices is directly proportional to the semantic authority that such descriptors have, that is, to the extent to which, for instance, "sexual harassment," "acquaintance rape," and "police brutality" are socially acknowledged as predicates that can be meaningfully applied to social experience. In this sense, the failure to protect the free exercise of this interpretive capacity – protection that is crucial for sustaining social and political agency – is itself an epistemic injustice.[6]

**Related chapters**: 3, 7, 9, 12, 25

## Notes

1 The affirmative invocation of the "culture of poverty" thesis by former vice-presidential candidate Paul Ryan in 2014 and the even more recent deployment of it in a *New York Times* column in May of 2015 (I make reference to this below.) are evidence of the continuing currency of this idea.
2 There are, of course cases where agency is inculpably compromised not because of a lack of awareness of options but rather when there is a veridical awareness of a lack of options. Though the remedies will differ, in both cases a fair assessment of agency will require hermeneutic access to the agent's web of beliefs.
3 This oblivion is a symptom of the epistemic gap between the first-person perspective of the agent and the third-person perspective of the judging observer, and it can assume at least two forms: oblivion to the perhaps inculpably compromised hermeneutic horizon of the agent and/or to the unjustly distributed material resources that occasion the unacknowledged *true* beliefs such an agent may have about that unjust distribution, i.e., the agent's realization that "the game is rigged."
4 See also Nagel (1979: 92–93).
5 The account of semantic authority that I invoke here can be found in Simpson (2001: 103, 110–111, 114). See also Fricker (2007: 147 ff). My account presumes that the scope of recognition demanded by newly emergent interpretations is more general than is apparent in Fricker's treatment.
6 Here I am referring to necessary, but of course not sufficient, conditions of agency. For an agent may well recognize, say, that she is being sexually harassed but may nevertheless find herself unable to actively counter it because of her other beliefs concerning socially available options.

## References

Delbanco, Andrew (2015) "Our Universities: The Outrageous Reality," *The New York Review of Books*, 62(12) (July 9, 2015): 38–39.
Fricker, Miranda (2007) *Epistemic Injustice: Power and the Ethics of Knowing*, Oxford: Oxford University Press.
Khader, Serene J. (2011) *Adaptive Preferences and Women's Empowerment*, Oxford: Oxford University Press.
Locke, John (1979) *An Essay Concerning Human Understanding*, Oxford: Oxford University Press.
Loury, Glenn C. (1985) "Beyond Civil Rights," *The New Republic* (October 7, 1985): 22–25.
McCarthy, Thomas (2009) *Race, Empire, and the Idea of Human Development,* Cambridge: Cambridge University Press.
Meyers, Diana Tietjens (2000) "Feminism and Women's Autonomy: The Challenge of Female Genital Cutting," *Metaphilosophy*, 31(5): 469–491.
Nagel, Thoms (1979) "The Policy of Preference," in Mortal Questions Cambridge: Cambridge University Press.
Obama, Barack (2015) Remarks by the President in the Eulogy for the Honorable Reverand Clementa Pickney. *The White House Office of the Press Secretary* June 26, 2015. Available at: https://obamawhitehouse.archives.gov/the-press-office/2015/06/26/remarks-president-eulogy-honorable-clementa-pinckney
Simpson, Lorenzo C. (2001) *The Unfinished Project: Toward a Postmetaphysical Humanism,* London and New York: Routledge.
Simpson, Lorenzo C. (1987) "Values, Respect and Recognition: On Race and Culture in the Neoconservative Debate," *Praxis International* 7(2): 164–173.

# 25
# EPISTEMIC AND POLITICAL FREEDOM

*Susan E. Babbitt*

The question of epistemic injustice arose in Latin America before it did in North America. Two hundred years ago, an intense philosophical debate in Cuba addressed the very issue. Armando Hart, who led Cuba's literacy campaign in 1961–2, unmatched in the world, says no one who disregards the Cuban Philosophical Polemic, 1838–40, understands the Cuban Revolution in the twentieth century (2006: 60). It has to do with epistemic freedom.

This will surprise some. Epistemic injustice itself explains the surprise. Part of the issue, as I suggest below, is that evidence and argument are ineffective against deep-seated expectations. Epistemic injustice includes such expectations, constituting identity. It includes personal investment in such identity. The Cuban debates matter for political freedom, which counters expectations in the North about national identity.

I note two implications of epistemic injustice, so considered: first, epistemic freedom is about how to live, morally and politically. It might seem to be principally about thinking on one's own. Yet "one's own" thinking needs discovery. And such discovery depends upon conditions, which often need to be brought about through moral, political and even personal action. Second, it requires faith, or believing what we cannot prove. I explain below.

## 1

Cuba in the 1830s was threatened by four global institutions (Conde Rodríguez 2000: 36; Hart Dávalos 2006: 49): Spain took Cuba to define its "national integrity", slavery was a "necessary evil", the US considered Cuba its manifest destiny, and England was gaining influence in the Caribbean. All four implied submission for Cuba. All four were dehumanizing.

Cuban philosophers, Félix Varela and José de la Luz y Caballero, had an insight about thinking (Conde Rodríguez 2000: 20; Torres- Cuevas 2004: 329f). They noticed that all thinking, even the supposedly most private, depends upon universals. Universals are general terms like "love", "freedom", and "tree". My thinking may be private, in some sense, but universals are not. They are social. They are shared. In the analytic tradition, we call them *kinds* (e.g. Wilson 1999). They are general terms unifying particular instances. Non-identical entities form a unity; for example, two books are of the *same kind* even though they are different colours, shapes, and sizes. When we do not know an entity's kind, we not only do not know that entity, we sometimes do not see it (e.g. Kuhn 1970: 66).

All knowledge involves judgments about kinds. Any act of deliberation, moral and non-moral, private or social, depends upon kinds, which determine what we understand and how we act (Searle 1995). Some kinds are more empirically rooted than others, but all depend upon social, historical, political, economic and cultural conditions (e.g. Boyd 2010). This is now well-known in analytic philosophy.

It was known earlier to Varela and Luz. They knew imperialism's "logic" (Rodríguez 2012: 13). As Frantz Fanon argued, European colonialism was not, after all, illogical: if the "natives" are considered non-human, their brutal exploitation does not contradict humanist values (Sartre 1963: 15). His point needs greater attention. Political action, like any action, depends upon kinds – some philosophical – determining what we see and how we know.

Under imperialism, Cubans were non-persons. Understanding universals and imperialism, Varela and Luz knew Cubans' very thought was a vehicle for oppression. This was because universals arise, as noted, from circumstances and conditions. They were deeply dehumanizing. If activists wanted *human* liberation, their political movement, to be radical, required understanding thinking.

The philosophical debates of 1838–40 urged the priority of epistemology in school curricula (e.g. Luz y Caballero 1947: 113). Participants in the debates were credited by historians with teaching Cubans how to think (e.g. Torres-Cuevas 2004: 329f). This doesn't mean they provided ideology. Rather, they clarified the *nature* of critical thought: it depends upon universals. More adequate universals require political and personal work.

## 2

Noam Chomsky remarks that although George Orwell criticized the Soviet Union, the original preface of *Animal Farm* is about England. Public opinion, Orwell argues, damages free thought and expression more than authoritarian government (Orwell 1943). Thus, those formed in "good schools" have fewer options: precisely due to their formation, they are less able to imagine, let alone live, options counter to social convention.

Varela and Luz, and later José Martí, took the point further. Social orthodoxies constrain individual imagination but so do global structures: The division of the world into persons and non-persons made human liberation, for Latin Americans, hard to expect. It also promoted a view of human beings, including about freedom, which made human liberation, once expected, hard to know (Conde Rodríguez 2000).

It was a view of freedom ignoring the nature of thought and its dependence upon cause and effect. In the early nineteenth century, European philosophers somehow conceived human beings as non-natural, our thinking mythically unaffected by imperialist conditions. The universe is governed by natural laws, but human beings are not, or at least thinking is not.

The upshot was that we live best, non-morally at least, "from the inside", hearing an "inner voice". We are free, roughly, if no one gets in our way, an idea called "negative freedom". That the "inside" is largely a product of the outside, because of causation and kinds, was ignored (Hart Dávalos 2006: 64–5, 129–44). For Cuban philosophers, knowing imperialism, European liberalism was naïve. Martí warned Latin Americans not to be "slaves of Liberty!" (1882/2002a: 50–1), falsely conceived.

According to Fina García Marruz, Martí is distinct among revolutionaries in urging "double redemption" (1968/2011: 406): *political* freedom required liberation from selves, not for moral reasons but for the sake of knowing human potential. Looking to oneself, Martí wrote, is like being "an oyster in its shell, seeing only the prison that traps him and believing, in the darkness, that it is the world" (1887/2002b: 187). The freedom of European liberals, at the time, was a preposterous elevation of that very prison.

Herein lay epistemic injustice: a way of conceiving oneself that blocked pursuit, or even imagination, of real political freedom. The challenge for Latin America, Martí argued in his famous "Our America", was that Latin Americans identified with the US. Imperialism, he noted, is like a tiger on velvet paws: It shapes how one sees oneself, giving rise to kinds that are unreliable, at least for human liberation. And it does so unnoticed: "When the prey awakens", Martí wrote, "the tiger is upon him" (1891/2002c: 292–3).

## 3

Martí predated analytic philosophers on an important insight: all aspects of knowing are radically contingent upon circumstances and conditions. To know the world *as it is*, not just as we expect it to be, depends upon causal connection. We gain knowledge when causal forces act upon us to change our orientation, values or interests. Occasionally, we even possess knowledge before we can articulate it, through feelings and intuitions. Philosophers today call it non-propositional or tacit knowledge.

Martí saw political implications of what some call "embodiment", the idea that the body thinks. For him, as for Marx, it means we must change the world, even ourselves, to know real human needs. Whether our beliefs about such needs are true depends upon how we act and for what purpose. Martí knew thinking, resulting in knowledge, is "reliably regulated" by cause and effect, to use the jargon of recent (philosophical) times.

We are "herd animals", as Marx said, because of how we think. "The human being is in the most literal sense a political animal, not merely a gregarious animal, but an animal that can individuate itself only in the midst of society" (1857–58/1978: 223). The radical contingency of knowledge upon circumstances and conditions means individual freedom and self-understanding are not achievable by individuals alone. This is because kinds depend, in part, upon politics.

Even Simón Bolívar, not a philosopher, knew the problem for liberalism as a problem, importantly, about knowledge. He was a liberal, a man of the Enlightenment. But he knew European philosophers were ignorant of what it meant to be "even lower than servitude . . . lost, or worse, absent from the universe" (1815/2003: 19–20). Bolívar raised a question that would not occur to most Europeans: If one is lost or absent from the universe, how is one known? It was not by living from the inside.

Bolívar emphasized strong central government and regional unity, defining direction. "Is it conceivable that a newly liberated people can be launched into the sphere of freedom without their wings disintegrating and hurling them into the abyss, like Icarus?" Bolívar wondered (1815/2003: 23). Real human freedom, because it depends upon thinking, which depends upon institutions, requires real human community. Knowing imperialism, Bolívar knew it had to be fought for.

Martí followed, abandoning liberalism in his youth. Latin American leaders, he argued, must bring about "by *means and institutions* . . . the desirable state in which every man knows himself and is active" (emphasis added, 1891/2002c: 290). The state in which individuals know themselves, as human beings, needs to be created, fought for, and discovered, through politics and philosophy. This is because of how we think, involving kinds, generated by practises.

## 4

Two arguments in recent analytic philosophy explain why revolutionary Latin Americans cared about knowledge. The same arguments explain why North Americans should care about knowledge, politically. We should care about knowledge *before* we care about ethics and politics, and we should do so for the sake of learning about epistemic freedom by looking toward the South.

First, the nature of knowledge is such that imagination is limited by circumstances and conditions, necessarily. Reason works this way. We make choices within a small range of possibilities, dependent upon expectations. Second, science involves faith: it involves believing without sufficient evidence.

To start with the first: in science, natural and social, we investigate events judged plausible. Indeed, all aspects of knowing involve plausibility judgments (Boyd 1999, 2010): If the lights go out, no one asks whether aliens are to blame. Instead, we investigate a small set of options, according to background conditions. This means creativity, giving rise to new options, requires challenging such conditions, including social practises that give rise to expectations and kinds.

For example, in an insufficiently appreciated argument of the 1970s, Hilary Putnam argued that no amount of empirical evidence alone could have displaced Newton before Einstein reconceptualised mass and energy (1975). Although empirical evidence against Newton existed before Einstein, Einstein's thought experiments – his ideas – made the evidence plausible.

Well-established beliefs cannot be displaced by evidence alone. Counter evidence is explained away. It makes sense. If I release an object and it fails to fall, no one concludes that I have disproved the law of gravity. Instead, observers seek an alternative explanation, such as the existence of an opposing force. If they discover no such force, reasonable people keep looking. They don't abandon the belief.

Beliefs about people, and non-people, can be similarly deep-seated, insensitive to evidence. It was no wonder, then, that Martí's independence movement had to be a "revolution in thinking" (Rodríguez 2012: 10). Like his predecessors, Varela and Luz, he took the nature of thinking to be a political priority. Extraordinarily, the Montecristi Manifesto (1895), political statement of the Cuban Revolutionary Party, names "the nature of ideas" an objective of the liberation war (Martí 1895/2002d: 343–4).

Indeed, the Manifesto raises an ancient philosophical question: how to know what it means to be human, and how to know that we know what it means. It is not so odd considering the objective was human liberation. Martí didn't assume that humanness was known, although it was surely *thought* to be known. Thus, he claimed that independence was not about "civilization and barbarity" (or "developed" and "developing") but instead against the "false erudition" that claims to tell us what these are (1891/2002d: 290).

It was about knowledge. Significantly, just before the statement above, Martí writes that "weapons of ideas are more powerful than weapons of steel". Political freedom required reconceiving human beings and how to live as such. Thus, he urged "una nueva cultura" – a new way of being (Rodríguez 2010: 5). The movement was political but also personal (Rodríguez 2012: 139–40) for the sake of imagination. Given the circumstances, the very conceivability of freedom required new sorts of practises, including individual day to day practises.

## 5

The second argument, from analytic philosophy, is that discovery requires faith. It involves believing what cannot yet be fully proved (Kitcher 1982; Eagleton 2009). Scientists, natural and social, believe in the existence of events and phenomena before they have sufficient evidence to justify the belief. They do so to get the evidence.

Fundamental social change, affecting how people live and think, also involves faith. This is because of the point above. In dehumanizing conditions, known as such, liberation involves challenging institutions, including philosophical institutions, or popular conceptual frameworks. But "una nueva cultura", supporting more adequate concepts may not be fully defensible *before* we start to live it.

Marx knew this to be true. He did not provide a vision of the new communist society: such a vision only comes clearly into view as collaborative efforts are made to work toward it. Early Buddhist thinkers referred to *saddha,* or faith, as one of the central cognitive faculties. It has nothing to do with religion. *Saddha* is a feeling of enthusiasm that arises in the mind when we perform certain actions and experience the results for ourselves. Such faith, or motivation, comes not from belief but from action.[1]

It means we sometimes have to live differently *first* to know *why* we should. Cubans have lived differently. Even US political conservatives know it. When Fidel Castro resigned in 2006, many predicted internal squabbling and chaos. Yet Julia Sweig, US Rockefeller senior fellow, noted a "stunning display of orderliness and seriousness", indicating the Cuban Revolution "rests upon far more than the charisma, authority and legend of [Raul and Fidel Castro]" (Sweig 2007, cited in Veltmeyer & Rushton 2013: 301).

More significant in this regard, though, is Cuban foreign policy, particularly internationalism (e.g. Gleijeses 2002). Cuba sent 300,000 volunteers to Angola between 1975 and 1991 to defeat the racist South African army. In Pretoria, a "wall of names" commemorates those who died fighting apartheid. Many Cuban names are there. No other foreigners are named (Gleijeses 2013: 521). In 1991, Nelson Mandela asked, "What other country can point to a record of greater selflessness than Cuba has displayed in its relations to Africa?" (Gleijeses 2013: 526).

In 2014, the *Wall Street Journal* reported that "[f]ew have heeded the call [to fight Ebola], but one country has responded in strength: Cuba". Cuba responded without hesitation, sending more than 450 doctors and nurses, chosen from more than 15,000 volunteers, by far the largest medical mission sent by any country. Why did 15,000 medical workers volunteer? There is an explanation. It has to do with the "far more" referred to by Sweig.

It is partly philosophical. A truth about motivation is known to economists (e.g. Pink 2010). We are not mostly motivated by material incentives but, instead, by what we receive back from an activity. Martí argued that "through the wonderful dispensation of nature, whoever gives of himself grows" (1894/1999: 46–7). At least 15,000 medical workers that year believed him. It would have been because they themselves experienced such "wonderful dispensation of nature", personally.

Martí defended a view expressed elsewhere – e.g. Marx, the Buddha, some indigenous traditions – but not dominant in Europe: human beings are part of nature, and we depend upon nature, including other human beings. On such a view, there is no mystery that so many medical workers would risk their lives in West Africa: We live better, and freely, when others live better, and freely. It is not about morality but about the nature of reality. It's about cause and effect.

In the 2000s, I introduced a philosophy course at my university, taught at the University of Havana by Cuban philosophers. I wanted students to know that *ideas* come from Cuba, not just culture. I wanted them to know the ideas were about *them*, about how to live and about the nature of reality. The course was quickly moved to Development Studies, which is a Social Sciences department. It was as if a course in Cuba could not be Philosophy. It had to be Geography or Sociology.

The course was renamed a course on culture. I had wanted it to be a philosophy course to counter a stereotype: ideas come from the North, culture from the South. When North Americans talk about freedom, we are talking about the human condition. When Latin Americans talk about freedom, it is about them, about "others". It gets studied, if it does, as ethnography. In the more than twenty years I have been going regularly to Cuba, I can't remember a single researcher in Cuba specifically to know its philosophical traditions. Their existence is not plausible.

Some suggest there are no alternatives to liberalism (Mills 2007: 102). There are plenty. But they are mostly from the South, and finding the evidence requires faith, of the sort that arises from action in a certain direction. The evidence is there, but commitment to philosophical liberalism makes it useless. It is explained away as "culture". Epistemic injustice of this sort requires "una nueva cultura" challenging expectations not just about who exists as persons but about who can think and what they think about.

## 6

Epistemic injustice applies to Latin American independence movements at two levels. First, the independence movements of the nineteenth century and the Cuban revolution of the twentieth were about epistemic injustice, long before it was discussed in the US. They did not use the term, but they knew two facts: thinking depends upon universals, which are shared, and imperialism is dehumanizing. A revolution, involving and perhaps initiated by the Philosophical Polemic of 1838–40, was about what epistemic freedom really means.

Second, epistemic injustice explains why the significance of such struggles for political freedom, especially epistemic freedom, are ignored in the North. Martí scholar, Pedro Paulo Rodríguez, writes that even Latin Americans ignore the political relevance of their philosophical traditions (2012: 177). The reason may be implausibility, generated by the globalization of Northern philosophical views, particularly liberalism. It makes counter evidence as potentially destabilizing as the idea that aliens caused the lights to go off.

We gain in two ways by considering the two points noted above. I refer to the philosophy of science here because it is about the nature of knowledge and not about morality, at least not directly. In analytic philosophy, we separate (unfortunately) epistemology and metaphysics, and ethics and political philosophy. The fact/value distinction still motivates. It didn't motivate Martí: that Latin Americans are persons is a matter of fact, directly relevant to what *ought* to be.

He gave priority to the nature of knowledge because before talking about ethics and politics, we must know people exist *as persons* and know that we know. We must know what it means, realistically. The Philosophical Polemic was about why it matters, politically, that we know how to know. Ignorance about knowledge, about universals, would undermine the struggle against imperialism, for political freedom. Indeed, they argued, such ignorance would end up justifying imperialism (Conde Rodríguez 2000).

On occasion, I meet North American researchers in Cuba. They say they are there to listen, to hear stories, any stories. They want to be non-judgmental. But when I ask whether they've collected stories of Communist Party members, they say no, not deliberately. They also admit to not seeking out members of the government. Their listening is judgmental, after all, unwittingly so. The moral judgment, defining direction, lies embedded in a worldview, unacknowledged, determining without argument who is free and who is unfree.

Such researchers may not know that social and natural sciences depend upon kinds. Such ignorance will mean their work is ultimately conservative, a vehicle for that very worldview. It was precisely this consequence that concerned the Polemicists. The first point above, regarding plausibility judgments, explains why they were correct. Self-conception, including national identity, is part of the "Background" (Searle 1995) explaining such judgments. It can include a view of both individual and political freedom, determining the results of research on such topics, before any empirical investigation.

Early Buddhist philosophers referred to *sakkāyadiṭṭhi,* or personality-belief. It includes national identity, opinions, loyalties, as well as petty likes and dislikes. Burmese monk, Ledi Sayadaw considered it a deep and pervasive evil (1999: 256–7), preventing freedom: We invest ourselves in personality belief, expecting it to ground human well-being, non-morally at least, and it cannot do so. For, it is largely arbitrary, explained by parents, teachers, social context and the media, among other factors.

Investment in *sakkāyadiṭṭhi* is explained by ignorance, particularly of cause and effect. The Buddha, like Martí, did not assume the fact/value distinction: precisely as I understand the nature of reality, constantly changing, I begin to understand myself and others. That *sakkāyadiṭṭhi* is arbitrary is a matter of fact. It should matter, and it did to Martí, that it not be a foundation for defining individual freedoms. For Martí, such freedoms involved a "Herculean struggle" against oneself (1882/2002a: 49). It was a striking view set against European liberalism.

But it was in synch with Eastern philosophers who acknowledged that human beings, like the rest of the universe, are subject to cause and effect, and dependent upon such for self-knowledge and freedom. If, like the oyster in its shell, we take personality-belief, including national identity, for granted, we don't notice that it can be ultimately dehumanizing, because the world is that way. The risk was eminently clear to Varela and Luz, who were not politically radical. The risk is evident today, if we care to notice.

## 7

The second point above, regarding the epistemic significance of faith, or *saddha,* tells us what to do about the epistemic injustice perpetuated by *sakkāyadiṭṭhi* and inevitable attachment to it. Martí emphasized what García Marruz calls "double redemption", as noted above, recognizing a naturalistic, causal conception of knowledge. The dialectical nature of knowledge, Martí argued, as did Marx, means how we think depends upon how we live.

J. M. Coetzee's *Disgrace* describes a male dog beaten when, on sensing a bitch, he became excited and unmanageable (1999: 89–90). With "Pavlovian regularity, the owners would beat it". The result was that the "poor dog didn't know what to do . . . it would chase around the garden . . . whining, trying to hide". Coetzee comments that a dog can be punished for wrongdoing – for chewing a shoe, for example – but not for going against its nature. The result is despair and confusion, a dog that punishes itself.

Human beings are punishing ourselves. Charles Taylor writes that we live in an "age of authenticity" in which happiness is having choices, the more the better (2007: 470–9). Scientifically, such a view cannot be right. Desires have causes, like everything else. They have no special status regarding human well-being unless of course we equate human well-being with doing what we want. Considered realistically, though, this makes well-being an enslavement to habit patterns.

That's how Martí saw it. So did Eastern philosophers (Hart 1987). It shouldn't be surprising, considering cause and effect, that on such a view of well-being, we experience despair and confusion, like the dog in Coetzee's example. The greater risk, though, is that we *don't* experience despair and confusion.

Eugène Ionesco had this worry. His 1959 play, *Rhinoceros,* is about a small town where people turn into rhinoceroses. At first, everyone is horrified by the rhinoceroses but eventually the change becomes seductive. Even the town's logician becomes a rhinoceros, happily, wanting to "move with the times" (Ionesco 2000:102–3).

Ionesco's play is about totalitarianism, but not the political sort. Instead, he meant totalitarianism of reason when no questions are raised about how human beings (and monsters) are individuated, the dilemma with which the play closes. In the end, Berenger, the only human remaining, reminds himself that "[a] man's not ugly to look at, not ugly at all!" However, a few sentences later he says, "I should have gone with them while there was still time" (Ionesco 2000: 104).

Berenger's conviction wavers, and we wonder whether his *self*-understanding (that he is "not ugly at all") will sustain his broader social understanding (that rhinoceritis is "disgusting"). He might, after all, go with the rhinos without regret, suggesting that rhinoceritis is not as serious a problem as identifying it as a problem, once everyone is a monster. Rhinoceritis, like everything else, is about kinds.

Rhinoceritis was the concern of the early Cuban activists and later Martí. Political domination was one issue. Dehumanization was another. The tiger of imperialism, Martí wrote, crouches "behind every tree, in every corner . . . his claws unsheathed" (1891/2002c: 293). Neither Martí nor his predecessors thought the tiger was easily known, or even identified. Their preoccupation with the reality of the ideas was motivated by personal experience with rhinoceritis (1895/2002d: 343–4).

Ironically, when we consider the reality of ideas, as Martí did throughout his entire body of work, religious philosophical traditions are useful. A dialectical, causal account of knowledge challenges how we live, as Martí argued. It implies, for example, the epistemic significance of self-dispossession. It also implies the significance of silence, specifically mental silence, needed to receive back from the world. Both ideas are prevalent in religious traditions, and little discussed in analytic philosophy.

Indeed, Terry Eagleton urges progressive philosophers to consider religious traditions, since they no longer read Marx (2009: xii). One reason is that religious philosophers often express the more Marxist idea that "freedom thrives only within the context of a fundamental dependency" (Eagleton 2009: 16). We need to live such "fundamental dependency", and some people do, within the North. North American activism has a history of looking South for inspiration and ideas (e.g. Gosse 1993). It just doesn't extend to philosophy, at least not in Cuba, and certainly not regarding political freedom.

## 8

Political freedom, for Martí, Varela and Luz, motivated thorough-going rejection of philosophical liberalism. Those in the North, arriving belatedly to the question of epistemic injustice, might follow suit. Cuba's battle for ideas, centuries old, was and is about the nature of ideas. It is consistent with some philosophical ideas in the North, mostly confined to the philosophy of science. The causal, naturalistic character of knowledge suggests epistemic freedom is undermined when injustice, even epistemic injustice, is named and analyzed without also transforming – politically, social and personally – conditions explaining it: capitalism and imperialism. This takes faith, "una nueva cultura".

**Related chapters** 9, 13, 24, 37

## Note

1 For those who think a cognitive faculty does not involve affect, or who are inclined to the Buddha's writing (as opposed to the institutions that have emerged from them) as religion, see my *Freedom and Death: Philosophical Reflections on Dhamma (Cause and Effect)* (forthcoming).

## References

Bolívar, Simón. (2003). The Jamaica letter: Response from a South American to a gentleman from this Island. In David Bushnell (Ed.), Frederick H. Fornoff (Trans.), *Simón Bolívar, el libertador*. New York: Oxford University, pp. 12–30.

Boyd, Richard N. (1979). Metaphor and theory change: What is "Metaphor" a Metaphor for? In A. Ortony (Ed.), *Metaphor and Thought*. Cambridge: Cambridge University Press, pp. 348–408.

Boyd, Richard N. (1999). Homeostasis, species and higher taxa. In Robert A. Wilson (Ed.), *Species: Interdisciplinary Essays*. Cambridge, MA: The MIT Press, pp. 141–86.

Boyd, Richard N. (2010). Realism, natural kinds and philosophical methods. In Helen Beebee & Nigel Sabbarton (Eds.), *The Semantics and Metaphysics of Natural Kinds*. New York: Routledge, pp. 212–34.

Coetzee, J. M. (1999). *Disgrace*. London: Secker and Warburg.

Conde Rodríguez, Alicia. (2000). Ensayo introductorio: Para una teoría crítica de la emancipación cubana. In Roberto Agramonte (Ed.), *La polémica filosófica cubana 1838–1839*. Havana: Clásicos Cubanos, pp. 3–66.

Eagleton, Terry. (2009). *Reason, Faith and Religion*. New Haven: Yale University Press.

García Marruz, Fina. (2011). La edad de oro. In Cintio Vitier & Fina García Marruz (Eds.), *Temas Martianos*. Havana, Cuba: Biblioteca José Martí, pp. 385–402. (Originally published 1962).

Gleijeses, Piero. (2002). *Conflicting Missions: Havana, Washington, and Africa, 1959–1976*. Chapel Hill, NC: University of North Carolina Press.

Gleijeses, Piero. (2013). *Visions of Freedom: Havana: Washington, Pretoria and the Struggle for Southern Africa, 1976–1991*. Chapel Hill, NC: University of North Carolina Press.

Gosse, Van. (1993). *Where the Boys Are: Cuba, the Cold War and the Making of the New Left*. New York: Verso Press.

Hart, William. (1987). *The Art of Living*. New York: Harper Collins.

Hart Dávalos, Armando. (2006). *Ética, cultura, y política*. Havana: Estudios Martianos.

Ionesco, Eugène. (2000). *Rhinoceros*. trans Derek Prouse. New York: Penguin.

Kitcher, Philip. (1982). *Abusing Science: The Case Against Creationism*. Boston, MA: MIT Press.

Kuhn, Thomas. (1970). *The Structure of Scientific Revolutions* (2nd ed.). Chicago, IL: University of Chicago Press.

Luz y Caballero, José de la. (1947). *La Polemica filosófica*, Volume 5. Havana: University of Havana.

Martí, José. (1999). Wandering teachers. In Deborah Shnookal & Mirta Muñez (Eds.), *José Martí Reader: Writings on the Americas*. New York, NY: Ocean Books, pp. 46–50. (Originally published 1894).

Martí, José. (2002a). Prologue to Juan Antonio Pérez Bonalde's poem of Niagara. In Esther Allen (Ed. and Trans.), *José Martí: Selected Writings*. New York, NY: Penguin Books, pp. 43–51. (Originally published 1882).

Martí, José. (2002b). The poet Walt Whitman. In Esther Allen (Ed. and Trans.), *José Martí: Selected Writings*. New York, NY: Penguin Books, pp. 183–94. (Originally published 1887).

Martí, José. (2002c). Our America. In Esther Allen (Ed. and Trans.), *José Martí: Selected Writings*. New York, NY: Penguin Books, pp. 288–96. (Originally published 1891).

Martí, José. (2002d). The Montecristi manifesto. In Esther Allen (Ed. and Trans.), *José Martí: Selected Writings*. New York, NY: Penguin Books, pp. 337–45. (Originally published 1895).

Marx, Karl. (1978). Grundrisse. In Robert C. Tucker (Ed.), *The Marx-Engels Reader* (2nd ed.). New York: Norton, pp. 221–93.

Mills, Charles. (2007). The domination contract. In Carole Pateman & Charles W. Mills (Eds.), *Contract and Domination*. Cambridge, UK: Polity Press, pp. 79–105.

Orwell, George. (1943). The freedom of the press. [Orwell's proposed preface to *Animal Farm*] Retrieved from http://orwell.ru/library/novels/AnimalFarm/english/efpgo [Accessed November 18, 2012].

Putnam, Hilary. (1975). The analytic and synthetic. In *Mind, Language and Reality: Philosophical Papers*, Volume 2. New York, NY: Cambridge University Press, pp. 33–69.

Rodríguez, Pedro Pablo. (2010). "Una en alma y intento": Identidad y unidad latinoamericana en. In José Martí (Ed.), *De los dos Américas: Aproximaciones al pensamento martiano*. Havana, Cuba: Centro de estudios martianos, pp. 3–48.

Rodríguez, Pedro Paulo. (2012). *Pensar, prever, server: El ideario de José Martí*. Havana, Cuba: Ediciones Unión.

Sartre, Jean-Paul. (1963). Preface. In Frantz Fanon (Ed.), Constance Farrington (Trans.), *Wretched of the Earth*. New York, NY: Grove Press, pp. 7–31. (Originally published 1961).

Sayada, Ledi. (1999). *Manuals of Dhamma*. Igatpuri, India: Vipassana Research Institute.

Searle, John. (1995). *The Construction of Social Reality*. New York: Free Press.

Sweig, Julia. (2007). Fidel's final "victory". *Foreign Affairs* 86:1 (January–February), 39–56.

Taylor, Charles. (2007). *A Secular Age*. Cambridge, MA: Belknap Press of Harvard University Press.

Torres-Cuevas, Eduardo. (2004). *Historia del pensamiento cubano: Volúmen 1, Tomo 1*. Havana, Cuba: Editorial de ciencias sociales.

Veltmeyer, Henry, & Rushton, Mark. (2013). *The Cuban Revolution as Socialist Development*. Chicago, IL: Haymarket Books.

Wilson, Robert. (Ed.). (1999). *Species: Interdisciplinary Essays*. Boston: MIT.

# 26
# EPISTEMIC COMMUNITIES AND INSTITUTIONS

*Nancy Arden McHugh*

In the late twentieth-century the question 'Who is an epistemic agent?' began to challenge mainstream epistemology, whose 'neutral' epistemic agent mirrored those dominating the halls of the academy – white, middle to upper class, western, heterosexual males. Sandra Harding in *The Science Question in Feminism* (1986); Gayatri Chakravorty Spivak in 'Can the Subaltern Speak?' (1988); Helen Longino in *Science as Social Knowledge* (1990); Patricia Hill Collins in *Black Feminist Thought* (1991); Lorraine Code in *What Can She Know?* (1991), and Susantha Goonatilake in 'Modern Science in the Periphery' (1993) critique this homogenous and privileged view of epistemic agency. Harding, Longino, and Code critiqued the male-centered nature of the epistemic agent. Collins' analysis furthered this discussion by also questioning the dominant view that privileges white bodies as the assumed generic epistemic agents. Spivak's and Goonatilake's work significantly repositioned the epistemic agent through critical questions about dominant knowledge centered on western colonial productions of ideas and practices, and how these silence, objectify, and ignore colonized epistemic agents. These arguments presented a critical lens for generating questions regarding epistemic justice and injustice. For example, Spivak's argument in 'Can the Subaltern Speak?' is a question of epistemic justice: can colonized subjects have the autonomy to speak and be heard in situations of epistemic violence, when one's knowledge and voice are utterly denied by another culture?

Although these feminist and post-colonial critiques challenged dominant assumptions in mainstream epistemology, like mainstream epistemology they also start from the assumption that the epistemic agent is an individual. This individualistic view of epistemic agency makes it challenging to understand how communities, especially oppressed communities, experience epistemic injustice and how these communities collectively engage in epistemic resistance. Fortunately there have been alternative models of epistemic agency proposed that recognize the epistemic agency of communities. These present pathways through which one can generate insights about how epistemic communities can be formed under conditions of oppression and how communities engage in resistant epistemic strategies.

The chapter begins by developing an understanding of epistemological communities and how they form under conditions of oppression. I then explore how these epistemic communities become 'communities of epistemic resistance'. From there I engage work on epistemic justice, tying these to arguments about epistemic resistance to make the claim that if we take seriously the idea that communities are epistemic agents, this provides a more robust understanding of epistemic injustice and illuminates how individuals and communities actively resist epistemic injustice. I finish with an example of a community of epistemic resistance generated via a prison writing group.

## Forming communities

The epistemic agency of communities and the formation of communities have played an important role in late twentieth- and twenty-first-century philosophy by raising critical questions about how knowledge is constituted, who counts as a legitimate knower, and how conditions of epistemic injustice shape communities and individuals. Lynn Hankinson Nelson initiated this discussion in contemporary feminist epistemology by arguing in 'Epistemological Communities' that 'it is communities that construct and acquire knowledge' and thus 'epistemological communities', not individuals, should be recognized as 'the agents of epistemology' (1993:123). She claims that it is communities who develop standards of evidence, practices, and methodologies that lead to knowledge. Knowledge is experiential, social, and built holistically, where the knowledge one acquires is interdependent upon and interconnected with the knowledge others acquire (1993:141). Thus, 'you or I *can* only know what we *know* (or could know), for some "we"' (1990:124).

Although Nelson was perhaps more explicit in her formulation of the epistemic agency of communities, writing in the mid-twentieth-century W.E.B. Du Bois and John Dewey were prescient in their writings about how epistemological communities are formed. In *The Public and Its Problems*, Dewey argues that communities are not loose associations of individuals but are formed by pertinent conditions that create meaningful linkages among people (1954:38). Furthermore, according to Dewey, we are not members of a community by virtue of birth, though this can contribute to our belonging to a community; '[w]e are born organic beings associated with others, but we are not born members of a community. The young have to be brought within the traditions, outlooks, and interests which characterize a community by means of education: by unremitting instructions and by learning in connection with the phenomenon of overt association' (154). We become members of a community by being 'brought within' or experiencing the pertinent conditions of that community. Although it is tempting to see the use of 'education' in a positive light, this was not Dewey's intention. 'Education' is descriptive of particular situations – negative, positive, or both given the conditions in which it is taking place. Furthermore, he uses it more broadly than how 'education' is normally conceived. Thus, education and acquiring knowledge are not primarily done in academic settings; they are what happen when we live and experience the world. 'Education' should be seen not only as a set of practices that can lovingly confer tradition, but also as practices that confer habits of privilege, experiences of marginalization, ways of viewing our own and others' bodies, practices that sediment social relationships and interactions, and an epistemic lens through which to experience and know the world.

Nelson frames this process in a similar way, arguing that although sensory experience might be an individual experience in the limited sense, that it is happening in and through a body; that experience is a social experience, an experience shaped by the communities in which one is immersed. Any experience and any knowledge that arises from these experiences is shaped by the history, culture, physical location, standards of evidence, methods, and ontologies of the communities through which one lives (1993:138). Knowledge is the product of communities, not only in the sense of the explicit and implicit collaboration necessary to acquire a new piece of knowledge, but also that epistemic communities set the conditions so that particular types of knowledge and particular interpretations are accepted.

In 'What is Africa to Me?', Du Bois' understanding of 'social heritage' drives home the significance of epistemological communities and how these are formed through conditions of oppression. He describes the process of forming communities as occurring through 'social heritage', indicating how one learns to be a member of a community through the habituation, experience, or education of being in that community and how that shapes the way one comes to develop knowledge and action in the world (1995:655). Like Dewey and Nelson, Du Bois emphasizes the experiential and epistemic nature of communities, but much more explicitly shows how the 'social heritage' of oppression shapes and links individuals into epistemological communities. Thus, although Nelson and Dewey note that oppression contributes to the formation of epistemological communities, Du Bois views it as fundamental in how it shapes and links oppressed communities together, even those that are geographically distant from each other. Du Bois' use of 'social heritage' in his essay is key. Du Bois states that prior to the Trans Atlantic slave trade, people of the African continent lived in small communities, tied together by face-to-face interactions. Yet, as he argues,

> one thing is sure and that is the fact that since the fifteenth century these ancestors of mine and their other descendants have had a common history; have *suffered common disaster and have one long memory*. The actual ties of heritage between the individuals of this group, vary with the ancestors that they have in common and many others: Europeans and Semites, perhaps Mongolians, certainly American Indians . . . [T]he real essence of this kinship is its *social heritage of slavery*.
>
> *(655, my italics)*

Slavery, he argues, created 'one long memory' – an epistemological connection that crosses the immediacy of local contact to form a community in which African Americans are united more broadly by a 'social heritage of slavery', an experiential and epistemological heritage providing ongoing 'education' that creates and recreates global systems of racism and racist exploitation.

An understanding of how epistemological communities are formed under the experiential nature of oppressive conditions can be further developed through Benedict Anderson's *Imagined Communities* (1983) and Chandra Mohanty's *Feminism without Borders* (2003). Benedict Anderson argues that *all* communities that are larger than those that can sustain face-to-face interaction are imagined communities. Much like Du Bois' formulation of social heritage, Anderson is articulating a view of community that is joined together not by immediate geographical bonds like a neighborhood or university, but by overarching and shared epistemological, political, and experiential conditions. Mohanty builds on this conception to consider how Third World women are imagined communities that can constitute 'communities of resistance'. Mohanty argues that imagined communities suggest a 'political rather than a biological or cultural bases for alliance. It is not color or sex that constructs the ground for these struggles. Rather, it is the *way we think* about race, class, and gender' (47). Thus, these communities are not formed based on biology or primarily physical location, though location can be significant, but instead how bodies–minds are conceived, enacted, and acted upon, in and through social, political, and epistemological structures. These conditions instigate what Mohanty calls 'communities of resistance'. Like Du Bois' understanding of communities arising out of a shared social heritage, 'communities of resistance' are those that are formed out of resistance to persistent, systemic domination and oppression (47). These communities of resistance reformulate and counter the dominant framework that dehumanizes them, that denies the significance and validity of their experience and knowledge, and that speaks for them and frames the groundwork for knowledge and epistemic legitimacy such that the voices of oppressed people are invisible, silenced, and discredited. As I will point to later in the chapter, oppressed groups resist these conditions through a number of epistemic strategies, including epistemic separatism, i.e., refusing to engage in dialogue and knowledge generating projects with oppressors; proposing alternative epistemic frameworks and practices; creating strategic alliances with other oppressed groups and/or allies with epistemic resources; and learning to use the epistemic skills of the dominant framework to develop epistemic strategies to counter the framework. These provide openings for new knowledge that reflects the experience of oppressed groups, new practices that meet their needs, and collaborations that give witness and legitimation to the voice and knowledge of oppressed groups.

Thus, if we bring together Anderson and Mohanty with Nelson, Dewey, and Du Bois, we can see that oppression creates pertinent conditions and social heritages, systems of education/experience, that link similarly affected people into epistemological communities. When we understand epistemological communities in the sense that epistemological communities can and frequently do arise from persistent oppression, the 'unremitting' 'education' that arises from the shared social heritage of this oppression, it becomes clear that communities experience epistemic injustice in virtue of being an oppressed community. Furthermore, this understanding provides the clarity that they resist epistemic injustice as an epistemological community. Following Chandra Mohanty's lead, I am going to describe such communities as *communities of epistemic resistance*.

## Communities of epistemic resistance and epistemic injustice

Focus on epistemic justice has developed from theorizing primarily about the role of epistemic justice in its relationship to individuals to theorizing about the role of epistemic injustice with communities. Given what I develop in the previous section, this move is critical for putting epistemic justice into action, since much of the social and epistemic *injustice* that people experience is in virtue of the *community* to which they belong. Among the important contributions to this area is work by Miranda Fricker, Elizabeth Anderson, Rebecca Mason, José Medina, and Gaile Pohlhaus, Jr.

In her initial formulation of epistemic agency and epistemic virtue in *Epistemic Injustice*, Miranda Fricker's approach was an individualistic one, even though she acknowledges that hermeneutical injustice results from the ignorance of communities' and institutions' lack of collective understanding of the experiences of oppressed communities (2007:130, 154). Fricker states

> [t]he wrong of testimonial injustice [when individuals are not considered to be reliable or trustworthy informants resulting from 'identity prejudice'] is inflicted individual to individual . . . By contrast hermeneutical injustice is not inflicted by any agent, but rather is caused by a feature of the collective hermeneutical resources – a one-off blind spot (in incidental cases), or (in systemic cases) a lacuna generated by a structural identity prejudice in the hermeneutical repertoire.
>
> *(168)*

Even though hermeneutical injustice is the result of collective ignorance of the sort that Charles Mills describes in *The Racial Contract* as an epistemology of ignorance, '*a particular pattern of localized and global cognitive dysfunctions*' (1997:18, my emphasis), Fricker argues that 'as with testimonial justice, the virtue [of hermeneutical justice] is to be individuated at its mediate end . . . The mediate end of the virtue, then, is *to neutralize the impact of structural identity prejudice on one's credibility judgment*' (173, original emphasis). This does not preclude 'collective exercise' or that 'it takes group political action for social change' (174). But that '[t]he primary ethical role for the virtue of hermeneutical justice, then, remains one of mitigating the negative impact of hermeneutical injustice on the speaker' (174).

In 'Can There Be Institutional Virtues?' (2009) and 'Group Testimony: The Making of a Good Collective Informant' (2012), Fricker seeks to develop a more social account of epistemic virtues. She argues that institutions can possess collective epistemic virtues and vices, which are more or less desirable based on the needs of the institution and those that the institution serves (2009). Furthermore, these epistemic virtues and vices are not necessarily properties of any one individual in the collective, but are properties of the overall institutional functioning. Thus epistemic virtues of institutions, such as trustworthiness, must be cultivated at the institutional level to promote democratic ideals (2012).

In 'Epistemic Justice as a Virtue of Social Institutions' (2012), Elizabeth Anderson also seeks a more social account of epistemic virtues and argues for an expanded structural account of testimonial injustice, which must be remedied through the development of structural virtues (2012:169). In recognizing that social institutions, such as judicial, educational, political, and medical bodies, function as epistemic institutions, Anderson argues that an institution is testimonially just when its members 'jointly commit themselves to operating according to institutionalized principles that are designed to achieve testimonial justice, such as giving hearers enough time to make unbiased assessments' (2012:168–169). When practicing in an unjust manner, these epistemic institutions can create and sustain structural 'group-based credibility deficits: differential markers of credibility; ethnocentrism; and "the shared reality bias"' (2012:169), even though when analyzed from the level of an individual epistemic agent, there was no individual epistemic failing. Thus, to create sustainable epistemic justice, epistemic institutions need to be constructed or reconstructed to prevent epistemic injustice (2012:171).

While Anderson's and Fricker's analyses of epistemic injustice engage the failings of epistemic institutions and means for remedying these failings, there has also been important work on epistemic injustice that focuses on the effects of epistemic injustice on oppressed communities and the ways communities resist epistemic injustice. In my description of how epistemic communities are formed, I used the phrase 'communities of epistemic resistance', building from Mohanty's work on communities of resistance. In what follows I characterize arguments by José Medina, Rebecca Mason, and Gaile Pohlhaus, Jr. as those in the area of communities of epistemic resistance. These writers develop arguments that recognize: 1) the epistemic injustice inflicted upon communities because of their oppressed status, 2) how epistemic injustice furthers and maintains the oppression of communities, and 3) how communities resist epistemic injustice. I am going to engage the last of these three approaches.

One critique of Fricker's work is that her account of epistemic injustice silences the agency and resistance of marginalized communities. Mason argues that Fricker 'pays insufficient attention to non-dominant hermeneutical resources to which members of marginalized groups have access in order to render their social experiences communicatively intelligible' (2011:298). Because Fricker does not identify these epistemic resources, she does not recognize how marginalized epistemic communities resist dominant epistemic frameworks to make meaning and to actively change their material and epistemic conditions; instead on Fricker's account marginalized communities appear to have little epistemic agency and to share a collective and symmetrical ignorance with dominant knowers (Mason and Pohlhaus, Jr.).

Medina in *The Epistemology of Resistance* (2013) explicitly formulates arguments that point to the epistemic agency of communities and how they resist dominant epistemologies. Medina argues that epistemic virtues, the sort needed to be epistemically just and to resist epistemic injustice – humility, diligence/curiosity, and open-mindedness – are developed when members of oppressed groups engage in 'positive epistemic resistance' (2013:50). Positive epistemic resistance results from engaging critically both internally and externally to 'unmask prejudices and biases, react to bodies of ignorance' and 'to be self-critical, to compare and contrast one's beliefs to meet justificatory demands, to recognize cognitive gaps' (2013: 50). When oppressed groups develop epistemic virtues out of this practice, they are able to develop a subversive lucidity. This epistemic clarity has a high level of epistemic agency, such that the epistemically virtuous subject has 'the potential to question widely held assumptions and prejudices, to see things afresh and redirect our perceptual habits, to find a way out or an alternative to epistemic blind alleys, and so on' (2013:45). As Pohlhaus, Jr., along with Du Bois and Mohanty, argues, these epistemic resources develop out of critically engaged shared experiences of oppression 'that stand outside or beyond any one individual' (2012:718) such that knowers do not develop this level of epistemic agency merely as individuals in an oppressed community, but within a community with a shared social heritage through which they have developed collective epistemic resources that are resistant to epistemic oppression. Thus, although experiences of oppression may be necessary for subversive lucidity, they are not sufficient.

Communities function as communities of epistemic resistance in spite of and frequently without the notice of dominant epistemic frameworks because oppressed epistemic communities have 'non-dominant hermeneutical resources to draw upon to interpret their social experiences' such that they have 'shrewd comprehension of their experiences' that are frequently 'inaudible from dominant social locations' (Mason 2011:300). When this 'shrewd comprehension' is enacted in a subversively lucid manner, these communities are able to 'recalibrate and/or create new epistemic resources for knowing the [dominant and marginalized] world more adequately' (Pohlhaus, Jr. 2012:720). One 'community' notable for their ability to develop alternative and subversive epistemic resources is the carceral community.

## Epistemology of incarceration

An oppressed community develops into a community of epistemic resistance through the intentional development of a subversive lucidity that reformulates the epistemic terrain. This is well-evidenced in the collective work of the LoCI-Wittenberg University Writing Group, of which I am a member. We write from behind the walls of London Correctional Institution, a men's prison in London, Ohio. In 'An Epistemology of Incarceration: Constructing Knowing on the Inside',[1] we argue that in spite of the oppressive and dehumanizing conditions that exist in the carceral system, people who are incarcerated can develop a type of subversive lucidity that we describe as an 'epistemology of incarceration'. An epistemology of incarceration is a 'strategic epistemology such that people make knowledge and meaning for themselves even under conditions of incarceration' (10).

For those living outside of prison, developing a critical epistemic consciousness is an achievement of hard, self-reflective work done in concert with a community that productively challenges, questions, and nurtures this work by resisting dominant communities that oppress, deny, and obstruct such a subversive consciousness. An epistemology of incarceration also is the result of hard, critical work. Our group argues that developing subversive lucidity may be even more challenging in prison than on the outside 'because of the high level of control and management that people experience in prison and because survival in prison requires a level of numbness, that regardless of one's epistemic acuity, is necessary to survive prison' (13). Even with the epistemic obstacles people who are incarcerated face, which we detail in our article, many inmates develop the epistemic acuity necessary for an epistemology of incarceration.

This epistemic stance, unique to those that have served time in prison, exemplifies a community of epistemic resistance in three primary ways. First, members of this community have developed a shared heightened consciousness, what we describe as a liminal consciousness, that is the result of 'the prisoner's internal and internalized perception of self as both once free and now incarcerated; the bureaucratic, historical, and social structure of the prison; and prisoner's knowledge of the deeply entrenched perceptions, attitudes and practices of people and institutions on the outside' (11).

Second, inmates with liminal consciousness engage in positive epistemic resistance by generating possibilities for developing epistemic virtues in themselves and in others. Among the ways they do this are: 1) Developing reading and study groups honed on particular topics. 2) Engaging ideas that are inside and outside of the dominant epistemic frameworks, strategically recognizing that 'to appear to know' one must be able to reflect and critique dominant frameworks, but in order 'to know' they must also study and understand alternative frameworks. 3) Practicing somaesthetics, such as yoga, martial arts, and meditation, and teaching or practicing these with other inmates, to develop resources for calm reflection, balance, and equanimity, making their lives in prison more bearable and preparing them for challenges they face on the outside. These practices create opportunities for developing 'the humility to recognize one's cognitive gaps; the diligence to engage in critical self-assessment; curiosity about what is out there to learn and experience; and open-mindedness to put one's self in a new learning situation and make one's self epistemically vulnerable' (18).

These practices are collective, done not only for the development of one's own knowledge and one's own epistemic virtues, but intentionally through an epistemic community that resists the demands of prison life. For example, while I am teaching outside of the U.S. in 2016, some members of our writing group have formed a class on philosophy of science and critical thinking to prepare new students for our class the next academic year. In doing so, they are exercising a level of agency and epistemic subversivity that benefits the collective more so than the individual leaders. This indicates a level of cooperative resistance and clear understanding of the communal nature of knowledge and education that many of us on the outside fail to recognize in our culture, which valorizes individual achievement, recognition, and compensation. The leaders of these groups don't receive pay, reduced time served, or any material benefits for this service. However, these practices help this community prevent or mitigate a 'shutting down one's intellectual and epistemic resources' through the embodiment of the emotional, epistemic, and physical demands of the carceral system (16).[2]

Although on the outside many think of education as a limited epistemic strategy because we tend to minimize its ability to create sustained, meaningful change, in prison education is viewed by many inmates as a prime means to create change for oneself, inside and hopefully outside of prison, and to create change for the overall social structure of the prison. Moreover, because people who are incarcerated 'are caricaturized in popular and political culture as unable to control themselves and as intellectually empty, cultivating an intellectual life that promotes epistemic virtues that most people on the outside don't possess' is a method to resist the dehumanization of incarceration (16). In organizing and participating in these epistemic strategies, the inmates develop shared epistemic resources that not only changes their situation, but that of others.

Third, through their epistemology of incarceration, these inmates function as a community of epistemic resistance by engaging in individual and collective resistance. This can occur through developing epistemic strategies that the LoCI-Wittenberg University Writing Group refers to as 'doing a bit' and 'picking your shots', which are shared, but frequently subtle, strategies for physical, emotional, and epistemic survival in prison.[3] Some are resistant by overt displays of heightened consciousness, such as student projects that challenge the view of prison life and the experiences of people who are incarcerated. For example, a student made a poster board for our class using materials taken from prison bulletin boards showing that the posted rules and practical and administrative structures of prison create a 'prison habitus', which works to ensure that inmates will not develop the epistemic autonomy to survive well on the outside. It is important to note that this student could have been put in solitary confinement for taking materials from bulletin boards. He was highly aware of this, yet felt these materials were critical for painting a full picture of his argument.

What these points about the epistemology of incarceration show is that people who are incarcerated, who arguably are those who are the least likely to have their voices and experiences heard and understood by those on the outside, who experience significant levels of epistemic injustice, are also among those who are most actively resisting such injustice. They are actively and collectively creating and articulating meaning in multiple formats for themselves and others similarly situated.

What is important to take away from this chapter is that when we acknowledge that marginalized communities resist epistemic injustice, we can recognize that although epistemic injustice *is* an injustice, it is not an epistemic dead end. Looking through the lens of epistemological communities allows us to understand not only how communities form under conditions of persistent injustice, but also how they resist this injustice by creating meaning, knowledge, and change.

**Related chapters**: 1, 2, 3, 4, 5, 7, 8, 17, 20, 21

## Notes

1 All references in this section are to this chapter.
2 Our group refers to this type of shutting down as being 'institutionalized'.
3 'Doing a bit' is a term used by people who are incarcerated to doing one's time/sentence (a bit of time) in prison and how one does her/his time. 'Picking your shots' is a term used to describe making conscious choices if, how, and at what cost one is going to resist prison's institutional structure.

## References

Anderson, Benedict (1983) *Imagined Communities*, New York: Verso.
Anderson, Elizabeth (2012) 'Epistemic justice as a virtue of social institutions,' *Social Epistemology*, 26 (2): 163–173.
Code, Lorraine (1991) *What Can She Know?* Ithaca, NY: Cornell University Press.
Collins, Patricia Hill (1991) *Black Feminist Thought*, 1st edition. New York: Routledge.
Collins, Patricia Hill (2000) *Black Feminist Thought*, 2nd edition. New York: Routledge.
Dewey, John (1954) *The Public and Its Problems*, Athens, OH: Swallow Press.
Du Bois, W.E.B. (1995) 'What Does Africa Mean to Me?', in David Levering Lewis (ed.), *W.E.B. Du Bois: A Reader*, New York: Henry Holt and Company, 655–659.
Fricker, Miranda (2007) *Epistemic Injustice*, Oxford: Oxford University Press.
Fricker, Miranda (2009) 'Can There Be Institutional Virtues?', in Tamar Gendler and John Hawthorne (eds.), *Oxford Readings in Epistemology (Special Issue: Social Epistemology)*, vol. 3. Oxford: Oxford University Press, 235–252.
Fricker, Miranda (2012) 'Group testimony: The making of a good collective informant,' *Philosophy and Phenomenological Research*, 84 (2): 249–276.
Goonatilake, Susantha (1993) 'Modern Science in the Periphery: The Characteristics of Dependent Knowledge', in Sandra Harding (ed.), *The Racial Economy of Science*, Bloomington, IN: Indiana University Press, 259–274.
Harding, Sandra (1986) *The Science Question in Feminism*, Ithaca, NY: Cornell University Press.
LoCI-Wittenberg University Writing Group (2016) 'An epistemology of incarceration: Constructing knowing on the inside,' *philoSOPHIA*, 6 (1): 9–26.
Longino, Helen (1990) *Science as Social Knowledge: Values and Objectivity in Scientific Inquiry*, Princeton, NJ: Princeton University Press.

Mason, Rebecca (2011) 'Two kinds of unknowing,' *Hypatia*, 26 (2): 294–307.
Medina, José (2013) *The Epistemology of Resistance: Racial and Gender Oppression, Epistemic Injustice, and Resistant Imaginations*, New York: Oxford University Press.
Mohanty, Chandra (2003) *Feminism without Borders*, 2nd edition. Durham: Duke University Press.
Nelson Hankinson, Lynne (1990) *Who Knows? From Quine to Feminist Empiricism*, Philadelphia: Temple University Press.
Nelson Hankinson, Lynne (1993) 'Epistemological Communities', in Linda Alcoff and Elizabeth Potter (eds.), *Feminist Epistemologies*, New York, NY: Routledge, 121–160.
Pohlhaus, Jr., Gaile (2012) 'Relational knowing and epistemic injustice: Toward a theory of willful hermeneutical ignorance,' *Hypatia*, 27 (4): 715–735.
Spivak Chakravorty, G. (1988) 'Can the Subaltern Speak?', in Cary Nelson and Lawrence Grossberg (eds.), *Marxism and the Interpretation of Culture*, Chicago: University of Illinois Press, 271–313.

# 27
# OBJECTIVITY, EPISTEMIC OBJECTIFICATION, AND OPPRESSION[1]

*Sally Haslanger*

## 1. Kinds of objectivity

The term 'objective' is used in multiple ways.[2] To begin, it is important to distinguish at least three different candidates for objectivity: objective *reality*, objective *discourse*, and objective *knowledge*. Here is how the terms are standardly (though controversially) used in current debates:

> Objective *reality* = what is 'out there', in some sense independent of us; how things are, regardless of how we think or speak about them.
> Objective *discourses* = discourses within which we can express facts.
> Objective *knowledge* = knowledge that can be justified in terms that are accessible to any rational agent.

There may be discourses that enable us to express facts that are not to be found in objective reality. For example, some would argue that secondary qualities, such as color, are not part of objective *reality* because color 'depends on us'. Nevertheless there are objective *facts* about whether a stop sign is red or blue. In contrast to color discourse, however, discourses about what's funny (allegedly) aren't even in the business of expressing facts. Color is not objectively real, but color discourse is objective; funniness isn't objectively real, and its discourse isn't objective either.

Objective knowledge, in turn, is distinguishable from objective discourse for, of course, knowledge requires not just the possibility of expressing facts, but getting the facts right, and more. After all, it is *knowledge*. The thought, however, is that not all knowledge is *objective* knowledge. The demand for objectivity imposes a higher (or different) standard than what is required for other sorts of knowledge. For example, if one gained knowledge of God through mystical experience or revelation not available to all rational inquirers, this would not be objective knowledge. But if God is real, then presumably God is objectively real. So objective knowledge can't just be understood as knowledge of objective reality.

I describe these distinctions not to endorse them, but to consider how what might seem to be a politically neutral set of distinctions can function (along with other background assumptions) to sustain systems of subordination. The project in this essay is not to ask how we should best understand objectivity (in its various forms). Rather, it is to consider how idea of objectivity embedded in evolving social practices.

I am interested especially in cases of what we might call *epistemic objectification*. These occur when a group's actual or imagined epistemic weaknesses are wrongly taken to be due to their nature, or essential to them as a group. Epistemic objectification is often bundled with other forms of objectification that essentialize or naturalize subordinated statuses. It is important to identify how such moves discredit the voices of the subordinate or marginalized so their resistance is muted or distrusted. This discrediting is a form of testimonial injustice. But the injustice of epistemic objectification is more than testimonial. Certain models of objectivity, or objective reality, support what I call *status quo* reasoning that works, under conditions of oppression, to justify subordinating practices quite generally. Status quo reasoning is both an epistemic injustice – since it is one factor in the perpetuation of epistemic marginalization – and also an epistemic tool of oppression.

Miranda Fricker has demonstrated vividly not only how prejudice gives rise to epistemic injustice, but how epistemic injustice is part of a loop such that it is both caused by *and* gives rise to injustice:

> Systematic testimonial injustices, then, are produced not by prejudice *simpliciter,* but specifically by those prejudices that 'track' the subject through different dimensions of social activity . . . when such a [tracker] prejudice generates a testimonial injustice, that injustice is systematically connected with other kinds of actual or potential injustice.
> *(Fricker 2007, 27)*

As I see it, epistemic objectification is typically an important part of this loop. Individuals are subordinated and denied epistemic resources; this causes epistemic harms, sometimes in the form of epistemic deficits; contingent epistemic deficits within the group are then objectified, i.e., treated as normal or natural, so not requiring or even allowing intervention; this rationalizes the denial of epistemic resources and epistemic credibility, thus perpetuating epistemic harm and, given the significance of knowledge both as an instrumental and final good, causing injustice broadly understood.

## 2. Normal, natural, and good[3]

Let's begin with the idea that objective reality is structured: there are objective divisions between some kinds of things, these divisions aren't up to us, and the way the world works depends on these divisions. For example, there is an objective difference between hydrogen and oxygen. The difference between hydrogen and oxygen matters to the causal structure of the world. If we want to know how the world works, we should seek knowledge of chemistry, among other things.

Presumably the difference between hydrogen and oxygen is not an accidental or contingent difference. It's not as if a hydrogen atom could have had eight protons (though we might have called the element with eight protons 'hydrogen'). Each element has a nature that is responsible for how it interacts with other things, giving rise to regularities in its behavior. For example, oxygen dissolves in water, oil does not, due to the chemical composition of each. This leads to a common assumption:

> *Essentialist Assumption*: Robust regularities are not accidental. They are due to the natures of things.[4]

But how do we determine which regularities are 'robust'? After all, oxygen doesn't dissolve in frozen water. And how much oxygen dissolves in a quantity of water depends on temperature, pressure, etc. Typically, to learn the natures of things we look for regularities under 'normal' conditions. Water is 'normally' a liquid, and oxygen dissolves in liquid water.

However, the idea of 'what's normal' has two importantly different uses.

1) 'What's normal' is a statistical concept: what's normal is what is statistically probable. (Normally, barns are red. Normally, November is a rainy month.)
2) 'What's normal' is a normative concept. What's normal is how things "ought" to be, or how things are when circumstances are "favorable". (Normally, humans begin to use language before age two. Normally, we respect others' property.)

The notion of a nature (or essence) provides a link between the statistical sense of normal and the normative sense: Things manifest their nature under normal conditions. And what happens by nature is fitting or right. Or sometimes, what happens by virtue of an X's nature is fitting for Xs.[5]

This line of thought allows that what's natural for something isn't inevitable. Accidents happen. The natural course of things can be disrupted. In some conditions, things manifest a 'deformity', their nature isn't fully expressed, e.g., a normal pregnancy will result in a normal offspring, but not all pregnancies or offspring are normal. A claim that something is abnormal is not just a statistical claim about how rare it is. If high lead levels are found in a water supply and, as a result, the majority of the children are born with cognitive challenges, we would not conclude that these challenges are normal for children. So the link between the statistical and normative senses of 'normal' relies on a further assumption:

> *Normative Assumption:* Things should express their natures, and under normal/favorable circumstances they will. Abnormal/unfavorable circumstances are not good and should be avoided or changed.

Note, however, that the epistemic value of the link between what's normal and what's essential is questionable. If we know what is essential to X, we can determine the normal/favorable conditions for X because those are conditions under which X reveals its essence and behaves in ways that are natural for it. But if we don't know what is essential to X, it is not clear what conditions are normal/favorable for it. There is a temptation, then, to fall back on the statistical sense of normal, for that may be our best evidence of X's nature.

The problem, however, is that what's statistically normal for a kind is *not* always due to the nature of that kind because it may be caused by unfavorable or socially manipulated circumstances. For example, under conditions in which women are denied access to formal education, it will be unsurprising if they are ill-equipped to compete intellectually in the public sphere: their vocabulary and conceptual repertoire may be stunted, their reasoning may make reference to considerations that are not considered relevant. This may be interpreted, however, as 'natural' for women, not a result of their contingent social circumstances; as a result, arguments that they should be given access to formal education fall flat, for women don't display the cognitive capacities that would make efforts to educate them fruitful.

Moreover, what's due to the nature of the kind is *not* always good or worth protecting (what *ought to be*), because we are sometimes in a position to improve on what's natural. For example, on one interpretation the whole point of society (cooperation, education, medicine, etc.) is to improve upon the natural. So both the essentialist and the normative assumptions are misguided. In short, what's 'normal' is not always natural, and what's natural is not always best. The corollary is also important: what is abnormal or unnatural is not always bad.

## 3. Status quo reasoning

The *Essentialist* and *Normative Assumptions* provide excellent resources to reinforce the status quo. Suppose we aren't in a position to make assumptions about the natures of things. But the natures of things (in chemistry and also politics) matter. If we make policies that require people to behave in ways that are contrary to human nature, it is a problem. Aiming to 'stick to the facts', suppose we note that on the whole, Fs are G, e.g., that women are nurturing. Suppose we also note that very often when we try to change Fs to be non-G, we fail, e.g., when we put women in highly competitive environments, they are unhappy and unsuccessful. It is tempting, then, to conclude that Fs are G by nature: Fs being G is not only statistically normal, but also normatively normal, e.g., that women are by nature nurturing. Or at least, we conclude that this "way things are" should be accommodated. If being G really is part of the nature of Fs, then if some Fs are not G, we should regard those Fs as defective and in need of correction, or we should anticipate that they will revert to their nature when circumstances normalize.

This observation about the naturalizing of the social world is not new: if the social world is a certain way (statistically), it must be due to nature, so good and right, and we shouldn't attempt to change it. This has implications for both objectification and marginalization.

### *a. Objectification*

The term 'objectification' is used in multiple ways (Papadaki 2015). The most common use occurs in moral theory in the context of a Kantian prohibition against treating individuals as means only and not as ends. To fail to recognize someone as a moral subject and to use them, against their will, simply to satisfy one's needs or desires, is to treat them as an object and do them a moral wrong. Objectification in this sense is connected with other morally problematic features of one's action including denial of the other's subjectivity and agency; belief in their instrumentality, fungibility, violability, claims of ownership (Nussbaum 1995), reduction to body or appearance; and silencing (Langton 2009).

However, 'objectification' is also used in a more general sense for a process of projection whereby an object is taken to have certain properties inherently that one only experiences or desires it to have (Langton 2004). For example, according to Hume, we objectify color, the necessity of causation, and value. In the case of persons, such objectification often depends on a desire-driven or projective illusion about the object of one's desire. Wanting someone or something to be a certain way, one comes to believe it is through processes such as 'phenomenological gilding', wishful thinking, and pseudo-empathy. Perpetrators who use another as a sex object, often do so under a projective illusion, i.e., they objectify the individual in both a Kantian sense and a projective sense.

There is another wrong, however, that can also be considered a form of objectification (Haslanger 2012, Ch. 1; Langton 2000). The *Essentialist* and *Normative Assumptions* entail that, in general, things have natures that call for a certain sort of treatment. For example, it may be that human beings are, by nature, rational, and their rationality calls for respect. As we saw above, a problem arises when we don't have knowledge of the natures of things and take statistical regularities to be evidence of natures. We are then apt to take accidental features of things to be 'given' by nature, or essential to them. In this sense of objectification, a group of things is (wrongly) viewed and treated as a kind of object, and the accidental properties in question are taken to be part of its nature. For example, this occurs in the 'naturalizing' of social roles: the characteristic roles that members of a group occupy are taken to be an expression of their kind's nature.[6]

Consider sexual objectification. In paradigm cases of sexual objectification, one person is treated merely as a sex object for the other's pleasure. This is plausibly a violation of the Kantian principle that persons should not be treated as mere means. But it would be wrong to understand sexual objectification simply as one-off occurrences or even a form of relationship between individuals. Typically, sexual objectification is a cultural phenomenon, and the vivid examples we are usually asked to reflect upon are manifestations of it.[7] The objectification of women, for example, involves a cultural interpretation of what women are *for*. Women are *for* satisfying men's desires. (In the case of sexual objectification, *for* satisfying men's sexual desires.) Even if the majority of people in the culture in question do not explicitly hold this belief, it may reasonably be postulated as an interpretation of the background ideology in a culture that regularly positions women as the caretakers (sexual or otherwise) of men. This form of objectification occurs as an organizing cultural frame: women have a nature (to serve and please men), and their nature suits them to function in particular social roles (wives, mothers, girlfriends).

The objectification of women plausibly combines both a projective and naturalizing error (women are *for* the satisfaction of men's needs) and a Kantian error (so we may treat them as tools). As suggested above, once a system of subordination is in place, naturalizing of social roles can happen just through what might appear to be a harmless, even objective, generalization from the evidence. For example, we might ask: are women or men better suited to nurture the young? Look around. Women are still overwhelmingly the primary caregivers of children (in addition to the sick, aged, disabled). Statistically, that's normal. And given this work, women have, in fact, developed abilities to nurture infants that most men have not developed. Of course there are women who are not mothers, who don't have nurturing tendencies, and who function well in competitive environments, but they are not 'normal'. If the actual world supports the idea that women are better suited to nurture the young, the *Essentialist* and *Normative Assumptions* easily kick in. So even if women appear to be effective competitors in business, industry, science, their nature may exert itself to override these 'unnatural' inclinations at any time, and it is a risk to include them fully. Moreover, the struggle that mothers in fact have in the workplace just proves that our sense of what's right and good for women is correct. If a working mother's life were easy, that would be unnatural given her nature to nurture. This is status quo reasoning at its most powerful. The world supports what we expect because we have made it that way. (Wittig 1993, 11–12)

This exemplifies the 'looping effect' of social kinds. Hacking (1995) describes the looping effect this way:[8]

> New sorting and theorizing induces changes in self-conception and in behaviour of the people classified. Those changes demand revisions of the classification and theories, the causal connections, and the expectations. Kinds are modified, revised classifications are formed, and the classified change again, loop upon loop.
>
> *(370)*

Note, however, that Hacking's loops always involve agents appropriating the classification as part of their intentional actions and even identity. An agent is labeled a 'refugee' and enacts the behavior taken to be characteristic of refugees, eventually incorporating the status of refugee in her identity; if refugees organize and change how refugees are viewed and treated, the theory of refugee must update to accommodate this (Hacking 1999, 9–10).

But the causal mechanism of looping need not always proceed through the activity of classification or theorizing or the identity and intentionality of the agents involved (Haslanger 2012 Ch. 3; cf. Mallon 2015), and the looping may occur in different directions. As social institutions and structures evolve, material opportunities shift so that the patterns of action and interaction change. We can unintentionally 'make people' be a certain way through large structures that are not under anyone's control and are not conceptualized, e.g., the interactions between educational, employment, and residential opportunities, together with transportation, health care, and judicial systems, can create social regularities, and notably inequalities, that are not intended or even apparent to us (Tilly 2002, 28). In objectification, the failure to recognize the structures that give rise to the regularities leads us to attribute the regularities to something intrinsic to the agents (Haslanger 2014a). The *Essentialist* and *Normative* Assumptions take hold. The 'labels' that we then apply to those socially positioned in the structures may *or may not* be taken up as identities.

This is clearly relevant to the issue of epistemic injustice (Haslanger 2014b). During oral argument in a recent affirmative action, *Fisher v. University of Texas*, before the Supreme Court,[9] the late Justice Antonin Scalia said:

> There are those who contend that it does not benefit African Americans to get them into the University of Texas, where they do not do well, as opposed to having them go to a less-advanced school, a slower-track school where they do well.[10]

It is tempting to read Scalia as engaged in a kind of epistemic objectification of African Americans: African Americans have not done well at the University of Texas (he claims); this reveals something about the epistemic potential of African Americans (as opposed, e.g., to the workings of bias or stereotype threat at the University of Texas). As a result, a school that is less demanding is more 'fitting' for African Americans.

Epistemic objectification comes in a variety of forms; in each case, one's status as a knower is conditioned by assumptions concerning one's proper social role or function. For example, in the case of women, objectification has historically depended on the projection of male desire: women are *for* meeting men's (sexual, childbearing, domestic) needs. In the case of African Americans, objectification is about labor: Blacks are *for* menial labor or domestic work; they are the 'enslaveable' (Smith 2006, 67). Robert Moses has argued that even now, in the United States, African Americans are provided only a 'sharecropper education'.

> A sharecropper education is an education of lowest expectations. Because people do a certain kind of work, their education is directly tied to this kind of work; they learn no more than is necessary to complete the task.[11]

In the contemporary economy, 'sharecropper education in the age of cotton has been transported alive and kicking into the age of information'.[12] This, of course, is an epistemic injustice: Blacks who are granted only a sharecropper education within the context of a knowledge economy are prevented from developing the epistemic capacities and confidence that are essential to full participation, thus rendering them systematically vulnerable to injustice.

The educational system creates looping effects, even if those upon whom the needs are projected do not identify with the characteristics attributed to them. For example, stigmatizing meanings of the Black body generate mistrust that alienates Black teens from school; the lack of education and access to professional success reinforces the racially stigmatizing meanings (Haslanger 2014b). But such looping does not depend on Blacks identifying with their role in providing menial labor, or dis-identifying with educational achievement per se. Alienation is from a school system that demeans and degrades them. We should never assume that people don't want what they can't have.

As was true of the southern civil rights movement, where sharecroppers, maids, day workers, and others who were expected to be silent found their voice, meaningful school reform will require the voices of students and communities demanding the quality education that too many assume they can't handle and don't want.

*(Moses and Cobb 2001, 12)*

Objectification, then, has multiple forms that support each other. Society is structured so that those occupying certain social positions exhibit regularities of behavior (or other features) whose social origin is invisible; cultural explanations of these regularities take them to flow from the natures of those occupying the social positions. This is what we might call naturalization or, more generally, ideological objectification. This, in turn, can support a projective fantasy that the structures we are aware of are actually fitting for those so-positioned; the structures are apt for those with such natures. This is projective objectification. And if the fantasy is that the world (and the nature of those socially positioned as our partners, workers, etc.) is such as to satisfy our desires, then the subjectivity and autonomy of the other is eclipsed as we treat them as a tool for such satisfaction, while thinking this fitting. This is Kantian objectification. Each of these leads to significant epistemic injustices:

1) *Ideological objectification* obscures the contingent social origins of our social (and epistemic) structures, impairing our capacity to identify *gaps* in shared hermeneutical resource (and the *causes* of those gaps).
2) *Projective objectification* promotes a sense that people are where they belong and the epistemic status quo is just or fair or inevitable.
3) *Kantian objectification* deprives those thus positioned of the subjectivity and autonomy constitutive of genuine epistemic agency.

*(See Fricker [2007, 44] and Pohlhaus, Jr. [2014] on 'truncated subjectivity')*

When one is treated badly and told that it is fitting, and the treatment is supported by both the institutional and ideological structures that dominate one's milieu, no wonder people come to accept it and conform their behavior: loop upon loop.

## *b. Marginalization*

Inferences supported by the *Essentialist* and *Normative Assumptions* are key to marginalization. In a milieu dominated by White people, a Black person is not normal. If the outlier is not normal, then they, or the circumstances, are unnatural, and there is need of correction. Of course, one's racial ancestry cannot be corrected, but the situation calls for adjustment. The effort to correct may focus on behavior or attitude. Or perhaps, since race itself cannot be changed, the conclusion is that Blacks are inherently defective and appropriately marginalized. Substitute for 'Black person' in the argument any non-dominant group descriptor. The world doesn't always reinforce our judgments of what's natural and right with perfect regularities, but that poses no challenge to an ideology that includes the *Normative Assumption*. Rather, the world's imperfections provide us opportunities to set nature on its proper path.

In the case of the disabled, the *Normative Assumption* has particular power to rationalize intervention. The very definition of disability seems to cast disabled persons as (normatively) abnormal. They are defective and so require treatment. Moreover, local impairment is often generalized to the whole individual: recently in an airport next to my husband who is in a wheelchair, an airline employee asked me: 'What is your husband's name'? as if the fully alert individual in the wheelchair in front of him couldn't answer even that simple question on his own. Looping again: prejudice against the disabled together with the *Essentialist* and *Normative Assumptions* renders them as 'by nature' incompetent, which denies them credibility and epistemic respect, which deprives them of resources and access to meaningful engagement, which fosters further prejudice. The problem is both testimonial and hermeneutic; the disabled are not only ignored or discredited, but typically their experiences of illness or disability are interpreted through the lens of the medical profession rather than in terms that are meaningful to the individual affected. (See also Carel and Kidd 2014).

The implications of such assumptions of 'abnormality' have prompted some theorists and activists to adopt the social model of disability. The social model distinguishes 'impairment' from 'disability'. *Impairment* consists of the disabled person's physical 'defect' or 'limitation'. *Disability* consists in the ways in which society allows or causes an individual's impairment to disadvantage them unjustly. For example, on the social model, being myopic is an impairment, but for most of us it isn't a disability because we have access to prescription glasses or contacts. But myopia is a disability for those who are poor and uninsured because their myopia goes uncorrected due to a lack of economic and social resources, and this has consequences for their ability to function fully in society. (See also Cooper 2007.)

The advantage of the social model is that it locates the condition to be changed in the social context rather than the disabled person's body. However, the social model seems to accept the idea that disabled bodies are impaired in a way that makes them inherently defective. But this is far from obvious. Shelley Tremain (2001) argues that, contrary to the assumptions of the social model, impairment is not a purely natural state. Even what counts as an impairment depends on the social context and, more specifically, is managed through a social/governmental/medical process that 'reads' bodies in terms of what can and cannot be treated. In particular, the very idea of an impairment arises through what she calls a 'diagnostic' mode of reasoning that focuses attention on features of individuals that are assumed to be in need of being fixed or managed. But by whose lights, and for what purposes? Elizabeth Barnes (2009, 2014) convincingly argues that to assume that disability (or impairment) is inherently bad depends on a skewed conception of human health and well-being. She argues, in keeping with many disability rights activists, that 'being disabled isn't something that's bad for you. Disability is, rather, a natural part of human diversity – something that should be valued and celebrated, rather than pitied and ultimately 'cured' (2014, 88; also Barnes 2016). Both the diagnostic paradigm and the misunderstanding of well-being impose substantial hermeneutic injustices.

In the case of disability, both the *Essentialist* and *Normative Assumptions* function in rather complex ways. If we assume that it is not just statistically but also normatively normal for adult humans to, say, walk without assistance, then walking is natural and fitting, and those who cannot without assistance are not just different, but defective. Likewise for cognitive disabilities: those who cannot process information quickly or who are challenged by complex social interaction are defective, even though such differences can also be advantages (Grandin 2006). The *Normative Assumption* provides the evaluation of the condition as a 'defect', and the *Essentialist Assumption* locates the defect in the individual.

Disability is usually considered a defect with respect to human nature, but it is worth noting that human conditions, understood as natural conditions, can be objectified too. Consider multiple sclerosis. It is statistically normal for those with multiple sclerosis to have difficulty with walking and balance. If we take these challenges to be a normal consequence of MS, then the *Essentialist Assumption* takes this to be indicative of a nature – but what nature? It seems to be the nature of MS to cause people difficulty with walking and balance. But this can seem to license two conclusions: 1) people who have MS and don't have difficulty with walking and balance don't *really* have MS (which is false), or 2) it is fitting for people with MS to have difficulty walking, so we shouldn't expect otherwise. This has the result that if you have MS, either you exemplify the nature of MS and can't avoid it without (invasive?) intervention, or you don't really have it at all.

These patterns of inference also apply to other social categories. Recall above that we considered that race (or sex) might be considered a defect: Blackness is abnormal and so a defective way of being human. Suppose we consider Blackness as a human condition, something like a disability. If we look for statistics about Blacks, they may seem to support conclusions about the nature of Blackness. Under social conditions in which Blacks are systematically subordinated, the 'nature' of Blackness will look pretty grim. Suppose the conclusion is that being Black carries with it being disposed to criminal activity. Then if we follow the pattern of inference outlined in the previous paragraph, we should draw two conclusions: 1) Blacks who aren't disposed to criminal activity aren't *really* Black, and 2) it is fitting for those who are Black to be disposed to criminal activity, and we shouldn't expect otherwise, at least not without (invasive?) intervention. This has epistemic consequences as well, for example, in education: 1) Blacks who do well in school aren't *really* Black, and 2) it is fitting for those who are Black to do poorly in school, and we shouldn't expect otherwise.

Thus, ideological objectification relying on the *Essentialist* and *Normative Assumptions* can help us explain two kinds of loops: loops in which what we have created is entrenched, and what we have disvalued is either marginalized or 'legitimately' changed. Objectification doesn't just affect what's in our heads; it affects what exists, what regularities are to be found, what types of things there are, and even what natures are manifested in the world. The material world reinforces our tutored dispositions. Racial classification and stigmatization reinforces racial segregation, which reinforces racial identity, which reinforces racial classification and stigmatization. Social structures, good or bad, constitute our lived reality; they also affect how the world evolves, what is and isn't in it.

## 4. Epistemic objectivity, epistemic injustice, and social critique

I've already suggested that our efforts to be (epistemically) objective, to 'stick to the facts', are implicated in the process of objectification. According to the dominant model of epistemic objectivity, we are objective in our inquiry if and only if our beliefs are justified in terms accessible to any rational inquirer. If one also assumes that we cannot have objective knowledge of value, then to be objective, our inquiry should be value-free.

Interestingly, the *Normative Assumption* seems acceptable even within inquiry that seeks to be objective. If the sense of goodness at issue is just what's 'fitting" for something given the nature of its kind, then the thought is that we have a naturalized form of value that is knowable through rational inquiry. Biologists can tell us what is normatively normal for mammals and marsupials: we can tell when a cat or a kangaroo is deformed and even identify possible causes of the deformity. So why not think that if we investigate human beings empirically, we too can determine what is natural and so fitting and good for them?

My own view is that empirical investigation is crucial for understanding what is good for humans and other things, and I'm even sympathetic to some claims about natures. But 'empiricist' moves that draw inferences to natures from statistical regularities are clearly not valid. And as feminists and others have argued for several decades, we should resist the claim that objective inquiry must be value free. (For example, Anderson 1995; Intemann 2010; Longino 1990; Mills 1988). A full discussion of epistemic objectivity would take us well beyond the limits of this chapter. Focusing on the issue of objectification, however, the task is to determine when a regularity is something that can and should be disrupted (which isn't simply a question of its naturalness!), and when it is one that we should accommodate.

There are two tendencies embedded in the *Essentialist* and *Normative Assumptions* that should be resisted in order to make progress on these tasks. The first is an individualism that locates the source of social patterns in individuals and ignores or rejects structural explanations of those patterns (Haslanger 2015). The second is bias towards stability and the status quo, in particular, the presumption that if this is the way things really (naturally) are, it is good (or good enough). Social critique must be prepared to destabilize the individual and the 'normal' conditions in which individuals interact, if it is to be successful in undoing the objectification that has made the social world what it is. Epistemic justice is not just about hearing the testimony of others or expanding our hermeneutical resources (though both are important), but also undertaking to dismantle the structures through which we objectify epistemic agents to suit the purposes of capitalist, ableist, White supremacist patriarchy.

**Related chapters**: 11, 16, 22, 23, 26

# Notes

1 Thanks to Abby Jaques, Rae Langton, and Stephen Yablo for helpful conversations, and to Ian James Kidd, José Medina, and Gaile Pohlhaus, Jr. for excellent comments on earlier drafts.
2 My understanding of these issues has been greatly enhanced by teaching a graduate seminar on objectivity with Stephen Yablo (Fall 2015). Thanks to him and to the seminar participants for their insights.
3 I've discussed some of these issues in connection with generics in Haslanger (2012, Ch. 1 & 17) and Haslanger (2014a).
4 Ron Mallon (2007) has offered compelling arguments that 'essentialism' is both too strong and too weak a view to capture the target of social constructionist critique, because a contingent causal homeostasis amongst a cluster of properties is sufficient for a natural kind (Boyd 1999; Mallon 2003, 2007). Of course the argument depends on what conception of essence one has in mind. In contemporary metaphysics, certain assumptions are common, viz., essences can, in principle, be captured by necessary and sufficient conditions for being that (kind of) thing, not all properties that something has necessarily are part of its essence, a thing's existence depends on its satisfying the conditions for its essence (it couldn't exist without having the relevant essential properties), and everything that is a member of a kind has an essence (Fine 1994, 1995). 'Essence', however, is sometimes treated as synonymous with 'nature', as in a *thing's* (or *kind's*) *nature*. I use the term 'nature' instead of 'essence' because it is more flexible and allows for kinds of variation not permitted by 'essence'. I have kept the term 'essentialism' because of its historical significance in these debates, but do not commit to the theses just listed. 'Naturalism' is not an adequate substitute because it has very different connotations.
5 There are actually two different claims at issue here. We sometimes use the term 'kind' for substance kinds such as *horse* or *human*, and sometimes for qualitative kinds such as *liquid* or *living*. Social kinds are confusing because they function in some ways like substance kinds, but are not essential to their members, so are more like qualitative kinds, e.g., *mother, professor*. In considering the nature of an individual (me), what's at issue is the substance kind (*human*). But I am also a mother and a professor, and insofar as there is something it is to be a mother, and a professor, these too have natures. They are qualitative natures or natures of the relevant properties/relations. But they are not part of my nature. And it may not be fitting for me to be either a mother or a professor. This is a source of much confusion, but I won't elaborate on it here.
6 There are two ways this might happen. For example, the characteristic roles that women occupy may be taken to be part of what it is to be a woman. If one is essentially a woman, then these characteristic roles become part of one's nature or essence. Or the characteristic roles that mothers occupy may be taken to be conditions on what it is to be a mother. Even if one is not essentially a mother, those who are mothers can be 'real' mothers only if they satisfy these conditions. See also fn. 3.
7 On the general idea of objectification, or reification, as a social, even structural, phenomenon, see also Honneth (2006), e.g., p. 100.

8 Also Hacking, "Making Up People," *London Review of Books* 2006, www.lrb.co.uk/v28/n16/ian-hacking/making-up-people
9 www.scotusblog.com/case-files/cases/fisher-v-university-of-texas-at-austin-2/
10 www.cnn.com/2015/12/09/politics/scalia-black-scientists-scotus/
11 www.ascd.org/publications/educational-leadership/oct01/vol59/num02/Algebra-and-Activism@-Removing-the-Shackles-of-Low-Expectations%E2%80%94A-Conversation-with-Robert-P.-Moses.aspx
12 www.qecr.org/press/17-robert-p-moses-we-tolerate-a-sharecroppers-education

# References

Anderson, Elizabeth. 1995. "Knowledge, Human Interests, and Objectivity in Feminist Epistemology." *Philosophical Topics* 23(2): 27–58.
Barnes, Elizabeth. 2009. "Disability and Adaptive Preference." *Philosophical Perspectives* 23(1): 1–23.
Barnes, Elizabeth. 2014. "Valuing Disability, Causing Disability." *Ethics* 125(1): 88–113.
Barnes, Elizabeth. 2016. *The Minority Body*. Oxford: Oxford University Press.
Boyd, Richard. 1999. "Homeostasis, Species and Higher Taxa." Robert A. Wilson (ed.), *Species: New Interdisciplinary Essays*. Cambridge, MA: MIT Press, pp. 141–186.
Carel, Havi and Ian James Kidd. 2014. "Epistemic Injustice in Healthcare: A Philosophical Analysis." *Medicine, Healthcare and Philosophy* 17(4): 529–540.
Cooper, Rachel. 2007. "Can It Be a Good Thing to Be Deaf?" *Journal of Medicine and Philosophy* 32(6): 563–583.
Daston, Lorraine and Peter Galison. 2007. *Objectivity*. Cambridge, MA: MIT Press.
Fine, Kit. 1994. "Essence and Modality." *Philosophical Perspectives* 8 (ed. J. Tomberlin): 1–16.
Fine, Kit. 1995. "Senses of Essence." Walter Sinnott-Armstrong, Diana Raffman, and Nicholas Asher (eds.), *Modality, Morality, and Belief: Essays in Honor of Ruth Barcan Marcus*, Cambridge: Cambridge University Press, pp. 53–73.
Fricker, Miranda. 2007. *Epistemic Injustice: Power and the Ethics of Knowing*. Oxford: Oxford University Press.
Grandin, Temple. 2006. *Animals in Translation: Using the Mysteries of Autism to Decode Animal Behavior*. New York: Harcourt.
Hacking, Ian. 1986. "Making Up People." Thomas C. Heller, Morton Sosna, and David E. Wellbery (eds.), *Reconstructing Individualism: Autonomy, Individuality, and the Self in Western Thought*. Stanford: Stanford University Press, pp. 222–236.
Hacking, Ian. 1995. "The Looping Effects of Human Kinds." Dan Sperber, David Premack, and Ann James Premack (eds.), *Causal Cognition: A Multi-Disciplinary Debate*. New York: Oxford University Press, pp. 351–383.
Hacking, Ian. 1999. *The Social Construction of What?* Cambridge, MA: Harvard University Press.
Haslanger, Sally. 2012. *Resisting Reality: Social Construction and Social Critique*. Oxford: Oxford University Press.
Haslanger, Sally. 2014a. "The Normal, the Natural and the Good: Generics and Ideology." *Politica & Società* 3: 365–392.
Haslanger, Sally. 2014b. "Studying While Black: Trust, Opportunity and Disrespect." *DuBois Review* 11(1): 109–136.
Haslanger, Sally. 2015. "What Is a (Social) Structural Explanation?" *Philosophical Studies* 173(1): 113–130.
Honneth, Axel. 2006. *Reification: A Recognition-Theoretical View*. The Tanner Lectures on Human Values, March 14–16, University of California, Berkeley. http://tannerlectures.utah.edu/_documents/a-to-z/h/Honneth_2006.pdf.
Intemann, Kristen. 2010. "25 Years of Feminist Empiricism and Standpoint Theory: Where Are We Now?" *Hypatia* 25(4): 778–796.
Langton, Rae. 2000. "Feminism in Epistemology: Exclusion and Objectification." M. Fricker and J. Hornsby (eds.), *The Cambridge Companion to Feminism in Philosophy*. Cambridge: Cambridge University Press, pp. 127–145.
Langton, Rae. 2004. "Projection and Objectification." Brian Leiter (ed.), *The Future for Philosophy*. Oxford: Clarendon Press, pp. 285–303.
Langton, Rae. 2009. "Autonomy-Denial in Objectification." *Sexual Solipsism: Philosophical Essays on Pornography and Objectification*. New York: Oxford University Press, pp. 223–240.

Longino, Helen. 1990. *Science as Social Knowledge*. Princeton: Princeton University Press.
MacKinnon, Catharine. 1989. *Towards a Feminist Theory of the State*. Cambridge, MA: Harvard University Press.
Mallon, Ron. 2003. "Social Roles, Social Construction, and Stability." F. Schmitt (ed.), *Socializing Metaphysics*. Lanham, MD: Rowman and Littlefield, pp. 327–353.
Mallon, Ron. 2007. "Human Categories Beyond Non-Essentialism." *Journal of Political Philosophy* 15(2): 146–168.
Mallon, Ron. 2015. "Performance, Self-Explanation, and Agency." *Philosophical Studies* 172(10): 2777–2798.
Mills, Charles. 1988. "Alternative Epistemologies." *Social Theory and Practice* 14(3): 237–263. Special Issue: Marxism-Feminism: Powers of Theory/Theories of Power.
Moses, Robert P. 2010. "Constitutional Property and Constitutional People." Theresa Perry, Robert P. Moses, Joan T. Wynne, Ernesto Cortés, Jr., and Lisa Delpit (eds.), *Quality Education as a Constitutional Right*. Boston: Beacon Press, pp. 70–92.
Moses, Robert P. and Charles Cobb, Jr. 2001. "Organizing Algebra: The Need to Voice a Demand." *Social Policy* 31(4): 4–12.
Nussbaum, Martha. 1995. "Objectification." *Philosophy and Public Affairs* 24(4): 249–291.
Papadaki, Evangelia (Lina). 2015. "Feminist Perspectives on Objectification", *The Stanford Encyclopedia of Philosophy* (Winter Edition), Edward N. Zalta (ed.), URL = <http://plato.stanford.edu/archives/win2015/entries/feminism-objectification/>.
Pohlhaus, Jr., Gaile. 2014. "Discerning the Primary Epistemic Harm in Cases of Testimonial Injustice." *Social Epistemology* 28(2): 99–114.
Rousseau, Jean Jacques. 1979/1762. *Emile: Or on Education*. Allan Bloom (ed. & trans.). New York: Basic Books.
Smith, Andrea. 2006. "Heteropatriarchy and the Three Pillars of White Supremacy." Incite! Women of Color Against Violence (ed.), *The Color of Violence: The Incite! Anthology*. Boston: South End Press, pp. 66–73.
Tilly, Charles. 2002. "The Trouble with Stories." *Stories, Identities, and Political Change*. Lanham, MD: Rowman and Littlefield, 25–41.
Tremain, Shelley. 2001. "On the Government of Disability." *Social Theory and Practice* 27(4): 617–636.
Wittig, Monique. 1993/1981. "One is Not Born a Woman." *The Straight Mind*. New York: Basic Books, 9–20.
Wollstonecraft, Mary. 1999/1792. *A Vindication of the Rights of Men, a Vindication of the Rights of Woman, An Historical and Moral View of the French Revolution*. Oxford World's Classics. Oxford: Oxford University Press.

# PART 5
# Case studies of epistemic injustice

# 28
# EPISTEMIC JUSTICE AND THE LAW[1]

*Michael Sullivan*

In criminal law the choice of what (and who) to punish and how much to punish has consequence for the kind of activities and lives that thrive or fail to thrive in our society. Of course, this is a complicated story that must include consideration of those who make the law, enforce the law, prosecute the law, judge the law, and apply the judgments of courts. All of these actors and many more not explicitly named contribute to the social meaning of the law in our society. Testimony, by experts and laypersons, is a central ingredient in the formulation of law and the adjudication of disputes. We use it to determine the motivation and intention of those who are accused of violating the law. At many turns, opportunities for epistemic injustice abound in the practices of our legal system because our institutions and ourselves are not up to the challenges of understanding the experiences of others in difficult situations foreign to our own and because we remain unaware of the role that unexamined prejudice and bias play even in our best efforts to be impartial.

We have laws against murder, assault, and stealing but also against financial fraud, drug possession, prostitution, littering. Many of these laws are unevenly enforced. There has been almost no criminal prosecution of bankers, for example, stemming from fraudulent loans or financial misreporting antecedent to the 2008 economic collapse. When activities are made illegal, enforcement agencies sometimes pursue one side of the criminal enterprise rather than the others – drug dealers rather than users, prostitutes rather than their clients. When laws are enforced and offenders convicted, it is often hard to explain disparities in sentencing among offenders even within the same jurisdiction. These disparities in sentencing are not unrelated to issues of social power and epistemic authority.

## Courts, judges, and juries

Courts are tasked with hearing contested cases and deciding their outcome. It might not be quite right to put it this way, but we often say that the courts are supposed to determine the truth of the matter. Courts make determinations regarding the contested facts in a case, and they apply the law to those facts. Often these decisions are made by juries with the assistance of judges. The United States models its court system primarily according to a theory of an adversary system. According to this theory, the two sides to a dispute make their case before a disinterested and impartial judge and/or jury. The central idea is that given fair rules, the competition between adversaries should help the truth come out. There are various depictions of the lady of justice sitting blind before the scales of justice. The blindness speaks to her impartiality and the scale to her task of weighing the strength of the competing sides of the case before her. When this image is interpreted in the context of the adversary system, it is said that if the two sides are given equal opportunity to present their case against each other, then the truth will emerge and tip the scales in favor of justice.

How well this theory works in practice has been the subject of extensive critical debate. There is no shortage of examples that raise questions about the impartiality of judges and juries and even about the suitability of impartiality as an ideal in light of mounting evidence that, for cognitive reasons, it may be impossible to achieve.[2] There is great worry that differences in skill among the attorneys contesting a case does more to tip the scales than the underlying truth of the matters ever will. An issue compounded by the fact that differences in the quality of attorney representation seem often correlated to the amount of money a client is able to spend. There are also deep concerns that the rules of evidence, even when they are primarily intended to assist the discovery of truth, often do the opposite.[3]

The rules of evidence are a complicated affair, not always geared toward prioritizing truth over other goals of the court system. We let individuals take the 5th Amendment in criminal proceedings rather than compelling them to testify against themselves. Also, in such proceedings, we let spouses invoke a special privilege to avoid testifying against their husband or wife. We exclude otherwise reliable evidence if it was collected as a result of an unlawful search and seizure. These, and other commitments, show that while determining the truth may be central, it is not the only matter of concern for constitutional, moral, and other reasons.

Yet, it is impossible to deny that our justice system is predicated on the idea that to do justice, the courts must seek the truth. Juries are asked not "who would you prefer win," but "who did what" and, in light of that, "who is entitled to what under the law?" Some of the oldest derivations of the word *justice* focus upon the idea that to do justice is to give to each what they are due. In our system, answering that question requires figuring out what has and has not been done and what the law proscribes in light of those facts. For the most part, it is held that judges and juries act appropriately only in so far as they make a good faith effort to answer these questions.[4]

## Truth and epistemic justice

Getting at the truth of contested facts is at the heart of our court system. It is and must be, at least *prima facie*, a central goal and value, perhaps the central one. To say this is not in any way to deny the salience of many excellent critiques of our justice system that highlight the ways in which appeals to truth mask systematic features that illegitimately privilege some groups and individuals rather than others. And yet, part of the reason such critiques are trenchant is precisely because our court system does, and must, claim that the verdicts it reaches are, given the tools available to it and qualified at times by the need to curtail the fact finding process to protect individual rights, good faith efforts motivated by a desire to get to the truth.

Accordingly, recent attention to epistemic injustice is of special interest to those concerned with the law. The discourse around epistemic injustice is connected with several authors, but especially to Miranda Fricker's (2007) book, *Epistemic Injustice: Power and the Ethics of Knowing*.[5] Fricker focuses principally on two injustices that she views as epistemic in nature: first, *testimonial injustice* wherein a speaker's credibility is undermined improperly because of prejudice, and second, *hermeneutical injustice* "when a gap in collective interpretive resources puts someone at an unfair advantage when it comes to making sense of their social experience" (1). Hermeneutical injustice is a complicated affair, but it also impacts the intelligibility of marginalized speakers. On Fricker's view, it is not a harm perpetrated by an agent (159) but "the injustice of having some significant area of one's social experience obscured from collective understanding owing to a structural identity prejudice in the collective hermeneutical resource" (155).

In *The Epistemology of Resistance*, José Medina contributes to the discussion and debate started by Fricker.[6] He argues that, in some ways, the kind of harms that Fricker characterizes as hermeneutic are harms for which some agents deserve to be blamed. He notes that there are several epistemic vices, often possessed by subjects in positions of social power, that have the effect of *actively* perpetuating their ignorance. These vices include arrogance, laziness, and close-mindedness, and they lead to the production of active ignorance. This approach wants to hold people accountable for what it sees as creating and maintaining an active ignorance with respect to the lives of others. Epistemic laziness manifests itself in a lack of curiosity about the contexts of the lives of others. Epistemic arrogance is often possessed by those who become accustomed to having their speech recognized socially as authoritative, whose speech is seldom challenged or treated as marginal. Imagine the difficulties involved when the conduct of someone in a marginal social position is assessed primarily by those in social positions at high risk of epistemic arrogance.

The debate over how best to think about the deficiencies that are described as forms of epistemic injustice is robust and far from settled. However, even as key issues continue to be vigorously debated, the general trajectory of the discourse surrounding epistemic injustice broadly speaking can be read as a call to raise critical consciousness regarding the shortcomings of our truth finding and legal practices along with some suggestions for improving them. Here are four ways we might combat epistemic injustice in trials: (1) Identify and establish structures, practices, and procedures that can mitigate the effect of such biases and maximize the truth-seeking power of trials. In particular, increase the collection and disclosure of more evidence to support testimony, such as the footage from police and city surveillance cameras. (2) Increase efforts to make judges and juries more representative of our democratic community and cognizant of its diversity. (3) Increase efforts to make judges and juries more self-aware of the role of implicit bias in judgment, and importantly but especially difficult. (4) Increase efforts to make judges and juries more aware of the assumptions they bring to their interpretation of the meaning of our social practices, the grounds for competing interpretations, and the ways that what appear to be judgments of common sense factual matters can look otherwise when different aspects of our contested social history and practices are highlighted.

*(1) Encourage collection and use of evidence that will help throw light on testimonial bias and hermeneutic capacities. The point is increasing the availability and disclosure of the kinds of information that help establish broader consensus on what occurred in particular cases, which taken together shine light on what is occurring more generally, and which compel recognition of facts at odds with readymade narratives that all too often serve as the grounds upon which present power structures remain complacent with respect to serious harm.*

It is extremely hard to defend the court process as good even in individual cases when it becomes *obvious* that truth has been ignored, and it is clearly impossible to do so if one seeks to judge the system as a whole. Such cases rightly provoke outrage in the larger community. However, the key qualifier here is "obvious." When it is not obvious that truth has been frustrated, when it is at least possible that the system performed well, red flags are not raised, and our larger democratic community tends to give the system a pass, which is another way of saying that we defer to dominant narratives. Intense scrutiny by smaller subsets of the community are read as either sour grapes from those in some way connected to the losing parties, or as strategic efforts on behalf of narrow interest groups to craft a narrative that serves their mission.

Rodney King, a black man, was beaten by baton wielding officers of the Los Angeles Police department in the course of an arrest in 1991. The arrest was videotaped by a man from a nearby apartment who later released that video to a local television station. Although King resisted arrest, giving the officer some cause to use force, the video shows the officers continuing to beat King as he lay on the ground. In a state trial, three of the four officers charged were acquitted on all charges. The remaining officer was acquitted on the charge of assault with deadly force, but the jury deadlocked on the charge of using excessive force, meaning he could go free for the time being. The incongruity between the acquittals and the video tape showing King being beaten as he lay on the ground made it impossible for a great many people not to reach the conclusion that something had gone terribly wrong in this trial's quest to get to the truth.

This is not to say that there weren't other views, or that there was universal support for the idea that the officers should have been convicted. Far from it, and yet there can be little doubt that the fact of the video evidence in this case was the reason why this case received such widespread publicity and why the officers were tried for crimes arising out of the same incident at the federal level, this time successfully. Without that tape, of course, the case would not have received national publicity. And even if it had, the public would have heard two sides to the story, perhaps producing strong convictions in those inclined to either believe or doubt police officer testimony, but it would not have produced the sense of outrage among that community that was produced when they struggled to square the verdict of acquittal with the image of officers beating a helpless suspect on the ground.

To this end, increasing the use of police body cams is a good idea. The Department of Justice reports that about 25% of 17000 police agencies use such devices as of 2014. The devices may help keep police accountable. They may also help police to defend their actions among communities that are highly skeptical of police testimony. Importantly, they provide context in which to assess often significantly different first-person testimony.

In a recent Op-Ed for the *New York Times*, John McWhorter, a black linguist at Columbia, reflects back on his disappointment that the jury at OJ Simpson's trial, a jury composed of nine black members, acquitted Simpson.[7] He was disappointed because he thought it unlikely that Simpson was innocent. Upon reflection, however, he came to see that: "The case was about much more than bloody gloves and bloody footprints. It was about the centrality of police brutality to black Americans' very sense of self." He observes, however, with a somewhat hopeful eye toward the future that:

> Amid the round-the-clock cable coverage of the Simpson case, America learned the difference between what the cops mean to black people versus what they mean to most others. Too few got the message at the time. But after the killings of Walter Scott, Eric Garner, Tamir Rice, Freddie Gray and other unarmed blacks by the police over the past two years, the conversation has changed. Many non-black Americans who were disgusted by the Simpson verdict have become more aware of the ubiquity of police brutality in black lives.[8]

One of the key factors, however, in producing the shift in the conversation that McWhorter acknowledges is the existence in many of these cases of video evidence. The point is not that such evidence is dispositive, or that absent such evidence there is nothing of value to rely on. Rather, the existence of such evidence helps to draw attention to the ways that testimonial and hermeneutic injustices have likely operated in the absence of such evidence and to add this awareness to our deliberations going forward. Video evidence can provide the larger public useful information about what kind of things are going on in law enforcement. This helps the fight against epistemic injustice not only be buttressing testimony of individuals that otherwise can be improperly deflated, but also by providing context for understanding why different groups see matters so differently.

(2) *We should increase efforts to make judges and juries more representative of our democratic community and cognizant of its diversity. Our judges should not only better represent the diversity of the larger democratic community but also insure that this diversity informs the interpretive and meaning making tasks they undertake.*

In 1987 the Supreme Court reviewed the case of Warren McCleskey, a black man who had been convicted of murdering a white police officer. He had been sentenced to death by a Georgia jury composed of eleven white jurors and one black juror.[9] On appeal, his defense team argued that a charging and sentencing study by Iowa Law Professor David Baldus should compel the court to make a finding of discriminatory intent on the part of the jury.[10] The Baldus study examined 2484 homicide cases in Georgia and concluded that the death penalty was given in cases with white victims eleven times more often than in cases with black victims, and that when the defendant was black and the victim white, over 21% of the time the defendant received the death penalty compared to only 8% of the time when both victim and defendant were white.[11] On the bases of this significant racial disparity, McCleskey's lawyers sought to have his death penalty overturned. The Supreme Court denied his appeal. The majority decision noted that even if they accepted the Baldus study at face value, its finding could not give rise to the inference that the particular Georgia jury in question acted with discriminatory purpose:

> To prevail under that Clause, the petitioner must prove that the decisionmakers in *his* case acted with discriminatory purpose. Petitioner offered no evidence specific to his own case that would support an inference that racial considerations played a part in his sentence, and the Baldus study is insufficient to support an inference that any of the decisionmakers in his case acted with discriminatory purpose.
> *(McCleskey v. Kemp, 481 US 279 (1987), 280)*

It would be wrong, the Court says, to attribute discriminatory purpose to any members of the jury absent specific evidence. This finding makes sense if one starts from the presumption that juries are sufficiently fair and impartial and then one asks what kind of evidence would be needed to rebut this presumption in the case of a particular jury. So everything depends on the way the burdens of proof get set up. It is assumed that McCleskey's jury did not racially discriminate unless shown otherwise. The law that McCleskey needs to overturn his sentence requires him to show conscious discriminatory purpose on the part of his particular jury, but the Baldus study doesn't do that. First, it just shows there are disturbing racial disparities in sentencing, but it doesn't show conclusively what the cause of these disparities are. It raises the disturbing possibility that racism could be responsible, and it investigates and controls for many other variables, but like all social science, it is unable to exclude with certainty all other possible non-racist explanations. Second, even if one were to embrace the conclusion that racism is the best explanation for the sentencing disparity, that still doesn't show that that the jurors intended to be racist. But to get his sentence overturned, that is precisely the burden that McCleskey must meet as the majority of the Court saw it. The Baldus study just doesn't talk about McCleskey's particular jury, so given the presumptions of fairness and impartiality, it is not sufficient to rebut them.

However, perhaps the Baldus study should be read as grounds not for rejecting McCleskey's sentence in particular, but for rejecting the presumptions of the possibility for sufficiently fair and impartial juries in general, or at least in death penalty sentencing cases in Georgia. If these disturbing disparities are taken to show unfairness sufficient for overturning McCleskey, it is because the jury system in general, or at least in Georgia, does not deserve the presumption that juries can behave fair and impartially. Seen in this light, and coupled with the history of Supreme Court jurisprudence, it's not difficult to anticipate that the Court would resist such a conclusion. Indeed, the effect of reaching it, by analogy, would be to put the entire jury system under a deep cloud of suspicion that would require immediate and substantial change. But one has to wonder if the binary that the McCleskey decision commits us to is complicit with a kind of epistemic injustice.

The traditional framing of the issue is that McCleskey didn't meet his burden of proof in demonstrating that his right to a fair trial was violated. It doesn't follow logically from this that he did get a fair trial but, all things considered, that's precisely what it encourages us to imagine. The decision effectively says that no matter how many Baldus type studies the Court gets, no matter how well documented general racial disparity in sentencing is, the Court will not do anything about it in any particular case unless there is evidence of discriminatory purpose.

Imagine if we told victims of car accidents that injurers were only responsible for harm that resulted from purpose or intention and not from negligence, and absent such purpose let the cost of accidents fall entirely on the victims. Victims would rightly point out that their injuries are no less injuries for having been caused unintentionally, and they would wonder why the cost is left to fall entirely upon them simply because the injurer didn't mean to cause harm. The victim didn't mean to be injured either. But the injury and harm from the accident is obvious and recognized. It doesn't disappear if we decide that the injurer didn't intend to cause it. However, in the absence of finding discriminatory purpose on the part of the jury, the McCleskey decision invites us to imagine that there was no harm.

We should reject this invitation. Indeed, in some ways the more disturbing question is not whether the members of the jury intentionally discriminated but whether they discriminated unintentionally. What if they acted in good faith, putting forth their best efforts to be fair and impartial, but were guided in their reasoning by implicit biases that operate unconsciously in ways that skew testimonial and hermeneutical sensibilities despite those efforts?

*(3) We should increase efforts to make judges and juries more self-aware of implicit bias in judgment.*

Beyond bias in juries, there has been a tremendous amount of work on the role of implicit bias generally. Do implicit racial stereotypes and attitudes, of which individuals are not consciously aware, impact their judgment? UCLA Law Professor Jerry Kang and his co-authors, Kristin Lane and Mahzarin Banaji, have summarized the findings:

> [S]everal aspects of the nature of implicit social cognition are now regarded as well established. Such results primarily include the pervasive and robust implicit favoritism for one's own groups and socially dominant groups . . . Legal scholarship and judicial opinions are beginning to consider how the law can and should adapt to such findings, in particular how they call into question existing assumptions regarding the notion of intent.[12]

There have been many inquiries into prejudice in general and jury bias in particular since McCleskey. According to Sommers and Marotta, both mock jury data and actual cases "have identified a significant, but small, relationship between race and trial outcomes."[13] If we conjoin evidence of racial disparity in trial outcomes with the implicit bias research on how subconscious stereotypes impact judgment, then even in the absence of discriminatory intent, we should begin with the presumption that there is a problem of unfairness in our jury system.

I am aware, of course, that such a recommendation may hurt rather than help the cause it is intended to recognize. As Medina points out with reference to the work of Iris Marion Young

> Claims that many of us participate in producing injustices and we ought to stop (or try to change our ways) are often misheard because they are understood under the conception of responsibility as blame or liability; and thus, instead of producing any fruitful dialogue, such claims typically provoke blame-shifting and excusing responses.
> *(Medina, 161)*[14]

This mishearing is especially acute if two other conditions obtain. First, when the group being blamed is both powerful and privileged by the putatively unjust regime. In Hollywood most bad characters are presented as knowing they're evil, but in the everyday world nobody admits they're evil, even to themselves (because that's not how they see themselves). If recognizing the claims of injustice entail affirming one's responsibility for it, the odds of that recognition diminish accordingly. Second, when the means of addressing the problem that gives rise to the injustice are in doubt or appear to be of high cost, then there is added incentive to ignore or otherwise dismiss the problem. On this analysis, claims of injustice stemming from judgment biased unintentionally by reliance on implicit racist stereotyping or attitudes are ripe for mishearing.

How are they misheard? They are heard as demanding too much, as guided by unrealistic standards for fairness. We can't ask jurors to do more than make their best efforts to be fair. As Kant remarked, ought implies can. So if the standards of impartiality are too high, if we can't meet them, then they can't be morally obligatory. If people made their best efforts, then they don't deserve to be blamed. Bias may be regrettable, but it is, alas, inevitable in human judgment, and we have, at least so far, failed to come up with anything better. The alternative would seem to be to decline to pass judgment altogether thereby leaving "criminals" free to inflict harm as they wish. But while we can't ask jurors to do more than their best, maybe we can help to make their best better.

What does it mean to say of a juror that they tried to be fair? It means in our present practice that they didn't try to be unfair. They didn't intentionally ignore evidence or defer to improper motives or preferences in formulating their conclusions. Although jurors are repeatedly cautioned that matters are serious and instructed they must be fair, and although they can be struck for cause during the *voir dire* process, the structural message sent to the impanelled jury is affirmative: the community trusts your judgment. You were asked if you could be fair, you said yes, and you have been placed on the jury. In other words, welcome to the jury, we take you as you are: representative, fair, and reasonable member of the community. Even if one doesn't typically occupy a position of social authority or privilege, this institutional design encourages the kind of epistemic arrogance that Medina worries about. And if one does typically occupy such privileged position, this approach reinforces it.

The prosecution and defense will now wage an all-out war to secure the judgment of the jury. They will do their best to frame their arguments in such a way as to find favor with the jury. In many cases, they will spend a lot of time with various jury experts, demographically representative mock juries, and focus groups in an effort to determine how to persuade the jury. Which words will resonate with the jury? How should the events be described? What kind of arguments will this jury find appealing? How should the lawyers dress, nod, smile, and wink to build rapport? The lawyers will not ask themselves "what arguments do I find compelling," but rather "what language, arguments, or other behavior, will help me get this jury to judge in my client's favor?" They will subordinate their entire strategy to the goal of convincing not some abstract rational decision maker, but that particular jury with all of the biases and predispositions that their experience and consultants help them identify.

*(4) Increase efforts to make judges and juries more aware of the assumptions they bring to their interpretation of the meaning of our social practices.*

But in the interest of fighting epistemic injustice, why not ask the jury to do something beyond taking up the posture of a passive judge? Why not ask them before they judge to actively think about themselves as judges. In light of the evidence that casts doubt on the jury's ability to be impartial, we shouldn't send such an entirely affirmative message to them encouraging excessive self-confidence. Why don't we tell them when they show up for jury duty that our whole justice system depends on juries, that we haven't found any better way to serve the community's needs, but that nonetheless there are deeply concerning racial disparities in sentencing. We should have them all take an anonymous implicit association test. There is evidence that people made aware of their implicit biases are able to correct for them to some degree. Let the jury know that in making their good faith judgments they should also judge themselves as judges; they should consider the possibility that given their life experiences they could have a tendency to undervalue or overvalue particular testimony. Obviously, much work would have to be done to investigate the particulars and assess how this could work in practice. Calls for self-monitoring alone will surely prove inadequate absent introducing other structural changes into the practice of jury deliberation that reinforce the goals that such monitoring seeks, but the idea of trying to help jurors become aware of their own cognitive challenges deserves attention. The point is not to reproach the jurors, or single them out for criticism, but to encourage more critical self-awareness.

This is often done in an implicit structural way when there are efforts to ensure a demographically diverse jury. Of course, it is a crucial strategy in democracy to let representational bodies deal with issues that deeply divide the community. If we don't all agree on a decision, at least we can say that we were all represented. And this scheme is also at work to some degree when we reflect upon the need for diverse juries. But, as Sommers and Marotta point out, "beyond perceived legitimacy, racial composition can also affect a jury's actual performance . . . Once more, the pressing question is why. A straightforward explanation is that jurors of different racial backgrounds often have different life experiences, perspectives about crime and policing, and other viewpoints that shape deliberations and a jury's final verdict."[15] It's not just that members of a jury judge differently because they bring different life experiences with them into the jury room, it's that those difference make for more robust discussions and deliberations. One explanation for this is that it is precisely because those differences play a key role in producing different epistemic sensibilities. There is some evidence for this in mock jury studies:

> Awareness that they were on a racially heterogeneous jury led White mock jurors to be more skeptical of a Black defendant's guilt, to make fewer factually inaccurate statements when discussing the case, and to be less resistant to talking about controversial issues during deliberations (compared with Whites on all-White mock juries).[16]

Diverse juries are not just important to counteract the tendency to deflate testimony by offsetting the biases among members, they are important because they can also help members become aware of some of the background experience and assumptions that inform their judgment precisely by the way they see some things differently from other members.

This is achieved structurally when diverse juries engage one another in the jury room, but it might be profitably pursued much earlier. At present, juries are questioned by lawyers during *voir dire* when they can be struck for cause; this is usually some aspect of their background or answers that suggest they cannot be fair and impartial in the case at hand, or they can be struck by peremptory challenges for which the lawyers need give no reason. If they are not excluded after *voir dire*, they are impanelled and instructed not to discuss any aspects of the case with each other until the trial is concluded. Again, this approach encourages them not to have any self-critical thoughts about their own role as a judge, and it doesn't expose them to the question of how some of the key narratives upon which their social understanding rest have been formed. If we put them in group discussions, not necessarily with the future jurors they would serve with, but with other future jurors, and facilitated robust discussions around topics that would get them thinking about how they came to hold some of their core beliefs, that may change the confidence level with which they hold the conclusions they reach on the basis of those beliefs. The point is to emphasize their role not just as members of a jury who bring to the jury in their person the community's belief, and not just as diverse persons who taken together contribute to the collective judgment of the jury, itself a small community, but also as members of the community who bring judgment about their role as a judge to their act of judging.

The retraining and wide-ranging dialogue needed for an assessment of the objectivity of our beliefs would require a significant investment of time and energy. But that doesn't mean that smaller gains might not be reached by beginning to tweak our institutional designs. If we are to rely upon the good faith of jurors, let us rely upon them and develop structures to assist them in confronting the possibility of implicit bias in their judgments. Let us tell them not that we call them to the jury because we have unwavering faith in their fairness and ability to discern the truth but because we have faith in their willingness to undertake the responsibility of judging and confront some of the epistemic risks and challenges that underlie that task. Following the evolving debate and discussion on epistemic injustice, we should begin to take seriously the notion that as ignorance of law is so often no excuse from the binds of law, active ignorance of our own ignorance and the epistemic lives of others should be no excuse from the demands of objectivity, fairness, and justice that making good law requires.

**Related chapters**: 1, 2, 3, 22, 26, 34

## Notes

1 I would like to thank Jonathan Gray, a distinguished graduate of Emory University with a major in philosophy and a JD candidate at the Yale Law School, for valuable research assistance.
2 For a more detailed discussion of the cognitive roadblocks to impartiality, see Saul (2017).
3 Paul Feyerabend (1975) notes a similar problem for the conduct of science: principles and methods adopted to advance progress in science will at times actually inhibit progress instead.
4 The exception that proves the rule is the practice of jury nullification, when the jury acquits a defendant even though they believe beyond a reasonable doubt that the defendant committed the crime charged. The usual reason given is because the jury believed that the state acted unjustly in criminalizing the activity for which the defendant was charged. For an account of the deficiencies on both sides of this debate, in support of and against the legality of jury nullification, see Kenneth Duvall, *The Contradictory Stance on Jury Nullification*, 88 N.D. L. REV. 409 (2012).
5 See Fricker (2007).
6 Medina (2012).
7 McWhorter (2016).
8 McWhorter (2016).
9 McCleskey v. Kemp, 481 US 279 (1987).
10 Baldus, Pulaski, and Woodworth (1983).

11 The Study is usefully summarized on various death penalty information websites: www.capitalpunishmentincontext.org/issues/race:

> Fewer than 40% of Georgia homicide cases involve white victims, but in 87% of the cases in which a death sentence is imposed the victim is white. White-victim cases are roughly eleven times more likely than black-victim cases to result in a sentence of death.
>
> When the race of the defendant is added to the analysis, the following pattern appears: 22% of black defendants who kill white victims are sentenced to death; 8% of white defendants who kill white victims are sentenced to death; 1% of black defendants who kill black victims are sentenced to death; and 3% of white defendants who kill black victims are sentenced to death. (Only 64 of the approximately 2500 homicide cases studied involved killings of blacks by whites, so the 3% figure in this category represents a total of two death sentences over a six-year period. Thus, the reason why a bias against black defendants is not even more apparent is that most black defendants have killed black victims; almost no cases are found of white defendants who have killed black victims; and virtually no defendant convicted of killing a black victim gets the death penalty.)

www.deathpenaltyinfo.org/death-penalty-black-and-white-who-lives-who-dies-who-decides

> Two of the country's foremost researchers on race and capital punishment, law professor David Baldus and statistician George Woodworth, along with colleagues in Philadelphia, have conducted a careful analysis of race and the death penalty in Philadelphia which reveals that the odds of receiving a death sentence are nearly four times (3.9) higher if the defendant is black. These results were obtained after analyzing and controlling for case differences such as the severity of the crime and the background of the defendant. The data were subjected to various forms of analysis, but the conclusion was clear: blacks were being sentenced to death far in excess of other defendants for similar crimes.

12 Lane, Kang, and Banaji (2007).
13 Sommers and Marotta (2014).
14 For an example of this phenomenon, consider the reaction to a recent piece in the opinion pages of the *New York Times* by the philosopher George Yancy (2015). In it Yancy points out that one can be racist or sexist without intending to be racist or sexist: "What if I told you that I'm sexist? Well, I am . . . Let me clarify. This doesn't mean that I intentionally hate women or that I desire to oppress them. It means that despite my best intentions, I perpetuate sexism every day of my life." Yancy makes the case for the myriad of ways in which racism and sexism can inform one's judgments and actions even when one explicitly rejects them. His piece received thousands of comments, and a great many of them demonstrated precisely the kind of challenges to fruitful dialogue that Medina's discussion develops with reference to Iris Marion Young's work.
15 Sommers and Marotta (2014).
16 Sommers and Marotta (2014).

# References

Baldus, Charles Pulaski and George Woodworth (1983) 'Comparative review of death sentences: An empirical study of the Georgia experience', *Journal of Criminal Law and Criminology* 74.3: 661–753.
Feyerabend, Paul (1975) *Against Method: Outline of an Anarchistic Theory of Knowledge* (London: Verso).
Fricker, Miranda (2007) *Epistemic Injustice: Power and the Ethics of Knowing* (Oxford: Oxford University Press).
Lane, Kristin A., Jerry Kang, and Mahzarin R. Banaji (2007) 'Implicit social cognition and law', *Annual Review of Law and Social Science* 3: 427–451.
McWhorter, John (2016) 'Op-Ed: What O. J. Simpson taught me about being black', *New York Times*, 3 February.
Medina, José (2012) *The Epistemology of Resistance: Gender and Racial Oppression, Epistemic Injustice, and Resistant Imaginations* (Oxford: Oxford University Press).
Saul, Jennifer (2017) 'Implicit Bias, Stereotype Threat, and Epistemic Injustice', in Ian James Kidd, José Medina, and Gaile Pohlhaus, Jr. (eds.), *The Routledge Handbook of Epistemic Injustice* (New York: Routledge).
Sommers, Samuel and Satis Marotta (2014) 'Racial disparities in legal outcomes on policing, charging decisions, and criminal trial proceedings', *Policy Insights from the Behavioral and Brain Sciences* 1.1: 103–111.
Yancy, George (2015) 'Dear White America', *New York Times*, 24 December.

# 29
# EPISTEMIC INJUSTICE
## The case of digital environments

*Gloria Origgi and Serena Ciranna*

### 1. The Internet as a source of epistemic injustice

In her insightful and worldly acclaimed work on epistemic injustice, Miranda Fricker argues that people can be distinctively wronged in their capacity as knowers. Much of the discussion around the notion of *epistemic injustice* has revolved around power relations between different groups of people. In this chapter we would like to take a different perspective on epistemic injustice, by applying it to the context of human/ICT interactions. New technologies may be a source of epistemic harm by depriving people of their credibility about *themselves*. The massive gathering of big data about our own identity and behaviour creates a new asymmetry of power between algorithms and humans: algorithms are perceived today as *being better knowers of ourselves* than we are, thus weakening our entitlement to be credible about ourselves. We argue that these new cases of epistemic injustice are, under many aspects, *more centrally epistemic* than other cases described in the literature because they wrong us directly in our epistemic capacities and not only in our dignity as *knowledge givers*. The examples of epistemic harm we will discuss undermine our epistemic confidence about our self-knowledge, a kind of knowledge that has been considered for a long time as markedly different from all other kinds of knowledge because of its infallibility and self-presentness. We are diminished as knowers, especially in the most intimate part of our epistemic competence. This is the case for both kinds of injustice that Fricker defines: *testimonial* and *hermeneutical*. But, before presenting a specific case, we would like to explain why we think that the ICT examples are more centrally epistemic than other case analyses in the literature and how they may help to contribute to answer some objections raised about the "epistemic" nature of the *injustice* committed towards knowledge givers and to illustrate in a clearer way the idea of *epistemic objectification*.

### 2. To what extent epistemic injustice is truly "epistemic"?

While it is very clear how people are epistemically wronged when they are denied access to knowledge on the basis of discrimination (for example, women, blacks and other groups who were not admitted to higher education until the second half of the twentieth century), it is less clear – as many authors have pointed out[1] – to what extent being wronged in your capacity as a *knowledge giver*, as in the cases Fricker names *testimonial injustice,* is a genuinely *epistemic* harm. As she writes: "The capacity to give knowledge to others is one side of that many-sided capacity so significant in human beings: namely the capacity for reason. So wronging someone as a giver of knowledge – by perpetrating testimonial injustice – amounts to wronging that person as a knower, as a reasoner, and thus as a human being".[2] But is this wrong an epistemic wrong? Who is epistemically hurt? It seems that the receiver of information, due to her biases and prejudices, will end up with less information than she would have had if she had considered the speaker at her face value instead of applying biased filters to her credibility assessment.[3] Thus, in a sense, the hearer inflicts on herself an epistemic offence by consciously or unconsciously deciding to underestimate the (potentially true) testimony of a certain person. By harming herself *epistemically*, she clearly harms also the speaker *morally* or *socially*, lowering her status as a less authoritative knowledge giver. However, she does not harm her *epistemically*, because if the informant knows the truth and she is not believed, she will go on knowing the truth, that is, her knowledge would not be diminished. Someone who knows who raped her in that library that night can be denied the right to be believed because of prejudices about her sex or her ethnicity, but this doesn't change the facts: if she knows who was the rapist, she will go on knowing this fact, and those who are epistemically hurt are the skeptics who turned down her testimony.

The same goes for hermeneutical injustice. Fricker defines this second type of injustice in the following way: Wherein someone has a significant area of their social experience obscured from understanding owing to prejudicial flaws in shared resources for social interpretation. The situation here is quite different than that of testimonial injustice. It is much less "asymmetrical": there is no inquirer and informant with asymmetrical information to share. There is a social group where everybody is "cognitively disadvantaged" for lack of a hermeneutical resource that would benefit especially one part of this social group, the less powerful, to make sense of a painful social experience. Fricker herself insists on this dimension of shared understanding:

> Our shared understandings as reflecting the perspectives of different social groups [. . .] Relations of unequal power can skew shared hermeneutical resources so that the powerful tend to have appropriate understandings of their experiences ready to draw on as they make sense of their social experiences, whereas the powerless are more likely to find themselves having some social experiences through a glass darkly, with at best ill-fitting meanings to draw on in the effort to render them intelligible.[4]

The "shared understanding" of a society is shaped by power relations and may hide the domination of one group on another. Yet, the lack of "shared resources of social interpretation" affects the society as a whole, not only the victims of domination. And Fricker acknowledges this in chapter 7 of her book, when she describes sexual harassment as the central case of hermeneutical injustice: "The lack of proper understanding of women's experience of sexual harassment was a collective disadvantage more or less shared by all. Prior to the collective appreciation of sexual harassment as such, the absence of a proper understanding of what men were doing to women when they treated them like that was ex hypothesi quite general".[5]

Women who were hurt by sexual harassment were clearly wronged but not *epistemically* wronged as a social group, because the whole society lacked these hermeneutical resources. Fricker argues that, even if it is true that some cognitive disadvantages are shared by the whole society, only some of them are *injustices*: "For something to be an injustice, it must be harmful but also wrongful, whether because discriminatory or because otherwise unfair. In the present example, harasser and harassee alike are cognitively handicapped by the hermeneutical lacuna – neither has a proper understanding of how he is treating her – but the harasser's cognitive disablement is not a significant disadvantage to him".[6]

One may argue that the harasser's cognitive disablement is a clear disadvantage to him. Take the example of the "collective harassment", which took place in Germany in the evening of the New Year 2016 in the city of Cologne:[7] the attacks on women at the city's central railway station shocked Germany and the rest of the world. About 1,000 drunk and aggressive young men were involved in various forms of harassment, rape in one case, and various robberies. The behaviour of those men, mainly immigrants from North Africa, were then used as an argument against immigration in Europe by many reactionary parties in Europe. The lack of hermeneutical resources of the perpetrators of the acts was something that clearly wronged not only the victims but also themselves.

Fricker's solution is to appeal to the work of Edward Craig (1999) and Bernard Williams (2002) and to count being treated as an informant – as a respectable epistemic agent – among the central features of the cognitive distribution of labour on which societies are based. Being an epistemic subject is also being considered as a reliable informant.

Yet, the importance of virtuous behaviour in order for knowledge to thrive in a society seems to be crucial for both parties: the society as a whole will be damaged by not considering informants at their value. The epistemic wrong seems to be distributed within the whole group, although the victims will be harmed by a special moral wrong, that is, a lack of respect and of consideration. Conceived in this way, cases of epistemic injustice need a socio-epistemological approach to knowledge to be identified.

In the case we are going to present in our contribution, victims are clearly wronged as epistemic subjects, without need to extend the essential properties of epistemic subjects to the social dimension. People are epistemically diminished as *individual* knowers: the knowledge of themselves *objectifies* them in a new way. Their identity becomes a virtual object, a "statistical double" that companies can buy and sell without people being able to have their voice heard in this process. What we are mainly concerned with here is the way in which we deal with our online identities and the possibilities that the production of these new identities create for *new kinds* of epistemic injustice, which deserve a closer analysis. Given that this may seem too big a departure from the central tenets of the ongoing debate – which focuses on the social dimension of our epistemic life and the power relations between groups – we hope to convince the reader that our "extended application" of the concept to these cases may open an interesting new line of debate and a number of relevant case studies.

## 3. Online identity prejudices

One of the major cognitive, social and epistemic revolutions of the last 20 years is the massive immersion of our cognitive life in digital environments. The transition to an Internet-mediated society of knowledge poses new challenges to epistemology. How is information searched, used, communicated and assessed on the web? What are the roles and effects of search engines, cognitive outsourcing, online monitoring and trust on our cognitive life and on our status as "competent informants"? These are very broad questions that we don't want to tackle within this short essay. Rather, we will concentrate on those aspects of our new "digital condition" that impinge upon the very idea of epistemic injustice.

Consider this case. I'm trying to find the address of a restaurant I had lunch at a few days ago. I activate my *Google Maps Timeline*, an application of Google Maps that helps you find the places you have been at and the routes you have traveled by recording all the chronology of your movements. I realise with surprise that Google has recorded a car trip I don't remember having made. I do not have a car and usually use my bicycle and public transports to move around the town. Also, Google indicates a trip out of town, and I don't have memories of a recent day trip to the countryside. I make an effort, maybe I am confused and I am just forgetting something: Where was I on Sunday, whom was I with? Did we take Paul's car to go the Parc de Sceaux? Or was it two weeks ago? I feel uneasy; a sort of short-circuit is going on in my mind: I go back and forth from the information Google is giving me and the ones I have stored in my memory; I don't know which one I should trust more. In a sense, I trust the accuracy of Google reports more than I trust my own epistemic capacities of retrieving memories of the places I have visited recently. But is it infallible? And how fallible is my own introspective access to my mental states? Do I have to give up my first-person privileged access to my memory on the basis of an act of deference to the authority and infallibility of Google? I am hesitant. What would be the interest of Google to attribute to me a fake memory? I don't want to become paranoid. From an objective point of view, it is far more probable that I had forgotten about this event, that a sort of "blank" in my mind made me overlook this short trip, rather than that Google had recorded by mistake an event that occurred to someone else. Yet, this puzzles me. I know that Google is a neutral witness of my movements. It has recorded all these details about my locations along the years just because I have asked it to do so, or because I simply have not modified the *default options* of my Google account when I started using it. In this sense, I have a reason to trust it. But the infallibility argument is a little too strong, especially when it conflicts with my own memories and the authority I have on my mental states. If I have myself hesitated in this case about whom to trust, what would this have been in the case of a third person who had to decide between Google's accuracy and the accuracy of my memory? What about a testimonial use of this situation? If that trip out of town happens to be the piece of evidence that condemns me for a crime, who should the judge trust? My word or Google's? In the context of testimony, let's say for example in a trial, this is clearly a case that opens the possibility of a huge testimonial injustice: a judge who should decide between the testimony of Google and ours would surely prefer the first one, and even use it as a piece of convicting evidence, even if we are sure we did not make that car trip. Our certainty as knowers of ourselves is undermined, and our word is not taken as reliable compared to the reliability of an automatic system.

Let us consider another example. This is not a fictional illustration but a real case example we found on a blog.[8] A manager asks on a blog how to behave in the following awkward situation: while interviewing some candidates for a job, she "googled" one of the shortlisted candidates and found some naked pictures on her MySpace account. The manager asks herself and on the blog: is this girl aware of her "image" on the web? Did she make these images spread intentionally or wasn't she aware of the fact that on MySpace they were not private? Should the manager talk to the girl about this? Is this legitimate or is it a violation of her privacy, of "her space"? It seems plausible to think that, if the candidate will be excluded from the race without further explanation, this could be perceived as unfair. The candidate would be deprived of the right to justify herself and explaining the presence of these pictures on the web. Maybe she did not put them there, someone else did. The candidate might just be unaware of her reputation on the web and also on the ways of dealing with it and withdrawing data she doesn't want to show, or doesn't want to show anymore. What to do?

As the examples above show, we lack knowledge of our own online identity and behaviour. This lack of knowledge is due at least to two factors:

1) By simply being present online, each web user generates a huge number of avatars and statistical profiles that constitute his/her online identity.
2) The data generated belong to various platforms with different normative frameworks in terms of the rights of the users to control these data. The users are very often unaware of the policies of the platforms and of their rights with respect to them.

This may cause actual epistemic harm because the representation and the selection of the raw data gathered in order to be intelligible to the users is done through algorithmic procedures that are determined by the owners of the platforms according to their specific interests. This results in a representation of the profile of the users that is inevitably biased and partial and does not reflect in an "objective" way what the users want to be known about themselves. More precisely, the use of big data may create a systematic *informational prejudice* against the subjects concerned. According to Hookway (2010), informational prejudice occurs when a person is prejudicially judged to lack the ability to provide information relevant in a given context and hence as being an unsuitable participant in collective epistemic activity. In this case, the informational prejudice concerns the capacity of a person to provide relevant information about *herself*.

Furthermore, the ability to determine the demographic traits of individuals through algorithms and aggregation of online data has the potential downside of systematic discrimination of groups. As a 2014 research paper on Big Data states: "Approached without care, data mining can reproduce existing patterns of discrimination, inherit the prejudice of prior decision-makers, or simply reflect the widespread biases that persist in society. It can even have the perverse result of exacerbating existing inequalities by suggesting that historically disadvantaged groups actually deserve less favorable treatment".[9]

If algorithms for data mining are seen as ways of eliminating human biases about themselves and their capacity of decision making, the way in which the data are collected may largely reflect existing prejudices within a society and have also the effect of "rigidifying" social categories by making it more difficult to change them.

## 4. Statistical döppelgangers: who owns them?

In 2009, Google announced on its blog a revolution on the web: *personalisation*.[10] The content of the webpages and of the advertisements started to be adjustable to the users' interests. In order to achieve this breakthrough result, *Google* adapted some viral marketing strategies of gathering data about the users through the "tracks'" they leave spontaneously on the Web and create profiles. Google is able today to provide services that are more and more coherent with the users' *center of interests*, because, as its CEO, Eric Schmidt, declared to the *Wall Street Journal* in 2010, "Google knows more or less who we are, what are our interests and who are our friends".[11] To achieve this result, Google exploits a number of *indicators*: localisation, browser, chronology of the pages visited by the user.[12] The algorithmic processing of these indicators makes targeted advertisement possible. This is why gathering users' data has become such a huge market opportunity in the digital economy. The *centers of interest* of the users are determined through a "profiling" process that uses as raw material the tracks that users spontaneously leave on the web. The accuracy of profiling is due to the automatic storing and archiving of a mass of data such as browsing history, IP addresses, social network activity, email content, keywords used in searching the web. This "immaterial capital" constitutes what is called *Big Data*. Some of them are just *observed*, that is, automatically gathered by the platform, which keeps them stored. Some are *communicated* to the users. Although the users' active behaviour is the very "substance" of these data, it should be noted that the user is "passive" in the data gathering process: most information stored about himself is deduced from his actions and automatically extracted. Once the users' tracks are gathered, the *data-mining process*, that is the interpretation and processing of the data, makes emerge a number of correlations through which the interests of the users are individuated in order to anticipate their future actions. In some cases, this processes ends up with the creation of a sort of "statistical double" of the user, a sort of *alter-ego* that is modified and refined through each new action. These "predictive profiles" are the essential ingredient of online marketing strategies: from the most visited webpages, an algorithm can deduce localisation, sex, age and nationality of a user. The algorithmic profiling, as it has been shown,[13] is not infallible: false predictions are possible and an incomplete or too biased treatment of the data may end up with an ill-targeted advertisement. Although predictive profiling has been mainly used in marketing, there are other areas in which these techniques become more and more relevant: education, risk management, insurance, health and finance. The possible uses and misuses of our statistical doubles, their correspondence to who we are and what we know about ourselves, the rights and duties we have towards them are a new area of investigation in which considerations of epistemic injustice are central.

An example of possible epistemic injustices generated by the lack of ownership of our personal doppelgänger is the one raised by the case of a young girl who started receiving from the big retailer Target a series of targeted coupons that are usually sent to pregnant women in their second trimester of pregnancy. Her father, who discovered the advertisings in his daughter's mail, got upset, went to Target, and asked to talk to the manager, in order to clarify why they were sending those coupons to his daughter. The young girl, the father explained, was still in high school. He asked if Target was trying to encourage her to get pregnant. The manager apologised: he didn't know why Target had sent such advertisements to the man's daughter. When, a few days later, the manager called him to apologise again, the man said that he had finally talked to his daughter and that she had confessed to him that she was pregnant.[14] Using data to predict a woman's pregnancy can provoke an epistemic harm to the targeted person by anticipating information she doesn't want to know at that time or she doesn't want to share. The level of informational disclosure about ourselves should be something we keep control of.

## 5. The hermeneutical injustice of algorithmic profiling

Algorithmic profiling is a source of statistical knowledge whose main objective is to obtain information about the users in order to anticipate their behaviour. The algorithmic and statistical nature of this form of knowledge makes of it a new standard of "objectivity" and "impartiality": the statistical doubles generated by this process are in a sense a more objective representation of ourselves than that we would be able to produce intentionally. It is our opinion that this claimed "objectivity" can be a source of epistemic injustice.

Let us first elaborate more about the problematic role of the users in the algorithmic profiling, a process that is made possible by one's own intentional interactions with the web. First of all, in the production of his digital double, the user is deprived of his intentionality: he is no more an intentional subject; his intentional actions are interpreted by the algorithms as traces of something else, and treated as a "symptom" of some hidden pattern of behaviour that is statistically relevant. This lack of intentionality is accompanied by a poor understanding of the terms and conditions of data sharing on a certain platform. These conditions are written in standard forms that have to be accepted in order to register to a platform, but data show that most people accept them by default without reading the details, thus without a proper awareness of the various treatments of data that the platform allows for itself. Second, the user is "alienated" from the data he has furnished: he doesn't have access to them anymore, he does not know how they will be used and, in those cases in which he can access the data, it is through the applications the platform provides to visualise these data he receives, a "biased" statistical information that has been algorithmically treated in a way that is inaccessible to him.

A recent survey[15] showed that 59% of the users declare that they are not able to deal with their personal data online due to lack of knowledge about the methods of data gathering and the rights they have to access their own data. Some of the most popular uses of algorithms, like for example the automatic selection of job applications through algorithms that use a series of parameters to "evaluate" the eligibility of the application (length, consistency, keywords, etc.) is often unknown to the applicants. The use of big data by companies in order to inspect their employees is also massively unknown. Roughly, there is a tension between the *explicit profile* the users produce and think they have control over and the *predictive profile* their statistical avatar produces and companies and platforms have control over. This creates a possible ground for epistemic injustices, as the example below shows.

Take the case of Google we mentioned earlier. Google offers a variety of services that allow it to deal with both our explicit profile and our predictive one. Recently, it has created a new application, *Google Take Out,* which allows the users to "export" their data in a file. *Take Out* is a simple interface from which the users can select some of the services (*Maps, Gmail, Photos*) that have gathered data on them and obtain those data. However, the procedure is opaque: what is accessible and what is not is very unclear, and the way the data are presented to the users are in a form of a new *explicit* "statistical double", while the *predictive* statistical double is hidden by the company.

Many users feel uneasy and sometimes paranoid, to the point of withdrawing their profiles from some platforms, about some sort of possible "harm" that the use of the big data generated by their own behaviour may cause to themselves without being exactly aware of what kind of dangers they are facing and which are their options (legal, technological, behavioural) to avoid them. As we have said, this is due mainly to three factors:

1) They ignore the systematic data gathering by the companies and are surprised – even frightened – by some "mysterious" correlations that emerge through their interaction with the platform (like showing advertisements that are more and more related to their interests and present concerns).
2) They don't know clearly who owns their predictive algorithmic double: the platforms? The advertisement companies who buy these data from the platforms? Internet? The State? Other entities?
3) They are not familiar with the techniques of data mining.

The impossibility for the subject to manage his own online identity, the fears and fragilities that this lack of control generate is a form of *hermeneutical injustice*. The very fact that a category such as "*predictive online profile*" or "*predictive statistical double*" doesn't exist and thus it cannot be the object of a debate and of an attribution to rights and duties is a hermeneutical gap in our contemporary digital societies. We feel uneasy about the fact that our data can be exploited in a way we do not control and, on the other hand, there are no hermeneutical resources to talk about this and to develop an awareness of what are our rights not only on our own online identity, but also on our online statistical double which is, at the moment, wholly in the hands of the platforms that control it. It has also been argued that the way in which we are represented by our statistical doubles may create a "representational crisis" in the subjects of whom they are doubles.

This creates a double hermeneutical injustice:

1) The inability of most people to manage their online identities can make it difficult for them to retain hermeneutical control over their online (and, by extension, "real-world") identities.
2) Many people lack the appropriate hermeneutical resources to discuss the epistemic implications of new digital realities.

In a recent article, the French sociologists Antoinette Rouvroy and Thomas Berns argue that in the digital age our form of representation is going from a "modern rationality in which we try to understand phenomena by reconstructing their causes" to a "post-modern rationality in which we don't try to understand phenomena, just to anticipate and predict their eventuality".[16] This may have a backlash on the way in which people represent themselves: the predictive statistical double is a sort of "anticipation" of our future behaviours, instead of an understanding of our past trajectory that may deeply change our autobiographical memory and our narratives of autobiographical narration.

Furthermore, the many uses of a *quantified self* in a series of successful applications (hours of sport, numbers of kilometres per day, variations of weight) can represent a new form of insight on ourselves but also a loss of control of the subject on his self-knowledge. Here we go back to the potential epistemic harm of being considered less reliable than algorithms about ourselves that we have discussed in Section 2. In terms of "hermeneutical injustice", we face the problem of dealing with a statistical double of ourselves that can harm our self-directed hermeneutical practices, either by "trivialising" them and making us feeling as part of a general category – such as "people who are underweight" or "people who have a cardiac fragility" – or by "alienating" us from the hermeneutical practices regarding ourselves that help us to make sense of who we are.

Again, the lack of the necessary hermeneutical resources in our societies to be able to talk about these new phenomena creates new forms of epistemic injustice which, in our analysis, are truly epistemic because they harm subjects in their very capacities as knowers of themselves. How can these resources be generated within our societies? Why can an "online generation" as the generation of people born after 1990 still live with such an opacity with respect to the management of our statistical doubles generated by big data? Instead of encouraging forms of "resistance" that imply a withdrawal from the social media and other useful applications, we prefer to suggest that a policy of "transparency" and "disclosure" about the use of our statistical doubles should be reinforced by new legislations and strongly requested by citizens. This requires also the work of intellectuals and academics to elaborate new hermeneutical resources around which new forms of awareness can be raised, as we are trying to do even in this modest contribution, by putting forward and inspecting the ideas of "predictive self" and "statistical doppelgänger".

## 6. Testimonial injustice online: whom to believe?

Many online interactions are testimonial in nature (we give information to others) but often in ways that are unstructured by more usual "real-world" norms and practices; online epistemic exchanges are often unregulated and unstructured, and highly prone to stereotype, prejudice and bias, and so on. And, as we have seen in the reports on Big Data, even in the case of more regulated interactions, such as the ones with online retailers or websites of job offers, the risks of reinforcing existing societal biases instead of "rationalising" society are many. Whereas data mining is often considered a way of eliminating human biases from the decision-making process, it may reinforce many societal prejudices and "naturalise" them in their pretended objectivity.

One of the primary objectives of data-mining techniques[17] is the anticipation of our behaviour. The anticipation of our behaviour is a rich market for different kinds of companies, such as companies that want to target their sales to insurance companies and other service companies. For example, many insurances companies are trying to establish partnerships with the companies that produce quantified self data in order to extract health profiles of their clients in a much more efficient way.[18] The potential discriminations and injustices that the use of predictive data may create in the future is something that should be socially and politically addressed. And also epistemically. The use of our predictive statistical doubles in order to infer our state of health in 10 years may harm our credibility as informants about ourselves and our expectations concerning our future. If a company has to choose between trusting the results of an algorithmic profiling and trusting the words of their clients (even if based on a traditional collection of evidence), it is easy to guess what it will prefer. The testimonial injustice we are facing in the digital age is that our testimony about ourselves could be discredited in favour of a more "objective" and quantified representation of our biography.

## 7. Conclusion

Much of our testimonial and hermeneutical practice is now done online. This implies that online environments constitute not only new spaces in which epistemic injustices can be perpetrated, but also they can generate and sustain new and distinctive sorts of epistemic injustice. Given the lack of control over the identities we produce by interacting on the web, the fast development of data-mining techniques to track our actions and predict our behaviours harms our capacity of making sense of ourselves and our control on our self-knowledge. This results in new forms of hermeneutical and testimonial injustice. The forms of injustice we analyse here are *essentially epistemic:* they harm us in our capacity for knowledge and self-knowledge and make us less credible as witnesses of our own lives.

**Related chapters** 1, 2, 4, 27, 30

## Notes

1 See Engel (2016) and Hawley (2010).
2 Cf. Fricker (2007:44).
3 This objection has been raised by Pohlhaus, Jr. (2014:101): "The difficulty of detailing testimonial injustice as an intrinsic epistemic harm lies in the fact that if we take away all of the secondary harms that may happen to someone who is not believed when she ought to be and we look at the situation strictly from an epistemic point of view, we are left with at least one person who remains ignorant of some piece of information and another person who has the information that the first one lacks. So wherein lay the intrinsic epistemic harm to this second person, to the one who knows"?
4 Fricker (2007:148).
5 Fricker (2007:151).
6 Fricker (2007:151).
7 For a report on the events, cf: www.bbc.com/news/world-europe-35231046
8 See Green (2012).
9 See Barocas and Andrew (2016).
10 See Horlig and Kulig (2009).
11 See Holman (2010).
12 Eli Parisier, *The Filter Bubble: What The Internet is Hiding from You*, New York: Penguin Press, 2011.
13 "La publicité ciblée en ligne", Cnil, Communication présentée en séance plénière le 5 février 2009 Rapporteur M. Peyrat www.cnil.fr/sites/default/files/typo/document/Publicite_Ciblee_rapport_VD.pdf
14 See Duhigg (2012).
15 See Serda Lab (2014).
16 See Rouvroy and Berns (2013).
17 See Duhigg (2012).
18 See Parisier (2011).

## References

Barocas, S., Andrew, D.S. (2016) "Big data's disparate impact", *California Law Review* 104: 671–732.
CNIL. (2009a) "Marketing ciblé sur Internet: vos données ont de la valeur", *www.cnil.fr* (Accessed: August 17, 2016).
CNIL. (2009b) "La publicité ciblée en ligne" *www.cnil.fr* (Accessed: August 17, 2016).

Craig, E. (1999) *Knowledge and the State of Nature*, Oxford: Clarendon Press.
Duhigg, C. (2012) "How companies learn your secrets", *The New York Times Magazine*, February 16, (Accessed: August 22, 2016).
Engel, P. (2016) *La fable de l'injustice épistémique*, unpublished manuscript.
Fricker, M. (2007) *Epistemic Injustice: Power and the Ethics of Knowing*, New York: Oxford University Press.
Green, A. (2012) "Should I tell a job candidate that near-nude shots on her MySpace page are hurting her prospects?", *Ask a Manager* [Blog], March 6, (Accessed: August 17, 2016).
Hawley, K. (2010) "Knowing How and Epistemic Injustice", in Bengson, J., Moffett, A., (eds.) *Knowing How: Essays on Knowledge, Mind, and Action*, New York: Oxford University Press.
Hookway, C. (2010) 'Some varieties of epistemic injustice: A response to Fricker', *Episteme* 7: 151–163.
Horling, B., Kulick, M. (2009) "Personalized search for everyone", *Google Official Blog*, December 4, (Accessed: July 29, 2016).
Jenkins, Holman W., Jr. (2010) "Google and the search for the future: The Web icon's CEO on the mobile computing revolution, the future of newspapers, and privacy in the digital age", *Wall Street Journal*, August 14, (Accessed: August 03, 2016).
Parisier, E. (2011) *The Filter Bubble: What the Internet Is Hiding from You*, New York: Penguin Press.
Pohlhaus, G., Jr. (2014) "Discerning the primary epistemic harm in cases of testimonial injustice", *Social Epistemology* 28/1: 99–114.
Rouvroy, A., Berns, T. (2013) "Gouvernementalité algorithmique et perspectives d'émancipation", *Réseaux* 31: 177.
Serda Lab. (2014) "Données personnelles, comprendre la nouvelle donne", *www.serdalab.com*, (Accessed: August 10, 2016).
Williams, B. (2002) *Truth and Truthfulness: An Essay in Genealogy*, Princeton, NJ: Princeton University Press.

# 30
# EPISTEMIC INJUSTICE IN SCIENCE

*Heidi Grasswick*

## Science and epistemic injustice

Scientific practices offer powerful forms of knowing, and there is no question that in the twenty-first century, they are a dominant force in knowledge production and circulation. Scientific practices are powerful both in the sense of producing immense amounts of knowledge that can be harnessed for use, and in the more basic sense of shaping contemporary life and material conditions of existence through resultant technologies, science-based policies, and science-based decision-making. Though the specifics of how the practices of science shape life vary tremendously around the globe and across social positions, it would be difficult to make the case that anyone remains untouched by their influence. Given their epistemic strength and political influence, scientific institutions and their practices need to be investigated as possible sites and sources of epistemic injustice.

That racism and sexism, among other forms of oppression, have significantly shaped the practices and results of science is by now well documented by postcolonial science and technology studies scholars, feminist theorists and philosophers of science, and critical race theorists alike. Historically, formal and informal barriers to the participation of women and racial minorities in scientific enterprises have had the effect of disproportionally favoring white males' presence and influence in science (Gornick 1990; Harding 1991, 1993; Schiebinger 1989, 1999). Internal to scientific communities, cultural climates hostile to women and racial minorities have been identified as key factors in making the progression of careers more difficult for members of these groups (Angier 1991; Fehr 2011; Harding 1993; Valian 1998).

Additionally, the ways in which scientific research on humans has been done and how research subjects have been treated have been influenced by racist attitudes and practices. Although protocols and regulations concerning the ethical treatment of human subjects in experimentation have evolved over time, some of the most egregious historical examples of the ethical abuse of research subjects have involved racial minorities or the poor. One of the most famous cases is the Tuskegee syphilis experiment from 1932–1972 in which the progression of the disease was studied in African-American men. Long after penicillin was discovered and became the standard treatment for syphilis, the Tuskegee study continued, with the men being denied treatment for their disease (Reverby 2009). Research directions themselves have also at times been motivated by racism and sexism. Long periods of scientific racism have been identified in which scientific research has been undertaken in order to justify whites' 'superior' place in the social and natural order (Gould 1996; Harding 1993). Research programs on behavioral links with biological sex differences have at times been developed and used to justify scientifically the underrepresentation of women in top positions in business, politics, and science (Fausto-Sterling 1992; Jordan-Young 2010).

Though many racist and sexist-motivated research projects have been discredited and strongly criticized for their use of poor methodologies, their place in the history of science makes it far from clear that scientific practices can be accurately characterized as generally aiming to benefit all of humanity. Historically, some groups have driven and benefitted from scientific research to a greater degree than others. As Shannon Sullivan and Nancy Tuana point out in the introduction to their collection, *Race and Epistemologies of Ignorance*, "a lack of knowledge or an unlearning of something previously known often is actively produced for the purposes of domination and exploitation" (Sullivan and Tuana 2007: 1).

More subtly, beyond the motivations and social applications of scientific research, background assumptions about social groups have shaped the generation of scientific knowledge. Because science is a human practice that takes place in a social context (Rouse 1996), it is not surprising that background assumptions about the social order are reinscribed within specific scientific practices as scientists generate scientific hypotheses, employ scientific reasoning, and eventually produce scientific results. Feminist science studies scholars have pointed to numerous examples where androcentric assumptions have shaped research design, such as the case of heart disease research. For years heart disease was studied on male subjects only, working with the assumption that male bodies were the norm and that the disease would present similarly across the sexes. This led to the specific manifestation of heart disease in women being underfunded and understudied (Rosser 1994). Gendered and racialized assumptions also play a role in the analogies, metaphors, and even structures of reasoning that are used to understand scientific processes. For example, gendered stereotypes associating masculinity with activity and femininity with passivity led to a dominant yet inaccurate understanding of the comparative role of egg and sperm in human reproduction, casting the sperm as active and the egg as purely a passive receptacle (Martin 1996).

Many of these intersections of scientific practices and the forces of oppression exemplify clear ethical injustices. It is an ethical injustice to discriminate against women and racial minorities in the entry to and participation in science; it is an ethical injustice to mistreat research subjects and exercise lower standards of care for particular groups; it is an ethical injustice to ignore the needs of certain segments of the population in scientific research, directing it instead toward the interests of the dominant. Strikingly, in spite of such historical patterns of ethical injustices in science, philosophy of science itself has paid comparatively little attention to questions of the ethics of science when measured against the wealth of philosophical material generated on the metaphysics, epistemology, and logic of science. While such ethical issues are important to attend to for their own sake, they also have more epistemic significance than traditional philosophers of science have supposed.

Many of these noted intersections of science and ethical injustice either constitute or contribute to cases of *epistemic* injustice. Epistemic injustices are those injustices where a wrong is "done to someone specifically in their capacity as a knower" (Fricker 2007: 1). 'Knowers' needs to be understood in a broad sense here, encompassing those who seek to know and understand the world around them, not just those who already know or claim to know. Epistemic injustice, then, includes unjust impediments to one's capacity as an *inquirer* (Anderson 2015). It involves obstacles to activities that are "distinctly epistemic" (Hookway 2010: 155). Appreciating the distinctively epistemic nature of such injustices is necessary if we are to have a thorough understanding of the social nature of our epistemic pursuits and correspondingly, the social conditions required in order to flourish epistemically.

*Injustices* deal in social relations and interactions. *Epistemic* injustices exist because large portions of our epistemic lives are social. Scientific inquiry in the twenty-first century is one of the most socially complex forms of knowing, due to its intense cognitive division of labor; this social complexity means that biases and stereotypes can influence epistemic interactions, just as they can any form of social interaction. Moreover, because scientific knowledge production is tightly intertwined with social needs and goals for its development and application, social injustices can push science in certain directions such that it creates new forms of understanding that can then serve as sources of further injustices. For example, research might be undertaken to legitimate certain gender or racial biases that in turn come to be relied upon both in the generation of further knowledge and in interactions with other knowers. Both science's internal nature and its connections to the rest of society make it particularly vulnerable to epistemic injustices.

The first wave of extensive discussions of epistemic injustice focused on and further developed the two forms of epistemic injustice – testimonial and hermeneutical – that were introduced and analyzed in Miranda Fricker's (2007) landmark, *Epistemic Injustice*. *Testimonial injustices* concern credibility deficits that members of subordinated groups experience due to social prejudice. In the case of scientific practices, evidence of testimonial injustices can be found in the documented experiences of racial minorities and women within science who have had to confront a model of the ideal scientist as a white male in a white lab coat, and have had to struggle to have their claims heard and taken seriously in the classroom and the lab (Keller 2002; Sands 1993; Weisstein 2002). Or consider cases where medical researchers and physicians perceive female patients and research subjects as being overly emotional and unreliable observers of their embodied experiences, given cultural stereotypes regarding femininity, perceptions that lead to either a dismissal of their symptoms or an increased likelihood of interpreting their medical complaints as having a psychological dimensions (Carel and Kidd 2017; Sherwin 1992; Wallen, Waitzkin and Stoeckle 1979).

*Hermeneutical injustices* concern the inability of subordinated groups to adequately understand their experiences due to the poverty of conceptual resources available for such understanding. When scientific research programs are directed toward the needs of the privileged, as historically they have been, structural gaps in conceptual and empirical resources evolve resulting in hermeneutical injustices that disadvantage subordinated groups in their ability to come to understand their experiences and convey that understanding to others.

Both testimonial and hermeneutical injustices play significant roles in scientific practices. However, in what follows, I frame my discussion in terms of two broad forms of epistemic injustice that scientific practices are especially prone to given the history of science's evolution within a social context of racial and gender oppression: *participatory* and *epistemic trust injustices*. These injustices track two broad categories of epistemic encounters: engagement as participants in knowledge generation and as receivers of knowledge. I focus primarily on racial and gender oppression, but epistemic injustices threaten to emerge wherever there is oppression, and scientific practices can be examined for evidence of epistemic injustice along any axis of oppression and at the intersections of multiple axes of oppression.

## Participatory epistemic injustices in science

Testimonial injustices are crucial to understanding the unjust impediments to the central epistemic activities related to knowledge transmission, yet epistemic injustices can also afflict many other core epistemic activities concerning the generation of knowledge itself. Christopher Hookway makes this point when he emphasizes the central importance of cooperative epistemic endeavors and argues that there is a wide variety of types of participant contributions that lead to the success of cooperative epistemic pursuits, contributions well beyond offering or seeking testimony

(Hookway 2010). Discussion and deliberation about epistemic matters, such as asking relevant questions or offering counterexamples to a proposal, are crucial to forwarding cooperative epistemic inquiry (Hookway 2010: 160). Taking such activities as central to cooperative epistemic pursuits, Hookway argues that if someone fails to be taken seriously in their contributions to joint epistemic inquiry due to the forces of oppression (such as through the mechanisms of prejudices and stereotypes), an epistemic injustice occurs. He offers the example of a teacher who, although willing to take student's informational questions seriously in their role as student, does not give a student uptake when they ask a question that is intended as a contribution to the inquiry itself. What happens in such cases is that someone who wishes "to be recognized as a member of a community of people collaborating in the attempt to improve understanding or advance knowledge" fails to be so recognized (Hookway 2010: 155). Their capacity to contribute to cooperative inquiry as an epistemic agent is stymied. When this happens as a result of systematic forces of oppression, a *participatory epistemic injustice* results.[1] Testimonial injustices are key examples of this broader category of epistemic injustice; suffering a credibility deficit due to social prejudice when making a relevant knowledge claim within the context of a joint inquiry is one obvious way to have one's participation in a joint epistemic endeavor stymied. But the category of participatory injustice is set out to include additional cooperative epistemic activities such as querying the assumptions, methods, and results at stake, being taken seriously in a brainstorming session, or being sought out by others to critique a novel theory or idea in its early form. None of these activities fit under a narrower model of testimonial injustice where the focus is on credibility assigned when one is making an assertion of knowledge. Hookway also notes that there can be far-reaching consequences from participatory injustices, as they can affect additional epistemic capacities of the recipient. When one is not taken seriously as a participant in inquiry, one can lose epistemic confidence or self-trust, becoming too tentative in one's contributions (Hookway 2010: 159). When one's questions are ignored, one may develop a habit of silencing oneself, not asking relevant questions that might forward the investigation (Hookway 2010: 156).[2]

As is well recognized by many philosophers of science, scientific practices are paradigms of cooperative inquiry. Thomas Kuhn famously emphasized the shared theoretical structures and methodological orientations that make collaboration and progress in periods of 'normal science' possible (Kuhn 1970). Karl Popper articulated the role of criticism in the collective endeavor of science (Popper 1962). Michael Polyani drew attention to the 'tacit' dimension of science with its shared sets of practices (Polyani 1958). Particularly in a contemporary context where scientific work is highly specialized, research progress depends upon a strong cognitive division of labor (Kitcher 1990). Scientists rely on the research activities and testimony of other scientists whose specialities differ from their own (Hardwig 1991). Even within small lab teams that may not require different specialists testifying on different topics, discussion and deliberation amongst team members is crucial to the development of theories, techniques, and ultimately, results and their interpretation.

Classic work in the sociology of science has detailed many of the ways in which social interactions amongst scientists and especially patterned dynamics within and across groups of scientists affect scientific outcomes and important decisions regarding the status of results (Galison 1987; Keller 1985; Latour and Woolgar 1986; Pickering 1984). The centrality of such social elements to the core activities of science make participatory epistemic injustices highly relevant to understanding scientific practices and the ways in which oppression can be implicated in them. Participatory epistemic injustices capture both obvious and not so obvious ways in which one's capacity to contribute to scientific knowledge-making can be stifled by the effects of oppression.

The denial of equal educational opportunities of the kind required for participation in scientific communities offers a clear example of a participatory epistemic injustice (see Kotzee 2017).

This extends not only to specific training for careers in science, but also to skills acquired through quality education that serve as markers for credibility, such as standardized grammar. As Elizabeth Anderson notes, "in societies that systematically deprive disadvantaged social groups of access to a decent education, the use of such markers in assessing credibility will tend to exclude those groups from further participation in inquiry" (Anderson 2012: 169). In the case of science, the significance of such participatory epistemic injustices is exacerbated because of the high degree of cognitive authority placed in the institutions of science. When society as a whole relies on and privileges the institutions of science to direct and produce knowledge that will have social relevance, the impact of participatory epistemic injustices that prevent or deter access to these communities of knowledge generation is more pronounced than in other areas of knowledge production.

Participatory injustices are of course also experienced by members of subjugated groups who are a part of a formal scientific community – for example, a credentialed scientist or graduate student acting as a member of a research team, a member of a different research team working in a similar area, or a peer reviewer of others' work. In any of these situations, the scientist's potential to contribute to and influence the research process depends on how they and their contributions to dialogue and deliberation are received by other scientists. Members of underrepresented groups who have managed to 'make it' into the formal scientific community are not necessarily always treated with the same respect and granted the same level of cognitive authority as other similarly talented members of the community. When members of underrepresented groups are taken less seriously and given less uptake in their intellectual interactions with their peers because of such biases, they suffer participatory epistemic injustices. Implicit biases of other researchers concerning race and gender in relation to 'smartness' and scientific creativity can affect how a wide variety of types of contributions of members of underrepresented groups are perceived, with cascading epistemic effects. Participatory injustices can occur when, due to such implicit biases, members of certain groups are not invited or encouraged to submit work to important conferences or publication venues to the same extent as others, or when their names are simply not thought of when members of the profession are soliciting peer reviewers. Furthermore, when members of certain groups are taken less seriously in the classroom, in the lab, at conference venues, and in the grant proposal process, one effect can be that the researcher does not receive the level of rigorous criticism that might be required in order to strengthen their work or help them identify in what positive direction the work needs to be developed. This too is a participatory injustice.

It is these types of dynamics that Helen Longino seeks to identify as problematic when she articulates communal requirements for objectivity and explicitly includes conditions of equality of intellectual authority[3] and community responsiveness to criticism (uptake) (Longino 2002). The goal of scientific objectivity as Longino understands it necessarily conflicts with participatory epistemic injustices. As she writes, "the social position or economic power of an individual or group in a community ought not determine who or what perspectives are taken seriously in that community" (Longino 2002: 131).

It is also possible to experience a participatory epistemic injustice with respect to science without formally being a member of any scientific community or striving to become one. Specifically situated laypersons can be in possession of local knowledge that is not directly accessible to professional scientists yet is highly relevant to a research project.[4] Local knowledge comes in various forms. It could be additional data or observations that are gathered simply in the course of living in the particular environment of interest: scientists from southern Canada interested in wildlife management in Canada's Arctic, whose field season often consists of only a few summer weeks, may have much to learn from observations of Inuit who live in the vicinity of the wildlife ranges through all seasons (Nunavut Wildlife Management Board 2000). Similarly, interviews with Iñupiat elders on the western Arctic Coastal Plain of northern Alaska have proved scientifically valuable in filling in historical information on local landscape change (predating aerial photographs and satellite imagery) (Eisner et al. 2009). Yet it is only relatively recently that such input from indigenous groups has been solicited, and the lack of such solicitation due to biases regarding what such groups could offer to the research process constitutes a participatory injustice.

Local knowledge can also take the form of nuanced understandings of the environment of study and practical 'know how' that may be valuable for determining the most useful research techniques and interpreting the research results of a study. For example, amongst post-Chernobyl concerns of radio-active fall-out and the contamination of sheep in the United Kingdom, Cumbrian sheep farmers developed frustration with scientists, who were ignorant of the practical difficulties of gathering sheep from open fells for testing, and the nuances of successful hill-sheep farming – ignorance that led to poorly formed policy regulations with severe financial losses for the farmers (Wynne 1992). Local knowledge from those outside the scientific community is often required to understand fully a problem that science aims to address, as well as to craft a solution that will be viable within the local context (the details of which may only be understood by locals).

Referencing archaeology and sociology in particular, Alison Wylie has stressed the importance of collaborative research with marginalized communities, arguing that in many contexts, such communities have valuable theoretical, methodological, and empirical insights to offer, as well as the possibility of a critical perspective on the assumptions of the scientific work (Wylie 2014).[5] Yet often, scientific communities do not seek such insights from the marginalized and commit participatory injustices in the process. It is all too easy for scientists' biases concerning traits associated with a group to affect their willingness to engage with and find value in the potential contributions of specific lay communities. The unjust influence of such stereotypes often ends up being coupled with the effects of an assumption of epistemic privilege (in comparison with 'untrained laypersons') that many scientists already carry. This can result in a collection of participatory injustices: testimonial injustices that dismiss attempts of lay communities to contribute knowledge relevant to the research, failures to take seriously the questions that these communities may be asking about the research, and failures to solicit input from such communities.

Patient advocacy groups from the Women's Health Movement (Tuana 2006) to AIDS advocacy groups (Epstein 1996) offer examples of resistance to such participatory injustices involving those outside of scientific communities. Such advocacy groups have fought for the inclusion of relevant lay communities in decisions about the direction of research and the choice of research methodology. They have argued for not just the correction of testimonial injustices, but also the correction of broader participatory injustices that have prevented such groups from contributing to the shape of research agendas and priorities when their understandings of the epistemic needs may differ from the perspective of the scientists. For example, as the race for AIDS treatments was unfolding, AIDS advocacy groups fought for a place at the scientific table, arguing that they understood the needs of AIDS patients better than many of the researchers and had a right to contribute to decisions about experimental treatments and the kinds of trials that were most likely to serve AIDS patients well (Epstein 1996; Hood 2003).

## Epistemic trust injustices[6]

Unjust obstacles to one's abilities to directly or indirectly contribute to scientific practices and the development of scientific knowledge do not exhaust the kinds of epistemic injustice that occur with respect to the sciences. All members of society, including scientists themselves, are positioned as non-experts with respect to most (and for some of us, all) scientific fields. Epistemic injustices can be inflicted upon non-experts who do not participate directly in the relevant inquiry but instead rely on others as sources of knowledge and understanding. In a social world, core epistemic activities extend not only to participation in the generation of knowledge and our communication of that knowledge, but also to our actions and judgments as potential *receivers* of knowledge and understanding. Social conditions have to be right for one to be able to receive claims from scientists (or other inquirers) in an epistemically responsible way. While many characteristics of social institutions (from poor science education, to interest groups propagating poor quality science, to poor media coverage of science) can interfere with one's capacity for epistemically responsible reception of scientific knowledge, conditions of oppression are significant in their potential to unjustly impede this ability, placing a greater epistemic burden on the marginalized.

For laypersons, the route to acquiring some degree of knowledge and understanding in an area in which they lack expertise lies in *trusting* the appropriate experts. To not trust scientists is to do without the knowledge they might be able to convey and suffer an epistemic opportunity loss in the process (Kitcher 2011). Laypersons need to trust scientific communities in order to benefit from the very best and most relevant scientific results along with the scientists' professional judgments of the status of scientific research, including its uncertainties. With this necessary epistemic role of trust comes the possibility of what I call *epistemic trust injustices*. Epistemic trust injustices occur when, due to the forces of oppression, the conditions required to ground one's trust in experts cannot be met for members of particular subordinated groups.[7]

The need for trust makes each of us vulnerable to others who claim expertise. It would be epistemically unwise to offer blanket trust to anyone and anything purporting to be scientific or that one takes to be scientific. One can be too gullible and lack discernment in one's placement of trust. For ideal epistemic success, the degree of trust one grants would always be balanced by the trustworthiness of the source. Problematically, however, one is never in a position to fully determine the trustworthiness of one's source. But it remains possible to distinguish *responsibly-placed trust* – trust granted in cases in which one has a preponderance of evidence for the trustworthiness of the source – from irresponsibly-placed trust in which the preponderance of evidence should lead one instead toward an attitude of distrust (Grasswick 2014).

*Responsibly-placed trust* is what is required in order for an agent to be able to receive knowledge and understanding from others in an epistemically virtuous way. Yet an epistemic community's trustworthiness, as well as the evidence available supporting that trustworthiness may vary, depending on the situation of the potential truster and their relationship with the knowledge provider. Trustworthiness is *situated*. In the case of a subjugated group that has experienced a history of oppression, a preponderance of evidence against the epistemic trustworthiness of scientific communities (leading to responsibly-placed distrust rather than responsible trust) can result when those scientific communities have participated in and contributed to that very history of oppression. In such circumstances, an epistemic trust injustice occurs, wherein members of the group are unable to satisfy the conditions of responsible trust.

One kind of evidence that speaks against the trustworthiness of a scientific community for a particular group is a history of scientists having gotten things wrong, especially with respect to areas of knowledge that are of particular relevance for the group. For example, female sexuality is of obvious interest to women, yet feminists have demonstrated how sexist biases and background assumptions have played a significant role in the history of research on women's sexuality, resulting in mistaken understandings and areas of ignorance that can be damaging to women (Lloyd 1993; Tuana 2006). Similarly, projects of scientific racism have purported to explain away economic disparities between those of European descent and those of African descent, suggesting no changes in social policy need to be made, yet repeatedly these projects have come to be discredited (Gould 1996; Harding 1993). Such evidence proves that scientists have repeatedly produced theories and results that turn out to be mistaken, a pattern that occurs more frequently with respect to particularly relevant knowledge for a specific group, offers reasons for the group's distrust.[8]

But other kinds of evidence can also contribute to an attitude of responsible distrust in scientific communities and their results. Naomi Scheman has explicitly argued for the link between histories of oppression and the epistemic untrustworthiness of scientific communities and institutions without focusing on instances of 'bad science' that gets things wrong. Instead, Scheman emphasizes the "systematically trust-eroding effects of various forms of social, political, and economic injustice" (Scheman 2001: 34), all of which can be identified in the institutions and practices of science. Histories of one's group having suffered ethical abuses as research subjects, being discriminated against in the entry to and participation in the institutions of science, and having had one's epistemic interests ignored while scientific institutions have appeared to serve the interests of the dominant, all contribute to the untrustworthiness of scientific institutions for members of such groups. Scheman writes, "the credibility of science suffers, and, importantly, *ought* to suffer . . . when its claims to trustworthiness are grounded in the workings of institutions that are demonstrably unjust – even when those injustices cannot be shown to be responsible for particular lapses in evidence gathering or reasoning" (Scheman 2001: 36). Her point is not that such ethical injustices imply that scientific institutions cannot serve as reliable truth trackers, but rather that what matters for grounding trust is whether or not variously situated laypersons outside of science can justifiably think they can serve as such (Scheman 2001: 35). Being at the receiving end of ethical injustices that are deeply connected to how these institutions and communities produce knowledge undermines reasons for trust in their knowledge claims.

This is a somewhat controversial connection to draw. However, it rests on a recognition that trust is a social relation, with an attitudinal dimension. Well-placed epistemic trust depends on the sincerity of the testifier toward a potential truster in a particular context, and a shared understanding of the goals of the particular epistemic enterprise that drive some of the decisions throughout inquiry (Wilholt 2013). Evidence of historical mistreatment by a scientific institution, especially if coupled with a lack of evidence that the institution's practices have changed significantly, does not foster confidence that the institution will be able to provide honest and meaningful knowledge for a member of a group that has suffered such mistreatment.

Though her work is not framed in terms of epistemic injustice, Scheman's arguments support the claim that members of subordinated groups can suffer epistemic trust injustices with respect to science. This is not a blanket claim that applies to all subordinated groups with respect to all scientific communities and institutions. Rather, the occurrence of epistemic trust injustices depends on the specific history of relations between scientific institutions and subordinated groups. Anthropology, for example, is a field whose origins were premised on the subordination of certain peoples and has a troubled history with many of these groups (Tsosie 2017). Where there is a poor track record of a particular scientific institution's interactions with a subordinated group, often alongside a poor record of the institution's ability and commitment to produce high quality knowledge that matters for the group, the conditions required to ground trust in the institution for epistemic matters cannot be met, and the group's epistemic abilities to gain knowledge and understanding through trust in scientific institutions are compromised.

Additionally, there are participatory repercussions of epistemic trust injustices. If certain groups do not trust an area of scientific research, they are unlikely to want to participate in it. For example, in the attempt to diversify the pool of research subjects in medical research and correct some of the racist and androcentric assumptions of the past, it has at times been challenging for researchers to encourage increased participation amongst certain demographics due to historical distrust (Epstein 2007).

## The significance of epistemic injustice in science

If science were just one among many equally influential ways of knowing in society, the epistemic injustices perpetrated through them would be far less serious. This is because there would be other ways in which to exercise one's epistemic agency (and have that agency recognized by others); so, although the epistemic injustices perpetrated through science would still interfere with one's capacities as a knower, whether that be through direct participation in it or through one's trust in it, the significance of these interferences to one's overall capacities as a knower would be less. However, the sheer dominance of scientific ways of knowing, and the cultural and cognitive authority that they carry, have worrisome effects (Feyerabend 1975, 1978).[9] Among them, the epistemic injustices experienced through science and its dominance result in serious losses in epistemic agency for those who are subjected to them. This applies both to those who struggle against structural barriers and implicit biases within scientific communities to participate fully in the practices, as well as those who are in positions of simply trying to acquire knowledge through trust in those institutions that have produced scientific knowledge.

Addressing epistemic injustices in science is no small task. Because these injustices deal with institutions – institutions that are intermeshed with and interact with a host of other cultural and social institutions including government agencies, educational institutions, corporations, and media outlets – structural remedies are required (Anderson 2012). More challenging still, the mechanisms of multiple institutions are not infrequently put to use by those who seek to actively generate distrust in science for their own purposes, such as through viciously generating doubt in climate change (Oreskes and Conway 2010). In the case of participatory injustices in science, the mechanisms of implicit biases and stereotypes held by members of scientific communities play a major role, yet both the source of those mechanisms and their remedies lie outside the individuals involved; they are situated, within a long history of scientific practices evolving within a culture of oppression. In the case of epistemic trust injustices, remedies will only come when scientific institutions find ways of becoming more accountable to those positioned outside of science, and begin the very difficult work of building better trust relations with those who arrive at the window of science with both histories of distrust and reasons for that distrust. The analysis of epistemic injustices in science provided here is a necessary first step in being able to envision scientific practices that help foster people's epistemic agency, both inside and out of formal scientific institutions.

**Related chapters** 6, 11, 20, 21, 26, 31, 32, 34, 35

## Notes

1 Hookway does not explicitly name these as participatory epistemic injustices. He instead refers to epistemic injustices that can "only be detected from the participant perspective" (Hookway 2010). Kwong (commenting on Hookway) uses the phrase 'participant-based injustices' (Kwong 2015: 339).
2 Kristie Dotson makes a similar point concerning testimonial injustices, arguing that when testimonial injustices occur, a coerced self-silencing can follow that she calls 'testimonial smothering.' In testimonial smothering, the victim comes to testify only with respect to things that they think will be understood and taken seriously (Dotson 2011).
3 In her 2002 book, Longino notes this must be understood as a 'tempered' equality of intellectual authority, in order to allow for differences in native ability and schooling.
4 Harding has argued that rather than only considering modern western scientific practices as 'science', we need to consider classifying a multiplicity of culturally specific yet reliable ways of knowing (traditional knowledges or local knowledges) as 'sciences' (Harding 2008).

5 This is not to say there are not challenges and limitations to the extent to which scientists are able to incorporate assumptions of lay communities that may severely challenge the basic premises of a scientific approach to their work and their commitments to certain standards of evidence. For a discussion of such limitations that face archeologists, see Cooper (2006).
6 Material in this section is based upon work supported by the National Science Foundation under Grant No. 1230600.
7 The concept of 'epistemic trust injustices' that I am using should not be confused with the idea of 'trust injustices' put forth by Gerald Marsh (Marsh 2011). Marsh's trust injustices are ethical injustices that occur when one fails to trust another for prejudicial reasons.
8 Even beyond concerns of specific groups, arguments in contemporary philosophy of science have suggested that our current scientific theories may not be the best, given the problem of as yet unconceived alternative theories that would likely be adopted over our current theories if they were to be so conceived (Stanford 2006).
9 For a sympathetic and insightful reading of the development of Feyerabend's thoughts on the relationship between science and society, see Kidd (2015).

# References

Anderson, E. (2012) 'Epistemic justice as a virtue of social institutions,' *Social Epistemology*, 26: 163–173.
Anderson, E. (2015) 'Feminist Epistemology and Philosophy of Science,' *The Stanford Encyclopedia of Philosophy* (Fall 2015 Edition), Edward N. Zalta (ed.), URL = <http://plato.stanford.edu/archives/fall2015/entries/feminism-epistemology/>.
Angier, N. (1991) 'Women join the ranks of science but remain invisible at the top,' *New York Times*, May 21.
Carel, H. and I.J. Kidd (2017) 'Epistemic Injustice in Medicine and Healthcare,' in I.J. Kidd, J. Medina, and G. Pohlhaus, Jr. (eds.) *Routledge Handbook of Epistemic Injustice*, New York: Routledge.
Cooper, D.E. (2006) 'Truthfulness and "Inclusion" in Archaeology,' in C. Scarre and G. Scarre (eds.) *The Ethics of Archaeology*, Cambridge: Cambridge University Press, 131–145.
Dotson, Kristie (2011) 'Tracking epistemic violence, tracking practices of silencing,' *Hypatia*, 26: 236–257.
Eisner, W.R., C.J. Cuomo, K.M. Hinkel, B.M. Jones, and R.H. Brower, Sr. (2009) 'Advancing landscape change research through the incorporation of Iñupiaq knowledge,' *Arctic* 62: 429–442.
Epstein, S. (1996) *Impure Science: AIDS, Activism, and the Politics of Knowledge*, Berkeley: University of California Press.
Epstein, S. (2007) *Inclusion: The Politics of Difference in Medical Research*, Chicago: University of Chicago Press.
Fausto-Sterling, A. (1992) *Myths of Gender: Biological Theories about Women and Men*, (2nd Ed.), New York, NY: Basic Books.
Fehr, C. (2011) 'What's in It for Me? The Benefits of Diversity in Scientific Communities,' in H.E. Grasswick (ed.) *Feminist Epistemology and Philosophy of Science: Power in Knowledge*, Dordrecht: Springer, 133–155.
Feyerabend, P. (1975) *Against Method*, London: Verso.
Feyerabend, P. (1978) *Science in a Free Society*, London: New Left Books.
Fricker, M. (2007) *Epistemic Injustice: Power and the Ethics of Knowing*, Oxford: Oxford University Press.
Galison, P. (1987) *How Experiments End*, Chicago: University of Chicago Press.
Gornick, V. (1990) *Women in Science*, New York: Simon & Schuster.
Gould, S.J. (1996) *The Mismeasure of Man*, New York, NY: W.W. Norton and Company Inc.
Grasswick, H. (2014) 'Climate change science and responsible trust: A situated approach,' *Hypatia*, 29: 541–557.
Harding, S. (1991) *Whose Science? Whose Knowledge?*, Ithaca, NY: Cornell University Press.
Harding, S. (1993) *The 'Racial' Economy of Science: Toward a Democratic Future*, Bloomington: Indiana University Press.
Harding, S. (2008) *Sciences from Below: Feminisms, Postcolonialities, and Modernities*, Durham, NC: Duke University Press.
Hardwig, J. (1991) 'The role of trust in knowledge,' *The Journal of Philosophy*, 88: 693–708.
Hood, Robert (2003) 'AIDS, Crisis, and Activist Science,' in R. Figueroa and S. Harding (eds.), *Science and Other Cultures*, New York, NY: Routledge, 15–25.
Hookway, C. (2010) 'Some varieties of epistemic injustice: Reflections on Fricker,' *Episteme*, 7: 151–163.
Jordan-Young, R. (2010) *Brain Storm: The Flaws in the Science of Sex Differences*, Cambridge, MA: Harvard University Press.

Keller, E.F. (1985) *Reflections on Gender and Science*, New Haven: Yale University Press.
Keller, E.F. (2002) 'The Anomaly of a Woman in Science,' in J.A. Kourany (ed.), *The Gender of Science*, Upper Saddle River, NJ: Pearson Education Inc., 66–74.
Kidd, I.J. (2015) 'Feyerabend on politics, education, and scientific culture,' *Studies in History and Philosophy of Science*, 57: 121–128.
Kitcher, P. (1990) 'The division of cognitive labor,' *The Journal of Philosophy*, 87: 5–22.
Kitcher, P. (2011) *Science in a Democratic Society*, Amherst NY: Prometheus Books.
Kotzee, B. (2017) 'Education and Epistemic Injustice,' in I.J. Kidd, J. Medina, and G. Pohlhaus, Jr. (eds.) *Routledge Handbook of Epistemic Injustice*, New York: Routledge.
Kuhn, T.S. (1970) *The Structure of Scientific Revolutions*, (2nd Ed.), Chicago: University of Chicago Press.
Kwong, J. (2015) 'Epistemic injustice and open-mindedness,' *Hypatia*, 30: 337–351.
Latour, B. and S. Woolgar (1986) *Laboratory Life: The Construction of Scientific Facts*, Princeton, NJ: Princeton University Press.
Lloyd, E. (1993) 'Pre-theoretical assumptions in evolutionary explanations of female sexuality,' *Philosophical Studies*, 69: 139–153.
Longino, H.E. (2002) *The Fate of Knowledge*, Princeton: Princeton University Press.
Marsh, M. (2011) 'Trust, testimony, and prejudice in the credibility economy,' *Hypatia*, 26: 280–293.
Martin, E. (1996) 'The Egg and the Sperm: How Science Has Constructed a Romance Based on Stereotypical Male-Female Roles,' in E.F. Keller and H.E. Longino (eds.) *Feminism and Science*, Oxford: Oxford University Press, 103–117.
Nunavut Wildlife Management Board (2000) *Final Report of the Bowhead Knowledge Study, Nunavut Canada*, Iqaluit: Nunavut Wildlife Management Board.
Oreskes, N. and E. Conway (2010) *Merchants of Doubt*, New York: Bloomsbury.
Pickering, A. (1984) *Constructing Quarks: A Sociological History of Particle Physics*, Chicago: University of Chicago Press.
Polyani, M. (1958) *Personal Knowledge: Towards a Post-Critical Philosophy*, Chicago: University of Chicago Press.
Popper, K. (1962) *Conjectures and Refutations: The Growth of Scientific Knowledge*, New York: Basic Books.
Reverby, S.M. (2009) *Examining Tuskegee: The Infamous Syphilis Study and Its Legacy*, Chapel Hill: The University of North Carolina Press.
Rosser, S. (1994) *Women's Health – Missing from U.S. Medicine*, Bloomington: Indiana University Press.
Rouse, J. (1996) *Engaging Science: How to Understand Its Practices Philosophically*, Ithaca: Cornell University Press.
Sands, A. (1993) 'Never Meant to Survive: A Black Woman's Journey,' in S. Harding (ed.) *The 'Racial' Economy of Science: Toward a Democratic Future*, Bloomington: Indiana University Press, 239–248.
Scheman, N. (2001) 'Epistemology Resuscitated: Objectivity as Trustworthiness,' in N. Tuana and S. Morgen (eds.) *Engendering Rationalities*, Albany: State University of New York Press.
Schiebinger, L. (1989) *The Mind Has No Sex*, Cambridge, MA: Harvard University Press.
Schiebinger, L. (1999) *Has Feminism Changed Science?*, Cambridge, MA: Harvard University Press.
Sherwin, S. (1992) *No Longer Patient: Feminist Ethics and Health Care*, Philadelphia: Temple University Press.
Stanford, P.K. (2006) *Exceeding Our Grasp: Science, History, and the Problem of Unconceived Alternatives*, Oxford: Oxford University Press.
Sullivan, S. and N. Tuana (eds.) (2007) *Race and Epistemologies of Ignorance*, Albany: State University of New York Press.
Tsosie, R. (2017) 'Indigenous Peoples, Anthropology, and the Legacy of Epistemic Injustice,' in I.J. Kidd, J. Medina, and G. Pohlhaus, Jr. (eds.) *Routledge Handbook of Epistemic Injustice*, New York: Routledge.
Tuana, N. (2006) 'The speculum of ignorance: The Women's Health Movement and epistemologies of ignorance,' *Hypatia*, 21: 1–19.
Valian, V. (1998) *Why So Slow? Women's Advancement*, Massachusetts: Institute of Technology, MIT Press.
Wallen, J., H. Waitzkin and J.D. Stoeckle (1979) 'Physician stereotypes about female health and illness: A study of patient's sex and the informative process during medical interviews,' *Women and Health*, 4: 135–146.
Weisstein, N. (2002) 'How Can a Little Girl Like You Teach a Great Big Class of Men?,' in J.A. Kourany (ed.) *The Gender of Science*, Upper Saddle River, NJ: Pearson Education Inc., 60–65.
Wilholt, T. (2013) 'Epistemic trust in science,' *British Journal of Philosophy of Science*, 64: 233–253.
Wylie, A. (2014) 'Community-Based Collaborative Archaeology,' in N. Cartwright and E. Montuschi (eds.), *Philosophy of Social Science: A New Introduction*, Oxford: Oxford University Pres, 68–84s.
Wynne, B. (1992) 'Misunderstood misunderstanding: Social identities and public uptake of science,' *Public Understanding of Science*, 1: 281–304.

# 31
# EDUCATION AND EPISTEMIC INJUSTICE

*Ben Kotzee*

## 1. Introduction

In the history of philosophy, education is a somewhat forgotten issue. Plato and Aristotle were both deeply occupied with the contribution of education to ethics and politics, and many major philosophical questions in, for instance, Locke, Rousseau, Kant, Hegel and Mill concern what and how the young should be taught. (For perspectives, see Rorty, 1998)

Happily, education is receiving new attention in epistemology. This is especially so in the fields of social epistemology (e.g. Goldman, 1999) in which the social arrangements by which knowledge is transmitted are studied and in virtue epistemology (e.g. Baehr, 2011) that studies the character of the individual knower and the experiences and practices through which good intellectual character develops. Both social and virtue epistemology have a strong normative focus and see epistemology's task not only as understanding what knowledge is, but as promoting good knowledge gathering practices. Furthermore, both these fields are deeply sensitive to the sub-optimality of many of our ingrained epistemic habits and practices (on the individual and social level).

In her account of epistemic injustice, Miranda Fricker draws explicitly on both social and virtue epistemology to develop her account of epistemic injustice. (See, e.g. Fricker, 1998; Fricker, 2007: 72–81) In particular, she sees the virtues of epistemic justice as developing through a process of individual and social 'training' and locates the source of the vices of epistemic injustice in sub-optimal or downright bad epistemic training. (Fricker, 2007: 82–85) Amongst those who consider themselves education scholars first and foremost, it is these critical perspectives on the epistemic dimensions of inequality and exclusion and how they operate in the classroom that have struck a particular chord.

In this chapter, I will give a brief account of some work on epistemic justice in education. I open with a discussion of epistemological thought about education to map the terrain (Section 2) before outlining features of the educational context, specifically, that make educational justice such a pressing concern (Section 3). Next, I outline some responses to problems of educational justice in education (Section 4) before concluding with a discussion of three challenges for thinking about epistemic justice in education (Section 5). Discussion of these challenges can fruitfully structure further research in the area.

## 2. The concept of 'education'

To most, 'education' means a social system organised to deliver teaching – in this sense, education is most often associated with schooling. Alternatively, 'education' may refer to a process or practice – in this sense, the word means something close to 'teaching'. In both senses, it is important to note, 'education' means more than being schooled in the formal sense. According to R.S. Peters, education is a normative concept: calling something an education involves the idea that something worthwhile is changed about a person (Peters, 1966: 24–25) that would not have occurred through purely natural development or growth.

Let us turn to the *activity sense* of education in particular. What we call 'teaching' happens in many contexts, not only in schools. Teaching goes on whenever one person intentionally brings it about that another person learns something. According to John Passmore (1980: 22), teaching is a triadic relationship of the following sort: in any situation in which teaching takes place, there is always a teacher $T$ who teaches a learner $L$ something $W$. A number of important philosophical points about education can be deduced from this very bare definition.

First, the something $W$ – the object of what is taught – can be many things. It can be a piece of factual knowledge (such as that Toussaint Louverture led the Haitian Revolution) or an element of skill or know how (such as how to tie a reef knot). It can be some other epistemic good like understanding (understanding trigonometry), or it can be a whole range of moral, aesthetic, political or economic objects (e.g. how to be good, what is beautiful, how to be a citizen, how to work, etc.)

A second point to notice is that for genuine teaching to occur, there must be an element of wittingness and willingness on the part of both teacher and learner. The teaching must be purposeful on the part of the teacher – there is no teaching going on if the teacher is not trying to teach something. Similarly, for $L$ to be taught something, they must learn it as a consequence of what $T$ teaches (or how $T$ organises a learning opportunity) and not by mere accident.

A third important point about teaching as triadic relationship is that it has an obvious success condition, namely, *learning* on the part of the learner $L$. The teacher $T$ succeeds in teaching the learner $L$ what is taught $W$ only if the learner learns $W$.[1] Teaching may fail due to a number of reasons, because of something $T$ does or does not do, because of something $L$ does or does not do, because of the availability of time or resources, or a number of other things.

This brings us to a fourth matter. One way in which teaching can be unsuccessful is if $T$ is not *competent* to teach $W$, that is, if $T$ does not know $W$ well enough or is not otherwise well-enough equipped regarding $W$. The teaching relationship assumes that the teacher has some degree of *epistemic authority* with regards to $W$ (Shalem, 1999; also see Cooper, 2008). Teaching of $W$ goes on when $T$ knows (or in some other way comprehends or has mastered) $W$ sufficiently well whereas $L$ does not know $W$ sufficiently well and $T$ then manages to move $L$ from their lesser knowledge or mastery of $W$ to greater knowledge or mastery of $W$. If $T$ does not know $W$, or perhaps if L already knows $W$, $T$ cannot be said to be teaching $L$ $W$. $T$'s authority over $W$ need not be complete – we need not imagine that 'teachers always know everything'. However, when $T$ does not have sufficient epistemic authority with regards to $W$, then teaching is either liable to be unsuccessful or, *in extremis*, cannot even be called teaching.

The question of the epistemic authority of the teacher is important, because the theory and practice of education has had such a difficult time with it. As Michael Hand holds:

> Anxiety about the teacher-pupil relationship is a key motivator of the rejection of transmission models of teaching and learning, scepticism about school curricula, and the emphasis on children as constructors or co-constructors of their own knowledge.
> *(2015: 328)*

The trouble is particularly acute for critical educators. As Carmen Luke drily notes (about feminist scholars):

> [A]lthough feminist educators may claim to have dismantled the master(teacher)/slave(student) power dichotomy of pedagogical relations . . . [f]eminist educators, as any academic on the university payroll, *are* institutionally authorized because they are judged and named, at the moment of tenure or hiring, as authorities of knowledge.
>
> *(1996: 293)*

In fact one can summarise the dispute between traditional and progressive educational thinkers in terms of how they view and are willing to enact epistemic authority in the classroom. Traditionalists, one may say, are comfortable with the teacher possessing epistemic authority and are inclined to see the teaching relationship as one where that authority plays a crucial role in making learning happen. Progressives, one may say, are uncomfortable with the view that it is the epistemic authority of the teacher that drives the teaching and learning relationship. For progressives, the role of the teacher is not to be the epistemic authority about a certain subject matter, but to be the facilitator or midwife for the student's learning (admittedly this, too, requires a certain form of knowledge or at least skill – pedagogical knowledge). Both traditionalists and progressives, one must admit, hold that both teacher and learner effort is necessary in the teaching situation (this is the third point above). Yet many theoretical debates in education are conducted in terms of how much the teacher's epistemic authority with regard to what she teaches matters.

## 3. Specifically educational dimensions of epistemic justice

Epistemic authority is, in itself, an entirely normal feature of our cognitive lives. About many things, someone else knows better than I do – because they have been there as an eyewitness whereas I have not, have tried something for themselves whereas I have not, have studied a matter in more depth than I, etc. Knowledge exchange is driven by the very fact that some know more about certain matters than others do. Fricker (2007) acknowledges this point and sketches an account of epistemic justice that is not without the notion of epistemic authority, but in which the main concern is that appraisals of epistemic authority are made correctly and fairly. This has both testimonial and hermeneutic elements. Epistemic justice requires both that testimony is given the appropriate credit and that our culture's modes of thinking and speaking about the world be so as to give everyone the communicative resources to understand and articulate both their own experiences and those of their social peers.

There are a number of dimensions along which one can evaluate educational institutions and practices for epistemic justice or injustice.

### *The level of credibility assigned to learners (or to children)*

Most obviously, one must evaluate whether teachers in a given educational environment give learners enough epistemic credit. Epistemic injustice would occur if teachers systematically gave learners less epistemic credit than they deserve due to some negative identity prejudicial stereotype pertaining to learners in a particular setting (or perhaps to children, in general). This may be because teachers take learners' testimonies less seriously than they deserve to be taken, or it may be that the dominant culture or the way educational institutions are arranged may privilege 'adult' modes of thinking and talk, leaving children at an unfair epistemic disadvantage.

### *Which particular learners teachers credit*

Teachers may give more epistemic credit to the views of students from epistemically privileged groups. On the testimonial level, they may believe or praise such students more often due to their identity as member of an epistemically privileged group. On the hermeneutic level, teachers, but, more so, the school's culture, language and ethos may give more credence to such students' perspectives, engage more naturally with these perspectives and fail to comprehend the perspectives of less privileged students.

### *What teachers teach*

On the testimonial level, teachers may teach the books and scientific, historic and cultural achievements of actors from privileged groups more often than those from less privileged groups. In the testimonial sense, one may regard this as teachers giving more credence to actors from privileged cultures; however, in the hermeneutic (and particularly *educational* sense), the selection of what is taught – what makes it onto the curriculum – has a deeper significance. Teaching a canon of ideas and works by actors from a particular cultural tradition makes that form of culture accessible to students; conversely, not teaching other cultural traditions forecloses students' understanding of that cultural tradition. Educationalists alert to epistemic injustice ask how decisions about the curriculum enable or block students' understanding of particular social experiences and encourage or inhibit the ability of students from particular cultures to express their particular understanding of the world.

### *Which students are admitted to certain courses of study*

Where schools, universities and other educational institutions operate selective policies of admission, there is the danger that fewer students from less privileged backgrounds will be allowed to study there. Excluding those from less privileged backgrounds from a given educational institution as 'unfit' to be educated there is, if unfair, a testimonial injustice; it would be an example of students from some backgrounds being undervalued in their capacity as knowers (the beneficiaries being students from privileged backgrounds who already benefit from credibility inflation). It also has a more subtle hermeneutic working. Judgements regarding knowledge or expertise of a subject is often – and quite properly – made on the basis of academic credentials. However, if it is a feature of the educational system that more members of privileged social groups are admitted to particular courses of study in the first place, this may mark out some endeavours as being 'for' members of those groups and not 'for' others (compare the over-representation of men in fields like mathematics and philosophy).

### *Who becomes teachers and scholars*

The question of who is admitted to certain courses of study both at school and, later, at university level translates directly into who becomes the teachers, scholars, researchers, leaders and figure-heads in academic fields. If members of a certain privileged group are admitted as students in certain fields more often or are admitted to elite educational institutions in greater numbers, they have a much better chance of becoming a teacher or an academic in that field. Again, we may find that, testimonially speaking, the voices of some teachers are heard (literally!) in classrooms and conference halls more often. Hermeneutically, their experiences and concerns may dominate and shape the character of those fields more readily, making it harder for those with unfamiliar voices to be heard.

### Which *teachers students* credit

It is common that, when teachers hail from a less privileged background, they are regarded as less effective as a teacher or are held to irrelevant standards. (It is well known that female academics, for instance, are evaluated more severely than male academics on their looks or dress by their own students in post-course evaluation exercises.) Teachers and students *both* are subject to the same common implicit biases.

### Which *students* other *students* credit

Issues may arise as to which students occupy positions of leadership (such as student leaders or sports captains, which students are asked to represent others in sports teams, debates, plays and artistic performances, and so forth).

Above, I have provided some examples of educational injustices that arise specifically in educational settings. Because educational settings have many actors – teachers and pupils, but also school administrators, parents, etc. – a very large number of possible epistemic relationships exist between members of these groups, and in each of these different relationships it is possible that people are assigned the wrong amount of epistemic credit based not on how much epistemic credit they deserve, but on who they are. When negative stereotypes and biases lead to people being undervalued in their capacity as knowers, this is clearly prejudicial. When positive stereotypes and biases lead to some others' capacity as knowers being inflated, this may seem less injurious; however, those not accorded the same epistemic status may yet be harmed by comparison. In the educational setting, where comparisons regarding what both teachers and students know and can do are constantly being made (in student exams, teacher evaluations, etc.), it follows that the possibility of epistemic injustice in both directions should be a matter of real concern.

## 4. Approaches to epistemic justice in the education literature

In the education literature, issues to do with epistemic justice have received attention in a number of different forms.

### *The credibility assigned to children*

A number of authors are concerned about the credibility assigned to children by adults, quite generally speaking. Murris (2013: 245), for instance, holds that the '[h]earer's prejudices cause them to miss out on knowledge offered by the child', and Carel and Györffy (2014)[2] hold that children, especially, are prone to suffer certain forms of epistemic injustice. Murris offers a radical answer to achieving epistemic justice in education. She holds that the relationship between teacher and learner needs to be conceived in more symmetric terms. In particular she holds that, given the right circumstances, the child can be an educator as much as the adult (Murris, 2013: 249–250). Rather than conceiving education as a process by which knowledge is passed on from teacher to learner, Murris (and others, for instance Biesta, 1994) insist that one must see teacher and learner as making meaning together in the classroom.

Hand (2015) disagrees. As we saw above, Fricker stresses that epistemic justice does not demand epistemic equality between speaker and hearer (Fricker, 2007: 19; Hand, 2015: 329). That some people know more than others is unthreatening in itself; it is when our judgements on who is a proper authority in some area become distorted through identity prejudice that injustice occurs. For the same reason, Hand holds that the mere fact that teachers know more than their students or pupils is not in itself a problem.

As we saw above, epistemic authority is a principle that underpins the possibility of teaching as a triadic epistemic relationship. If a teacher does not have epistemic authority[3] regarding some content at all, we may question whether they are in a position to teach it. Importantly, the opposite is true too: if one assumes that a learner is in no position to *learn* what is being taught, one may question whether what is going on is teaching. Take this example: a teacher of mathematics appears to 'teach' a group of three-year-olds calculus. The teacher knows full well that the three-year-olds are just starting to count. Would one seriously consider it to be teaching if the teacher knew that nothing of what she says or demonstrates is likely to be absorbed by the children? Just as the teacher needs a degree of epistemic authority to teach, so the learner needs to have and be accorded a degree of epistemic receptivity – itself a form of epistemic authority! – in order to be liable to be taught.[4]

Rather than questioning the very basis of epistemic authority, what deserves to be investigated are (a) what *is* the appropriate level of epistemic authority that must be accorded to teachers and learners to make teaching at all possible?, (b) how are such judgements about epistemic credibility to be made?, (c) what departures from this ideal are unjust and which not? and (d) how does the way that our educational institutions are arranged contribute to (or perhaps prevent) such injustices? As Sayles-Hannon holds, students (and, one may add, their teachers) need to tread a line between gullibility (blindly accepting the words of others) and extreme scepticism to 'develop a set of tools for examining the reliability of testifiers'[5] (Sayles-Hannon, 2012: 381). Epistemic justice in the teaching situation would consist in teachers being accorded the right amount of authority and learners the right amount of receptivity that they deserve in order to make teaching possible. On the longer term, one may hold that the very point of education is to make it the case that learners can begin to assign the right amount of epistemic authority to speakers generally and that, in those cases in which they are *themselves* the epistemic authorities, they assume this responsibility and discharge it well. From a social epistemological perspective, one may say that part of the point of education is to prepare people to take part appropriately, fairly and *justly* in knowledge exchange.

## *The value of epistemic diversity*

Questions around epistemic justice also surface in debates about the value of epistemic diversity in education. The question is whether there are differences in the epistemic orientation of people from different cultural groups and whether epistemic justice requires that we either make special arrangements for those who hail from (putatively) different epistemic cultures or actively seek to include more diverse epistemic perspectives within our educational institutions. Indeed, since the US Supreme Court's decision in Grutter v. Bollinger (2003), 'affirmative action' or 'positive discrimination' in university admissions is often justified in terms of the *epistemic* benefits of fostering an educational community that includes many perspectives.

Siegel (2006) holds that there is already much diversity in the practice and study of education. Siegel does not equate 'diversity' with 'cultural diversity'. What is of epistemic relevance, he holds, is the diversity we find in educationists' beliefs and belief systems, research methods and methods of inquiry, and research questions and cultures. While applauding the epistemic value of this diversity, Siegel takes issue with those who hold that we should accept incommensurability between the different beliefs, questions, methods and general research cultures that scholars bring to the study of education (Siegel, 2006: 7). He holds that the benefit of epistemic diversity is best felt when these different positions enter into debate, thereby unearthing the strong and weak questions, claims, methods, etc. in each other's armouries. For critique of other positions to be possible, however, shared epistemic standards are needed (Siegel, 2006: 9). What goes for debate in educational research, Siegel holds, also goes for pedagogy, practically speaking: diverse views are extremely welcome in the classroom, but for anyone to be able to learn something from classroom debate, it presupposes that certain rationally binding conclusions are reached. For this reason, Siegel (1995) holds that even quite radical pedagogy requires realist epistemology. Carmen Luke agrees. She asks:

> How can we sustain critiques of injustice, subordination, imperialism, or exploitation without reference to some forms of normativity, benchmarks, or feminist 'master narratives'? This . . . illustrates the paradox of feminism's relation to authority – its anti-foundationalist stance and commitment to contingent identities and knowledge, and yet at the same time its political and theoretical mission of critique and transformation.
>
> *(1996: 295)*

Jeff Frank (2013) connects Siegel's views on debate between diverse perspectives to questions of epistemic justice. Frank agrees that relativism leaves clashing perspectives unable to influence one another (and, so, undermines debate, as well as teaching itself). However, Frank holds that Siegel's realism also leaves an important question unanswered: why is it that, despite the fact that it has available a good set of critical logical tools, members of the dominant culture often do not realise their own prejudices? As Frank writes, of the ignorance of the dominant male culture *vis-à-vis* something like sexual harassment:

> [W]e need to more effectively understand the reasons behind dismissals of harassment as a step to creating strategies that address this dismissal in epistemologically justified and politically effective ways.
>
> *(2013: 362)*

Rather than seeing epistemic *diversity* as a particular good, Frank holds that we should strive for epistemic *justice* (2013: 365). For Frank there is no general benefit to hearing many different voices as such, but the field of education must remain aware of the influence of power on who is heard and must take due cognisance of the perspective of those without power. For this reason Frank suggests that epistemic diversity is not a good in itself, but is valuable insofar as it can lead to epistemic justice.[6]

## *Distributional concerns*

Ben Kotzee (2013) holds that debates about educational justice have mostly addressed questions to do with the *distribution* of educational opportunities, such as places at particular schools or universities or funding of certain educational opportunities. The literature on educational justice often sees education in terms of finite goods, the distribution of which is zero sum: granting a certain education to someone denies someone else that same education. While this may be true as far as, say, school or university places go, the distribution of knowledge is not zero sum as an in principle infinite number of people can share the same knowledge. The only limits on sharing *knowledge* would be the (still difficult) ones of how effectively to communicate this knowledge in ways that are not so resource heavy as to make the acquisition of this knowledge zero sum practically speaking. Where access to certain forms of knowledge require long, intensive or expensive education, access to educational goods may begin to appear zero sum; however, advances in information technology already makes much knowledge more widely available than ever before.

Kotzee (2013) holds that educational justice should be reconceived not as distributive justice, but as epistemic justice. He holds that epistemic justice in education does not imply that one needs to embrace equality of either educational inputs or educational outputs. Rather, he follows Elizabeth Anderson (2007) and Debra Satz (2007) in holding that the education system should be sufficient to a given level. For Anderson and Satz, that level is the education that makes it possible to take part in the politics of the country as an effective citizen; for Kotzee, the level is that of possessing sufficient facility with science, broadly conceived, that a person may comprehend and, where appropriate defer to, scientific expertise formulated for public consumption.[7]

While Kotzee holds that a sensible epistemic division of labour may result in even quite marked inequalities in knowledge between people, one may well take a more egalitarian line and argue that it would be impossible to achieve hermeneutic justice in society at large without providing substantively equal educational input to all. In particular, achieving hermeneutical justice through education may well involve an attack on elite forms of education that provides the children of some (but not of others) with disproportionate cultural influence in our society and that, at the same time, holds up a certain culture as a pinnacle of education and refinement. Further debate is likely over whether it is epistemically just for certain educational institutions to expand the boundaries of science (to the possible detriment of equality) or must pursue a more egalitarian agenda in the name of hermeneutical epistemic justice.

## 5. Epistemic justice in education: particular challenges

As we saw above, the nature of education as an enterprise makes possible distinct forms of epistemic injustice that can (only) take place there. However, the relationship between teacher and learner is – no matter how kindly the teacher – one of epistemic authority, and this raises tricky questions for the very notion of epistemic justice. To conclude, I will briefly discuss three such questions.

### *(1) What is the difference between 'uneducatedness' and suffering from hermeneutical injustice?*

According to Fricker, one suffers from hermeneutical injustice when one lacks the conceptual resources to express one's experiences. Those who are 'uneducated' (or perhaps not yet educated – I simply mean those who have not undergone an education, because they are young, have not had the opportunity, etc.) lack the conceptual resources to express their experiences: does this mean that all those who are uneducated suffer from hermeneutical injustice? Admitting so would erase the difference between those who have not (yet) been educated and those who suffer an active epistemic injustice. One could say that the reason why the plain uneducated do not suffer from hermeneutical injustice is because, in principle, the resources are available to express their experiences. Society does not deny these resources, the uneducated simply have not acquired them yet.

The problem is this. After years of rights struggles for less privileged groups (e.g. the struggles for black rights, women's rights, gay rights, disability rights, etc.), there *are* now much more refined conceptual resources available for articulating the experience of belonging to one of these groups. While we need not think the struggle for women's rights, for instance, is close to complete, today there exists a body of feminist scholarship that, once mastered, helps women to understand and articulate their experiences of oppression (and similarly for other identity issues). Does this mean that women, now, do not suffer epistemic injustice any longer, but should simply educate themselves in feminist scholarship in order to find the conceptual resources to express their experiences? No. Many people who belong to disadvantaged social groups cannot effectively articulate their experiences due to having been educated in a dominant culture in which they do not come into contact with critical scholarship of the sort described above. If we do not call this hermeneutical injustice, but say that people in this situation are simply *uneducated* in the politics of their respective identity groups, we are losing something from the picture.

The question is this. How easily should we admit that a person suffers from hermeneutical injustice in an educational setting? On the one hand, everyone has a degree of responsibility to *acquire* the conceptual resources necessary to participate in politics; education demands that learners, of whatever identity group, must engage in intellectual struggle to become capable of self-expression. As has become clear, however, achieving self-expression is made easier for some than for others by the education system. The question is how much responsibility rests on society to ensure that everyone can articulate their experiences and how much responsibility rests on the individual student to educate themselves in those strands of practical politics that will give them a voice.

Perhaps a thornier question is whether *all* learners' experiences deserve the possibility of articulation. What if the experiences in question are wrong or bad? Would we demand of the teacher of the white male skinhead who despises immigrants that she makes available to him the conceptual resources or argumentative space to articulate his views better? No. Most likely we would see the teacher's task as that of disabusing the learner in question of his malign view. The same would hold if a learner's experiences were not wrong as such, but were merely of poor quality. Take, for instance, the example of the art student from a developing country who paints nothing but shallow and sentimental representations of life in her home country (farm animals, sunsets, national heroes, etc.) Is it necessarily an hermeneutical injustice if her art teacher instructs her not always to paint 'life back home' but to broaden her subject matter and mode of expression? Doing so would be a crucial part of practical education in art and can be done without denying the basic validity of expressing a sense of place or rootedness through art. The point is that we will need criteria to distinguish between when someone is suffering a hermeneutical injustice and needs to be helped to express their point of view and when they simply stand in need of what we have always called 'education' and to help them *develop* their point of view in a positive direction.

### *(2) How do we change the epistemic social imaginary without dishonesty?*

José Medina holds that epistemic credibility is not a zero-sum matter, but that it is not entirely non-positional either. According to Medina, the 'social imaginary' that governs who is accorded epistemic credit makes the experiences of some more readily visible than that of others and makes the experiences of others unintelligible or invisible (2011: 22–23).

The point is well-known to education theory and critical pedagogy, which stresses how important it is not only to scrutinise and criticise the claims of the dominant culture to possess unbiased knowledge, but also to carve out curriculum time to teach about different cultures and to *valorise* their achievements *performatively* (by the example of what culture the teacher holds up or enacts in the classroom). In the multicultural classroom, one can easily imagine a teacher who, attempting to shift the 'social imaginary' pertaining to knowledge, treats the views of students from the dominant culture in a critical, questioning fashion (in order to encourage criticism of that culture) and treats the views of students from non-dominant cultures generously (inviting admiration of that culture). The question naturally arises when such politics in the classroom (however well-motivated) lapses into dishonesty or simply replaces one facile interpretation of a culture with another. David Cooper, for instance, cautions that, were one to demand that teachers must always respect and accept the point of view of the student, this would lead to an automatic disrespect for the teacher's own point of view and an abandonment of the ideal that the teacher should be truthful to her subject as she understands it (2008: 83).

Is treating the views of members of the non-dominant culture with kid gloves (i.e. too generously) not itself unjust? Some may hold that the less privileged cannot possibly receive too much epistemic credit. The problem is that part of the aim in the educational context is to teach respect for evidence and respect for the strength of the argument over personality. Teachers may do those who are given too much respect a disservice by failing to teach this basic lesson. Students from the dominant culture, subjected to criticism in ways others are not, again, may complain of hypocrisy and, likewise, find their respect for argument and evidence undermined. The question is how to reconcile efforts to shift the social imaginary through the performance of teaching with the duty to judge students' epistemic contributions individually and not in terms of their culture.

### *(3) The question of education's double epistemic function*

Thus far, we have regarded the goods that an education promotes as epistemic in the sense of true beliefs, justified beliefs, knowledge or understanding. However, education not only makes available certain cognitions to people, but can also shape peoples' epistemic character – education can be *transformational* in the agential sense. (For more on what he calls the 'edificationist' conception of education, see Kidd, 2015.)

Education's double epistemic function can lead to the following sort of puzzle. Normally, when speaking about epistemic justice, we hold that a person should not receive too little epistemic credit, nor too much, but just the right amount of credit that is due to them (Fricker, 2007: 19). In educating children, we do, though, sometimes have reasons to give children *more* credit than they are due. This is if we want to motivate them to learn (compare how we sometimes tell average or poor students that they are doing well or working hard or that they are making good progress to keep them motivated). More darkly, teachers also sometimes give their students' ideas *less* credit than they are due for some pedagogical purpose (this is the approach of the 'hard task master' who motivates their student to better work by constant criticism). We may even employ such pedagogical tactics in the service of promoting epistemic justice. In the social justice classroom, for instance, the teacher may deflate the credibility of those from epistemically advantaged backgrounds in an attempt to 'teach them how it feels', or she may inflate the credibility she assigns to those from epistemically disadvantaged backgrounds in order to provide a sympathetic account of their self-understanding.

Admitting that it is a possible pedagogical trick to give a student *less* credit than they deserve is not to endorse oppressive or demeaning teaching methods. Philosophy knows the type of the hard task master teacher all too well, and while the subject has its share of mean-spirited teachers, even the kindest philosophy teacher routinely holds up their students' arguments to far higher levels of scrutiny and criticism than anyone would encounter in real life. Likewise, admitting that one may, for pedagogical purposes, give a student *more* credit than they deserve is not to advocate mollycoddling. Both approaches will be attended by some successes and some failures. Overindulgence can lead to complacency or arrogance. Nitpicking can lead to a loss of confidence or aversion to learning. Even so, it is in the realm of possibility that teachers can either over- or under-value the opinions voiced by students based on what they think is in the long-term best interests of the epistemic character development of the student. Departing from giving due credit to a student's views may even be in the long-term epistemic interest of society as a whole. If a kindly teacher (or a hard task master!) motivates a young prodigy to genius by over- (or under-) valuing what they say on occasion, this may be in all of our interests. What departures from strict epistemic justice in the classroom should be allowed and which not is an interesting question for future debate.

**Related chapters** 1, 2, 3, 26, 30

## Notes

1 The relationship does not go the other way, because *L* can learn *W* independently. Learning is a success condition rather than a necessary condition for teaching because it is also possible for *T* to teach *W* perfectly well, without *L* ever learning *W*.
2 Carel and Györffy (2014) write about the medical context, but the point generalises. See also Burroughs and Tollefsen (2016).
3 In the proper sense of the term – this does not mean real or perceived power over another, but proper, rational authority regarding some matter *vis-à-vis* someone else.
4 In the context of the distribution of education, Kotzee and Martin (2013) hold that the right to receive an education means little if it is not 'exercisable' – what will be taught must be matched to what the learner can learn.
5 For a more critical view, see Stengel (2012).
6 For more on the epistemic diversity debate in education, see Ruitenberg and Phillips (2011), Robertson (2013) and Smeyers (2013).
7 Compare Kitcher (2011).

## References

Baehr, J. 2011. *The Inquiring Mind: On Intellectual Virtues and Virtue Epistemology*. Oxford: Oxford University Press.
Burroughs, M. and Tollefsen, D. 2016. 'Learning to Listen: Epistemic Injustice and the Child', *Episteme* 13, 359–77.
Carel, H. and Györffy, G. 2014. 'Seen but Not Heard: Children and Epistemic Injustice', *The Lancet* 384, 1256–7.
Frank, J. 2013. 'Mitigating Against Epistemic Injustice in Educational Research', *Educational Researcher* 42 (7), 363–70.
Fricker, M. 2007. *Epistemic Injustice: Power and the Ethics of Knowing*. Oxford: Oxford University Press.
Goldman, A. 1999. *Knowledge in a Social World*. Oxford: Clarendon Press.
Hand, M. 2015. 'What Do Kids Know? A Response to Karen Murris', *Studies in Philosophy and Education* 34, 327–30.
Kidd, I. 2015. 'Educating for Intellectual Humility', in J. Baehr (ed.) *Intellectual Virtues and Education: Essays in Applied Virtue Epistemology*. London: Routledge, 54–70.
Kitcher, P. 2011. *Science in a Democratic Society*. Amherst, NY: Prometheus Books.
Kotzee, B. 2013. 'Educational Justice, Epistemic Justice, and Levelling Down', *Educational Theory* 63 (4), 331–49.
Kotzee, B. and Martin, C. 2013. 'Who Should Go to University: Justice in University Admissions', *Journal of Philosophy of Education* 47 (4), 623–41.
Luke, C. 1996. 'Feminist Pedagogy Theory: Reflections on Power and Authority', *Educational Theory* 46 (3), 283–302.
Medina, J. 2011. 'The Relevance of Credibility Excess in a Proportional View of Epistemic Injustice: Differential Epistemic Authority and the Social Imaginary', *Social Epistemology* 25 (1), 15–35.
Passmore, J. 1980. *The Philosophy of Teaching*. Cambridge, MA: Harvard University Press.
Peters, R.S. 1966. *Ethics and Education*. London, UK: George Allan and Unwin.
Robertson, E. 2013. 'The Epistemic Value of Diversity', *Journal of Philosophy of Education* 47 (2), 299–310.
Rorty, A. (ed.) 1998. *Philosophers on Education: New Historical Perspectives*. London: Routledge.
Ruitenberg, C. and Phillips, D. 2011. *Education, Culture and Epistemological Diversity*. Dordrecht: Springer.
Sayles-Hannon, S. 2012. 'On Whose Authority? Issues of Epistemic Authority and Injustice in the Social Justice Classroom', *Philosophy of Education* 380–8.

Shalem, Y. 1999. 'Epistemological Labor: The Way to Significant Pedagogical Authority', *Educational Theory* 49 (1), 53–70.
Siegel, H. 1995. '"Radical" Pedagogy Requires "Conservative" Epistemology', *Journal of Philosophy of Education* 29 (1), 33–46.
Siegel, H. 2006. 'Epistemological Diversity and Education Research: Much Ado about Nothing Much?', *Educational Researcher* 35 (2), 3–12.
Smeyers, P. 2013. 'Making Sense of the Legacy of Epistemology in Education and Educational Research', *Journal of Philosophy of Education* 47 (2), 311–21.
Stengel, B. 2012. 'Imagining Epistemic Justice', *Philosophy of Education* 2012, 389–92.

# 32
# EPISTEMIC INJUSTICE IN MEDICINE AND HEALTHCARE

*Havi Carel and Ian James Kidd*

## 1. Introduction

This chapter explores the relation of epistemic injustice to medicine and healthcare as they arise from epistemic asymmetries and differential power relations. Healthcare systems rely on complex structures of epistemic norms and expectations, both implicit and explicit, that create *knowledge asymmetries* – for instance, privileging the knowledge derived from medical training and theory, rather than that potentially rooted in patient experience, which effectively limits epistemic authority to healthcare practitioners. The privileging of certain forms of experience amplifies this by creating *experiential asymmetries*: phenomenologists of illness have disclosed how ill persons experience both their illness and the social world, including healthcare environments (Toombs 1987). Chronically ill patients, in particular, experience their illness not as localized biological dysfunction, but as *ongoing, pervasive*, perhaps *all-encompassing* – a definitive 'mode of being'. Although illness may be only one aspect of that 'mode' or way of life, it can come to dominate their identity either as they conceive it, or, more significantly, as others do.

By contrast, most practitioners can leave the world of illness, at the end of the day, physically and psychologically, experiencing it through the context of a professionalised domain (see Kalanithi 2016; Klitzman 2007). The power structures of healthcare systems can also indirectly affect the epistemic confidence and capacities of ill persons. Many are vulnerable and fragile in various ways – physically, emotionally, socially – as a result of their condition and treatment, and the difficulties of life as an ill person in an often uncooperative, uncompassionate social world. Such fragility is apt to challenge the autonomy and dignity that epistemic agency requires – for instance, patients often require *permission* for everyday tasks, such as receiving a visitor or eating certain foods.[1] Similarly, epistemic agency can be challenged through one's being complexly dependent on friends and family, healthcare staff, or even strangers.

We suggest that such asymmetries, dependencies, and power relations can increase the vulnerability of patients to epistemic injustice. In this chapter, we describe some of the relevant structural and epistemic features of medicine and healthcare, and indicate some potential ameliorative strategies (see Carel and Kidd 2014; Kidd and Carel 2016).

## 2. Epistemology, illness, and healthcare

Epistemically toned criticisms of healthcare systems are not new, but analysing them using the concept of epistemic injustice is.[2] Such criticisms take two forms. The first are *patient complaints*, made by ill persons, especially those with prolonged and involved experience of healthcare, who report, *inter alia*, that their doctor does not listen to their concerns, or that their reports about their condition are marginalised during examinations, or that they encounter substantial difficulties in their efforts to make themselves understood to the healthcare professionals (HCPs) charged with their care.

The second are *health professional complaints*, made by practitioners, including nurses, doctors, surgeons, and consultants, often but not always directed towards the perceived epistemic failures of patients ('not always', since the epistemic hierarchies among medical staff could generate injustices – for instance, the knowledge a nurse has from daily interactions with patients may not be appreciated by a doctor who only checks periodically). Practitioners often report that patients tend to provide medically irrelevant information, offer odd observations, or otherwise fail to contribute epistemically to the collection of medical data – a bad thing in a culture of deadlines, targets, and time pressure.

Such complaints conspire to create a situation in which neither group can engage in effective reciprocal testimonial and hermeneutical relations. This has the result of complicating, and in some cases compromising, the epistemic relationship between ill persons and HCPs. Such breakdowns can have serious practical consequences. Patients may become unable or unwilling to give complete or accurate reports of their symptoms. Compliance with treatments falters. Hospitals become perceived as places of silencing and isolation, as well as sickness. HCPs may experience frustration and increased communication difficulties.

It is clear that these epistemic problems are systematic and longstanding features of healthcare systems, rather than isolated, incidental cases of atypical failure. There is an abundant body of empirical evidence – historical, sociological, and anecdotal – that documents the many forms of epistemic problems in healthcare. In the late 1960s, for instance, paediatrician Barbara M. Korsch *et al.* (1968, 1969), now an expert in medical communication, describes various 'gaps in doctor-patient communication'. Her aim was not just diagnostic, but therapeutic: once the causes of these gaps are identified, one can work out how to close them – by reforming doctor training, say.

Our claim is that the sorts of epistemic problems described so far are grounded in contingent features of healthcare systems, resulting in epistemic and non-epistemic harms to patients, who are not 'heard', or treated as subjects of knowledge, in ways that can affect their treatment and care. Such problems can, we propose, be understood and ameliorated if analysed using the concept of epistemic injustice. That concept is needed, because previous and current attempts at resolving these problems have, so far, met with little success: a vast pathographic literature – books, blogs, diaries, narratives – continues to include epistemic complaints of exclusion, 'silencing', and marginalisation (Frank 2010) and, to take one example, the UK Patients' Association reports that complaints about *communication* are among the most frequent it receives.[3] Clearly many ill persons will be epistemically and communicatively impaired, often as a consequence of their condition. An epistemic injustice will only occur when agential and structural factors erode or impair the testimonial and hermeneutical capacities of ill persons. Our focus is chronically somatically ill adults, setting aside paediatric and acutely ill patients and mental illness, which have their own complexities and therefore require separate treatment (on these, see Burroughs and Tollefsen 2016; Carel and Györffy 2014; Crichton, Carel, and Kidd 2016; Lakeman 2010; Scrutton 2017).

## 3. Testimonial injustice in healthcare

Ill persons can experience testimonial injustice during interactions with HCPs in medical contexts or with non-practitioners within the wider social world – a distinction increasingly blurred within medicalised societies, in ways liable to exacerbate the vulnerability of ill persons to epistemic injustice (see Wardrope 2014). Ill persons can suffer prejudicial credibility deflations and hermeneutical marginalisation at the hands of medical staff, strangers, colleagues, friends and family, and, perhaps more surprisingly, other ill persons. Their epistemic vulnerability *qua* ill person can intersectionally amplify other prejudices (see Collins 2017; Smith 2010). *Agential testimonial injustice* occurs when a hearer (a HCP, say) allows a negative stereotype of illness to prejudice their perception and evaluation of the credibility of an ill speaker – a patient, say. *Structural testimonial injustice* occurs when certain types of testimonial practice suffer exclusion or marginalisation due to a socially and epistemically authoritative discourse, such as that of scientific medicine.

### *Stereotypes, credulity, and illness*

Agential testimonial injustice is generated by culturally prevalent stereotypes of ill persons, the majority of which build in negative accounts of their epistemic abilities. The ill are often stereotyped as, *inter alia*, cognitively impaired, overwrought, unable to 'think straight', existentially unstable, anxious, morbid, and so on, due either to their condition or their psychological response to it. Such attributions are liable to prejudice how others perceive and evaluate their epistemic abilities.

Some illnesses are also positively stereotyped, such as the 'autistic genius', but the overwhelming majority are not. An ill person may be perceived to necessarily lack the qualities characteristic of a credible epistemic agent – cool, calm, rational, detached, and objective (Goldie 2012). Moreover, testimonies ordinarily taken to be indicative of credibility, like steady, articulate speech, are liable to be interpreted as the exception – that one 'got them on a good day', a lucky one-off for the patient.

Many HCPs evince instances of prejudicial credibility judgment. One complained to us that patients 'say a lot of irrelevant things, like, "When I eat lettuce, my elbow hurts", [so] I have to listen carefully for the important stuff and ignore the rest'.[4] But patients tell different stories:

> I asked a professor whether being exposed to reduced oxygen levels long-term, the way I am, would have any detrimental effects on cognitive function e.g. would that explain why my memory had rapidly become much worse? He just laughed off my genuine and serious concern by saying he had the same problem and sometimes couldn't even remember his wife's name. I never did get a proper reply to that question
>
> I don't mention problems because though they are real for me, they're minor in the grand scheme of things[5]

A more graphic historical example, offered by Daniel Dennett, concerns the use in the 1940s of curare, a paralytic poison, as a general anaesthetic:

> The patients were, of course, quiet under the knife [. . .] but when the effects of the curare wore off, complained bitterly of having been completely conscious and in excruciating pain. The doctors did not believe them. (The fact that most of the patients were infants and small children may explain this credibility gap.) Eventually a doctor bravely

committed to an elaborate test under curare and his detailed confirmation of his subjects' reports was believed by his colleagues.

*(1981: 209)*

The agential/structural distinction is complicated in these cases, because they involve not only individual agency, but also a complex background of culturally prevalent stereotypes and structural features of healthcare systems – time pressure, routinisation of tasks, formalisation of diagnostic practice, to mention a few. An optimal epistemic interaction needs supporting conditions, which healthcare systems often fail to provide. Indeed, healthcare commentators, practitioners, and policymakers are engaged in vigorous debates about these problems. A good example is the emphasis currently given to the solicitation and inclusion of 'patient perspectives' (Coulter and Ellins 2009; Greener 2009; McIver 2011).

Unfortunately, epistemically toned complaints by patients and practitioners persist despite many reports, initiatives, studies, and reforms. A vast literature now exists on 'listening to patients', 'patient perspectives', 'cultural literacy', and so on, much of it overtly concerned with enhancing the prospects for effective testimonial and hermeneutical practice in healthcare (see, e.g. Rudd 2015; Srivastava 2007). Such initiatives are not always taken seriously by medical students, which is unfortunate, not least since they arguably express a latent aspiration to epistemic justice: '[a]ny component of a curriculum upon which interns slap the "touchy-feely" label is doomed in terms of attendance' (Ofri 2013, 4).

## *Information and participation: two perspectives*

The testimonial injustices that ill persons suffer can have both an agential and a *structural* character, as they are the result of the organisation of social communities, as well as the activity of agents. A healthcare practice or system can be informed or shaped by epistemic prejudices in a way that confines the testimonial possibilities available to ill persons. And an agent's decisions and actions can also be informed by such prejudices. If an agent can deflate the credibility of a speaker, structural factors can prevent a person from *being* a speaker in a thick sense by 'shutting them out', before silencing can even begin.

The prejudicial credibility deficits characteristic of testimonial injustice occurs during social-epistemic interactions with others. Christopher Hookway (2010) argues that such deficits can occur even before those interactions begin. Prejudices can impair a person's ability to engage in shared epistemic practice, constituting pre-emptive forms of testimonial injustice.[6] Hookway suggests that two perspectives enable us to reveal the full extent of the epistemic damage caused by such prejudice: a participatory perspective and an informational perspective. We discuss these each in turn.

The starting point is the fact that our participation in shared epistemic practices, such as debating or enquiring, is necessarily premised upon certain presuppositions about our epistemic peers. These presuppositions take the form of implicit or explicit expectations about the sorts of capacities and dispositions that our epistemic peers should typically exhibit.

Hookway focuses on two presuppositions. First, that participants will have a *sense of relevance*, a capacity to determine which ideas are worth taking seriously, which objections are meritorious, and so on. A person who lacks a sense of relevance is likely to undermine the efficiency of any epistemic community by failing to properly judge the relevance of their and others' contributions. Second, that participants have a *capacity to provide information* that can meaningfully contribute to the epistemic task, for instance to provide factual corroboration or correction, or to have sufficient background knowledge of the subject. Hookway identifies two forms perspectives attached to these two presuppositions, which uncover the variety of ways in which certain persons and groups can be excluded from participation in shared epistemic activities (Hookway 2010).

The *participatory perspective* reveals how a person or group are prejudicially judged to lack capacities required for having a *sense of relevance*, and hence as not being suitable participants for collective epistemic activity. Certain negative prejudices hamper participation because their social and epistemic consequence is that one is prevented from 'recognising [a potential participant] in debate or discussion' (Hookway 2010, 156). In such cases, a well-placed concern with epistemic efficiency is corrupted by being placed in the service of an often-unconscious epistemic prejudice.

We think that ill persons are vulnerable to participatory prejudices for two reasons. The first is that ill persons are supposed to lack the training and experience needed for the possession of a robust sense of relevance required for the epistemic practices of medicine. Since ill persons generally lack medical training, they may be judged to lack the prerequisites for a sense of relevance in medical contexts. This judgment relies upon the implicit co-definition of a sense of relevance with medical expertise, but this excludes the overwhelming majority of ill persons from potential possession of a sense of relevance. This form of participatory prejudice would be a structural feature of contemporary healthcare practice. The notion of 'the patient expert' and acknowledgement of the importance of patient perspective in co-design methodologies are examples of first steps towards tackling the problem. However, in so far as the discourse and the decision making are continued to be taken to be primarily medical, the power of such prejudices may continue to exert itself.

The second reason ill persons are vulnerable to participatory prejudices is that they are typically regarded as the *objects* of, rather than as *participants* in, the epistemic practices of medicine. A patient's participation may be confined to confirming basic biographical details or reporting symptoms by answering questions of the 'what sort of pain is it?' type. If one's stance towards a certain social group incorporates the perception of them as providers of information only in this minimal sense, then it will be difficult for one to regard them as participants in a more epistemically substantive sense.

Hookway also suggests we view the problem from an *informational perspective*. This perspective reveals how a person or group are prejudicially judged to lack the ability to provide information relevant in a given context and hence as being an unsuitable participant in collective epistemic activity. This problem can arise in two mutually reinforcing ways. First, a *refusal to concede* the significance of the information being offered by a particular individual or group. This is especially liable to occur in cases where the type of information in question is not reflected in or recognised by the experience of the dominant social group, in our case, the healthy. An epistemically dominant group may therefore refuse to concede that certain forms of information (such as qualitative reports of illness experiences) are relevant and significant to the epistemic task at hand, and therefore prevent it from informing the established epistemic practices; this also rules out the possibility of that information prompting *reform* of those practices (see Wainwright and Macnaughton 2013 for a critique of the exclusion of qualitative data from feeding into guideline creation).

Second, we may see a *refusal to consider* presuppositions about the significance and types of information that are legitimate and admissible. An epistemic community will typically operate with a range of informational presuppositions for legitimate practical and cognitive reasons. The informational perspective can reveal how members of that community refuse to periodically reconsider those presuppositions, especially in the face of vigorous and sustained calls by groups who argue for the significance of other forms of information. Hookway argues that because the excluded forms of information do not inform current practice, it will generally be the case that an informational lacuna can only be detected from the 'participant perspective' (2010, 158). The absence of social and epistemic resources can often only be identified and appreciated by those marginalised individuals and communities who suffer from their absence – a core sentiment of standpoint epistemology (Wylie 2004).

We think that ill persons are vulnerable to such prejudice in the two ways described. Ill persons are subject to refusals to concede the relevance of the types of information that they typically offer, such as information concerning their sense of bodily estrangement or worries about social isolation. Such information is not widely integrated into modern healthcare practice, and when it is, it tends to be classified as 'subjective' or 'non-medical', and does not trigger action. Ill persons are also subject to refusals to consider the possible significance of the forms of information that are being excluded, for instance by accepting that existential changes that accompany experiences of illness are important. Despite persistent testimonies from ill persons, psychologists, philosophers, and phenomenologists, the epistemic norms of medicine remain focused on 'objective' quantitative information (Frank 2010; Toombs 1987).[7]

## 4. Hermeneutical injustice in healthcare

A patient is vulnerable to hermeneutical injustice if they struggle to access, employ, or share the resources necessary to create or share the sense of their experiences. This can take two different forms. First, *semantically-based hermeneutical injustice*: a patient finds that the required resources do not exist, exacerbating a painful sense of the 'ineffability' of illness – a frustrating sense of being unable to 'get across' or 'put into words' the lived experience of being ill (see Carel 2016).

Second, *agency-based hermeneutical injustice*: a patient is denied hermeneutical agency by being prevented or discouraged from participating in meaning-making practices, maybe within healthcare contexts dominated by the epistemic resources and practices of biomedical science (see Blease et al. 2016). Or, of course, these two could occur together, with patients being unable to make sense of their experiences or to work to create resources that might help them to. And consider, too, the more general sorts of difficulties that illness, across most of its forms, can impose on our epistemic and social agency.

In the case of illness, hermeneutical injustice arises because the resources required for the understanding of the social experiences of ill persons are not accepted as part of the dominant hermeneutical resources. Most ill persons are capable of describing their experiences in non-expert terms, but such experiences are often considered inappropriate for public discussion and play little role in clinical processes. Such experiences are seen as private, if not shameful, and are also stigmatising (see Goffman 1963). Talking about them can exact a social and personal cost from the ill person – for example, disclosing one's HIV status can lead to social exclusion in certain groups.

Ill persons' accounts are often dismissed as 'moaning', idiosyncratic, or as part of the 'warm-up' to the legitimate epistemic activities initiated by a healthcare practitioner. Unless constituting a formal complaints procedure, such experiences often remain unnoted by HCPs and healthcare institutions. Despite initiatives such as patient and public involvement (PPI), co-design methodologies, and patient-centred care, by and large such experiences still play little role in the design of clinical services, performance review, or production of clinical guidelines. The qualitative nature of such accounts makes them difficult to quantify and they are often considered inadmissible evidence by medical bodies (Wainwright and Macnaughton 2013). Recent attempts in the UK to shoehorn the diversity of illness experiences into the 'friends and family test' further reduce the richness of such experiences.[8]

Hermeneutical injustice can arise through two sorts of social and epistemic practices, which act to prevent the promotion of non-dominant hermeneutical resources. The first are *strategies of exclusion*, which take the form of excluding a currently hermeneutically marginalised group from the practices and places where social meanings are made, such as professional committees or legislative bodies. This can take agential or structural forms. Such exclusion can take different forms, from physical exclusion to subtler forms such as employment of legal or medical terminology and conventions, resulting in the exclusion of those who are not members of those groups from participating in deliberative processes.

The second are *strategies of expression*, in which a social group is excluded because, as Fricker argues, its 'characteristic expressive style [is not] recognized as rational and contextually appropriate'; if, for instance, adopting an 'intuitive or an emotional expressive style means that one cannot be heard as fully rational' (Fricker 2007, 160–161). If so, the style that a marginalised group uses in its efforts to make the case for the recognition of its hermeneutical resources can serve to undermine those very efforts. This can lead to a vicious circle of increasing frustration, leading to more extreme styles of expression, which in turn lead to further epistemic disenfranchisement.

Are ill persons especially vulnerable to hermeneutical injustice? Our suggestion is that they are: ill persons typically have non-dominant hermeneutical resources that are not recognised or respected by the epistemically dominant medical profession, but which are essential to the understanding of the experience of illness. Ill persons can be, and often are, victims of strategies of exclusion: they report that they are forced to adopt an epistemically marginal role in consultative exercises, or that their preferred expressive styles are derogatively interpreted as irrational, perhaps as a 'difficult patient' or the various patients who provoke 'heartsink' – feelings of 'frustration, irritation, dislike', and so on – including those labelled by Clark and Croft as 'clingers', 'incommunicatives', or 'self-destructives' (see Wilson and Cunningham 2014, ch.5).

Such pejorative judgments of those expressive styles is reflective of a wider philosophical prejudice that contrasts rationality and emotionality, thereby encouraging a sense that reason ought to be expressed dispassionately (Burley 2011; Nussbaum 1990). This prejudice is especially apposite in illness because illness typically has an intense impact upon a person's life and so invites expression in emotive and anecdotal styles. A person operating with the rationalistic prejudice will find it difficult to regard the expressive styles that ill persons find both natural and appropriate as rational – a difficulty that can be resolved if one adopts a more pluralistic view of what counts as an appropriate expressive style, sensitive to the particularities of experiences of illness (Kidd forthcoming). Indeed, it may be a form of epistemic justice to *trust* that ill persons who narrate their experiences do often employ styles appropriate to their experiences.

These expressive styles may be overtly emotional and display socially unaccepted emotions such as anger, envy, and fear. The expression may be nonlinear and confusing, jumping between different events and times. It may be repetitive, as part of a process of acceptance. Or the expression may centre on themes that are difficult to accept, such as mortality, pain, and isolation. The new areas of research and practice, such as 'arts and health', medical humanities, music and dance therapies, as well as the phenomenology of illness, are a critical challenge to this set of prejudices about expression, aiming to legitimate varied forms of expression. They can be seen as attempts to combat hermeneutical injustice by providing expressive means to both make sense of and communicate the experience of illness.

The hermeneutical injustice that ill persons are particularly susceptible to generally takes the form of a double injury, because the marginalisation of their resources and expressive styles exacerbates the already considerable hermeneutical challenges that ill persons commonly face. Many experiences of illness evince two hermeneutical features. The first is *inarticulacy*, the difficulty of communicating certain aspects of the experience of illness (Carel 2013). The second is *ineffability*, the sense that certain aspects of those experiences cannot be communicated to others through propositional articulation because understanding is premised upon a person's having had the requisite bodily experiences. Typical examples of experiences that are hermeneutically accessible only to those who have had the corresponding personal experiences include childbirth, extreme pain, and religious experience (see, *inter alia*, Biro 2013; Heyes 2013; Wynn 2005). Indeed, a striking theme of many pathographies by trained healthcare practitioners testify to shock at the inability of medical-epistemic resources to articulate the experience of illness (see Gawande 2014; Kalanithi 2016).

## 5. The harm to patients

With the phenomena of testimonial and hermeneutical injustice in place, we can now examine the nature of the primary epistemic harm they suffer. Fricker characterises that harm in terms of *objectification*, but more recently Gaile Pohlhaus, Jr. (2014) has suggested that it is more fully understood in terms of *truncated subjectivity*. Pohlhaus, Jr. argued that the 'primary harm of testimonial injustice' should be defined as 'being relegated to the role of epistemic other, being treated as though the range of one's subject capacities is merely derivative of another's' (2014). The victim is not seen as capable of contributing to epistemic practices from her own standpoint:

> Consequently, her epistemic labour contributes to the community via which epistemic interests are pursued, but she is not permitted to contribute in ways that would redirect epistemic practices toward those parts of her experienced world that extend beyond or trouble the veracity of the dominantly experienced world. Any contribution that might do so is summarily denied epistemic support and uptake by dominant members of the community.
>
> *(2014, 107)*

Patients seem to occupy the position of 'other' in Pohlhaus, Jr.'s sense, in that their testimony is regularly solicited and indeed essential (e.g. in reporting symptoms or side effects of a drug), but nonetheless they remain a 'derivatised subject', i.e. a subject whose capacities are reduced to attending only to what stems from the perpetrator's perspective (2014, 105). Patient testimonies are sought as sources of factual information, but testimony about the lived experience of illness and the clinical encounter, which may challenge the medical view, is excluded from consideration and plays no formal role in decision-making and service design. Thus in cases of testimonial injustice, patients are perceived as 'somewhere between an epistemic subject and object' (2014, 107).

Pohlhaus, Jr.'s account accurately captures the epistemic plight of many ill persons in healthcare contexts: first, they are afforded limited capacities to epistemically contribute, usually by providing factual *information*, but not by offering their distinctive *experiences*. Second, their epistemic labour contributes to the epistemic practices of healthcare systems, but they are not permitted to contribute in ways that redirect the interests or concerns of those systems. One may call this an infringement of patients' epistemic autonomy. These two points can only be uncovered by an epistemic analysis; this shows both the theoretical efficacy and practical significance of such an analysis, which can open the way to reforming healthcare practices in order to address this issue.

Both empowering patients' epistemic practices and autonomy and tackling epistemic injustice by combating negative stereotypes are required (Carel 2012).

## 6. Summary

This chapter explored epistemic injustice in medicine and healthcare. Howsoever, several issues that may also point towards future work remain unresolved. The recent 'narrative turn' in medicine has had profound influence on medical education and professional development.[9] Medical students, trainees, and practitioners have been invited to learn how to listen to patient narratives and how to utilise those narratives in clinical practice. We suggest that this development needs to be underpinned with a call for reflection on 'ground floor' conceptions of the nature of health and of what counts as medically relevant knowledge and understanding. This kind of reflection is distinctly philosophical and thus complements the literary and applied work of narrative medicine.

Perhaps we also require a deeper sense of *structural epistemic injustice*: forms of injustice generated by systems, institutions, and practices. Certain conceptions of health may contain latent prejudices about nature of credibility, understanding, and explanation in medical and healthcare contexts. Think, for instance, of 'naturalistic' characterisations of health and disease as biological dysfunctions, best understood using the concepts and practices of biological science (see, e.g. Boorse 1975, 1977). On this model, epistemic relevance is confined to science and scientifically trained HCPs in a way that may generate epistemic prejudices against patients. Yet the door may swing both ways: Jeremy Wardrope (2014) has argued that medicalisation may illuminate, rather than occlude, the experiences of patients. If so, then subtle analyses of the nature of authority and credibility are needed, as they feed into our concepts of epistemic 'peerage' in healthcare (see Freeman 2015).

We hope that research on these sorts of issues will give a better account of how to enable and enrich the testimonial and hermeneutical capacities of ill persons, healthcare practitioners, and the public.[10]

**Related chapters:** 1, 2, 3, 4, 5, 6, 10, 18, 20, 22, 26, 33

Havi Carel's work on this paper was generously funded by a Wellcome Trust Senior Investigator Award (grant no. 103340).

## Notes

1 Of course this is done for good medical reasons, but is still a radically different experience for most adults, and leads to a sense of diminished autonomy and disempowerment.
2 A classic example of the former is Illich (1975).
3 See www.patients-association.org.uk/patient-stories/ (accessed on 11 July 2016).
4 Personal communication.
5 These examples are taken from responses to a query we posted on a patient mailing list in 2012.
6 Fricker has recently developed the notion of 'structural testimonial injustice' to clarify the preemptive character of certain testimonial injustices. See (or, rather, hear) her keynote lecture, 'Epistemic Injustice Revisited', delivered at the conference *Understanding Epistemic Injustice*, University of Bristol, 26 June 2014, available to download at www.bristol.ac.uk/philosophy/research/epistemic-injustice-/
7 Although many healthcare practitioners argue that such detachment is essential for emotional reasons, many recent writers protest this. See, for instance, (Groopman 2008; Ofri 2013).
8 See www.england.nhs.uk/statistics/statistical-work-areas/friends-and-family-test/friends-and-family-test-data/ (accessed on 11 July 2016).

9 A good resource is the Columbia University Medical Centre Program in Narrative Medicine, which hosts *Intima: A Journal of Narrative Medicine*: www.narrativemedicine.org/index.html
10 We are grateful to José Medina and Gaile Pohlhaus, Jr. for very helpful comments on an earlier draft of this chapter. A bibliography of work on epistemic injustice and illness is maintained at www.academia.edu/30136837/Epistemic_Injustice_and_Illness_Bibliography

# References

Biro, David, 'When Language Runs Dry: Pain, the Imagination and Metaphor', in L. Folkmarson Käll (ed.), *Dimensions of Pain*, London: Routledge, 2013, 13–26.
Blease, Charlotte, Havi Carel, and Keith Geraghty, 'Epistemic injustice in healthcare encounters: Evidence from Chronic Fatigue Syndrome', *Journal of Medical Ethics*, doi:10.1136/medethics-2016-103691 (2016).
Boorse, Christopher, 'On the distinction between disease and illness', *Philosophy and Public Affairs* 5.1 (1975): 49–68.
Boorse, Christopher, 'Health as a theoretical concept', *Philosophy of Science* 44.4 (1977): 542–573.
Burley, Mikel, 'Emotion and anecdote in philosophical argument: The case of Havi Carel's *Illness*', *Metaphilosophy* 42.1–2 (2011): 33–48.
Burroughs, Michael and Deborah Tollefsen, 'Learning to listen: Epistemic injustice and the child', *Episteme* 13.3 (2016): 359–377.
Carel, Havi, 'Phenomenology as a resource for patients', *Journal of Medicine and Philosophy* 37.2 (2012): 96–113.
Carel, Havi, *Illness: The Cry of the Flesh*, London: Routledge, 2013.
Carel, Havi, *Phenomenology of Illness*, Oxford: Oxford University Press, 2016.
Carel, Havi and Gita Györffy, 'Seen but not heard: Children and epistemic injustice', *The Lancet* 384.9950 (2014): 1256–1257.
Carel, Havi and Ian James Kidd, 'Epistemic injustice in healthcare: A philosophical analysis', *Medicine, Healthcare and Philosophy* 17.4 (2014): 529–540.
Collins, Patricia Hill, 'Intersectionality and Epistemic Injustice', in Ian James Kidd, Jose Medina, and Gaile Pohlhaus, Jr. (eds.), *The Routledge Handbook of Epistemic Injustice*, New York: Routledge, 2017.
Coulter, Angela and Jo Ellins, *Patient Focused Interventions: A Review of the Evidence*, London: The Health Foundation, 2009, available at www.health.org.uk
Crichton, Paul, Havi Carel, and Ian James Kidd, 'Epistemic injustice and psychiatry', *Psychiatry Bulletin*, 1–6, doi: 10.1192/pb.bp.115.050682.
Dennett, Daniel, *Brainstorms*, Cambridge, MA: MIT Press, 1981.
Frank, Arthur, *The Wounded Storyteller: Body, Illness, and Ethics*, Chicago: University of Chicago Press, 2010.
Freeman, Lauren, 'Confronting diminished epistemic privilege and epistemic injustice in pregnancy by challenging a "panoptics of the womb"', *Journal of Medicine and Philosophy* 40.1 (2015): 44–68.
Fricker, Miranda, *Epistemic Injustice: Power and the Ethics of Knowing*, Oxford: Oxford University Press, 2007.
Gawande, Atul, *Being Mortal: Illness, Medicine, and What Matters in the End*, London: Profile Books, 2014.
Goffman, Ervin, *Stigma: Notes on the Management of Spoiled Identity*, New York: Simon & Schuster, 1963.
Goldie, Peter (ed.), *The Oxford Handbook of the Philosophy of the Emotions*, Oxford: Oxford University Press, 2012.
Greener, Ian, *Healthcare in the UK: Understanding Continuity and Change*, Bristol: The Policy Press, 2009.
Groopman, Jerome, *How Doctors Think*, Boston: Houghton Mifflin Company, 2008.
Heyes, Cressida J., 'Child, Birth: An Aesthetic', in L. Folkmarson Käll (ed.), *Dimensions of Pain*, London: Routledge, 2013, 132–141.
Hookway, Christopher, 'Some varieties of epistemic injustice', *Episteme* 7 (2010): 151–163.
Illich, Ivan, *Medical Nemesis: The Expropriation of Health*, London: Calder & Boyars, 1975.
Kalanithi, Paul, *When Breath Becomes Air*, New York: Random House, 2016.
Kidd, Ian James, 'Exemplarism, ethics, and illness narratives', *Theoretical Medicine and Bioethics*, forthcoming.
Kidd, Ian James and Havi Carel, 'Epistemic injustice and illness', *Journal of Applied Philosophy* 33.2 (2016): 172–190.
Klitzman, Robert, *When Doctors Become Patients*, Oxford: Oxford University Press, 2007.
Korsch, Barbara M., Ethel K. Gozzie, and Vida Francis, 'Gaps in doctor-patient communication: Doctor-patient interaction and patient satisfaction', *Pediatrics* 42 (1968): 855–871.
Lakeman, Richard, 'Epistemic injustice and the mental health service user', *International Journal of Mental Health Nursing* 19 (2010): 151–153.

McIver, Shirley, 'User Perspectives and Involvement', in Kieran Walshe and Judith Smith (eds.), *Healthcare Management*, 2nd ed. Maidenhead: Open University Press, 2011, 354–372.

Nussbaum, Martha, *Love's Knowledge: Essays on Philosophy and Literature*, Oxford: Oxford University Press, 1990.

Ofri, Danielle, *What Doctors Feel: How Emotions Affect the Practice of Medicine*, Boston: Beacon Press, 2013.

Pohlhaus, Jr., Gaile, 'Discerning the primary epistemic harm in cases of testimonial injustice', *Social Epistemology* 28.2 (2014): 99–114.

Rudd, Rima E., 'The evolving concept of *health literacy*: New directions for health literacy studies', *Journal of Communication in Healthcare* 8.1 (2015): 7–9.

Scrutton, Anastasia, 'Epistemic Injustice and Mental Illness', in Ian James Kidd, José Medina, and Gaile Pohlhaus, Jr. (eds.), *The Routledge Handbook of Epistemic Injustice*, London: Routledge, 2017.

Smith, Susan, *Sick and Tired of Being Sick and Tired: Black Women's Health Activism in America, 1890–1950*, Philadelphia: University of Pennsylvania Press, 2010.

Srivastava, Rani, *The Healthcare Professional's Guide to Clinical Cultural Competence*, Toronto: Elsevier Health Sciences, 2007.

Toombs, Kay, 'The meaning of illness: A phenomenological approach to the patient – physician relationship', *Journal of Medicine and Philosophy* 12 (1987): 219–240.

Vida, Francis, Barbara M. Korsch, and Marie J. Morris, 'Gaps in doctor-patient communication II: Patients' response to medical advice', *The New England Journal of Medicine* 280 (1969): 535–540.

Wainwright, Megan and Jane Macnaughton, 'Is a qualitative perspective missing from COPD guidelines?', *The Lancet Respiratory Medicine* 1.6 (2013): 441–442.

Wardrope, Alistair, 'Medicalization and epistemic injustice', *Medicine, Healthcare, and Philosophy* 18.3 (2014): 341–352.

Wilson, Hamish and Wayne Cunningham, *Being a Doctor: Understanding Medical Practice*, London: The Royal College of General Practitioners, 2014.

Wylie, Alison, 'Why Standpoint Matters', in S. Harding (ed.), *The Feminist Standpoint Reader: Intellectual and Political Controversies*, London: Routledge, 2004, 339–351.

Wynn, Mark, *Emotional Experiences and Religious Understanding: Integrating Perception, Conception, and Feeling*, Cambridge: Cambridge University Press, 2005.

# 33
# EPISTEMIC INJUSTICE AND MENTAL ILLNESS

*Anastasia Philippa Scrutton*

## Introduction

The first part of this chapter looks at epistemic injustices that can take place in the context of psychiatric diagnosis and treatment. I argue people diagnosed with mental illnesses are often stereotyped in such a way as to deflate their credibility, and that the authoritative and even exclusive status accorded to third-person, medical perspectives on experiences of mental illness leads to hermeneutical marginalization and silencing. The second part of the chapter takes as its starting-point the idea that epistemic injustice can be countered by a recognition of the ways in which the marginalized person is in fact epistemically privileged. I argue that recognizing the ways in which people diagnosed with mental illnesses have access to distinctive and/or unique forms of knowledge can correct our testimonial sensibilities and provide us with new hermeneutical resources, and is therefore a route to epistemic justice. I explore ways in which this might be the case in relation to experiences of mental illness, focusing on two kinds of knowledge: knowledge of what the experience is like, and knowledge of what is good for the person. I conclude with some implications for clinical practice and more general ethical behaviour.

Before beginning, a few caveats. First, by using terms such as 'mental illness', 'depression' and 'schizophrenia', I do not mean that these are things that exist 'out there', independently of the way in which our society makes sense of them, as natural kinds. Rather, people have a diverse range of experiences, which are consistent with what have developed to be the medical criteria for these things and which in certain contexts would be diagnosed and interpreted as mental disorders. This is important since the idea that mental illness, depression and schizophrenia are natural kinds is problematic metaphysically, because no physical or phenomenological essence or set of necessary and sufficient conditions have been identified to distinguish them from other experiences (Bentall and Pilgrim 1999; Davidson 2004: 158; Kendell and Jablensky 2003: 5; Littlewood 1997: 67). It is also problematic ethically, since essentializing these experiences in medical terms tends to deflect our attention away from causal and contributory social injustices, and can diminish both hope and meaning (Blazer 2005: 6; Kvaale Gottdeiner and Haslam 2013; Scrutton 2015a; 2015b). While the ontological status of mental illness terms is not the focus of this chapter, a central contention of the chapter is that experiences are shaped in no small degree by the categories into which we put them, and that interpreting the experiences we associate with mental illness in purely medical terms (as a natural kinds view tends to do) gives rise to epistemic injustices (see Kidd and Carel 2017).

Second, by virtue of the topic of this book (epistemic *in*justice), this chapter will focus on problematic assumptions and practices, and ways of addressing them, and will put to one side existing positive experiences and practices. However, this is also not an exercise in psychiatry-bashing: epistemic injustice takes place sometimes because of, but sometimes in spite of, formal psychiatric policies. More importantly still, the subject matter should not lead us to lose sight of the fact that many psychiatrists and mental health professionals are compassionate, intelligent people, who frequently have a positive impact on those with whom they work. Much epistemic injustice in mental healthcare arises as a result of factors beyond professionals' control: lack of time, training or resources, or responsibility for responding to situations that in fact require a far more systemic, societal response.

Third, while I am focusing on epistemic injustice in the context of psychiatry, there are other problematic attitudes perpetrated towards people diagnosed with mental illness in non-medical contexts. For example, a voluntaristic or moralising model of depression, according to which people could stop being depressed by pulling themselves together, looking on the bright side and adopting a different lifestyle is epistemically problematic because a frequent experience in depression is of diminished free will, and this is disbelieved and denied in voluntarist accounts (Scrutton forthcoming [a]). This would seem to be a form of hermeneutical injustice, since the people who disbelieve people with depression about their experience of diminished free will lack insight into certain experiences and empathy towards those who have them. These and other problematic attitudes are not the focus of this chapter, but the ways of addressing epistemic injustice I explore in the latter part of the chapter are also relevant to them.

## 1. Epistemic injustice

In a famous experiment published in 1973, psychologist David Rosenhan and seven mentally healthy collaborators made appointments with a range of psychiatrists and feigned having had auditory hallucinations. Following hospitalization, Rosenhan and the other collaborators kept notes on their treatment in the hospitals, reporting that attendants would behave verbally and even physically abusively towards patients in front of other patients, but that this behavior would terminate abruptly if other staff were known to be coming. Reflecting on the experience, Rosenhan writes, 'Staff are credible witnesses. Patients are not' (1973: 256).

Much has changed for the better in mental healthcare, particularly in relation to the more humane treatment of patients – and yet service users and reflective service providers alike report that mental health patients are still deemed to have diminished credibility such that cognitive biases are applied and confirmed. For example, Larry Davidson reflects that in diagnosis, 'In the form of a tautology, once I know that you experience psychosis, I feel entitled to question the credibility of your experiences. Then, once I establish the lack of legitimacy of your experiences, I am able to infer from this that you have a psychotic disorder' (Davidson 2004: 154). This is perhaps particularly the case in relation to diagnoses involving psychosis, since delusion (and thus actual diminished credibility) is one form of psychosis. Yet, as the quotation from Davidson highlights, presuppositions about what psychosis involves can give rise to circular reasoning, so that a person with some psychotic symptoms does not begin with a clean slate, but is suspected of having a constellation of symptoms commensurate with a psychiatric disorder.

In addition to confirmation biases, part of the reason for testimonial injustices lies, far more simply, in the diminished authority accorded to medical patients in a medical context. This, of course, cuts across all diagnoses. Thus, Richard Lakeman notes the disparity between his perceived credibility in his role as a doctor and as a patient in the context of drugs used for treating mood disorders:

> I recall feeling profoundly affected by a small dose of a commonly prescribed psychotropic drug. When I reported this to the prescriber, my claims were met with incredulity, as the reaction I experienced was quite unusual. As a professional, the veracity of my reporting of the symptoms or behaviour of others had never been called into question in the manner that it was when I was in the position of patient.
>
> *(Lakeman 2010: 151)*

Mental health diagnoses are particularly 'sticky': a past diagnosis can result in a confirmation bias that leads to ongoing testimonial and other forms of epistemic injustice. Richard Bentall reports the case of Andrew, whose past diagnosis made Andrew's upset behaviour at his grandmother's funeral immediately pathologizable. Bentall reports that, in the absence of any irrational behaviour or a report by Andrew of pathological experiences, his detainment in a psychiatric ward was justified on account of his being 'excessively polite', and his decision to wear a suit interpreted as evidence that he was 'grandiose' (Bentall 2010: 111–112). As in this case, epistemic injustice might involve not only being disbelieved, but also not even being listened to due to prior perceptions, or even repeatedly and systematically misinterpreted. This forms a meeting point for testimonial injustice and hermeneutical marginalization.

Two distinct but related forms of hermeneutical injustice are particularly conspicuous in the context of diagnosis. First, experients are treated as sources of data rather than participants in the diagnostic process (see Carel and Kidd 2014). Second, experiences reported can be forced into an existing mold to the exclusion of other aspects of the experience that are important to the patient. As Giovanni Stanghellini puts it:

> The nosological [disease-classifying] approach based on operational criteria for discrete disorders may force researchers and clinicians to commit 'procrustean errors' [...], in which the patient's symptomatology is stretched to fit pre-existing diagnostic criteria. Diagnostic categories are conceptualised as boxes ('category' originally means 'box', 'container') in which similar objects should find their place (dolls with dolls, candies with candies). The 'meaning' of a symptom is reduced to the properties that correspond to one category or box [...]. There is little space for personal meanings and personal narratives, as well as for meanings and narratives negotiated during the psychiatric interview.
>
> *(Stanghellini 2004: 183–184, my parentheses)*

Because of the (pre-formed and medically defined) structure of a psychiatric or other medical interview, the ability to interpret the experience correctly is perceived as lying with the physician, the health expert. More problematically still, because of the perceived authority of medicine as a branch of science in western society, the medical perspective is regarded not only as authoritative but often even as exclusive of other perspectives, such that medical diagnosis effectively constitutes a monopoly on the way the experience is interpreted. In a 2012 study of the way in which interpretations and contextual factors can affect experiences such as hearing voices, one voice hearer, Holly, gives the following account of the reaction of psychiatrists:

> [I] relayed this experience to psychiatrists in the [hospital] and was sent for EEG tests, was told that I was hallucinating, was, this guy just didn't listen to, just obviously hadn't heard anything really that I'd said... I just felt that this really positive experience was just scrutinised and just not, just liked mocked. I didn't feel offended, I just thought they were being really stupid, and disregarding this kind of, yeah, really important thing.
>
> *(Holly, cited Heriot-Maitland, Knight and Peters 2012: 46)*

This indicates that by virtue of hermeneutically marginalizing Holly (not listening to her interpretation of her experience), the psychiatrists suffered epistemically: they became 'stupid' because they did not have the hermeneutical resources to understand the experience fully. Unlike paradigmatic forms of hermeneutical injustice, here it is not the case that an experience is not understood at all on account of the absence of a valid interpretation for it. Rather, one valid perspective on an experience is lost because another valid perspective is dominant and exclusive, giving rise to a one-sided interpretation (see Mason 2011). This is problematic, in part because other perspectives may give rise to a richer and more therapeutic interpretation than a purely biomedical perspective can do on its own. Thus, in a study of people who experience voice-hearing positively, Lana Jackson, Mark Hayward and Anne Cooke note that:

> Most participants felt that their voice-hearing experiences were meaningful and therefore sought alternative understandings (often spiritual) to an illness-based medical view. Those who had received a diagnosis of mental illness tended to view their voices as more than just 'a bunch of symptoms that need fixing' (Rachel). This often conflicted with the medical approach they were offered.
> *(Jackson, Hayward and Cooke 2010: 149)*

In these cases, a medical perspective was often found to conflict with a 'meaningful' one; when medical models are presented as non-exclusive (and depending on the 'meaningful' narrative adopted), they could instead supplement it. While these people evidently had the confidence and support required to reject a biomedical model, other people might instead lose confidence in their own, potentially therapeutic, interpretation. As Miranda Fricker notes:

> When you find yourself in a situation in which you seem to be the only one to feel the dissonance between received understanding and your own intimated sense of a given experience, it tends to knock your faith in your own ability to make sense of the world, or at least the relevant region of the world.
> *(Fricker 2007: 163)*

This could be detrimental, since changing the way an experience is interpreted in turn changes the way in which it is experienced: if an experience ceases to be interpreted in positive or meaningful terms, it may cease to be so (Scrutton 2015c; Scrutton forthcoming [b]). In addition, whether or not the person's perspective would have been helpful, the silencing that is a structural facet of psychiatric diagnosis and treatment is, in and of itself, deflating, and likely to effect a transition from experients being active agents to being passive recipients – in other words, becoming healthcare consumers rather than participants, and objects rather than subjects.

These cases focus on situations in which people have been disadvantaged by virtue of a particular diagnosis being imposed upon them. There are also situations in which people have felt advantaged by a medical diagnosis but disadvantaged by its removal. For example, DSM-5's decision to collapse what was previously called Asperger's into the autistic spectrum has led to distress on the part of patients, not only because it will have a negative impact on the services available, but also because it undermines the positive 'Aspie' identity and community formed around the diagnosis (Giles 2014). What is problematic here is that patients have not been asked to participate in discussions of how their experiences are interpreted and defined, and interpretation has been perceived as entirely the prerogative of a third-person body. As with the examples cited earlier, this is part of a more deep-rooted problem relating to medical diagnosis of 'mental disorders' as currently understood. The idea that a medical expert must legitimate certain experiences by defining them as 'real illnesses' may currently be a necessity in terms of people receiving certain kinds of care and providing justification to employers and insurance companies for time needed away from work. However, it is also an idea that reinforces an unjust distribution of epistemic credibility, suggests biomedical treatments as the default solution to a person's mental distress, and deflects attention away from the social issues at the heart of many of the experiences we term 'mental disorder'.

## 2. Epistemic justice

As Havi Carel and Ian James Kidd argue, one way of countering epistemic injustice in healthcare is to recognize that patients, as well as medical professionals, are epistemically privileged in distinctive ways. Broadly speaking, medical professionals tend to be experts primarily in third-person forms of knowledge, while patients are likely to be experts primarily in first-person forms of knowledge. That said, there is no reason that the expertise of each should not come to be extended to the other form of knowledge (Carel and Kidd 2014: 535). In this section, I will focus on two distinct though related forms of knowledge experients have: knowledge of the experience itself, and, in some cases, conscious or unconscious knowledge of what is good for them.

Attention to first-person accounts of mental illness experiences tends to reveal some surprising characteristics that are not captured by medical literature on it. For example, in relation to depression, in addition to revealing its sheer heterogeneity, facets such as an altered sense of time, an experience of diminished or annihilated free will, and altered bodily experience come to the fore. Our understanding of experiences we already associate with depression are sharpened and deepened: impaired social function seems *(pace* DSM-IV) not only to be a side effect of depression, but integral to it; guilt and loss of hope take a variety of forms (Ratcliffe 2014). These aspects can be surprising to the experient, the clinician and the medical world more generally (Carel and Kidd 2014: 538). In addition to understanding depression experiences more clearly, understanding these experiences also leads to a better understanding of 'normal' or 'non-pathological' human experience (Carel 2012; Ratcliffe 2014).

Listening to experients is accompanied by practical epistemic problems that need to be surmounted. First, many experients do not have the education, abilities or opportunities needed to articulate their experiences, thus giving rise to the fact that studies of the phenomenology of mental illness often focus on the experiences of highly educated sufferers. This can result in the empowerment of more educated sufferers but to the further marginalization of less-educated sufferers and to intersection of different kinds of discrimination and negative stereotyping (Crenshaw 1989). A second practical epistemic problem is that the person's experiences may be described in such a way as to fit recognized symptoms of depression due to perceived expectations, thus leading to a skewing of the description (Paterson 2003: 991; Ratcliffe et al. 2014). Listening to experients is therefore unlikely to be sufficient unless the experient first has the resources needed for describing them, including, where relevant, breaking away from received medical and social descriptions of the experience. Facilitating linguistic and non-linguistic ways of expressing the experience in which the idea that the experience is an objective belief entity is bracketed can enable other, under-described aspects of the experience to come to the fore (Carel 2012: 107). Crucially for our discussion, this process presupposes the validity of a plurality of perspectives on the experience, thus countering the dominating tendencies of medical approaches to mental illness described above. Where service users' experiences are listened to and their perspectives upheld, distress such as that caused by the removal of Asperger's from DSM-5 may be avoided or diminished, whether because removal would not take place or because the dialogical process is likely to make it less disempowering.

In addition to having unique knowledge of what an experience is like, experients can also, in some cases, have insight into what is good for them. As in Lakeman's case, this might take the form of being aware of side-effects that make a particular treatment inadvisable. Or, as Holly hints, it might take the form of being aware that a 'pathological' experience has positive value. A notable example of the latter case is provided by Frederick Frese, retired director of psychology at a public psychiatric hospital and an advocate for people diagnosed with schizophrenia. Frese was diagnosed and involuntarily hospitalized with schizophrenia in the 1960s, and continues to have intermittent episodes. These episodes, he writes, add valuably to his ability as a psychologist, making him a sign of hope for others with schizophrenia, by showing them that they can also integrate their condition with a successful job and happy family life. They also give him better insight into how people with schizophrenia think and behave than he would have were he just another 'chronically normal' person, and enable his patients to trust him as a fellow sufferer. Frese's form of schizophrenia includes imbuing certain numbers with particular mystical values. While his earlier episodes lacked insight and were often frightening, his later experiences have been marked by a sense of peace, wonder and joy. In the conclusion to one article written in 1994, he describes his then-present psychological state:

> When, in Milwaukee, I was breaking the code of the universe, I discovered the power of the Trinity as I have come to know it. My experience taught me that directly to approach the Deity in such a presumptuous manner can be fraught with terror and disaster. Such a thing is far too powerful an experience for a mere mortal to handle. I still have a code, of course. You may have noticed that I have used a generous sprinkling of sevens, twelves, and forties, as well as threes, as I constructed this narration. These religiously oriented mystical numbers give me little bits of joy as I go about any of my work. I know that this does not make rational sense, but I am most confident that neither I, nor anyone else, is a totally rational being. And my 'secret code' unlocks innumerable joys for me throughout each day.
>
> (Frese 1994: 25)

Frese's and others' accounts point to the positive value experiences such as psychosis can have, in spite of psychiatry's tendency to view them as purely negative phenomena (see Scrutton 2015c). Listening to the ways in which experients evaluate their experiences may provide information about what is likely to be good for them. At times, as in Frese's case, this may imply that a positive interpretation should not be overridden by a biomedical one, though it may be held alongside it. At other times, it may make medical diagnosis and treatment inappropriate or even unhelpful and pathogenic (see e.g. Roxburgh and Roe 2014).

A further intriguing possibility about the way in which experients can have insight into what is good for them concerns 'motivated delusions': delusions that develop because they play a defensive function such as preventing loss of self-esteem, and help manage negative emotions (see Bortolotti 2015). In this case, the insight involved seems to be unconscious. Motivated delusions sometimes occur in the context of Reverse Othello syndrome, in which the person believes their partner to be faithful to them, despite strong evidence to the contrary. Consider the following example:

> Butler's patient was a talented musician who had sustained severe head injuries in a car accident. The accident left him quadriplegic, unable to speak without reliance on an

electronic communicator. One year after his injury, the patient developed a delusional system that revolved around the continuing fidelity of his partner (who had in fact severed all contact with him soon after his accident). The patient became convinced that he and his former partner had recently married, and he was eager to persuade others that he now felt sexually fulfilled.

*(McKay, Langdon and Coltheart 2005: 313)*

Over time, and roughly coincident with his physical rehabilitation, the man realized that his girlfriend had in fact broken up with him and moved on, and no other symptoms were observed. Peter Butler argues that the delusion alleviated the man's sense of loss (Butler 2000: 90). Other possible examples of motivated delusion include cases of erotomania (in which the person irrationally believes someone is in love with them) and anosognosia (in which the person believes they are not missing a limb, are not disabled, or are not ill, when in fact they are). Motivated delusions can of course have costs as well as benefits: for example, in anosognosia, they may prevent people from seeking help, and in general they can alienate the person by creating a gap between their and others' perceptions of reality (Bortolotti 2015: 493). They are also more likely to become counter-productive if held over a longer period of time. Nevertheless, as Lisa Bortolotti argues, they may provide psychological defence against more serious harm during times of intense distress by guarding against severe negative emotions and even by enabling the person in other ways to function epistemically (Bortolotti 2015). Crucially, as Bortolotti argues, it might not be possible for the severe negative emotions to be headed off or for epistemic functionality to continue, by any other means. The person with motivated delusions is, I suggest, both epistemically compromised, since she holds a belief that is both false and irrational, and also epistemically privileged, since she (and probably she alone) has a particular, if unconscious sort of insight into what is needed in order for her to survive a traumatic event.

## 3. Conclusion

Reflection on reports by patients and physicians indicates that a variety of epistemic injustices are found in psychiatric mental healthcare. I have argued that these are founded upon and perpetuated by the prioritization of objective, third-person accounts to the detriment and even exclusion of subjective, first-person ones. In order for these injustices to be overcome and epistemic justice practiced, mental health professionals need to be cognizant of the ways in which experients are epistemically privileged – for example, in having unique knowledge of what their experiences are like and, in some cases, of what might be best for them. This provides medical professionals, and the family and friends of people diagnosed with mental illnesses, with reasons for listening closely to people diagnosed with mental illnesses. It does so in a way that does not make false claims about the kinds of knowledge people diagnosed with mental illness have, and that does not whitewash the fact that some people diagnosed with some forms of mental illness have problematic epistemic states (such as delusions). While the focus of this chapter has been on epistemic injustice in psychiatry, recognition of experients as epistemically privileged helps to counter other problematic forms of epistemic behaviour in relation to mentally ill people more generally. For example, in relation to the moralizing attitudes noted at the beginning of the chapter, cultivating a recognition of the ways in which experients are epistemically privileged would enable greater understanding of the immutability of some experiences and the difficulties experients face in relation to them. More generally, adopting an attitude of listening rather than 'knowing best' would help to counter the stigma and sense of alienation and diminished agency that people with mental illness often experience.

**Related chapters** 1, 2, 3, 4, 16, 18, 32, 34, 36

# References

Bentall, Richard, *Doctoring the Mind: Why Psychiatric Treatments Fail*. London: Penguin, 2010.
Blazer, Dan, *The Age of Melancholy: "Major Depression" and Its Social Origins*. New York: Routledge, 2005.
Butler, Peter, Reverse Othello syndrome subsequent to traumatic brain injury, *Psychiatry: Interpersonal and Biological Processes* 63.1 (2000): 85–92.
Carel, Havi, Phenomenology as a resource for patients, *Journal of Medicine and Philosophy* 37 (2012): 96–113.
Carel, Havi and Kidd, Ian James, Epistemic injustice in healthcare: A philosophical analysis, *Medicine, Healthcare, and Philosophy* 17.4 (2014): 529–540.
Crenshaw, Kimberlé W., Demarginalizing the intersection of race and sex: A black feminist critique of antidiscrimination doctrine, feminist theory and antiracist politics, *Chicago Legal Forum, special issue: Feminism in the Law: Theory, Practice and Criticism* 1 (1989) Article 8: 139–167.
Davidson, Larry, Phenomenology and contemporary clinical practice: Introduction to special issue, *Journal of Phenomenological Psychology* 35.2 (2004): 149–162.
Frese, Frederick J., A calling, *Second Opinion* 19.3 (1994): 11–25.
Fricker, Miranda, *Epistemic Injustice: Power and the Ethics of Knowing*. Oxford: Oxford University Press, 2007.
Giles, David, 'DSM-V is taking away our identity': The reaction of the online community to the proposed changes in the diagnosis of Asperger's disorder, *Health* 18.2 (2014): 179–195.
Heriot-Maitland, Charles, Knight, Matthew, and Peters, Emmanuelle, A qualitative comparison of psychotic-like phenomena in clinical and non-clinical populations, *British Journal of Clinical Psychology* 51 (2012): 37–53.
Jackson, Lana, Hayward, Mark, and Cooke, Anne, Developing positive relationships with voices: A preliminary grounded theory, *International Journal of Social Psychiatry* 57.5 (2010): 487–495.
Kendell, Robert and Jablensky, Assen, Distinguishing between the validity and utility of psychiatric diagnoses, *American Journal of Psychiatry* 160 (2003): 4–12.
Kvaale, Erlend, Gottdeiner, William, and Haslam, Nick, Biogenetic explanations and stigma: A meta-analytical review of associations among laypeople, *Social Science and Medicine* 96 (2013): 95–103.
Lakeman, Richard, Epistemic injustice and the mental health service user, *International Journal of Mental Health Nursing* 19 (2010): 151–153.
Littlewood, Roland, Commentary on spiritual experience and psychopathology, *Philosophy, Psychiatry and Psychology* 4.1 (1997): 67–73.
Mason, Rebecca, Two kinds of knowing, *Hypatia: A Journal of Feminist Philosophy* 26.2 (2011): 294–307.
McKay, Ryan, Langdon, Robyn, and Coltheart, Max, 'Sleights of mind': Delusions, defences and self-deception, *Cognitive Neuropsychiatry* 10.4 (2005): 305–326.
Paterson, Barbara, The koala has claws: Applications of the shifting perspectives model in research of chronic illness, *Qualitative Health Research* 13 (2003): 987–994.
Pilgrim, David and Bentall, Richard, The medicalisation of misery: A critical realist analysis of the concept of depression, *Journal of Mental Health* 8.3 (1999): 261–274.
Ratcliffe, Matthew, *Experiences of Depression: A Study in Phenomenology*. Oxford: Oxford University Press, 2014.
Ratcliffe, Matthew, Broome, Matthew, Smith, Benedict, and Bowden, Hannah, A Bad Case of the Flu? The Comparative Phenomenology of Depression and Somatic Illness, in Matthew Ratcliffe and Achim Stephan (eds.), *Depression, Emotion and the Self: Philosophical and Interdisciplinary Perspectives*. Exeter: Imprint Academic Ltd., 2014, 163–182.
Rosenhan, David, On being sane in insane places, *Science* 179.4070 (1973): 250–258.
Roxburgh, Elizabeth and Roe, Chris, Reframing voices and visions using a spiritual model: An interpretative phenomenological analysis of anomalous experiences in mediumship, *Mental Health, Religion and Culture* 17.6 (2014): 641–653.
Scrutton, Anastasia Philippa, Two Christian theologies of depression, *Philosophy, Psychiatry and Psychology* 22.4 (2015c): 275–289.
Scrutton, Anastasia Philippa, 'Interpretation, meaning, and the shaping of experience: Against depression being a natural entity and other forms of essentialism. *Philosophy, Psychiatry and Psychology* 22.4 (2015a): 299–301.
Scrutton, Anastasia Philippa, 'Is depression a sin or a disease?' A critique of moralising and medicalising models of mental illness, *Journal of Religion and Disability* 19.4 (2015b): 285–311.

Scrutton, Anastasia Philippa, Is depression a sin? A philosophical consideration of Christian voluntarism, *Philosophy, Psychiatry and Psychology* (Forthcoming [a]).

Scrutton, Anastasia Philippa, Can being told you're ill make you ill? A discussion of psychiatry, religion, and out of the ordinary experiences, *Think: Philosophy for Everyone* (Forthcoming [b]).

Stanghellini, Giovanni, The puzzle of the psychiatric interview, *Journal of Phenomenological Psychology* 35 (2004): 173–195.

# 34
# INDIGENOUS PEOPLES, ANTHROPOLOGY, AND THE LEGACY OF EPISTEMIC INJUSTICE[1]

*Rebecca Tsosie*

### Introduction

Of all the Western academic disciplines, anthropology has had the most enduring impact on the lives of Indigenous peoples, framing them in various 19th and 20th century texts as the cultural 'Other' according to their allegedly 'primitive' character.[2] This cultural construction was based on an earlier philosophical lexicography that developed the trope of 'civilization' as a mode to justify rights to land, resources, and human labor within the colonial empires claimed by the European monarchs.[3] The cultural constructions of the past continue to inform Western law and policy and are profoundly linked to both testimonial and hermeneutical forms of epistemic injustice. Although the more overt racism of the past has been carefully sanitized from contemporary usage, the theoretical framework of epistemic injustice provides a powerful new mechanism to understand the historic wrongs, as well as the contemporary harms that Indigenous peoples continue to experience. In addition, the theory of epistemic injustice can enhance the dynamic interaction between law and ethics that is currently reshaping the social context of work within anthropology and archaeology.[4]

I was asked to write on epistemic injustice and anthropology, and I do so with respect. Much of anthropology merely replicates categories of knowledge that are deeply embedded within all Western intellectual disciplines, including law, philosophy, and the social sciences. There are many critiques of these academic disciplines, and many anthropologists have critiqued the origins of their own discipline and attempted to incorporate a more just set of guidelines into their practice.[5] This chapter is not an attack on anthropology. Rather it is an effort to show how the cultural construction of the 'Other' extended into the law that continues to govern Indigenous rights, and how that law is now portrayed as 'fair and neutral', masking many forms of epistemic injustice.

This chapter first describes the historical context necessary to understand epistemic injustice as it concerns Indigenous peoples and anthropology and situates that discussion within several contemporary case studies. The chapter then engages the theoretical literature to see how theories of epistemic injustice can accurately describe the historical harms to Indigenous peoples, as well as the continuing harms that arise from inadequate legal and policy responses.

## 1. The historical context

From the date of contact to the formation of the modern nation-states, such as the United States, the European nations relied on the Doctrine of Discovery within the Law of Nations to claim their colonial empires in the New World.[6] The Doctrine of Discovery originated during the Crusades but was later used by the European nations to claim ownership of lands in the Americas occupied by 'uncivilized' and non-Christian peoples. The first European nation to 'discover' and 'settle' lands occupied by 'uncivilized' peoples could claim good title to the lands. The Doctrine of Discovery was premised upon Christian theology and natural law, and as a legal construct, it relied upon the tropes of 'civilization' and 'savagery' to distinguish the respective mode of land acquisition.[7] Lands occupied by Indigenous peoples were considered available for 'discovery' and 'settlement', whereas lands occupied by other civilized Nations could only be claimed by political 'conquest'.

In 1830, Chief Justice John Marshall imported the Doctrine of Discovery into U.S. federal law when he settled a title dispute between two non-Indian claimants. In Johnson v. McIntosh, Marshall ruled that the United States had conveyed a valid title to defendant (McIntosh) because Great Britain had transferred its title by 'discovery' to the United States, enabling the U.S. to extinguish the Indians' 'right of occupancy' and exercise its preemptive right to full ownership.[8] The plaintiff (Johnson) claimed title from earlier pre-Revolutionary War purchases directly from the Chiefs of the Piankeshaw Indian Nation, who were the undisputed first possessors of the lands. However, Marshall said that the Indians merely held a 'right of occupancy' because they lacked the 'civilized' character necessary to claim a full legal title to land. This justification for limiting property rights to Europeans was based on the allegedly 'primitive' character of the Indians, who Marshall described as 'fierce savages, whose occupation was war, and whose subsistence was drawn chiefly from the forest. To leave them in possession of their country was to leave the country a wilderness'.[9] Taken in historical context, the opinion effectuated a triple injustice. Native peoples were considered too 'savage' to merit legal rights or to engage in a reasoned discourse about the nature of their rights. As nonparties to the action, they had no way to contest the development of the doctrine. Indeed, they were deemed incapable of understanding the nature of their juridical status. The federal government maintained full authority to direct legal actions on behalf of Indian tribes until 1967, when Congress finally granted Indian tribal governments the right to independent representation in American courts by their own legal counsel.[10]

The Doctrine of Discovery is a legal fiction developed by the European nations to claim ownership of land, resources, and human labor in the New World, and it was premised upon the view that Europeans held superior rights because of their status as the most civilized peoples in the world. The Enlightenment philosophers legitimated that view within their accounts of political theory, to the clear disadvantage of Indigenous peoples. As John Stuart Mill reasoned in *On Liberty*, civilized peoples merited the greatest level of political rights.[11] Thomas Hobbes wrote that the Indigenous peoples of the Americas were 'savages' living in the 'state of nature'. Because of this, the Europeans had a 'perfect right' to capture the 'insufficiently populated' lands that they 'discovered'.[12]

Similarly, in the *Second Treatise of Civil Government*, John Locke remarked that 'in the beginning all the world was America', a wilderness and commons ripe for settlement of land and cultivation of private property rights. While Locke did not endorse genocide of Indigenous peoples, he clearly believed that Indians lacked the capacity to own property because they 'roamed' over their vast wilderness instead of 'cultivating' the land as did the 'civilized' Europeans.[13] Locke also used Indigenous peoples to support his epistemological theories concerning the origin of knowledge.[14] Locke considered Native people to possess a primitive form of knowledge, similar to that of 'children, idiots, and the illiterate'.[15] According to Locke, their heads were filled with 'love and hunting', and they had 'vulgar conceptions of the divine', which rendered their religions nothing more than superstition or atheism.[16]

Hegel agreed, writing that Native Americans 'are like unenlightened children, living from one day to the next, and untouched by higher thoughts or aspirations'. According to Hegel, the Indians suffered from their encounters with Europeans because of the 'weakness of their physiology', which made them susceptible to disease, and from their inability to engage the 'arts of the Europeans,' including 'brandy drinking'.[17] These views ultimately supported the view that Indigenous peoples should be treated as the 'wards' of the civilized government. As the benevolent guardian, the civilized government had the power to constrain Indigenous peoples' autonomy through the exercise of a fostering paternalism. John Stuart Mill sanctioned this treatment in his book, *On Liberty*, observing that because Indigenous peoples lacked the capacity to think for themselves, the government could rightfully subject them to 'civilization' programs.[18]

The philosophical constructions were justified by reference to 19th century science, which held that Europeans were at the apex of civilization, while Africans were at the lowest rung.[19] Indigenous peoples were somewhere in between, and it was hoped that they would eventually become more like the more favored 'White race'.[20] The field anthropologists of the day were working with evolutionary theory and social hierarchies. Thus, the science of craniology sought to measure the skulls of all races to determine which one was the most 'civilized'. Not surprisingly, Europeans came out on top.[21]

Interestingly, the political practice of the European governments toward Indian Nations was a bit different. Both Great Britain and the United States used treaties to negotiate their place on Indigenous lands, as they did with their counterparts in Europe and Asia. However, during the latter half of the 19th century, U.S. Indian policy turned from treaty negotiations to overt political domination. Congress acted in 1871 to bar the Executive from negotiating any further treaties with Indians, although it confirmed the legal status of the existing Indian treaties (which numbered over 500). After the Civil War ended, the United States sent its troops to the frontier to deal with the 'Indian problem'. Although the Indians experienced some victories (most notably, the Battle of the Little Bighorn), they were few and short-lived. By the end of the 19th century, the Native population of the United States plummeted to its nadir, due to warfare, disease epidemics, and the appropriation of tribal lands and food resources for the benefit of a burgeoning settler population.

During the late 19th century and early 20th century, Federal policymakers employed the image of the 'savage' as they endorsed a paternalistic view of Native peoples as primitive wards and sought to forcibly assimilate American Indians and Alaska Natives to Anglo-American cultural norms. Federal officials removed Native children from their homes to federal boarding schools, where they were precluded from speaking their language or learning tribal customs. The federal agents also punished the active practice of Native ceremonies and cultural traditions on the reservation, often appropriating sacred objects from practitioners and selling them to various museums and collectors. Ironically, as federal officials actively worked to destroy Indigenous cultures, anthropologists invaded Native communities to document their languages, music, dances, and ceremonies before they 'vanished' altogether.[22]

The hermeneutical consequences of these appropriations were massive and enduring. Indigenous peoples lost the authority to interpret their own history and culture, as well as their authority to protect themselves from further appropriation. Indigenous peoples lost physical possession of vast amounts of their cultural heritage, and they were also subjected to the imposition of alien hermeneutical schema. Indigenous peoples were foreclosed from participating in the creation of epistemic practices and excluded from the institutions where meaning is made. The interpretation of Indigenous culture shifted to the expertise of anthropologists within museums and academia, and Indigenous peoples became the *objects* of the epistemic practices of anthropology. Needless to say, this history is replete with instances of testimonial and hermeneutical injustice, and Indigenous peoples continue to suffer from participatory prejudice and informational prejudice as they seek to repatriate cultural objects within domestic and international forums.[23]

Despite the dire predictions of federal policymakers at the turn of the century, Indigenous peoples survived this brutal past. Within the United States, contemporary tribal governments possess jurisdiction to govern their reservation lands and their members under the prevailing federal policy of 'self-determination'. Although federal law and policy now recognizes and confirms tribal authority, the Supreme Court has judicially restricted tribal jurisdiction over non-members and outside the reservation. This can frustrate the efforts of tribal governments to preserve and protect their cultural heritage.

There are continuing issues about which tribes constitute legitimate governments, as well as the credibility of tribal claims to ownership of their tangible and intangible culture heritage. Not surprisingly, in the legal narratives that resolve such claims, contemporary anthropologists and archaeologists hold the power as 'experts', while the perspectives of Indigenous peoples are often dismissed as biased, uninformed, or otherwise lacking in credibility. This dynamic is best analyzed under the principles of epistemic injustice.

## 2. Epistemic injustice

In an earlier article, I drew upon Miranda Fricker's work to explain how 'epistemic forms of injustice', that is, injustices relating to the categories of knowledge and experience, affect Indigenous peoples.[24] Western knowledge systems are typically built upon a rationalist, secular epistemology that elevates the importance of science, economics, and technology. These forms of knowledge are seen as principled, fair, and neutral. In comparison, Indigenous knowledge systems are often seen as deficient because they are perceived as faith-based 'religious systems' and or as the more primitive forms of cultural knowledge associated with 'tribal' groups. Western knowledge systems, on the other hand, are seen as universally superior to these forms of local knowledge as a mechanism of understanding our world and developing policy innovations. In addition, the attribution to "secularism" conveniently disregards the Protestant Christian roots of Western European knowledge and attributes religiosity to less civilized cultures, including indigenous peoples.

In a sense, this history can be equated with a form of 'epistemic imperialism' in which the epistemic values of efficiency, instrumental value, and domination of nature come to stand in for what is valid and true, privileging science and technology as objective and therefore 'value-free'. Although contemporary scholars within postcolonial studies and global feminism have questioned this supposed objectivity,[25] the discourses of science and technology continue to dominate the domestic policy arena, as demonstrated by public land management, agricultural production, public health administration, and the management of environmental and cultural resources.

This colonial and imperialist history continues to harm Indigenous peoples because the legal and policy structures that determine their contemporary rights, as well as their ability to gain redress for historic wrongs, are built upon a model that disregards indigenous values and excludes them from full participation in the social and epistemic practices of the dominant culture. This exclusion is largely invisible to other constituent members of society because the injustice to Indigenous peoples as 'epistemic communities' is masked by the pervasive view that American Indians and Alaska Natives are now 'equal citizens' under the United States Constitution.[26] Although Indigenous peoples are themselves 'epistemic agents', uniquely embodied and historically and socially situated within their identity as the First Nations of this land, their actual experience is one in which others define the narratives that construct their rights.

As Fricker points out, we share a collective space as members of a society, and our basic social interactions center upon knowledge and social experience. We convey knowledge to others by telling them, and we make sense of our own experience by interacting with others within the social spaces we share, including domains of governance, the job market, educational institutions, and the like. I will here be discussing the legal system, as a social institution that broadly invokes power relations between the U.S. government and its citizens, and between the U.S. government and Indigenous Nation. My argument is that forms of epistemic injustice permeate the legal system and reflect the long-standing cultural construction of Indigenous peoples as 'Others'. I will first describe the essence of epistemic injustice and then develop several case studies to illustrate its impact upon Indigenous peoples.

Federal law controls the lives of Indigenous peoples within the United States because of the 19th century case law that articulated their legal status as 'domestic dependent nations' with a 'trust relationship' to the United States.[27] This status is unique. In the 19th century, Indians were considered 'wards' of the United States and were not 'citizens' within the meaning of the U.S. Constitution, even after enactment of the 14th amendment. However, Congress ultimately naturalized American Indians to citizenship in 1924. As a result, contemporary Native Americans share an identity with other citizens as individuals, but they are also citizens of their tribal governments, whose political identity is both pre-Constitutional and extra-Constitutional. To the extent that the emphasis is placed on shared identity, Indigenous peoples are vulnerable to the forms of 'identity harm' that Fricker discusses. Indigenous rights derive from their aboriginal occupancy of the land and from the political bargains they made with the United States as separate sovereign nations. Consequently, the rights of Indigenous peoples to land and resources, including cultural heritage, depend upon the continuing ability of Indigenous Nations to assert their group identity as culturally and politically distinct from that of the United States.

Epistemic forms of injustice can suppress an Indigenous nation's ability to articulate its own identity. This can occur in the form of 'testimonial' or 'hermeneutical' injustice. Under Fricker's framework, testimonial injustice arises when someone is wronged in his or her capacity as a giver of knowledge, while hermeneutical injustice occurs when someone is wronged in his or her capacity as a subject and source of understanding.[28]

Of the two forms of epistemic injustice, testimonial injustice is most aligned with legal theory and practice. Lawyers routinely invoke the testimony of witnesses to prove that something happened, or did not happen. Similarly, we 'qualify' the witnesses to ensure that they have the requisite knowledge and are capable of delivering their testimony. Ultimately, the judge and jury decide what testimony is most credible and persuasive. Within this structure, as Fricker and other theorists observe, there is a vast capacity for episodic forms of injustice to occur. For example, the listener may assess a credibility deficit to certain speakers, based on their race, class, gender, or appearance. They may also privilege speakers based on those characteristics. In fact, there is a growing body of literature indicating that 98% of human beings (including jurors and judges) harbor implicit racial biases that unconsciously affect their perception, memory, judgment, and action.[29]

The forms of testimonial injustice that Fricker and others identify may become incorporated into the legal system, in which case they become structural forms of injustice. Gaile Pohlhaus, Jr. argues, correctly in my view, that the primary harm of testimonial injustice can be described in terms of the 'subject/other' relationship that 'circumscribes the victim's subjectivity within the confines of the perpetrator's subjectivity'.[30] For Indigenous peoples, the 'subject/other' relationship has always defined their nature in relation to Europeans, defining their identity as sovereigns, as knowledge-holders, or as property holders. In this sense, Indigenous peoples have been deemed 'deficient' in comparison with Europeans. Their governmental status is frequently described as 'quasi-sovereign', while their aboriginal right to property is merely 'a right to occupancy', and not a full property interest for purposes of the Constitutional law regulating government takings. In addition, both tangible and intangible forms of Indigenous cultural heritage have been pillaged and appropriated on the theory that Indigenous cultural property does not merit the same protection accorded to owners or authors and artists within Western society.[31]

Testimonial forms of epistemic injustice privilege Western knowledge, even with respect to the most fundamental issue of whether a group is, in fact, an 'Indian tribe'. For example, a tribe who is petitioning for 'recognition' through the federal acknowledgement process must generally 'prove' its identity by reference to written documentation produced by 'objective' experts, including historians and anthropologists. Similarly, tribes who seek to 'prove' the existence of a sacred site on aboriginal lands now under state or federal ownership must generally rely on the testimony of an anthropologist who can document the group's belief system and its historical occupancy on particular lands.[32] This type of testimonial injustice may not immediately discount the assertion of a tribal witness, but the truth of the assertion is contingent upon validation by a qualified 'expert' who is culturally 'neutral' and has the scientific training necessary to be 'credible'.[33]

Hermeneutical injustice, on the other hand, is 'the injustice of having some significant area of one's social experience obscured from collective understanding' because the group in question suffers from epistemic marginalization.[34] This can occur because the group lacks the same hermeneutical resources to define viable categories of experience or because the group is not certified as having the same epistemic authority as the dominant group.[35] In both cases, the dominant society draws upon its understanding of the historical circumstances and its assumptions to discount the experience of the indigenous group, and it also normalizes an epistemology that was created precisely to exclude other groups. Within the law, hermeneutical injustice commonly occurs when there is no recognized legal category for the category of harm experienced by an Indigenous group. For example, following the 1989 Exxon Valdez oil spill, several Native Alaskan communities sued Exxon for the destruction of their traditional subsistence way of life caused by the massive oil spill.[36] The federal court described culture as an 'internal' state of mind, which could not be destroyed unless a person lost 'the will' to pursue a given way of life.[37] The harm to the Indigenous group was multiple, disrupting longstanding practices, customs, and ceremonies that integrated the people with their environment. The people could not 'live' their culture or transmit it to their children because of the destruction of the environment and associated wildlife resources. However, the court found this type of harm to not be cognizable under any theory of tort law, which is not surprising given the fact that the British common law would not reflect harms to land-based Indigenous cultures. What is disappointing, however, is that this obvious hermeneutical gap did not even register an inquiry regarding the justice of limiting indigenous claims to the standard categories of Anglo-American common law.

Similarly, the United States Supreme Court has routinely failed to find a 'substantial burden' on Indigenous religious practitioners for purposes of the First Amendment of the U.S. Constitution when some 'neutral' federal law or policy impedes their ability to practice their religion. Hence, in *Lyng v. Northwest Indian Cemetery Protective Association*, the Court held that the federal government could permissibly extend a logging road through a site held sacred by several Indigenous groups in Northern California because the government was merely developing 'its' land for the public benefit and had no intent to coerce the Indigenous peoples into giving up their 'belief' that the land was 'sacred'.[38] Again, the experience of the 'sacred' was evaluated at the individual level of what is in the 'mind'. So long as individual Indians are free to 'believe' the site is sacred, it is irrelevant that the conduct of the government will remove the ability of the group to practice ceremonies that it feels are vital to sustain its existence. The Court failed to find a 'substantial burden' even after assuming, for the sake of argument, that development would foreclose practice of the religion altogether.

The 9th Circuit Court of Appeals, sitting *en banc*, used a similar logic in *Navajo Nation v. United States Forest Service*, which upheld the use of reclaimed sewage wastewater to manufacture artificial snow for a company leasing land for recreational skiing on the San Francisco Peaks.[39] The San Francisco Peaks are a very sacred site for the Navajo Nation, the Hopi Tribe, and at least a dozen other tribal Nations in the Southwest. Although the Native practitioners argued that spraying sewage effluent over the area would desecrate the mountain and its associated spirit entities, as well as contaminate the herbs used by practitioners for healing ceremonies, the Court found that the federal agency was merely maximizing the value of the land for the 'public benefit' and had no duty to give weight to the subjective beliefs of the affected Native peoples.

Each of these cases illustrates hermeneutical injustice because the harms asserted include cultural and spiritual claims that do not map onto an available category of experience or thought within the Western legal system.[40] The experience of cultural harm cannot be measured by Western empirical standards and witness testimony is often the only way to present the claim. In this respect, Indigenous peoples also suffer from testimonial injustice because they are often not perceived as credible when they attempt to convey their beliefs. For example, in the *Lyng* case, the Court noted that 'not all Indians' agreed that the site was sacred (and it is true that not every Indian person is a practitioner of his or her traditional culture) and also expressed the view that if the Forest Service had to cater to this belief, this would result in the Indigenous group claiming '*de facto* ownership' of a vast area of public land.

Because the Indigenous claim must be addressed under Western standards, there is no ability to gain recognition for the unique harm suffered. In fact, the Constitutional right to freedom of religion is based upon what Ian James Kidd terms 'cosmopolitan secularism,' which dismisses Indigenous metaphysical beliefs as 'false', holding instead that:

> '[T]here are no supernatural entities,' like gods and ancestor spirits and sacred places and creatures, nor transcendent realities, and so no sense to be made of 'accounts of the good life that are grounded in the idea that a "significant existence" requires some contribution to the cosmos'[41]

Under this view, the religious practitioners in the *Lyng* case could not 'prove' that their 'World Renewal' ceremony was in fact necessary to preserve the world. Nor could the Hopi practitioners in the San Francisco Peaks case prove that the ancestral spirits known as 'Kat'sinas' in fact 'live' on the San Francisco Peaks. This is not because of a lack of proof of sufficient quality or quantity, but because such claims are automatically considered 'false' because they are outside the realm of reasonable belief.[42] No proof is possible and even sincere belief in what is 'incredible' constitutes a marker of epistemic dysfunction. The Indigenous reality cannot be articulated within the Western legal system because indigenous metaphysical views are dismissed as 'false' and because they are excluded from co-creating doctrines that could protect them from harm (for example, by using an intercultural definition of what constitutes a 'substantial burden on religious practice').[43]

## 3. Case studies: anthropologists, archeologists, and epistemic injustice

The protection of Native cultural heritage is vitally important to tribal cultural survival.[44] However, for most of U.S. history, the legal protections that exist for burial sites, tangible property, and intellectual property were generally held not to extend to Indigenous peoples because of their cultural differences. State laws protecting marked graves within consecrated Christian cemeteries were held not to extend to tribal burial sites. Similarly, tribal songs and designs were not protected by doctrines of U.S. copyright law that offer limited protection for 'original creative works' by an author. In the text that follows, I will offer additional case studies demonstrating the continuing existence of hermeneutical injustice and testimonial injustice. The debate over ownership and control affects the tangible cultural heritage of Native peoples, including ancestral human remains, funerary objects, sacred objects, and objects of cultural patrimony that are held by various institutions throughout the nation and the world.

Throughout much of the 19th and 20th centuries, anthropologists and archaeologists looted Native villages, battlefields, and cemeteries to acquire Native peoples' personal effects, as well as their remains.[45] The leading anthropologists in the country (such as Kroeber) maintained possession of Native American remains for study. In the late 19th century, the United States military issued an order authorizing servicemen to dismember Native American bodies recovered from battlefields, and send the remains to a medical repository in Washington, D.C. for 'scientific' analysis of Indian crania. In addition to these official policies, Indian bodies were routinely plundered and desecrated by frontier vigilantes.

As a legacy of this gruesome past, Native American human remains and cultural objects were openly traded on the market as historical artifacts or relics until 1990, when Congress passed the Native American Graves Protection and Repatriation Act.[46] As of 1990, there were over 150,000 Native American human remains held by federal agencies and federally-funded museums, as well as hundreds of thousands of funerary objects, objects of cultural patrimony and sacred objects. NAGPRA authorized culturally affiliated tribes to request repatriation of the remains and cultural objects on the theory that the remains and objects were rightfully under the control of the communities of origin. The statute also prohibited commercial sale or trade of Native American human remains or cultural items.

Despite these advances, the statute did not resolve all of the battles. Under NAGPRA, the burden is on the Native American claimant to demonstrate its status as a 'federally recognized' Indian tribe that is 'culturally affiliated' to the remains or cultural objects at issue. Although the statute explicitly identifies cultural narratives and tribal histories as permissible methods of proof, the courts have developed more restrictive standards of 'genetic similarity'. This has precluded some tribal communities from gaining repatriation of 'ancient' Indigenous remains. Archaeologists have asserted that ancient human remains should be considered the 'property' of science because they cannot be 'culturally' affiliated to modern day Indian tribes. In *Bonnichsen v. United States*, the federal court agreed, with reference to skeletal remains that washed up on the banks of the Columbia River in Washington and were estimated to be 9000 years old.[47] The Court said that the tribal claimants were relying on their tribal narratives to demonstrate cultural affiliation, rather than scientific proof of shared 'genetic or cultural identity'. According to the Court, the tribal testimony was insufficient to show 'where historical fact ends and mythic tale begins,' and thus the tribe failed to prove that the 'Kennewick Man shares special and significant genetic or cultural features with presently existing indigenous tribes, people, or cultures'.[48] The Court's ruling restricted the permissible standard for determining cultural affiliation to what was scientifically provable, thereby negating indigenous conceptions of cultural affiliation and indigenous constructions of kinship. Interestingly, after years of legal wrangling, scientists secured the right to do DNA testing of the remains and found that there was genetic similarity to the contemporary tribes holding ancestral occupancy rights in this area.[49]

Native claims can also be obscured by the legal categories that pertain to commercial trade of 'cultural heritage' on the international market.[50] There is still no international law regulating museum collections of Indigenous human remains and cultural objects. Many of the world's leading museums in countries such as England, Germany, and Australia house collections of Indigenous remains and cultural objects from all of the former colonies. Do they 'own' these Native ancestral remains and sacred objects?

In an era where self-determination is understood to be a fundamental and inherent human right of all Indigenous peoples, Indigenous claimants have filed repatriation claims for return of their ancestral remains.[51] However, there is no legal right to repatriation across international lines. Rather, such claims are usually treated as opportunities to craft voluntary ethical relationships between Indigenous peoples and museum professionals. For example, in April 2013, the Museum of Medical History in Berlin, which houses numerous exhibits of human body parts, returned '33 skulls and skeletons to Australia and to members of tribes from the Torres Strait Islands between northern Australia and Papua New Guinea'.[52] Ned David, the leader of the Torres Strait Islander group, expressed their sense of relief at 'bringing their ancestral remains home', but said that the 'moment is tinged with sadness for what was involved with the removal of the remains'.[53] The German Museum Association's ethical guidelines recommended that the museums 'study provenance systematically and return human remains that had been collected as part of a violent conflict'.[54]

In the United States, members of the Fort McDowell Yavapai Nation within the state of Arizona experienced a similar set of emotions when the community repatriated the remains of tribal members from the British Museum in 2014. The remains had been sold to the British Museum in the early 20th century after the infamous massacre of a group of unarmed and innocent Yavapai Indians in Arizona. It was not until 2014 that the tribe learned that the remains were in the British Museum's collection, and the tribe subsequently made a repatriation request, which was honored on the moral principle that takings of Indigenous remains from episodes of historical violence ought to be returned to the communities of origin in accordance with basic moral principles honoring human dignity and equal respect.

The Hopi Tribe of Arizona did not merit the same standard of ethical treatment when it sought to enjoin the auction of 70 sacred objects known as Kat'sina, but popularly described as 'masks'. The sacred ceremonial objects dated to the 19th century and had been stolen from the tribe prior to passage of the federal repatriation statute in 1990, and they were ultimately placed for sale in a French auction house in April 2013. The Hopi Tribe's Constitution precludes removal of sacred items from tribal lands, and the Hopi Tribe sought repatriation of the items, invoking diplomatic assistance from federal officials and the support of anthropologists, such as the Museum of Northern Arizona's director, Robert Breunig, who wrote a letter to the Paris auction house urging return of the objects to the Hopi Tribe and the other affected Pueblo Nations at Acoma, Zuni, and Jemez. Breunig wrote:

> I can tell you from personal knowledge that the proposed sale of these katsina friends and the international exposure of them, is causing outrage, sadness and stress among members of the affected tribes. For them, katsina friends are living beings . . . To be displayed disembodied in your catalog, and on the Internet, is sacrilegious and offensive.[55]

The French court rejected the claim that the objects should be treated as 'living beings' and also the premise that the objects were 'sacred'. The court ruled that French law did not prohibit the sale of the items because they were the 'private property' of a collector, and American law did not apply in France.[56] The French auctioneer expressed 'concern' about 'the Hopi's sadness' but said that when such objects become part of 'private collections' in Europe – or the United States – they 'are desacralized'.[57] Of course, it is hard to find that a category of objects has been 'desacralized' without acknowledging that they *were* (and perhaps still are) 'sacred'. This case illustrates the most egregious form of hermeneutical injustice – what Gaile Pohlhaus, Jr. terms 'willful hermeneutical injustice' – because the dominant group refuses to concede the possibility of certain interpretations of objects or experiences by the community of origin, even as it acknowledges that this experience may have once existed, but no longer does (again, according to the standards of the dominant group).[58]

All of these cases are very recent, and they are all troubling because the contemporary conduct is considered lawful, despite the acknowledged harm to the Indigenous groups. The appeal to epistemic injustice is firmly grounded in the historical and contemporary claims of Indigenous peoples.

The injustice continues with respect to intangible cultural resources, such as tribal songs, symbols, ceremonies, and designs. During the late 19th and early 20th centuries, anthropologists documented and recorded tribal ceremonies and songs, often in graphic detail. Today, many tribal communities claim those sound recordings and archives as the 'cultural and intellectual property' of the community of origin. However, other citizens view these repositories as part of a rich cultural commons, free for appropriation. For example, in 2004, the hip-hop duo known as 'OutKast' was heavily criticized by Native Americans when the group performed 'Hey Ya' at the Grammy Awards. The song 'borrows' from a sacred Dine (Navajo) Beauty Way song, and the performance featured women in 'buckskin bikinis' who were imitating a Plains 'War Cry'. The combination of stereotyping and cultural appropriation was deeply offensive to the Lakota and Dine people, as well as other Native Americans. There is a continuing and active debate over who 'owns' the historic sound recordings and archives and who ought to have the power to govern the use of them. These archives are important because they are the most complete documentary resource of Native epistemologies. They are important to Native peoples and they are important to anthropologists, which sets up a continuing tension over preservation and use.

Each of these case studies raises instances of identity harm, as well as testimonial and hermeneutical injustice. Year after year, these cases go into the American courts, and very rarely are they decided in favor of Indigenous peoples. The only route to 'justice' in the United States for Indigenous peoples is by appeal to Congress for a political solution. However, even that avenue is in jeopardy due to the current instability of the political process.

## 4. Conclusion: unpacking injustice: 'the epistemology of resistance'

In the words of José Medina, 'we need a theory of injustice more than a theory of justice'.[59] As Medina observes, this is true because our 'idealizations about our epistemic interactions' minimize the daily hermeneutical and testimonial injustices that surround us in our everyday practices.[60] For Indigenous peoples, the consequences are severe. Native Americans constitute less than 1.6% of the U.S. population, and yet they have aboriginal and treaty-guaranteed rights to land and resources that are distinct from any other group or population. Because they are the smallest of any domestic minority group, it is relatively easy for a rogue group of lawmakers to disregard Indigenous peoples' rights in service of the economic or political goals of the majority. This recently occurred in Arizona when Congress attached a rider onto a huge defense Appropriations Bill transferring title to federal public lands to a private mining company in order to facilitate development that will have catastrophic cultural consequences for the San Carlos Apache Tribe and other Apache people. The Apache people had the prior possession of those lands, and they still access a sacred site at 'Oak Flat' for ceremonial purposes. So long as these lands were under federal control, the agency was bound by federal law to consult with culturally affiliated tribes and consider Native American cultural rights when developing management plans. This process can be neatly by-passed once the lands are titled to a private mining company.

The public process of lawmaking is designed to allow citizens within democracy to debate, consider other perspectives, and act only after achieving a full understanding of the issues. The effort to privatize the public lands at Oak Flat through legislation was defeated on numerous occasions after testimony by the Apache people and their supporters, including environmental groups. In that sense, the larger society embraced the sort of 'network solidarity' that Medina endorses at the conclusion of his book. However, the closed-door 'deal' that resulted in a midnight 'rider' to the Defense Appropriations Bill negates any sense of shared responsibility for epistemic interaction. Going forward, the law gives a stamp of approval for what really constitutes a wholesale silencing of the Apache people.

The developing scholarship on epistemic injustice is important because it illuminates forms of injustice that are generally invisible to all except for the affected groups. In that sense, Indigenous peoples truly have developed the 'meta-lucidity' that Medina references, which allows them to 'see the limitations of dominant ways of seeing' and to 'reconceptualize' the ways in which we must relate to others.[61] By naming what is occurring and refusing to allow members of the dominant society to slip into what Pohlhaus, Jr. terms 'willful hermeneutical ignorance', Indigenous peoples have an opportunity to participate in an intercultural understanding of what is 'sacred' and how we are connected to one another.[62] Indigenous people understand time and place differently from Europeans. They possess a unique form of knowledge that is rooted in these lands. As the peoples that belong to these lands, we can make visible that which informs our mutual reality. It is the responsibility of the encompassing society to make this space available as a matter of law and public policy.

**Related chapters**: 3, 28, 30, 35, 36, 37

# Notes

1 I am very grateful for the helpful editorial comments of Ian James Kidd and Gaile Pohlhaus, Jr. on earlier drafts of this chapter. Their scholarly work has illuminated my understanding of the issues that I discuss, and their thoughtful responses to the text enhanced the quality of my arguments and analysis. I am also thankful for the exceptional support of Tara Mospan, the law librarian who assisted me when I was on the faculty of the Sandra Day O'Connor College of Law at Arizona State University, working on the initial draft of this chapter.
2 See Smith (2012: 70).
3 See Smith (2012: 68–69) on the ways that various academic disciplines developed in relation to colonialism.
4 See Soderland and Lilley (2015).
5 See, e.g., Swidler, Dongoske, Anyon, and Downer (1997) – a compilation of essays, including essays by Native American archaeologists, such as Dorothy Lippert, who critique the colonial forms of thinking within the discipline but point out the beneficial work that archaeologists can do on behalf of Indian tribes.
6 See Williams, Jr. (1996).
7 See Williams, Jr. (2012).
8 Johnson v. McIntosh, 21 U.S. (8 Wheat.) 543 (1823).
9 Johnson v. McIntosh, 21 U.S. at 558–59.
10 Public Law 89–635 – Oct. 10, 1966. A law authorizing tribes to bring suits on their own behalf in federal court for federal question cases: 28 U.S.C.A. § 1362.
11 See Mehta (1999) for a discussion of Mill's *On Liberty*, as well as the impact of other philosophical works during this era.
12 See Hobbes (1651).
13 Of course, these views were uninformed by reality. In fact, many Indian nations, including the Pueblo Nations of the American Southwest were settled in villages that predated European arrival by several thousand years, and they maintained huge agricultural fields.

14 See Squadrito (1996).
15 Squadrito (1996).
16 Squadrito (1996).
17 Quoted in Tibebu (2011: 89–91).
18 J.S. Mill, *On Liberty* [1859], at p. 9 (I am using Elizabeth Rapaport (ed.) (1978).
19 See Gould (1981).
20 See Jefferson (1785).
21 See Gould (1981).
22 I discuss the legacy of these policies in Section 3 of this chapter.
23 I am grateful to Ian James Kidd for this observation as well as the reference to Hookway's account of participatory and informational prejudice.
24 See Tsosie (2012a).
25 See, e.g., Daston and Galison (2007), Harding (2006, 2008), and Douglas (2009).
26 Here I am loosely relying on the argument that Pohlhaus, Jr. (2014b: 47) makes about the sociality of interdependence, namely that 'epistemic communities' precede epistemic individuals and therefore the individual necessarily must rely upon the help of others as he or she seeks to know about the world.
27 This construction also dates to the 19th century in the two other foundational cases within Federal Indian law written by Chief Justice John Marshall. See Cherokee Nation v. Georgia, 30 U.S. (5 Pet.) 1 (1831); Worcester v. Georgia, 31 U.S. (6 Pet.) 515 (1832).
28 Tsosie (2012a: 1154), citing Fricker.
29 The 'state of the art' in implicit bias research is surveyed in Staats, Capatosto, Wright, and Contractor (2015).
30 Pohlhaus, Jr. (2014a).
31 See Young and Brunk (2012).
32 Tsosie (2012a: 1155 and ns. 141 and 142) describes the process of identifying 'traditional cultural properties' under the National Historic Preservation Act.
33 I am grateful to Ian James Kidd for differentiating these two different forms of testimonial injustice. The first assesses a credibility deficit to the speaker, based upon some imagined racial/cultural deficiency, while the second questions the entire epistemic framework of the indigenous speaker unless and until validated by an appropriate 'objective' framework of knowledge. In either case, the same outcome attaches, but they constitute conceptually distinct forms of prejudice.
34 Tsosie (2012a: 1158), citing Fricker.
35 See Carel and Kidd (2014), discussing the ways in which hermeneutical injustice can arise.
36 In re Exxon Valdez, 1994 WL 182856 (D. Alaska), affirmed 104 F.2d 1196 (9th Cir. 1997).
37 1994 W.L. 182856 at *4.
38 Lyng v. Northwest Indian Cemetery Protective Ass'n, 485 U.S. 439 (1988).
39 Navajo Nation v. U.S. Forest Service, 535 F.3d 1058 (9th Cir. 2008).
40 Tsosie (2012a: 1161).
41 See Kidd (2014).
42 I thank Ian James Kidd for this insight and also his observation that 'there is a conceit in cosmopolitan secularism, reflecting a tension between the titular terms: one claims to be cosmopolitan – open to learning from a diversity of traditions – but at the same time, one denies the self-understanding of every religious tradition, reducing them to "options" on a "menu" of religions.'
43 Peter Winch discusses the complexity of this in 'Language, Belief and Relativism', as he queries how a European anthropologist can make sense of a practice described by a member of the Zande people. The anthropologist describes the practice as 'witchcraft' in the sense of the Zande belief system. However, it may be the case that the Zande are using their language to describe a different reality, rather than merely holding a different belief about the same reality. See Winch (1987: 195–6).
44 See Tsosie (2009).
45 See Trope and Echo-Hawk (1992).
46 It should be noted that NAGPRA does not apply to the sale or trade of Indigenous cultural heritage outside the United States. There is an active global market for all categories of Indigenous cultural heritage, including human remains.
47 Bonnichsen v. United States, 367 F.3d 864 (9th Cir. 2004).
48 Bonnichsen v. United States at 882.
49 See Preston (2014).
50 See Tsosie (2012b).

51 See U.N. Declaration on the Rights of Indigenous Peoples, art. 3 (providing that Indigenous peoples have the right to self-determination); art 13 (providing that Indigenous peoples have the right 'to the use and control of their ceremonial objects and the right to repatriation of their human remains').
52 See Carvajal (2013).
53 See Carvajal (2013).
54 See Carvajal (2013).
55 See Wagner (2013).
56 Moore (2013: 107).
57 Moore (2013: 107).
58 See Pohlhaus, Jr. (2012).
59 Medina (2012: 12).
60 Medina (2012: 13).
61 Medina (2012: 47).
62 See Pohlhaus, Jr. (2012).

# References

Carel, Havi and Ian James Kidd (2014) 'Epistemic injustice in healthcare: A philosophical analysis', *Medicine, Healthcare, and Philosophy* 17.4: 529–540.
Carvajal, Doreen (2013) 'Museums confront the skeletons in their closets', *New York Times*, May 29.
Daston, Lorraine and Peter Galison (2007) *Objectivity* (New York: Zone Books).
Douglas, Heather (2009) *Science, Policy, and the Value-Free Ideal* (Pittsburgh: University of Pittsburgh Press).
Gould, Stephen Jay (1981) *The Mismeasure of Man* (New York: Norton & Company).
Harding, Sandra (2006) *Science and Social Inequality: Feminist and Postcolonial Issues* (Urbana and Chicago: University of Illinois Press).
Harding, Sandra (2008) *Sciences from Below: Feminisms, Postcolonialities, Modernities* (Durham, NC: Duke University Press).
Hobbes, Thomas (1651) *Leviathan: Or, the Matter, Forme, & Power of a Common-Wealth Ecclesiasticall and Civill* (St Paul's Churchyard, London: printed for Andrew Crooke).
Jefferson, Thomas (1785) *Notes on the State of Virginia* (Paris: privately published).
Kidd, Ian James (2014) 'Emotion, religious practice, and cosmopolitan secularism', *Religious Studies* 50.2: 139–156.
Medina, José (2012) *The Epistemology of Resistance: Gender and Racial Oppression, Epistemic Injustice, and Resistant Imaginations* (Oxford: Oxford University Press).
Mehta, Uday Singh (1999) *Liberalism and Empire: A Study in Nineteenth Century British Liberal Thought* (Chicago: University of Chicago Press).
Mill, John Stuart (1859) *On Liberty* (London: Longman, Roberts, & Green Co.).
Moore, Steve C. (2013) 'Sale of Hopi masks a desecration', *Museum Anthropology* 36.2: 107–108.
Pohlhaus, Jr., Gaile (2012) 'Relational knowing and epistemic injustice: Toward a theory of willful hermeneutical ignorance', *Hypatia* 27.4: 715–725.
Pohlhaus, Jr., Gaile (2014a) 'Discerning the primary epistemic harm in cases of testimonial injustice', *Social Epistemology* 28.2: 99–114.
Pohlhaus, Jr., Gaile (2014b) 'On subjects, objects, and others', *Social Epistemology Review and Reply Collective* 3.6: 44–50.
Preston, Douglas (2014) 'The Kennewick Man finally freed to share his secrets', *Smithsonian Magazine*, September 2014.
Rapaport, Elizabeth (ed.) (1978). *J. S. Mill, On Liberty* (Indianapolis and Cambridge: Hackett Publ. Co.).
Smith, Linda Tuhiwai (2012) *Decolonizing Methodologies: Research and Indigenous Peoples* (New York: Zed Books).
Soderland, Hilary A. and Ian A. Lilley (2015) 'The fusion of law and ethics in cultural heritage management: The 21st century confronts archaeology', *Journal of Field Archaeology* 40.5: 508–522.
Squadrito, Kathy (1996) 'Locke and the dispossession of American Indian', *American Indian Culture and Research Journal* 20.4: 145–181.
Staats, Cheryl, Kelly Capatosto, Robin A. Wright, and Danya Contractor (2015) *State of the Science: Implicit Bias Review 2015* (Kirwan Institute for the Study of Race and Ethnicity), http://kirwaninstitute.osu.edu.

Swidler, Nina, Kurt E. Dongoske, Roger Anyon, and Alan Downer (eds.) (1997) *Native Americans and Archaeologists: Stepping Stones to Common Ground* (Walnut Creek: Altamira Press).
Tibebu, Teshale (2011) *Hegel and the Third World: The Making of Eurocentrism in World History* (Syracuse: Syracuse University Press).
Trope, Jack F. and Walter R. Echo-Hawk (1992) 'The Native American Graves Protection and Repatriation Act: Background and legislative history', *Arizona State Law Journal* 24: 35–77.
Tsosie, Rebecca (2009) 'Who Controls Native Cultural Heritage? Art, Artifacts, and the Right to Cultural Survival', in James A. R. Nafziger and Ann M. Nicgorski (eds.), *Cultural Heritage Issues: The Legacy of Conquest, Colonization, and Commerce* (Leiden: Martinus Nijhoff Publishers), 3–36.
Tsosie, Rebecca (2012a) 'Indigenous peoples and epistemic injustice: Science, ethics, and human rights', *Washington Law Review* 87: 1133–1152.
Tsosie, Rebecca (2012b) 'International Trade in Indigenous Cultural Heritage: An Argument for Indigenous Governance of Cultural Property', in Christoph B. Graber, Karolina Kuprecht, and Jessica C. Lai (eds.), *International Trade in Indigenous Cultural Heritage: Legal and Policy Issues* (Cheltenham: Edward Elgar Publishing), 221–245.
Wagner, Dennis (2013) 'French plan to auction Hopi masks stirs furor', *The Arizona Republic*, April 3.
Williams, Jr., Robert A. (1996) *The American Indian in Western Legal Thought: The Discourses of Conquest* (Oxford: Oxford University Press).
Williams, Jr., Robert A. (2012) *Savage Anxieties: The Invention of Western Civilization* (New York: St Martin's Press).
Winch, Peter (1987) *Trying to Make Sense* (Oxford: Basil Blackwell).
Young, James O. and Conrad G. Brunk (eds.) (2012) *The Ethics of Cultural Appropriation* (Oxford: Wiley-Blackwell).

## Legal cases
Cherokee Nation v. Georgia, 30 U.S. (5 Pet.) 1 (1831); Worcester v. Georgia, 31 U.S. (6 Pet.) 515 (1832).
Lyng v. Northwest Indian Cemetery Protective Ass'n, 485 U.S. 439 (1988).
Navajo Nation v. U.S. Forest Service, 535 F.3d 1058 (9th Cir. 2008).
Bonnichsen v. United States, 367 F.3d 864 (9th Cir. 2004).

# 35
# EPISTEMIC INJUSTICE AND CULTURAL HERITAGE

*Andreas Pantazatos*

### Introduction

Epistemic injustice has become a hot topic in philosophical debates recently, reminding us that little attention has been paid to the consequences in our societies when epistemic injustice occurs. Given that epistemic injustice shapes and informs human action, its impact expands beyond the economy and politics of knowledge. Epistemic injustice plays a role in ethical decision making and thus the social harmony of our societies. To marginalize and silence voices in the name of lack of credibility, lack of conceptual resources and lack of intellectual ability is not synonymous with ethical practice and democratic institutions.

One of the areas in which marginalization of communities has been discussed during the last two decades is heritage and our relationship with the past. Surprisingly the debate about marginalized communities in heritage has not been linked straightforwardly with philosophical accounts of epistemic injustice. As a result, little work has been done on the relationship between heritage and accounts of epistemic injustice.[1] And the conceptual framework, which accounts of epistemic injustice offer for the analysis of marginalization in society, has not been utilized in heritage discourse.[2]

Heritage is constantly under negotiation, and its meaning is under evaluation. Given that different people develop different associations with heritage, the meaning of heritage changes over time, and what counts as heritage is under constant interpretation. During this process, those who are considered legitimate heirs of heritage claim priority over the interpretation of heritage and the decision making structures about what is preserved and what is sustained for the benefit of future generations. One of the issues that has been debated for some time is why and how some communities have a stronger stake in heritage than others. And more importantly, why communities with more social and epistemic power tend to marginalize and ignore other communities with less power in the interpretation of heritage and the decision making structures about its future. Although this debate touches upon the borders of epistemic injustice, it has ignored one of the most significant aspects of heritage and heritage institutions broadly construed. Heritage and its institutions are significant places for epistemic interaction and to a large extent they set a conceptual framework for our epistemic interactions.[3] This is from where I start my argument.

In this essay, my aim is to defend the idea that there is a kind of epistemic injustice, namely participant perspective epistemic injustice, drawing upon Hookway's work (2010), which is highly relevant to heritage if we accept that heritage and its institutions are unique areas of *epistemic interaction*, and if we adhere to the idea that part of what heritage institutions broadly construed do is to distribute epistemic goods. It follows from this that as distributors and interpreters and preservers of epistemic goods, heritage institutions should act in the light of the ethics of sharing.

Sharing is subject to power relations and can be *more just* or *less just*. Sharing is grounded on participants, their engagement and acknowledgement of what is shared, and negotiation between participants about what is shared and how they are engaged with what is for sharing. In this process participant perspective epistemic injustice plays an important role. If heritage institutions do not take seriously the participants' perspective, their engagement and acknowledgement of what is for sharing and their negotiation abilities are severely undermined. As a result, they become marginalized. However, in the case of heritage, not to take someone's interpretation and understanding seriously means that the significance of what is transited from past to future is distorted.

My essay is divided in three sections. In the first section I shed light onto the relationship between heritage and epistemic injustice. I argue that participant perspective epistemic injustice is more relevant to heritage than other accounts of epistemic injustice (see Fig. 35.1). In the second section, I defend the claim that if participant perspective epistemic injustice occurs in heritage institutions, then it distorts the distribution of epistemic goods. In the third section, I address the ethics of sharing (see Fig. 35.2), and I argue that participant perspective epistemic injustice also affects the sharing of knowledge that takes place at heritage institutions.

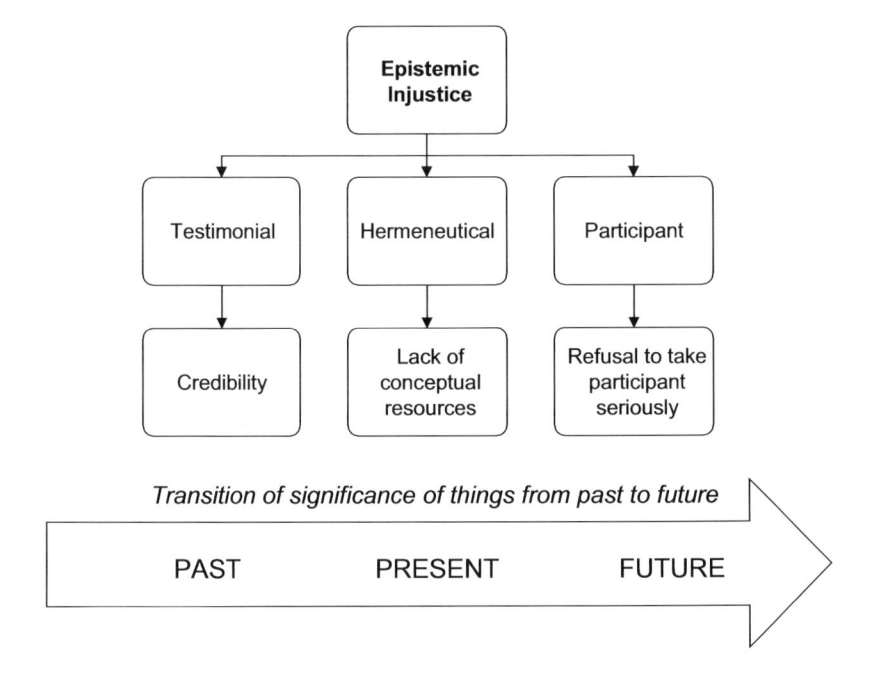

*Figure 35.1*

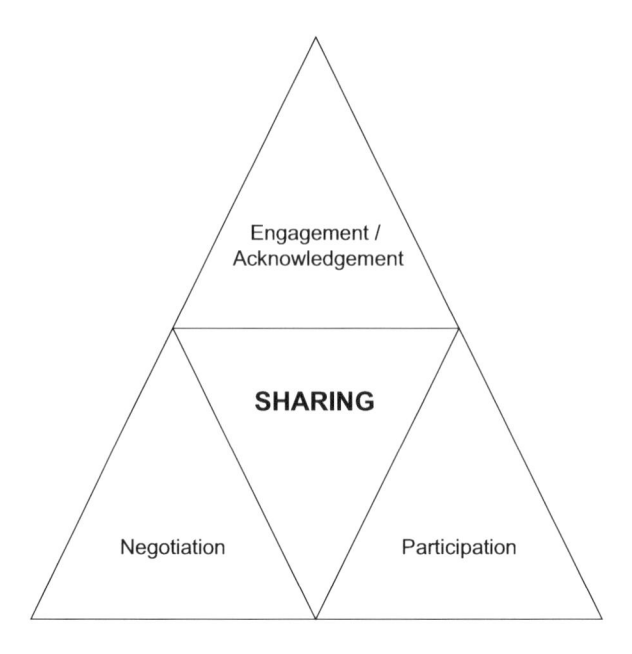

*Figure 35.2*

## 1. Heritage and accounts of epistemic injustice

Places, landscapes, monuments, ancient buildings and archaeological sites can be nominated to UNESCO's World Heritage List under the condition that they fulfil at least one of the six cultural criteria defined in the 1972 World Heritage Convention (including its revisions through periodically issued Operational Guidelines).[4] All sites must manifest 'Outstanding Universal Value', that is to say, value that is shared by all people, purportedly beyond cultural differences, to justify their preservation for future generations.

One of the World Heritage Sites (WHS) is found in Durham City, located in north-east England.[5] The great attraction of the city is its magnificent Cathedral, which is situated atop a peninsula of the River Wear, thereby giving it a remarkably dramatic location and spectacular view. The ancient Cathedral and Castle (historically the house of the Prince Bishops of Durham, subsequently donated to the University and now functioning as University College) were inscribed on the List thirty years ago. The Palace Green between them was later added to the inscribed property.

Although the WHS can be appreciated visually by all, to find out more information about the heritage site, one needs to visit Durham's World Heritage Visitor's Centre.[6] The Centre primarily provides information about the Durham World Heritage Site and the significance of UNESCO's programme for World Heritage Sites all around the world. There is also a short official video that provides visitors with useful information about Durham's World Heritage Site.

During one of my recent visits to the Centre, I realized that I had never taken time to watch this informative video, although I walk through the site almost every morning on my route to work at Durham University. So one weekend, I watched it. What I observed is that although the video supplies important information about the site, its buildings and its many years of history, almost nothing is said about the variety of stakeholders who are related to the site, their associations with the heritage site, their interpretations and their multifaceted understandings of Durham's heritage site. For instance, there is no reference to the historic centre of Durham City and its residents whose lives have been closely linked with the life of the Cathedral. As a friend of mine who watched the video with me put it succinctly: 'where is the city here?' Traders and residents of Durham City have developed associations with the heritage site which, to a large extent, have shaped the perception of Durham's World Heritage site. Their contribution is muted, if it is present at all.

The same concern can be raised for the association with different kinds of heritage, such as industrial heritage, which have co-existed in Durham for many years. The County of Durham was a prominent mining area for many years, before the abrupt closure of the mining industry during the 1980s. The mining communities have developed a strong regional and cultural identity, as well as developing associations with Durham Cathedral. It is not by accident that during the Durham Miners' Gala every July, the new banners of the miners' unions are blessed at a special ceremony at Durham Cathedral, the centre of the World Heritage Site. These communities have developed their associations with the World Heritage Site, and they have contributed new layers of meaning, which defines their interpretation of the site and therefore their relationship with it. If their voices are muted or silenced without any presence in the official information which has been selected with visitors, our understanding of the World Heritage Site is insufficient and, to some extent, distorted.

An injustice against some of the stakeholders of the heritage site is therefore manifested in the official scripting of the WHS. The stake of some groups in Durham's World Heritage Site is weakened because their associations with, testimonies to, and interpretations of the heritage site are not communicated in the official epistemic interactions between the World Heritage Site and the public. As a result, their contribution to the future shaping of the heritage site is constrained and constantly undermined. To understand how stakeholders of heritage can be victims of epistemic injustice, we need to shed light onto the relationship between heritage and epistemic injustice.

Heritage, broadly construed, is what we inherit from the past. This includes material traces such as ruins, objects, structures of buildings of different purposes (i.e. religious and/or military), monuments and landscapes. We also inherit intangible things from the past, such as values, beliefs, traditions and social structures.

Heritage has many different sorts of value: cultural, epistemic, historic, financial, religious, just to mention some.[7] It is not by accident that countries with rich heritage invest in their heritage infrastructure and increase visibility for their heritage. They anticipate great numbers of visitors and tourists, whose presence will contribute to the local economy and to the country's economic development as a whole. Beyond its financial value, heritage is valuable because it is a great source of knowledge. Heritage can provide knowledge about forms of past lives, civilizations and circles of lives around the globe, which, although they have been lost, are highly relevant for us who live in the present. It is often assumed that all human beings have an interest in heritage and more generally in the past because it helps us to understand who we are today and how we got here. In addition, attempting to connect with the distant past has the potential to help us to connect with distant others in the present. Following from this, heritage has historic value, but it is different from history, which refers to the past. Heritage is what we inherit from the past, but its significance is relevant for us in the present, and it is sustained for the future. Heritage is multifaceted and a dynamic process: what is understood as heritage today might be altered tomorrow.[8] It is open to interpretation, and the different associations people develop with it add new layers on its meaning. Hence, heritage does not convey 'frozen' knowledge and merely information about what took place in the past. Heritage sets in motion, via our interactions with what we have inherited from the past, a set of questions about our self-understanding, our engagement with others and our understanding of the world. Given that our interaction with what we have inherited from the past is central to the epistemic role of heritage, constraints that obstruct this interaction undermine the epistemic role of different stakeholders of heritage.

To a large extent, heritage institutions facilitate our interactions with heritage. Heritage institutions, broadly construed, include such things as heritage interpretation centres, heritage site information offices and visitor centres, museums of different kinds, national and international authorities whose main concern is the protection of heritage. These institutions act as custodians, stewards of heritage by exercising their duty of care for it. In their capacity as stewards of the past, heritage institutions play a significant role in the acquisition and transmission of knowledge by employing epistemic practices. Epistemic practices include collecting, presenting and educating. It is worth noting that these institutions are subject to all sorts of non-epistemic factors. For instance, entrance fee in some institutions make it difficult for those who live with minimum wage to visit them. Or, some of the institutions are dominated by middle-class white people. In some other cases the state uses these institutions to promote their political ideas as it happens with totalitarian governments.

We can distinguish between *first order* and *second order epistemic practice*. Take, for instance, a set of Roman terracotta lights. How do we acquire knowledge of them? We raise questions about their materials, their size, their shape, method(s) of manufacture, who made them and for what purpose(s). We also raise questions about how this particular piece reached us in the present, who found it, who excavated it (if it is a product of an archaeological excavation), where was it found and what this means for this object. All these questions, insofar as they ask about the materiality and material history of the piece, come under the umbrella of first order epistemic practice.

There is, however, a slightly different set of questions that we can ask while we try to build our knowledge for this set of Roman terracotta lights.[9] What is the biography of this set and its parts? Has it been used differently over the years? What kind of associations and interpretations have been developed about it? Has the set acquired new layers of meaning that call for different modes of understanding? If the set is exhibited at a museum or an art gallery, we can ask why has this set been displayed in relation to other objects from the same era? Or, why has it been displayed at all? These questions, insofar as they ask about the history of meanings and values conferred on the piece, refer to the category of second order epistemic practice.

This brief sketch of the epistemic practices of heritage institutions reveals an aspect of their role in the economy of knowledge that has been ignored. Heritage institutions do not merely aim at the preservation of what has been inherited from the past and the furtherance of knowledge. Heritage institutions also play an active role in the distribution of knowledge and other epistemic goods. By epistemic goods here, I mean those goods that help us to achieve our epistemic aims. Understanding, for instance, is a good candidate for what we call epistemic goods. When we claim that we understand something in terms of knowledge, we communicate that we are in position to perceive the meaning of that thing, and we are able to use it to draw inferences in our reflections.

Recall now what I said about the catalyst role of heritage in the economy of knowledge. Heritage institutions employing first and second order epistemic practices facilitate our interaction with what we have inherited from the past, and distribute epistemic goods. Epistemic goods enhance this interaction by enabling us to play a role in the constant negotiation of the future shaping of heritage. One of the constraints that can hinder our interaction with what we have inherited from the past is the marginalization of stakeholders in the economy of knowledge. Marginalization takes place when different stakeholders are not acknowledged and engaged as equals in the acquisition and transmission of knowledge. For example, local communities can give initial information about a heritage site, but they do not play a role in later practices of interpretation of the site. As a result, marginalized stakeholders do not feature in the distribution of epistemic goods, given that the voices of marginalized stakeholders do not appear almost anywhere in the interaction between us and what we have inherited from the past. In what follows, I argue epistemic injustice hinders the distribution of epistemic goods, and this is one form that epistemic injustice can take in relation to cultural heritage.

A common thread of argument in the ethics and politics of heritage is that communities whose own histories are excluded or not represented by the official interpretation of heritage are marginalized, and their silencing leads to alienation from their own heritage.

As a result, social injustices might occur that are rooted in the abuse of rights over place and misrepresentation of the identity of marginalized communities. The core of the argument is that communities in one way or another are not provided with space to tell their own story and supply their own interpretation of heritage, and this excludes them from the economy of knowledge.[10] This description sketches how epistemic injustice features in debates about heritage. However, this sketch does not provide a sufficient insight into the relevance of different accounts of epistemic injustice in heritage. One should not forget that it is significant to take into consideration the different accounts of epistemic injustice (testimonial and hermeneutical) because this is how we can reveal the epistemic role of stakeholders in their relationship with heritage. Different epistemic roles designate different accounts of epistemic injustice, and this entails a different relationship with heritage as resource of knowledge.[11] The general sketch of epistemic injustice in relation to cultural heritage overlooks the role of heritage institutions in the economy of knowledge.

'Testimonial injustice occurs when the testimony of an individual or collective is perceived as less credible owing to an identity prejudice' (Fricker 2007: 28). For instance, one's capacity to provide testimony is undermined on the basis of being a woman or being a foreigner in a country. Hermeneutical injustice (Fricker 2007) happens when an agent's assertions are not given attention because of a lack of the requisite conceptual and other resources that "are required for formulating important problems or for addressing them systematically" (Hookway 2013: 178). The main difference between the two accounts of injustice is that for testimonial injustice the agent is treated as someone who cannot be a credible informant in exchanges of knowledge. Whereas for hermeneutical injustice the agent lacks the conceptual resources to contribute to the understanding of certain claims and thus is not capable of making them. Both accounts, however, highlight the role of agent as an informant. Her/his capacity to provide information in obtaining and transmitting knowledge is what is undermined when the agent suffers testimonial or hermeneutical injustice. While Fricker primarily focuses on the lack of self-knowledge as the harm of hermeneutical injustice, we can also highlight that this lack of self-knowledge is necessarily accompanied by an inability to transmit the knowledge one lacks, making it similar to testimonial injustice in this way: in both cases epistemic agents are hindered in their capacity to transmit knowledge.[12]

There is, though, a different form of epistemic injustice that is not captured by Fricker's account (Fricker 2007). Christopher Hookway (2010) puts forward what he understands as participant perspective epistemic injustice. Although Hookway's account starts from the role of the agent in obtaining and transmitting knowledge, he points out that there are different epistemic roles that one can take in the economy of knowledge. Hookway distinguishes between being an informant and being a participant. According to Hookway (2010), those who act as participants do not exchange information as informants do, they contribute to knowledge by asking questions and putting forward alternative possibilities for consideration. So, incidents of what I want to call participant perspective epistemic injustice occur when an agent tries to participate in an epistemic practice but her/his contribution is not taken seriously because he/she is prejudicially judged to lack the relevant abilities or credentials to ask interesting and/or relevant questions. Hookway succinctly points out that participant perspective epistemic injustice results in a phenomenon that can undermine knowledge transmission. Silencing agents under participant perspective epistemic injustice entails that their questions or contributions broadly speaking are not used as pillars for the furtherance of knowledge, and this can lead to lack of epistemic confidence on the parts of agents. It is Hookway's account (2010) that I argue seems to be more relevant to heritage (see Figure 35.1).

I have argued elsewhere (Pantazatos 2016) that heritage institutions are in a unique position to account for the transit of objects between past and future in such a way as to secure the transfer of their significance, broadly construed. By 'transit', I mean that heritage institutions not only convey the physical objects in their collections, but they are also conveyors of the objects from one stage of the objects' lives to the next. Given that this is the *modus operandi* for heritage institutions, the duty of care for heritage institutions includes a concern for how the transit from past to future is accomplished.

In heritage institutions, what is in transit from past to future is more than just the physical objects themselves. What can also be transmitted includes the significance of objects, their meanings, associations, allusions, which have been shaped by the different stages of their lives and by their relationships with communities. A wide variety of participants who are related to an object ought to contribute to what is preserved from the object's significance, which stage of its life is given priority, and what reasons recommend the secure transfer of the object with this particular significance to the future.

What is inherited from the past and what is in transit from past to the future via the present is under interpretation and negotiation. Heritage is in continuous flux. What is inherited and at the same time is in transit from past to future is shaped by the contributions of different stakeholders who have developed associations with it. These stakeholders can act both as informants and as participants following the distinction proposed by Hookway (2010). It seems that their role as informants contributing to the exchange of knowledge is more appropriate to the transit of objects from past to present. Stakeholders can offer testimony about what they know about an object, and enabling their conceptual resources they contribute to how this object might be understood in the present. Hence, heritage stakeholders can be victims of testimonial or hermeneutical injustice while they become epistemically involved in the transit of the object and its significance from past to the present. Non-expert stakeholders are usually victims of epistemic injustice because they are charged with lack of the conceptual resources to provide adequate interpretations of what is in transit from past to present.[13] Given that heritage is a dynamic process, and it is open to interpretation, expertise is one of the ways in which one can become epistemically involved with heritage. Stakeholders who are not experts might have developed associations and thus different kinds of knowledge from experts, but their information is highly relevant to heritage and plays a role in how things from the past can be understood. On a similar note, Indigenous communities have been victims of testimonial injustice because their epistemic contributions to what has been inherited from the past and its significance have been prejudicially judged to lack credibility because of prejudices and stereotypes rooted in race and identity (Tsosie 2017).[14]

## 2. Participant perspective epistemic injustice and the distribution of epistemic goods

A central aspect of heritage institutions is the transit of the significance of what is inherited from the past to the future. The significance of what is inherited from the past and its transit to the future are not defined merely by the role of stakeholders as informants (sometimes there is limited information about what is inherited from the past), but also by the role of stakeholders as participants in the economy of knowledge. Participants can 'float ideas' and ask 'pertinent questions' about how the significance of what is inherited is captured. Stakeholders as participants shape heritage and its significance because participants can add new layers of meaning and inquire for alternative interpretations. Stakeholders as participants in the economy of knowledge of heritage are entangled with an important aspect of heritage and the role of heritage institutions in the future.

I have pointed out earlier that the transit of the significance of the object is from past to the future. So heritage and future go hand in hand. Stakeholders in their role as participants are in a position to float ideas about the future of heritage and more importantly to consider alternative possibilities for heritage and how it should be treated. Participation in obtaining and transmitting knowledge tends to be forward looking, and thus the participant perspective epistemic injustice indicated by Hookway (2010) is more relevant to heritage. When participant perspective epistemic injustice occurs, the participant is silenced, and their alternative consideration for the future of heritage is not taken on board. As a result, the participants are prevented not only from shaping the future of heritage but also from participating in the stewardship of it.

Recall the example of Durham's World Heritage Site. The official narrative of the significance of the World Heritage Site focuses primarily on the main building structures such as the Cathedral, the Castle, the Palace Green and the drama of the peninsula. The site has acquired significance over hundreds of years with the participation of different stakeholders. However, there seems be nothing on the site as a witness of the interpretation of the different stakeholders. More importantly, there seems to be no evidence where the interpretation of different stakeholders of the intangible heritage aspects of the site has initiated a starting point for developing a narrative of the site that will probably add new features to the official narrative.[15] Hence, the significance of the site, which is in transit from past to future, is shaped by the official narrative of the site, and any alternative possibilities that would add a new layer to the significance of the site are not considered. The patina of time adds new episodes to the life of the site, but it also fades the participants' perspective, who have not been taken into consideration as equal interpreters of the site.

For the victims of participant perspective epistemic injustice, this refusal to be taken seriously is one consequence that is coupled with the exclusion from the distribution of epistemic goods. The nature of participation in the acquisition and transmission of knowledge can be associated with different epistemic goods. For instance, if there is no room for questions to be taken seriously, how it is possible to achieve understanding?

'Intellectual activities, like other human activities, have aims' (Roberts and Wood 2007: 32). Similarly, intellectual activities aim at some epistemic goods. Epistemic goods are both instrumental and constitutive to knowledge and to the furtherance of knowledge. Epistemic goods are instrumental because they are means which guarantee to some extent what we call knowledge. For instance, to be knowledgeable of the division of political powers in England, one should be familiar with some facts about Magna Carta and have some understanding of the reasons that led to its publication. One might know the facts about Magna Carta, but this is not necessarily sufficient to claim knowledge about the role of Magna Carta in the division of political powers in England. To claim knowledge about the role of Magna Carta in the political history of

England, one should be able to make an inference from those facts to claims about the division of political powers in England.

Given the catalytic role of heritage institutions in the economy of knowledge, these institutions are in a unique position to fulfil their role by distributing epistemic goods. Although we can recognize a variety of epistemic goods, the following three items are the most relevant to heritage institutions: acquaintance, understanding and curiosity.

Heritage institutions disseminate information about the past broadly construed. However, it is usually difficult to have warranted knowledge of what happened at those times because as Lowenthal (2015) points out 'the past is a foreign country', and we cannot really have access to it. In the majority of the cases, the closest we can get is to become familiar with some events, memories and texts. Hence, heritage institutions enable their multiple stakeholders to be acquainted with aspects of what has been inherited to us from the past. Heritage is not fixed, and it is not static. Heritage is assembled from a wide and varied mixture of past events, folk memories, mythologies, physical relics and landscapes and possible symbolisms associated with them. So, to be acquainted with heritage, we mean that one is not in 'immediate contact with it' because one is not necessarily in a position to have some or full knowledge of what has been inherited from the past and how this has developed. Acquaintance with the past entails that one tries to establish cognitive contact with the past. This is carried out by one's memory and personal stories, attitudes related to the past, forms of recognition, modes of appreciation, and understanding that occurred on earlier contact. Acquaintance with heritage can be distorted if stakeholders suffer from participant perspective epistemic injustice.

Acquaintance depends on asking pertinent questions about what has been inherited from the past, floating ideas, and drawing connections between different aspects of heritage. If heritage stakeholders are not taken seriously while they float their ideas and raise questions, acquaintance becomes fragmented and sometimes impossible. If stakeholders are not encouraged to participate actively and their questions are not taken seriously as standpoints, which can initiate new responses for what has been inherited from the past, their confidence to become acquainted with the past is seriously undermined. A good example here to illustrate my point is Hadrian's Wall in the north of England. By visiting and walking along the wall, one is able to see where the wall has been and the material from which it was made, but one cannot be assured how the wall was and how it functioned for the Roman soldiers who used to reside at that area. One cannot make confirmed judgements about the relationship between the wall and its local residents on both sides of the wall at those times. And of course, the wall and the landscape around it have acquired their own life in contemporary times, including many different associations developed over the last two centuries. All these cannot be provided by one set of recognizable, objective and universal criteria, which can be applied to supply us with knowledge about the wall during Roman times and beyond. Different stakeholders can only familiarize themselves with some aspects of Hadrian's Wall by asking questions that aim to capture the picture of what the Wall used to be like at the time, and how it has been developed during the times that followed its foundations, use and later excavation. This kind of acquaintance puts us in a position to enquire and float ideas about many aspects concerning the Wall and of course our own relationship with the people of Roman times who lived in that area. For instance, if you are a tourist who does not live in the area, you might start asking information about how travelling was made possible to this end of the Roman Empire during times where transport was not so comfortable and quick as it has been after the second half of the twentieth century. These different forms of cognitive contact with the past are blocked if relevant questions and ideas remain silenced because the stakeholders' participation is constrained. And it is constrained because participants might be judged to lack the capacities to ask interesting questions.

Beyond acquaintance, heritage institutions can also facilitate understanding of how we can begin to grasp details of the past even though I have pointed out that our insight into the past might be limited. Our understanding of what we have inherited from the past entails a grasp of the continuous significance of the past for the present and the future. What is inherited from the past is *fabricated* and so understanding of the past and its significance seems to be a difficult task. One should not forget that the knowledge associated with heritage is situated in particular social and intellectual circumstances, and it thus depends on a large context. Consequently, it is open to alteration and interpretation. Knowledge associated with heritage is under constant negotiation. We are not called to understand merely what past life used to be. We are called to understand what is in transit from the past and make sense of its significance. Recall the example of Hadrian's Wall. Understanding of Hadrian's Wall is expanded beyond the process of gathering information about how the wall was built and the life of Roman soldiers there. This information is sufficient to enable us to make inferences from a wall guarded by soldiers to one of its use and major interpretations that the wall was the physical frontier of the Roman Empire. An important part of the significance of Hadrian's Wall is that it was the final frontier of the Roman Empire. This can provide the basis for further inferences about what frontiers mean for contemporary countries in a world of major migration, and what kind of landscape contexts frontiers shape for those who live on both sides of those frontiers. What 'frontier' means depends on context. Context is open to multiple interpretations and different associations; it is also a source for a variety of explanations and inferences one can draw from. Hence, understanding Hadrian's Wall as a 'frontier' moves beyond facts about the wall per se; it demands to grasp the significance of what has been in transit and central to it is that it marked a frontier. Similarly with acquaintance, setting questions and floating ideas about what Hadrian's Wall has been is core to the process of understanding. Understanding is diminished if there are no questions asked or if new ideas which provide alternatives for further deliberation and reflection are not pursued. In the case of Hadrian's Wall, any participant brings questions from their own background and float ideas which can be drawn from their own forms of knowledge and experiences. We undermine the participants' interpretations of the site if their questions and ideas are constrained. And we end up with a limited understanding of the significance of Hadrian's Wall from past to future. More importantly, participants are discouraged from building a confident interaction with heritage, and this consequently leads to narrow understanding of what heritage is and how it should be treated in the future. If participant perspective epistemic injustice sets constraints to acquaintance and understanding, it can also be a hindrance for one more epistemic good such as *curiosity*.

Curiosity is entangled with heritage institutions. Let us not forget that the precursors of encyclopaedic museums were called 'cabinets of curiosities' (Bennett 1996). These were collections of unrelated things, including archaeological remains, ethnographic objects, plants and animals from all around the world. The exhibition of these unrelated items aimed to reveal the interconnectedness between things, and between people and things from different parts of the world. Hence, these 'curiosities' initiated a kind of wonder about the world providing the first step into an inquiry about them and their environment, broadly construed. Following from this, curiosity as distributed by heritage institutions can be understood as a reflective form of wondering, which may involve a process of questioning. Asking questions is a necessary condition for inquisitiveness, but it is not for curiosity (Miscevic 2007 and Watson 2015). Both curiosity and inquisitiveness are concerned with 'getting inquiry off the ground'. However, for inquisitiveness one is required to ask questions, and one must also be good at asking questions because one's questioning aims at improving their epistemic standing. Curiosity does not necessarily aim at the improvement of one's epistemic standing. For example, one who is curious about ancient statues might ask questions about its material and how they were crafted, but this does not entail that one aims to improve one's epistemic standing about sculptures. One simply enjoys seeing ancient statues and would like to find out more about them. It is like a wish to understand more about ancient statues.[16]

Curiosity, broadly construed, is more akin to heritage institutions than inquisitiveness. Heritage institutions are more concerned with providing diverse stimuli for wonder than providing a framework that elicits good questions and requires from their stakeholders to be able to ask good questions. Heritage institutions are spaces where epistemic interactions take place, and they thus aim to make sure that there is an atmosphere where different stakeholders feel confident to wonder and to start asking questions. Given that heritage is both subject to negotiation and open to interpretation, then to exercise curiosity within heritage institutions is to give participant stakeholders the chance to unlock the multiple possibilities of heritage. By doing this, stakeholders can reveal aspects of heritage and its future because they can consider alternative possibilities for the significance of what will be inherited in the future.

Consider, for instance, the Throne of Weapons at the British Museum, a chair made out of parts of rifles (mainly AK-47s) and other weapons welded together.[17] The chair is made as part of the 'Swords into Ploughshares' project from weapons collected after the civil war in Mozambique. Wondering about this object, we can ask questions about how it was assembled or why people chose this object to talk about war. Even if we are not interested in these questions, by wondering about them we can get answers that might lead us to a different set of topics, such as what happens in civil wars or how civil wars are relevant to the development of contemporary Africa. These ideas are part of the significance and the interpretation of the heritage of the Throne of Weapons.[18] What is inherited in the future is more than the object itself: it is its significance. And the significance of heritage is unlocked by being in a position to exercise our curiosity about things from the past. This is how we can push the boundaries of our acquaintance and understanding of the past, given that we have fragmented information about what happened then. It is important for heritage institutions to allow and actively invite different stakeholders to wonder about alternative possibilities for the future of heritage. This is how audiences become interlocutors and evaluate whether their participation can shape the future of heritage.

A good example here is the Abraham Lincoln Presidential Library and Museum at Springfield in Illinois.[19] Towards the end of the museum exhibition, visitors are asked to participate voluntarily via an interactive screen to choose which of Lincoln's ideas from his major speeches are relevant for USA today. The museum collects the data, and the results will be released when this project finishes. This interactive activity motivates people to exercise their curiosity about the importance of what has been inherited from the past and its significance for today and tomorrow. Inviting stakeholders to exercise their curiosity and taking on board their views is to engage actively with their participation. However, if there are stakeholders who are victims of participant perspective epistemic injustice, they are not provided with space to float questions, their suggestions for alternative possibilities of heritage are not taken on board and they are thus not encouraged to exercise their curiosity. In this case, not only do we undermine epistemic confidence, but also we encourage alienation from heritage. If one's contribution is not taken on board for the future of heritage, one might lack motivation and ambition to get involved with heritage. As a result, stakeholders can withdraw altogether from any epistemic interaction with heritage, and their interpretations of heritage will remain silenced.[20]

So far, I have argued that participant perspective epistemic injustice undermines the distribution of epistemic goods such as acquaintance, understanding and epistemic curiosity, and it can thus distort the epistemic role of heritage. Let me clear the ground from an objection to my argument, before I move to my next point about the relationship between participant perspective epistemic injustice and the sharing of knowledge in the context of heritage.

Although there might be some cases where heritage institutions obstruct the distribution of epistemic goods and alienate people, insofar as heritage institutions are, generally speaking, open to the public, they do (at least in principle) include multiple perspectives by way of the many interactions that take place with those who visit them.[21] A good example in support of this line of argument is to take into consideration the World Heritage Convention. According to the World Heritage Convention, there are some heritage sites across the world that have exceptional value, that is, outstanding universal value as it is defined by the list of the six criteria of the World Heritage Convention. Central to the understanding of the outstanding universal value is that sites that manifest outstanding universal value can be acknowledged as such by all irrespective of economic, social, cultural and geographical differences. World Heritage sites possess exceptional value, and they thus should be preserved for the benefit of humanity. So, they can be shared by all humanity. Although the idea of universal value hinges upon common and shared understandings of heritage, it leaves space for 'interpretation and translation' of the universal framework into different cultures (Lambadi 2013b). Each local participant at a World Heritage site is able to make her/his own understanding, meaning and interpretation of the site. The ascription of outstanding universal value does not constrain participants from making their own associations with World Heritage sites. By contrast, it welcomes participation and contribution to the making of the meaning of the site. In 1999, UNESCO recognised that without the understanding, support and daily care of local communities, who are the true stewards of World Heritage, 'no amount of funds or army of experts' (Lambadi 2013a) will be able to protect World Heritage sites.

Although participation is encouraged and celebrated by the World Heritage Convention and the framework of outstanding universal value, this does not entail that the participant perspective is taken into consideration from an epistemic point of view. I argued earlier that participant perspective epistemic injustice occurs in heritage when heritage institutions do not take on board the participants' perspective for the significance of what is in transit from the past to the future. This happens because the participants are judged incompetent in asking relevant and pertinent questions about heritage, and they thus cannot add anything important in the debate. The World Heritage Convention does not seem to offer a solution to the participant perspective epistemic injustice for heritage. Sites that have acquired the status of World Heritage tend to be iconic structures and places that over the centuries have accumulated value, and they have become important for various reasons (historic, religious, aesthetic, environmental) for the whole of humanity. They are recognized as sites of outstanding universal value, and they thus should be preserved in their initial historical state so that their authenticity remains intact. World Heritage sites, however, narrate an 'official history', which is usually written and narrated by experts.

Official histories of heritage rarely allow space for the participant perspective. A reason for this might be the danger of incoherent representation of the site. If there is no official history and there are multiple narratives, it will not be clear what the significance of the site is. The demand of a coherent representation of the site does not strike me as a strong reason to overlook the participant perspective point of view. Given that the epistemic role of the participant is to consider new possibilities for how we interact with remains from the past, and to float new ideas about our relationship with the past, they are not distorting the representation of any site. By contrast, they add new layers to its perception. If this is not allowed, then World Heritage sites are not successful in distributing epistemic goods because they commit participant epistemic injustice. Official histories of heritage can provide some acquaintance and some understanding of what remains from the past. They can also inspire some curiosity. These epistemic goods, however, will be limited to those participants who share the official history. For those participants who, for a variety of reasons, are not related to the official history, the distribution of epistemic goods is not possible, and they thus feel alienated from heritage. More importantly, their epistemic role does not feature in the significance of what is in transit from past to future. Hence, they become people without a voice for what is understood as common inheritance.

## 3. Participant perspective epistemic injustice and the ethics of sharing

In the previous section I argued that if heritage institutions commit participant perspective epistemic injustice, the distribution of epistemic goods is distorted and thus heritage participants can be marginalized and silenced. The distorted distribution of epistemic goods has a consequent impact for the sharing of knowledge which is central to the function of heritage institutions. In what follows, I argue that participant perspective epistemic injustice is related to the ethics of sharing because it undermines the sharing of knowledge.

A significant role of heritage institutions is to share knowledge with diverse publics of what is under their custody. Sharing depends on reciprocity between the participants in sharing and negotiation between them of what is to be shared. In cases of participant perspective epistemic injustice where the participants' perspective is not taken seriously, participants cannot enter into a reciprocal relationship between one part of the relationship that judges the other part as inadequate to contribute to the relationship and thus into negotiation into what is to be shared. Here, those who suffer from participant perspective injustice are not acknowledged as those who have the capacity to participate, and they are thus not engaged in negotiating what is being shared. As a result, they are judged as non-competent to play a role in the negotiation of what is being shared and thus their views are marginalized or silenced. If this is the case, reciprocity that is a condition for sharing is undermined and therefore one could argue that any obligations which are rooted in the ethics of sharing are not fulfilled. Let me illustrate my sketch of the ethics of sharing with an example.

One of the interesting cases about participant perspective in relation to heritage is the reconstruction of monuments after war and/or civil conflict. Let us accept for the sake of the argument that the civil war in Syria comes to an end, and there is a decision for the reconstruction of the sites that were damaged during the conflict. One of the chosen monuments for reconstruction is one of the six UNESCO World Heritage sites, the Great Mosque of Aleppo with the great minaret, which was destroyed in April 2013.[22] Any heritage institution that is in charge of sharing knowledge about this monument should acknowledge and engage with all relevant participants and take seriously how they think about the reconstruction of the monument. So, those who float ideas about the reconstruction of the minaret and the consequent commemoration of its destruction as part of the monument's heritage should be acknowledged, and their participation should be encouraged. This is how they will actively play a role in the negotiation of what is shared in relation to the heritage of the minaret between the past and the future generations. What future generations will know about the minaret of Aleppo depends on those who participate in the negotiation of what is shared about the heritage of this destroyed site. Hence, if heritage institutions do not take on board the voices of those who claim that part of the heritage of the monument and its significance is also the *destruction* of the monument, not only do they commit participant perspective epistemic injustice on them, but they also deny their role in the sharing of knowledge for the future.

Similar examples can be brought from museums where the display of ethnographic objects do not provide any space for those who would claim legitimate right to participate in the sharing of knowledge of the ethnographic objects in question. For instance, the display of the Aboriginal Bark Shield at the Enlightenment room of the British Museum provides information about how it was moved from Australia to the United Kingdom, but there is no sufficient information given about the Aboriginal perspective in relation to the Bark Shield.[23] What is shared in terms of knowledge and what is inherited to future generations about the Bark Shield and its significance does not include the Aboriginal perspective.

So, heritage institutions are in the position to share epistemic goods and knowledge, this means that they are by default in the position of a custodian, a steward of what is to be shared. For those who might claim that heritage institutions are already custodians of the past, I remind them that being a custodian of the past and being in a position to share what has been under custody are two different kinds of stewardship. We might want to call this a *two-tier stewardship*. The first-tier of stewardship has to do with taking care of what has been inherited from the past. The second-tier has to do with being in a position to choose and collect and share what has been under your stewardship with significant others. In the second-tier stewardship, your duty is not simply to take care of what has been inherited, it is to choose what will be shared in terms of knowledge with others. Here, heritage institutions are in a position of power, and they decide what to share and how to share. If they do not create an atmosphere of epistemic confidence that will enable members of the public to act both as informants and participants in the sharing of knowledge, then heritage institutions abuse their position of power. The ethics of sharing is abused when the previous condition is not met. And the condition is not met when incidents of a particular kind of epistemic injustice, that is, participant perspective epistemic injustice occurs.

**Related Chapters:** 5, 7, 26, 34, 37

## Notes

1. The only article that makes a direct reference to the term epistemic injustice in the context of heritage without going into details is by Sophia Lambadi (2013: 310–330).
2. What is worth noting is that cultural heritage and epistemology have shared interests. For instance, both are concerned with knowledge and repositories of knowledge, they are also concerned about testimony (presentation, selection), social and epistemic practices (debating, learning, questioning) and the social and epistemic role of institutions. Both cultural heritage and epistemology are also interested in the interpretation of our experiences, seeking for arenas to make this possible. For the connection between heritage and social practices, please see: Smith (2006).
3. Museums as representatives of heritage institutions accommodate a variety of epistemic interactions. Museums do not merely distribute epistemic goods, they *select* information via collecting things, they *frame* them and they *display* them to the public. In these there is a danger to commit epistemic injustice. For instance, they fail to attend the perspective of Indigenous communities, they might adapt to popular stereotypes about the display of historical events, or they might display a nation in the world in a triumphalist and nationalistic manner. Also see Duncan and Wallach (2004: 51–70).
4. http://whc.unesco.org/en/conventiontext/ (accessed 21 July 2016) and http://whc.unesco.org/en/guidelines/ (accessed 21 July 2016).
5. For Durham World Heritage Site, see http://whc.unesco.org/en/list/370 (accessed 18 July 2016).
6. http://whc.unesco.org/en/search/?criteria=Durham (accessed 17 July 2016).
7. For a discussion of value of heritage, see Hamilakis and Duke (2008).
8. A good example here is the abandoned industrial buildings in places like Detroit. At the start of the current financial crisis, these buildings were seen merely as abandoned ruins. Nowadays, they are considered significant industrial and urban heritage.
9. For the idea of biography of objects see: Kopytoff (1986: 69–94).
10. A good example here is homeless people and immigrants who are not given space for their own interpretation of heritage. For the heritage of homeless people, see: Zimmerman and Welch (2011: 67–85). For ethics of heritage and immigration, see Holtorf, Pantazatos and Scarre (2016).
11. For example, I understand that many Indigenous peoples want both testimonial and hermeneutical roles: they will not testify about their cultural heritage unless they are also allowed to ensure that it is interpreted in the right ways.
12. I am grateful to Gaile Pohlhaus, Jr. for this point.

13 David E. Cooper (2006) explains sufficiently this occurrence of epistemic injustice, arguing that it is not without difficulties to accept non-experts' accounts for the interpretation of the past.
14 One should note here that there have been strenuous efforts to acknowledge the testimonies of Indigenous communities and engage with them as credible informants about their past. The Burra Charter code of best practice, which has been adopted by archaeologists, anthropologists and heritage practitioners in Australia, signals the effort to fight epistemic injustice. For Burra Charter code of practice, see: http://australia.icomos.org/wp-content/uploads/The-Burra-Charter-2013-Adopted-31.10.2013.pdf (accessed 10 July 2016).
15 Although there seems to be an official narrative of the site, there seems to be no clear evidence of it.
16 My understanding of curiosity here is closer to Miscevic's (2007) account of curiosity.
17 See www.britishmuseum.org/research/collection_online/collection_object_details.aspx?objectId=575651 &partId=1 (accessed 9 September 2016).
18 For an interpretation of the Throne of Weapons, see: McGregor (2010).
19 See www.illinois.gov/alplm/Pages/default.aspx (accessed 8 September 2016). I was able to participate in this activity during my visit at the Abraham Lincoln Museum on the 21st of September 2015.
20 For instance, for many people the rock of Acropolis where the Parthenon is located has always been primarily the legacy of the ancient Athenians to the future. However, part of the heritage of the rock of Acropolis and its interpretation as a heritage place is the buildings and structures (including Roman buildings, Christian churches and mosque minarets), which disappeared under the axis of neoclassicism.
21 I am grateful to Gaile Pohlhaus, Jr. for making this point clearer.
22 See http://en.unesco.org/news/unesco-director-general-deplores-continuing-destruction-ancient-aleppo-world-heritage-site (Accessed 9 September 2016).
23 One should bear in mind that museums such as the British Museums have huge collections, and it takes time to change their modes of display.

# References

Bennett, Tony. 1996. *The Birth of the Museum: History, Theory, Politics*. New York: Routledge.
Cooper, David E. 2006. 'Truthfulness and "Inclusion" in Archaeology', in Chris Scarre and Geoffrey Scarre (eds.), *The Ethics of Archaeology: Philosophical Perspectives on Archaeological Practice*. Cambridge: Cambridge University Press, 131–145.
Duncan, Carol and Alan Wallach. 2004. 'The Universal Survey Museum', in Bettina Messias Carbonell (ed.), *Museum Studies: An Anthology of Contexts*. Oxford: Blackwell, 51–70.
Fricker, Miranda. 2007. *Epistemic Injustice: Power and the Ethics of Knowing*. Oxford: Oxford University Press.
Hamilakis, Yannis and Phillip Duke. 2008. *Archaeology and Capitalism: From Ethics to Politics*. Walnut Creek, CA: Left Coast.
Holtorf, C., A. Pantazatos and G. F. Scarre (2016) *Cultural Heritage, Ethics and Contemporary Migrations* London and New York: Routledge.
Hookway, Christopher. 2010. 'Some varieties of epistemic injustice: Reflections on Fricker', *Episteme* 7: 151–163.
Hookway, Christopher. 2013. 'Freedom of Mind, Self-Trust, and the Possession of Virtues', in Tim Henning and David Schweikard (eds.), *Knowledge, Virtue, and Action: Essays on Putting Epistemic Virtues to Work*. New York: Routledge, 175–187.
Kopytoff, Igor. 1986. 'The Cultural Biography of Things: Commoditization as Process', in Arjun Appadurai (ed.), *The Social Life of Things: Commodities in Cultural Perspective*. Cambridge: Cambridge University Press, 69–94.
Lambadi, Sophia. 2013a. 'The National Museum of Immigration History (Paris, France), neo-colonialist representations, silencing, and re-appropriation', *The Journal of Social Archaeology* 13: 310–330.
Lambadi, Sophia. 2013b. *UNESCO, Cultural Heritage, and Outstanding Universal Value*. New York: Altamira.
Lowenthal, David. 2015. *The Past Is a Foreign Country*. New York: Cambridge University Press.
McGregor, Neil. 2010. *A History of the World in 100 Objects*. London: Allen Lane.
Medina, José. 2013. *The Epistemology of Resistance: Gender, and Racial Oppression, Epistemic Injustice and Resistant Imaginations*. Oxford: Oxford University Press.
Miscevic, Nenad. 2007. 'Virtue-based epistemology and the centrality of truth (towards a strong virtue epistemology)', *Acta Analytica* 22: 239–266.

Pantazatos, Andreas. 2016. 'The Ethics of Trusteeship and the Biography of Objects in Philosophy', in V.S. Harrison, A. Bergqvist, and G. Kemp (eds.), *Philosophy and Museums: Ethics, Aesthetics and Ontology*. Cambridge: Cambridge University Press, 179-197.

Roberts, Robert and W. Jay Wood. 2007. *Intellectual Virtues: An Essay in Regulative Epistemology*. Oxford: Clarendon Press.

Smith, Laurajane. 2006. *Uses of Heritage*. London: Routledge.

Watson, Lani. 2015. 'What is inquisitiveness?', *American Philosophical Quarterly* 52: 273–287.

Zimmerman, Larry and Jessica Welch. 2011. 'Displaced and barely visible: Archaeology and the material culture of homelessness', *Historical Archaeology* 45: 67–85.

# 36
# EPISTEMIC INJUSTICE AND RELIGION

*Ian James Kidd*

## 1. Introduction

This chapter charts various ways that religious persons and groups can be perpetrators and victims of epistemic injustice. Religious persons and communities can commit, or can suffer, epistemic injustices. Miranda Fricker, for instance, mentions religion as a 'dimension of social activity' that prejudices could track but does not focus upon it (2007, 27). A religious identity can invite others' prejudice and entail activities and experiences that others might find difficult to make sense of, while also shaping a person's epistemic sensibilities. The practices of testifying to and interpreting experiences take a range of distinctive forms in religious life – for instance, if the testimonial practices require a special sort of religious accomplishment or if proper understanding of religious experiences is only available to those with authentic faith. But it is also clear that religious communities and traditions have been sources of epistemic injustice – for instance, by conjoining epistemic and spiritual credibility in ways disadvantageous to 'deviant' groups. I explore the ways that epistemic injustice and religion can interact and focus mainly on the major monotheistic religions that are culturally dominant in the modern West.

## 2. Epistemic injustice and theologies

The literature on epistemic injustice and religion is modest and mostly represented by the work of the eminent feminist philosopher of religion, Pamela Sue Anderson (2004, 2012). She focuses on ways that gendered prejudices in Western religious traditions has damaged the spiritual development and self-understanding of women. The epistemic aspect of these critiques lies in the erosion and distortion of the testimonial and hermeneutical credibility and confidence of religious women. The transposition of gendered stereotypes into the epistemic practices of theism can and has excluded women from religious discourses, which, if left unchecked, corrupts the concepts, symbols, and other epistemic resources of the religious imaginary, a concept Marije Altorf (2009) adapts from Michèle Le Doeuff (1989). If a religious woman lacks the confidence and credibility needed to articulate and make sense of her experiences, then she suffers a spiritually-toned epistemic injustice.

A striking feature of Anderson's more recent work on epistemic injustice are potent criticisms of the ways that the practice of mainstream philosophy of religion might promote certain forms of epistemic injustice. A sensitivity to gender, race, 'epistemic location', and an expansive engagement with the many forms of religiosity are needed for just understanding of 'thinking subjects', and religious persons, who are marginalised epistemically and socially within the academy (see Anderson 2012, 2015). It is too soon to tell whether philosophers of religion will engage with the ethico-epistemic issues that Fricker's concept captures, but one can look elsewhere for work exploring their relation to religion. The trick is to not to look for discussions couched in Fricker's own terms, but rather for the sorts of concerns and topics they track. One can talk about epistemic injustice without using that term, and lack of a term ought not to be confused with lack of sensitivity to the underlying phenomenon.

Several significant movements in theology engage with issues of epistemic injustice, and I consider two – *feminist* and *liberation* – in detail, making occasional remarks on *queer* theologies along the way.

At their broader, the many varieties of feminist theology share a concern to identify and reconstruct gender prejudices in religious thought and practice. Its relation to epistemic injustice turns on the conviction, voiced by the late Rita Gross (2002, 63), that 'adequate theology cannot be done on the basis of erasing many voices', such as those of women and aboriginal peoples. Feminist theologies explore the fact that the institutional and intellectual structures of many, if not all, religions are shaped by androcentric biases, in different ways, at different levels. For a start, women may be characterised negatively in the relevant terms in a religious tradition, perhaps as *earthly* or *bodily*, or as loci of craving and desire, even if the characterisations are more nuanced and less fixed than was once supposed (Coakley 2000). If a dominant theological anthropology assigns to women a derogatory status, then the very possibility of their enjoying epistemic credibility and authority is denied or impugned. Next is the related promotion of overwhelmingly male religious exemplars, often coupled to explicit denial that women are apt for religious exemplarity, although this varies by tradition; there is, for instance, a long Indian tradition of men recognising, indeed esteeming, female spiritual exemplars (Frazier 2009). If, in a religious culture, epistemic and spiritual status are connected, then to deprive women of religious exemplarity in effect deflates their credibility and authority, at least in religious matters.

If there are general ways that religions could generate epistemic injustices, there are other ways peculiar to distinctive traditions. One is that theistic traditions can conceptualise God or the divine using typically masculine terms, like power or reason, thereby presenting a conception of epistemic authority defined relative to men. Such conceptualisations project a sexist social order onto a transcendent reality, explicitly or not; for instance, the Wisdom tradition of Hebrew Scripture insisted that God is beyond gender, while the Church Fathers denied that woman was theomorphic, able to 'image' God (Ruether 1990). Another specific way to impose epistemic injustices onto women within a religious tradition is to privilege the use of gendered language, metaphors, and images in quotidian and theological discourse – a default to the male pronoun for God, 'the Father', say. And another would be nomination of women as the sources of epistemic and spiritual corruption, whose best example is likely the Christian postlapsarian doctrine by which Eve is the 'embodiment of sin and corruption' (Yee 2003, 1).[1]

Feminist theologies offer at least three ways to understand the unjust epistemic effects of entrenched religious sexism. The first is to show the *silencing* of the experiences, thoughts, and reflections of women of spirit, not least their accounts of their marginalisation in and by the traditions to which they belong – a theme reflected in the subtitle of Ursula King's influential collection, *Women and Spirituality, Voices of Protest, Voices of Promise* (King 1989). Second, to document and protest occlusion of the social and spiritual experiences of religious women, including the ways they are 'shut out of theological reflection' (Ruether 1983, 13) and denied a role in the 'formation of . . . theological meaning' (Loades 1990, 4). And third, feminist theologies offer powerful ways to identify and interdict systems of doctrinal and social power that deprive religious women of their epistemic authority – for instance, by detailing the 'disastrous' effects on Christian women's 'self-understanding' of their tradition's 'fundamentally ambivalent' conceptions of the moral and metaphysical status of women (Loades 1990, 2). These systems must also be sensitive to the intersections of gender and race (see Armour 1999).

Alongside such critical ways, constructive projects for a diversification of our conceptions of religion and theology can be offered. Though a standing concern of feminist theologies, positive projects are clear in the efforts by queer theologians, such as Marcella Althaus-Reid, to create 'a new space for a theological dialogue for and from heterosexual dissenters', able to exploit theological insights latent in the 'elements of consciousness' of their 'loving relationships' (2003, 4, 115), which offer new 'discourses of the sacred' (2000, 3). This requires overcoming the credibility deficits and hermeneutical marginalisation imposed on queer religious communities, a project whose relationship to 'orthodox' theologies is highly contested (see Cornwall 2011).

I suggest that epistemic injustice is a deep, latent theme in feminist and queer theologies. A religious life is only possible if one can engage in testimonial practices and draw upon rich hermeneutic resources within an epistemically nourishing tradition. But such abilities to participate in those practices and access those resources can be corrupted by a variety of prejudices, generating testimonial silencing and smothering (Dotson 2011), and hermeneutic marginalisation. If so, such corrupted traditions perpetuate epistemic injustices that prevent women and others of being able to report and make sense of their spiritual experiences.

## *Liberation theologies*

Early critics of feminist theologies called attention to a neglect of other marginalised social and religious groups, insisting that the 'struggle for justice for women' ought be extended to the 'liberation of humankind' (Grey 1999, 89). Perhaps the most influential manifestation of this call is the 'liberation theology' movement that emerged in the Latin American Catholic Church in the 1970s. True to its Marxist inspirations, 'liberation' has social and economic as well as epistemic aspects, of which two stand out. The first is a profound association of epistemic and material oppression, of a sense that effective oppression of people requires restriction of epistemic opportunities, for education, criticism, and debate. Second, a more theologically charged conviction reflected in the title of Gustavo Gutiérrez's 1986 book, *The Truth Shall Make You Free*, taken from John 8:32. The aspects converge in a conviction that epistemic and spiritual oppression are mutually reinforcing, since enforced failures to create and share in truth and knowledge are spiritually deleterious. Crucially, however, social and economic realities in modern societies ensure that this afflicts the illiterate poor more than a literate elite. If so, argues Gutiérrez, theological thought and practice should make epistemic justice a central aim – not the abstract grasp of 'cold, warehoused truths', but liberatory actions with truth and love as their *'criteria for discernment'* (1986, 102, original emphasis).

The tacit ambition of epistemic justice is warranted by appeal to the epistemic lessons of Jesus' own ministry, devoted to tending and attending to the marginalised. At the heart of liberation theology is the positive promotion of an 'ethical and intellectual orientation' towards those people and groups 'marginalized by and within theology' (Rowland 1999, 3). The related critical aim is to encourage materially and epistemically privileged theologians to revise what Kwok Pui-lan describes as their 'suspicion' of those on the social and theological 'margins' (2005, 126). If so, there are two ways that liberation theology engages issues of epistemic injustice. One is drawing attention to the social, material, and theological structures that marginalize the testimonies and experiences of certain religious groups, or what Gayatri Chakravorty Spivak dubs the 'itinerary of silencing' (Spivak 2013).[2] Such efforts include interrogating established theological economies of credibility, taking seriously marginalized voices, and cultivating a virtuous willingness 'to listen and to be challenged and to respond' (Noble 2014, 9). Second, liberation theologies can show the fruits of more epistemically just modes of theological practice and how they 'liberate' previously occluded forms of religious experience and understanding. Interestingly, this is presented not as an ideological intrusion into Christian theology, but as an overdue realization of its latent imperatives – hence why many liberation theologians quote Jeremiah 22:13–17, 'To know God is to do justice', in its fullest spiritual, material, and epistemic senses.

The conjunction of epistemic and spiritual liberation is also evident in other religious traditions as feminist, postcolonial, and queer insights flowed through other traditions. A systematic study could focus on religious movements alert to (i) the articulation of the latent epistemic aspects of religious concepts of justice – particularly in Judaism (Stone 2004) and Islam (Shaikh 2013) – and (ii) the appreciation of the ways that prejudices distort judgments of epistemic and spiritual credibility and authority within the historical and current forms of those traditions. A promising possibility is Mahatma Gandhi's concept of *satyāgraha*, built from Hindu materials, that promotes both personal 'insistence' on truth and the creation of social and epistemic conditions receptive to its acquisition and debate – ones unmarred by gender and caste prejudice, for instance. In effect, this is a call for epistemic justice, rooted in a religious tradition noted for its entrenched syncretic and pluralistic tendencies (see Gandhi 1996, part I, Parekh 2001).

## 3. Religion as a source of epistemic injustice

A vigorous literature exists devoted to the epistemic, as well as moral and social, harms that can be generated by and within religious institutions and traditions, criticisms often offered from their own members. Can these criticisms be articulated in the terms of epistemic injustice?

### *Religious aliens*

Paul J. Griffiths (2010) defines a 'religious alien' as anyone who seems to inhabit a religious form of life that one does not take oneself to inhabit. To a nonreligious person, all religious people are aliens, as theists are to atheists, while to a religious person only the people who inhabit a different form of life are religious aliens, as Sikhs do to Zen Buddhists, say. Griffiths describes a set of 'families of responses' to them, including 'domestication', 'shunning', and 'love's embrace', each of which can be analysed using the concept of epistemic injustice. It is clear, for instance, that our responses to religious aliens invoke complex questions of testimonial and hermeneutical engagement of sorts that bring the possibility of injustice. Are religious aliens negatively stereotyped – as godless, profane, or pagan – in ways that are credibility-deflating? Do religious people have the hermeneutical practices and resources needed to be, as Griffiths (2010, 123) says, 'receptive to the . . . alien's particular otherness'? Can one even regard aliens as epistemically credible if their conception of reality is regarded as metaphysically and spiritually false or flawed?

Such questions invoke complex issues of epistemic injustice, confidence, and power that are ripe for systematic investigation. A good starting point would be Anderson's (2015) work on feminist perspectives on religious diversity and the discussion of how aliens can provoke crises of epistemic confidence in one's tradition offered by Griffiths (2001, chs. 2–3). Those less sympathetic to religious concerns might also consider the ways that non-religious aliens were, historically, epistemically stigmatised. During the Middle Ages, atheism was an indisputable 'sign of ignorance' and 'immorality', such that listening to them was a tangible risk to one's moral and spiritual integrity. If so, testimonial and hermeneutical injustice may sometimes be latent in a whole culture or picture of the world (see Weltecke 2013).

## *Christian mysticism*

Feminist philosophy of religion affords rich materials for studies of epistemic injustices that were facilitated and legitimated by religious traditions. Grace Jantzen offers the case of the marginalisation of women in the Western Christian mystical tradition in her influential book *Power, Gender, and Christian Mysticism*. To retrieve and 'celebrate' those women mystics is to contribute to the feminist project of 'deconstructing patriarchal paradigms' that led to the occlusion of their testimonies and experiences (1995, 3, 347). It is also to challenge modern philosophical approaches to mysticism that continue that legacy of marginalisation, not least by reactivating debates about 'who counts as a mystic' within cultures averse to the idea of women having an 'authoritative' status. If women mystics' experiences were accepted, then their attainment of union with God would undermine their spiritually derogated status and force a 'reconsideration of the categories' of spiritual and social order (Jantzen 1995, 2, 15, 16). The women's testimonies and experiences could transform the entire religious imagination.

Jantzen's study of the gendered injustices perpetrated against women mystics in the Christian medieval tradition is complex and has been contested.[3] But it addresses the issues definitive of epistemic injustice, such as the hermeneutical marginalisation of certain groups, for instance, and the abuse of social power to distort credibility economies. Similar themes are developed by Sarah Coakley, who recently argued that analytic philosophy of religion has tended to 'trivialise' the 'epistemic significance' of St. Teresa of Avila's mystical experiences. Although she does not explicitly invoke the concept of epistemic justice, it flows through her suggestion that, by taking lessons from feminist thought, philosophers of religion can 'do richer justice hermeneutically to the texts of mystical theology' (2009, 283).

## *The soul-making theodicy*

The project of theodicy has been subjected to morally inflected criticisms that offer another possibility for detecting subtle forms of epistemic injustice generated by religious traditions. I focus on the soul-making theodicy, developed by John Hick in *Evil and the Love of God*, and the epistemically-inflected criticisms of it developed by moral anti-theodicists.

The core claim that Hick develops is that experiencing and engaging with suffering is necessary to the cultivation of moral and spiritual virtues. Since God desires our perfection, He places us into a world whose abundant suffering makes it an optimal environment for the exercise of those virtues – a 'vale of soul-making'. Influential as it is, the theodicy is criticized on many fronts, but I focus on objections of a feminist character.

Marilyn McCord Adams (1999) is perhaps the most famous critic of the soul-making theodicy, challenging its central claim by arguing that certain human experiences of suffering are so terrible – extensive and intensive – that, as Hick puts it, they 'crush [one's] character' (2010, 330–331). Such 'horrors', as Adams dubs them, not only 'fail to advance' the sufferer's moral and spiritual 'progress', but are so 'damaging' that progress becomes 'virtually impossible' (1999, 53). Indeed, such 'horrors', far from being soul-*making*, are irreversibly *soul-breaking* – a religiously-inflected form of what José Medina calls 'epistemic death', that occurs as a result of harm to one's epistemic capacities and agency, 'so deep as to annihilate one's self' (see Medina 2017, 108).

If certain experiences of suffering result in 'epistemic death', then that is one way to base a critique of the soul-making theodicy in epistemic injustice. But two others are worth mentioning.

The first arises from Hick's appeal to *mystery* as a response to horrendous evils (which he calls 'dysteleological evils'). The deep problem of evil, he argues, lies in the fact that evils and suffering are 'distributed in random and meaningless ways', for which we can provide no rationally and morally compelling explanation (2010, 333). Although Hick invokes such 'mysteriousness', arguing that it is conducive to the process of soul-making, the claim is false and – I argue – a source of epistemic injustice. It is false because the distribution of evil and suffering is not 'random', but obviously socially and materially conditioned. Evils track individuals and groups along the lines of sex, gender, race, and social-economic situation, in the case of both natural and social evils. If the distribution is explicable, it is not mysterious – a point obvious from historical and sociological investigation, and neglected by philosophers of religion who, as Morny Joy (2010) complains, talk blandly and vaguely of how *people* suffer, rather than admit that certain groups of people – women and the poor, say – suffer more intensely and extensively from evils, including group-specific evils (like female genital mutilation), and are also less able, socially and epistemically, to protest and interdict their suffering. If epistemic injustice is a sort of evil, then its distribution is not 'random'.

An appeal to mystery, of the sort Hick offers, is a source of epistemic injustice in two ways. First, it is apt to distract attention away from the empirical realities of suffering, not least the social identities of the sufferers, thereby occluding the testimonies and experiences of the sufferers by removing any sense that it is relevant or imperative to attend to them. It adds silencing to the experience of suffering, hence the 'refusal' of feminist philosophies of religion to 'distract attention' away from the social identities and voices of the suffering (Jantzen 1998, 264). Second, appeal to mystery tends to divert intellectual attention away from concrete empirical realities onto a transcendent domain, usually to speculations about God's reasons for allowing evil. This has the hermeneutical consequence that *understanding evil* becomes a task of abstract theorizing rather than sensitive engagement with the lived experiences of the sufferers (see Burley 2012a). Understanding evil becomes a matter of ratiocination informed only minimally by an empathetic engagement with the testimonies and experiences of sufferers – a criticism that is central to *moral anti-theodicy*, which emerged, over the last fifty years, to challenge styles of theodicy judged to encourage morally opprobrious forms of detachment from, and insensitivity to, suffering. Moral anti-theodicy has a latent epistemic aspect, closely related to concerns about injustice. D.Z. Phillips, for instance, argued that theodicies 'betray the evils that people have suffered', and thereby 'sin against them' (2004, xi). Among its aspects, this 'betrayal' includes a failure to assign a central role to the testimonies of those who suffer – a betrayal by silencing. Indeed, a grim irony is that suffering is silenced by the very people who confidently assume the task of making sense of the experiences of the suffering. Theodicies, as critics put it, are complicit in 'dehumanising victimization without reconciliation', objectionable insofar as it 'averts its gaze from the cruelties that exist in the world', including the human perspectives of those living those cruelties (quoted and discussed in Trakakis 2008, ch. 2).

Theodical projects can be sources of epistemic injustice if they fail to encourage the development of the resources and sensitivities needed to attend humanely to the testimonies of religious people of their experiences of suffering. If so, such projects will, however inadvertently, be epistemically unjust.

## 4. Religion and vulnerability to epistemic injustice

Debates about the epistemological status of religion in late modern societies are arguably shaped by two background convictions – inherited from the Enlightenment, operating at the level of a *sensus communis*, rather than explicitly affirmed doctrine. One is that religious belief is epistemically suspicious, reflective of ignorance, superstition, or of the persistence of a set of psychosocial needs. Another is that religious beliefs, institutions, and traditions have been and continue to be epistemically deleterious at the individual and social levels – a claim that is developed and explored by political theorists, cultural critics, and many others. If so, then religion is liable to be interpreted as the source, not the victim, of epistemic injustices. These are deep waters – historically, culturally, intellectually – and there is little work on the ways that the concept of epistemic injustice could be used to navigate them.

Certainly the central concerns captured by the concept of epistemic injustice can be found in influential recent works, including Charles Taylor's recent study, *A Secular Age*, that interprets modern secularism in terms of a change in the prevailing 'conditions of belief' of modern societies. Religious belief, once 'axiomatic', is now 'one . . . possibility' among others, 'eligible' for some, but not for others, such that different groups within a culture 'experience their world very differently' (2007, 3, 14). Such contexts complicate judgments of credibility and interpretation because epistemic possibilities that are crucial to one group are ruled out by another – for instance, if talk of a sense of love of or union with god can only be heard as symbolic or expressive at best, or 'outmoded' or literally senseless at worst, then there is a space for epistemic injustice (see Cottingham 2005, ch. 6, Kidd 2014). Or religious groups might be negatively stereotyped in ways that prejudicially deflate their credibility or find the activities and experiences constitutive of their faith rendered hermeneutically opaque within a religiously illiterate society (see Anderson 2013, Svartvik and Wirén 2013).[4] Or the non-religious social peers might not only be ignorant of basic knowledge – of doctrines, dietary rules, and so on – but also have a hermeneutically inadequate *approach* to religion.

Contemporary philosophers of religion of many different stripes nowadays advocate richer ways of making sense of the diversity of forms of human religiosity – historical, cross-cultural, and phenomenological, for instance (see, *inter alia*, Burley 2016, Wynn 2005, Zagzebski 2007). Underlying such work is a call for an enriched hermeneutical sensibility of a sort that relates to what Fricker calls epistemic injustice – for instance, an appreciation that 'taking a religious belief seriously' means locating it within a 'form of life', rather than isolating it from its supporting context of thought and sensibility, thereby consigning it to unintelligibility. This is difficult if the beliefs and practices seem absurd or unintelligible, but the virtue lies in seeing that such appraisals are products of a contingently inherited sensibility, rather than exercise of an epistemically privileged perspective on reality (see Burley 2012b).

The idea that our contingently inherited epistemic sensibilities can act as deep sources of epistemic injustice is a complex one – sketched, in part, by Kidd (2013) and Ratcliffe (2008, ch. 10). But the idea is best explored in the context of religion where epistemological issues are complicated by the very fact of significant differences in how human beings experience and conceive the world.

## *Naturalism and religious experiences*

The deep roots of epistemic injustice are usually contingent prejudices against certain social groups – women, blacks, the disabled, and so on – that are explicable in psychosocial terms. But a further possibility, at least in the case of religion, is that the roots of such injustice can be something akin to a worldview or conception of reality. Certainly certain philosophers of religion have argued that certain religious claims and experiences are deprived of credibility and intelligibility by a naturalistic worldview (see, for instance, Cottingham 2005). Central to that worldview – or set of related views – is a denial of the existence of supernatural entities and realities – gods, soul, karma, and other components of many religious ways of life. Since they are judged not to exist, belief in them must be evidence of epistemic fault, usually to be explained in the terms of psychological and evolutionary terms (see De Cruz and De Smedt 2015, Dennett 2006).

Most cases of epistemic injustice involve deficiencies of epistemic goods – credibility and intelligibility – that stem from negative prejudice or lack of hermeneutical resources. I want to suggest that, in certain cases, the very possibility of credibility or intelligibility is removed, and that this can result from adoption by an epistemic agent of a certain worldview. Call this a *deep epistemic injustice* and consider as an example the project of 'spiritual neuroscience', which used to be called 'neurotheology'. Critics make various empirical and methodological objections to such projects, but a deeper worry is that spiritual neuroscience presupposes a naturalistic framework that implicitly rules our certain epistemic possibilities – specifically, it rules out the possibility of a veridical interpretation of religious experiences, of their being what their experients report and interpret them to be.

Although 'religious experiences' is a broad and elastic one, within religious communities it is typically taken to refer to some sort of experience of absorption in, union with, sense of or a something whose reality is not only denied but also excluded by a naturalistic picture of the world (see Katz 2012). But, as David E. Cooper argues, such a picture necessarily 'denies truth or sense to . . . such experience[s]' and 'entails that the experience cannot be taken at face value' (2002, 337–338). If so, people who adopt it are *de facto* prevented from regarding as credible any testimonies to such religious experiences that are regarded, at least if they are interpreted to be, *inter alia*, perception of a divine being, 'union' with the 'grounds of being', or whatever. In such cases, the person's credibility is not deflated, but definitively *denied*, at least concerning those experiences.[5]

The idea of deep epistemic injustices of this sort is contestable, of course, because it depends on fundamental metaphysical convictions. Naturalists will likely reject talk of their illegitimately ruling out the possibility of veridical interpretations of religious experience by denying that they are legitimate. If the blunt fact is that there are no transcendent realities, then rejecting reports of experiences of one is not an injustice, but what informed scientific reason requires. Yet the critics' response will be to reject the naturalistic confidence in that picture of the world; perhaps, like the later Wittgenstein, they think *Weltbild* cannot be proven or refuted, since any practices and criteria of proof and refutation would presuppose the very picture whose status is being questioned. Or perhaps they follow the position of the existential phenomenologists: that naturalism takes for granted a tacit sense of reality that it cannot epistemically justify (see Ratcliffe 2003, 2013).

Since exploration of the points of contact between epistemic injustice and the deep philosophical issues sketched here is in its early days, these remarks are necessarily brief. It is striking, though, that those who develop them evince a consistent concern with issues of our testimonial and hermeneutical capacities. Ratcliffe argues that neurotheologians fail to grasp that their commitment to methodological naturalism, their 'definitive refusal' to admit theistic possibilities into scientific enquiry, entails implicit ontological commitments, that are 'antagonistic to theism'. Confident in its own sense of neutrality, neurotheology 'implicitly rules out the possibility of certain coherent, theistic ontological claims' (2003, 234, 327). The epistemic consequence is that the naturalist cannot but withhold the possibility of credibility and intelligibility from people's reports of religious experiences, which will be naturalised and pathologised (see Kidd 2017). If one agrees with the critique of the naturalism, then this may seem like a case of deep epistemic injustice – a denial of the possibility of testimonial credibility and intelligibility to those who report experiences incompatible with a naturalistic metaphysics. But naturalists, of course, will reject the critique and hence the charge of deep epistemic injustice.

Since the possibility of deep epistemic injustices will ultimately turn on a larger debate about philosophical naturalism, it is best not to hold one's breath for solutions. But it does point to the potential fruits of exploring cases where religious persons might feel that they are victims of epistemic injustice. Certainly we can use it to pose interesting questions. Is it a testimonial injustice to deny credibility to religious persons who report experiences of a sort that, though profoundly significant to them and their communities, can only be found incredible (in a technical, literal sense) by others? Is it a sort of hermeneutical injustice if the education and culture of secular societies fail to provide their members with the sensibilities and resources needed to make sense of religious people's experiences? Is epistemic justice a political and civic virtue within modern societies where a premium is placed on debate and understanding between diverse religious and non-religious communities? And if our pictures of the world fundamentally structure our sense of what sorts of testimonies and experiences can be regarded as credible and intelligible, then is there a deeper – 'metaphysical' – aspect to the possibility of epistemic justice in the context of religion in modern societies?

A sense of what sorts of experiences can be credibly reported and cogently made sense of may be rooted in a picture of the world. But this may be a vision some social peers may not share; indeed, one that many may regard as *absurd*.

## 5. Conclusions

This chapter has surveyed several points of contact between epistemic injustice and religion. Although this study is in its very early stages, there are rich existing resources within various forms of theology – feminist, liberation, and queer – and various current debates within the philosophy of religion and wider philosophical thought. One can think of religious doctrines, communities, and systems of thought as sources of epistemic injustice, or one can think of religious agents as victims of epistemic injustice; or – of course – one can recognise that the options are mutually compatible and consider both together. There are various possibilities available, and given the epistemic and cultural complexities attending religion – in its widest sense – in modern societies, there should be great interest and urgency in exploring them.[6]

**Related chapters:** 1, 2, 3, 10, 18, 22, 26, 33, 34

## Notes

1 This is a large theme, explored by, among many others, Daly (1973), Ruether (1983), and Schüssler Fiorenza (1993).
2 See 'Reading Spivak', Donna Landry and Gerald MacLean's introduction to Spivak (2013), for useful context and criticisms of her work.
3 Useful critical discussions of Jantzen's book, and its relation to wider scholarship on medieval Christian mysticism, can be found in the reviews by Stanley Hauerwas in *Modern Theology* 13.3 (1997), 399–421, and Anneke Mulder-Bakker in *Gender and History* 10.2 (1998), 316–318.
4 A disturbing example of a morally obnoxious hermeneutical failure in the context of religion is discussed by Medina (2012, §4.2.1).
5 I give a fuller account of how adoption of a naturalistic stance can occlude a person's capacity to engage epistemically with religious claims and experiences in Kidd (2012).
6 I am grateful to José Medina and Gaile Pohlhaus, Jr. for comments on an earlier draft, to Rachel Muers and Tasia Scrutton for encouraging my early interest, and to David E. Cooper and Matthew Ratcliffe for inspiring my ideas.

# References

Adams, Marilyn McCord (1999) *Horrendous Evils and the Goodness of God* (Ithaca: Cornell University Press).
Althaus-Reid, Marcella (2000) *Indecent Theology: Theological Perversions in Sex, Gender, and Politics* (London: Routledge).
Althaus-Reid, Marcella (2003) *The Queer God* (Abingdon: Routledge).
Altorf, Marije (2009) 'Feminists and Fools: Imagination and Philosophy of Religion', in Pamela Sue Anderson (ed.), *New Topics in Feminist Philosophy of Religion* (Dordrecht: Springer), 3–16.
Anderson, Pamela Sue (2004) 'An Epistemological-Ethical Approach to Philosophy of Religion: Learning to Listen', in Pamela Sue Anderson and Beverley Clack (eds.), *Feminist Philosophy of Religion: Critical Readings* (London: Routledge), 87–102.
Anderson, Pamela Sue (2012) *Re-Envisioning Gender in Philosophy of Religion: Reason, Love, and Epistemic Locatedness* (Farnham: Ashgate).
Anderson, Pamela Sue (2013) 'Love, Sexual Stereotypes and Confidence', in Jesper Svartvik (ed.), *Religious Stereotyping and Interreligious Relations* (Basingstoke: Palgrave Macmillan), 33–44.
Anderson, Pamela Sue (2015) 'A Feminist Perspective', in Chad V. Meister (ed.), *The Oxford Handbook of Religious Diversity* (Oxford: Oxford University Press), 405–420.
Armour, Ellen T. (1999) *Deconstruction, Feminist Theology, and the Problem of Difference* (Chicago: University of Chicago Press).
Burley, Mikel (2012a) 'Contemplating Evil', *Nordic Wittgenstein Review* 1: 35–54.
Burley, Mikel (2012b) 'Believing in Reincarnation', *Philosophy* 87: 261–279.
Burley, Mikel (2016) *Rebirth and the Stream of Life: A Philosophical Study of Reincarnation, Karma, and Rebirth* (London: Bloomsbury).
Coakley, Sarah (2000) *Religion and the Body* (Cambridge: Cambridge University Press).
Coakley, Sarah (2009) 'Dark Contemplation and Epistemic Transformation: The Analytic Theologian Re-Meets Teresa of Avila', in Oliver D. Crisp and Michael C. Rea (eds.), *Analytic Theology: New Essays in the Philosophy of Theology* (Oxford: Oxford University Press), 280–312.
Cooper, David E. (2002) *The Measure of Things: Humanism, Humility, and Mystery* (Oxford: Clarendon).
Cornwall, Susannah (2011) *Controversies in Queer Theology* (London: SCM Press).
Cottingham, John (2005) *The Spiritual Dimension: Religion, Philosophy, and Human Value* (Cambridge: Cambridge University Press).
Daly, Mary (1973) *Beyond God the Father: Toward a Philosophy of Women's Liberation* (London: Women's Press).
De Cruz, Helen and De Smedt, Johan (2015) *A Natural History of Natural Theology: The Cognitive Science of Theology and Philosophy of Religion* (Cambridge, MA: MIT Press).
Dennett, Daniel (2006) *Breaking the Spell: Religion as a Natural Phenomenon* (New York: Viking).
Dotson, Kristie (2011) 'Tracking Epistemic Violence, Tracking Practices of Silencing', *Hypatia*, 26: 236–257.
Fricker, Miranda (2007) *Epistemic Injustice: Power and the Ethics of Knowing* (Oxford: Oxford University Press).
Gandhi, Mahatma (1996) *Selected Political Writings*, edited by Dennis Dalton (Indianapolis: Hackett).
Grey, Mary (1999) 'Feminist Theology: A Critical Theology of Liberation', in Christopher Rowland (ed.), *The Cambridge Companion to Liberation Theology* (Cambridge: Cambridge University Press), 89–105.
Griffiths, Paul J. (2010) *Problems of Religious Diversity* (Oxford: Wiley-Blackwell).
Gross, Rita M. (2002) 'Feminist Theology as Theology of Religions', in Susan Frank Parsons (ed.), *The Cambridge Companion to Feminist Theology* (Cambridge: Cambridge University Press), 60–78.
Gutiérrez, Gustavo (1986) *The Truth Shall Make You Free: Confrontations* (Maryknoll, NY: Orbis).
Hick, John (2010) *Evil and the God of Love*, 2nd ed. (Basingstoke: Palgrave Macmillan).
Joy, Morny (2010) 'Rethinking the "Problem of Evil" with Hannah Arendt and Grace Jantzen', in Pamela Sue Anderson (ed.), *New Topics in the Philosophy of Religion* (Dordrecht: Springer), 17–32.
Katz, Steven T. (2012) *Comparative Mysticism: An Anthology of Original Sources* (Oxford: Oxford University Press).
Kidd, Ian James (2012) 'Receptivity to Mystery', *European Journal for Philosophy of Religion* 4.3: 51–68.
Kidd, Ian James (2013) 'A Phenomenological Challenge to "Enlightened Secularism"', *Religious Studies* 49.3: 377–398.
Kidd, Ian James (2014) 'Emotion, Religious Practice, and Cosmopolitan Secularism', *Religious Studies* 50.2: 139–156.

Kidd, Ian James (2017) 'Phenomenology, Neurology, Psychiatry, and Religious Commitment', in Alasdair Coles and Fraser Watts (eds.), *Neurology and Religion* (Cambridge: Cambridge University Press), forthcoming.
King, Ursula (1989) *Women and Spirituality: Voices of Protest, Voices of Promise* (Basingstoke: Macmillan).
Kwok, Pui-Lan (2005) *Postcolonial Imagination and Feminist Theology* (Louisville, KY: Westminster John Knox Press).
Last Stone, Suzanne (2004) 'Feminism and the Rabbinic Conception of Justice', in Hava Tirosh-Samuelson (ed.), *Women and Gender in Jewish Philosophy* (Bloomington, IN: University of Indiana Press), 263–288.
Le Doeuff, Michèle (1989) *The Philosophical Imaginary*, translated by Colin Gordon (Stanford, CA: Stanford University Press).
Loades, Ann (1990) *Feminist Theology: A Reader* (London: John Knox Press).
McCord Adams, Marilyn (1999) *Horrendous Evils and the Goodness of God* (Ithaca: Cornell University Press).
Medina, José (2012) *The Epistemology of Resistance: Gender and Racial Oppression, Epistemic Injustice, and the Social Imagination* (Oxford: Oxford University Press).
Medina, José (2017) 'Varieties of Hermeneutical Injustice', in Ian James Kidd, Gaile Pohlhaus, Jr., and José Medina (eds.), *The Routledge Handbook of Epistemic Injustice* (New York: Routledge), 107–132.
Noble, Tim (2014) *The Poor in Liberation Theology: Pathway to God or Ideological Construct?* (London: Routledge).
Parekh, Bhikhu (2001) *Gandhi: A Very Short Introduction* (Oxford: Oxford University Press).
Ratcliffe, Matthew (2003) 'Scientific Naturalism and the Neurology of Religious Experience', *Religious Studies* 39: 323–345.
Ratcliffe, Matthew (2008) *Feelings of Being: Phenomenology, Psychiatry, and the Sense of Reality* (Oxford: Oxford University Press).
Ratcliffe, Matthew (2013) 'Phenomenology, Naturalism, and the Sense of Reality', *Royal Institute of Philosophy Supplement* 72: 67–88.
Rowland, Christopher (ed.) (1999) *The Cambridge Companion to Liberation Theology*, 1st ed. (Cambridge: Cambridge University Press).
Ruether, Rosemary Radford (1983) *Sexism and God-Talk: Toward a Feminist Theology* (London: SCM Press).
Ruether, Rosemary Radford (1990) 'The Liberation of Christology from Patriarchy', in Ann Loades (ed.), *Feminist Theology: A Reader* (London: John Knox Press), 138–147.
Schüssler Fiorenza, Elisabeth (1993) *In Memory of Her: A Feminist Theological Reconstruction of Christian Origins* (New York: Crossroad).
Shaikh, Sa'diyya (2013) 'Feminism, Epistemology, and Experience: Critically (En)gendering the Study of Islam', *Journal for Islamic Studies* 33: 14–47.
Spivak, Gayati Chakravorty (2013) *The Spivak Reader: Selected Works of Gayati Chakravorty Spivak*, edited by Donna Landry and Gerald Maclean (London: Routledge).
Svartvik, Jesper and Wirén, Jakob (eds.) (2013) *Religious Stereotyping and Interreligious Relations* (Basingstoke: Palgrave Macmillan).
Taylor, Charles (2007) *A Secular Age* (Cambridge, MA: Harvard University Press).
Trakakis, Nick (2008) *The End of Philosophy of Religion* (London: Continuum).
Weltecke, Dorothea (2013) 'The Medieval Period', in Stephen Bullivant and Michael Ruse (eds.), *The Oxford Handbook of Atheism* (Oxford: Oxford University Press), 164–178.
Wynn, Mark (2005) *Emotional Experience and Religious Understanding: Integrating Perception, Conception, and Feeling* (Cambridge: Cambridge University Press).
Yee, Gaile E. (2003) *Poor Banished Children of Eve: Woman as Evil in the Hebrew Bible* (Minneapolis: Fortress).
Zagzebski, Linda (2007) *The Philosophy of Religion: An Historical Introduction* (Oxford: Blackwell).

# 37
# PHILOSOPHY AND PHILOSOPHICAL PRACTICE
## Eurocentrism as an epistemology of ignorance

*Linda Martín Alcoff*

> ... even philosophical systems are facts of history.
>
> *Kwame Nkrumah (1964:3)*

Why would it be surprising that the work of philosophers would be affected by their cultural and historical and national contexts? In this chapter I want to suggest that avoiding and denying the contextual influences on philosophical systems and trends is the work of an epistemology of ignorance. That is, transcendental illusions about the creation of philosophical ideas and the progression of philosophical debates must be cultivated and protected. Such illusions have been and continue to be functional for certain groups of philosophers, not to mention the empires that house them.

Perhaps the most important way in which western philosophy protects and maintains its ignorance about the effects, and limitations, of its geographical location is through the perpetuation and defense of Eurocentric practices and curricula. We should understand Eurocentrism in philosophy as the exclusive or nearly exclusive attention to a European canon of philosophical writing. Given the intellectual wealth of the world, an exclusive focus on the European tradition requires an intentionality and some manner of justification. Oftentimes justifications are quite explicit, as Amy Olberding (2015) has recently argued. Non-western philosophies have to merit inclusion by presenting distinct lines of argumentation one cannot find in the Western canon, yet they must also pass a test of intelligibility, not being so distinct that they are beyond comprehension. These demands have an air of methodological common sense about them (e.g. 'we cannot know what we cannot make sense of, nor do we need to know from new sources what we already know'). Yet they remain forms of Eurocentrism by assuming the non-negotiable legitimacy of a Western measuring stick, holding Western judgments, sensibilities, assumptions, norms, and conventions in place as the gatekeepers for philosophical inclusion. The capacity to judge whether an idea is distinct from Western traditions is itself a philosophical task that should not be left to one side of the dialogue. Indeed, such approaches brook no dialogue: Westerners are judging whether other traditions are worthy, but not putting themselves in the position to be taught.

I want to suggest that such forms of Eurocentrism indicate that it is a species of an even larger pathology I will call the *transcendentalist delusion*: a belief that thought can be separated from its specific, embodied, and geo-historical source. Philosophical ideas and arguments, on this approach, can be discerned and assessed without attending to the location of their genesis. The genealogy of an idea is a concern of intellectual historians, perhaps sociologists, but neither appropriate nor germane to philosophy.

The transcendentalist delusion is both a cause and a symptom of Eurocentrism. It has legitimated the long persistence of exclusionary intellectual practices that were initiated in the midst of the first era of European empire building. Starting with the empires of Spain and Portugal during the Renaissance, new discursive formations had to be spawned in order to manage, explain, and justify these ambitious, and violent, projects. Conquerors such as Cortes reported in their journals of finding marvelous cities equal or greater than any in Europe, and the subsequent mandate from Christian monarchs and Church officials to kill elites, enslave populations, and build bonfires out of their intellectual and cultural products required some subterfuge. Enrique Dussel has suggested that what the Europeans did in the Americas was less of a discovery than a covering over or *encubrimiento* (Dussel 1995). Eventually, new theories developed about the existence of natural geographical hierarchies and typologies of peoples, cultures, and religions that claimed to justify and explain Europe's domination of the world (see Eze 1997).

Central to the discursive formation emerging around the formation of European colonial empires was the idea that Europe was at the vanguard of human culture, achieving the highest successes in every domain of human inquiry and endeavor, but especially the domain of knowledge. Colonialism required such beliefs. As Ghanaian philosopher Kwame Nkrumah explains, 'To say that each man was able to contribute to the truth would require at the social level that each man should have political rights. To say that each man was *equally* capable of contributing to the truth would require that each man should have equal political rights' (1964:44). Ramon Grosfoguel (2013) has named this a form of *epistemicide*, explaining that it was a necessary aspect of conquest. The knowledges of the peoples subject to colonization had to be rendered harmless to the colonial project. This could occur in multiple ways: by denying that these were true knowledges, or by claiming that they were epistemically inferior to European knowledges, or by outright theft of a knowledge and then repackaging it as a European invention. Destroying and deriding the intellectual traditions of a people altered the sense of self for both colonizer and colonized, enabling hubris for the one and inhibiting resistance for the other. And as Nkrumah notes, thwarting demands for political democracy required incapacitating the idea of epistemic democracy, or the ability of all to contribute equally to human knowledge. Projects of conquest could then justifiably pursue non-dialogic processes of engagement, epistemic and otherwise.

In the beginning of Europe's rise, domination was given a decidedly Christian cast. A major example of this was in the Spanish monarchy's doctrine of 'Requerimiento.' This doctrine required that the indigenous peoples of the Americas submit to religious conversion, and further declared that upon conversion they immediately became subjects of the (divinely sanctioned) crown. By such means Christianity provided not only a cover for colonialism but a bureaucracy for surveilling and managing populations. The interpretation of Christian doctrine such practices relied on was contested from within the Church, most effectively by Bartolome de las Casas. As strong secular tendencies emerged across northern Europe in the 17th century, the legitimation of colonial practices was again put to the test, and yet, interestingly, the rise of secularism did not lead to a general repudiation of empire-building except among a small minority (most notably, Denis Diderot). Instead, followers of Enlightenment ideas began to develop putatively scientific and philosophical forms of argumentation that would legitimate colonial rule on the basis of rational superiority rather than religion. Theories began to proliferate about the intellectual and moral effects of climates and the subsequent hierarchies of cultures and peoples. Yet the political utility of these new theories was just as useful: just as before, when a refusal of Christian conversion justified force, so the rejection of European governance proved one's backwardness and resistance to progress (McCarthy 2009).

In an impressive sleight-of-hand, these new philosophical justifications established Europe as *both* the vanguard of the human race *and* as achieving a universal form of thought. The values, epistemology, and scientific methodology that *could only* emerge from the cooler latitudes of the conquering societies were universally true and applicable to all (Zea 1988–89; Zea 1992; Dussel 1995; Wynter 2000; Wynter 2003). Herman Melville sets up a character in his slyly seditious 1850 novel, *White Jacket*, to explain that

> We are the pioneers of the world, the advance-guard . . . the political Messiah has come in us, if we would but give utterance to his promptings. And let us always remember that with ourselves, almost for the first time in the history of the earth, national self-ishness is unbounded philanthropy; for we cannot do a good to America but we give alms to the world.
>
> *(1850:151)*

Ingeniously, the origin of an idea in 'America', or Europe, established its ability to achieve universal scope.

What also follows from this idea is that the cultural achievements of the advance-guard reflects on the outermost capacities of the human race. Hence, what other cultures do reflects their current developmental state, while the achievements (or missteps) of the United States and Europe showcases the fundamental capacities of the human species.

With this orientation in place, modern European epistemologies had no need to consider the limited applicability of their justificatory norms or the advisability of enlarging the dialogic space of philosophical debate. Though they recognized the geographical specificity of their endeavor, they believed it to have a global reach, without need for contextual reflection. Quite obviously, such delusions emerged out of an experience of empire, which spawned several important philosophical trends and, in fact, philosophical errors. These errors included the inattention to philosophical genealogy or the relationship between ideas and their cultural contexts, as well as idealist and non-dialogic conceptions of justification and truth. A whole edifice of framing assumptions such as nature/culture, mind/body, civilized/savage, and public/private served to sequester particularist, embodied, and material issues away from the sight, and sites, of philosophers. These framing assumptions also helped to conceal the particularity, embodiment, and materiality of philosophical projects.

The transcendental delusion, then, was born out of a very specific European experience that it then had no tools to analyze, reflect upon, or correct.

Women's studies scholars discovered more than a generation ago that one cannot simply add women and stir as a way to introduce scholarship and research on women into the academy, given the dominance of such framing assumptions and concepts as I've discussed, as well as naturalized ideas about families and gender that render women's (or any non-male) experience outside of the sphere of analysis. Just so, one cannot simply add non-Western philosophy or topics such as race and colonialism to the existing field of philosophy, its canon and curriculum, without subverting the mainstream periodization, the existing canon, even questioning what is meant by 'philosophy.'

In some respects the challenges posed by race and colonialism are even more intransigent than those posed by gender and sexuality. As Genevieve Lloyd wrote in 1984, feminism has required (and still requires) attending to the Other of reason, that is, to the abjected realm of bodies, desires, and particularities of affective commitments that have been positioned as outside of, and obstacles to, the rational faculties of judgment. Feminism cannot simply be included alongside without refiguring some of the central features of the existing discipline and its ideas about its best practices. Both feminism and decolonial theory call out for dismantling such basic terms of identity as 'man' or 'human.' Yet some have imagined feminist philosophy itself as transcendent of its own time and place, able to stay within the domain of Eurocentric theoretical resources without attending to their geographical genealogies. On such a view, only part of the transcendental delusion would require reform for such feminist philosophy to carry on. Such a partial reform is not possible for the work of decolonial and critical race philosophy, since it would not mandate an expansion of the geographical boundaries. Eurocentric theory is going to be called out, and worse, put in context as a limited, partial, often delusional perspective, and not in any sense the underlying key to the riddle or the mainspring of critical and liberatory philosophy.

Critical race and decolonial theory forces us to attend to the colonial context in which the European canon of rational thought has been and continues to be produced. This project involves uncovering the Eurocentrism embedded in the way in which philosophy is defined, conceptualized, and taught, and this requires placing Western philosophy, most of which occurred in what the discipline defines as the modern period beginning in the late Renaissance, squarely within its context of the long *duree* of European and U.S. global empire building. The societies that spawned our modern philosophers were not inessential backdrop but constitutive of the available meanings and conceptual repertoires, the reaches of intelligibility, and the central problematics of this tradition. Examples include debates over freedom and individual sovereignty, the sphere of legal rights and property rights, and the nature of human understanding (Mehta 1999; Bernasconi 2003). And this is just as true for the liberatory and radical tracks of European modern philosophy, such as Rousseau, Hume, Kant, Marx, Mill, and others, as it was for the more conservative thinkers. Both groups had intra-European debates and social struggles in mind, but these were themselves formulated against a contrast class drawn from 'new world' indigenous cultures, Asian cultures, African cultures, and non-Christian societies, all of which were constructs sometimes fashioned by little more than travelogues (Coronil 1996; Mignolo 2011).

Modern European philosophy emerged from a context of epistemic injustice toward non-European societies, and this injustice is perpetuated by legitimating ideas about intellectual superiority of European-American philosophy. To correct this injustice, and avoid its repetition, philosophy must develop, as Zea, Dussel, Nkrumah, and so many others have argued for more than half a century, greater reflexive capacities as a part of its normal work. It must come to be understood as deeply connected to its context, and this requires working from and within the decolonial studies now emerging in geography, history, anthropology, sociology, and so on (i.e. the assortment of derided social sciences that too many philosophers, from all persuasions, have summarily ignored) that explore the intellectual contours and effects of the context of European colonization (e.g. Gordon 1995; Maldonado-Torres 2006). Perspectivism, as I will argue, will prove insufficient if it implies a setting of philosophies alongside one another, as if Anglo-European philosophy must simply begin to make way for others, or make a space for other philosophical traditions alongside itself, to the side, if not to the back. Rather, instead of a pluralist perspectivism, what is required is a decolonizing of the way in which we interpret, and teach, Western philosophy and, indeed, every form of philosophical thought.

In what follows I will focus on the need to think through the geography of epistemology, or what some have called shifting the geography of reason.

## The geography of epistemology

The idea of geography here involves the practice or orientation of *spatialization*. What geographers study is not simply the coordinates of entities in a domain, but the constitution of the domain itself, including its borders and its internal and external relations. In order to observe the workings of European meaning systems, we must rethink the imagined ground upon which Western philosophy locates itself. Here is how Walter Mignolo puts this point:

> The important observation to make here is not simply whether there are other perspectives about the 'same event' but that another paradigm emerges across the epistemic colonial difference. The dominant theo- and ego-politics is being contested by the emerging shift to the geo-politics and body politics of knowledge: knowledge produced from the geo-historical and bio-historical perspective of racialized locations and people.
> 
> *(Mignolo 2005:48)*

What Mignolo makes clear is that the solution cannot be an 'add alongside' or happy multiculturalism. Perspectivism may imply contrasting points of view and the capacity to access different sorts of empirical evidence, lending support for aggregation models of knowledge that would build from the acknowledgement of multiplicity and difference to a more expansive, comprehensive account. Yet Mignolo and others have argued that the overarching frames of Eurocentrism are intrinsically imperialist and insusceptible to compatibilism or an adequate inclusivity. This does not entail or imply that every single claim or theory in the traditional European canon of philosophy is untrue and unusable, but that the overarching framework constitutes its domain via a paradigm that cannot play well with others.

Mignolo's reference to 'theo-politics' has to do with the way in which, as I described earlier, 15th and 16th century Christianity began to systematically destroy all of its competing sign-systems, expelling peoples, committing genocide, burning temples and books en masse, and redrawing universal maps of location, history, and value in its own terms. The people of Africa came to be viewed as the descendants of Ham, the disobedient son in the Bible who, by his disobedience, deserved his fate of being made a servant to his brothers. And so all peoples who remain ignorant of the word of God became classified as heretics and, for that reason, barbarians (a word continually in use in public discourses today). For the Greeks the term *barbaros* was used to designate non-Hellenophones, though in the Christian era the contrast class came to be predictably defined as one who is heathen, meaning non-Christian. In both cases the concept designates by negation without identifying any substantive alterity. Thomas Aquinas defined the barbarian as one whose manner of life defies common sense (what later came to be called natural law) and, as such, their lives do not accord with human nature (Las Casas, quoted in Mignolo 2005:18) But this again works via negation, denying the *Other* a substantive difference. One needs to know nothing about them, their beliefs or practices, except *what they are not*. Hence, the contrast class for establishing the boundaries of civility or humanity is defined in terms not of self/Other, but in terms of self/*not-self*. Difference is reduced to a question of one's relation to the norms and belief systems of the dominant Christian European society. Barbarians are those who have repudiated Christianity, and their own belief-systems and ways of life have no bearing on this judgment. Unlike the Inca and followers of Islam, for example, who recognized an overlap between their own belief-systems and those of other theists, the Christian Church could tolerate no commonality.

The division of the Iberian peninsular and subsequently the entirety of the Americas into binary maps of Christian/Heathen or Christian/not-Christian produced this binary of Self/not-Self in which the other is reduced to a negative, comparative feature. This is what spurred debates about whether the indigenous were human beings, capable of personhood, endowed with even a modicum of rationality or even self-regard. Such a construction constitutes a radical form of epistemic injustice, as it follows from one's very identity or being. This is what José Medina

(2017) has called 'epistemic death': when one experiences both testimonial and hermeneutic exclusion and thus shut out completely from contributing to the production of meaning and knowledge. In reality, of course, productions of meaning and knowledge never stop occurring, even among the most abject conditions, yet will be unacknowledged by the Masters, or appropriated without attribution.

Such a construction of barbarian identity removes any motivation to learn other ways or creeds. The claim that those designated are inferior and inadequate thinkers is not justified by a study and evaluation of different practices, customs, forms of religiosity, institutions, beliefs, and the like, but simply on the observation that a group is not-Christian or not-rational or *not-self*.[1] This is an epistemology of ignorance born of imperial and colonial projects of plunder that legitimates a lack of investigation and study beyond one's own domain. Hence Eurocentrism has no need to apologize, much less correct itself. On the contrary, Eurocentrism has a need *not to know*, a motivation *not to learn*, in the service of its material and discursive conquests.

The language of 'human nature' has an implicit normativity and capacity for comparison built into it, since if there is a human nature, then there is at least the possibility of an inhuman nature. Such inhuman natures are continually attributed to differently abled bodies as well as different cultures and practices. If we want to ward off the possibility of this kind of conclusion, or, in other words, if we wish to maintain a normative idea about human nature without thereby producing a class of sub-humans, we will need to develop a capacity for the sort of reflexive analysis that decontextualizing philosophical thought makes all but impossible.

Decolonial theory by figures such as Mignolo, Dussel, Wynter, Grosfoguel, Coronil, and Nkrumah provide the tools to begin such philosophical reflection on Western philosophy and in particular Western epistemologies, although they are almost completely absent from required curricula, and even optional curricula. An important piece of this reflection must be the way in which the domain of the 'secular' is understood, in order to draw the links between the foundations of European colonialism, the Enlightenment, and conceptions of modernity. This is the point of Mignolo's concept of 'theo-politics': that the teleological and exclusivist conceptions of intellectual, cultural and scientific development that are used to rank varied global achievements and contributions are still operating within a political world view with significant elements of theology. Thus, the transition from Spanish-Christian discourses of colonialism to Enlightenment secular ones, referenced earlier, should be understood to be at least in some important respects superficial, since the overarching framing assumptions and teleology remained operational. Whether it has an associated God or not, there is a theological resonance in a teleological frame that moves from a state of grace (or state of nature); a fall (into mob democracy, for example, or authoritarian scholasticism, or submission to tyranny); a developmental trajectory of salvific, philosophical enlightenment (or scientific progress alongside industrialization); and a period of divine or transcendental punishment and judgment (which could become the task, of course, of the philosophers). Western philosophy is imagined always as a light or gift brought to the *hoi polloi* by a talented and profound individual or small group, never as something emerging from the mass. If the mass rejects the gift of philosophy, or doesn't value its contributions, this act alone is often sufficient to define them as barbarians. Hence, there are those who can cohabit the garden of ethical life, if they willingly follow the Teacher, and those who must be shunted out. For those inside the garden walls, there is a set of political protocols for the protection of rights, and altogether different treatment for those outside the walls.[2]

Mignolo's point is that secularism simply adopted and adapted a prior Christian theological mapping with all of its trappings of a universal system of truth that judged resisters blameworthy for their exile and suffering. If Christianity organized the peoples of the world fundamentally into those who see the light and are saved and those who are unwilling or incapable of salvation, current ideas about modernity continue this schema. What is new in the modern period is that the categories of demarcation between the self and the not-self become racialized and associated with land mass.

There is a wonderful geographical doublespeak in the philosophy profession, where the salience of location is both avowed and denied. On the one hand, it is bad form to locate a philosophical idea as having a national lineage. We don't speak in polite society of French ideas or German theories: this would sound too much like Nazism's idea of Jewish science and art. Yet the principle reason given for rejecting the relevance of lineage is methodological: because this would obviate the distinction between philosophy and intellectual history, and reduce ideas to arbitrary features of their formation that cannot sustain causal claims. Even if it can be established that an origin of an idea played a causal role in its formation, philosophers are said to be interested in reasons, not causes. Neither the meaning nor the validity of an idea is determined by its genealogy.

On the other hand, our curricula continue to operate with implicitly colonial historiographies that organize the canonical periodizations of western philosophy and its geographical borders. The canon periodization we use misnames particulars as universals. Still today the history of philosophy is grouped within the following categories: Ancient (meaning 4th century Greece), Early Modern (meaning 17th century northwestern Europe, excluding Spain and Portugal), Modern (meaning the same area in the 18th century), and Nineteenth and Twentieth Century (including here England, Scotland, Germany, Austria, France, and the U.S. and Canada). These time-maps represent modernist frames about the progression of reason. If anything, the last few decades have witnessed a further narrowing of the field, cutting out Chinese and Indian philosophy from so-called top departments. The history of philosophy is itself on the ropes in many analytic departments, losing its market share of courses and faculty lines, so one may imagine that this solves the problem of the colonial narrative, but in reality it only further ensures a decontextualization of thought. The canon at least gives us a historical trajectory for current debates and preoccupations.

The idea here is not that philosophies are reducible to their context, and dismissable on those grounds, but that without understanding philosophical systems and trends in their context we cannot hope to adequately interpret or assess them. It is not that the origin of an idea is all-determinative, but that we should stop assuming it has no effect without exploration. Context can explain why a weak argument gained favor and came to be representational of a sub-field, but it also can explain why the question was formulated just so, even if the answer given was rather brilliant. Thankfully, the situation is beginning to improve in the history of philosophy, where a larger range of contemporary interlocutors are taken up alongside canonical figures, as well as historical, social, and political events (good examples: Solomon, Beiser, O'Neill, Potter). And such work is helping to reshape periodization and geographical boundaries, as we come to understand, for example, the influence of the learned Arab world on early Modern philosophers. It is not simply that they helpfully kept Aristotle in their libraries for us, but that their disputations on numerous topics set the terms of discussion. I'll shortly give an example related to this point.

Yet in other sub-fields of philosophy, there has not been as much methodological progress, and questions continue to be portrayed as timeless and transcendent of their context. Such approaches leave intact and unchallenged the geographic imaginary that privileges the West as the origin and principal location of Philosophy. In this imaginary, which is regularly reinforced, if not policed, by our departmental curricular requirements, philosophy is a practice invented by the ancient Greeks, re-emerging (as if from a dream) in modern Europe, and primarily flourishing in those countries influenced by the West. This is a time-map, and it allows those of us who locate ourselves in the western tradition to rest assured that those behind us, even if they start on the path we have charted, will never catch up.

Thus, the idea of 'theo-politics' helps name the teleological framing of philosophical history that legitimates geographical narrowness. Just as once the world was divided between Christians and non-Christians, today there are those who do philosophy (or who do philosophy properly) and those who don't, and these divisions correspond to geographical locations. Next I want to turn to the other term Mignolo refers to in the passage above, which is the idea of 'ego-politics'. This is a reference to René Descartes, and in particular, to Enrique Dussel's analysis of the role Descartes played in the formation of western epistemology's colonial narrative about its own emergence as an uncaused cause.[3] The philosophical scholarship on Descartes has taken some very productive turns of late, benefitting from the newly expansive contextual trends in the history of philosophy, as I noted. This has helped to place Descartes' work in relation to earlier periods, and there have also been multi-layered readings of his nightmarish meditations (see e.g. Bordo, Scheman, Brown, Lee). But what remains too often neglected is the link between Descartes and the Jesuitical tradition in which he was educated. Understanding this link challenges received ideas not only about the development of early modern European epistemology but also about how modernity is continually defined today.

The Jesuit order, or Society of Jesus, was founded only in 1536, 60 years before Descartes' birth. The order was quickly distinguished by its willingness to proselytize under difficult conditions, including as one of its four vows the promise of engaging in missionary work, and they soon became some of the most active missionaries in the New World. In some cases Jesuits sought to protect indigenous populations from abuse, but they also operated as overseers of indigenous labor in the mines and plantations and owned significant numbers of African slaves.

As early as 1549, Jesuits began missionary work in the wide expanses of the New World. Thus the evolution of the order tracked their colonizing projects in the service of Spain and France as they began to develop the institutions and practices that would help them manage the populations under their patronage throughout the Americas, including the job of efficiently extracting labor. The innovation of the Jesuits was to proselytize not primarily by forced memorizing of the catechism but, rather, by inviting others to join in their personal relationships with Christ by performing self-examination as individuals and developing a capacity for reflection on their beliefs, meanings, values, and the relation of these with the divine purpose.

From the age of 10 until he graduated at 17, Descartes was enrolled in the Jesuit Collège Royal Henry-Le-Grand at La Flèche. He then went onto the University of Poitiers, where he earned a degree in Canon Law, or the body of Christian laws. His subsequent quite numerous travels took him to the papal nuncio in Italy, where it was Cardinal Berulle who first urged Descartes to write philosophy.

Descartes' association with the Jesuits links him securely to Spain (whose philosophy in this period is too often ignored) but also to the New World. The flow of people and of intellectual influences across the Atlantic was intense starting in the 16th century, and so it was not at all odd that Descartes studied logic from a work written by the well known Mexican philosopher of that period, Antonio Rubio.

The Jesuit belief in a thorough and sustained 'examination of conscience' maps easily onto the *Meditations on First Philosophy*, first published in 1641, in which Descartes (1993) provides an uncanny reportage of his innermost doubts and debates. Such self-examination is also clearly evident in his *Passions of the Soul*, published in 1646 (see Descartes 1990).[4] Dussel and other historians of philosophy have traced Descartes' formative influences also back to Fonseca, the Portuguese philosopher who influenced a generation of Jesuits known as the Coimbrian school. Here the principal topic of discussion was the concept of method, identified as 'the art of reasoning about whatever probable question' (quoted in Dussel 2014:15). Another Portuguese influence on Descartes that Dussel tracks is Francisco Sanchez, who proposed a means to arrive at certainty through a process of doubt.

In standard intellectual histories, Descartes' influences are listed as the late works of Aristotle, the Stoic school of Greek philosophy, and St. Augustine. Augustine's influences on Descartes are thought to be less theological than involving his self-examining, reflexive practice and his logical approach to questions of time and reality. Hence all of Descartes' influences are taken to be secular. One of the interesting implications of this new contextualization of Descartes' ideas is that the move from religious to secular philosophy is not as sharp a break as it is often made out to be. Nor is secularism a necessary component of the self-critical reflections associated with rational modernity.

Dussel suggests, in fact, that we should locate the emergence of modern thought with Las Casas rather than with Descartes. In this shift, modernity is the emergence of a critical reflection on difference and material conditions rather than a conquering and isolated ego. It is a reflection directed toward the ideas and practices that inhabit one's social and historical context, and not simply directed at one's self or one's own personal beliefs. As Mignolo suggests, the differences between such definitions of modernity are not compatible: we cannot place such perspectives alongside one another but must shift registers. Descartes's aim is for each individual to achieve absolute or indubitable certainty, just as the Jesuits aimed for. Hence, he finds the route of perceptual sensation too defeasible for this purpose, nor can it disprove his eventual conclusions. By contrast, Las Casas works through a direct perception of his material surroundings, the real world conditions of the Indians and their cultural achievements, using this to test dogmatisms of Church interpreters and their use of syllogistic reasoning. But unlike traditional empiricists, Las Casas recognizes the particularism and thus perspectivism of his own location – a perspective that provides the criteria necessary to identify the strange and barbarous. Because he recognizes it as a perspective, he is able to see the Other as having a substantive difference, and not simply as a 'not-self.' Las Casas then goes on to engage in reflective social critique of his own society's doxastic conventions.

Descartes' habitus was very much unreflectively informed by the theo-politics of Christian conquest, producing an ego-politics with the imperialist mind-set that rejected all external influences out of hand. The progress of Western philosophy continues to be hobbled by this approach, insistently ignorant of potential interlocutors. Las Casas, by contrast, is visibly groping toward a different self-understanding, in which one's own inclinations are analyzed in relation to their social context. With this approach, dialogic models of philosophical thought, especially those that can span cultures and belief-systems, are non-negotiable necessities for the achievement of understanding.

What theo- and ego-politics have in common is an imperial design on time and space. Where theo-politics proposes a singular historical developmental trajectory of progress and redemption, ego-politics proposes a spatial mastery from a singular nodal point. Descartes' procedure requires no dialogic interlocutors, no collective process, and yet can achieve a truth for all. Without speaking to all, it is a truth that speaks for all.[5] Against these Mignolo proposes 'a geo-politics and body politics of knowledge: knowledge produced from the geo-historical and bio-historical perspective of racialized locations and people.' This is not a reversal but a decentralization: in place of a singular trajectory of successive events in which every culture can be located as either 'ahead' or 'behind,' he and others propose a pluriversality of heterogeneous historico-structural nodes. Las Casas moves us closer to this ideal by deflating the concepts that would legitimate hermeneutic closure, turning away from dialogue.

## Conclusion

My argument has been that Eurocentrism is more than simply a preference for a particular tradition of philosophical thought, but a practice of ensuring ignorance that perpetuates the sort of epistemic injustices that came to be consolidated in many European intellectual trends during its extended efforts to colonize the globe. Continuing to separate philosophical practice from its context obscures this fact, disabling critical reflexivity, justifying exclusivity, indeed, justifying a rather appalling ignorance about others and other intellectual traditions.

There has always been a resistance both within and outside the philosophical traditions emerging from Europe. Within the West, feminist and post-colonial and critical race and decolonial philosophies have recently increased in scope and vigor, but they are not entirely new. Outside of the West, the critique has been persistent. Decolonial thought emerged to contest European intellectual mono-lingualism as soon as the Conquest began; it's just that this rich tradition of counterpoint has been all but excluded from the Western curriculum. Western philosophy's long overdue engagement with its non-Western critics is the only solution to the epistemology of ignorance.

In his essay 'What is Enlightenment?' Michel Foucault (1984) makes an interesting observation about Kant's own writings on the French Enlightenment. He looks at two of Kant's essays, the 1798 essay on the French Revolution, 'Contest of the Faculties,' and his 1784 essay whose title Foucault unabashedly stole. Rather than considering Kant's characterization of the content of the Enlightenment, Foucault notes another interesting feature of these texts. He points out that Kant is venturing to make a commentary on his own present moment, a rare move for a philosopher. This has the effect of positioning philosophical reflection in a specific temporality, as emerging in a here and now, in relationship to the present.

Both the French revolution and the Enlightenment were events in space and time, often given starting dates and geographical locations. Thus, Foucault suggests, in commenting on such events, 'the philosopher presenting his philosophical discourse cannot avoid the question of him being part of this present . . . about his membership of a particular 'we,' if you like, which is linked to a greater or lesser extent to a cultural ensemble characteristic of his contemporary reality. This 'we' has to become, or is in the process of becoming, the object of the philosopher's own reflection' (2010:13). I suspect that for Foucault, the 'cultural ensemble characteristic of his contemporary reality' is a reference to the particularity of a group identity, as German or European, for example.

Kant's commentary, and Foucault's perception of it, is a small opening to contextual self-reflection, and, as Foucault points out, for Kant it is an opening as yet unfulfilled. Contrast this with Dussel's reading of Las Casas as a better candidate for the paradigm shift of European modernity in philosophy. Las Casas is also taking note of his surroundings, his present, the 'we' of which he is a part, but he is also attentive to his material surroundings in the context of peoples and labor and the uses to which these are put, and thus he is not only cognizant of the elite 'we' at the upper strata. Las Casas is mostly considering the philosophical justifications (what Foucault might call the matrix of rationality) that operate in regard to this organization of the material field. Against this, Las Casas offers assessments and criticisms, considering the 'we' and 'them' of Europeans and Indians (or indigenous) in relation to the concept of barbarism. For this reason, Dussel suggests retaining 'modernity' as a normative ideal in the sense of reflective critical engagement with the material context of thought, despite the fact that he vigorously contests the usual teleology of modernity. For Dussel, this is the sort of philosophical practice that might resuscitate the moribund philosophical traditions that remain willfully ignorant of their transcendentalist delusions.[6]

**Related chapters**: 1, 3, 9, 10, 11, 13, 25, 34

## Notes

1 We could understand the self/Other distinction as inclusive of, or even identical with a self/not-self distinction, but Mignolo's point is that there is a conceptual distinction between being an Other, and being simply defined in terms of a negation.
2 This intellectual and secular bifurcation maps onto older Christian ones, but its characteristic megalomania is not found everywhere. The ancient Chinese under the long Zhou dynasty defined themselves as the Middle Kingdom, a form of jurisdiction that acknowledges boundaries and neighbors. Islam understands itself to have a constitutive relationship with Jews and Christians, distinct religions practiced by 'the people of the book,' whose teachings Muslims must respect. Numerous indigenous groups describe their genealogy as place-based rather than as deriving from a source or value that transcends place (which is why their displacement can destroy identity). Group names (e.g. Murrawarri people of what is today called Australia) are often identical to place names. It is a mistake to jump to the conclusion that Eurocentrism is a universal problem or innate human tendency.
3 Some of the following borrows from Alcoff (2013).
4 Rene Descartes, *The Passions of the Soul: An English translation of Les Passions de L'Ame* Trans by Steven H. Voss Cambridge Ma.: Hackett Publishing Co, 1990.
5 Descartes engaged in vigorous dialogues with others, as we know, and yet the 'Method' he propounds requires no such dialogues nor does it even encourage them.
6 My sincere thanks to Gaile Pohlhaus, Jr., José Medina, and Ian James Kidd for their thorough critique and fruitful suggestions.

## References

Alcoff, Linda Martín. 2013. 'Philosophy, the Conquest, and the Meaning of Modernity: A Commentary of "Anti-Cartesian Meditations: On the Origin of the Philosophical Anti-Discourse of Modernity" by Enrique Dussel', *Human Architecture* 11.1: 57–66.
Bernasconi, Robert. 2003. 'Will the Real Kant Please Stand Up: The Challenge of Enlightenment Racism to the Study of the History of Philosophy', *Radical Philosophy* 117: 13–22.
Coronil, Fernando. 1996. 'Beyond Occidentalism: Toward Nonimperial Geohistorical Categories', *Cultural Anthropology* 1.1: 51–87.
Descartes, René. 1993. *Meditations on First Philosophy: In Which the Existence of God and the Distinction of the Soul from the Body Are Demonstrated.* Trans. Donald A. Cress, 3rd edition. Cambridge, MA: Hackett.
Descartes, René. 1990. *The Passions of the Soul: An English Translation of* Les Passions de L'Ame. Trans. Steven H. Voss. Cambridge, MA: Hackett.
Dussel, Enrique. 2014. 'Anti-Cartesian Meditations: On the Origin of the Philosophical Anti-Discourse of Modernity', *Journal for Culture and Religious Theory* 13.1: 11–52.
Dussel, Enrique. 1995. *The Invention of the Americas: Eclipse of 'the Other' and the Myth of Modernity.* Trans. Michael D. Barber. New York: Continuum.
Eze, Emmanuel Chukwudi, ed. 1997. *Race and the Enlightenment: A Reader.* Cambridge, MA: Blackwell.
Focault, Michel. 2010. *The Government of Self and Others: Lectures at the College de France, 1982–1983*, F. Gros, ed., trans. G. Berchelle, New York: Palgrave McMillan.
Foucault, Michel. 2003. *Society Must Be Defended.* Trans. David Macey. New York: Picador Press.
Foucault, Michel. 1984. 'What is Enlightenment?' in Paul Rabinow, ed., *The Foucault Reader.* New York: Pantheon.
Gordon, Lewis. 1995. *Fanon and the Crisis of European Man: An Essay on Philosophy and the Human Sciences.* New York: Routledge.
Grosfoguel, Ramón. 2013. 'The Structure of Knowledge in Westernized Universities: Racism/Sexism and the Four Genocides/Epistemicides of the Long 16th Century', *Human Architecture* 11.1: article 8, 73–90.
Maldonado-Torres, Nelson. 2006. 'Post-Continental Philosophy: Its Definition, Contours, and Fundamental Sources', *Worlds and Knowledges Otherwise* 1.3: 1–29.
McCarthy, Thomas. 2009. *Race, Empire and the Idea of Human Development.* Cambridge: Cambridge University Press.
Medina, José. 2017. 'Varieties of Hermeneutical Injustice', in Ian James Kidd, José Medina, and Gaile Pohlhaus, Jr., eds., *The Routledge Handbook of Epistemic Injustice.* (New York: Routledge).
Mehta, Uday Singh. 1999. *Liberalism and Empire: A Study in Nineteenth Century British Liberal Thought.* Chicago: University of Chicago Press.

Melville, Herman. 1850. *White-Jacket: Or, the World in a Man-of-War, with an Introduction by William Plomer*. New York: Grove Press.
Mignolo, Walter. 2011. *The Darker Side of Western Modernity*. Durham, NC: Duke University Press.
Mignolo, Walter D. 2005. *The Idea of Latin America*. New York: Wiley-Blackwell.
Nkrumah, Kwame. 1964. *Consciencism*. New York: Monthly Review Press.
Olberding, Amy. 2015. 'It's Not Them, It's You: A Case Study Concerning the Exclusion of Non-Western Philosophy', *Comparative Philosophy* 6.2: 14–34.
Wynter, Sylvia. 2003. 'Unsettling the Coloniality of Being/Power/Truth/Freedom: Towards the Human, After Man, Its Overrepresentation: An Argument', *The New Centennial Review* 3.3: 257–337.
Wynter, Sylvia. 2000. 'The Re-Enchantment of Humanism: An Interview with Sylvia Wynter by David Scott', *Small Axe* 8 (September): 119-207.
Zea, Leopoldo. 1992. *The Role of the Americas in History*. Edited by Amy A. Oliver. Translated by Sonja Karsen. Savage, MD.: Rowman and Littlefield.
Zea, Leopoldo. 1988–89. 'Identity: A Latin American Philosophical Problem', *The Philosophical Forum* 20.1–2: 33–42.

# INDEX

ability: bodily change and 84–6; epistemic features beyond and entangled in 82–4; know how and 79, 81–2
ableism 126, 164
Addams, Jane 209
agency, epistemic and political 201–2, 254–60; of communities 274–5
agential components of hermeneutical injustice 42, 201–2
agential power 187–9
Ahmed, Sara 163
AIDS patients 318
Alcoff, Linda 240
algorithmic profiling 308–10
Allendé, Salvador 151
Althaus-Reid, Marcella 388
Althusser, Louis 100
Altorf, Marije 386
American Medical Association 215
Amin, Samir 151
Anderson, Benedict 272–3
Anderson, Elizabeth 56, 244, 246, 273–4, 317; on education system 331; on structural testimonial justice 33–4
Anderson, Pamela Sue 386–7, 389
Andrews, Julie 84, 86
androcentrism 125–6
anger, hard to handle 128
Anglo-American epistemology 93, 95, 97; indifference to more "politicized" approaches 102
Angola 265
anthropology of Indigenous peoples 356; epistemic injustice in 359–62; epistemology of resistance and 365–6; historical context of 357–9; protection of sacred places and 362–5

Anzaldúa, Gloria 41, 50, 135, 149, 165; on mestiza consciousness 163–4; on modes of consciousness 155
Aristotle 198, 405
aspectival captivity 15–16
assimilationism 142
asymmetries, knowledge and experiential 336
atheism 389
Atlanta School 110
attributability-blameworthiness 229–30
Austin, J. L. 144
authority, epistemic 325
Ayotte, Kevin 128–9

Baehr, Jason 226
Baier, Annette 70
Bailey, Alison 133–4
Baldus, David 297
Baldwin, James 50
Balfour, Lawrie 110
Bambara, Toni Cade 116
Banaji, Mahzarin 298
Bandaranaike, Sirimavo 151
Bandung Era 151–2
Barnes, Elizabeth 286
Bartky, Sandra 201
being-in-the-world 198–9
belief-sets as forms of social consciousness 103–4
Bentall, Richard 349
Berenstain, Nora 22
Bettcher, Talia Mae 170
bias, implicit: in criminal justice system 298–300; hermeneutical injustice and 239–40; remedies for 240–1; testimonial injustice and 236–7
Biernat, Monica 75

black feminism: excluded by white feminists 141; intersectionality and 115–17; quieting and smothering of testimony and 120–2; standpoint epistemology and 120, 163
Black Lives Matter (BLM) movement 139–40, 143; hermeneutical injustice and 146; hermeneutical marginalization and 140
blameworthiness 229–30
*Blyew v. U.S.* 17
bodily change and ability 84–6
Bolivar, Simón 263
Bonilla-Silva, Eduardo 141, 145
Bonjour, Laurence 89
*Bonnichsen v. United States* 363
Boroditsky, Lera 145
Bortolotti, Lisa 353
Boxill, Bernard 142
Braudel, Fernand 150
breadth of hermeneutical injustices 46–7
Breunig, Robert 364
Brown, Kendrick 167
Brownmiller, Susan 177
Brownstein, Michael 236, 241
Buddhism 265–7, 389
Burge, Tyler 197
Butler, Judith 127, 129, 161, 195
Butler, Peter 353

California Proposition 54 145
Canada 317–18
Cardoso, Fernando Henrique 152
caste segregation 107
Castoriadis, Cornelius 3, 94–5, 97
Castro, Fidel 265
categorical connections 28
Central Park Five 22
Chambati, Walter 131
Chen, Mel 165
Chernobyl accident 318
choice: agency and 254; of belief, free 89–90; trust as matter of 75–7
Chomsky, Noam 262
Christianity: Eurocentrism and 401–3; gendered language in 387; Jesuit order 404–5; mysticism 390
classificatory pluralism 45–8
class studies and social justice 116–17
Coakley, Sarah 390
Code, Lorraine 3, 17–18, 126, 135, 270; on rhetorical spaces 50, 133
coercion, conceptual 133
Coetzee, J. M. 267
cognition-truth axis 190–1
cognitive authority 18
collective harassment 305
collective identity politics 120
Collins, Patricia Hill 4, 15, 235, 270; on black feminist standpoint 163; on controlling images 21; on exclusion of Black women's voices in knowledge production 141; on feminist theorizing and women's standpoint 125; on oppositional consciousness 127–8
colonialism 149–51, 262, 356–9; postcolonialism, coloniality, and the Bandung Era 151–2; *see also* anthropology of Indigenous peoples; Eurocentrism
coloniality 151–2; of power 152–3
Combahee River Collective 116, 119
communities 270–1; epistemology of incarcerated 275–7; forming 271–3; of resistance 272–5
complicity with hermeneutical injustices 42–3
conceptual coercion 133
Conde Rodriguez, Alicia 268
condition, epistemic 214
consciousness: being-in-the-world 198–9; intentional 201; liminal 276; perception and 198–200; as relational 196; subversive 275
constitutive power 187–9
contributory injustice 20, 133–4
controlling images 21
Cooke, Anne 350
Cooper, Anna Julia 13, 141
Cooper, David 332–3, 393
coordinated ignorance and social contract 16–18
Coronil, Fernando 402
cosmopolitan secularism 362
courts, judges, and juries 293–301
Craig, Edward 29–31, 33, 72–3, 305
credibility 72, 236, 249; deficit 76; grammar and education and 33–4; judgments 197–8; level assigned to learners (or to children) 326, 328–9; social imaginary and 332–3; testimonial injustice and 62; *see also* trust
Crenshaw, Kimberle 117, 119–20, 122, 128
criminal law: courts, judges, and juries 293–4; truth and epistemic justice in 294–301
crip epistemologies 164–5
crisis of homo/heterosexual definition 159–60
critical race theory 49, 217, 400
critical theory 100
Cuba: imperialism in 261–2; Revolution 151, 261, 265
Cudd, Ann 102
culture of justification 14, 92
culture of poverty 255

Darwell, Stephen 245
Darwin, Charles 208
Daukas, Nancy 130, 249
David, Ned 364
Davidson, Larry 348
death, epistemic 390, 401–2
death, hermeneutical 2, 47, 49; defined 41–2; fighting against hermeneutical injustice and 48–50
de Beauvoir, Simone 95

de Bruin, Boudewijn 238
decentered of epistemic injustices 154–5
decolonial praxis 149–55
decolonial theory 400, 402, 406
deep epistemic injustice 393
degrees of change and/in epistemic systems 19–21
delusions, motivated 352–3
Dennett, Daniel 338–9
dependentistas 152
depth of hermeneutical injustices 47
Descartes, René 404–5
determined ignorances 132
de Tocqueville, Alexis 110
Dewey, John 6, 205, 207–10, 271–3
Diderot, Denis 398
disability: conceptually knowing the apparatus of 175–6; identity 164; initially knowing the apparatus of 182; *To Kill a Mockingbird* and 178–82; marginalization and 285–7; politically knowing the apparatus of 176–8; social model of 286
discourse-power axis 191
discriminatory epistemic injustice 2–3, 53, 61
discursive injustice 73, 130, 144
disobedience 49–50, 134
distribution: of educational opportunities 330; of epistemic goods and participant perspective epistemic injustice 377–82
distributive epistemic injustice 61–6
distrust 70–1
diversity, epistemic 329–30
Doctrine of Discovery 357
Dotson, Kristie 14–16, 19–20; on contributory injustice 20, 133–4; on culture of justification 92; on epistemic resources 86; on epistemic violence 120, 129; Plato's Cave and 108–9; on testimonial smothering and quieting 73–4, 169, 235
double epistemic function of education 333–4
Douglas, Frederick 134
Du Bois, W.E.B. 107–10, 141; on epistemic communities 271–3, 275
Durham World Heritage Site 372–3
Dussel, Enrique 398, 400, 402, 404–6
dynamics, hermeneutical injustice 46
dysfunction 57

Eagleton, Terry 268
education: activity sense of 325; concept of 325–6; dimensions of epistemic justice 326–8; distributional concerns in 330–1; double epistemic function of 333–4; literature, approaches to epistemic justice in 328–31; particular challenges with epistemic justice in 331–4; renewed attention in epistemology 324; value of epistemic diversity in 329–30; what teachers teach and 327; which particular learners teachers credit in 327; which students are admitted to certain courses of study 327; which students other students credit in 328; which teachers students credit in 328; who becomes teachers and scholars and 327
effects-vice 225
egalitarianism, hermeneutic 65
ego-politics 404–5
Einstein, Albert 264
eliminativism 142–3, 145
embodiment: being-in-the-world and 198–9; consciousness and 196; political implications of 263
emotions, outlaw 128
Engels, Friedrich 106
Enlightenment, the 100, 102, 263, 391, 398, 402
epistemic agency 201–2, 254–60
epistemic authority 325
epistemic condition 214
epistemic death 390, 401–2
epistemic disobedience 49–50, 134
epistemic diversity 329–30
epistemic exclusions of ideology 109
epistemic exploitation 21–2, 247–8
epistemic friction 18, 93, 161
epistemicide 398
epistemic imaginaries 3, 94–5
epistemic injustice: agency and 254–60; in anthropology 356–66; Black Lives Matter movement and 139; branches of philosophy within 13; communities of resistance and 273–5; criminal justice system 293–301; cultural heritage and 370–83; dangers of defining the field of 14–16; decentered as decolonial praxis 154–5; decolonial praxis and 149–55; defined 1; degrees of change and 19–21; digital environments 303–11; discriminatory 2–3, 53, 61; distributive 61–6; education and 324–34; Foucault and 187–94; gaslighting as 168–70; harms of 210–11, 244–5, 343–4; implicit bias, stereotype threat, and 235–41; interpersonal as political and 57–8; intersectionality and 115–23; knowledge and 80–1; lenses 22–3; in medicine and healthcare 336–44; mental illness and 347–53; new terrains of social experience in 58–9; normative ethics and 243–4; participatory 315–18; phenomenology and 195–203; political agency and 254–60; political freedom and 261–8; queer epistemology and 158–65; religion and 386–94; in science 313–21; social contract and coordinated ignorance in 16–18; social epistemology and 213–19; topic depth and scope 1–2; as truly "epistemic" 303–5; two main varieties of 104; unintended 54–7
epistemic: insurrection 49–50; justice 294–301; labor and knowledge production 21–2; objectification 73, 246–8, 280; objectivity 287–8; othering 131–2; privilege 131; psychology 35; recognition 248–50; relations

and interdependence 18–19; resistance and social injustice 122–3; resources and implicit understanding 86–7; responsibility 89
epistemic significance of other minds 6
epistemic trust 71–2; injustices 318–21
epistemic vice 223–30; ethical and 245–6
epistemic violence 13, 122, 128; within intersectionality 119–20
epistemic virtue 202–3, 223–30
epistemology 13; geography of 400–5; of ignorance 132–4, 243–4, 273; of incarceration 275–7; queer 158–65; representation 205–7; of resistance and liberation 106, 134–5, 365–6; social 93–4, 97, 213–19; standpoint 119–20, 162–4; trans★ 167–73; transactional 207–10; vice 223–30; of victims 133
essentialist assumption 280, 287–8; marginalization and 285–7; objectification and 282–4
esteem 248–50
ethical vice 245–6
ethics 13; normative 243–4; of sharing 382–3
Eurocentrism 125–6; as epistemology of ignorance 397–406; *see also* colonialism
exclusive reading 139
existential harm of hermeneutical injustice 201–2; pragmatism and 205–11
expansiveness, hermeneutical 49
expectations, normative 215–19
experiential asymmetries 336
exploitation, epistemic 21–2, 247–8
extracted speech 22

Faletto, Enzo 152
Fanon, Frantz 6, 95, 141, 201–3, 262
Feagin, Joe 105
Fehr, Carla 216
feminist epistemology 125–6, 399–400; epistemologies of ignorance and 132–4; epistemologies of resistance and liberation and 134–5; systematic epistemic silencing and 128–32; Who knows? question in 126–7; Whose knowledges? question in 127–8
feminist philosophy 18; black 115; education and 331–2; epistemic resources and 86; intersectionality and 115–23; Marxism and 55; "personal is political" 57; science and 216–17; standpoint theory and 125, 162–3; transcendental orientation and 196–7; women's standpoint and 125; zeitgeist and 55
feminist theologies 387–8
first order agency 256–7
first order epistemic exclusion 19–20
first person authority and trans★ epistemology 170–1
*Fisher v. University of Texas* 284
Foucault, Michel 5–6, 55–7, 94, 178, 193–5, 406; on apparatus 176; conception of power 188–9; on power/knowledge 190–2; on power/knowledge/resistance 192–3; queer theory and 158–9; as theorist of epistemic injustice 187
Frank, Andre Gunder 152
Frank, Jeff 330
Frankfurt School 100
free choice of belief 89–90
freedom, political 261–8
French revolution 406
Frese, Frederick 352
Fricker, Elizabeth 92–3
Fricker, Miranda 2–3, 38, 41, 96, 101, 126, 168, 171, 207, 273, 315, 359; on apparatus of disability 176–8; on blameworthiness 229; on collective space in society 360; on credibility 62–4, 72, 76, 236; differentiation of two main varieties of epistemic injustice 104–5, 132, 140, 195, 294–5; on distributive epistemic injustice 61; on epistemic authority 326; on epistemic ignorance 132; on epistemic injustice 213; on epistemic objectification 247–8; on faith in the speaker's competence 72; Foucault and 187, 191–2; on hermeneutical injustice 42, 45–9, 86, 105–6, 202, 217; on hermeneutical marginalization 64–5; on *To Kill a Mockingbird* 63, 179–82; on localised hermeneutical practices 44; on marginalized communities 274; on ontological or existential implications of epistemic injustice 201; queer theory and 159; on racially motivated concept-suppression cases 45; on relativistic outlook of postmodernism 102; on religion 386; on remedies to implicit bias and stereotype threat 240–1; representational epistemology 205–7; on roots of testimonial injustice 246; on shared pool of hermeneutical resources 43–4; on social perception 197–8; on steadying the mind 198, 201; on systematic identity prejudices 75; on testimonial injustice 28–35, 61–2, 227–8, 280, 303–5; on uneducatedness 331
Friedan, Betty 132
Frost-Arnold, Karen 130, 134
Frye, Marilyn 132
Fuller, Steve 214

Gandhi, Mahatma 389
Garcia Marruz, Fina 262, 267
Garner, Eric 296
*Gaslight* 168
gaslighting 127; defined 168; as epistemic justice 168–70; as hands of "allies" 167–8; no more "allies" and 171–3; trans★ epistemology and first person authority and 170–1
gender: language in Christianity 387; reason and 126–7; social justice and 116–17
genital excision 257

geography of epistemology 400–5
geopolitics of knowledge 4, 150; articulating an academic 152–4
Gestalt theory 198
Gines, Kathryn 141–2
Glaser, Jack 240
global eliminativism 145
global justice 254–5
Goguen, Stacey 239–40
Goldin, Claudia 75
Goldman, Alvin 214
Gooding-Williams, Robert 110
Google 307, 309; Maps 305–6
Goonatilake, Susantha 270
Gordon, Lewis 202
Gramsci, Antonio 100
grand narratives 55
Gray, Freddie 296
Great Britain 357–8; Durham World Heritage Site 372–3; Hadrian's Wall 378–9; Magna Carta 377–8; Throne of Weapons 380
Grice, H. P. 249
Griffiths, Paul J. 389
Grosfoguel, Ramón 131, 398, 402
Grosforguel, Ramón 152
Gross, Rita 387
*Grutter v. Bollinger* 329
Gutiérrez, Gustavo 388

Haack, Susan 92
Hacking 283
Hadrian's Wall 378–9
Halberstam, Jack 164
Hall, Kim Q. 5
Hamilton, Patrick 168
Hand, Michael 325
Haraway, Donna 95, 126–7
Harding, Sandra 17, 56, 97, 125–6, 162–3, 270
hard to handle anger 128
harmful consequences of epistemic injustice 210–11, 244–5, 343–4
Hart, Armando 261
Hartsock, Nancy 125
Hartz, Louis 110
Havis, Devonya 133
Hayward, Mark 350
healthcare *see* medicine and healthcare
health professional complaints 337
hegemony 100
Heidegger, Martin 85, 95, 195
Heil, John 90
Heldke, Lisa 21, 128
heritage 370–1; and accounts of epistemic injustice 372–6; participant perspective epistemic injustice and distribution of epistemic goods 377–82; participant perspective epistemic injustice and ethics of sharing 382–3

hermeneutical death 2, 47, 49; defined 41–2; fighting against hermeneutical injustice and 48–50
hermeneutical expansiveness 49
hermeneutical imperialism 49
hermeneutical injustice 86, 104, 132; breadth of 46–7; classificatory pluralism and 45–8; defined 41–2, 238; depth of 47; difference between uneducatedness and 331–2; distributive terms and 64–6; dynamics 46; existential harm of 201–2; fighting against hermeneutical death and 48–50; hermeneutical participation and 140; hermeneutical responsibilities and 42–5; implicit bias, stereotype threat, and 238–40; lived experience of 201; midway cases of 47, 106; non-fatal 42, 49; post-racial ideal and 145–6; post-racialism and 141–3; science and 315; semantically produced 45–6; social epistemology and 217–18
hermeneutical insurrection 48–50
hermeneutical marginalization 43, 49, 55, 64, 87, 140–1
hermeneutical privacy 49
hermeneutical resistance 48–50
hermeneutic egalitarianism 65
Hick, John 390–1
Hoagland, Sarah Lucia 133–5
Holton, Richard 70, 76
homophobia 163
hooks, bell 131
Hookway, Christopher 32–3, 307, 315, 339–40, 371, 375–7
Hornsby, Jennifer 129–30, 144
Howard School of international relations 109–10
Hume, David 282, 400
Hurtado, Aida 134
Husain, Mary 128–9
Husserl, Edmund 6, 195–8

identity: barbarian 401–2; disability 164; politics 119–20, 131; prejudices, online 305–7
ideological objectification 285
ideological state apparatuses 100
ideology: concept as crucial tool for Western progressives 100; epistemic injustice and racist 104–10; in Marxism 101–3; racism as an 103–4
ignorance: coordinated 16–18; determined or willful 17, 132–3, 365–6; epistemologies of 132–4, 243–4, 273; Eurocentrism as epistemology of 397–406; loving, well-intentioned 131; pernicious 119–20, 129; reliable 120; white 44, 246
illness *see* medicine and healthcare
illocution 143–5
illocutionary acts 144
illocutionary disablement 129
impairment 286

## Index

imperialism 268, 398, 401; European colonialism and 262; hermeneutical 49
implicit bias: in criminal justice system 298–300; hermeneutical injustice and 239–40; remedies for 240–1; testimonial injustice and 236–7
implicit understanding 86–7
impossibility and hermeneutical injustices 43
incarceration, epistemology of 275–7
inclusive reading 139
Indigenous peoples *see* anthropology of Indigenous peoples
individualism 3, 90
informational perspective in healthcare 339–40
informational prejudice 307
injustice, epistemic *see* epistemic injustice
injustice, hermeneutical *see* hermeneutical injustice
Institute of Management Consultants 215
instituting imaginary 95
institutional incorporation 117–18
insurrection 48–50; of knowledges 192
intentional consciousness 201
*inter alia* 94
interdependence and epistemic relations 18–19
interpersonal as political 57–8
interpretive-hermeneutical resources in philosophy 95
interpretive injustice 73
intersectionality 4; black feminism and 115–17; defined 115; epistemic injustice and 118–19; epistemic violence within 119–20; institutional incorporation 117–18; testimonial practices of quieting and smothering in 120–2
inverted world 17
Ionesco, Eugène 267–8
Islam 128–9, 389

Jackson, Frank 79
Jackson, Lana 350
Jaggar, Alison 128
Jantzen, Grace 390
Johnson, E. Patrick 161–2
Johnson, Meri Lisa 164–5
*Johnson v. McIntosh* 357
*Journal of Literary and Cultural Disability Studies* 164
*Journal of Race Development* 110
Judaism 389
justice, epistemic 294–301

Kafer, Alison 164
kaleidoscopic sensibility 16
Kang, Jerry 298
Kant, Immanuel 195–6, 243–4, 247, 324, 400, 406; Kantian objectification 283–5
Keet, André 131–3
Kidd, Ian James 8, 9, 58, 351, 362, 392
King, Martin Luther, Jr. 140

King, Rodney 296
King, Ursula 387
know how and ability 79, 81–2; profound bodily change and 84–6
knowledge: after experiencing profound bodily change 84–6; asymmetries 336; epistemic features beyond and entangled in ability 82–4; epistemic imaginary and 3, 94–5; epistemic resources and implicit understanding 86–7; geopolitics of 4, 150, 152–4; and ignorance about women of color 131; insurrection of 192; judgments involved in 262; know how and ability 79, 81–2; local 317–18; objective 279; oppositional 164; power and 190–2; production and epistemic labor 21–2; propositional 79, 82; reconceptions of place and purpose of responsibility in 95–6; subjectivity 90; subject of 125–6; subjugated 134
Knowles, Eric 240
Kobrynowicz, Diane 75
Kornblith, Hilary 89–90
Korsch, Barbara M. 337
Kotzee, Ben 8, 330–1
Kuhn, Thomas 94, 214, 316
Kukla, Rebecca 73–4, 130, 144
Kyratsous, Michaelis 58

labor, epistemic 21–2
Lakeman, Richard 348–9, 352
Langton, Rae 129–30, 144
language: as common ground between self and other 200; as complex social practice 143–4
Larrabee, Mary Jeanne 135
Latin America: Catholic Church in 388; epistemic injustice in 266; political freedom in 261–3, 265, 268
Lee, Harper 5, 62, 176, 178–82
Li, Peizhong 240
liberation, epistemology of 134–5
liberation theologies 388–9
liminal consciousness 276
linguistic terrorism 41
listening, virtuous 48, 54–5
Lloyd, Genevieve 126–7, 399
localised hermeneutical practices 44
local knowledge 317–18
Locke, John 256, 324, 357–8
locutionary acts 144
Longino, Helen 270, 317
looping effect 283, 286
Lorde, Audre 41, 50, 141
love 248–9
Lowenthal, David 378
Lugones, Maria 128, 131, 134–5
Lukács, Georg 100–1
Luke, Carmen 326, 330

Luz y Caballero, José de la 261–2, 264, 267
Lyotard, Jean-François 55

MacIntyre, Alasdair 96
MacKinnon, Catharine 129
Magna Carta 377–8
Maitra, Ishani 21, 144, 238
Mandela, Nelson 265
Manley, Michael 151
marginalization: hermeneutical 43, 49, 55, 64, 86–7, 140–1; objectification and 285–7
Marotta, Satis 298
marriage, traditional definition of 66
Marsh, Gerald 74–5
Marshall, John 357
Martí, José 262–3, 265–8
Martin Alcoff, Linda 9, 17, 131
Marx, Karl 106, 265, 268, 400
Marxism 55–6; blind spot on colonialism 150; hope for class consciousness 106–7; ideology 100–3
Mason, Rebecca 273–4
May, Vivian 13, 118, 128
McCarthy, Thomas 254–5
McCarthyism 100
McCleskey, Warren 297–8
McCord Adams, Marilyn 390
McDowell, John 246
McGary, Howard 141–2
McGowan, Mary Kate 129–30, 144
McGrath, Ben 85
McHugh, Nancy Arden 7
McKenzie, Mia 167
McKinney, Rachel 22, 158–9
McKinnon, Rachel 5
McRuer, Robert 164
McWhorter, John 296
McWhorter, Ladelle 161–2
medicine and healthcare 336; epistemic injustice harm to patients 343–4; epistemology, illness, and 337; hermeneutical injustice in 341–3; structural epistemic injustice in 344; testimonial injustice in 338–41; *see also* mental healthcare
Medina, José 1, 16, 62, 64, 118, 189, 273, 295; on epistemic agency of communities 274–5; on epistemic credibility 332; on epistemic death 390, 401–2; on epistemic friction 161; on epistemology of resistance 106, 134–5; Foucault and 193; on *To Kill a Mockingbird* 179–82, 228; on language of social imagination 94; on meta-lucidity 244; on mistake of intellectualism 96–7; on social ignorance and responsibility 95
Melville, Herman 399
memory, politics of 254–60
Menchú, Robert 153
Mendieta, Eduardo 134–5

mental healthcare 347–8; epistemic injustice in 348–51; epistemic justice in 351–3; *see also* medicine and healthcare
Merleau-Ponty, Maurice 6, 95, 195, 197–200
mestiza consciousness 163–4
meta-perspectives 107
micro-resistance 50
midway cases of hermeneutical injustice 47, 106
Mignolo, Walter 4, 125, 131, 152–3, 155, 405; decolonial theory 401–2; on epistemic disobedience 134; on knowledge generation 149
Mill, John Stuart 244–5, 324, 358, 400
Mills, Charles W. 3, 16–17, 49, 217, 249, 273; on epistemologies of ignorance 132–4, 243–4; on white ignorance 246
Minghella, Anthony 28, 63
*mirabile dictu* 109
Mitchell, Claudia 84–6
modernity 149–50, 153
modes of consciousness 155
Mohanty, Chandra 272–5
monologism of the colonizer 131
Monteith, Margo 240
Montmarquet, James 226
Moraga, Cherríe 135
Morales, Mario Roberto 153
Morris, Aldon 109
Moses, Robert 284–5
Moskowitz, Gordon 240
motivated delusions 352–3
Murchison, Bill 139
MySpace 306
mysticism, Christian 390

Narayan, Uma 21
narrative 96
Native American Graves Protection and Repatriation Act 363
Native peoples *see* anthropology of Indigenous peoples
naturalism 392–4
*Navajo Nation v. United States Forest Service* 362
Ndlovu-Gatsheni, Sabelo J. 131
Nelson, Lynn Hankinson 126, 271–3
neo-Nazis 65–6
neo-racism 255
Newton, Isaac 264
Nkrumah, Kwame 397–8, 400, 402
Noë, Alva 81–2
non-fatal hermeneutical injustices 42, 49
normative assumption 281, 287–8; marginalization and 285–7; objectification and 282–4
normative ethics 243–4
normative expectations 215–19
Nozick, Robert 66
Nussbaum, Martha 246

Obama, Barack 141, 142, 255
objecthood 201–2
objectification 73, 246–8, 280; ideological 285; Kantian 283–5; looping effect 283; marginalization 285–7; projective 282, 285; sexual 283; status quo reasoning and 282–5
objectivism 102
objectivity: epistemic 287–8; kinds of 279–80; normal, natural, and good 280–1; in transactional epistemology 208–10
Occidentalism 4
Ohio Women's Rights Convention 45–6
Olberding, Amy 14, 21–2, 397
oppositional consciousness 127–8
oppositional knowledge 164
*Orientalism* 151–2
Origgi, Gloria 8
Ortega, Mariana 131
Orwell, George 262
Ostrove, Joan 167
Other, the 4, 128, 131–2, 343, 356, 360–1, 399–400, 405
outlaw emotions 128
Owen, David 15–16

Pantazatos, Andreas 8–9
Park, Robert 109
participation: exclusion from 216–17, 375–6; perspective epistemic injustice and distribution of epistemic goods 377–82; perspective epistemic injustice and ethics of sharing 382–3
participatory epistemic injustices in science 315–18
participatory perspective in healthcare 339–40
particularities 95
Passmore, John 325
patient complaints 337
Pavlovian response 267
Peet, Andrew 73
perception: consciousness and 198–200; as inherence in things 199; phenomenology of social 197–8
performatively produced hermeneutical injustices 45–6
perlocutionary acts 144
pernicious ignorance 119–20, 129
personalist-vice 228–9
perspectivism 401, 405
Peters, R. S. 325
phenomenology: existential harm of hermeneutical injustice 201–2; method 195–7; "settling the mind" through the body 198–200; of social perception 197–8
Phillips, D. Z. 391
Pitts, Andrea J. 4
Plato 324
Plato's Cave 107–9

pluralism, classificatory 45–8
Pohlhaus, Gaile, Jr. 1–2, 43–4, 360; on epistemic communities 273–5; on epistemic exploitation 247–8; on Fricker's analysis of *To Kill a Mockingbird* 108; queer theory and 159; on resistance of epistemic domination 106; on rhetorical spaces 50; on truncated subjectivity 343; on willful hermeneutical ignorance 133, 170, 365–6
Polemicism 266
police brutality 296
political activism and social justice 116–18
political agency 254–60
political eliminativism 142, 145
political freedom 261–8
political philosophy 13
politics of memory 254–60
Polyani, Michael 316
Popper, Karl 316
Portugal 398
postcolonialism 151–2
postmodernism 100, 102, 187
post-racialism 141–3; ideal and hermeneutical injustice 145–6
post-racism 143
poverty, culture of 255
power: agential 187–9; coloniality of 152–3; constitutive 187–9; knowledge and 190–2; queer theory and 158–9; resistance and 192–3; trust and social 69–70
powerlessness, experiences of 57–8
practical trust 71–2
pragmatism 55–6; harms of epistemic injustice and 210–11; representational epistemology and 205–7; transactional epistemology and 207–10
prejudicial credibility in healthcare 339–41
prejudicial over-generalisation 58
privacy, hermeneutical 49
profiling, algorithmic 308–10
profound bodily change, effects of 84–6
projective objectification 282, 285
propositional knowledge 79, 82
psychiatry *see* mental healthcare
psychic alienation 201
public eliminativism 142, 145
Pui-lan, Kwok 388
Putnam, Hilary 264

queer epistemology 158–9; crip epistemologies and 164–5; question of standpoint and 162–4; self-knowledge and 161–2; and sexuality as a problem for truth 159–61
queer theory 158
quieting and smothering 120–2, 129, 169, 235
Quijano, Aníbal 152

## Index

race: post-racialism and 141–3; social justice and 116–17
*Racial Contract, The* 16–17, 132, 273
racism: as an ideology 103–4; Black Lives Matter movement and 139–40; epistemic 131; ideology and epistemic injustice 104–10; neo- 255; post- 143; science and 313–14, 319–20
rape 209–10, 304–5
Ratcliffe, Matthew 392–3
Rawls, John 101, 105, 110
reason and gender 126–7
reasoning, status quo 282–7
recognition, epistemic 248–50
reduction, phenomenological 196
Reid, Thomas 197
reliable ignorance 120
religion: as dimension of social activity 386; feminist theologies of 387–8; liberation theologies 388–9; naturalism and 392–4; protection of Indigenous persons' 362–5; soul-making theodicy 390–1; as source of epistemic injustice 389–91; and vulnerability to epistemic injustice 391–4
representational epistemology 205–7
resistance: communities of 272–5; epistemology of liberation and 106, 134–5, 365–6; hermeneutical 48–50; power and 192–3
responsibilist-vice 226–7
Reverse Othello syndrome 352–3
rhetorical spaces 50, 133
rhetoric of beginnings 15
Rice, Tamir 296
Rich, Adrienne 127
"Robinsonades" 101
Rodriguez, Pedro Paulo 266
Rolin, Kristina 216
Rooney, Phyllis 127
Rorty, Richard 55–6, 205, 207
Rosenhan, David 348
Rouse, Cecilia 75
Rousseau, Jean-Jacques 324, 400
Ruben, David-Hillel 101
Rubio, Antonio 404
Ryle, Gilbert 80

*saddha* 265
Said, Edward 150–2
*sakkayadithi* 266–7
Salamon, Gayle 14
Sanati, Abdi 58
Sanchez, Francisco 405
Sartre, Jean-Paul 95
Satz, Debra 331
Saul, Jennifer 6, 236
Sayadaw, Ledi 266–7
Scalia, Antonin 284

Scheman, Naomi 127, 320
schizophrenia 352
Schmidt, Eric 307
science: epistemic injustice and 313–15; epistemic trust injustices in 318–21; participatory epistemic injustices in 315–18; racism and sexism shaping 313–14, 319–20; significance of epistemic injustice in 321
Scott, David 151
Scrutton, Anastasia 8
second order agency 254, 256–7
second order epistemic exclusion 19–20
Sedgwick, Eve 158–60
self-censorship 122
self-conscious awareness 31, 37
self-knowledge and queer epistemology 161–2
self-regulation 240
self-trust 18
Seller, Anne 90
semantically produced hermeneutical injustices 45–6
semantic authority 254
"settling the mind" through the body 198–201
sexism 216–17; science and 313–14
sexual objectification 283
shared cognitive labor 165
shared reality bias 274
sharing, ethics of 382–3
Shelby, Tommie 3, 103–4, 108
Sheth, Falguni 141
Shotwell, Alexis 3
Siegel, H. 329–30
Sikhism 389
silence as resistance 134
silencing: in healthcare 337; illocution and 143–5; itinerary 389; systematic epistemic 128–32
Simpson, Lorenzo C. 7
Simpson, O. J. 296
sincerity silencing 129–30
"Situated Knowledges" 126
situatedness of knowers 127
slavery 47, 261, 404; social heritage of 272
Smith, Linda Tuhiwai 129
smothering and quieting 120–2, 169, 235
social consciousness 103–4, 108
social contract and coordinated ignorance 16–18
social epistemology 93–4, 97, 213–19
social experience, new terrains of 58–9
social heritage 272
social imaginary 332–3
social justice: epistemic resistance and 122–3; from epistemic virtue to 202–3; political activism and 116–18; testimonial relationships and 121
social movement frameworks 116
social perception, phenomenology of 197–8
social power and trust 69–70

social practice 27
Sommers, Samuel 298
Sosa, Ernest 89, 225
soul-making theodicy 390–1
spatialization 400–1
Spelman, Elizabeth 135
Spivak, Gayatri Chakravorty 13, 128, 150, 270, 389
standpoint epistemology 119–20; queer epistemology and 162–4
standpoint theory 125
Stanghellini, Giovanni 349
Stanley, Jason 80–1, 86
statistical döppelgangers 307–8
status quo reasoning 282–7
stereotype threat: in healthcare 338–9; hermeneutical injustice and 239–40; remedies for 240–1; testimonial injustice and 237–8
Stewart, Maria 41
Strawson, P. F. 70
structural epistemic injustice 344
structural testimonial injustice 28, 30, 33–5, 38; in healthcare 338
subalternity 13, 153, 270
subjectivity/subjectivities 90, 94–5
subject of knowledge 125–6
subjugated knowledge 134
sub-knowers 17
subversive consciousness 275
Sullivan, Jesse 84–5
Sullivan, Michael 7–8
Sullivan, Shannon 5–6, 314
Sundstrom, Ron 141, 143
systematic epistemic silencing 128–32
systematic uptake failure 129

Target stores 308
Taylor, Charles 267, 392
Taylor, Paul C. 141, 146
testimonial betrayal 2, 28, 35–8
testimonial bias in criminal justice system 295–7
testimonial injustice 27–8, 61–4, 104, 132, 140, 280; defined 28, 235; as epistemic 303–5; epistemic vice and 223–30; Fricker's account of 28–30; in healthcare 338–41; implicit bias and 236–7; *To Kill a Mockingbird* and 178–82; as objectification 73; online 310–11; stereotype threat and 237–8; structural 28, 30, 33–5, 38; transactional 28, 30–5, 38, 56–7
testimonial quieting 129
testimonial smothering 73
testimony 27; bias in criminal justice system 295–7; information perspective 32; quieting and smothering 120–2, 169, 235; systematic class of sub-knowers and 17; trust in 72–3
theo-politics 401, 403–5

thick and thin trust relations 37–8
third-order epistemic exclusion 19–20
*To Kill a Mockingbird* 5, 62–3, 108, 176, 178–82, 223, 227–8, 236
Tolstoy, Leo 57
Tomlinson, Barbara 118
*Townhall* 139
transactional epistemology 207–10
transactional testimonial injustice 28, 30–5, 38, 56–7
transcendentalist delusion 397–9
transcendental orientation 196–7
trans* epistemology: "allies" and 167–8; first person authority and 170–1; gaslighting as epistemic injustice and 168–70; no more "allies" and 171–3
Tremain, Shelley 5, 286
trickster strategy 134
truncated subjectivity 343
trust: absence of 69; in action 74–5; distrust, and reliance 70–1; epistemic and practical 71–2; injustices in science 318–21; overlapping concepts of 69; social power and 69–70; in testimony 72–3; trustworthiness and untrustworthiness in 73–4; uniqueness, rationality, and choice in 75–7; *see also* credibility
truth: –cognition axis 190–1; epistemic justice and 294–301; epistemic social imaginary and 332–3; sexuality as a problem for 159–61; transactional 208–9
Tuskegee study 313
two-tier stewardship 383

unaided accomplishment 258–9
understanding, implicit 86–7
UNESCO World Heritage List 372
unintended epistemic injustice 54–7
uniqueness, rationality, and choice in trust 75–7
United States and Indigenous peoples *see* anthropology of Indigenous peoples
universal sisterhood 131
untrustworthiness 73–4

Varela, Félix 261–2, 264, 267
vice, epistemic 223–30; ethical and 245–6
virtue, epistemic 202–3, 223–30
virtue-reliabilism 224–5
virtue-responsibilism 225–6
virtuous listening 48, 54–5
Vitalis, Robert 109

Walker, Alice 49
Wallerstein, Immanuel 150
Walsh, Catherine 155
Wardrope, Jeremy 344

*Index*

Watson, Gary 229
white ignorance 44, 246
Wiggins, David 246
willful hermeneutical ignorance 17, 132–3, 159, 170, 365–6
Williams, Bernard 198–9, 201, 305
Williamson, Timothy 80–1, 86
Women's Health Movement 318
Woodson, Carter G. 141
World Bank 151

World Heritage Convention 381
World Heritage Sites (WHS) 372–3, 377, 382
Wylie, Alison 216, 318
Wynter, Sylvia 149, 154–5, 402

Yap, Audrey 238

Zagzebski, Linda 226
Zea, Leopoldo 400
zeitgeist 55

Printed in Great Britain
by Amazon